The operas of Benjamin Britten

The operas of
BENJAMIN BRITTEN

Edited by David Herbert

THE COMPLETE LIBRETTOS ILLUSTRATED WITH DESIGNS OF THE FIRST PRODUCTIONS

Preface by Peter Pears

Contributions by Janet Baker, Basil Coleman
Eric Crozier, Colin Graham, Hans Keller
John Piper, Myfanwy Piper, Andrew Porter

Columbia University Press
New York   1979

To Brenda

This book was designed and produced by
The Herbert Press Ltd
65 Belsize Lane, London NW3 5AU, England
Designer Gillian Greenwood

Printed in Great Britain by
Hazell Watson & Viney Ltd, Aylesbury, Bucks

Library of Congress Cataloging in Publication Data

Britten, Benjamin, 1913–1976.
  [Operas. Librettos. English]
  The operas of Benjamin Britten.

  Bibliography: p.
  Includes index.
    1. Operas–Librettos. 2. Britten, Benjamin, 1913–
1976. Operas. I. Herbert, David. II. Title.
ML49.B74H5   782.1'54   79–2052
ISBN 0–231–04868–8

Contents

Editor's note

My purpose in compiling this book is to provide both a permanent reference work and an evocative record of the original stage realizations of Britten's operas. All sixteen librettos have been included – carefully revised in the light of Britten's own scores; the texts that appear here are what he wanted sung on the stage. They are illustrated by set and costume designs (and occasionally performance photographs) of first productions. The main text consists of articles by some of those who collaborated most closely with Britten (as designers, librettists and producers) in the creation and first staging of the operas, together with an introduction by Hans Keller, a personal contribution by Janet Baker and two essays by Andrew Porter on the first and last operas.

I would like to thank the contributors. I would also like to thank all those who have helped to assemble the material, and particularly Donald Mitchell, Rosamund Strode, Myfanwy Piper and Julia MacRae, without whose encouragement, advice and constant assistance the book could not have appeared.

David Herbert

Acknowledgements

The editor is grateful to the many people and organisations who have allowed set and costume designs from their own private collections to be reproduced; namely, The Britten Estate, Richard Cyzer, Francis Durbridge, The English Music Theatre Company, Faber Music Ltd, Colin Graham, Christine Hare, Anne and Heydon Hill, Charles Knode, Cara Lancaster, John Lewis, Donald Mitchell, Tanya Moiseiwitsch, Sir Peter Pears, John Piper, Rosamund Strode, Annena Stubbs, Carl Toms, Theodor Uppman, and L. A. Yeats. Acknowledgement is also made to the Birmingham Museums and Art Gallery for their courtesy in allowing us to reproduce illustration 21, to the Theatre Museum, Victoria and Albert Museum (Crown Copyright) for permission to reproduce illustrations 17, 19, 20, 22, 45, 46, 84, 85, 88, and to Nigel Luckhurst, Sebastian Piper and Derrick Witty for photographing so many designs specially for the book.

THE TEXT

All excerpts from the letters and other writings of Benjamin Britten are reproduced by permission of the Executors of the Britten Estate, © 1979.
Not to be reproduced without the permission of The Britten Estate.

Acknowledgement is made to Secker & Warburg Ltd, London, and to Alfred A. Knopf, Inc., New York, for permission to include extracts from *The Letters of Thomas Mann* (trans. Richard and Clara Winston), 1971, in 'Writing for Britten' by Myfanwy Piper; also to Farrar, Straus & Giroux, Inc., New York, and Chatto & Windus Ltd, London, publishers of *Music of Three Seasons* by Andrew Porter, and *The New Yorker* for permission to include 'The First Opera: *Paul Bunyan*' and 'The Last Opera: *Death in Venice*' which are based on reviews written for *The New Yorker*.

THE LIBRETTOS

Acknowledgement is made to Faber Music Ltd and Boosey & Hawkes Publishers Ltd, publishers of the librettos (all of which are copyright works) and, for specific permission to reproduce individual librettos, to the following:
Paul Bunyan: Faber Music Ltd, London
Peter Grimes: The Bodley Head Ltd, London
The Rape of Lucretia: Ronald Duncan
Albert Herring: Hawkes & Son (London) Ltd and Eric Crozier
The Little Sweep: Hawkes & Son (London) Ltd and Eric Crozier
Billy Budd: The Society of Authors as the literary representative of The Estate of E. M. Forster, and Eric Crozier
Gloriana: Sir Rupert Hart-Davis on behalf of The Estate of William Plomer

The Turn of the Screw: Myfanwy Piper
Noye's Fludde: Hawkes & Son (London) Ltd
A Midsummer Night's Dream: Hawkes & Son (London) Ltd
Curlew River: Faber Music Ltd, London
The Burning Fiery Furnace: Faber Music Ltd, London
The Prodigal Son: Faber Music Ltd, London
The Golden Vanity: Faber Music Ltd, London
Owen Wingrave: Faber Music Ltd, London
Death in Venice: Faber Music Ltd, London

PHOTOGRAPHIC ACKNOWLEDGEMENTS
Cyril Arnold: 23, 24, 25
Condé Nast Publications Ltd: 40, 41
Dominic Photography: 94, 99, 100, 103, 104
Kurt Hutton: 68, 69
Nigel Luckhurst: 9–16, 18, 26–9, 57, 67, 70–81, 122
Angus McBean: 34, 65
Edward Mandinian: 30, 31
Bob Mates: 44
Sebastian Piper: jacket photograph, 38, 39, 48, 50, 51, 53–5, 82, 83, 121
Derrick Witty: 1–8, 17, 19, 20, 22, 32, 33, 37, 45–7, 56, 58–62, 66, 84, 85, 88–93, 95–8, 101, 102, 105, 108–17, 123–137, 139, 140
Roger Wood: 42, 43, 52

Peter Pears

Preface

Benjamin Britten's natural language was music; he was more at home with notes, pitches and sounds than he was with words, and while he was happy and ready to welcome the words which he was to clothe, it more often than not happened that the detailed design of the opera was clarifying in his mind long before the libretto was ready. Situations and characters started to ferment in his mind as soon as a story was settled in outline. Even when one was only discussing possibilities, it seemed that something was brewing. *King Lear*, for instance, was on its way to the front of his mind when public interest in the idea (leaked to the press) inhibited and froze it: Britten didn't need advice from unknown Shakespearians. There were many other librettos which arrived through the post but got no further than the back of a drawer. He had plenty of ideas of his own. An opera libretto which he would have dearly liked to include in this volume was *The Tale of Mr Tod*. The wonderful scene of Brock in bed and Mr Tod waiting, waiting . . . what we have lost! The snores, the fight, the clatter, the long silence . . . I wanted to be Mr Tod with Owen Brannigan as Tommy Brock, but the terms which the publishers demanded put it out of the question.

There were librettos just begun (*Mansfield Park*) and others finished but not accepted (*Anna Karenina*), and there was Prosper Merimée's *Matteo Falcone* which Britten was tremendously taken with for years, and of course there was the series of little Christmas stage cantatas which very nearly reached active composition but, owing to the passage of time, just failed. With his sixteen operas, by eighteenth-century standards Benjamin Britten was a moderate producer. By the standard of the twentieth century, his own century, he was incredibly fecund. He could be called the only British professional opera composer – and yet how much more! Here at least are all the librettos which he put to music.

Hans Keller

Introduction: Operatic music and Britten

Musicians – composers as well as listeners – like to hate or love opera, but few will admit to any hate-love, fewer still to its possible fruitfulness. Yet, no sooner does a great composer decide to *serve* a libretto and its underlying idea than he proceeds to take over, to *master* all the words involved – and control has never yet been the expression of love, though it readily indulges in protestations of love.

I MUSIC *v.* OPERA

Even though the Matthew Passion or the John Passion is easily as good a church opera as is any of Britten's three 'Parables for Church Performance', Bach can hardly be said to have shown any sympathy with operatic thought. The difference? It isn't so much that Britten's characters dress up and move around a bit; after all, musico-dramatically and, in particular, texturally speaking, Bach's dress up and move around at least as much, not to speak of those awe-inspiring moments when they stand still, one of them above all. No, Bach's attitude towards words themselves is ambivalent. In his own church operas or church parables, i.e. his passions and cantatas, the words have been mastered in the first place – by religion, which Bach's music *is* prepared and able not only to serve, but to convey more deeply and clearly than words can. In his secular cantatas, on the other hand, his contempt of words results in downright musical embarrassment, for us, anyway: the job wasn't worth wasting his real music on, and all his real music is sacred, whether it's a cantata or a Brandenburg Concerto or, yes, a suite – of sacred dances, if you hear what I mean. The counter-pole is Bach's coeval, Handel, who did respect opera, tried to serve the text, and finished up by mastering it, with music that went far beyond it, straight across it.

Where does that leave us? Right in the middle of the ambivalence: only in their worst music do Bach and Handel leave verbal drama, words, alone. Otherwise, why should they? You can't have your words and compose them, unless you are a Carl Friedrich Zelter, with whose respectful setting of the *Erlking* (as opposed to Schubert's) Goethe was delighted, and has remained the last to be delighted. And Schubert himself fought shy of opera, musical opera, even when composing one or the other: responsibly respectful towards the dramatic situations he was faced with, he adopted what he felt was the wisest course of action, in that he left his most characteristic music at home, safely and consistently so, throughout his operatic output.

In order to get a clear picture of this conflict-ridden area of love and hate affairs between music and opera, however, we have to go one steep step further than Schubert – remembering, at the same time, the instrumental part of his mature output, above all the three great quartets and the string quintet: it is the field of instrumental music pure and complex which, just because it has absorbed musical drama in its sonata thought, seems furthest removed from stage drama – and within that field, it is, of course, the string quartet and its relatives (such as the string quintet) which, *ceteris paribus*, present the richest and subtlest expression of sheer musical drama.

What I am leading up to is that with two downright sensational exceptions, no great string-quartet composer has been a continual composer of great operas, lastingly receptive to the fascinations of operatic thought – and that conversely, again with those two exceptions, no great and persistent opera composer has been a composer of great string quartets. The two exceptions are Mozart and Britten – of whom more anon.

Meanwhile, be it noted that I chose my words meticulously: Beethoven may be said to have written a great opera (though many say he didn't), Verdi a great string quartet (almost), Schoenberg more than one of each. But these very examples support my case: Beethoven's theatrical discomfort, first in *Leonora*, and then in its replacement *Fidelio*, all but equals Verdi's symphonic and textural discomfort in his Quartet, while Schoenberg's great stage works depend on their hostility to the stage – in view of which they are not always described as great. And even below this plateau, the confrontation, ambivalent and easily destructive, between operatic thought and symphonic-quartet thought makes itself felt: a Hans Pfitzner, great in at least one opera, *Palestrina*, is at his smallest in the string quartet, while I know from first-hand experience that Franz Schmidt, at first a passionate opera composer, deliberately turned his back on this art form – and deepened his symphonic-quartet thought in the process. Back on the high plateau, finally, that unique operatic symphonist, Wagner, coached Beethoven string quartets in private – but in his own active art, he had to content himself with the theatrical assimilation of those instrumental modes of thought which, as a listener, he seemed to place above all others – wide-ranging symphonic thought processes, in and outside the string quartet.

In the last resort, then, the conflict is not between words and music, but between drama and drama – the one human, or expressed through human (or, in Wagner's case, superhuman) metaphor, the other metaphysical, or expressed through unworldly – purely musical – metaphor. By way of religious drama and music drama (i.e. drama dictated by musical thought), Bach and Wagner, strangest of all bedfellows, had it both ways.

Britten and Mozart had it both ways, too – only more so: not content with absorbing extended instrumental thought into their operas, they proceeded to inject operatic thought, however limited in range (hardly ever throughout a movement) into their symphonic thought. The height of Mozart's symphonic thought is reached in the string quintet where, in the slow movement of the C major, he turns sonata form into duet form, or, conversely, accommodates a *continual* duet between the first fiddle and the viola in a sonata framework – to the extent of melodiously singing across the most unmelodic bit in a conventional sonata build-up, i.e. the so-called bridge passage between first and second subject. And the next danger point from the duet's point of view, the conventional development section, is here replaced by a seven-bar transition, still singing along with the sharpest operatic characterization, with a personalizing differentiation between the two instruments.

Now, the height of Britten's own symphonic thought is reached, without question, in his Third String Quartet which, composed thirty years after his Second, consummates what the earlier (though nowise early) work had foreshadowed, not only in terms of human drama made purely musical, but also in venturing, whole-mindedly, that decisive step beyond – into the Mozartian realm of the instrumental purification of opera.

If ever there was an operatic testament apart from *Tristan and Isolde* (which, in the end, Wagner decided generously to survive), one should have thought that it was the sixteenth of Britten's operas, *Death in Venice*: never before in the history of this uniquely problematic art form had universal significance and uncompromising personal statement – no longer interested, it already seemed at the time, in the reactions of an audience this side of the life barrier – coalesced without the slightest friction; in fact, one could never have as much as envisaged such a possibility – except, again, on the other side of the barrier, amongst composers in paradise. But then, that's precisely the great artist's (as distinct from the 'good' artist's) task, the realization of this particular brand of impossibility – the worldly capture of the other world. Great art, in short, makes a success of great philosophy's inevitable failure – a mission of which Wagner himself was only too aware, even before he discovered and incorporated Schopenhauer.

In any case, even if the common-sensical reader is not willing to follow me that far, preferring mental life this side of the barrier, where we all know what we mean by Clapham Common or Kensington Gardens, he will agree that after the last page of *Death in Venice*, we feel and think that this is it: it's been said, all of it, and left, without undue persuasion, to those who care. Thus the work far transcends that which it truly masters and controls – Thomas Mann's story, originally packed with personal complications without universal significance: Britten's conscious respect for Mann's literary achievement has always seemed to me a function of his unconscious respect for what he could do with it, about it.

Yet, after the fullest of stops at the end of *Death in Venice*, what happens in the finale of the Third Quartet? *Death in Venice* is complexly continued in its introductory, quasi-operatic recitative, and it is only when the body of the movement starts – a passacaglia which consummates not only the final chaconne of the Second Quartet but, far more specifically, every single *operatic* passacaglia which, from *Peter Grimes* onwards, Britten had written – that we realize how little we have yet known of his testament: it is now, in the quartet, between ourselves as it were, that he confides his last secrets to us, to those who want to listen – for again, he does not ask to be heard, as he would have done in a piece of orchestral symphonism. Take it or not, he says to us; in any case, I leave it. Nor is there a full-stop at the end: maybe life is not a period, it's not for me to say. A testament with a perfect cadence at the end would beg life's basic question – the nature of death.

When, decades ago, I first drew detailed attention to the fascinating and intriguing parallels between the creative characters of Britten and Mozart, I was not over-occupied with Britten's operas: after all, at that stage, he hadn't written all that many of them. Now I am: meanwhile, he wrote more than Mozart – as many as Mozart would have written in a normal life-span.

It is, in fact, only when one concerns oneself with their respective, specifically *operatic* techniques that one becomes alive to an operatic element in their symphonic thought which, until then, one had missed, because it is a bit of a negative element, and none the worse for that. Let's face it frontally: neither Mozart nor Britten was a natural, congenital developer, whereas, say, Haydn or Beethoven or Mendelssohn or Brahms or Schoenberg was.

In an opera, much of what would be the development's concern in a symphony or string quartet is at least mapped out by the action and the interaction of characters: Wagner alone refused to accept this difference between verbal drama and musical (symphonic) drama, and wrote symphonies for the stage instead – which, since they had to heed both the verbal drama's and the purely musical drama's requirements, tended to get rather long, with plenty of verbal repetition where the music – including its symphonic development – demanded it.

Mozart and Britten, on the other hand, though they did, of course, indulge in musical development in their operas, especially in the ensembles, never transcended the stage's requirements to the extent of developing their thoughts purely musically where, from an operatic point of view, such development did not make immediate and instinctive sense – there and then, in the theatre. Now, the primary reason was not just their much-lauded 'sense for the theatre', but that this very sense was, at least in part, a function of that *negative* quality I am trying to postulate – their aversion to, their inhibitions, or even innate hesitancy about, symphonic develop-ment: their greatest developments are second thoughts, not part and parcel of their first thoughts (as they are with a Haydn and a Beethoven). In other words, Mozart and Britten loved the stage not only for what it offered, but also for what, if you were no Wagner, it often tended to exclude.

So far as Britten is concerned, this observation may not come as a particular shock. But Mozart has been dead a little longer, and proportionately sanctified, his mature development sections are accepted as ultimate truth better than which, truer than which, nothing could be envisaged. Now, since a full understanding of Britten's operatic genius is promoted by a full understanding not only of Mozart's operatic genius, but also of his one extra-operatic limitation, I propose to make, at least, an *hors d'oeuvre* of it (remembering that in its strict French sense, the term also denotes a dish served in the interval of a meal).

For one thing, Mozart was fond of leaving the development section out of cer-tain sonata structures altogether, and not only in movements which, for reasons of overall balance, invited such an omission – pre-eminently slow movements, to which Haydn tended to confine his so-called 'abridged' sonata forms which, in any case, he used most sparingly. The reader need not be particularly learned in order to appreciate my case, which can immediately be supported by music he readily recalls, such as the *Figaro* Overture. For another thing, Mozart, in order to get out of developing, abbreviated not only some of his sonata forms, but also some of his development sections themselves, by making parts of them non-develop-mental: in the first movements of some of his B flat works, for instance (such as the 'Hunt' Quartet or the second Piano Trio in that key), he starts his development section not with actual development, but with a belated, complete, completely stable second subject in the dominant, as if we were still in the exposition.

For a third thing, however, not all the development sections in Mozart's greatest sonata structures are, in fact, great. Could there be a greater exposition and recapitulation than those of the first movement of the Clarinet Quintet? But its development section is merely good: it is uninspired, conventional, its predict-able modulating sequences trying (successfully, it must be admitted) to cover the developmental ground as painlessly and as straightforwardly as possible: Mozart gets back into the recapitulation as the crow flies, as it were.

And what has all this to do with Britten's operatic music? Everything – everything that has not yet been noted. Had I conducted this stage of my argument in terms of an analysis of his, rather than Mozart's, symphonic attitude, in order to show that amongst other things, he loved the stage for what it did *not* offer, I should have been guilty of *ignotum per ignotius*, an attempted illumination that would have left the scene darker than it was before I came in: Britten's symphonic thought is not sufficiently known, has not yet been sufficiently absorbed on a purely instinctive level, to make any such explanation meaningful without the help of a strictly comparable case that is spontaneously known or knowable to all of us.

But when I now say that Britten, as a developer and non-developer, is the closest of blood-relations of Mozart, the knowledgeable reader will easily supply his own evidence from that part of Britten's symphonic output which he happens to know intimately. All the same, it behoves me to complement my observations about Mozart's attitude to development with one or two concrete examples of Britten's own, equivalent reactions to this central symphonic problem.

Supreme masterpiece that it is, the Spring Symphony is 'abridged' symphonic form driven to its extreme: instead of cutting the development out of one continuous structure, he cuts it, wholesale, out of a long string of, proportionately, smaller-scale forms in which the human voice is used, often quasi-operatically. And upon those occasions when he does develop, he easily tends to fly across the danger area as crow-like as did Mozart in the opening movement of the Clarinet Quintet. In fact, the first movement of the afore-mentioned Second String Quartet, though perhaps his most successful symphonic structure at that point in his creative evolution, evinces discomfort at precisely the same juncture as does the corresponding movement of Mozart's Clarinet Quintet: the development section which, decades ago, I euphemistically called a 'free fantasia', shows the selfsame drop in inspiration and invention, the identical desire to get back – no, forward, to the recapitulation, whose deeply inspired difference from the exposition is at least as drastic as it is in Mozart's case (where, however, most of the difference is confined to the second subject).

The ultimate test case is, of course, the work which I have described as expressing the height of Britten's symphonic thought – the Third String Quartet of thirty years later (1975, a year before his death). I have drawn attention to its continuation of *Death in Venice* in the finale, but that's not the only operatic spot in the work: the first movement, by far the most symphonic of the five, is entitled, not 'Duos' (as it might have been if Britten had wanted to be purely factual rather than meaningfully metaphorical), but – 'Duets'! No harder evidence could be found for Britten's allegiance to opera on the one hand and, on the other, for my submission that his love of opera was inextricably bound up with his lifelong experience of the incisive, hurtful problem of symphonic development.

For the one movement which, wellnigh eccentrically, bears this operatic title is, paradoxically, the one movement which contains an unoperatic, downright anti-operatic development section – and perhaps the composer's greatest, profoundest, most far-reaching development to boot (reaching as it does far into, and beyond the recapitulation!), the one which can compare with Mozart's *great* development sections. Almost needless to add by now, the Third String Quartet's metaphorical opera, the 'duet' texture, is interrupted at the point where – unnoticed by analysts and critics – the development starts (or rather, two bars later, for there is transitional texture); and the duets are, of course, resumed in the recapitulation. In the development itself, that is to say, the title 'Duets' becomes quite meaningless: with the help of double and triple stoppings, the texture here extends well beyond a normal quartet sound – as far as a nonet. At the same time, the highly original inclusion of developmental material in the recapitulation and indeed the movement's final relaxation, the harmonization thus achieved between opera and symphonism, is a sublime, self-therapeutic reparative symptom of the healthy disease, the allergy to development, which Britten, Mozart-like, had suffered from all his life, and without which the musical world would have been the poorer: a musical testament if ever there was one. It may be unfair on the rest of us, but on the level of genius, limitation turns into its opposite, right down or up to Beethoven's deafness which, demonstrably, was an indispensable condition of his late works – music that could not have been conceived by an ear in touch with the outer world, the 'real' world, as they call it, i.e. the world of topical rather than timeless reality.

Likewise, Britten's (and, admittedly to a lesser extent, Mozart's) developmental limitations enabled, indeed forced the composer to explode into opera with an elemental musicality with which few other opera composers approached the stage: some of them were too developmental, too symphonic, to be genuinely operatic, while most of them were so unconcerned with pure music that they weren't concerned about development at all, didn't as much as notice its absence in their minds – with the result that they wrote all those countless operas that live on the opera lover's interest rather than the music lover's, whereas in aural view of many a Britten opera, many a pure-music lover finds himself able to accept, at the very least, an armistice in his conflict with the genre, without realizing that Britten's relative difficulties with what the purist cherishes most in his pure music, to wit, development, are in fact ultimately responsible for the musical substance of his operas – not solely responsible, to be sure, but at least a *conditio sine qua non*, nevertheless.

Near the beginning of the century, two of Freud's most brilliant pupils, Carl Gustav Jung and Alfred Adler, broke away from the master and founded their own schools of depth psychology or dynamic psychology. Everybody – especially many a thinker about music and the arts – knows what happened to C. G. Jung and his analytical psychology, but few people know what happened to one of the most interesting of the many Adlers they may have vaguely heard about, and his Individual Psychology. The chief reason for his neglect appears to be that he talked more than he wrote, so that relatively little survived. None the less, one of Alfred Adler's neologisms has penetrated all our western languages and behaves as if it had always been there – 'over-compensation': he postulated a simple psychological law according to which a defect or deficiency tended to be not merely compensated (as happens on the purely organic level), but over-compensated. I suggest that nothing could explain the intensely musical side of Britten's operatic genius more simply – nor can Mozart's operatic genius altogether escape this explanation!

Of course, genius has to be there in the first place – but once it is, over-compensation will produce the opposite of limitation to such a lavish extent that it needs a great deal of critical perception, and empathy as well, to discover the original limitation, especially if that limitation has not proved all that limiting in the first place, having often been overcome straightforwardly, without the help of over-compensation. Needless to add, the limitation has to be one of which the genius's mind is aware – has to limit something he is creatively interested in: Puccini's symphonic limitations, about which he couldn't have cared less if they struck him at all, did not produce any over-compensation in his operas; as a result, the level of their musical substance is more variable than that of the Britten operas.

And once the limitations are, themselves, so limited that they do not prevent a Mozart from writing his gigantic quintets, his great quartets, and all his other symphonic master-structures, just as they don't prevent a Britten from writing his operatically inspired, symphonic testament, i.e. the Third Quartet, it is these very limitations that have it both ways, for once – I mean, for twice: a defect is being over-compensated which, in the end, doesn't turn out to be a defect, any-way – merely *the deep consciousness of a hurdle*. It is one of the great fallacies of our time's common or garden dynamic psychology to conclude that only unconscious-ness can be 'deep', that 'mere' consciousness is superficial: the greater the genius, the deeper his conscious mind, his ego, his awareness of what other minds don't own up to, and hence can't over-compensate with anything like the same power, purposiveness, clarity, and realism – the same objective validity: we ordinary mortals, if we over-compensate at all, do it for our own sake; Benjamin Britten's operas do it for yours.

It is in this way that he enables the pure musician to agree to a temporary armistice with opera – because the composer himself has turned the armed con-flict between music and opera into a sublimely amorous confluence, mutually fructifying, whereas even on the level of *Fidelio, Tristan,* and *Moses and Aron,* three of the world's most uncompromising geniuses invite opera, the stage, to compro-mise, for pure music's sake. But then, the three just couldn't do without symphonic development: that was *their* limitation – one which could not be over-compen-sated, because it was not experienced as one. On the contrary, they felt jolly virtuous about it.

II BRITTEN'S OPERATIC CHARACTER

To the English-reading intellectual, Friedrich Schiller is a second-rate poet and a playwright who seems to have stimulated a great composer or two, and that's about it. To the Germans, Schiller is one of their two or three Shakespeare-like geniuses. The difference in evaluation is easy to explain: all English Schiller trans-lations are, at best, third-rate, and hence worse than nothing – one of many un-noticed literary tragedies, this, and one which isn't only literary; for Schiller was an important post-Kantian philosopher too.

In our present context, a closely-argued aesthetic differentiation he introduced is of fundamental significance, since it throws glaring light on the difference be-tween Britten's operatic character on the one hand and, on the other, that of the other three giants referred to at the end of section I. Schiller juxtaposed what he described as the 'naive' artist and what he proposed to call the 'sentimentalic' artist: I apologise for an awkward neologism – for which, however, Schiller him-

self is to blame, in that he invented the German word '*sentimentalisch*' for his purpose, which he derived from '*sentimental*': the latter word and its meaning are the
same in German and in English, whereas what Schiller means by 'sentimentalic'
is not immediately comprehensible in either German or English – so here goes.

The 'naive' artist is in tune with nature, expressing it, its laws, its truths spontaneously – the mouthpiece, as it were, of physical, metaphysical, and psychological truth. The 'sentimentalic' artist, on the other hand, is in search of lost
nature: he is the perpetual striver, who thinks it is better to travel than to arrive,
if only because one travels further that way. And just as C. G. Jung discovered his
personality types when he compared Freud's personality with his own, so Schiller
discovered his artistic personality types on the basis of what he felt to be the sharp
contrast between Goethe's artistic personality, which he thought 'naive', and his
own, which he knew to be 'sentimentalic', striving – forgetting in the process that
the entire history of art, any art, cannot boast any striver, either amongst its
creators or amongst the figures they created, who can remotely compare to that
striver *par excellence*, Goethe's Faust. Nor would it do for Schiller to retort that the
'sentimentalic' Faust is Goethe's 'naive' creation, for the poet's lifelong obsession
with his hero *cum* anti-hero was a measure of his autobiographical involvement:
the more we know about Goethe, the more we realize how much we can learn
about him, the character of his own mind, through Faust's.

Let that pass; Schiller's illusions about Goethe, his works and his psychology are
one thing; the searching validity of his thesis is another. For he did apply his
differential diagnosis not only to the artist but – aesthetically immeasurably more
important – to his art; his crucial essay is, in fact, entitled *On Naive and Sentimentalic Poetry*.[1] Again, the differentiation does not only apply to Schiller's chosen
art, literature, but also to music. I would, in fact, go much further than Schiller
did, in proportion as I am more musical than he was: I would suggest that his
eminently practical theory applies more purely to music than to any other art –
that it's music, alone amongst the arts, which is, in fact, the ideal touchstone for
any aesthetic theory, for the elementary and elemental reason that music cannot
contain anything inartistic, extra-artistic, without ceasing to be music altogether.

Words have strong and primitive extra-artistic involvements, as have pictures,
edifices, and indeed physical movements, whose 'beauty' is even appreciated in
sport, where they are called 'poetry' and 'rhythm' by the technically unreceptive,
because such spectators don't know what else to call them: they are only too well
aware that they are employing no more than an extravagant metaphor or two.
Notes and motifs, on the other hand, phrases, harmonies and rhythms, mean
nothing outside music: simple signals apart, they are music or mad – and that
nowadays, there is a lot of mad music around is not in question (and I don't
mean musical madness either, as depicted in the sanely composed 'Mad' Interlude from *Peter Grimes*).

So far is music as such removed from any pictorial or conceptual thought that
it is almost impossible to talk about it without distorting it – which is why I invented my wordless method of musical analysis called 'functional analysis';
significantly enough in the context of the present argument, Britten was so
enthusiastic about my method that he commissioned one such analysis from me –
of Mozart's last quartet. (I thus analysed his own Second Quartet too.) But long
before I go into the precise significance of his enthusiasm, I have to expose the

precise nature of my argument – which, with the help of Schiller, won't be too difficult. For if music is a successful touchstone for his theory, then his theory must be an equally successful touchstone for one particular aspect of music – its aesthetic typology: for once, one may hope that concepts, words, though by their nature static, will not distort the dynamic essence of music.

One aural glance at the best-known part of our history of music convinces us that an otherwise inexpressible, profound difference between musics and musics suddenly becomes verbally clear in the warm light of Schiller's theory, to wit, the fundamental characterological contrast between Mozart and Haydn, or Mozart and Beethoven, between Bruckner and Mahler, Britten and Wagner, or, of course, between Britten and Schoenberg – so much so that one need hardly spell it out: Schiller's theory applies, as it were, without our having to apply it – which is the highest and rarest compliment we can pay to any theory: the inevitability of its practice. There fall from our ears as it had been scales: the music of Mozart, Bruckner and Britten is 'naive', as indeed are the composers themselves in their creative attitudes; whereas Haydn, Beethoven, Mahler and Schoenberg are proto-typically 'sentimentalic'.

If I may resume and expand my medical metaphor, one simple pair of 'clinical' signs for Schiller's differential diagnosis emerges at once – at least, so far as everybody except for Britten is concerned, and even he partakes in this clinical picture so long as we *don't* think too much of his operas! What I am referring to is a difference which the naivest of listeners will happily accept, since it's one that operates in his own mind when he listens to these composers' mature music: when he hears two important works by a 'sentimentalic' composer whose music he has made his own, and even though he be quite ignorant historically and biographically, he will tend to know, instinctively, which is the earlier and which the later work, whereas two such works by a 'naive' composer may well baffle him chronologically.

Or, to put it yet more bluntly, other things being equal, 'naive' works tend to be more alike than 'sentimentalic' works: even the most knowing amongst us must confess that, say, amongst the ten great string quartets of Mozart, there are quite a few whose chronological place could not be guessed on the basis of purely musical evidence; and that formally, these masterpieces are far more alike than the mature quartets of Haydn or Beethoven – though Mozart's great string *quintets* aren't, an exception which will disclose its significance as we close in on Britten's *operatic* character itself.

Meanwhile, be it noted that what is true of the Mozart quartets – and you can play the same game amongst his immature works in this *genre* – is true of most of Bruckner's symphonies, only more so; as a matter of fact, music lovers who don't take to them, as well as those critics whom they lead, go so far as to maintain that Bruckner, very much unlike his beloved model Beethoven, always wrote the same symphony – a criticism which retains a point if you divest it of its negative evalua-tion: like the majority of Mozart's Ten Quartets, most of Bruckner's symphonies are variations on one and the same formal scheme. There is *more* than all the difference in the world between this creative attitude and that of a Haydn, Beethoven, or Schoenberg: we are, in fact, confronted with two contrasting creative worlds, to the extent of having to admit that if we didn't know that an early and a late work of Haydn, Beethoven, or Schoenberg was by the same com-poser, we wouldn't always be able to recognise the fact. We would, of course, identify relations between them and a remote influence of one on the other, but suchlike we identify in the works of different composers, too – where, moreover, the influence often isn't all that remote.

The difference is, straightforwardly, that between Schiller's 'naive' artist, his natural, and his striver: if you strive, you have to change drastically and all the time, whereas if you don't, you needn't. The 'naive' composer is there. He hasn't arrived; he is there in the first place: he reveals from his stable position. The 'sentimentalic' composer, on the other hand, is getting there: he considers it his sacred creative duty to communicate the continuous struggle, the striving search, to leave behind a potent picture of the soul of the seeker – if only for the sake of those who, thus stimulated, want to join the search. He will, ineluctably, play the role of the priest, always aware of his mission, whereas the 'naive' composer, simply offering his revelations, may not even be alive to the fact that he does: compare Beethoven's consciousness and Mozart's unconsciousness, Mozart's or Bruckner's stark statements with Beethoven's or Mahler's striving *developments*.

What have I said? At one fell (but fair) swoop of the pen, I have plunged Schiller's words right into the middle, the *developmental* middle of music – into music at its most wordless, its most unoperatic. The swoop is fair because music expresses the seeker's evolution, prototypically, in its unstable developments, while it discloses the seer's, the 'naive' artist's discoveries in its stable statements. Let's face it simply, without obsessional qualifications: there's nothing like a Bruckner theme, and there's nothing like a Beethoven development! Critics of Beethoven dislike his themes and deny their melodic significance (Stravinsky!), while critics of Bruckner dislike his developments and think they make his symphonies too long. In musical reality, Bruckner's symphonies *seem too long* because they *are too short* – because their developments just don't develop enough or with sufficient intensity. Lacking the slightest talent or inclination for the stage, Bruckner could not, of course, over-compensate as Britten did.

Now, Britten himself takes his place amongst the 'naive', the revelatory artists with the same admiration for the 'sentimentalic' artist which the two types have always shown for each other on the level of genius: we remember Mozart's productive admiration of Haydn, Haydn's of Mozart and, of course, Britten's own of Mahler.

Development in the strictly musical sense, then, is as 'sentimentalic' as is the artist whose compulsive search makes him continually develop; and in diatonic music, the paradigm of all development is, simply, incessant modulation, producing harmonic lability, while it is harmonic stability – the single-key statement in the diatonic world – that is the 'naive' composer's home ground: even the greatest Mozart developments don't reach the level of inspiration of, say, the sublime statement that is the modified recapitulation of the Clarinet Quintet's second subject. *Mutatis mutandis*, this difference can be observed throughout Britten's entire output and, given both his genius and his love of human drama, is responsible for his being one of our time's very few great opera composers, conceivably the only one. For once you cease to be naive in the theatre, you run the risk of writing oratorios for the stage – of which *Moses and Aron* is, of course, one of the very greatest of all times.

When I submit that Britten is one of our time's very few great opera composers, the implication is that amongst our time's great composers, including even those who have written great operatic music, there are precious few, perhaps none, that fall into the 'naive' category to any appreciable extent – and the possible combination, in the same creative personality, of 'naive' and 'sentimentalic' traits is not, of course, denied. Now, we have, so far, observed Britten's 'naivety', in fact everybody's 'naivety', without reference to his historical position. Schiller's antithesis, however, has to be applied along the historical as well as the individual coordinate: were he alive today, he would not fail to point out that at the present stage in the development or envelopment of our culture, great 'naivety' has become exceptional to the extent of feeling anachronistic: it is Britten's 'naivety', not his style or his alleged harmonic conservatism, that has given him the name of a reactionary amongst modish avant-gardists.

Naivety is not of our world – not of its culture and its civilisation, anyway: 'but now is my naivety not from hence', Britten might well have said. We are reaping the benefit, and suffering the sterilizing effects, of sophistication, which produces great art on the level of genius, and little more than artificiality on the level of mere talent. But even where sophistication is absent, naivety is not, for that reason, present – certainly not 'naivety' in Schiller's sense: the age pushes the artist – even many a potentially 'naive' artist – into a striving, searching role, for as opposed to the artist of the past, and especially its musician, the contemporary creator cannot even start before he has sought and found his means of expression: forced, historically, to be a seeker on the technical plane, he has to be very strong indeed if he wants to retain any naivety he may possess, in the usual sense or in Schiller's, for the purpose of his creative character formation. And this is the reason why our time teems with bad operas, non-operas, opera-substitutes, 'music theatre' which has it neither way, or theatre music which needs the stage in order to hide its musical inadequacy. When, on the other hand, the 27-year-old Britten writes a mere operetta in two acts and a prologue, i.e. *Paul Bunyan* (tolerantly revised in 1974, after the composer had intolerantly rejected it for decades), which is the very type of music that, normally, falls flat when experienced without the stage, its sheer musical substance is such that, in a radio broadcast, it even overwhelms antagonists who confess that they wouldn't have credited Britten with the ability to write an ultra-musical musical. A 'sentimentalic' composer would not have been prepared to face such a task five years before *Peter Grimes*, anyway – if he had been prepared to consider the proposition at all, at any stage in his development, his obligatory search.

At any previous historical juncture, Britten's 'naive' operatic character would have been exceptional in view of its musical substance; at the present, culturally obsessional stage with its compulsive, insecure searches and its cries for distant help, it is wellnigh unique. Britten does indeed seem to me the one twentieth-century opera composer of weight who is not of the twentieth century. Many may agree, for the wrong reasons: theirs is a negative criticism, mine a positive – timeless – evaluation. There is, in fact, no other opera composer around in this century who is so good and so 'naive' – and those who are as good, but 'sentimentalic' at the same time, aren't as good *qua* opera composers; for good, unapologetic opera needs Schiller's 'naivety': it doesn't need a priest, however inspired, using the theatre for his own ends – if there is an end to the developmental process he is reflecting (which there isn't if he is a proper striver).

It is at this point that I can explain what I think is the significance of Britten's enthusiasm for my own wordless method of analysis. For two reasons, that is to say, I take his reactions to functional analysis as unambiguous evidence of his profoundly 'naive' creative character. First, 'naive' composers can be shown to suspect words about music: Mozart's analytic remarks in his letters are few and very far between, whereas Beethoven verbalized a great deal; as for Haydn, he even put self-analytic remarks into his scores. Again, Mahler worried about a symphony representing a whole world, while Bruckner couldn't have cared less about what it represented, so long as it served – was expressive of? – God. His hero Wagner, on the other hand, never stopped theorizing, both in his writings and (as we now know)[2] in his conversation – nor, at subsequent stages in the history of composition, did Schoenberg. Brahms, a 'sentimentalic' giant who was everything that Britten was not and wasn't anything that Britten was, had even started collecting material for a book on when and why the great masters used forbidden progressions – consecutive fifths and consecutive octaves. And Britten himself suspected most words about music more deeply than any other 'naive' composer.

On the surface, my second reason for Britten's enthusiasm about functional analysis contradicts my first – for if the 'naive' composer can be shown to suspect verbal analysis, would we not expect him to react against *any* kind of analysis? We would be doubly wrong. For one thing, there is the 'naive' type's admiration for the 'sentimentalic' type – whose analytic reflections he will, quite often, happily accept so long as they leave his own music alone. But for another, more specific thing, just as he is fascinated by the 'sentimentalic' composer's developments without being over-anxious to emulate them, the 'naive' composer is intrigued by my wordless analysis *qua* 'developments': hearing them, I have heard more than one 'naive' listener exclaim that 'this is really a development', and Britten's successive quick grins when listening to such an analysis were indistinguishable from his facial reactions to a development section he liked: *the 'naive' artist loves watching the search he doesn't need*, whether the searcher is a seeker (composer) or a researcher (analyst).

While the evidence for Britten's anti-developmental, 'naive' creative character, and especially for the 'naive' framework of his operatic character, may now be considered complete, it shows a loose middle: when I discussed the relative anti-chronology of a 'naive' creator's works, his unconcern with developing from one work to the next, I did, after all, say that one *mustn't* think too much of Britten's *operas* in this respect – nor of Mozart's string *quintets*. Why not? Because there is drastic evolution, or at least progress, in either of these fields – not continuous, maybe, but rich in contrasts nevertheless. It is true that Mozart's last quintet, the one in E flat, is as little of a last or late developmental stage (at least as far as its outer movements are concerned) as *The Magic Flute* is a consummation; none the less, the differences between any two great Mozart quintets are far more fundamental than those between any of the Ten Quartets.

Likewise, the differences between Britten's operas are unmatched in the rest of his output, with the sole exception of the special, highly-charged area of the string quartet: within it, the Third is, as we have seen, at least as much of a contrasting testament as is *Death in Venice* within Britten's operatic world – which creative circumstance places both works in a special category outside the antithesis between 'naive' and 'sentimentalic' art; for in the face of death, the 'naive' composer naturally – supernaturally – discovers the seeker in himself.

What, then, produced this unparalleled commitment to contrast with which the Mozart quintets and the Britten operas surprise us? In Mozart's case, there is, in my opinion, a simple personal element – the player envisaged for the first-viola part, to wit, Mozart himself; in fact, *both* prospective viola players may have played a role in Mozart's imagination – Mozart and Haydn! We recall that the piano concertos, too, show richer contrasts, better-defined progress from at least some works to some later ones, than do successive creations in Mozart's other genres. In Britten's case, on the other hand, it clearly is a trans-personal element that makes his operas so different from each other – one which leads us straight to the heart of his operatic character. For let us not forget that his reluctance to 'develop' in the technical sense, and his 'naivety', are not the heart of the matter; rather, they are, artistically speaking, the biological conditions which make that operatic heart beat with such athletic strength.

At last, then, on top of drawing parallels between Britten and Mozart, we are getting down to identifying an – all the more meaningful – difference. True, what great artists have in common helps us to understand them – but it also hinders us, unless we insist on going on to discover what they do not have in common.

Mozart once said that the mere idea of an opera libretto could transport him into a state of white heat. It didn't really matter to him whether a libretto expressed the moralism of the German operas, *Die Entführung* and *The Magic Flute*, works admired by the 'sentimentalic' Beethoven, or whether it displayed what Beethoven considered the objectionable amorality of, below all, *Così fan tutte*.

Of Britten's own 'relationship to the text' (to steal a phrase from Schoenberg), Beethoven would have approved far more whole-heartedly – for Britten did not treat his librettos as mere material, which was the crime Mozart had perpetrated, whatever he may have thought or even said before the creative event. So what were Britten's conditions? The very fact that they changed to and fro in the course of his operatic life gives us a clue to the changeability of his operas and their musical styles, which are more comprehensive even than Stravinsky's. During the earlier stages, encompassing *Peter Grimes* (1945), *The Rape of Lucretia* (1946), *Albert Herring* (1947), *The Beggar's Opera* (1948), *The Little Sweep* (the children's opera of 1949), and *Billy Budd* (1951), various attempts had been made to find common themes and common aims, such as innocence betrayed or assaulted, the musical defence of the outsider (the not-so-odd-man-out), the injustice of all too human justice and its social consequences. Even Britten's homosexuality was drawn in in order to explain both such odd-women-in as Ellen Orford in *Peter Grimes* or Lucretia herself, or indeed his musical preoccupation with boys – for the pre-occupation is musical in *Peter Grimes* too, even though the boy himself does not sing: purely instrumental thought takes over. And indeed, though such critical whisper was not without malice and usually sprang from ill-repressed homo-sexuality on the part of observers who simply could not bear the sound of the music of a straightforwardly homosexual genius, it had at least this to be said in its undeserved favour – that it could not help drawing sane attention to Britten's conquest of new musical territory so far as the use of children's voices in and out-side the opera house was concerned, a conquest which, in 1954, contributed to what may be his greatest operatic achievement altogether – *The Turn of the Screw*.

Meanwhile, *Billy Budd* (1951) could still be included in the critical theme-song of the innocent individual misunderstood and maltreated by his social environment; with its all-male cast, moreover, the opera reinforced the strictly confidential, aesthetic witch-hunt against homosexualized art – an ironical perversion, this, of sober music criticism, since the opera's texture succeeds in unfolding contrasts within the self-imposed limitation of male voices the like of which the heterosexual Richard Wagner did not find easy to realize in all those hours of all-male *Siegfried* which precede – the Woodbird apart – the eventual, overwhelming explosion of musical femininity, when Brünnhilde at last wakes up: 'Hail thee, Sun!' indeed – the sun being feminine in German.

But before *The Turn of the Screw*, there was *Gloriana* (1953) – that criminally neglected opera whose intermittent inspirations are all the greater for the whole not being a facile masterpiece: *The Magic Flute* isn't either. Now, *Gloriana* could not be fitted into the themes the critics had devised for Britten: a reason perhaps, for its underestimation. And after the *Screw* came *Noye's Fludde* (1958) and *A Midsummer Night's Dream* (1960): at the very least, the critical theme-song had to be repeatedly interrupted, even though it could perhaps be resumed, so far as it was about 'morality' in both main senses of the noun, with *Curlew River* (1964), *The Burning Fiery Furnace* (1966), *The Golden Vanity* (1967), *The Prodigal Son* (1968), and *Owen Wingrave* (1971) – the televisual opera which, quite obviously, was planned, behind television's front, as a work that would, ultimately, be heard where all opera ought to be heard if it wants fully to retain its musical allegiances: in the opera house.

Yet again, the opera composer's last creative will, *Death in Venice* (1973), disappointed the 'morality' experts who, in fact, objected to what they felt to be its homosexual immorality operating under the thinnest of guises; the experts thus let this characteristic 'third-period' music suffer for what they couldn't take in the libretto. It is downright grotesque that we should need the present writer, who happens to be a heterosexual without homosexual interests, for the purpose of stressing the enormous creative advantage of Britten's homosexuality: however little Britten may have been alive to the fact, his psychosexual organization placed him in the privileged position of discovering and musically defining new truths which, otherwise, might not have been accessible to him at all.

At the same time, what, in psychoanalytic parlance, thus happened in Britten's ego and his id does not seem to help us towards distinguishing his attitude to the operatic text from Mozart's, and the fact that his operatic attitudes were so violently changeable raises the question whether they evinced any constant element at all. Now, when we look for constancy in the human mind, be it an ordinary individual's or a genius's, the psychic place where to look for it is not the id, which is wilful in the Schopenhauerian sense of the 'will', i.e. the instinctual sense, nor the ego – which is not deep enough to be unbending: it is in the ego that we 'change our minds'. Constancy, unchangingness, faithfulness in any sense can only be found where faith itself, again in any sense, must needs originate – in the unconscious as well as the conscious conscience, the psychoanalytic superego.

And once we ask ourselves what Britten had, musically speaking, a conscience about, the answer is not far to seek, even though it may be a little difficult to find the right words, for the simple reason that the commitment in question reached deeper than words do – as deep as music itself does, in fact, even though it was not a sheer commitment *to* music (as it was, pre-eminently, in Mozart's case). Rather, it was a commitment *of* his music, *to* something else.

What? It could be various things, and the moral, humanitarian, even political ideals that have been isolated are, of course, amongst them, as is a recurring religious, indeed Christian engagement, which even manifests itself in the unlikely, anti-historical circumstances of *The Rape of Lucretia*; Britten takes his religion into his secular music where the superficially orthodox Roman Catholic Mozart takes his secular music into the church.

I have chosen the word 'engagement' advisedly, and not merely because it alludes to the French concept of committed art, *art engagé*, which usually starts and finishes with political commitment anyway. However, when we engage somebody, we bind him by contract or promise, whether we hire a servant or indeed ourselves, thus being engaged to be married: the central element in any type of engagement, overt in the case of the servant and a trifle more covert in the case of the *fiancé*, is that of service, and it is a stark fact that Britten's operatic music invariably *serves*, ranging from religious or quasi-religious service through the service to one or the other of his superego's social causes to, again – what? What does *A Midsummer Night's Dream* serve? What indeed does the operetta *Paul Bunyan* serve – or, for that matter, *Death in Venice*?

At either end of Britten's multiply contrasted operatic output, which spans thirty-three creative years, we face works that could hardly be more different, and listening to which we almost have to remind ourselves that they are by the same composer – *Paul Bunyan* and *Death in Venice*. And yet these two, the operetta and the opera, have something essential in common – something they share, moreover, with that highly sensitive 'adaptation from William Shakespeare by Benjamin Britten and Peter Pears' that stands right at the centre of Britten's operatic life (but well beyond the middle, both chronologically and developmentally speaking). The firm common background of these three disparate works is emphatic 'poetry' in the wider sense, that of Schiller's '*Dichtung*' – truly creative words, literature, created by writers whom the composer admired – with W. H. Auden at one end, adapted Shakespeare at the centre, and Thomas Mann adapted by Myfanwy Piper at the other.

Service to the poet: the tendency is not confined to these three works, where it overtly manifests itself, but also plays a powerful role, *inter alia*, in what might prove Britten's ultimate operatic masterpiece, *The Turn of the Screw*; and across all the other ideas and ideals which Britten served in his operas, and which were allowed to vary, his respect for his chosen words remained, throughout his rich operatic evolution, a wellnigh mathematical constant – the one creative element that could always be foreheard before the first note was sounded. Time was when Ronald Duncan's poetry for *The Rape of Lucretia* was placed in sneering inverted commas, his pretentious language ridiculed, his retrospective Christian interpretation of pre-Christian drama (originally Britten's idea, we now know) considered downright journalistic; after all, Duncan was, at that stage, a proper journalist too. But those of us with ears to hear recognised the depth of that opera's approach immediately, the clarity of the music helping us across and below any ambiguities in the words. On the other hand, those without any such ears had to wait, patiently, for a change in cultural fashion: today, the youngest generation of poets and poetry lovers adopts a very different attitude towards Ronald Duncan

– and any moment now, the music critics will catch up with them, revaluing the music through the words, where they ought to have valued the words through the music in the first place.

Two final considerations flow from our recognition of the hard fact that Britten's operas *serve* – serve ethical ideals on the one hand, and ideal or idealized literature on the other. They are, perhaps, our most important considerations if we want to arrive at a comprehensive – rather than 'well-rounded' – picture of Benjamin Britten's operatic character.

His service to poetry first, since we have examined it last. It follows from what we have discovered about this unchanging element in Britten's attitudes to his texts that once he decides that he loves a text, whether it needs adaptation or not, he regards it as his duty to take the kind of binding step which, in our relations to people rather than to texts, has been firmly formalized: before he puts pen to paper, or (on his composing walks) musical thought to words, he inwardly declares himself engaged to be married to his text, with all the implications of faithful service and, yes, mastery which an engagement ineluctably carries.

Right at the outset of our argument, the alert reader became aware of a loose beginning, to which he has become ever more critically alive in the course of these past 10,000 words. How precisely, he asks, does Britten fit into this initial picture of 'music *v.* opera', of the weighty composer's ambivalence towards words? Does Britten not respect his chosen words the way that ridiculous light-weight, Carl Friedrich Zelter, respected Goethe's *Erlking*, to the poet's delight? Does Britten not suppress, or indeed simply lack, his beloved Schubert's creative aggression towards the text (of which English listeners with less than perfect German are blissfully unaware)? Did he not delight, Zelter-like, a W. H. Auden, a Ronald Duncan, when he had treated them without a trace of maltreatment? As a matter of fact, Auden told me, in private conversations that were immeasurably more substantial than was our public (radio) exchange of musical views, that he never ceased to regret the eventual break-up of their creative collaboration (which, incidentally, had nothing to do with any ambivalence between musician and poet); his unreserved admiration for Britten's art survived until his death.

The answer which, I suggest, ties up our loose beginning does indeed lie in our metaphor: not even a happy marriage is without ambivalence, but service easily outbalances, outshines mastery, which itself is robbed of its destructiveness by love: it's as elementary as that. The text is not material for Britten, but partner – yet he 'uses' it rather than merely supporting it; at the same time, any distortions of it are, invariably, this side of destruction. Of the many ways in which genius tends to have it both ways, Britten's simultaneous respect for, and use of his texts is one in which most, if not all operatic geniuses have failed – except when they wrote their own texts and thus contrived *mutual* love and respect between music and text. Britten does indeed make the text love his music *a posteriori*: by going beyond what the psychoanalysts call 'object love' and actually identifying with his betrothed, he makes us experience the text as if he had written it. Volumes could be filled with analyses of the musical results, tight-rope dances all of them – and 'dance' is the word: the tensions between verbal rhythm and musical rhythm, continual though they are (rather than continuous!), are never allowed to cause verbal death on the one hand, or musical death on the other.

But it is the other conclusion emerging from our recognition of Britten's uninterrupted *operatic service* that robs our character picture of its well-roundedness – thus, one hopes, contributing to its realism: the perfect circle describes mathematical truths and artistic truths, but never those of human psychology – nor even of that superhuman psychology we find at the back of artistic truths. In other words, there's no denying that our picture of the 'naive' Britten simplifies. There is no service without a search, without strife, Bruckner's service to God excepted, if you can call it a 'service' at all: he really had God living next door and therefore didn't even need a telephone service. To the extent to which Britten's music serves, that is to say, we must accept a 'sentimentalic' side to his operatic character – which, firmly though it is under the control of his dominant 'naivety', has produced his wide-ranging operatic development, with all its striking, sometimes almost shocking differences and contrasts from work to work, from phase to phase. So even here Britten has it both ways, as he 'naively' goes on his 'sentimentalic' operatic pilgrimage, which leads him as far as the personal involvement in change for the players' sake had led Mozart in his quintets and, to some considerable extent, his piano concertos. Given Britten's astounding talent, the ease with which he accommodates his 'sentimentalic' operatic search within his 'naive' asethetic position is indeed a measure of the depth and breadth of his genius.

Both texturally and structurally, these differences and contrasts between his operas range between extremes. No other opera composer has allowed himself comparable contrasts in scoring, instrumentation, orchestration, though it must be remembered that from the moment go, a chamber-musical attitude to the full orchestra can be demonstrated, and this paradox develops intensively together with Britten's creativity: the fuller the orchestra, the more chamber-musically is it likely to be treated. It had all happened thrice before, in the works of Mahler, Schoenberg, and another Austrian, Franz Schreker. There is no sign of the latter two having influenced Britten in this respect – and every sign of the 'sentimentalic' Mahler having done so.

More surprising is the influence of the 'sentimentalic' Wagner, clear to the naked ear at the earlier stages; the composer would probably never have admitted it. But the fact remains that the leitmotiv technique which, perhaps, celebrated its climax in *The Rape of Lucretia* held sway right to the end, even though it was employed in structural contexts – such as recitatives and numbers – which the later Wagner would have rejected, and though the modifications to which it submitted from work to work almost made it a new type of technique each time it was reintroduced. Stylistically and indeed musico-philosophically, Britten was an anti-Wagnerian, greatly enjoying both his conscious and his unconscious jibes at Wagner in *Albert Herring*, where the 'hero' drinks his lemonade secretly laced with rum to the accompaniment of the potion chord from *Tristan and Isolde* (conscious), while there is martial C major which, just because the parody is unconscious, cannot hide its subtle and multiple relations to *The Mastersingers*. But then, none of Britten's hates were without love, which was why they were liable to be used as dynamic (as distinct from static) models – not for what to do, that is, but for what to do about it, and about what one had done about it: a further contribution, this, to the operas' constant change and inconstancy.

The 'sentimentalic' Schoenberg was another such anti-model, helping Britten to serialize, anti-serialize, and trans-serialize – to discover and rediscover applications of the technique which Schoenberg might have dreamt of, but never realized.

The Turn of the Screw is neither the first nor the most original product of this particular search,[3] without which the heterophony in and beyond the Church Parables would, could never have come about – even though biographically and chronologically, Britten's visit to the Far East in 1956 seems 'the cause' of all later heterophonic ventures. *A* cause, yes, but *causa prima?* On the contrary, it was serial thought that was the *conditio sine qua non* of all later heterophonic developments.

The harmonic aspect of serial technique remained untouched so far as its atonality, its denial of the unifying function of key was concerned: a twelve-tone chord in *Billy Budd* immediately discloses its proper tonal (dominant) function; it is absorbed by the key structure. But within the tonal area, there are the most far-reaching excursions. Polytonality appears as early as *Peter Grimes* and, subsequently, undergoes contrasting developments – right to the end, beyond the last opera, or rather, *in* the last 'opera', that for string quartet – the Third. Modality and mixed modality evinced a similar fate. Like leitmotiv technique, modality climaxed in *The Rape of Lucretia* – never to be forgotten, nor just re-used.

But the last and most dramatic of all the 'sentimentalic' searches within 'naive' frameworks, the last stimulation which this greatest eclectic since Mozart unconsciously accepted with creative gratitude, he owed to – dare one say it? – John Cage. At this point, if Britten were alive, he'd kick or kill me, notwithstanding his unqualified pacifism. Yet that entire novel dimension of interpretative freedom in some of his later works, of the performer's own creative role, his actual contribution to composition – all those quasi-aleatoric devices used in the church operas, in *Death in Venice* and, again, in the 'opera for string quartet', are the traceable result, however indirect, of the war of liberation which our age's leading, imaginative unmusician has waged; in Britten, he produced a new type of ultra-musicality – and now *he* would kick me too, and vigorously deny being guilty of any such crime as having been responsible for musical meaning. But then, you never know what happens to your thoughts, or your studied thoughtlessness.

It is, in fact, when we examine the 'indeterminacy' (Boulez's term) of Gustav Aschenbach's – the protagonist's – recitatives in *Death in Venice*, their rhythmically unbridled notation, that this essay comes – no, not full circle but, if the extension of the well-established metaphor be permitted, ascending spiral. Let us see how Britten instructs his tenor:

> These Recitatives, which are conceived as interior monologues (or soliloquies) for Aschenbach, should be sung freely, with varying speeds, according to their meaning and dramatic text. They should always be declamatory in style, rather than lyrical. On the other hand, they should never be sung exclusively in the manner of *recitativo secco*, but always with some expression.
>
> It is further emphasized that these Recitatives form an integral part of the composer's conception of the opera, and their length and location have been precisely calculated in relation to the pace and development of the drama. Cuts should not be made, other than those optional cuts indicated by the composer in the score.

From this description, and without having had a look at the score, the tenor-reader would hardly glean that all he is going to be confronted with is pitched black dots within bar-lines. Britten talks about 'speed' and 'pace', it will be noted, but the word 'rhythm' does not as much as occur, even though the fundamental aleatory fact is that there isn't any – before the singer comes in: there are no note-values. Apart from everything else, a little unconscious dig at Schoenberg's 'speaking voice', perhaps? (*Not* 'speech-song', *Sprechgesang*, which is recitative.) For Britten's soliloquizing singing voice is exactly the opposite: where Schoenberg rhythmicizes and de-pitches, Britten pitches and de-rhythmicizes. For the rest, there is even more performing contribution here than meets the eye – in that Peter Pears, the dedicatee of the work and the first Aschenbach, was a joint creator of the pitches as well as the sole creator of the rhythms themselves: Britten is said to have picked up the pitch line from private declamation.

At the outset of our reflections, we submitted that 'no sooner does a great composer decide to *serve* a libretto and its underlying idea than he proceeds to take over, to *master* all the words involved.' But one of the chief results of our intervening reflections has been that Britten serves 'poetry' (creative writing) in general, and indeed Thomas Mann's in eventual – testamentary – particular. Now, by leaving the verbal rhythm of Aschenbach's recitatives alone until the performer comes to grips with it, Britten ensures that if there's going to be any master in the house, it's going to be the singer who, spontaneously, will identify with the protagonist and his words – an extreme effect of Britten's own identification with his betrothed: through impersonating the 'poet' (and Aschenbach himself is one!), the singer will neatly roll mastery and service into one homogeneous whole, as only happens in the happiest of marriages. I fear by now it's a bit late to stun the reader with the observation that the operatic Britten tends to have it both ways.

---

[1] *Über naive und sentimentalische Dichtung*: the last word is untranslatable, since the concept extends over the whole of creative writing.
[2] See Cosima Wagner's *Diaries* (*Die Tagebücher*) in two hefty volumes, Munich, 1976 and 1977.
[3] Needless to add, it produced demi-semi-parody, too, as did the unconfessed, ultra-ambivalent Wagnerian allegiance – though this time outside the field of opera, and well after *The Turn of the Screw*, i.e. in the *Cantata Academica: Carmen Basiliense* of 1960. Throughout his creative life, in fact, Britten misunderstood twelve-tone technique as such as an academic method - but he remembered it until *Death in Venice*.

Janet Baker

Working with Britten

Ben was a king. When he walked into a room the air began to crackle; everyone came alive, became more than themselves. When he left, he made us feel as though we had been better than our best, pleased with ourselves.

Approaching his kingdom, which begins for me where one leaves the A12 and makes that right turn 'to Aldeburgh', feels exactly like going home. It must have rained a lot over the years during Festival time but in my memory the town is everlastingly bathed in sunlight, the cornfield behind the old rehearsal hall is for ever gently moving in a soft breeze, and colleagues are sitting in shirt sleeves enjoying a coffee break in the open air.

They have been marvellous years. People would look at us, the young ones, as though we'd been given the Good Housekeeping 'seal of approval' if we were appearing at Aldeburgh; working with Ben did indeed 'seal' us – with quality. Once exposed to him a musician could never be quite the same again. It wasn't that Aldeburgh concerts were given endless rehearsal; on the contrary, I can remember a number of occasions when we felt decidedly pushed for time, but that's part of professional life in general; it was rather a widespread longing to do great things because Ben would be listening; after that it wasn't enough just to be at one's best for Aldeburgh, one tried to give the same dedication to every situation.

One of the most touching aspects of his personality was his deep understanding of performers and their problems. He was a performer of the very highest calibre himself and he knew from the inside exactly how we felt. This was the only level on which I could attempt to communicate with him. We talked once about the difficulty of the *Lucretia* rape scene; this is awkward for me since the tessitura lies just on the break in my voice around middle C. The entire scene is full of drama, which is hard for me to achieve so low in the voice. Ben's comment when we spoke of this was, 'Oh! dear, it's my fault, I've written it all wrong.' Of course he had not written it 'all wrong'; he had scored the piece for Ferrier whose voice was rich and full in that area but who had difficulty later in the opera where I felt more comfortable.

He once gave the cast of *Albert Herring* a piece of advice which I have never forgotten. He had watched a run-through which had not pleased him but which we all thought had gone well. He explained that in playing comedy one must not think the situation amusing oneself; that the characters were not in the least amusing or eccentric *to* themselves, which is precisely why an audience thinks them to be so. We must therefore take ourselves seriously and not try to make the characters funny; this fact is well known to actors but I had not come across the theory before and found it illuminating and true.

Ben was always ready to talk over problems. He discussed the character of Kate in *Owen Wingrave* at length as we were sitting among the tombstones in Blythburgh churchyard. He warned me that she was not an easy person to play but that he wanted me to tackle her because of my ability as an actress.

In my experience of the 'good' women, like Penelope, Dido, Savitri or Charlotte, there is in all of them a perverseness which is their saving grace; none of them is too good to be true, they each have a flaw. Penelope, that paragon of fidelity, from some sort of strange cussedness, does not look at Ulysses for a long time in the Peter Hall production; perhaps she is paying him back in that moment for all the empty years. Dido knew perfectly well that Aeneas had a special destiny to fulfil; nevertheless, she defied the gods, took him, and paid the penalty. Charlotte is a model wife but an adulteress in her heart; Savitri won her husband from Death by a sort of trick. Such flaws do not mar a wonderful character; they make the person more real, more moving, and more believable. In such contradictions lies the fascination of acting. It is exactly the same with bad girls. Dorabella, although only very mildly wicked, is young and thoughtless; Vitellia is indeed ruthless but she is also a very frightened lady and she bitterly regrets her behaviour; Kate is full of fear too, of insecurity and the vulnerability of youth, a product of an anxious mother, for whom she feels responsible; she behaves badly but there are reasons for her behaviour.

People would often say to me during the weeks of rehearsal for *Owen Wingrave*, 'Does Ben see you as this sort of character, because he has type-cast you all so carefully?' In that case, he must also have seen me as a teenager when I was already a woman of over thirty; that sort of logic is nonsense. What he did see was a singer who had to be capable of acting a difficult role and who looked right enough in shape and size to pass for a younger woman. The real key to Kate's character lies in the score at the moment when Owen's body is discovered and she realizes that she will spend her entire life suffering the most dreadful remorse for what she has done. Ben portrays Kate's anguish most vividly. A bad person feels no remorse; Kate is not a bitch and she is not bad; she is young, and she is without security of any kind, dependent upon the charity of the household, constantly and desperately mortified by her own mother.

To work under Ben's baton was a joy of a special kind. The clarity of his beat and the sureness of his tempi gave a rare security. One was upheld by his marvellous shaping of the phrase but at the same time given room, a sort of freedom, to yield to the inspiration of the moment. Only the very greatest conductors have this ability. I imagine his accompanying at the piano was the same but I never had the opportunity to sing Lieder with him on my own. There was an occasion during the English Opera Group's tour of Russia in 1967, when he played for Peter and me in a performance of *Abraham and Isaac*, which I shall always remember.

Whether he directed his own or the music of another composer, there was a feeling that the tempo he chose was the right one. The sheer kindness of his personality and the infinite patience with which he would iron out problems never made one feel restricted or dominated. People with his sort of charm allied to immense talent must find relationships easier than lesser mortals do. Of course there must have been a 'dark' side to him, after all, he was a genius, not a saint; all I can say with perfect honesty is that I never saw it.

Ben's personal magnetism drew everybody towards him. My own decision not to allow myself to approach too close too often is one which I do not regret. I must have appeared at most of the Aldeburgh Festivals since the early sixties except for the odd year when Glyndebourne performances made it impossible to make the journey to Suffolk. Ben would get a bit huffy about Glyndebourne interfering with his projects but I would grin to myself and think, 'It's a jolly good thing not to be always available at the Master's call!' He knew perfectly well that I considered Aldeburgh home and he knew also of the huge musical debt I owed both to him and to Peter. So did many musicians. One couldn't really do anything *for* him, though, except try to perform at one's very best, of course. But there was no way of returning a fraction of what he poured out to us and to his profession.

Now that he is gone, I feel very differently. The one thing he would ask is continued loyalty in every sense, to the place and to the School which is his superbly fitting memorial. That, at least, I can give; it is especially important that the musicians who fell under his spell and were polished by his methods of working should pass on as much as possible to the young people involved in the Snape project. It is very greatly Ben's doing that English musicians have become a truly important international force in the years since 1945. If it is possible to sum up the reasons for this tremendous flowering of talent it might be in the word 'Excellence'.

It is quality which divides the professional from the amateur, a dedicated, single-minded search for the best – in oneself – allied to the best in others. In work with Ben everyone was concerned with this search because it was his search too.

I have always believed that the creative person inhabits a world unknown to others. The gulf which exists between his world and that of the re-creative artist is wide indeed. Even at their most sublime, performers are still only able to go as far as the entrance and look from afar towards the land where the composer is perfectly at home. The suffering such a homeland exacts from an individual as the price he must pay for the original ideas he brings back to us is unimaginable. And yet, while there is no doubt that the composer wants no other country, it must be frightening and lonely there. Contact is far more easily made on the performing level and many people consider it to be as important as the creative one because performers bring a work to life. I cannot agree; even if a composition is never heard, the process of seizing an inspired idea, and shaping it into concrete form, makes the composer what he is. A woman is not less a mother because her child dies at birth; she has undergone the psychological and physical processes which make her so; the same with the creative genius, whether his music is heard or not, he has gone through the agony, and there it lies, the material for others to use.

I often used to wish I could communicate with Ben on his own level, the level of his creative work; an utterly futile wish. Yet when he was conducting and one gave him, heart and soul, of one's best in performance, the look in his eyes, the expression of gratitude on his face, made such moments memorable and the best sort of communication one could possibly wish for.

The last rehearsal I did with Ben was on *Phaedra* during the summer of 1976; this is the piece he wrote for me, a dramatic cantata. Dramatic indeed, full of passion and nobility. Phaedra – the words of the Robert Lowell translation which Ben used make her a woman who has loved, betrayed, suffered remorse – attempts to put right the terrible wrong she has done, and nobly dies; a character to glory in. Her music is towering, full of contrast, and the bars in which she announces the progress of the poison surging through her veins are among the most sublime of all Ben's music. I now have copies of the printed score but the much-thumbed, tatty, yellow-paper-bound, awkward-sized manuscript I had at first is more precious to me. I always revise from it. I began to memorize the score during my annual tour of the USA in January 1976, in a train going from New York to Washington. The first rehearsal was in the spring of that year and when Steuart Bedford and I met Ben in the library at the Red House the music was tucked safely away in my head; Ben was pleased I knew it so well at that early stage.

We worked for two hours that day. Steuart and I had run through the piece on our own the day before and he had started to play the first recitative section rather fast for me. It is marked 'agitated crotchets' and I could not manage the words 'My lost and dazzled eyes' clearly enough. I said to Steuart, 'I'm sure Ben will want me to sing the phrase at a speed which makes the words possible' and sure enough, the following day, Ben did comment on this very point. He would always see at once how to solve a difficulty according to the individual need. He also mentioned that the word 'Aphrodite' a little further on should be sung marcato, a marking which is not in the printed vocal score. I asked him if I could start the final phrase 'My eyes at last give up their light', on C, instead of E as he had written it, because it gives the voice a moment to relax before that extremely taxing end; this he immediately agreed to.

On the day of the first performance, Ben, who had been at the previous day's rehearsal, appeared at the final run-through. He saw I was without the score and said, 'You're a brave girl to do the first performance from memory.' I was suddenly terror-stricken and thought, 'My God! perhaps I'm not as brave as I think I am!' and then that night I thought of the five months of study and decided to trust my memory. Responsibility for the work of any composer is a heavy burden, but the premiere of a piece with the creator sitting in his box twenty feet away is a terrifying one. I opened my mouth and out rolled the words 'In May, in brilliant Athens', beautified by the perfect acoustic at the Maltings. The performance went very well and everyone was stunned by the power and passion of Ben's writing at a time when he was so frail physically.

The following year, we repeated the performance and this time Ben was not in his box. Somehow the first summer without him was not a sad one. The air, the fields, the buildings, were all filled with his joyous spirit, free of the frail body at last.

A composer belongs to the whole world; but a composer has to live at a specific time in a certain place and is a human being like the rest of us; so Ben is also the special property of his country, and of the people who knew him. As a man, a musician, and a friend he belongs particularly to those of us who were lucky enough to know him, to work with him, and to love him.

John Piper

Designing for Britten

I first met Benjamin Britten at a concert at the old Queen's Hall in 1932, when he was nineteen and I was twenty-nine. A bit later, we met often at a kind of advisory committee of the Group Theatre along with, among others, Wystan Auden, Christopher Isherwood, Robert Medley, the painter, and designer of most of the Group productions, and Rupert Doone, chief producer and father figure of the Group. He had been an admired dancer in the Diaghilev company and this as well as his impressive personality gave him lustre. He produced *The Ascent of F.6*, *The Dog Beneath the Skin*, MacNeice's translation of the *Agamemnon* of Aeschylus, and other plays, most of them designed by Medley, some of them with music by Britten. In 1938 came *Trial of a Judge*, by Stephen Spender (Unity Theatre) which I designed and painted.

A clearly announced, and accepted, aim of the Group was the achievement of a stage unity stemming from a close collaboration of the author (preferably a poet), the designer (usually a painter), the composer (if any) and the producer and cast, regardless as far as possible of individual prestige and personality. The unity wasn't always achieved, sometimes it wasn't even evident, let alone obvious, but it was an ideal; and clearly the origin of the ideal was the Diaghilev ballet. I believe it remained a stage-ideal for Britten all his life, and is traceable in all his works involving collaborators. I know that at that time, in our youthful bumptiousness, we believed that only dedicated artists working together could revitalize the stage.

In the mid-twenties, long before the war, I had been to all the Diaghilev ballets I could get to while working in my father's law office, and the excitement – the tinge of exultation – in the dancing married to modern music and modern art worked in my blood and bones as it did for many of my generation, not to mention those older and younger.

After *Trial of a Judge*, and after Britten's departure to America in 1939, he and I hardly communicated until his return and the triumphant Sadler's Wells production of *Peter Grimes*, produced by Tony Guthrie and designed by Kenneth Green. During the war, a year or so before Britten's return to England, I had designed a Sadler's Wells ballet (*The Quest*: choreography by Frederick Ashton, music by William Walton) and, with the Diaghilev bug still biting, I was passionate to do more work for the stage. *Oedipus Rex* for Laurence Olivier and the Old Vic followed in 1946. So that I was specially pleased when I was invited by Britten to design *The Rape of Lucretia* which was to re-open Glyndebourne after the war. Ronald Duncan was the librettist, Eric Crozier the producer. There is quite a loud echo of the former, Diaghilev-influenced, Group Theatre days in the last words of Britten's foreword to *The Rape of Lucretia* symposium (Bodley Head, 1948). 'The composer and poet should at all stages be working in the closest contact from the most preliminary stages right up to the first night.' He very soon came to realize (if he hadn't already) that this close contact also applied to the composer and his producer and designer. And as far as I am concerned, in the Britten operas that I designed, from *The Rape of Lucretia* onwards, this passionate insistence of his on the unity of the parts – that is, of all collaborating participants – only increased, through the 27 years that followed to *Death in Venice*. He came more and more to demand (always in the gentlest possible way) advance information. If you said 'I've done these sketches,' he might say: 'That's wonderful, that's marvellous, that's just how I hoped it would look.' But then, having done that, he would go much further and say: 'What's going to happen at the end of Act 1, when that turns round, you know, or this goes off the scene, what are we going to get next, because I can't compose the music until I know exactly what's going to happen.' Sometimes the music anticipated all production and design points and that could cause discussion. In *The Turn of the Screw*, for instance, at the first arrival of the Governess at Bly, he had already sketched 'arrival' music, before points of production had been decided. He said: 'Look, when she arrives, obviously she didn't come by train, she came by coach or something, a wheeled vehicle you see, at any rate to the outer gate at Bly. We must have a coach.' And I began to protest. I said: 'But the scenery is not like that, you don't have a coach in this kind of scenery.' We had all decided already on the actual *kind* of scenery wanted. Basil Coleman backed me up. A coach would be realistic in manner, foreign to everything else, foreign to the evocative and atmospheric sense of the scenery. Britten said: 'Well, I'm terribly sorry, I see a coach there; there must be a coach.' In the end there was no coach: the coach music (or coach-horse music) is so vivid and telling that a coach simply is not necessary, and he was finally convinced of this. It was not enjoyable at the time, but looking back on this contretemps I find it both pleasing and enlightening, and it was only one of frequent occasions when this kind of thing happened. He was forcing us to persuade him that this *was* so – that the music *worked* without this scenic help, that it came to life unillustrated. His ideas were precise and sound and positive in the way he saw them. They were often extremely practical too, on points such as the seating of a stage band for combined visual effect and audibility, or on the exact placing of a piece of scenery with acoustics in mind.

In a detailed historical work such as *Billy Budd* there had to be a degree of naturalism neither necessary nor desirable in the other Britten operas I worked on. The ship must be a positive ship of the right date and character, there must be authentic details in rigging, costumes and so on – evocation and atmosphere were largely created by lighting, black velvet and gauze hangings. This ship with its main deck scenes, under-deck and captain's cabin involved very careful modelling, and I think these models were probably quite helpful to Britten and to the producer, Basil Coleman (who helped greatly in working out the details of them), in providing a definite recognizable acting area. I remember only very few worries about the scenery of *Billy Budd*. It was complicated to build, but it was concrete in its statements and at any rate positive in its effects. Very unlike *Death in Venice*, 22 years later. I grumbled a great deal to myself (and sometimes aloud) in the intervening years, about the time-taking problems of designing for Britten operas. In fact, each one from *Albert Herring* (to mention those I worked on, but am not otherwise speaking of here) through *Gloriana* (with those myriad costumes about which Basil Coleman was untiringly helpful) to the stage version of *Owen Wingrave* – was a great, and new, experience.

The whole scenic gamut between stating facts and creating atmosphere was embodied in the range of works, and I tried in each case to relate the designs to my own immediate practice and experience as a painter, as well as to fulfil the composer's and producer's demands – in all this being a humble follower of my elders and betters: Picasso, Braque, Matisse, Léger and several other Diaghilev designers I had for long revered. The old principles (or, anyway, theories) of the pre-war Group Theatre – a united front by all participants from first note on paper to first night – still operated.

The three Britten operas I learned most from while working on them were *The Turn of the Screw*, *A Midsummer Night's Dream* and *Death in Venice*. The first and last of these were certainly experienced from first note to first night, as my wife Myfanwy wrote the librettos for them, and Britten was always in touch, if often only on the telephone about points on the words, or about what something might look like. About *A Midsummer Night's Dream* I had an idea. I thought that in most productions I had seen of the play the scenery was preponderantly green, though it was Midsummer *night*. I had been looking at a lot of Chinese and Japanese brush and wash drawings while hearing Britten's music in early stages on the piano, all of which seemed to me to suggest (as do summer nights) shades of diluted Chinese ink, with sometimes additions of Chinese white, making tones of silver grey. I still find that these, for me, marry reasonably well with this particular music.

Death in Venice is a supremely evocative opera. It must embrace the Venice of all time as well as Thomas Mann's Venice and our own Venice of the 1970s. Britten adored Venice. So do I. I had worked there with Britten in 1953 for three weeks during rehearsals of *The Turn of the Screw*, and while the scenery was being set up and costumes completed before the opening night at the Fenice opera house. In 1971 we all explored it together again, including the Lido, which I feared, because it had to be represented in some not too abstract or symbolic fashion in several scenes. There in late afternoon were the dreary deserted beach huts that I remembered, the litter hardly ever reached by high tide, and Aschenbach's colourless hotel. I had forgotten the gorgeous sweep of sand, melting when the tide was low to a wide slice of the Adriatic. As for Venice itself, I did dozens of small drawings on walks and gondola trips, not frameable drawings but notes of mouldings, of doors and windows, well heads in squares, bases of columns, reflections in water, bits of creeper hanging over fragments of wall which, when helped by Colin Graham's ingenious and quickly-changing production, might add up to a cumulative suggestion of the evasive city.

A conversation with Donald Mitchell prompted these notes. I am grateful to him for his encouragement and for his engaging questions which I have tried to answer here.

Myfanwy Piper

Writing for Britten

The three librettos that I wrote for Benjamin Britten were all based on highly developed literary works: works that depend on the poetic build-up of atmosphere and of mental apprehensions, on accumulated moments of word-filled suspense, on evocations of the authors' belief in the active magic of places to give force to the stories that they tell. But in the work of adaptation I discovered that, though the difficulties presented by each one were many and different, none was due to the richness of the original. The richness was, rather, a help.

There was a particular fitness for Britten in the idea of making *The Turn of the Screw* into an opera, not only because of the subject, corruption and innocence and their mutual effect, but because of Henry James's stylistic means. He tells the story with an elaborate fabric of words against which the action and the conversations that take the action further stand out to make the dramatic shape. But nothing that happens is significant without the accompanying density of offered feelings and facts, echoes and memories. Britten used the voice as an instrument that detaches itself from the orchestra to tell the story, but depends for its full dramatic, as well as musical, effect on its relation to the whole fabric of sound and of echoes and memories of sound. He builds up the weight of musical experience as James builds up the weight of evidence and fantasy. It was the overwhelming importance of the words between the actions that made everyone think how difficult, even impossible, it would be to turn the story into an opera. But it was precisely this that made it so apt for Britten. That it is fatal to go for the bones without the wordy tissue was demonstrated by the stage play *The Innocents* (which I saw after I had begun the libretto) in which, with great ingenuity, the story was shaped and tidied into a semblance of what the three unities demand. The intention, no doubt, was to concentrate the diffuseness and so increase, for the stage, the tension and horror. But, in spite of extraordinary performances by Flora Robson and the two children, in losing the sense of time passing, the shifting of places, the gaps in the action, the long months when nothing and everything happened, by laying it on thick *and* fast, it lost the ambience and the drama as well.

Britten had a passionate respect and love for words. Every word is set to be heard for its part in the unfolding of the story and for its quality as part of the human instrument. Speech articulated in sorrow or joy, in pain or ordinary conversational exchange is as much part of the music of the voice as the note itself: the word and the note is one thing, not two. Therefore, to use a word that is not true to the demands of the moment, or to distort language by using a wrong emphasis or an unnatural inversion is like striking a false note, it sticks out and offends. What is silly will sound sillier, what is commonplace more commonplace, what is awkward impossibly awkward. Nothing can be slurred over in a fine flourish of sound, nothing shrugged off as operatic licence. All this I learnt from going to rehearsals and performances of all Britten's operas from 1946 (*The Rape of Lucretia*) onwards, long before there was any question of becoming a librettist myself.

When, in 1953, I began to work on *The Turn of the Screw* I found that although I had learnt what kind of language sounded natural and inevitable, I did not always know how to achieve it. I also did not realize how easy it is to fall into the literary trap. When I showed the first tentative words of dialogue to Britten he said, 'Don't colour them, the music will do that.' This did not mean that they were to be colourless, or flat, but that they were not to be high-flown, over-descriptive, self-indulgent or imprecise. Except for the places where the action called for children's songs or moments of lyrical expansion the words had to illumine, by exactness and simplicity, and each one had to bear repetition when Britten needed it.

Many people also doubted the adaptability of *The Turn of the Screw* because of its supposed vagueness. In fact it is vague only in one thing: in what, if anything, actually happened between the children and the haunting pair. This vagueness does not affect the drama in any way, it only affects what people think of it. In every other particular Henry James is precise. He is precise about the Guardian, who does not appear; about Quint and Miss Jessel, what they looked like, what their characters in life were like; about the Governess, her inexperience, her innocence, her impressionable nature and her possessiveness; about Mrs Grose, her ignorant good nature and changeable credulity. He is precise about the number of times the Governess saw, or thought she saw the Ghosts, and the places where they were seen. He is precise about her state of mind and the changes that took place in her attitude. He is precise about every change of tempo and about every event that lead to the dénouement. When quite early in our discussions the idea of three acts was abandoned and Britten planned the opera in terms of short scenes linked by orchestral passages, the nature of these scenes, except for the first scene of Act II, was clearly dictated by an analysis of the text; what had to be invented were the details. And even for them there was, more often than not, some suggestion that could serve as a starting point: for example, James's '. . . Flora was playing very hard. We were on the edge of the lake, and, as we had lately begun geography, the latter was the Sea of Azof', gave me the idea of the list of the names of seas, only I made Flora call their lake the Dead Sea to load the recital a little more.

There was a lack, and that a very serious one; there was no suggestion anywhere of what the Ghosts might have said to the children, or to each other. Britten was determined that they should sing – and sing words (no nice anonymous, super-natural humming or groaning). I was so daunted that I tried to forget at once what words and concentrated on the place and time in the opera of their appearances and their kind of dramatic disposition on the stage. It was this being at a loss that made us plan the night scene at the end of Act I when the Ghosts mobilize their forces, and so effectively, combine the series of short confrontations the Governess has in the book. It also provided the only time when all six characters were on the stage together, something musically essential. It was perhaps in the organization of this scene that I became practically aware of how important it was to Britten to be able to visualize a scene while he was composing it. This need became particularly acute during the writing of *Death in Venice* because of the complicated journeys from the Lido to Venice and back and the elaborate walks in the streets. It is one of the reasons why he liked writer, producer and designer to work with him from the very first.

If the Ghosts were my cross, the fact that out of six characters two were children, one of whom, at least, was bound to have a small immature voice and comparatively little musical experience, was Britten's. He therefore asked that Miles should have a short, very simple song, the tune and echoes of which could steer him through the work. Long before the many attempts to find the right words had been written and discarded, and Britten himself had decided to use the Malo rhyme from an old-fashioned Latin grammar that an aunt of mine produced, I conceived the idea that the song, hitherto only sung in Miles's childish voice, should be sung in the mature and tragic accents of the Governess, when she discovers that he is dead.

Thus, at the very beginning, the difficulties themselves helped to set the boundaries of the piece. The first act was the unfolding of the situation. At the end of it the Governess was in possession of all the facts. She had wormed the history of the immediate past out of Mrs Grose; she had seen Miles with Quint and Flora with Miss Jessel; she knew that the children were aware of each other's secret and she knew that they sensed her anxiety; she had made her vow to win them from their familiars – to save them and to possess them. Each scene was planned to take the drama one step further and, at the same time to show some aspect of their daily life; in this way some indication of the passage of time could be given without holding up the action. The evening soliloquy, though interrupted by Quint, was a pattern of other summer evenings; the schoolroom scene, though disquietened by the Malo rhyme, a sample of many schoolroom days. The extraordinary interludes were at once timeless and urgent, both putting off and anticipating each inevitable crisis.

In March 1954 Britten had a rather painful operation and after his return to Aldeburgh he wrote '. . . in spite of all this I started the opera this morning and have quite good progress to report. I have got well into the first scene – I am quite pleased with it. So far there are not many alterations in the words to suggest – nothing that cannot be done by writing. The best plan seems to be for me to go on working and writing the suggestions of changes daily (or telephoning if they are urgent) and when it seems to need your actual presence I will write to you suggesting it and hope you may be able to fit it in.' This was more or less how we went on for all three operas although we got to rely more and more on telephone conversations for *The Turn of the Screw*. For the other two, many years later, it was easier for me to get away, since our children were grown up.

Before Britten started writing he had been getting very excited about the musical plan and at the end of the same letter he wrote, 'Thank you for your suggestions of titles. I do not feel we have arrived yet, although something to do with Bly is hopeful I think. I am not worrying about it until forced to, but I must confess that I have a sneaking horrid feeling that the original H.J. title describes the musical plan of the work *exactly*!!' I'm not sure why we were reluctant at first to call it *The Turn of the Screw* unless it was a certain scrupulousness toward Henry James.

It was not all smooth going and there were bombshells. On 12 April he wrote, 'It has been lovely having Basil [Coleman] here, we have done a lot of work together on the piece. We have had one major discussion which he will talk to you about. It arose out of a sudden fear that the work is going to be much too short. The first three scenes incidentally play only ten minutes. Please do not be shocked at his suggestions and give it a fair chance. When you have thought it over we must meet at once because it may affect some of the scenes a lot.' A postscript elucidated a little, 'I don't want it to sound as if the proposed alteration comes only because the piece might be too short, because it *has* been in my head for some little time. . . . a prologue? . . . the interview or the ghost story party? probably spoken?'

Difficult: I had tried to get all necessary information into the Governess's journey and I was afraid a prologue would be repetitive, unless I rewrote Act I scene i, but it had already been set and time was short. I tried various things. An undated letter said, 'The second version of the prologue has just arrived and my dear, I'm afraid I prefer the first, as the present idea stands I can't do the second version recitative, it needs fuller accompaniment to match the nice lyric quality.' It was a rather gay scene from Henry James's introductory ghost story party – but he was right as he almost always was. For literary as well as musical reasons it wouldn't have done, it had quite a different atmosphere from the rest, all right in James's story but wrong for the tightness of the recreated work. 'I feel the ideal is a *slightly* shorter version of the 1st. I can then start with a few loud chords and set it naturally as recitative.'

Later there was another insertion. We had decided to leave out the whole of the episode of the Governess's letter to the Guardian in Act II. It suddenly seemed absolutely necessary – an instance of Henry James's sure story telling; each event is essential. The beginning of the churchyard scene took a long time to get right. 'I'm sorry about the churchyard scene worry. I feel that one must for dramatic and musical reasons have a set piece for the kids at the beginning of it. What else can it be. I don't see how a gentle make-believe of a choir procession (unless done grotesquely) could offend anyone; and I don't see why the words should offend more than the music – most people would anyhow recognise the tune first especially if they start it off stage as I'd like.' I don't remember the tune or who thought it would be offensive. But I wasn't happy and could think of no way to parody a hymn until at last it was solved by a clergyman friend who said, 'It must obviously be a "Benedicite".'

The Turn of the Screw builds up a sense of evil without ever stating what that evil is. Without what James in a preface to the story calls 'the limited deplorable presentable instance'. Neither Britten nor I ever intended to interpret the work, only to re-create it for a different medium. 'There is', James goes on to say 'for such a case no eligible absolute of the wrong; it remains relative to fifty other elements, a matter of appreciation, speculation, imagination – these things more-over, quite exactly in the mind of the spectator's, the critic's, the reader's experience.' He seems to have been surprised at the success of his ingenuity in suggestion and complains that he has been 'assailed with the charge of all indecently expatiating. There is not only from beginning to the end of the matter not an inch of expatiating, but my values are positively all blanks. . . .'

But in creating this sense of evil he was greatly helped by the silence of Quint and Miss Jessel. This help we did not have. The Ghosts remained (and remain) my greatest worry. There is a hint in James that the evil that was in Quint arose in the first place out of his passion for power. It has been said that what he actually says to Miles in the opera is laughably lacking in evil. But I felt that the problem was not so much to show him as evil as to suggest what there could be about him that attracted so inexperienced and innocent a child. We had agreed that since the work was to be written in prose, except for the children's rhymes, here was the place for verse, so as to separate the dead, even more, from the living. One of the more obvious ways for evil to present itself to the innocent is in some form of siren song. What Quint sings is an expression of the kind of mystery that could surround a half-known grown-up in the thoughts of a romantic and isolated boy. I searched about for possibilities in books and dreams and remembered too being driven as a child into a state of high excitement and frustration by the sounds of adult life after I had gone to bed. Hence the lines:

> I am the secret life that stirs
> When the candle is out.

The words are intended as a way in which a clever and unscrupulous nature might play upon those imaginings and exploit them. It was even harder going with Miss Jessel as the only thing James tells us about her is, that, though attractive to Quint (and part of that attraction was that she was a lady), she was not attractive enough to hold his attention. And so, rather lamely, I invented the bitterness and the anti-male note.

Britten said that he must have a confrontation between Quint and Miss Jessel at the beginning of Act II and that I should look at Verlaine's *Colloque Sentimental*, in which two lovers taunt each other with their past. Except for the idea, it was not much help, and I could only emphasise their unhappy self-absorption.

What is absorbing and fascinating about *The Turn of the Screw* is not the sin that lies beneath the fine mist of evil, nor yet the Governess's unfulfilled love, which it was at one time the Freudian fashion to make responsible for the whole affair, but the vulnerability of innocence at all ages. The children's inquiring innocence is assailed from outside, the young woman's is attacked from within by her own fears and imagination and from without by the evidence of her bemused senses, which she constantly mistrusts.

When I discovered the line in W. B. Yeats's poem *The Second Coming* that I used in the Ghosts' colloquy:

> The ceremony of innocence is drowned.

it seemed to epitomize the story; and Britten gave it the theme of the whole work.

It was nearly fifteen years before we worked together again, on *Owen Wingrave*, an opera for television commissioned by the BBC.

Henry James saw 'a tall quiet studious young man' sitting on a seat near him in Kensington Gardens, 'presently he settled to a book with immediate gravity'. From this brief vision came the story of Owen Wingrave, the last of the Wingraves of Paramore, the last of generations of upright English men and women obsessed with the glory of war. The peaceful young man in the twopenny chair took on the battle of all conscientious objectors against the pressures of righteous aggression. When Coyle, Owen Wingrave's crammer for his entry to Sandhurst, went to Paramore (before the story opens) it was 'an occasion singularly tinged for him with the sense of bereavement and mourning and memory, of names never mentioned, of the far away plaint of widows and the echoes of battles and bad news. . . . Mr Coyle was made to shudder a little at the profession of which he helped to open the doors to harmless young men. Miss Wingrave might have made such a bad conscience worse – so cold and clear a good one looked at him out of her hard fine eyes and trumpeted in her sonorous voice.' Sir Phillip Wingrave, Owen's grandfather, was 'a relic rather than a celebrity. . . . The eyes of the imagination could glance back at his crowded Eastern past – back at episodes in which his scrupulous terms would only have made him more terrible.' Henry James himself asks whether it could all have sprung from the sight of his neighbour in the Park and certainly one feels that he must, in his extensive country house visits, have seen an 'impoverished Jacobean house, shabby and remarkably creepy', have observed ranks of rather bad portraits of military gentlemen and their wives, have encountered the narrow outlook of those dedicated to the military life. He may perhaps not have registered them at the time, but when he needed them they surfaced to be manipulated by him for the sake of his story.

One knows that there are people like these, de-humanized by their own strict and immovable code, but because James manipulates them they are in danger of becoming caricatures and this was one of the difficulties of turning the story into an opera. These difficulties were, perhaps, increased by the fact that it was commissioned as a television opera. People who work in a comparatively new medium (and this was ten years ago) are always very much obsessed by what can be done with it; they create a closed circle of experts, and they in turn create a mystique. At the same time, because the audience is unknown, invisible and very varied, there is a tendency to overdo things, to underline them, so that the subtleties of which the medium is capable can easily be thrown away in the interest of making something, already perfectly clear, obvious. There is a mixture of inventiveness and crudity in the approach. *Owen Wingrave* is the story of a house and family haunted by the past, and also by ghosts and their legend. These latter are shown, when they appear in the opera, in black and white, while the rest is in colour; it is very effective, and does away with the need for skeletons, transparencies or sheets. But one day we caught a man busily spraying cobwebs through an ingenious machine onto every surface on the set. That was out of character with our piece as well as James's story. Miss Wingrave's shabbiness would certainly have shone. But to the simple relationship (which must never be forgotten) between television and audience, Ghosts mean Cobwebs. This was an exaggerated and probably accidental happening, but it illustrates a finer point.

When we were planning the work our first discussions dwelt upon the visual, rather than verbal presentation of dramatic points. Scenes were conceived with the encouragement and technical knowledge of everyone concerned to make the full use of the resources of the medium. Several of these were very successful; the use of black and white for the Ghosts and the legend, already referred to; the dinner party where, when the general conversation stops, the head of each person is isolated in turn, while we hear what they are thinking as they battle with the unmanageable situation; the separate and combined attacks of the family, in various parts of the house, over a period of several days upon Owen; the part played by the house itself (in spite of its unsatisfactory appearance), soaked in the inviolable tradition of the family; the sequences of banners and portraits. When it came to the stage performance all these things, although they were extremely difficult to get right, did, in fact come off in spite of having been thought up specifically for television. They were, however, all comparatively simple effects. When we thought up something much more elaborate, it was not effective either on the screen or on the stage. This was the double scene in which Owen reads in the park and Coyle goes to tell Miss Wingrave in her London lodgings of his momentous decision. I had wanted both parties to catch a glimpse of the horse-guards in their red uniforms – Miss Wingrave out of her window, Owen in the park; for them both to be exhilarated by the sight; but for Owen, after being briefly seduced by its gaiety, to transform it in his imagination into a chaos of falling cavalrymen and horses on a battlefield. I think now that it was a typical amateur's idea, over-elaborate and impractical; but we had endless talks about it and were assured that it would be both possible and effective. I have no doubt that it could be done for a full-scale film where expense was no object, or even for a television piece in which built sets and outdoor locations could both be used. For an opera that is impossible. Unfortunately the difficulties were not faced up to until it was far too late and we spent fruitless hours, looking at film sequences of battlefields all the wrong scale, in the cinema at Aldeburgh. In the stage performance I would have been content to leave out the horse-guards altogether, avoid the unsatisfactory projection and rely alone on the music to suggest the general idea. But this was something that Britten could not bring himself to do – if he had written for horses there must be horses or a suggestion of horses.

When we turned our attention to the libretto, we went on much as before, analysing the text, getting to know the characters through James's descriptions so that even when he had no dialogue for a particular scene we knew enough about them to invent it.

On 14 May 1969 Britten wrote, 'I have been working a bit on the opera from a more musical point of view, and one thing does strike me. I think we need a sort of musical flowering bit for Coyle and Mrs C. in the first scenes and what has occurred to me could be a little number about *youth* for Coyle . . . (instead of "the boy is mad"). Something about rashness, madness, pomposity etc. of youth – a more general piece than we have now. And for Mrs Coyle (this is very tentative perhaps somewhere in Scene iii possibly in her retort to C. about favourites) . . . a rather lyrical bit about the attractiveness, excitement of youth.' Coyle's piece: 'I thought I knew them all, the foibles of the young', and Mrs Coyle's: 'So many boys come here, and I rejoice in all', came quite easily from James's convincing characterizations.

One of the characters who was unsatisfactory and over whom I had a great deal of argument was Kate. Kate was treated by James in the same slightly larger than life way as the rest of the household at Paramore: bigoted, unimaginative and unsympathetic, black against Owen's white, although he did allow her a certain brusque independence and strangeness, as well as an unconventional beauty. Britten took Mrs Coyle's view of her that she was an impossible and arrogant girl, not worthy of the thoughtful Owen. I felt that in spite of her insufferable behaviour she was as much a victim of her background as Owen, but lacked his opportunities to think again; that she must have had another side or he wouldn't have been attracted by her (though I don't believe he was much interested in anything except himself at the time of the tale). I felt that we needed a gentler, if not a sentimental passage between them to prepare us for her breakdown at the end: hence the lines beginning, 'I came to look for a jewel from my brooch'. Britten was convinced enough to give these few lines a marvellously lyrical tenderness. But Janet Baker, who played Kate, could never get over her dislike of the unfortunate girl.

As always Britten faced me with some stunners. I had begun my text straight in with the dialogue between Coyle and Owen, much of it only slightly adapted from James. But he saw at once that something was needed to precipitate the outburst and so wanted to begin with a lesson. 'I think it is important to establish the crammer's atmosphere before we break it up, and besides, I've thought of a nice way of doing it musically!'

Although the lesson was very short I had to do a great deal of reading in Memoirs and even in Clausewitz's *Art of War* to find the kind of thing I might use. But I was grateful for it because I became so immersed in Napoleon's battles and in tales of the Indian Mutiny that it became natural to me to use military metaphors and this led, I hope, to a certain poetic verisimilitude in the characters' use of language.

Henry James saw the dramatic possibilities of his story and turned it, himself, into a one act play, *The Saloon*. It was at first rejected, by the Stage Society, on the advice of Bernard Shaw, with whom Henry James had a heated correspondence. Shaw objected to Owen's death, saying that such noble intentions should have been rewarded with success. But James would have none of such optimism: it would have been aesthetically wrong, but also wrong in the psychology of such a family. Shaw retorted that it was as easy for an author to give victory to one side as to another.

Owen Wingrave was very near Britten's heart. He had thought of it as a subject for years and had spoken of it before he wrote the *War Requiem* (1961). When at last he wrote it it came as a very personal coda to follow up the Requiem. His own beliefs had been in conflict with the patriotism of all proper Englishmen in 1939, just as Owen's had been with his family. And so Owen's hymn to peace in Act II was deeply important. We talked a lot about it. However the words have come out, the music is an extraordinary affirmation of belief. It is, in a sense, the climax and the lesson of the piece – that Owen dies in the end does not, in spite of Shaw, invalidate the message.

Before the final shots of *Owen Wingrave* were taken at The Maltings Britten had begun to think about *Death in Venice* seriously (it had been in his mind for years) and one November day, just as I began to think that once again the intense months of working with Britten had come to an end, he asked me if I would consider working with him on a new opera. My first thought when I heard its subject was that it was impossible; the second that if Britten said so, it could be done.

In a letter to Wolfgang Born, an artist who had produced 'Graphic fantasies' for his novella *Death in Venice*, Thomas Mann wrote: 'For the writer it is always a flattering and moving experience to have a product of his mind taken up, reproduced, celebrated, glorified by an art that appeals more directly to the senses – graphic art or the theatre say.' It is interesting that his intellectual generosity should have accepted the possibility of a different dimension to his work, and especially to this one, for which he felt such a deep moral and artistic responsibility. '. . . it would be ungrateful if I were to complain', he continued, 'about the degree of sympathetic interest that my story has aroused and continues to arouse in the German public. And yet I have frequently been bothered by an element of sensationalism which attached to this interest and which was connected with the pathological subject matter. . . . Pathology can enter the realm of literary art only if it is used as a means for intellectual, poetic, symbolical ends.'[1] In reorganizing Mann's story for music and the stage it was even more important to keep a just balance between the passionate-erotic and the poetic-symbolic. As we worked from the first analysis to the last words and notes it became clear that what we were doing, what indeed we had to do to make this 'celebration' work at all, was to amalgamate the dual hero Aschenbach-Mann: Aschenbach, the imagined casualty of genius, with Mann, the acutely self-conscious young writer. Gustav von Aschenbach had to be a real figure, a distinguished middle-aged writer to whom the events of the story actually happened, but in portraying him Mann's self-knowledge and those personal fears of isolation in the creative life that haunt his early letters and works were crucial. In reply to criticism from a friend he wrote, 'I am an ascetic as far as my conscience directs me towards achievement. . . . I distrust pleasure, I distrust happiness which I regard as unproductive . . . one cannot serve both masters, pleasure and art. . . . You say that one of these days I will receive more cool respect than heartfelt affection. Dear friend that is simply not true.'[2] But he was afraid it might be. In the autobiographical short story *Tonio Kröger*, Tonio-Mann cries, 'I tell you I am sick to death of having to represent what is human without having myself a share in it.' Behind all this is the passionate interest of the romantic German philosophers (which Mann inherited) in the nature of genius. The dilemma of Tonio Kröger's life and also of Aschenbach's aptly illustrates Nietzsche's words: 'The perfect artist is forever shut off from reality. But on the other hand it is sometimes understandable that the artist should tire to the point of desperation of the eternal non-reality and falseness of his inner existence and try to venture into the most forbidden territory, the real, try in fact to exist in earnest.'

It took a little over two and a half years from our first conversation to the first night at Snape and although we were not working on it all the time during those months, I don't think it was ever out of our thoughts, nor did we cease to discuss it. The intention had been to produce the work in eighteen months and so we had to make our first analysis without very much preliminary research. This, I now think, was an advantage since we were forced to use the text to solve its own problems; to make ourselves so familiar with the symbolism and the reality, the realism and fantasy, with all their cross-references and echoes that even if we had not Mann's rich prolegomena, his *kind* of dramatic thinking became natural to us in the course of composition. So that when, for instance, we decided to make the Hotel Manager into one of the Death-Hermes characters, although he had little or nothing to say in the story, it was easy to provide him with the kind of allusive remark, both obsequious and knowing, that would once more underline the strangeness and the inevitability of Aschenbach's adventure. He does not manipulate, he merely takes verbal advantage, and presses home, like the others, his edgy insinuations.

The discoveries that we made were afterwards corroborated, and often (necessarily) elucidated by further reading in Mann's own works and in books about him and his background, but that first exploration of his dense and disturbing text was the basis of all that followed.

In Mann's story the order of events is essential: everything depends upon what went before, from the first walk in Munich to the last sighing breath upon the sands of the Lido. Tempting as it was to simplify for the sake of theatrical neatness we decided to keep this order with very few omissions or re-arrangement. We did omit the false start of his holiday (on the Adriatic coast) because although it underlines the interplay of chance and fate it adds nothing essential and its inclusion would not have justified the delay in the action. The most difficult problem in planning was that set by Tadzio and his family. Aschenbach has no communication with his own kind and although we know everything that he thought about Tadzio we know nothing of Tadzio's thoughts about him. The implication is that, beyond a certain pleased self-consciousness at being the object of so much attention, he thought very little. The important thing from our point of view was that, unlike the Ghosts in *The Turn of the Screw*, what he thought or said would have been of no interest to us. Here what needed to be underlined was not communication, but the lack, indeed the impossibility, of it. The decision to formalize this separateness into dance was neither an arbitrary, nor yet entirely an aesthetic one. It arose out of the nature of theatrical performance. Only dancers find it natural to be on the stage for any length of time in silence and only dancers can express the trivialities and pleasures of human behaviour without speech. By extending the number of dancers to include the children of the hotel guests and the beach attendants we were able to organize the childrens' games in the two beach scenes into ballets and so externalise Aschenbach's habit of poeticizing the events in which he could not partake.

When Aschenbach walked out into the street in Munich on that spring evening, frustrated and ill at ease, he had already set in train the events that were to end in tragedy. He soon encountered the first of the characters who play a double role: the realistic one that their names imply – the Traveller, the Young Old Man (or Elderly Fop), the Old Gondolier, the Leader of the Strolling Players – and a symbolic one. They are the figures who, albeit by their ordinary actions, lead him on his journey towards his fate. Nowhere does Mann suggest that they have supernatural powers, or that they are one and the same person, but he links them by endowing each with the snub nose and grin of Death and the broad-brimmed hat and staff of Hermes, the conductor of the dead across the Styx. The first description of the Traveller, too, seemed to me to have a specific reference to the posture given to representations of Death in medieval German woodcuts as well as the traditional pose of Hermes. 'In his right hand he held an iron-shod stick, and braced himself against its crook, with his legs crossed.' To make the symbolic point dramatically it made sense to think of these four characters, who never appear together, being sung by one person. And there seemed very good dramatic reasons why the list should be extended to include the Hotel Manager and the Barber who, by their ordinary actions, also were instrumental in his death. One other voice was eventually added, that of Dionysus, the stranger God. If these seven characters were to be sung by one singer it would make it possible to have a performer capable of creating an impressive role that contrasted and supported the long and taxing one of Aschenbach, who, it seemed would scarcely ever be off the stage. It would also occasionally add to the mystery of verbal and musical echoes that of gesture and of glance.

One of the first difficulties in making a libretto from *Death in Venice* was how to reconcile the comparative austerity of language required by the composer with the extreme wordiness of the text. And all those words of Thomas Mann at first seemed necessary for our full understanding. We need them to know what kind of a person Aschenbach was (only to such a person could the events of the story have happened). The action which is so often only intellectual re-action has to be described in words. Many of the words have several meanings – the obvious meaning within the terms of the action, and a symbolic one in terms of the loaded story and a literary, evocative one.

Some people have wondered why we did not use the device of a narrator who could have told us more about Aschenbach and at the same time have reduced the burden of the part? But Mann is God, the all-knowing of the novella and he is also Aschenbach, and therefore there is nothing that he knows that Aschenbach does not know too. The division is a matter of style and approach; of irony, self-parody, exhortation on the one hand and on the other the awkward taciturnity of a man unaccustomed to ordinary intercourse alternating with the spontaneous flow of poetical musing. The essence of the method and also of the tragedy is that we should be aware of Aschenbach's self-knowledge and also aware, as he is, that he will not profit by it.

There were three kinds of language used. The short rapid early recitative of the exchanges between Aschenbach and another or others; a lengthened measured line, which sometimes becomes verse; and the straight rather literary prose of the ironic comment. This last posed a great problem for Britten. From several points of view he would have liked to have these passages spoken. It would have underlined the dryness and the isolation of the incorrigible winter; it would have provided a rest from singing for Aschenbach and it would have done what we had in mind to do at the outset, create a music-drama in which speech, music and dance all had an integral place. Further it would have made it easier to get across the facts of Aschenbach's past and the working of his mind to an audience who might not be familiar with the book. But it didn't work. The change of projection from singing to speaking voice, its relation to the piano accompaniment, the licence to proliferate words because the singer did not have to be considered, the drop in dramatic tone all made Britten change his mind. In the end the Aschenbach of the notebook, the detached comment, came to play a very positive dramatic role. As Aschenbach, the protagonist, became less detached and more fatally involved in events the comments became fewer and less frequent – like Apollo's, 'I go, I go now', in the dream, the voice of his literary sanity fades away.

Not only this but no words or action are used in isolation; they all have back- and cross-references. Of course this is the essence of the musical score – but that needs direction and underlining from the script. So, again unlike *The Turn of the Screw* where I often had to search in the text for some hint that could be expanded, here I had to look for what could be left out. I had to concentrate upon what was essential in a given situation – and if more seemed essential than I could use in one place it had to be saved for another and that place be made appropriate to receive it. For the prose passage at the end of the first scene for example, I had originally used much more of Mann's first chapter in the attempt to plant the hero. But it was turgid and held up the action and so these bits of information about his moral and literary attitudes to life and living were inserted later, only to come back at the very end, just before the last Phaedrus song.

If my problem with the prose comments was selection, the other kinds of language were difficult in a different way. In *Death in Venice* there is a great deal of description, mingled with philosophic musing – it cannot be ignored since it is part of Aschenbach's relation to life as well as to events. Some passages were comparatively easy when the music and the words can create a mood which is a lyrical acceptance of the event which they follow: example, the passage that begins, 'Mysterious gondola. . . .' It is a matter of selection (once again), and balance. But what about Aschenbach's reaction to the beauties of Venice and his pleasure at being there again? 'City of Lion and Saint' is all very well in Mann's literary prose but I needed something much more immediate. Aschenbach-Mann had a positive relationship with Venice. When he first sets eyes on it after his journey all his mixed feelings as well as his love of the place need expression. Eventually I found what I wanted in a letter of 1932 from Mann to his children Erika and Klaus who were then staying at the Hotel des Bains on the Lido. 'In spirit I am with you, leading that magical life between the warm sea in the morning and the ambiguous city in the afternoon. Ambiguous is really the humblest adjective that can be applied . . . and for all the city's modern silliness and corruptness . . . this musical magic of ambiguity still lives or at least has hours in which it is victorious. . . .

'For certain people there is a certain melancholia associated with the name Venice. It is full of home atmosphere – nowadays a spiritually rather corrupt and staled atmosphere, I grant you . . . but still my heart would be pounding were I there again!'[3] I tried hard to get this pounding heart into the verse, but it refused to fit.

For the last scene of Act I we had to translate a chapter of very elaborate poetic prose into the terms of the stage. When Aschenbach returns to the Lido after his abortive departure he enjoys a brief period of untroubled bliss. He sees the world around him as an Hellenic idyll and expresses this vision in language that reaches extraordinary heights of neo-classical parody. Britten wrote to me just before the Aldeburgh Festival of 1971, 'I'm sure that my decision to put D. in V. in the safe till it's all over was the right one, and I'm sticking to it. But I can't stop thinking about it, and I have come to a conclusion. . . . . . . the scene in which I came to a grinding halt as you know, is the big final one of Act I, the idyllic one. I couldn't get the tone right, *relaxed* enough, after all that to-ing and fro-ing to Venice, and before the final climax; and *abstract* enough (a word you used in suggesting the naked boys), as if in Aschenbach's mind; and I wanted to save Aschenbach before the big set piece. What would your reaction be to having the "interpretation" of the boys' dances sung by the chorus as kind of madrigals (again your word)?' He then goes on to describe how he sees it visually. When writing the words of this scene I had not felt familiar enough with the German classical revival to attempt to imitate the style in English and yet it needed to be removed from the style of the rest of the work so as to give it the abstract quality that we had discussed. So I went to Elizabethan neo-platonic verse for inspiration. What I had already written for Aschenbach could be adapted for the chorus and the musical result did have the required formal abstraction that Britten looked for.

The most embarrassing task was to have to precis bits from Plato in the Phaedrus song and its tragic recapitulation in the last act. Mann was fascinated by the Dialogue and dwells at length on it. I cut his passage unmercifully short in

an attempt to get a dignified simplicity that was not philosophically unthinkable.
Incidentally the last line of the second Phaedrus song provides an example of how
a strong verbal line may be a weak musical one and vice versa. I originally wrote:

> The senses lead to passion Phaedrus,
> And passion to the pit.

but the alliterative ps were awkward and ugly to sing and so it became:

> And passion to the abyss.

It was when we were discussing the 'idyll' scene that the idea of introducing the
voice of Apollo occurred. At first I had thought of a boy's voice and then, after a
concert where James Bowman, the male alto, was singing, I became entranced by
the idea of introducing this extraordinary sound into the scene. Peter Pears had
suggested a counter-tenor to Britten almost at the same time. Once having introduced Apollo into this scene the problem of the dream in the second act, which we
had been shirking, had a possible solution: 'that night he had a fearful dream – if
dream be the right word for a mental and physical experience which did indeed
befall him in a deep sleep. . . . . . . its theatre seemed to be in his own soul, and
the events burst in from outside, violently overcoming the profound resistance of
his spirit. . . . . . . left the whole cultural struggle of a life-time trampled on,
ravaged and destroyed.' Reading this, and what followed, again and again and
reading also *The Bacchae* of Euripides, it seemed, to me, that however the producer and choreographer decided to stage the dream, the dialogue must be between the two sides of Aschenbach's nature; the Apolline and the Dionysiac. I was
very much helped in sorting out my ideas about this whole aspect of the story
(which I had arrived at in an uninformed and rather muddled way) by the
introduction and notes to a new German edition of *Death in Venice* edited by T. J.
Reed, and by subsequent conversations with him.

Although *Death in Venice* is full of strong visual excitement it seemed to be
essentially a work to be read. But, working on the libretto, it was surprising to
discover how theatrical much of it is. The events, the series of twists of the tale, of
which it is built up, all have a sharp extrovert front, behind which the mysterious
mental processes seethe. One of the scenes that was, of course, a gift to the opera
was the Players scene. Brilliant, sinister, embarrassing, it serves to contrast more
strongly than ever Aschenbach's incapability of taking part in ordinary pleasures
with the easy conviviality and laughter of the hotel guests. Mann tells us very little
about the songs: the first was a sentimental duet, the second popular and suggestive, the third 'a rowdy air with words in an impossible dialect. . . . The refrain
had neither words nor accompaniment. It was nothing but rhythmical, modulated,
natural laughter. . . .' *O mia carina* the first song I used was an early popular
number that had been rediscovered (and so it gave us a lot of copyright trouble).
It seemed particularly suitable with its suggestion of love pushed beyond the
bounds of good behaviour. I wrote a new verse translation from a literal one and
added a third verse which I was able to make appropriate for the listening
Aschenbach; 'For you forgotten honour work and duty'. The second song I re-
wrote in a rather raffish style from another popular joke song. The real facer was
the laughing song. What language could it be written in? Though incomprehensible, words here and there ought to be interpretable. I toyed with macar-

onics, using Italian, French and English or German perhaps, but my Italian was not good enough to play about with, my German almost non-existent and there seemed no excuse for French. I thought of nonsense verse but even if it had been possible, the Englishness of it would have been unacceptable. At last it occurred to me that the Venetian dialect would have been incomprehensible to the hotel guests, Aschenbach included, and that it would also be incomprehensible in whatever language the opera might be translated. So with the help of a book of old Venetian ballads and nursery songs, having decided with Britten what rhythmic shape was needed, I wrote a version of what was eventually used. It had no grammar and was all wrong but it said more or less what I wanted to say – then I showed it to a friendly professor of Italian (who wished to remain anonymous). He was amazed and amused at my unscholarly efforts, but saw what I was after, re-wrote it in proper dialect and added the brilliant and suggestive last verse himself.

Anyone who worked with Britten knew his gift for getting work and ideas out of people they did not know they were capable of. From the first conversation about *The Turn of the Screw* to Aschenbach's last cry in *Death in Venice* I could rely on his committed encouragement; whether it was to produce a whole scene or a small alteration for which he would often wait patiently while I gnawed my pen. Perhaps even more important for the final work was his sure dramatic instinct operating through his musical needs. Again and again he made me expand the text with a liveliness that my too-slavish attention to the original might have failed to do. Alterations or modifications were always evoked, never dictated. There was positive and continuing pleasure and pride in working with him and I am grateful to have enjoyed it.

The quotations from Thomas Mann's letters are from *The Letters of Thomas Mann* vol. I, selected and translated by Richard and Clara Winstan (Secker and Warburg, London, 1971, and Alfred A. Knopf, New York).
[1] To Wolfgang Born on 18 March 1921.
[2] To Kurt Masters in 1906.
[3] To Erika and Klaus Mann in 1932.

Andrew Porter

The first opera: *Paul Bunyan*

Paul Bunyan, which was first performed at Columbia University, New York, in 1941, is an opera about America by two young Englishmen. W. H. Auden's libretto is based on tales of the legendary giant logger, his clerk Johnny Inkslinger, his cook Hot Biscuit Slim, and the rest of his team. In two acts it traces the progress of the country from primeval forest to poisoned air, polluted rivers, and PWA. projects. It is a moral fable for an age when 'the aggressive will is no longer pure.' The action begins in virgin forest and closes 'as the frontier closes. Gone the natural disciplines / And the life of choice begins.' The theme is responsibility. It's easy to be honest, industrious, cooperative, social when you're a band of brothers together, taming nature; pioneer virtues are put to the test once pioneering days are done. Paul's foreman goes off to public-works administration in Washington, Slim to manage a mid-Manhattan hotel, Johnny to be technical adviser for a Hollywood movie about logging. Paul takes his farewell saying,

> Other kinds of deserts call   To that low instinctive cry
> Other forests whisper Paul,   There to make a way again
> I must hasten in reply   For the conscious lives of men.

The opera ends with a litany: 'From a Pressure Group that says I am the Constitution . . . From a Tolerance that is really inertia and delusion . . . From the theology of plumbers or the medical profession, From depending on alcohol for self-respect and self-possession, Save animals and men.' Once, it was men united in the struggle against nature; now, is it to be every man for himself, or man working for men? *Paul Bunyan*, composed at the same time that Orwell, in wartime England, was writing *The Lion and the Unicorn*, is a deeply serious work treated with a light touch that justifies the authors' calling it an operetta. On the surface, it is an idyll. The music is deft, charming, filled with captivating tunes; it displays Britten's genius for drawing sonority from a small orchestra and often adumbrates – in threnody, ballad, or dapper ensemble – his later compositions. The libretto is lightly strung, elliptical, understated, as revue-like in structure as *The Dog Beneath the Skin*. The lack of a clear plot and the conceits of leaving Paul as an offstage voice (but how could one represent onstage a hero as tall as the Empire State Building?) and of using Fido, Moppet, and Poppet, a dog and two cats, as commentators may have helped to keep *Paul Bunyan* in obscurity for thirty-five years. The BBC and then the English Music Theatre Company revived it in 1976; the Preparatory Division of the Manhattan School of Music staged it the following year. These were happy Bicentennial revivals; the attractions of the piece far, far outweigh its structural weaknesses.

Paul Bunyan got a bad press when it was first done. Its faults were evident:

Auden's libretto, clever, often slick and tiresomely literary, is at once simple and schematic in its groundplan and diffuse in its decorative details. The faults were pointed out in reviews not so much untrue as incomplete. (Some of them also implied that it was impertinent of two brilliant young Englishmen to tackle an all-American subject; they should be put in their place.) But when *Paul Bunyan* was revived, it became apparent that the 'choral operetta' is one of those early works of genius whose youthful freshness and abundance can set an audience's spirits soaring. The faults remain – there are still lines at which one flinches – but have been lessened by the removal of two of the most 'literary' numbers: a love-song cum rhyming game ('Appendectomy / 's a pain in the neck to me . . . Pyschokinesia / Never gets easier') and a sophisticated chorus of film stars and models who materialize while the lumberjacks dream. The specific social criticism in *Paul Bunyan* does not cut deep, and so it can be taken lightly. What matters is the general vision of unspoiled nature and men harnessing (and spoiling) that nature, of first love and first grief, of dreams, ambitions, and the compromises that life imposes. And what matters most of all is the world of lyrical, joy-giving music which Britten creates, a world one can go on living in for days after hearing the opera and then later, through memory's ear, re-enter at will.

Britten and Auden were not novices or strangers to one another when they created *Paul Bunyan*. The piece is not prentice work. From *Our Hunting Fathers*, in 1936, they had been collaborating on cantatas, songs, films, and plays. The *Variations on a Theme of Frank Bridge*, first heard at the Salzburg Festival of 1937, had already made Britten's international reputation. His felicitous mastery is apparent in every number of *Paul Bunyan*. There is a simple phrase in the pro-logue, 'Once in a while the odd thing happens', set in a way that seems to make the heavens open onto visions of strangeness and splendour. The effect is achieved by a leaping octave taken up by voice after voice, through the four-part writing, in a concealed canon; by an inspired control of diatonic dissonance and resolu-tion; and by the sure, unconventional spacing of the choral chords. On paper the passage looks simple – as simple as the magical bars that open Mozart's Clarinet Quintet. The sound of it in performance defies analytical description. One day, reading Bellow's *Henderson the Rain King*, I came across the words 'Once in a while' in a very different context, and suddenly the phrase sang out from the page as Britten had set it, to prompt reflections about the kind of composer whose music seems to break forth with heaven-sent spontaneity and inevitableness. *Paul Bunyan* is a lyrical and vocal opera, yet its orchestration is also marvellously deft, exact, and colourful; the spontaneous singer – Mozart, Schubert, Rossini – is often a skilful instrumental technician as well. Other inspirations are the poignant lament of Tiny, Paul's daughter, for her mother; Slim's song to the effect that, as Pinker-ton puts it in the old translation of *Butterfly*, 'the whole world over, the Yankee is a rover' (here Britten uses hemiolia – six beats divided now into twos, now threes – as buoyantly as if the device had just been discovered); and the large ensemble 'O great day of discovery', in which the great globe itself seems slowly to begin turning.

Paul Bunyan was written to be technically accessible to high schools. The Manhattan performers – mostly aged about sixteen, some much younger – put on a show whose enthusiasm, joyousness, dedication, and feeling of communal ac-complishment would have delighted Britten's heart.

Eric Crozier

Staging first productions 1

Benjamin Britten returned from America in spring 1942, bringing with him a contract for his first full-scale opera. The commission had been offered by Serge Koussevitsky, conductor of the Boston Symphony Orchestra, on the understanding that the first performances would take place in America. The subject was to be *Peter Grimes*.

In wartime England, where the opera-houses at Covent Garden, Sadler's Wells and Glyndebourne were closed 'for the duration', prospects for any large-scale musical venture looked bleak. Britten, nevertheless, invited his friend Montagu Slater to write the libretto. Slater was a novelist and playwright working in the Films Division of the Ministry of Information, and before the war Britten had composed incidental music for two short verse-plays of his.

Peter Pears, meanwhile, who had returned to England with Britten, applied to Sadler's Wells Opera for an audition. He had almost no previous stage experience, but his musicianship and intelligence ensured him a warm welcome from Joan Cross, director of the company since 1940. She and the musical director, Lawrance Collingwood, engaged him to sing various leading roles. From that time on Britten became a regular visitor to the opera whenever Peter Pears or Joan Cross was singing: it was then that he first had the opportunity of getting to know one or two of Verdi's operas really well, as he later acknowledged in an article written for the fiftieth anniversary of Verdi's death.[1] In another article, written in 1945, he acknowledged his debt to Sadler's Wells Opera, whose existence had been an incentive to him to complete *Peter Grimes* and the qualities of whose artists had considerably influenced both the shape and the characterization of his opera.

Since September 1940, when the London blitz had closed Sadler's Wells Theatre, the company had spent most of its time on tour, with a repertory that was limited to the more popular operas. Salaries were low, and the leading singers were allowed to accept outside concert-engagements, a system not conducive to the highest standards of opera-ensemble. As was inevitable in wartime, a large proportion of the singers were young and inexperienced: ingenious direction and animated stage-work had to compensate for vocal and orchestral shortcomings. Yet, whatever criticisms might be made on musical grounds, the company played a vital part in keeping opera alive during the war years.

The originality of Slater's libretto has not, I think, received adequate recognition. It is true that the basic outlines of the characters come from *The Borough*, Crabbe's immensely long *Poem in 24 Letters*. It is also true that Britten and Pears contributed largely to the shaping of the plot and especially to the crucial idea of transforming Grimes from a savage fisherman –

> One whose brute feeling ne'er aspires
> Beyond his own more brute desires

(as Crabbe approvingly quoted from Scott's *Marmion*) – into a very different kind of creature, a bold and aspiring hero at loggerheads with society. Yet the entire text, apart from six quatrains by Crabbe and the small phrase '*Grimes is at his exercise*', is Slater's own work.

He wrote it in a four-beat, half-rhymed, simply worded verse which expands at moments of heightened intensity into more formal verse-patterns and a richer vocabulary: the latter qualities are clearly recognisable in such climactic arias as Ellen's '*Let her among you without fault cast the first stone*', or '*Embroidery in childhood was a luxury of idleness*', and in Peter's '*What harbour shelters peace?*', or '*Now the Great Bear and Pleiades*'. The short interjectory sentences of the recitatives and the more expansive phrases of the arias both seem to me admirable for musical setting. Slater wisely jettisoned Crabbe's rhyming couplets along with his parsonical attitudes, and allowed his own text freely to reflect the diverse speech-rhythms of the individual Borough characters.

Crabbe had a reputation for harsh, unsparing realism, but his verse is not without humour, especially when he criticises young people or reports conversation. Slater's characters, however, have a humour all their own, as shown in the yearnings of the drunken lay-preacher Boles, in the panic of the two Nieces and Auntie's strict concern for the proprieties, and in Balstrode's comments on his fellow-citizens.

Most of 1944 was spent by Britten in his millhouse at Snape composing *Grimes*. As the work grew, so practical ideas developed about the first performances. When it seemed likely that Sadler's Wells Theatre would reopen in summer 1945, Serge Koussevitsky generously waived his claim to the world premiere. Reginald Goodall, a young conductor with the Opera Company, was invited to conduct, I was asked to produce, and Kenneth Green, a boyhood friend of Britten, was to be the designer. Green was art-master at Wellington College, and I made a number of visits to Berkshire to plan the sets with him. At other times I went to Snape, where there was the immense excitement of hearing each newly-completed act played and sung by Britten with unforgettable intensity.

Back in London we were having serious discussions about who was to sing Ellen Orford. It was clear that the part was modelled on the personality of Joan Cross and written with her qualities as singer and actress in mind, just as Grimes was written for Peter Pears. The two of them would make an unmatchable pair. Yet there were problems. The Opera Company had several younger sopranos under contract, one or two of whom might be eager to sing Ellen, even though they had nothing like the same experience vocally or dramatically as Joan Cross. Matters were complicated by the fact that Joan Cross was also director of the company. Various principal singers, for whom there were no parts in the new work, were showing increasing hostility to the idea of staging *Grimes* at all and had begun a serious agitation to get rid of the director and run the company by committee. In spite of these machinations (which seem endemic to opera companies), finally it was resolved that if the Wells was to give the best possible performance, the initial cast must include Joan Cross.

Britten had been inspired to write the opera by the genius of a particular place, the lonely coast of East Suffolk with its huge expanse of sky and marsh and its small communities huddling by the water's edge, dependent on, yet constantly threatened by, the sea. He evoked the place, the people, the landscape, the movement of wind and clouds and waves and birds and grasses, with a knowledge as detailed as that of Crabbe himself. Indeed, asked why he had not stayed on in America, Britten could well have answered in the words of his own hero –

> I am a native, rooted here.

Rooted by what –?

> By familiar fields,
> Marsh and sand,
> Ordinary streets,
> The prevailing wind.

My aim as producer – and in 1945, it should be recalled, Aldeburgh and the Suffolk coast were familiar to far fewer people than today – was to evoke those ordinary streets, the curiously distinctive shapes and textures and juxtapositions of Aldeburgh buildings and the particular quality of light that bathes them, and also to recreate something of the life that had filled the town in the early years of the nineteenth century. Kenneth Green and I attempted, by what might be called selective realism, to express the truth of that particular place and its people. Our characters were English provincials of the early 1800s, yet for modern audiences their power lay not in their historical period but in their humanity. Outwardly Grimes was a misfit in a very narrow form of society: inwardly, his significance came not from his strangeness but from the way in which he personified ambitions and frustrations that are latent in everyone.

Some critics felt that the visual idiom of the designs did not match the idiom of the music. There may have been some truth in this. But in the circumstances, remembering the element of risk inherent in staging a new opera for the re-opening of Sadler's Wells, we were probably right in our approach, which was, in any case, what the composer wanted.

The cramped conditions of the Sadler's Wells stage were against us. There was very little depth and all too little space in the wings. This presented serious difficulties and I had to tell Britten that, to be absolutely sure of changing the scenery in time between the second and third scenes of Act I, he must provide more music. He was always sensible about practical matters, but he looked very glum indeed when faced with this demand. I was, he said, like somebody who brings a huge block of stone along to an architect when he has just completed a cathedral and tells him to fit it in somehow. But finally he agreed.

Our stage rehearsals began on tour – at a Methodist Hall in Sheffield, at a gymnasium in Birmingham and in the Wolverhampton Civic Hall. They had to be fitted in with our normal touring schedule of eight opera-performances weekly, and in Wolverhampton we rehearsed all through VE Day because there was no time to spare for celebrations. Then we went to London for a final intensive fortnight of lighting, orchestral, and dress rehearsals in the theatre that had served as a rest-centre and scenery-store for the past five years.

The rest is history. Let me quote from an eye-witness of that memorable first night on 6 June 1945:

> The orchestra might be too small to do justice to the Interludes, the stage-space too cramped for the action, the idiom of the music unfamiliar . . . yet the impact was so powerful that when the final chorus reached its climax and the curtain

began to fall slowly, all who were present realized that *Peter Grimes*, as well as being a masterpiece of its kind, marked the beginning of an operatic career of great promise and perhaps also the dawn of a period when English opera would flourish in its own right.[2]

Some years earlier I had been greatly impressed by performances of La Compagnie des Quinze, a company of young actors founded by Jacques Copeau with the declared aim of bringing back truth, beauty and poetry to the French stage. I had talked about them to Britten and suggested that perhaps we could create an operatic equivalent – a small group of outstanding singers who would devote several months each year wholly to opera. This would have to be in summer, when singers were less in demand for recitals and oratorios. We could, I suggested, ask them to work together for five months annually and to refuse all other engagements during that period. There need be no chorus, and our orchestra could be a group of soloists. Britten thought that twelve players would be the minimum – string quintet, wind quartet, horn, harp and percussion.

The long-threatened palace revolution at Sadler's Wells had taken place exactly two weeks before the London reopening. A majority of singers had been persuaded not to sign contracts for the new season unless they were given control in place of Tyrone Guthrie and Joan Cross, with powers to hire and fire and decide what operas should be performed. The governors had accepted this ultimatum, and even before the first performance of *Grimes* it was plain that there would be no place at the Wells in future for Britten and his colleagues. If more new operas were to be composed and performed – and, having begun, Britten was immensely eager to continue – an independent company would have to be created for staging them. Very little money was available from CEMA (later, the Arts Council) or other public bodies: so the necessary funds would have to come from private sources.

Sometime in the winter of 1944 I had given Britten my copy of André Obey's play *Le Viol de Lucrèce* as a possible subject for his first chamber-opera. He gave the play in turn to Ronald Duncan, an old friend and a poet for whose verse-play *This Way to the Tomb* he had undertaken to provide incidental music. John Piper was invited to design the scenery and costumes, and I was to produce.

In autumn 1945 Britten and Duncan had their first discussions. The story of Lucretia in Obey's play is presented by two all-seeing narrators, the Male and Female Chorus, who set the drama in historical perspective. Clearly, these two roles would be excellent for Joan Cross and Peter Pears. The four central characters – Lucretia, Collatinus, Tarquinius and Junius – came straight from Shakespeare's poem, and for reasons of economy, both artistic and financial, only two additional characters – Lucretia's maidservants – were to be used.

Before plans had gone very far, I was invited to Glyndebourne to meet John and Audrey Christie. They were hoping to re-open their opera house in 1946 and they suggested that we might present the new opera there. This plan was agreed in the course of discussions with their general manager Rudolf Bing. The Christies undertook to set up a new company, the Glyndebourne English Opera Company, to present *Lucretia*, and to house us at Glyndebourne for one month of rehearsals and two weeks of performances. Since we would only be able to stage one opera in our opening season, we decided to have two alternating casts of singers, so that we could give six or seven performances weekly.

In early May 1946 (only eleven months after the premiere of *Grimes*) our company of singers gathered at Glyndebourne to begin stage-rehearsals. The conductors were Ernest Ansermet and Reginald Goodall: the two Lucretias were Kathleen Ferrier and Nancy Evans: Peter Pears and Joan Cross shared their parts with the Danish Lieder-singer Aksel Schiotz and the soprano Flora Nielsen.

Some critics were disappointed. The success of *Grimes* had been so unexpected and so exciting that audiences were predisposed to expect a similarly powerful and realistic work. What they saw and heard was totally different, and some were not sure that they liked it. The libretto was much criticised – partly because words are so clearly heard in chamber-opera that any weaknesses show up very plainly. A considerable amount of revision of the text was to prove necessary later.

The opera received 83 consecutive performances between June and October: 14 of these were given at Glyndebourne, 28 in London, 35 in five provincial cities, and 6 in Holland at the invitation of the Dutch Wagner Society. The performances at Glyndebourne and in Holland were sold out, those in London were well-supported, but those in Liverpool, Manchester, Edinburgh and Glasgow were half-empty. Despite the inherent weaknesses of the double-casting system (which we employed only for the first season), the quality of the performances improved markedly as the season went on. This was a great advance on the normal repertory system of opera, in which performances deteriorate steadily after the opening of any new production as less skilled artists are brought in to replace the stars.

By the end of that first season we were convinced that small-scale opera offered many advantages for the immediate future. The Christies were willing to continue their support at Glyndebourne but not elsewhere: so we resolved to establish a company of our own, the English Opera Group. Britten, John Piper and I, as artistic directors, issued a manifesto, in which we declared: 'We believe the time has come when England, which has never had a tradition of native opera but has always depended on foreign works, can create its own operas. Opera is as much a vital means of artistic expression as orchestral music, drama and painting, and the lack of it has meant an impoverishment of English artistic life.'

At the present day, when English operas and opera-singers are welcomed internationally, it seems strange that thirty years ago we found it necessary to be so explicit. The boldness of what we were attempting can, however, be measured by what was actually achieved in those early years. During its first five seasons the English Opera Group was to give no less than 488 stage-performances of Britten's first four chamber-operas, and – wrote the Earl of Harewood in respect of these figures, in 1951 – 'that the first four operas have all been by Britten is no more surprising than that the first works after Gluck's attempt to reform the theory of opera were by Gluck.'[3]

Our immediate problem in October 1946 was to plan an independent season for the following summer that would include *Lucretia* and a new chamber-opera. We knew roughly who our leading singers would be, but we had no story for the second opera. Britten had asked Duncan at one time to plan a libretto based on *Mansfield Park* with main roles for Kathleen Ferrier and Peter Pears, but this had not been successful. As always, we were in a hurry: there was only seven months in which to get the new opera written, raise money for its production and for the purchase of the *Lucretia* scenery and costumes from Glyndebourne, engage singers and orchestral players and technicians, book theatres for a five-month season and publicize our plans.

Thinking about the singers available to us, and remembering some of the excellent performances they had given at Sadler's Wells in recent years – Joan Cross as a splendidly stylish Fiordiligi and Margaret Ritchie as a delicious Dorabella, partnered by Peter Pears as Ferrando in *Così fan tutte* – and remembering, too, what a subtle comedian Pears had shown himself to be as Vasek in *The Bartered Bride*, I hit upon the notion of making a comic opera from Maupassant's short story, *Madame Husson's Rose King*, which some years previously had been filmed with Fernandel as the greengrocer's boy and Françoise Rosay as Madame Husson. Nothing could offer more of a contrast to *Lucretia*. Only a small cast would be required, and the settings were relatively simple – an important consideration when planning a theatrical tour. Moreover, the action could easily be transplanted from Maupassant's Normandy to Britten's Suffolk, and in particular to that small bit of East Suffolk around 'Ufford and Orford, Iken and Snape', within a ten-mile radius of Britten's mill, where I had spent many happy days working with him and his librettists during the past few years. This time, however, there was to be a difference, for when Britten had finished reading the Maupassant story, he gave it back and asked me if I would write the libretto. The result was *Albert Herring*.

We began, as always, by drawing up a list of essential characters and voices. Then we blocked out the action in three acts, and listed the probable contents of each scene. Britten went carefully through these lists with me, to establish what musical forms he would like to use at each point – plain or accompanied *Recitative*, *Arioso*, *Aria*, *Duet*, *Trio*, or *Ensemble*. Once we had decided the overall shape of each act, in terms of dramatic development and musical exposition and contrast, and once we were agreed about the voices (and in some cases the personalities) of each performer, it was time for me to make the imaginative leap from Gisors to Loxford and begin writing.

A particular difficulty of writing comic opera is the question of rhyme. Without rhyme, it is hard to achieve precision; but too much rhyming, or rhyme that is too elaborate, gives an impression of artificiality that chiefly attracts attention to the author's ingenuity. Since the days of the Savoy Operas, the writer of verse for singing is almost obliged to fall back on near-rhyme and assonance, and to shun what Verlaine in his *Art Poétique* called the 'phony jewel' of exact rhyme.

A Suffolk grandfather of mine had kept a shop. I used to help there sometimes in my holidays, and when I began my libretto it did not occur to me that a shop was an unsuitable setting for a comic opera or that the people of a small country town were unsuitable characters. But several people had misgivings about the result. On the first night at Glyndebourne in 1947, John Christie met his guests with an unhappy expression, saying 'This isn't *our* kind of thing, you know.' Had the opera been in Italian or German or Czech, he might not have been troubled – but because it was in English he found it common. So did the critic of *The Times*: in his view, the opera was a mere charade, 'a ghastly little work' as he subsequently told me, forgetting perhaps that I was its author. What he and Christie objected to cannot have been the music, which is witty, inventive, economical and swift-moving: it must have been the libretto. Certainly the story and the characterization are very simple, but what I think gave most offence was the lower-class speech of some of the characters, although what other idiom such characters could use I do not know.

Despite John Christie's forebodings, our comic opera met with great success. In 1947 we gave it more than forty times, and *Lucretia* had the same number of performances. It was surprising to find how enthusiastically audiences in Holland and Switzerland responded to what until then had seemed to us a strictly local comedy. We took our two operas to the Festival at Lucerne, and it was there that Peter Pears made a suggestion that brought us hurrying back to England as soon as the tour was over. Britten and I went straight to Aldeburgh, where we measured up the Jubilee Hall and inspected the church. After securing the approval of the Mayor and the Vicar (shades of *Albert Herring*!), we set about establishing a committee that would help us to launch our first Festival of Music and the Arts the following summer. The centrepiece was to be two performances of *Albert Herring* in the tiny Jubilee Hall, which had originally been built by public subscription as a reading-room and later used as a roller-skating rink. Opera at Aldeburgh! – the whole idea seemed extraordinary, and yet it was no more so (as Peter Pears had realized) than transporting singers and players and scenery and costumes right across Europe, at the price of a heavy subsidy from the British Council, to give performances in an overcrowded Festival city. In Aldeburgh, at a fraction of the cost, we would bring opera and concerts and exhibitions to a small community for whom nothing of the kind was available within a radius of many miles.

Britten's cantata *Saint Nicolas*, for which I wrote the text, received its first performances at the 1948 Festival. It was a logical development from that work, with its use of children's choirs and treble voices, to an opera for children. We had discussed this idea two years before, during a brief holiday at Zermatt; but, as so often happened, the idea did not harden into a definite plan until some practical occasion offered. Britten had a particular fondness for *Swallows and Amazons* and other adventure books by Arthur Ransome, and he was eager to base a children's opera on one of those; but when we made up our minds to write the new work for the 1949 Festival, a much simpler idea occurred to him – a lyric from Blake's *Songs of Innocence*:

> When my mother died, I was very young,
> And my father sold me while yet my tongue
> Could scarcely cry 'weep! 'weep! 'weep! 'weep!
> So your chimneys I sweep and in soot I sleep.

This is paralleled by that even more passionate and appalling lyric from the *Songs of Experience*, which begins:

> A little black thing among the snow,
> Crying 'weep! 'weep! in notes of woe!
> Where are thy father and mother, say?
> They are both gone up to the church to pray . . .

The foreword to the libretto describes how our ideas developed. Our original child performers came from the Ipswich Co-operative Society Choir, and the music that Britten gave them to sing has so much freshness and variety that over the past thirty years successive generations of children in Great Britain and abroad have enjoyed singing it. This small work was the forerunner of a whole series of operas that were to be written for Aldeburgh by Britten and other composers.

Albert Herring had been dedicated to E. M. Forster, an author for whom Britten felt considerable affection and admiration. He was then in his seventies, and he used to come over to Aldeburgh from Cambridge, where he had rooms at King's College. Britten hoped to persuade him to collaborate on an opera, but Forster hesitated because he had never previously attempted to write for the stage. In the end, I was asked to assist him. We met for a preliminary discussion, when Forster made two points plain – he did not care to write a comedy (as had been suggested) 'because comedy must be either satirical or nostalgic', nor did he want to write a chamber-opera: any opera with which he was connected must be on the grandest possible scale. Some time after this Britten was invited to provide a work for Covent Garden as part of the Festival of Britain celebrations in 1951. Obviously this would have to be a large-scale opera – but at that time no subject had been found.

A year or two earlier there had been a re-issue of Melville's posthumously-published story, *Billy Budd*, which previously had only been obtainable in the collected edition of the author's works. Forster greatly admired this story. '*Billy Budd*' – he had written in the chapter on Prophecy, in *Aspects of the Novel* – 'is a remote unearthly episode . . . [in which] Melville reaches straight back into the universal, to a blackness and sadness so transcending our own that they are indistinguishable from glory.' It was not Forster, though, who suggested *Billy Budd*: it was Britten. Who but a composer could have envisaged an opera that takes place entirely on a man-of-war, that has no women characters, and whose hero suffers from a paralytic stammer? The story's disadvantages are plain; but its advantages outweigh them. In terms of human action, it is a most powerful tale. It is also a parable – though what the parable means is debatable. One critic concludes that Melville's aim was to justify the ways of God to man: another considers the book 'his final protest against the nature of things and of fate': a third interprets it as a triumph of innocence and the recognition of the necessity of evil. The action illuminates the characters of three men, Billy Budd, Claggart and Captain Vere – but above and beyond them it seems to cast huge shadows of their human selves that wage an endless conflict beyond time and space. This quality of 'extension' in a story is of immense value to an opera-composer: he needs situations, characters and events that possess intensity in themselves and symbolize forces greater than themselves. In *Billy Budd*, for the first time since *Grimes*, Britten had found a subject that fulfilled these requirements and engaged his deepest sympathies.

Collaboration on an opera, like any artistic collaboration, is a creative process and hard to describe. Ours was governed from first to last by respect for Melville and the desire to interpret him faithfully – not an easy task with an author whose rhetorical language sometimes appears to conceal more than it expresses, even though, at his best, he is lucid and unforgettably powerful, as when he writes

> 'I have swum – I have been
> 'Twixt the whale's black fluke and the white shark's fin.'

The history of our collaboration can best be traced from the evidence of five manuscripts that I have preserved. The first can only be dignified with the name of manuscript as a courtesy-title: it consists of three small sheets from a jotting-pad, and is the sole record of our first working-session. In response to a telegram from Britten, I arrived at Aldeburgh at breakfast-time one cold winter's day late in

1948. He and Forster gave me some coffee and toast, then handed me a copy of *Billy Budd* and left me alone with it. Their eagerness for a favourable verdict was all too plain. As soon as I emerged, later that morning, serious discussion began of the great merits of the story and the problems that it presented for stage-adaptation. This went on through lunch and until tea-time when, after a short walk, we settled round the fire with Melville's book and a notepad. My first 'manuscript' includes two short lists in Britten's writing, one recording all the characters that Melville names, the second listing the dramatic episodes as they occur in the book. There is also a third sheet, which consists of a sketchy side-view of a sailing-ship, drawn by Britten, slightly modified by me, and annotated by Forster with place-names – *Main Deck*, *Quarter Deck*, *Captain's Cabin* – to help us find our way around.

Manuscript Two dates from a meeting in January 1949, when Britten had resolved to go ahead with the opera for Covent Garden and we made plans for setting to work in earnest. This is a kind of dry working-synopsis, a scenario in five main scenes, each one sub-divided into episodes.

Manuscript Three is more interesting. This one is labelled *Billy Budd, Opera: First Draft – March 1949*. It contains forty pages of typescript and represents several weeks of continuous work by Forster and myself. Throughout that period we lived in Britten's house at Crabbe Street in Aldeburgh, within a few yards of the sea, where we had been provided with a comfortable working-room at the far end of the corridor from Britten's study. After breakfast each day, and each afternoon after tea, Forster and I began work, discussing whatever scene was next to be written, questioning each other, making suggestions, referring to Melville or checking technical points in our reference-books, and finally agreeing to set down a draft of our joint ideas.

Britten was busy scoring his *Spring Symphony*, but midway through the morning he would visit us to see how things were going. We met at meals and talked about *Billy*: we went for walks and talked about *Billy*: friends came in the evenings and for politeness' sake we talked about other things, but our minds were still on *Billy*. By the end of March we had succeeded in drafting all the main scenes: our typescript is surprisingly complete and readable, but not yet a libretto – so much is clear from the number of alterations that had to be made later.

In August, Forster and I returned to Aldeburgh. Britten had been studying our typescript, meanwhile, and his musical ideas had been developing. He now invited us to spend a month with him to revise and simplify the text. From now on, he assumed the dominance in our partnership and led the discussions. He asked us, for instance, to omit Melville's flogging from the first act and to substitute a more lyrical episode. He wanted a big new chorus scene as climax to Act I. (This was one of the few occasions when we added anything not directly suggested by Melville: ten years later, when Britten compressed the original four acts into two, this scene was removed.) Melville's Afterguardsman, who tempts Billy with the guineas, was fused with the character of the terrified Novice. In addition to structural changes like these, we went through each scene word by word, line by line, checking, compressing, tautening. Since the libretto had inevitably fallen into prose, an important task was to provide small lyrical episodes wherever possible that would enable the music (as Britten expressed it) 'to flower'. A libretto in verse is half-way towards the condition of music, for the words are already shaped into formal and rhythmical patterns: a prose-libretto gives the composer the more difficult task of building his musical structures with fluid and unorganized material. After a month, our task was complete and we separated, taking with us copies of Manuscript Four, a libretto in 57 pages.

It was from this almost final text that Britten began to compose; 'almost final' – because no libretto can really be complete until the composer has finished the score. My Manuscript Five is basically the same as the previous one, but it contains a great many small alterations, the necessity for which arose from the composer's detailed work on the text during the following two years. This is something for which the librettist must always be prepared: his work is not complete, and may still need adjustment, right up to the final stages of rehearsal.

Britten had a stricter sense of discipline in writing music than any other composer I have known. His invariable practice was to do his creative work in the morning. This was in the form of some pencil sketches, from which a vocal score, and later a complete orchestral score, would be made. Lunch was often delayed if this work was going well, and Britten would return to his study between tea and dinner-time. After dinner, he would relax, either playing the piano or listening to music on the radio or seeing friends, except when he was pressed for time, and then he would go back to his desk for an hour or two's scoring.

Night work he mistrusted, but he had considerable faith in the capacity of his subconscious mind to solve problems while he slept – and, perhaps for that reason, his favourite reading before going to sleep was poetry. Despite his belief in the necessity for inspiration, he showed considerable mistrust of the artist who sits around waiting for inspiration to come. Composition, in his view, was a process of hard, regular, sustained work, a tilling of the soil in which the seed of inspiration might lodge and grow, and he would sometimes say that he had done all the work on a piece and now it was only a question of 'finding the right notes'. But the way he said this made plain that he regarded it as the most important stage and one not wholly under his control.

Britten had an instinctive capacity for engaging one's wholehearted interest in what he was planning to do, and he took a positive delight in meeting challenges and overcoming difficulties of every kind. He took his vocation with great seriousness, but in those early days when I knew him best he was full of gaiety and high spirits, and the most delightful of companions. He loved walking, swimming and outdoor games, and he always played to win, delighting in landing shots at tennis that were impossible for his opponent to return.

This enjoyment of the sheer physical pleasure of playing games, and of winning by swift intelligence combined with economy of effort, had its counterpart in his piano-playing and conducting. He was like a trained athlete beginning a race, poised, determined, nervously intense – and at such times he radiated a magnetism that inspired everyone performing with him. When he was composing, too, he was always concerned to challenge his singers and musicians to the limits of their abilities, whether he was writing for a school choir or an international virtuoso. It was partly this that so much endeared him to everyone who worked with him in the art to which he devoted his life.

[1] *Opera*, February 1951: *Verdi. A Symposium.*
[2] From Eric Walter White, *Benjamin Britten. A Sketch of His Life and Works* (Boosey & Hawkes Ltd, London 1948).
[3] Editorial, *Opera*, in May 1951 (pp. 273-5).

Basil Coleman

Staging first productions 2

One evening in 1948 all those involved in the staging of Britten's new version of *The Beggar's Opera* met for the first play-through of the work, with Britten himself at the piano. His playing of his brilliant settings of *The Beggar's Opera* tunes, frequently with marvellous indication of the instruments for which he had written them, was altogether dazzling. I reeled home full of fascinating new sounds, images and emotions, little knowing how important that first meeting with Britten was to be in my future life.

I must explain my reason for being there: *The Beggar's Opera* is usually performed by actors who can sing. Britten's far more musically demanding version requires singers who can act. Gay's dialogue is not easy, even for professional actors, and at the suggestion of Tyrone Guthrie who was to direct the opera, I was asked, as an out-of-work actor at the time, to help the singers with the spoken dialogue. Guthrie was unable to take the first week of rehearsals so he also asked me to become his production assistant.

Rehearsals for *The Beggar's Opera* were very exciting. The dialogue still presented problems, partly because for most singers speaking requires a quite different use of the voice from that used for singing, and the frequent alternating from one to the other can be a severe strain for them. Nevertheless there were many brilliant performances in Guthrie's production. Britten wanted the singers to slide in and out of the songs and dialogue in a seamless way, and in large measure I think they succeeded.

Britten's next opera was *The Little Sweep*, a children's opera with libretto by Eric Crozier, composed for the 1949 Aldeburgh Festival. As is well known now, it contains four songs to be performed by the audience. The story of Sammy the sweep is treated with such devotion and integrity that cast and audience become totally involved and concerned for him. Part of the work's great appeal, after the thrill of discovering the dirty little sweep up the chimney and the sympathy felt for him by his more privileged contemporaries, is the excitement of the young people out-witting the grown-ups in order to save him.

In the original score, at the end of the opera, the cast went off carrying Sammy to safety in a huge trunk, which the young people pass off as luggage belonging to the cousins who are returning home. However, the entire cast is then meant to sing the final song with the audience. I decided to dim the lights and have the cast return and build the departing coach from Sammy's trunk with the addition of a couple of chairs and the twins twirling the sweep's brushes as the coach wheels. (Later we changed the brushes for colourful parasols.) Sammy sat astride the rocking-horse in front, as if drawing the coach. This was subsequently written into the published score, though sometimes I wonder if it would have been better left out so that future directors could find their own ways of staging the end.

Britten attended as many rehearsals as his composing allowed, especially latterly when they took place in the Jubilee Hall at Aldeburgh. The rehearsals of this work had particular appeal for him as they involved so many young people. There was always added excitement when he joined us, as he and the children responded so well to each other.

We opened with a public matinee for Aldeburgh townspeople and children who otherwise would not have had a chance to see the show. Inevitably the only un-rehearsed part of the performance was that of the conductor working the audience in their four songs. There was no need for concern: Norman Del Mar made an instant success of it and contributed enormously to the audience's enjoyment.

The circumstances surrounding the next production I did for Britten could not have been more different: that of *Billy Budd* at Covent Garden in December 1951. I first heard the work in his Aldeburgh home in Crabbe Street together with Peter Pears and both librettists, E. M. Forster and Eric Crozier. As well as playing from the piano score, Britten half-sang all the vocal parts, giving a vivid idea of the characterizations he had in mind throughout. Gradually the new words and music built up a detailed picture of the sailing ship and all members of the crew, and as the daylight faded in the room round him and the terrible events of the story developed, Britten became more and more immersed in them himself. At the finish he was exhausted, physically and emotionally. It was very apparent how much the work meant to him and I did my utmost to hold onto those first images and impressions as they came flooding over us, for use in the production.

There was a last minute crisis when Josef Krips, who was to have conducted, withdrew from the production. Britten, the only other person who knew the score, was persuaded to take over. He always needed the security of sympathetic and like-minded people around him to work with. With John Piper as designer and Peter Pears, for whom he had written the part, as Captain Vere, he felt he had this. 'Now our team is complete,' he said.

Few opera companies carry a sufficient number of singers from whom to cast an all-male production, so additional singers were brought in to augment the resident Covent Garden Company. Britten very much wanted the young Geraint Evans to sing Billy Budd but he felt the part lay too high for his voice. Instead he sang the part of the Sailing Master, a performance full of individuality and character. There was no other young baritone in the country who readily fitted Melville's description of Billy so David Webster, the Administrator of the Royal Opera House, held auditions in America. He returned with Theodor Uppman, a happy choice; there was a naivety and an air of innocence about him which was both unusual and appropriate.

John Piper and I discussed the sets in great detail, visiting both HMS *Victory* at Portsmouth and the Greenwich Maritime Museum. Apart from the Prologue and the Epilogue, the entire story is being recalled by Vere in his old age; the forces of good and evil are at work, with Billy Budd as the innocent victim. The struggle is not confined to the particular characters we are witnessing. It is the universal question of good and evil, our own strengths and weaknesses and the moments of decision within ourselves with which we are being confronted. We felt therefore that too realistic an approach in the design would be unsuitable.

We started work on the under-deck scene as the most difficult one: how to suggest its great depth but lack of height and at the same time allow the performers to stand upright in order to sing and make sure that the set in no way muffled the sound. John Piper worked in model form for any units which would require construction. He made a series of long, low arches in balsa wood suggesting the ribs of the ship, a marvellously ghostly white skeleton which answered our purpose exactly. All we needed to add was a small cat-walk section of the upper deck leading to a gangway, by which Claggart and his men could descend when they interrupted the fight between Billy and Claggart's accomplice, Squeak. The arches were joined one to another and strengthened so that hammocks could be slung between them when the men retire for the night.

Lack of space determined that we made no attempt at 'setting sails' in view of the audience. Otherwise we tried to simulate all the action called for in the libretto, the holy-stoning of the main deck, pulling of the halyards, preparation of the guns and other equipment necessary for waging battle. The guns formed part of the main deck scenery, otherwise all properties were brought on and off by the cast during the course of the action. The scenes in the captain's cabin are in marvellous contrast with the big ones that take place on the main and lower decks and the set had to be small and confined to create a realistic effect. In order to focus attention on the cabin, Piper masked the set in with a black cloth all round. This helped the sound projection too, particularly for the opening to the first scene, with its calm and cultivated atmosphere in the midst of war.

We had planned the use of gauze across the front of the stage throughout the entire battle scene, on which to project the descending mist when the enemy ship is sighted. Unfortunately its presence had a bad psychological effect on some members of the cast who were convinced it would absorb a lot of the sound in the early part of the scene. The alternative was to let the gauze make a slow descent as if the mist were falling. At the dress rehearsal E. M. Forster slipped me a piece of paper on which he had written 'sluice gate of porridge!' For the revival of the work some years later I am glad to say it was agreed to re-instate the gauze at the beginning of the scene.

Although extra singers had been brought in for *Billy Budd*, we could have done with still more in the Chorus since they had to be divided into different groups for different ranks and occupations, and when a group had to sing on its own the sound was often thin. This is especially so in the first main deck scene where singers always find the long slow legato line very hard to sustain and keep in tempo while at the same time dragging holy-stones backwards and forwards across the deck. It is inevitable so early in the opera that they concentrate on the singing at the expense of the action, thus providing a field-day for some critics.

Britten was remarkable to work with and too much involved with the job in hand to worry about his image as conductor. He genuinely believed that interpreters are as necessary and important as creators. Everyone who worked with him was made to feel an equal, and this may partly account for his ability to make singers and instrumentalists do things of which they never knew they were capable before. He knew exactly what he wanted and how to get it, and provided the artist was serious he was most patient and encouraging.

At that time Britten's music and whole idiom were new to most singers and often made greater demands on their musicianship and intelligence than they had been used to. Gradually the cast responded to the words and music and became more and more involved in the moving story.

The entire cast, chorus and orchestra gave a fine performance on the first night but not all the critics were as generous as the one who wrote: 'Last night's performance must be accounted a major event both in English Music and in the London Theatre.' However, Britten, himself never entirely satisfied, seemed very pleased. In later life he rated *Billy Budd* highly among his operas; it was one of those most dear to him.

For some years after the war, when the Royal Opera House was re-opened, it was the seasons given by the Sadler's Wells Ballet Company, now the Royal Ballet, which were most successful. It was understandable, therefore, that they should have expected to do the Gala Performance for the Queen's Coronation, so when Britten's opera *Gloriana* was accepted, there was a certain hostility. In my opinion, part of Britten's satisfaction, when he was officially encouraged to write the new opera, derived from a feeling that by so doing he might also be helping the cause of English opera a stage further.

Britten asked another distinguished poet and novelist, William Plomer, to write the libretto for this work. It was to be based on one episode in the life of the first Queen Elizabeth. Britten always wanted to be involved in the activities of the English Opera Group, the preparation of its current productions, its future plans and, when time allowed, in performing himself with the company. In turn the Group was very dependent on him and not only for its repertory. It was when he was most involved in composing, especially works not intended for the Group, that his divided loyalties usually made things difficult for him. However, on one occasion, in answer to something I must have written to him at this time, he replied, 'It is unnecessary, and even dangerous, to tell me to be selfish! I *am* that naturally, I fear – for now the problem of writing a *good* opera is more in my mind than anything else – other problems seem remoter every day! It is going well, especially from the libretto problem . . . we have sketched out fully all the work except the last two scenes – and very satisfactorily sketched too. [Plomer] . . . is fine to work with: reasonable and skilful.' On another occasion he wrote, 'William is a treasure'.

Once again Britten wrote with certain singers in mind, most especially Joan Cross as Elizabeth and Peter Pears as Essex, also Geraint Evans as Mountjoy and Jennifer Vyvyan as Penelope Rich. John Piper was to design. The opera included two big scenes in which dancing played an important part. For diplomatic reasons the request for the choreographer of our choice was delayed for some time as 'the Ballet is up in arms because they are not doing the Coronation Gala.' Ultimately it was agreed that the inventive John Cranko should undertake it. He very much wanted Beriosova, who was a member of the Sadler's Wells Ballet Company, as Concord for the Masque in the Norwich scene, but repeated requests to use her were refused. Cranko asked me to accompany him in a final attempt to try and persuade Ninette de Valois to let her appear, but she continued to refuse him. At the end of nearly an hour's effort on both our parts she reluctantly gave in and Beriosova gave a beautiful performance.

The production was a big one and there was very little time for preparation. John Piper and I had to work on each scene separately as it arrived from the composer, which made it difficult until a fairly late stage to get an overall idea of the work, particularly from the point of view of the settings.

Organizing the production department of the Royal Opera House for the making of the costumes alone was going to be an enormous task. Quite apart from those for the principal characters, there had to be three costume changes for every member of the chorus for different state occasions, as well as those for the small chorus of Ladies-in-Waiting in the second of the Queen's ante-room scenes, and the Old Men's and Boys' Chorus in the Street Scene. The wardrobe of Elizabeth I is legendary, both for the number and the richness of the dresses. In the opera, apart from wearing the same dress for the first two scenes which take place on the same day, we decided she must have different clothes for the other four scenes in which she appears. There was also Lady Essex's dress in which the Queen makes her cruel re-entrance in the Whitehall Ballroom Scene, in order to shame the rightful owner, in public, for her tactless exhibitionism. This dress had to be made to mis-fit Joan Cross in order to be effective.

Basically the plot and the characters included in the opera are historically correct. Accordingly, we felt that the design, including the costumes, should attempt to give an authentic visual impression of the period. There is a relentless rigidity about the shape of the women's dresses, with their panniered skirts, and their size, especially when a number would have to appear together, had to be taken very much into account in our discussions about the different settings, of which the work calls for no less than seven. We were also conscious of the special occasion which the first performance was to celebrate, and the need for pageantry and display. In *Gloriana* there is no music linking scene with scene within an act, as in Britten's other operas, and so the onus was greater on the designer and director to keep the scene breaks as short as possible.

The final design was fairly simple in construction. The upstage part of the main acting area was slightly raised, right across the stage; this, together with steps down and additional raised sections added when required, formed the basic ground plan for the big formal scenes.

In the opening scene a group of colourful tents was arranged loosely in a semi-circle as if surrounding the tilting ground off-stage, with Cuffe observing the tournament in progress between them.

In the Norwich Scene (Act II scene i), in order to leave as much space as possible for the dances in the Masque, we tried to suggest that the action was taking place under a high canopy, supported by very slender carved wooden pillars. The members of the Chorus who sing the unaccompanied madrigals which form part of the Masque, were grouped and re-grouped on the back raised section of the stage to form a kind of scenic background to each of the dances. In order to make Elizabeth sufficiently important in the midst of all this, we brought her on in a canopied litter from which she watched the Masque. Piper achieved a re-markable spring-like freshness in the scene, partly by using a great deal of white, particularly in the costumes.

In the scene in the Palace of Whitehall (Act II scene iii), the music for the court dancing is provided by an on-stage orchestra. We decided to elevate these players above the Court, as if in a minstrels' gallery: this also gave them a very clear view of the conductor's beat from the orchestra pit. Elizabeth has very dramatically important moments in this scene. In spite of needing ample floor space for the performers, we felt it necessary to give her an eminent position by providing an extension to the raised section of the stage running down-stage centre. It was particularly useful when, for example, she at last agrees to let Essex go as Lord

Deputy of Ireland, and also for the Chorus to be able to sing downstage to her in the big ensemble which follows.

This scene had the feeling of a dark and richly panelled great hall with more slender pillars used to define architectural features, and most of the costumes were in the strong colours of medieval stained glass. It was a fitting setting for the uneasy scenes that take place between the Court Dances.

The Street Scene (Act III, scene iii) requires the use of the whole stage which creates problems as it precedes the final scene and a long scene change between the two would have been fatal. Piper used a minimum of two-dimensional pieces profiled to produce a three-dimensional effect, which could be brought on and off stage swiftly. Incidentally, the youthful player of the gittern who accompanies the Ballad Singer in this scene was Julian Bream. For the final scene Piper designed a cut-out cloth resembling a huge Tudor screen which hung in silhouette against the sky cloth beyond. Both sets were wonderfully dramatic and were achieved by relatively simple means. Piper's designs inevitably have a very 'painterly' quality and he himself would be the first to acknowledge the debt the whole production owed to the scenic department of the Royal Opera House for its superb realization of them.

It is in the Queen's ante-room (Act I scene ii, Act III scene i) that the characters of the Queen and Essex, and their extraordinary relationship, are most fully developed. To emphasise this intimacy we knew that we must set this scene close to the audience and moreover be able to bring it on and off stage quickly. I was also anxious that it should have a more personal, feminine character. The result suggested the interior of a marquee, with heavily gathered gauze painted with a bold foliage motif on a background of elusive colours, predominantly pale lavender. It had an ephemeral quality which added a further poignancy to the two scenes. In the second of these, Essex bursts in to try and justify his failure in Ireland to the Queen. She was at her dressing-table surrounded by a free-standing cubicle draped with fragile curtaining to give her a greater feeling of privacy while dressing. When the Ladies-in-Waiting tried to prevent Essex from intruding further, he tore down the curtain and exposed the ageing Queen, wigless and ugly. (Joan Cross's stillness after this happened, and while the full implications of it began to dawn on her, was one of the many great moments of her performance.) Planning the ante-room (in Act I scene ii) as near to the audience as possible enabled it to be set downstage of the opening Tournament Scene, so saving time on the scene change, desirable as it was the first one of the evening. Similarly it was necessary that the scene in the Garden of Essex's house in the Strand (Act II scene ii) could be set rapidly downstage of the Norwich set and allow for at least part of the change to the Great Room in the Palace of Whitehall (Act II scene iii) to be going on while the scene was in progress. Piper made use entirely of gauzes for this scene, staggered one behind the other wherever space allowed; painted in shades of green to suggest creeper and foliage. These could be flown in and out quite rapidly. Although it only involves four people, the scene is a complex one of frustration, changing loyalties and intrigue and unfortunately the space we had allowed it was insufficient for it to be played out satisfactorily.

During the period of preparation, a production meeting was called to discuss problems. It took place in David Webster's outer office and he himself attended. Before we disbanded at the end of the meeting Webster made a short speech. He said he wished to set on record that in his opinion it was a great mistake that the Gala performance of the new work would also be its first performance, implying that it should first be performed to an opera-going audience who would appreciate it as a work of art in its own right. In the event he was proved right, but it was, to say the least, a dispiriting send-off to a big production. Whether Webster, knowing that Britten would be interested to learn the outcome of our production meeting, had hoped that I might repeat his words while there was still time to change plans, I do not know. I held back from doing so to begin with. When eventually I did mention it to Britten he made no comment. He had never veered from his original idea that the first performance should celebrate the young Queen's coronation.

Rehearsals started at a disadvantage without the conductor John Pritchard. Previous commitments abroad had also prevented him from fully studying the work until after his return and Britten was still too involved in working on the orchestral parts to be with us much of the time. Both Joan Cross and Peter Pears were concerned that their voices were not big enough to ride the orchestra in some moments of the work. I tried to help by keeping them downstage whenever possible. In the intimate scenes there were fewer problems and we could fully enjoy their great artistry. Whilst Essex's arrogant and ambitious characteristics did not come naturally to Pears, he admirably suggested the hot-headedness of the spoilt favourite who was by turns devoted to his Queen and frustrated and exasperated by her. There was brilliant contrast in Joan Cross's performance of the Queen as she presented herself in public, then revealed herself in private; between the lonely woman's longing for a close human relationship and her fear of its possible consequences for her people and her country; between her sense of her own power and her humility before God. Cross's last scene, where the Queen recalls the aims and aspirations of her reign, alternately singing and speaking dialogue, as she quietly waits alone for death, was a fine ending to a great performance.

Visually the production made immediate impact on the first night audience and John Piper's beautiful sets and costumes received more than one ovation. It is sad but perhaps understandable, that the work itself, with all its remarkable richness and complexity, was less accessible to an audience predominantly comprised of Heads of State, diplomats and politicians. It is sadder and less understandable that so many critics appear to have been influenced by that response at the time. It is worth mentioning that Britten's reaction was '. . . if I had listened to the critics I would have given up writing music long ago.' The reception by subsequent audiences in London and the provinces was altogether more rewarding.

Britten's next opera was *The Turn of the Screw*, commissioned for the Venice Biennale in 1954. The idea of basing it on Henry James's ghost story came from Myfanwy Piper, whom Britten asked to work with him as librettist for the first time. Britten never liked leaving Aldeburgh especially when he was busy composing. In a letter he wrote: 'Goodness – how difficult it is to write an opera with the librettist so far away [Oxfordshire]! She is so good, but is so occupied with being a wife and mother!' However, the opera was on time and the collaboration a very happy and successful one. In spite of his previous achievements, Britten was much in need of encouragement. 'I have never felt so insecure about a work – now up, now down – and it helps a great deal to know that you, who know so instinctively what I'm aiming at, like it so much,' he wrote.

It was, in every sense, to be an English Opera Group production – a chamber work employing small forces, a form which Britten believed in and some critics had done their best to dissuade him from using. Three of the six parts were written for singers for whom he had the highest regard, Joan Cross, Jennifer Vyvyan and Peter Pears. The instrumental parts were written for members of the English Opera Group Orchestra and each was given a cadenza in Variation VIII at the beginning of Act II. The work itself was dedicated to all those members of the Group who were involved in the first production.

The Group, of which I had been an Artistic Director for some time now, was usually in debt but for once the fee for mounting this opera was adequate. It made possible a period of several weeks for coaching, a month of rehearsals and for the singers to forgo all other engagements during the rehearsal time – a unique situation. Britten was most concerned that rehearsals should take place in the quiet of Aldeburgh to avoid publicity and other distractions, and this too was agreed.

The casting of the parts of the two children was a considerable problem; they carry great responsibility, particularly that of Miles. The auditions were disappointing, leaving us with little choice. One of the few boys brought back for a second hearing was a very shy but quite personable little twelve-year-old, with a true but very small treble voice. Despite this it was decided to risk casting him, in the hope that the voice would develop and grow during rehearsals – the boy was David Hemmings.

Now Britten was more concerned than ever about the casting of Flora. After all, the first two performances were to form part of an important international festival. It was finally agreed to cast an experienced adult singer who would be able to hold a sure vocal line, particularly in scenes which the child characters carry on their own.

The design for the opera was a most challenging one; the first act contains a prologue and eight scenes linked together by a theme and set of seven variations for orchestra. The second act contains a further eight scenes similarly linked, the act this time beginning with a variation. It is necessary to stress the fact that there is no break in the music throughout each of the acts.

The action takes place in no less than eleven different locales – mainly in Bly, a country house and its surrounding park, set in east England. The scenes are often very short, the orchestral variations between even shorter, and this, together with the fact that the English Opera Group productions were conceived mainly for performance in medium-sized theatres and on tour, meant that large-scale or heavily built scenery of any kind was not possible, even if desirable. How to melt in and out of each of the scenes effectively with the changes causing as little distraction as possible during the variations between? The difficulties were further increased by the virtual impossibility of achieving a good black-out on stage. In a chamber opera of this kind, and especially one which includes at least one child singer, the action must be brought downstage as much as possible, thus making it very difficult to make scene changes without them being visible in light reflected from the orchestra pit. In most theatres a gauze right across the proscenium opening throughout would have been a solution, but again the singers were anxious about not being heard or seeing their beat clearly enough. The idea had to be abandoned except on two occasions: for The Journey, the first scene of all, with the Governess travelling in a coach to Bly. As she got nearer her destination light faded up on the gauze in front of her, revealing the Gateway to the Park. A gauze was also used for the first scene of Act II with the ghosts of Jessel and Quint, where it helped considerably to create an illusion of 'nowhere' called for in the libretto.

John Piper and I decided to try to 'save up' units which together would suggest the facade of the house, only revealing them as the story unfolded and when they were needed for the action. For the first scene, entitled 'The Welcome', only the front door of the house was visible, placed downstage on one side, with a rather fully gathered gauze hanging across the stage beyond it, painted to indicate foliage and park. For the following scene, 'The Letter', the gauze was pulled off-stage to reveal a three-sided Victorian-Gothic bay window next to the front door. For the third scene another gauze pulled off-stage above the window unit revealed the tower on which the ghost of Quint would appear, thus completing the facade of the house on one side of the stage. Interior scenes were suggested by door and window units and pieces of furniture brought on from the opposite side of the stage and backed by further gauzes, one painted to suggest wall-paper for example. For the Churchyard Scene the church porch and tombstones were also brought on from this side. Throughout most later scenes we were aware of the Park and Jessel's lake painted on the backcloth with another painted gauze hung in front of it to give greater depth and mystery. All built units and pieces of furniture were designed to be taken on and off stage as swiftly and quietly as possible. The pulling of the gauzes on and off stage worked very successfully and the designs helped to create a remarkable atmosphere of sinister beauty. Piper's response to Britten's operas is so sure that he has always found a way of realizing the essential texture and atmosphere of each of them in visual terms. *The Turn of the Screw* was no exception, and with the help of Michael Northen's clever lighting we got close to our original idea of making the scenes appear and disappear like a series of Victorian tinted vignettes, each lighting cue carefully timed with the music. We were not always successful in making Quint and Jessel ghostly enough, but when they were static, as on Quint's first appearance on the tower and Jessel's in the lake, the illusion was acceptable. It was much more difficult with a scene like the last of Act I where I felt it to be dramatically important that they should encroach nearer to the Governess and Mrs Grose in their desperate fight to keep a hold on the children. Even with different coloured lighting, the closer they came the more substantial they appeared. Yet, for musical reasons too, it was important that the singers should be near in order to help achieve the climax with which the act ends.

The scenes of the opera are most carefully shaped individually and in contrast with each other to establish character and slowly build up situation and atmosphere. Britten was well aware of the need for contrast when he wrote of the scene in the churchyard for instance, 'I feel so strongly, for the form and drama of the work as well as for the music's sake, that we *must* have something light and gay here, something for the children to be young and charming in (for the last time almost, in the work) – and I think the idea of the hymn (a kind of 'choir' procession) to be the best yet thought of.'

The rich and detailed characterization in the words and music given to each of the six parts has been realized with the utmost economy, like everything else in the work. This is not always easy to achieve in performance. There is no time in scenes of such short duration gradually to build a character, mood or situation; frequently these must be established immediately at the start of a scene. Again, the relationships between the characters are subtle and complex and depend entirely on ensemble playing for their realization.

I can think of no other opera where the performers are so dependent upon each other because the music and drama are so integrated. The closer we got to doing what seemed right dramatically the more everything fell into place musically. There was considerable satisfaction once this began to happen. The way David Hemmings's voice developed and strengthened was also a source of pleasure.

Before our departure for Venice we had a final rehearsal with orchestra. All costumes and what parts of the scenery we had been able to rehearse with were already on their way. The opera was performed where we had rehearsed it in the Workmen's Hall at Thorpeness, not on the tiny stage but in the main body of the hall with the orchestra to one side. Britten of course conducted. There were no means of indicating the lighting fades in and out for each scene to help the 'suspension of disbelief' on the part of the small audience of relatives and friends seated very close to the action, and props and bits of furniture had to be taken on and off the playing area in full view. For all that, the power with which the work came over to that first audience was unforgettable. They were quite overwhelmed by the experience. This was true of every performance Britten gave of any work. There was nothing routine about them or his rehearsals, each one was a unique experience.

We arrived in Venice a week before our first performance with what seemed like sufficient time for the singers to become acclimatized and for preparation of the stage. There was insufficient equipment in the theatre to work our elaborate lighting plot and a good deal of what we required had to be taken with us.

Every bit of available time was needed for its installation, for the assembling of the scenery for the first time and for the theatre staff to learn to work the complex lighting cues and unconventional scene changes. By this time Britten was getting very nervous about the opening and unfortunately was more than usually upset when things went wrong or were not timed as precisely as planned during those final rehearsals.

On our First Night the heavy air of the lovely theatre was made pleasanter by the scent of the roses placed in each box on gala occasions. In spite of the occasional noise of scene changes, the performance was a fine one, with Jennifer Vyvyan especially remarkable as the Governess. It is to the credit of Olive Dyer who played Flora, that some members of the audience asked to be taken backstage to meet the wonderful children! Apart from the work itself, it was the ensemble of the whole production that was frequently commented on and came in for much critical attention in the Italian Press.

Britten was in very good spirits after the highly successful reception accorded his new work and we had a memorable drive across Europe and back to England in his open car. He and Peter Pears took it in turn to drive, with Imogen Holst and myself as passengers. It was a perfect 'unwinding' before we got back for the first performance of the opera in London as part of the English Opera Group's new season.

Colin Graham

Staging first productions 3

In the twenty-four years I knew Benjamin Britten I directed seventeen of his nineteen stage works: of those seventeen I collaborated closely with him on fifteen, including eight of the last nine premieres. The two that have so far escaped me are the ballet *The Prince of the Pagodas* and *Billy Budd*. I would not have been able to equal Basil Coleman's brilliant productions on stage and television of the latter, and I do not so far regret this. In addition to the fifteen close collaborations were an opera, *Idomeneo*, which is not by Britten but is as important to his work on the stage as any of his own compositions, and another opera which, tragically, he was never to write. Ironically I feel that I worked with him in even greater depth on these two than many of the others.

Britten's influence over me began years before we met: in fact, I was seduced by some of his earlier works (*Peter Grimes*, *The Rape of Lucretia*, *Les Illuminations*, *Albert Herring*) well before I came to know the conventional operatic repertory, and even in those days I could recognise the theatrical strength of his work.

I came into opera after training and working as an actor. While I was still at RADA I landed a few months' work as a temporary Assistant Stage Manager at Covent Garden. In 1953 I became an ASM with the English Opera Group and in 1954 I was stage managing the premiere of *The Turn of the Screw* in Venice. During these two years I learned much from Basil Coleman, the Director of Productions of the EOG and, through his influence, I rehearsed the understudies of *The Turn of the Screw* cast. The worldwide success of the opera in his production almost coincided with his temporary emigration to Canada, and so the subsequent revivals were left to me. It was during this period of extensive rehearsal and touring that I got to know Benjamin Britten and, on the ship taking us all to the Stratford Festival in Ontario, he told me that he would like me to direct *Noye's Fludde*.

Noye's Fludde is taken from the Chester Miracle Plays, a copy of which was given to Britten by Eric Crozier. The opera was conceived primarily to entertain and exploit the talents of the wealth of young musicians in East Anglia; it was only natural that Britten's personal commitment to the area in which he lived should also find him creating suitable musical opportunities. Some of the forces required by the opera are now legendary: the handbells from Leiston Modern School, which heralded the appearance of the rainbow; the percussion group from Woolverstone Hall, with its set of slung mugs for the raindrops which start and end the storm; the recorders from Framlingham College which vie with the wind; the bugles from the Royal Hospital School, *Holbrook*, which play the Animals in and out of the Ark and end the opera so poignantly. And the Animals themselves, of course, who were auditioned (coincidentally in the presence of Aaron Copland) from schools right across the county of Suffolk.

The large orchestra (originally 150 players) includes strings, allowing for three grades of proficiency, and the whole lot, with the professional stiffening of a piano duet, string quintet, recorder and one percussion player were massed around the font of Orford church while the opera was played out on a stage erected at the end of the nave. The Aldeburgh Festival always depended on the use of local churches – in fact made a virtue of it – and the white simplicity of the twelfth-century church of Saint Bartholomew was ideally suited to this event. The jagged church tower, struck by lightning early in the 1880s (since rebuilt), has often watched a motley and sizeable crew struggling, in various stages of costume, across the old Town Square to the church below; the cast of *Noye's Fludde* were the first, the monks of the three Church Parables followed after.

The preparations for the first performance, given as part of the 1958 Aldeburgh Festival, were complicated and hilarious. The choirs (eighty Animals) and orchestra rehearsed in their separate groups all over East Anglia for some months before the concerted final rehearsals, to which they were ferried along the country roads in a fleet of charabancs. They were aided by a 'demo' record made with the composer at the piano, and with all the roles sung by him, Peter Pears, Imogen Holst, the composer's two sisters, and myself – a collector's item! John Schlesinger used the opportunity of *Noye* to make one of his early documentaries for BBC television's *Monitor* programme.

For the first production, the principal solo roles of Sem, Ham, Jaffett and their wives were given to boys and girls chosen from wide-held auditions; these supported the more experienced performances of Owen Brannigan as Noye and Gladys Parr (and later, Sheila Rex) as his drunken wife. Mrs Noye's gossips were to have come from a Suffolk school, but at the last minute the headmistress got wind of the innocently dissolute parts they were to play and had them withdrawn. Mrs Noye was Gladys Parr's last role before retirement, Owen Brannigan made Noye one of his most enduring and endearing characterizations, while Jaffett was sung by Michael Crawford, then a very recently broken-voiced young tenor.

The Chester plays were originally played on floats or carts at fairs and Britten was anxious to retain their basic naivety (though the music is far from naive). Trevor Anthony, the Welsh bass, was chosen (rather than a straight actor) to speak the Voice of God and, to achieve a similarly unsophisticated effect, it was decided that I should do the set. The ark was basically a combination of painted screens set by the Property Men around a flight of steps (Mount Ararat); they represented a galleon complete with waves and a cabin for Mr Noye in which the Raven and Dove sheltered. The design was taken from a medieval primitive painting of an ark in full sail. A palm tree was chopped down to use as the mast, from which the rigging slapped in the storm while Mrs Noye and a monkey were violently sick over the side.

At the climax of the storm the hymn 'Eternal Father strong to save' was sung by cast and audience; it was one of Britten's master-strokes, having additional significance on the storm-bound fishing coasts of East Anglia. This and the other two hymns provided much of the basic musical material.

One of the most ingenious features of the opera is that it can be performed by almost any group of musicians, using local resources as available. The same goes for the staging: Ceri Richards, the eminent Welsh painter, designed the original costumes for the principals and the set of masks and heads worn by the Animals over their school uniform, but many later productions have been as successful with simpler means. There is room even for a certain amount of extemporization in the orchestration: James Blades, the percussionist, rejoiced in helping Woolverstone Hall devise outlandish percussion instruments to be played alongside the slung mugs and the wind machine.

If I have written at some length about *Noye's Fludde*, it is because it represented my first, and most reponsible, work for Britten who, many felt, was taking some risk with a virtually untried director.

When Britten became involved with John Cranko's ballet *The Prince of the Pagodas* (one of the composer's most magical and neglected scores) he made some personal research into the music of the East. He was particularly affected by the Japanese Noh plays and by the music of Bali and Japan, and this influence is apparent in several succeeding works, notably the Church Parables, *Death in Venice*, and *A Midsummer Night's Dream*. It was natural that Cranko should become the director of this last: the scenario of the *Pagodas* ballet may have had its detractors, but the successful entente between composer, choreographer and designer (John Piper) cannot be belittled, nor its effect on the works to follow.

Like many of Britten's works, *A Midsummer Night's Dream* was written to celebrate a special occasion: the rebuilding and extension of Aldeburgh's Jubilee Hall, the scene of so many of the Festival's triumphs. There was to have been a new theatre: land had been bought and designs completed, but local politics and financial considerations got in the way and instead the stage of the Jubilee was enlarged.

The libretto was selected by Pears and Britten from Shakespeare: the condensation was cleverly accomplished with only one new line – 'compelling thee to marry with Demetrius' – which replaced the whole of Shakespeare's first act. This made it possible to open the opera with the Fairies, whose dissension controls the destinies of all the other characters.

Act I is preluded and interwoven with the mysterious music of the enchanted forest – a forest of shadows ruled over by their King, Oberon, and occasionally illuminated by Tytania as by a shaft of moonlight. Caught in a web thus woven, the poor mortals have no chance of escaping unaffected by all this magic. The act ends with Tytania (spelled thus to emphasise Britten's preferred way of pronunciation) going to sleep in her bower and the application of Love's juice to her eyes by the jealous Oberon.

The material and atmosphere of Act II is based on four shifting chords heard at the start – each one played by a different section of the orchestra and between them using up all twelve tones: strings for sleep and mystery, silver harp and percussion for the Fairies, woodwind for the benighted mortals, and brass for the mischief of Oberon and Puck and the Ass's bray. By the end of the second act, the lovers have quarrelled and been paired off more suitably, and Tytania sleeps, once again, in the arms of her beloved Ass.

The third act begins at dawn, with the dew on the ground bringing 'waking' in all its forms: the sun rises and the spells twine and intertwine with the translucent string music that underlies all the various revelations of the day. Transformation music – a joyous and ceremonial passacaglia (no Britten opera is without one) – translates the scene to the wedding celebrations at Theseus's palace and the Rustics' entertainment of 'Pyramus and Thisbe'. This is a delicious and wicked spoof of many operatic clichés – of music and performance: the EOG's three Flute-Thisbes (Peter Pears, Kenneth MacDonald and Bernard Dickerson) have vied with each other for the best rendering of a quasi-*Lucia* Mad Scene as performed by some well-loved Divas. Finally the opera is drawn to a close by the Fairies' nuptial blessing and Puck's Epilogue.

Britten wanted the Fairies to sound strange and unearthly, and so made the unconventional choice of a counter-tenor (Alfred Deller) for Oberon. There is no doubt in this version of the story that the Fairies control every happening with their whims and discord. It has been said by some critics that in the opera the humour of the lovers has been sacrificed to the element of magic and to the rumbustiousness of the comics. This may have been so in the original production, which took place at a time when Cranko was beset by personal and professional problems that inhibited his work on the opera (particularly his own preparation), and that finally resulted in his leaving the country. But in later productions, lovers, rustics and fairies have been shown to share equal measures of magic and wit, as they do in the play.

Shortly after the Aldeburgh premiere, the production, and the English Opera Group, were taken over by Covent Garden. Without the Royal Opera's administration and technical life-belt the EOG would never have survived, but it did mean the immediate demise of this original production. A new one was given, a few months later, at the Royal Opera House. It was conducted by Georg Solti, directed by John Gielgud, designed (quite differently) by John Piper, who had designed it at Aldeburgh, and had an almost entirely new cast.

Considering that the opera was conceived for the 'home team on its home ground' the sudden disappearance of the original production seems strange, and Britten and Aldeburgh had to wait until 1967 for a production of their own. This had a beautiful, kinetic set by Emanuele Luzzati and it christened the Snape Maltings operatically.

Snape, although built as a concert space, in fact lends itself well to opera, large-scale or small, and *A Midsummer Night's Dream* was to be followed by other successful productions: a guest performance of *Gloriana*, new productions of *The Rape of Lucretia*, *Albert Herring*, *The Turn of the Screw*, Mozart's *Idomeneo* conducted by Britten, and the Britten-Imogen Holst edition of Purcell's *Dido and Aeneas*. Britten's original version of Dido and Aeneas was first produced during the 1951 Festival of Britain EOG season; Imogen Holst came in as co-editor later.

It is worth mentioning, *en passant* while writing more or less chronologically, two 'variations of the original'. The 1963 production of the Britten version of *The Beggar's Opera* included a new Prelude to Act III. This was based by Britten on Lucy's air which opens the act but was orchestrated to represent the alarum bell which announces the escape of Macheath from Newgate at the end of Act II. This Prelude is in no printed score but it provides the opera with an impression of bells without which, along with horses, the sea, and a passacaglia, no Britten opera is complete. And, to keep the record straight and complete, the 1965 production at Aldeburgh of *The Little Sweep* included an entirely new play, also by Eric Crozier, to preface the opera – the old one being considered by then out of date and not representative of how operas are made today.

1964 saw the birth of *Curlew River*: it seemed as if my work of the previous six years, with the EOG and other companies in other fields, had all been an apprenticeship leading to this moment. The Noh play which had most affected Britten during his musical excursion to the Orient was *Sumidagawa*, written in the fifteenth century by the most revered playwright of the time, Juro Motomasa. It tells, very simply, of a Noblewoman who, driven mad by grief when her son is kidnapped, comes to a ferry. A boat waits to take pilgrims to a miracle-shrine on the further bank, but, because she is mad, the Ferryman refuses to carry her over until her despair moves him and the other pilgrims to feelings of guilt. During the journey he tells of the miraculous happenings at the shrine – the grave of a young child – and the Madwoman recognises her son from his story. At the tomb they are confronted by a vision of the boy and his mother is relieved of her madness.

The Noh plays are of Zen-Buddhist origin and were originally performed by the monks themselves: the action is extremely stylised and the women's roles were also played by the monks. (Some years later, on a visit to Kyoto, I was entertained at a monastery by the Abbot, who amazed me by reciting from memory long stretches of the Ferryman's role.) The play lay fallow in Britten's memory for nearly ten years until, with the help of William Plomer, librettist of *Gloriana*, who himself had spent many years in Japan, he was ready.

The problem was to preserve the simplicity and stylization of the Noh play while creating a style sympathetic to a present-day western audience; the text is extremely close to the original and at all costs pastiche had to be avoided. This was achieved by giving the story the framework of a performance by western monks (of indeterminate period), and transferring the story to the fens of East Anglia. At the opening of the opera (Britten preferred to call it a Church Parable) the Monks process through the church singing an appropriate plainchant melody (in this case 'Te lucis'), which provides the thematic basis for the whole work. The Monks include a group of seven lay-brother musicians who accompany the singers. After a simple address by the Abbot, to organ and drums, the Monks make preparation for the play.

While working on the opera in Venice, we attended mass given in their own chapel by the monks of San Giorgio Maggiore. We were impressed and moved by the ritual robing of the Brother of the Day who was to celebrate the mass – the robes were unfolded from a linen chest with extreme delicacy and reverence. This led Britten to follow the Abbot's address in the Parable with a robing ceremony: the orchestra is heard playing together for the first time and the passage is based on 'Te lucis'. During this the three monks chosen as the story's protagonists are prepared and robed for the assumption of their roles. At the end of the Parable, the whole process is reversed (with the orchestral music in mirror-image) for the recessional.

Britten carried many of the musical characteristics of *Sumidagawa* into *Curlew River*: slow flute trills echoed by the voice, groups of repeated notes on one syllable, the use of small hand percussion. But the music is unmistakably his own, and the seven players (flute, horn, organ, percussion, harp, viola and double bass) combine to give magical and full-bodied sounds. A melisma is frequently built into the orchestral and voice parts to create the effect of an echo or resonance even when the acoustic is dry.

A notable peculiarity of the work is that there is no conductor as such: at every point of the score the ensemble is led by one of the instruments, a singer, or even a gesture – these 'leaders' are clearly denoted in the score. This meant, during the composition, the most careful consideration of placing – the relative positions of the seated musicians to the singer at any given moment being very important. I was asked to design the set and to give Britten a model *before* he started composing so that he could have it by him at all times when working out the logistics and dynamic balances. He usually wanted to involve the director and the designer at the libretto stage of conception, so that production ideas could be included as he went and he himself could build up a visual picture at the same time. *Curlew* was an extreme case of this and my presence in Venice was necessary while he was writing so that we could discuss the staging of each section before and after he wrote it. (The peace of Venice was essential to him since the US Air Force had begun to use his house at Aldeburgh as a landmark for lining up their jet fighter trainees on the runway approach to their nearby air base.)

Preliminary work on the production did not end here: a style of movement had to be devised – by a director who, perhaps fortunately, had never seen a Noh play in the flesh – a style which, like the music, retained the distilled intensity of the original without attempting to copy it. The singers, and even the players to some extent, underwent a course of movement training before and during rehearsals. A vocabulary of hieratic gesture was devised which had to be truthful and not stilted: the watchpoints were control, clarity, and concentration.

The first night audience could have had no idea of what awaited them in Orford church: the suspense – for all of us – was heightened by a blackout and an electrical storm just as the performance was about to begin. For forty-five minutes they sat patiently in the dark and were to reward the eventual end of the piece with an extraordinarily receptive silence which seemed to last a very long time.

Once again Britten had broken new ground in the development of opera and this time with minute forces which belied the effect they created. He was to use many features discovered during the *Curlew River* experience in the works which followed the three Church Parables – notably in *Death in Venice*. Meanwhile, the following year saw a recording and a revival of *Curlew River* and the first steps taken toward its successor, *The Burning Fiery Furnace*.

On the way to the *Jours de Fête* at Tours, a visit to Chartres Cathedral impressed us all with the magnificent colours and imagery of the stained-glass windows. Here too, but in a sculpture, were Nebuchadnezzar and the Fiery Furnace, and here the second Church Parable was born. If *Curlew River* had been introvert in the Zen sense, *The Burning Fiery Furnace* was outgoing, fantastic and colourful. It follows the same pattern and convention and is also a story of faith. William Plomer developed the style 'authentically': here the Protagonist is threefold – Ananias, Azarias and Misael, the favourites of the King – and the Antagonist is dual and more dangerous – the mad Nebuchadnezzar and the Astrologer who pits his idolatrous beliefs against the steadfast faith of the three young Jews. The same triptych form is there: after the first clashes of will at the Feast, the three young men deliberate with anxiety on their future, at the same dramatic point as the Ferryman had told his tale in mid-stream, in a trio based closely on the opening plainchant melody 'Salus eterna'. The dramatic happenings at the tomb of the Madwoman's son and her faith's reward of peace and sanity are here paralleled by the raising of the Image of Gold and the appearance of the Angel in the

Furnace. Here the resolution is the conversion of Nebuchadnezzar.

Both the Acolytes (trebles) and the players take a more active part: the boys provide an entertainment at the Feast – thought by many to be unsatisfactory and unnecessary – as well as the dazzling Angel in the Furnace. The players, to whom is added an alto trombone, have a pagan march to play as they parade round the church while Merodak, the Image of Gold, is raised. The Parable ends, before the closing Ceremony, with a 'Benedicite' in which the Angel and the other trebles echo the men's voices in descant.

If the windows of Chartres provided an impetus for the Second Parable, Rembrandt's *Prodigal Son* at the Hermitage in Leningrad, visited during an English Opera Group tour of Russia, was one of the inspirations for the Third Parable. Although it followed the same format, deliberate and startling divergences from the pattern, established in the other two works, heightened the effect of *The Prodigal Son* and allowed it to stand high in its own right. It also demanded a greater complexity of staging. In *The Burning Fiery Furnace* the Abbot himself takes on the responsibility of performing the evil Astrologer; in this work the opening ceremonies and plainchant are interrupted by the appearance in the aisle of the Abbot, dressed and masked as the Tempter, mocking the Monks and their congregation. *His* 'sermon' intends to show how evil and greed will triumph. The first part of the story is quiet, idyllic and pastoral: the Chorus and the Elder Son work in the fields (slow motion and stylized mime) while the Younger Son is persuaded by his alter ego, the Tempter, to demand his patrimony from the Father. He leaves home: there is a transitory passage while the Son tramps through the sands of the desert, for which James Blades devised an unusual percussion effect. On his arrival at the City, the Son is greeted by the decadent Citizens, and the central section, far from being introspective, represents the temptations to which he succumbs: the sensuality and greed represented by wine, women, and gambling. (Here the orchestral addition is a high trumpet with a glorious, wild concerto-like prominence.) The Temptations were by far the hardest section of the three Parables to conceive and to stage; the words, music, and production were shaken up and altered more than once. The Tempter is triumphant in one of the most devastating moments of the three Parables. The return of the Prodigal, struggling wearily through the sand, mirrors his jaunty departure. The Father's greeting, arguably the most moving moment in all three Parables, prefaces the festal rejoicing, which is interrupted by the Elder Son and concluded with the Father's final moral. The lesson is taken up by the Abbot (as himself now) before the final Recession.

The three operas were all performed on the same wooden stage – a raked circle, high enough for sightlines in church, on one side approached by a spiral ramp and bounded by the orchestra on the other. The main circle's acting-area contains a highly polished upper circular level: a kind of 'sacred' Noh stage area which is only used by the principal characters in the stories. Behind the approach ramp, which itself provides yet another upper and lower level, and diagonally opposite to the orchestra, is a tall mast used in *Curlew River* for the sail during the journey, for the Image of Gold, Merodak, in *The Burning Fiery Furnace*, and for a sun which sets at the Prodigal's departure and rises again on his return. Each of the three works had its own individual language of movement while conforming to a certain basic vocabulary.

The first two pieces were revived and recorded in successive years until the *Prodigal* made it possible to present all three together as a cycle on successive evenings. The English Opera Group was once again given new life and possibilities as the triptych impressed audiences all over the world. Each opera was published in short score by Faber Music – Britten's publishers since 1964 when his previous long-standing arrangement with Boosey & Hawkes was allowed to lapse – accompanied by very full 'production notes'. I was doubtful about the wisdom of this idea, which I felt was redolent of Gilbert and Sullivan and the traditions of the D'Oyly Carte, but Britten was nervous of an 'operatic' style of production in other hands, and wanted the notes published, not as essential instruction but as an indication of the style in which he felt the operas should be performed.

In 1963, to celebrate Britten's fiftieth birthday, there was a semi-staged concert performance of *Gloriana* conducted by Bryan Fairfax at the Royal Festival Hall. In spite of the occasion's coinciding with the assassination of John F. Kennedy in Dallas – news filtered through in the interval – the opera was a great success, the Press eating the words of their colleagues of 1953. In 1966, Sadler's Wells Opera needed a last-minute substitute for a cancelled new production and it was decided to mount *Gloriana*. It had to be prepared at short notice but this added to the air of excitement that was felt by all the participants from the start of rehearsals. I proposed to Britten a simple, fluid and fast-moving production in the style of the Elizabethan stage – 'A prince is set upon a stage, in sight of all the world, and must not fail' (Act III scene iii). Sylvia Fisher's assumption of Elizabeth, a worthy successor to that of Joan Cross, brought her to a new peak in her career, and the opera has remained in the repertory ever since.

Shortly before our visit to Russia in 1964, Britten said two things of widely differing import: that he was greatly excited by the Russian soprano, Galina Vishnevskaya whom he had seen as Natasha in *War and Peace* at the Bolshoi (she was the wife of Rostropovitch, the cellist with whom Britten had already struck up a lasting friendship); and that he had been asked by the Vienna Boys' Choir to write them a short opera for their concert programmes – preferably one in which they would not have to play girls' parts – and that he had as yet no ideas for a project.

I suggested *Anna Karenina* as a subject for himself and Vishnevskaya. He did not at once disagree and a letter soon afterwards showed how his interest had quickly grown:

BB to CG 19 February 1965:

> It is a fabulous book and I have been very over-excited by it and had lots of ideas about the possible opera. But oh, – how *can* one completely compress it into one evening? The main difficulty as I see it is – how to convey the main ideas of the work, of these two couples, the one living only for 'self' (altho' brilliant, beautiful and occasionally touching) and the other, for God or Goodness – viz. the last section (although Levine and Kitty are never pompous or pretentious). Of course, the Anna-Vronsky story is famous, and useful as the impetus for the whole, and one must keep the main features. But can we find a way of doing the two strands side by side? One, one might typify by the city life, and the other by the country, but avoiding, of course, too much over-simplification and, above all, avoiding making the main characters abstractions – the moral, tho' clear, unexpressed. What a task! I hope we can do it, *because I can think of nothing more important in one's life than finding another medium (the operatic) for this wonderful story.*'

The following winter of 1965–6 I was at the Red House for an extended visit to work on the first draft. The task, an enormous challenge, was exhilarating and devouring. In odd moments we discussed possibilities for the Vienna Boys and came up with the old ballad of *The Golden Vanity*. Some few stanzas long only, this story of a treacherous captain (supposed by some to be Francis Drake) who lets his cabin boy drown rather than reward him with his daughter's hand for sinking the Turkish pirate-ship, contained the kernel of an idea.

The spring of 1966 saw Britten in hospital and the composition of *The Burning Fiery Furnace* interrupted. As a convalescence present I gave him the completed first drafts of both *Anna* and *The Golden Vanity*, the latter now expanded into a short opera. The plot is considerably extended, with much more conflict and involvement for the 'Turkey pirates', and the new material – some twenty stanzas – a pastiche of the original four or five. This saw its way into a second version in the ballad form, broken up for the introduction of recitative – a kind of miniature *Billy Budd*, complete with sea-battle.

BB to CG 14 August 1966:

> . . . I sit slogging away at the 'Lowland Sea'. I am enjoying it quite a bit – it's not too easy to do, but I think it's working out all right. The words are excellent and stimulating. Things crop up of course as one goes along . . . I've wanted a bit *more* on several occa.ions and so I have either invented myself (to be corrected by you later!) or gone back to Version I and picked out some discarded bits . . .

When the opera was completed (for double boys' chorus – the crews of *The Golden Vanity* and the *Turkish Galilee* – and soloists) I was despatched to Vienna to rehearse the boys. Although an excellent German translation had been provided by Hans Keller, I was glad at the Choir's decision to do it in English for the sake of their American and British tours. Rehearsals were fun (with two long benches to represent the ships – even in performance – and suitable flags) and clearly quite different from anything else they were used to!

The premiere was at Snape on 3 June 1967. The eighteen-minute opera was such a success that they immediately repeated the whole thing. Once again Britten had provided what the performers were best at.

Meanwhile *Anna* had reached her second draft and Britten had started discussions with Galya and Slava Rostropovitch. Plans were made for a Bolshoi premiere with Galya as Anna and Slava as translator and conductor. However, from now, like some other composers' best intentions (notably Verdi's *Il Re Lear*), Nemesis was to stalk this project. The first bombshell came with the Russian invasion of Prague. We were engaged on a production of *Peter Grimes* for Scottish Opera at the Edinburgh Festival when we heard the news on the radio at lunchtime. Galya and Slava were with us and were devastated. This was a great setback, and even the Foreign Office took pains to point out tactfully that a Bolshoi commission was now surely out of place.

Galya herself temporarily disappeared from the operatic scene at this moment and other sopranos were considered; also the idea of scaling the subject down to a more economical scale for production at Snape. The distillation could have been an advantage, but now I had my own worries. The shape of the adaptation, we felt, was successful: it maintained the relationships and contrasts referred to in Britten's letter above – it would be a long opera but no longer than some and it would not require huge forces, Bolshoi or no Bolshoi. But I was not happy with the quality of the actual words. These excerpts from letters speak for themselves:

CG to BB 26 November 1967:

> I feel that in trying to be faithful to Tolstoy's 'everyday' way of speech on one hand, and not to be too pretentiously 'poetic' on the other, I have fallen between two stools. The bits that seem best to me are the very ones that are original and not adapted from Tolstoy's dialogue.
> Would you mind if I sent the libretto as it now stands to William [Plomer] to ask what he thinks? I would very much value his 'reader's opinion' and hope he will feel able to give advice . . .'

Britten agreed and Plomer was willing to assess the libretto.

WP to CG 10th January 1968:

> I have carefully read, re-read and brooded over your third draft of Anna K. I am worried about your wish to re-write the whole thing again. I find the whole construction of the piece markedly ingenious, and intensely dramatic, but what we are concerned with is the language. I *don't* find the language 'banal', but I do find it plain. And I feel this is right. I don't believe that flowery paraphrasing of Tolstoy's plain, lifelike directness and naturalism would do any good. The plainness, the very plainness of the language is often touching, moving, or even exciting to read, in your libretto I mean. So think what it will be like when the music carries it away.

I never had the opportunity of discussing this impasse with Britten: we became very involved in preparation for *The Prodigal Son* and then, another blow. Britten had always been sensitive about premature public discussion of his work, particularly before composition had begun. Unfortunately so many people were now involved in this project that it was difficult to keep it dark, and too much interest was now being shown by the Press and even by foreign impresarios for Britten's liking. It was enough to inhibit him.

Then came the offer from the BBC to commission a television opera – which happened when Britten was feeling strongly about the Vietnam War and the shooting of students at Kent University.

Although Britten never actually stated he had shelved *Anna*, I believe it was this series of events, from Prague onwards (including his own ill-health), that put paid to the project. The textual problem might well have been resolved with Plomer's help, but he died in 1973. Naturally, it was a disappointment to me, and I still feel sad at the loss of this opera he might have written – one which I believe would have shown a range of passions and emotional depths different to those he had yet charted.

Britten had been very impressed by Basil Coleman's television production of *Billy Budd*. Many people thought it a perfect opera for television, perhaps even more suited to that medium than the stage. His one criticism was the bad balance and rapport between singers and conductor when he and the orchestra had to be in another studio. Accordingly, when Britten agreed to conduct a special television production of *Peter Grimes* it was filmed at Snape, all under the one roof whose acoustics had now been tried and tested in many sound recordings. The success of *Billy Budd* was also to lead indirectly to Britten's acceptance of the commission for his television opera.

Basil Coleman was the obvious choice for director of *Peter Grimes*, but he felt unable to do the work justice in Snape without the full technical resources of a television studio. Finally a BBC staff producer was appointed (Brian Large, who had been having considerable success with his imaginative visualization of concerts and some oratorios, notably *The Dream of Gerontius*), and Joan Cross was asked to take charge of the acting performance. The cast foregathered for a long and wintry period of filming at Snape in February 1969.

Appreciation of the final product was mixed, and Britten was not entirely happy with the great distance between him and the singers even in the same area. But the film sold well and all was set fair for the commissioned work.

I believe *Owen Wingrave* was sold in advance to as many as seventeen international television companies for simultaneous transmission. The massive audience was a wonderful opportunity for Britten to make his personal statement about war and the empty glory of heroism, in the context of the Vietnam War and the shooting of the students demonstrating against it on Kent campus. The story, by Henry James, was particularly apposite. Owen, the last scion of a traditionally military family, rebels against the gory tradition of his ancestors and suffers humiliation, and finally death, at the hands of his nearest and dearest and the spirits of his forebears. He dies 'the bravest of them all'.

Myfanwy Piper, librettist of *The Turn of the Screw*, wrote the text, and the opera was given an all-star cast of singers most closely associated with Britten's work: Sylvia Fisher, Janet Baker, Heather Harper, Jennifer Vyvyan, Benjamin Luxon, John Shirley-Quirk, Nigel Douglas (a 'newcomer') and Peter Pears. Brian Large was in charge of the cameras and administration, and I was supposed to direct the production and be in 'overall artistic control'. Understandably this was an important venture for the BBC, and their arrangement was not without its problems. To begin with, I found it difficult to keep tabs on the advance preparations, since all matters, artistic and administrative, inevitably passed through channels within the BBC where the opinions of 'outsiders' were not made welcome. By the time we went into rehearsal, I felt that I was there very much on sufferance, at Britten's request, and that I had had little or no influence on the artistic conception.

All rehearsals went well at Snape in spite of the arctic weather of November 1970 – particularly the scenes at Paramore, seat of the Wingraves. But the filming itself was complicated by Britten's ill-health, which eventually kept him away from the gruelling daytime camera rehearsals at a time when he most needed to be there to see how the scenes would develop on the screen. By the time he arrived in the evenings for the filming sessions, he was inevitably presented with *faits accomplis* very often not to his liking.

In spite of an excellent performance and Brian Large's brilliant camera work, the final effect of the opera on the screen lacked impact. Although the opera was conceived for television, Britten constantly had the theatre in mind for the work's final homecoming. While he was composing, he said he feared *Owen* would finally be completely successful only on the stage. Maybe the camera had too selective an eye for a work which relies very much on the accumulative effect of ensemble reaction. The short tele-script-type scenes at the start of the opera, before Owen goes down to Paramore, dilute the drama; some of Britten's later stage works were inclined to linger overmuch in a state of prologue, and the real pace of this drama is delayed until the characters assemble in the haunted Paramore – where the atmosphere (and the musical invention) engenders quickly and powerfully and the precipitous second act is gripping.

We gave the stage premiere at the Royal Opera House, Covent Garden, two years later with basically the same cast. It had a magnificent and eerily transparent set by John Piper, which made possible the constant atmospheric changes which were conspicuously absent in our television production. Again the preliminary scenes came off least well and left one with the feeling that all the necessary information could have been integrated to better effect into the scenes at Paramore. Britten's surmise that the opera would come off better in the theatre was right. In spite of these strictures I believe *Owen Wingrave* to be an underrated work, perhaps because of its long slow start, perhaps because of the topical connotation of its genesis. Its precepts, nonetheless, remain constantly apposite and the music has great power and brilliance. Britten cannot have been entirely disillusioned with the medium of television as, in his last months, he was discussing the possibility of setting the Chester Christmas Plays for live performance by Pimlico School with a later performance by them on television.

At the American premiere at Santa Fe Opera, the audience and Press were enthusiastic. The identification of the audience with Owen's feelings was undoubtedly much stronger than in England because of personal involvement in the situation of the Vietnam War. Even in the preliminary scenes some remarks were greeted with applause, and the American cast put the work over with driving conviction and commitment.

Paradoxically, the script of *Death in Venice* reads even more like a film-script than *Owen Wingrave* and makes greater 'cinematic' demands on staging than its predecessor. Britten managed to keep the early discussions of *Death in Venice* under wraps for some time. He had mentioned the idea from time to time and, a few weeks after the filming of *Owen*, I presented him with a scenario to suggest how Thomas Mann's novella might be adapted as an opera for the stage. He gave me a funny look, and it turned out that he had already discussed the idea with Myfanwy Piper, whose libretto is a masterly achievement of a very difficult task.

Perhaps of all his works, this one went deepest into Britten's own soul: there are extraordinary cross-currents of affinity between himself, his own state of health and mind, Thomas Mann, Aschenbach (Mann's dying author-protagonist), and Peter Pears, who must have had to tear himself in three in order to reconstitute himself as the principal character.

The central situation concerns a distinguished author who fears his inspiration has dried up: he turns from a coldly classical attitude to art and beauty to a sensual and painful self-involvement which finally destroys him. At an early stage of the opera's composition, Britten was told a heart operation was essential if he was to live for more than two years. He constantly expressed the fear (not for the first time) that he might not live to finish his opera. After a slow start, it was written with extreme urgency – a white heat which is very evident in the second part of the opera, in parallel with Aschenbach's own illness.

The forces of the opera are unusual. The orchestra, apart from a large percussion section, is standard. (It is similar to that of *Owen Wingrave*, which was the first full-scale opera, orchestrally, since *Gloriana*, eighteen years its senior.) There are three principal protagonists: Aschenbach, the author; the ambiguous Traveller who recurs in seven different guises during the course of the opera; and Tadzio, the

Polish boy. The Traveller is a fate-figure represented by all the characters in the story who are responsible for turning Aschenbach towards Venice and eventually to his death. In the book many of these have features in common – a certain shape of hat, a skull-like aspect, bad teeth – and to them the librettist has added the enigmatic Hotel Manager who becomes Aschenbach's principal antagonist. This role was written especially for John Shirley-Quirk, who provided a *tour de force*. Tadzio was not as easy to find: not only had he to be 'perfect', but also a good dancer.

The dance aspect was crucial. All of us who had seen it, found the relationship between Tadzio and Aschenbach too sentimental and salacious in Visconti's film. Britten himself, who did not see it, was nevertheless certain that a convention had to be found which would keep these protagonists separated on different planes. One of the more poignant aspects of the story is that Aschenbach finds it impossible to make contact with the boy.

Britten had wanted to work with Frederick Ashton again ever since he directed the premiere of *Albert Herring*. Now he approached him to explore the possibility of containing Tadzio's world in dance and stylized movement. Tadzio, his Mother – the Lady of the Pearls – and the rest of his family and friends all became dancers. It was important to find someone with the right qualities of personality and looks for Tadzio. Eventually Ashton discovered Robert Huguenin in the ranks of the Royal Ballet, and Deanne Bergsma performed the role of the Lady of the Pearls.

The cast is completed by an ensemble of twenty-seven young soloists who fill all the other roles, large and small, of the citizens of Venice and her foreign visitors, and also act as 'chorus' when necessary.

Musically, the opera uses three distinctly different styles: the 'black-and-white', piano-accompanied recitative, in which Aschenbach examines his emotions in the light of his literary precepts; the 'coloured' orchestral sections, which accompany the development of the plot and represent the atmosphere of Venice and the Lido; and the silvery percussion, which attends Tadzio and the dance and which again shows an oriental influence.

Britten had been growing away from conventional forms of staging ever since *Gloriana*, and he was at first particularly keen on finding an unconventional way to stage *Death in Venice*. The filmic approach to the libretto made it difficult for John Piper and me to find the right convention. Britten had first to be persuaded that no scene had to be presented in a literal way; there had to be some expressionistic form of stylization. This was compounded by the use of dance.

Snape seemed to lend itself to various unconventional shapes of stage, which were tried, but eventually and inevitably it was the musical convention that dictated our final solution. We set the whole in a black box like the inside of a camera whose retina opened to reveal the constantly shifting pattern of colour and images of Aschenbach's mind. The recitatives were placed in a sharp horizontal shaft of white light which isolated and lifted Aschenbach from the black recesses of his mind. The dance sections were presented in a different colour-quality of light or against a gleaming white background to highlight the Greek classical aspect. These walls could also change to John Piper's depiction of Venice during the author's visits to La Serenissima. His striking paintings were complemented by Charles Knode's evocative costumes and the lighting of John B. Read, which played as important a part as the staging or the rest of the design.

The second act, as I have indicated, was written with an urgency which encompasses Aschenbach's despair and dissolution and the composer's own desperation to complete the opera. It is in this act that the libidos of Britten, Mann, and Aschenbach coalesce. The hysteria rests for a moment towards the end with one of the most poignant and unforgettable moments of Britten's works when Aschenbach, at the end of mental and physical tether, remembers Socrates's farewell to Phaedrus; Pears's performance was particularly moving. It is impossible to ignore the connection with Britten's last String Quartet, which was first played at Snape, by the Amadeus Quartet some months after Britten's death. Finished in Venice shortly before his death, on a last visit without Pears, this stands as a very personal and final message.

The first act of *Death in Venice* takes Aschenbach to the city and to 'the warm and lovely South' where, against his better nature, he becomes involved with Tadzio. The act is not without its problems, not least in the many extended recitatives. In the second act these are fewer, shorter, and more subjective. It is significant that the Overture ('The Arrival in Venice') is heard after the prologue, some twenty minutes after the beginning of the opera. The long dance sequence which ends the act – 'The Feasts of Apollo' – set a series of problems once the composer and librettist had decided to base the scene on a pentathlon. Although set to some exquisite music, five events are too many and dilute the impression made by Tadzio in Ashton's choreography. Even Ashton was somewhat stumped when confronted by long-jumps and sprinting races. When Britten eventually saw the opera at a special performance at Snape some months after the premiere, he was dissatisfied with the shape of this scene. He made small cuts, but I feel he might have reconsidered its shape more drastically had he been able to be present at rehearsals; it would not have been the first occasion that he found subsequent alterations necessary. He nearly always had one sticking point; the scores of *The Rape of Lucretia* and *Billy Budd* were considerably revised after their first production, and the climax of *Curlew River* was rewritten five times during rehearsals before he was satisfied.

To say that we missed the composer during rehearsals would be an understatement. He was always a remarkable colleague on these occasions, and his interpreters were here trying to realize what was perhaps the most difficult assignment he had ever set them. Peter Pears was working on the most arduous and personally-involving role of his career at the same time that Britten was under surgery in hospital; his professional devotion and application had never been greater. In spite of the strain, perhaps because of it, Aschenbach is arguably his finest interpretation to date.

It was typical of Britten that, at the special performance when he saw his opera for the first time, he was more nervous on his colleagues' behalf than on his own, knowing how we would have felt had he not liked it. Since the designs were completed he had seen and heard nothing, and he can have had no idea how he would find his own work when presented with it so objectively. Happily he made only a few minor adjustments – mostly involved with 'The Feasts of Apollo'.

The wheel of Britten's stage works came full circle with the British premiere of *Paul Bunyan*. The operetta which was his first stage work had waited more than thirty years for another production, and this was also to be the last of Britten's involvements in the theatre. Since the death of its author, W. H. Auden, tantalizing bits and pieces of this amazing score had emerged in various light-hearted concerts. Finally permission was granted to the BBC for a full sound production. Although a few revisions were made, the work was heard virtually as it was first written, and triumphantly.

Based on the legendary exploits of an American backwoods giant, Paul Bunyan, the operetta borrows freely from various music-theatre styles and also provides interesting pre-echoes of works which were to follow. It was written by Britten and Auden in response to a demand for semi-serious works of musical quality suitable for performance on campus. It was first given by Columbia University, New York in 1941. Britten was disillusioned by the staging of the piece and disheartened by critical reaction. His old friend Auden had not been easy to work with and their friendship was strained when Britten returned to England in 1942. This is history. So is the creation of *Peter Grimes* which followed. All or none of these things may have been contributory factors, but *Paul Bunyan* was withdrawn.

. By the late 1970s, the underpinning motives of the story – ecology, the brotherhood of man, the end of an era – were once again topical in the world and for Britten personally. Even so it took a great deal of persuasion – and of his own courage – before he allowed it to be staged again. Many objections were raised beyond the obvious one – that this might be the painful revival of a flop. He particularly did not want it thought of as an opera, let alone the successor to *Death in Venice* which he must have considered his final statement for the stage.

At this point, the English Opera Group had made way for the creation of the English Music Theatre, whose purpose was to develop the versatility and facilities of young singers in a wide spectrum of music theatre. Steuart Bedford and I were the Artistic Directors: Bedford had conducted the BBC performance and we were naturally eager to have *Paul Bunyan* in our first year's repertory. The BBC performance had given much pleasure and received great critical acclaim. I think it was this, and the final efforts of Donald Mitchell, Britten's friend and publisher, and his wife Kathleen, which persuaded him to let us have a go. It opened the 1976 Aldeburgh Festival in the presence of the composer who, although not able to be at rehearsals, had been much involved in the conception of the production. Shortly before *Paul Bunyan* paid a return visit to Snape that Christmas, Britten died. He had always found the final scene, Paul's Farewell at the end of the Christmas Party, personally moving, and this Christmas performance, only a few days after his death, affected everyone present:

CHORUS	The campfire embers are black and cold,
	The banjos are broken, the stories are told,
	The woods are cut down and the young are grown old . . .
	No longer the logger shall hear in the Fall
	The pine and the spruce and the sycamore call. . . .
PAUL	Goodbye, dear friends,
CHORUS	Goodbye, Paul
INKSLINGER	Paul, who are you?
PAUL	Where the night becomes the day
	Where the dream becomes the fact,
	I am the Eternal guest
	I am Way
	I am Act.

The last opera: *Death in Venice*

Thomas Mann's novella *Der Tod in Venedig*, published in 1912, is a highly wrought composition that lends itself to musical setting. It employs a technique of motivic repetition, variation, and cross-reference probably suggested by the musicians' leitmotiv system. It is rich in recurrent and developing imagery and in allusions: Plato, Platen, and Plutarch, Socrates and Schiller, Homer, Virgil, and Nietzsche all play upon it. At moments, the chiselled German prose even moves into classical metres. Benjamin Britten's last opera, performed at the Aldeburgh Festival in 1973, was *Death in Venice*, to a libretto skilfully drawn from Mann by Myfanwy Piper. If Mann had written his work especially to inspire Britten, he could hardly have made it more apt for Britten's music. Uncannily, its images are those that the composer had been using throughout his career. In Mann's first chapter, his protagonist, Gustav von Aschenbach, has a vision of the exotic, menacing East (birthplace of both Dionysus and the cholera that between them are to destroy him) and of a tiger's eyes gleaming through the steamy forest; we recall the tiger that lurked in the forest of Lucretia's dreams in Britten's opera *The Rape of Lucretia* and burned bright in his Blake settings. The sea is another symbol important in Mann's tale and in many of Britten's works. Aschenbach's 'love of the ocean had profound sources: the hard-worked artist's longing for rest, his yearning to seek refuge from the manifold shapes of his fancy in the bosom of the simple and the vast; and another yearning – for the unorganized, the immeasurable, the eternal.' This theme Britten had already sounded, before *Death in Venice*, in *Peter Grimes* and *Billy Budd*. The beauty and innocence of childhood had long attracted him, who wrote the finest children's music of our day. The children in *Death in Venice* do not sing, but they dance to a bright percussion patter and iridescent gamelan timbres that recall *The Prince of the Pagodas* and the child-fairy consort of *A Midsummer Night's Dream*. Mann's central image, of a youth who seems to embody the world's grace and beauty, is one that had long troubled and inspired the composer of the *Michelangelo Sonnets*, *Les Illuminations*, *Billy Budd*, and the *Nocturne*.

For the mysterious, prowling menace, for the limitless sea, for the innocent children, and for Tadzio, the lovely youth, Britten found themes, timbres, rhythms, and harmonies that can play upon one another. Through a clear rising octave followed by a chain of thirds, triad-accompanied, we behold the sea itself. Death, Dionysus, and sweet, sultry threat from the East stalk through the stricken city, and through the stricken Aschenbach's increasingly fevered fancies, in thirds no longer open but clogged and sinister. Often enough, Mann himself seems to have prescribed the musical treatment – when, for example, Aschenbach sits contemplating the sea, 'dreaming deep, deep into the void' as Britten and his heroes have so often done, and suddenly a human form disturbs the horizon; 'he withdrew his gaze from the illimitable, and lo!, it was the lovely youth who crossed his vision.' In the opera, Aschenbach spins serene melismas around the 'sea' motif, and then, across the quiet-glowing calm, the 'Tazdio' motif, radiant on the vibraphone, casts not a shadow but a different, shimmering, more immediate kind of light. At the close of both book and opera, there is a transformation and reconciliation of images. Hitherto, the attendant figures urging Aschenbach along each stage of his journey have borne the attributes of Hermes, conductor of souls; but now, in a passage that draws on the *Symposium*, Tadzio himself is seen as the young Hermes. Aschenbach's last sight as he dies is of the 'lovely psychogogue' beckoning toward Plato's 'vast sea of beauty' – on whose shore the man whose love of the beautiful has transcended the particular 'will create many fair and noble thoughts, grow and wax strong.' In the score, the 'Tadzio' motif, as heard here, seems to provide an answer to Peter Grimes's question, 'What harbour shelters peace?' (A similar musical shape, a recurrent Britten motif, accompanied the inflamed Tarquin when he plunged into the cooling waters of the Tiber, and Billy Budd in his dream of long ocean sleep.) Frederick Ashton, in his sensitive choreography for *Death in Venice*, mirrored the classical allusion by basing this final sequence on the attitude of the Giambologna Mercury.

In his work-notes for the novella (as we learn from T. J. Reed's careful, perceptive edition of it), Mann transcribed the *Symposium* passage and underlined the phrase '*an die Ufer des grossen Meeres der Schönheit*'. His reference to it in *Der Tod in Venedig* is oblique, but then much about the tale, and particularly its close, is by intention ambiguous. The author's first impulse was to make of a real-life experience (what purports to be the real-life Tadzio's account of the event was published in the German magazine *Twen* in 1965) an 'intoxicate song' – in which, presumably, Aschenbach would have found new inspiration beneath the touch of Dionysus. But then, when the Apollonian pressures of thought, study, reason, and careful craftsmanship were brought to bear on the emotional adventure, the intoxicate song became, as its author somewhat ruefully confessed, a 'moral tale'. Although homosexuality, he said, was a way of feeling that he honoured, and although there could be more essential *Geist*, or inspiration, in it than in 'normality', in the novella it had finally been rejected, not hymned, because the moral and social responsibilities of a novelist should outweigh an individual's lyrical, private enthusiasm. Within *Der Tod in Venedig* lie the preoccupations and unresolved paradoxes of Mann's unfinished essay on *Geist und Kunst*. The work itself, though much admired, he deemed a 'secret failure'. Its author had shown himself not a *Dichter* but a *Schriftsteller*; the selfconscious, calculating artificer had conquered the aspirant poet.

But Mann was wrong, and Britten's opera shows it. Opera is the medium in which music can answer questions and resolve paradoxes when words alone must fail. Consider the last scene of *The Ring*, whose sense Wagner felt to be sufficient, though he could never verbalize it. Consider the penultimate scene of *Death in Venice*, when a passage from the *Phaedrus* – Socrates' reflections on the path, from beauty appreciated by the senses, that may lead to wisdom, or to the abyss – is quoted by Aschenbach. In Mann, the sentences are 'shaped in a disordered brain,' murmured and muttered from 'a rouged and flabby mouth'. So, too, in the opera – but they are set to one of the most limpid, tenderly beautiful melodies that Britten ever composed and are followed by a brave, splendid paean built from the 'limitless sea' motif. The essential, dithyrambic quality that the novelist feared had been lost during the 'sobering, corrective process' of his writing has by the composer been revealed.

Aschenbach, of course, is not a simple mask for Mann, any more than he is for Britten (or, *pace* the Visconti film, for Gustav Mahler, who lent only his forename and physical appearance to Mann's hero). Though *Der Tod in Venedig* is one of a series of tales in which Mann explored the techniques by which life is made into art, here the 36-year-old author projected himself forward, imagining the plight of an established, honoured author whose rigorous dedication to purity of form has been extreme. One who has followed only Apollo is destroyed at the last by Dionysus. Britten approached the experience from, so to speak, the other side. Older than Aschenbach, established and honoured, author of a recent opera, *Owen Wingrave*, whose musical manners and gestures, timbres, and tricks of utterance were commonly judged masterly but somewhat disappointingly familiar, he may have been struck by some sentences in Mann's account of Aschenbach: 'His later style gave up the old sheer audacities, the fresh and subtle nuances; it became fixed and exemplary, conservative, formal, even formulated. . . . Not that he was doing bad work. So much, at least, the years had brought him, that at any moment he might feel tranquilly assured of mastery. But he got no joy out of it – not though a nation paid him homage. To him, it seemed that his work had ceased to be marked by that fiery play of fancy which is the product of joy and which, more potently than any intrinsic content, forms in turn the joy of the receiving world.' Most creators pass through such dark hours. (Mann imagined one of Schiller's in another of his tales, *Schwere Stunde*.) It would be impertinent to impute any such reflections to Britten had not *Death in Venice* made it plain that audacity, freshness, and the fiery play of fancy had not left him, were not the opera the product of joy in which the receiving world has rejoiced. Dionysus and Tadzio are here not rejected. The opera embraces at once fidelity to the events of the printed tale, a marvellous musical realization of its intricate, delicate facture, and that lyrical, 'hymnic' celebration of beauty leading to 'many fair and noble thoughts' which Mann reproached himself for not having sung.

After that has been said, some details of the technical mastery may be noted. There is perhaps a shade of naughtiness in the opening phrases. To voice the sterility ('unyielding, unproductive') Aschenbach is experiencing, the singer climbs a twelve-note row and then limps down its inversion. His line moves with dragging, painful gait, leaping only once, from B to E. The note-row does not recur, but proud declamation on and around E characterizes Aschenbach in his aspect as the famous writer. B and E underpin his involuntary avowal at the end of Act I, 'I love you,' and form the long pedal-point of the Act II prelude, through which the notes of 'love you' ('hackneyed words . . . ridiculous but sacred too and no, not dishonourable even in these circumstances'), like dancing, teasing points of light, dissolve each attempt at a resolute, connected phrase into confusion. The main themes of the music are distinct and memorable. Broad, picturesque strains conjure up a vision of Venice, the fabulous city rising from the sea. Lulling barcaroles accompany passages between the Lido and the Piazza; the gondoliers' strange, ringing cries later insinuate themselves into Aschenbach's musings. In piano-accompanied recitative – as if thinking aloud or jotting down reflections in a diary or writer's notebook – Aschenbach voices observations that on the page the novelist can tell us. It is a successful musical device for keeping narrative levels apart, although as a result Mrs Piper's and Britten's Aschenbach becomes an even more selfconscious creative artist than Mann's. Mann can preserve the distinction between his own and his protagonist's accounts of events and appearances. Music, however, is a better medium than prose for communicating the emotions that fill the hero during his approach to Venice, on his first glimpse of the sea, and at his first sight of Tadzio. Another device in Mrs Piper's skilful libretto – casting Tadzio, his family, and his friends as dancers – reflects the fact that, in Mann, Aschenbach never speaks with them.

The opera is in two acts, the first lasting about eighty minutes and the second about an hour. Formally the score is divided into seventeen scenes, but several of them are scenes of shifting location. The ninth, for example, begins in a gondola, traverses the Piazza, settles for a while in a café, moves into St Mark's, then down the Merceria, across to the Lido by gondola, into the hotel, to the door of Tadzio's bedroom (in the words of Plutarch's *Erotikos*, the lover whose quest of beauty has not transcended passion for a particular person 'pursues by day and haunts the door by night'), and finally to Aschenbach's own room. The work is nearly a monodrama for Aschenbach, a tenor, and was composed for Peter Pears, who created Peter Grimes in 1945 and has taken leading roles in Britten's operas ever since. At the age of 64, Mr Pears made his Metropolitan début, as Aschenbach. Reviewing it, I repeated what I wrote after the Aldeburgh premiere. 'As Aschenbach, Peter Pears is beyond praise. His voice seems tireless. It can be full and proud, sweet, tender, sorrowful, ringing, angry. His placing of tone and word and his control of accent and timing are as affectingly precise as in a performance of *Winterreise*. His singing carries at all dynamic levels. His acting of the part is superb. It is a great performance of a great role.' The other important part is for a baritone, who in multiple incarnations plays all the figures conducting Aschenbach on his journey, and sounds the Voice of Dionysus in his Act II nightmare. John Shirley-Quirk in these linked roles was very subtle, very deft. The offstage Voice of Apollo is a countertenor or high tenor. Otherwise there are just the dancers – the part of Tadzio, that 'mortal child with more than mortal grace' has proved hard to cast – and a large group of soloists with small roles who combine to form the chorus. The Aldeburgh performance of the opera was recorded; although *Death in Venice* has proved enthralling in theatres both large and small, the discs should be heard as complement to any large-theatre production. The richness and passion of this beautiful, detailed score are perhaps most fully enjoyed in closeup.

'The first opera: *Paul Bunyan*' and, 'The last opera: *Death in Venice*', based on reviews written for *The New Yorker*, appear here by permission of its editor and of Farrar, Straus and Giroux, Inc., and Messrs Chatto & Windus, publishers of *Music of Three Seasons*, a collection of Andrew Porter's *New Yorker* writings.

Paul Bunyan

*An operetta in two acts
and a prologue*

by W.H.Auden

BENJAMIN BRITTEN OP. 17

FIRST PERFORMANCE

5 May 1941   *Columbia University, Brander Matthew Hall*
New York

In the Prologue

Old Trees	Chorus
Young Trees	Ellen Huffmaster, Jane Weaver, Marlowe Jones, Ben Carpens
Three Wild Geese	Harriet Greene, Augusta Dorn, Pauline Kleinhesselink

In the Interludes

Narrator	Mordecai Bauman

In the Play

The Voice of Paul Bunyan	Milton Warchoff
Cross Crosshaulson	Walter Graf
John Shears	Leonard Stocker
Sam Sharkey	Clifford Jackson
Ben Benny	Eugene Bonham
Jen Jenson	Ernest Holcombe
Pete Peterson	Lewis Pierce
Andy Anderson	Ben Carpens
Other Lumberjacks	Alan Adair, Elmer Barber, Arnold Jaffe, Marlowe Jones, Charles Snitow, Robert Zeller, W. Fredric Plette Thomas Flynn, Joseph Harrow
Western Union Boy	Henry Bauman
Hel Helson	Bliss Woodward
Johnny Inkslinger	William Hess
Fido	Pauline Kleinhesselink
Moppet	Harriet Greene
Poppet	Augusta Dorn
The Defeated	Ben Carpens, Eugene Bonham, Adelaide Van Way, Ernest Holcombe
Slim	Charles Cammock
Tiny	Helen Marshall
The Film Stars and Models	Eleanor Hutchings, Ellen Huffmaster, Ben Carpens, Lewis Pierce
Frontier Women	Marie Bellejean, Eloise Calinger, Irma Commanday, Alice Gerstz Duschak, Marian Edwards, Elizabeth Flynn, Rose Harris, Ethel Madsen, Jean Phillips, Evelyn Ray, Irma Shocken, Adelaide Van Way, Jane Weaver, Ida Weirich, Marjorie Williamson

Conducted by Hugh Ross   *Produced by Milton Smith*

CHARACTERS

Chorus of old trees	*In the Prologue*	SATB
Four young trees		SSTT
Three wild geese		MS.MS.S
Narrator *In the Ballad Interludes*		BARITONE OR TENOR
The voice of Paul Bunyan		SPOKEN PART
Johnny Inkslinger *bookkeeper*		TENOR
Tiny *daughter of Paul Bunyan*		SOPRANO
Hot Biscuit Slim *a good cook*		TENOR
Sam Sharkey	*two bad cooks*	TENOR
Ben Benny		BASS
Hel Helson *foreman*		BARITONE
Andy Anderson		TENOR
Pete Peterson	*four Swedes*	TENOR
Jen Jenson		BASS
Cross Crosshaulson		BASS
John Shears *a farmer*		BARITONE
Western Union Boy		TENOR
Fido *a dog*		HIGH SOPRANO
Moppet	*two cats*	MEZZO SOPRANO
Poppet		MEZZO SOPRANO
Quartet of the Defeated (Blues)		CONTRALTO, TENOR, BARITONE, BASS
Four cronies of Hel Helson		4 BARITONES
Heron, Moon, Wind, Beetle, Squirrel		SPOKEN PARTS
Chorus of lumberjacks, farmers and frontier women		

SYNOPSIS OF SCENES

Prologue	In the forest
Act one	
Scene one	A clearing in the forest
Scene two	The camp
Act two	
Scene one	A clearing in the forest
Scene two	The Christmas party

No 1 **INTRODUCTION**

No 2 **Prologue**
In the forest

CHORUS OF OLD TREES
Since the birth
Of the earth
Time has gone
On and on:
Rivers saunter,
Rivers run,
Till they enter
The enormous level sea
Where they prefer to be.

But the sun
Is too hot
And will not
Let alone
Waves glad-handed
Lazy crowd,
Educates them
Till they change into a cloud
But can't control them long.

For the will
Just to fall
Is too strong
In them all;
Revolution
Turns to rain
Whence more solid
Sensible creatures gain:
In falling they serve life.

Here are we
Flower and tree,
Green, alive,
Glad to be,
And our proper
Places know:
Winds and waters
Travel; we remain and grow;
We like life to be slow.

FOUR YOUNG TREES
No. No. No. No.

CHORUS
O.

YOUNG TREES
We do *Not* want life to be slow.

CHORUS
                        Reds.

YOUNG TREES
We are *bored* with standing still
We want to see things and go places.

CHORUS
Such nonsense. It's only a phase.
They're sick. They're crazy.
[*Enter Two Wild Geese*]

TWO WILD GEESE
Ooh!

O how terrible to be
As old-fashioned as a tree:
Dull old stick that won't go out;
What on earth do they talk about?
    Unexpressive
    Unprogressive
Unsophisticated lout.
How can pines or grass or sage
Understand the Modern Age?
[*Enter Third Wild Goose*]
Ooh!
What's up, eh? Do tell us quick.

THREE WILD GEESE
That's the best I ever heard!
Shall we tell them? Now?
You are all to leave here.

CHORUS
What?
                It's a lie!

YOUNG TREES
                        Hurrah!

CHORUS
                            Don't listen!

YOUNG TREES
                                    How?

THREE WILD GEESE
Far away from here
A mission will find a performer.

CHORUS
A mission?
What mission?

THREE WILD GEESE
To bring you to another life.

YOUNG TREES
What kind of performer?

THREE WILD GEESE
                            A Man.

YOUNG TREES
What is a man?

CHORUS
What is a man?

THREE WILD GEESE
A man is a form of life
That dreams in order to act
And acts in order to dream
And has a name of his own.

YOUNG TREES AND CHORUS
What is that name?

THREE WILD GEESE
Paul Bunyan.

CHORUS
                        How silly.

YOUNG TREES
When are we to see him?

THREE WILD GEESE
He will be born at the next Blue Moon.

CHORUS
  It isn't true,
  I'm so frightened.
                    Don't worry
  There won't be a Blue Moon in our lifetime.
  Don't say that. It's unlucky.
  [*The moon begins to turn blue*]

YOUNG TREES
  Look at the moon! It's turning blue.

CHORUS
  Look at the moon! It's turning blue.

THREE WILD GEESE
  It isn't very often the conservatives are wrong,
  Tomorrow normally is only yesterday again,
  Society is right in saying nine times out of ten
  Respectability's enough to carry one along.

CHORUS
  But once in a while the odd thing happens,
    Once in a while the dream comes true,
  And the whole pattern of life is altered,
    Once in a while the moon turns blue.

SEMI-CHORUS OF OLD TREES
  We can't pretend we like it, that it's what we'd choose,
  But what's the point in fussing when one can't refuse
  And nothing is as bad as one thinks it will be,
  The children look so happy – Well, well, we shall see.

YOUNG TREES
  I want to be a vessel sailing on the sea,
  I want to be a roof with houses under me,
  I've always longed for edges – I'd love to be a square –

TUTTI
  How swell to be a dado and how swell to be a chair.

    But once in a while the odd thing happens,
      Once in a while the dream comes true,
    And the whole pattern of life is altered,
      Once in a while the moon turns blue.

    NO 2a FIRST BALLAD INTERLUDE

NARRATOR
  The cold wind blew through the crooked thorn
  Up in the North a boy was born.

  His hair was black, his eyes were blue,
  His mouth turned up at the corners too.

  A fairy stood beside his bed;
  'You shall never, never grow old', she said,

  'Paul Bunyan is to be your name';
  Then she departed whence she came.

  You must believe me when I say,
  He grew six inches every day.

  You must believe me when I speak,
  He gained 346 pounds every week.

  He grew so fast, by the time he was eight,
  He was as tall as the Empire State.

The length of his stride's a historical fact;
3.7 miles to be exact.

When he ordered a jacket, the New England mills
For months had no more unemployment ills.

When he wanted a snapshot to send to his friends,
They found they had to use a telephoto lens.

But let me tell you in advance,
His dreams were of greater significance.

His favourite dream was of felling trees,
A fancy which grew by swift degrees.

One night he dreamt he was to be
The greatest logger in history.

He woke to feel something stroking his brow,
And found it was the tongue of an enormous cow.

From horn to horn or from lug to lug,
Was forty-seven axe-heads and a baccy plug.

But what would have most bewildered you
Was the colour of her hide which was bright bright blue.

But Bunyan wasn't surprised at all,
Said, 'I'll call you Babe, you call me Paul'.

He pointed to a meadow, said, 'Take a bite
For you're leaving me for the South tonight'.

Over the mountains, across the streams
They went to find Paul Bunyan's dreams.

The bear and the beaver waved a paw,
The magpie chattered, the squirrel swore.

The trappers ran out from their lonely huts
Scratching their heads with their rifle-butts.

For a year and a day they travelled fast
'This is the place', Paul said at last.

The forest stretched for miles around,
The sound of their breathing was the only sound.

Paul picked up a pine-tree and scratched his shins,
Said, 'This is the place where our work begins'.

Act one

Scene one
A clearing in the forest

NO 3 BUNYAN'S GREETING

VOICE OF PAUL BUNYAN
It is a spring morning without benefit of young persons.

It is a sky that has never registered weeping or rebellion.

It is a forest full of innocent beasts. There are none who blush at the memory of an ancient folly, none who hide beneath dyed fabrics a malicious heart.

It is America, but not yet.

Wanted. Disturbers of public order, men without
    foresight or fear.

Wanted. Energetic madmen. Those who have thought
    themselves a body large enough to devour their
    dreams.

Wanted. The lost. Those indestructibles whom defeat
    can never change. Poets of the bottle,
    clergymen of a ridiculous gospel, actors who
    should have been engineers and lawyers who
    should have been sea-captains, saints of
    circumstance, desperados, unsuccessful
    wanderers, all who can hear the invitation of
    the earth. America, youngest of her daughters,
    awaits the barbarians of marriage.

NO 3a CALL OF LUMBERJACKS

LUMBERJACKS' CHORUS [*gradually approaching*]
Timber-rrr. Down the Line. Timber-rrr.

NO 4 LUMBERJACKS' CHORUS

FIRST SOLO
My birthplace was in Sweden, it's a very long way off,
My appetite was hearty but I couldn't get enough;
When suddenly I heard a roar across the wide blue sea,
'I'll give you steak and onions if you'll come and work for
    me'.

LUMBERJACKS' CHORUS
            We rise at dawn of day
            We're handsome free and gay,
                We're lumberjacks,
                With saw and axe
            Who are melting the forests away.

SECOND SOLO
In France I wooed a maiden with an alabaster skin
But she left me for a fancy chap who played the violin;
When just about to drown myself a voice came from the
    sky,
'There's no one like a shanty boy to catch a maiden's
    eye'.

CHORUS
We rise at dawn etc.

THIRD SOLO
O long ago in Germany when sitting at my ease,
There came a knocking at the door and it was the police;
I tiptoed down the backstairs and a voice to me did say
'There's freedom in the forests out in North America'.

CHORUS
We rise at dawn etc.

In Piccadilly Circus I stood waiting for a bus
I thought I heard the pigeons say 'Please run away with
    us';
To a land of opportunity with work and food for all
Especially for shanty boys in Winter and in Fall.

We rise at dawn etc.

NO 4a BUNYAN'S WELCOME

PAUL BUNYAN
Welcome and sit down, we have no time to waste.
The trees are waiting for the axe and we must all make
    haste.
So who shall be the foreman to set in hand the work
To organise the logging and see men do not shirk?

NO 5 QUARTET OF SWEDES

FOUR SWEDES
I. I. I. I.
CHORUS
Why?

FOUR SWEDES
Swedesh born and Swedish bred,
Strong in the arm and dull in the head.
Who can ever kill a Swede?
His skull is very thick indeed,
But once you get an idea in
You'll never get it out again.

PAUL BUNYAN
What are your names?

FOUR SWEDES
Cross Crosshaulson
Jen Jenson
Pete Peterson
Andy Anderson

PAUL BUNYAN
In your opinion which of you, which one would be the
    best
To be the leader of the few and govern all the rest?

FOUR SWEDES [*fighting*]
Why?
Who?
You?
O.
No.
Me.
He?
Yah!
Bah!

PAUL BUNYAN
None of you, it seems will do,
We must find another.

CHORUS
>   Yes, but who?
> [*Enter a Western Union Boy, on a bicycle*]

No 6   WESTERN UNION BOY'S SONG

WESTERN UNION BOY
>   A telegram, a telegram,
>   A telegram from oversea
>   Paul Bunyan is the name
>   Of the addressee.

>   [*Exit across stage*]

CHORUS
Bad News? Good News? Tell us what you're reading.

PAUL BUNYAN
I have a message that will please you from the King of
Sweden.
[*Reads*]
>   Dear Paul
>   I hear you are looking for a head-foreman, so I'm
>   sending you the finest logger in my kingdom, Hel
>   Helson. He doesn't talk much.
>   Wishing you every success.
>   Yours sincerely
>   Nel Nelson. King.
[*Enter while he is reading Hel Helson*]

PAUL BUNYAN
Are you Hel Helson?

HEL HELSON
Aye tank so.

PAUL BUNYAN
Do you know all about logging?

HEL HELSON
Aye tank so.

PAUL BUNYAN
Are you prepared to be my head-foreman?

HEL HELSON
Aye tank so.

PAUL BUNYAN
>   Then I think so too.
>   Now for one to cook or bake
>   Flapjacks, cookies, fish, or steak.
[*Enter Sam Sharkey and Ben Benny*]

SAM SHARKEY
Sam Sharkey at your service.

BEN BENNY
Ben Benny at your service.

No 7   COOKS' DUET

SAM SHARKEY
>   Sam for Soups

BEN BENNY
>   Ben for beans

SAM SHARKEY
>   Soups feed you

BEN BENNY
>   Beans
>   For Vitamins

SAM SHARKEY
>   Soups satisfy
>   Soups gratify

BEN BENNY
>   Ten beans a day
>   Cure food-delay

SAM SHARKEY
>   Soups that nourish
>   Make hope flourish

BEN BENNY
>   Beans for nutrition
>   Beans for ambition

SAM SHARKEY
>   The Best People are crazy about soups

BEN BENNY
>   Beans are all the rage among the Higher Income
>   Groups

SAM SHARKEY
Do you feel a left-out at parties, when it comes to
promotion are you passed over, and does your wife
talk in her sleep, then ask our nearest agent to tell you
about soups for success.

BEN BENNY
You owe it to yourself to learn about Beans and how
this delicious food is the sure way to the body
beautiful. We will mail you a fascinating booklet
Beans for Beauty by return of post if you will send us
your address.
[*Enter Johnny Inkslinger*]

INKSLINGER
Did I hear anyone say something about food?

SAM SHARKEY
What about a delicious bowl of soup?

BEN BENNY
What would you say to a nice big plate of beans?

INKSLINGER
I'll have a double portion of both, please.
>   [*Exeunt Sam Sharkey and Ben Benny*]

PAUL BUNYAN
Good-day stranger. What's your name?

INKSLINGER
Johnny Inkslinger.

PAUL BUNYAN
Can you read?

INKSLINGER
Think of a language and I write you its dictionary.

PAUL BUNYAN
Can you handle figures?

INKSLINGER
Think of an irrational number and I'll double it.

PAUL BUNYAN
>   You're just the man I hoped to find
>   For I have large accounts to mind.

INKSLINGER
Sorry I'm busy.

PAUL BUNYAN
What's your job?

INKSLINGER
O, just looking around.

PAUL BUNYAN
Who do you work for?

INKSLINGER
Myself, silly. This is a free country.
[*Enter Sam Sharkey and Ben Benny*]
Excuse me.

SAM SHARKEY
Your soup.

BEN BENNY
Your beans.

BOTH
Just taste them.

PAUL BUNYAN
Wait a minute.
[*Sam Sharkey and Ben Benny stand back*]
Have you any money?

INKSLINGER
Search me.

PAUL BUNYAN
How are you going to pay for your supper?

INKSLINGER
Dunno. Never thought of it.

PAUL BUNYAN
If you work for me
You shall eat splendidly
But no work, no pay.

INKSLINGER
No sale. Good-day.   [*Exit Inkslinger*]

CHORUS
Now what on earth are we to do
For I can't keep accounts, can you?

PAUL BUNYAN
Don't worry, he'll come back
He has to feed.
Now what else do we lack
Who else do we need?

SAM SHARKEY
I'd like a dog to lick up all the crumbs
And chase away the salesmen and all the drunken
  bums.

BEN BENNY
I'd like a pair of cats
To catch the mice and rats.
[*Paul Bunyan whistles – enter Fido, Moppet, Poppet*]

No 8 ANIMAL TRIO

FIDO
Ah!

MOPPET AND POPPET
Miaou!

FIDO
The single creature lives a partial life,

Man by his eye and by his nose the hound;
He needs the deep emotions I can give,
Through him I sense a vaster hunting-ground.

MOPPET AND POPPET
Like draws to like, to share is to relieve,
And sympathy the root bears love the flower;
He feels in us, and we in him perceive
A common passion for the lonely hour

FIDO
In all his walks I follow at his side,
His faithful servant and his loving shade;

MOPPET AND POPPET
We move in our apartness and our pride
About the decent dwellings he has made.

No 8a BUNYAN'S GOODNIGHT (i)

PAUL BUNYAN
Off to supper and to bed
For all our future lies ahead
And our work must be begun
At the rising of the sun.

                                        [*Exeunt*]

No 8b EXIT OF LUMBERJACKS

LUMBERJACKS' CHORUS
Down the line. Timber-rr.

No 9 THE BLUES: QUARTET OF DEFEATED

PAUL BUNYAN
Now at the beginning
To those who pause on the frontiers of an untravelled
  empire
Standing in empty dusk upon the eve of a tremendous
  task, to you all
A dream of warning.
[1, 2 AND 4 MEN: 3 A WOMAN]
1 Gold in the North came the blizzard to say
  I left my sweetheart at the break of day,
  The gold ran out and my love grew grey.
       You don't know all, sir, you don't know all.

2 The West, said the sun, for enterprise,
  A bullet in Frisco put me wise,
  My last words were, 'God damn your eyes'.
       You don't know all, sir, you don't know all.

3 In Alabama my heart was full,
  Down the river bank I stole,
  The waters of grief went over my soul.
       You don't know all, sir, you don't know all.

4 In the streets of New York I was young and well,
  I rode the market, the market fell,
  One morning I found myself in hell.
       I didn't know all, sir, I didn't know all.

ALL
       We didn't know all, sir, we didn't know all.

4 In the saloons I heaved a sigh
1 Lost in deserts of alkali I lay down to die
3 There's always a sorrow can get you down
2 All the world's whiskey can never drown,

ALL
>   You don't know all, sir, you don't know all.

3 Some think they're strong, some think they're smart,
>   Like butterflies they're pulled apart,
>   America can break your heart.

ALL
>   You don't know all, sir, you don't know all.
>   [*Enter Inkslinger*]

PAUL BUNYAN
>   Hello Mr Inkslinger. Lost anything?

INKSLINGER
>   I want my supper.

PAUL BUNYAN
>   What about my little proposition?

INKSLINGER
>   You win. I'll take it. Now where's the kitchen,
>   Mr Bunyan?

PAUL BUNYAN
>   Call me Paul.

INKSLINGER
>   No. You're stronger than I, so I must do what you ask.
>   But I'm not going to pretend to like you. Good night.
>   [*Exit Inkslinger*]

NO 10 BUNYAN'S GOODNIGHT (ii)

PAUL BUNYAN
>   Good night, Johnny, and good luck.

NO 10a SECOND BALLAD INTERLUDE

NARRATOR
>   The Spring came and the Summer and Fall;
>   Paul Bunyan sat in his binnacle.

>   Regarding like a lighthouse lamp
>   The work going on in the lumber camps.

>   Dreaming dreams which now and then
>   He liked to tell to his lumbermen.

>   His phrases rolled like waves on a beach
>   And during the course of a single speech

>   Young boys grew up and needed a shave,
>   Old men got worried they'd be late for the grave.

>   He woke one morning feeling unwell,
>   Said to Babe; 'What's the matter? I feel like Hell'.

>   Babe cocked her head, said; 'Get a wife;
>   One can have too much of the bachelor life'.

>   And so one morning in the month of May
>   Paul went wife-hunting at the break of day.

>   He kept a sharp look-out but all
>   The girls he saw were much too small.

>   But at last he came to a valley green
>   With mountains beside and a river between.

And there on the bank before his eyes
He beheld a girl of the proper size.

The average man if he walked in haste
Would have taken a week to get round her waist.

When you looked at her bosom you couldn't fail
To see it was built on a generous scale.

They eyed each other for an interval;
Then she said 'I'm Carrie' and he said 'I'm Paul'.

What happened then I've no idea
They never told me and I wasn't there.

But whatever it was she became his wife
And they started in on the married life.

And in a year a daughter came
Tiny she was and Tiny her name.

I wish I could say that Carrie and Paul
Were a happy pair but they weren't at all.

It's not the business of a song
To say who was right and who was wrong.

Both said the bitter things that pain
And wished they hadn't but said them again.

Till Carrie said at last one day:
'It's no use, Paul, I must go away'.

Paul struck a match and lit his pipe,
Said: 'It seems a pity but perhaps your're right'.

So Carrie returned to her home land
Leading Tiny by the hand

And Paul stayed in camp with his lumbermen
Though he paid them visits now and then.

One day Tiny telegraphed him: 'Come quick.
Very worried. Mother sick'.

But the doctor met him at the door and said:
'I've bad news for you, Paul; she's dead'.

He ran upstairs and stood by the bed:
'Poor Carrie', he murmured and stroked her head.

'I know we fought and I was to blame
But I loved you greatly all the same'.

He picked up Tiny and stroked her hair,
Said: 'I've not been much of a father, dear.

But I'll try to be better until the day
When you want to give your heart away.

And whoever the lucky man may be
I hope he's a better man than me'.

So they got ready to return
To the camp, of which you now shall learn.

Scene two
The camp

CHORUS (WITH JOHNNY INKSLINGER)
1 Nothing but soups and beans
2 Mondays, Wednesdays and Fridays soup
3 Tuesdays, Thursdays and Saturdays beans
1 Sundays, soup *and* beans.
2 Soup gives me ulcers
3 I'm allergic to beans.
1 Have you seen the chief about it, Johnny?

INKSLINGER
He's not back yet from his wife's funeral.

2 Well, something's gotta be done about it, and done
   quick.
3 You'll have to speak to them, yourself.

ALL
Things have gone too far.

NO 11 FOOD CHORUS

CHORUS
Do I look the sort of fellow
Whom you might expect to bellow
      For a quail in aspic, or
Who would look as glum as Gandhi
If he wasn't offered brandy
      With a Lobster Thermidor?

Who would howl like some lost sinner
For a sherry before dinner
      And demand a savoury;
Who would cricitize the stuffing
In the olives, and drink nothing
      But Lapsang Suchong tea?

Our digestion's pretty tough
And we're not particular
But when they hand us out to eat
A lump of sandstone as the sweet
Then things have gone too far.

O, the soup looks appetising
Till you see a maggot rising
      White as Venus from the sea;
And a beetle in the cauli-
Flower isn't very jolly
      Or so it appears to me;

Flies have interesting features
And, of course, they're all God's creatures,
      But a trifle out of place
In a glass of drinking water
And it makes my temper shorter
      If I meet one face to face.

Our digestion's pretty tough
And we're not particular.
But when we're even asked to crunch
A rat or cockroach with our lunch
Then things have gone too far.

INKSLINGER
Iron, they say, is healthy,
And even wood is wealthy

In the essential vitamins;
But I hate to find a mallet
Tucked away in the fruit salad
      Or a hammer in the greens.

There are foods, so doctors tell you,
With a high nutritious value
      That the Middle Ages never knew;
But I can't secrete saliva
At the thought of a screw-driver
      Or a roasted walking shoe.

CHORUS
Our digestion's pretty tough
And we're not particular
But when the kitchen offers one
A rusty thumb-tack underdone
Then things have gone too far.
[*Enter Sam Sharkey and Ben Benny*]

SAM SHARKEY AND BEN BENNY
Anything wrong?

INKSLINGER
Please don't think for a moment we want to criticize.
Your cooking's wonderful. We all know that Sam's
soups are the finest in the world and, as for Ben's beans,
why there isn't a dish like them anywhere. But don't you
think that just occasionally, say once a month, we could
have something different?

SAM SHARKEY
I can't believe it.

BEN BENNY
It's not possible.

SAM SHARKEY AND BEN BENNY
After all we've done for them.

SAM SHARKEY
Haven't you stayed awake all night thinking how to
please them?

BEN BENNY
Haven't you worked your fingers to the bone?

SAM SHARKEY
Day in, day out.

BEN BENNY
Week after week, month after month.

SAM SHARKEY
Year after year.

BEN BENNY
Not a word of thanks.

SAM SHARKEY
Just grumble, grumble, grumble.

BEN BENNY
Treating us like dogs.

SAM SHARKEY
I can't bear it any longer.

BEN BENNY
You don't know how much you've hurt us.

SAM SHARKEY
My nerves.

BEN BENNY
My art.

SAM SHARKEY AND BEN BENNY
Very well. Very well. From now on you shall do the cooking yourselves.

INKSLINGER
O but please. We didn't mean to upset you.

SAM SHARKEY
It's alright. We understand perfectly.

INKSLINGER
Sam. Ben. Please listen. I'm sorry if . . .

BEN BENNY
Don't apologize. We're not angry.

SAM SHARKEY
Just a little sad, that's all.

BEN BENNY
One day perhaps you'll realize what you've done.
Come, Sam.

SAM SHARKEY
Come, Ben.

[*Exeunt*]

No 12 CHORUS ACCUSATION

CROSS
There now look what you have done.

INKSLINGER
What I did, you asked me to.

JEN
You know I only spoke in fun.

PETE
I never understood what you
Meant to do.

ANDY
                I said it wouldn't do
You heard me, didn't you?

INKSLINGER
What would you have done instead?

CHORUS
Never mind. Beyond a doubt
You have put us in the red
So you'd better get us out.

No 12a SLIM'S SONG

SLIM [*Off*]
In fair days and in foul
    Round the world and back,
I must hunt my shadow
    And the self I lack.
[*Slim rides on*]

INKSLINGER
Hullo stranger. What's your name?

SLIM
Slim.

INKSLINGER
You don't look like a logger. Where do you come from?

SLIM
I come from open spaces
    Where over endless grass
The stroking winds and shadows
    Of cloud and bison pass;
My brothers were the buffalo,
    My house the shining day,
I danced between the horse-hoofs like
    A butterfly at play.

In fair days and in foul etc.

One winter evening as I sat
    By my camp fire alone,
I heard a whisper from the flame,
    The voice was like my own:
'O get you up and get you gone,
    North, South or East or West,
This emptiness cannot answer
    The heart in your breast.

'O ride till woods or houses
    Provide the narrow place
Where you can force your fate to turn
    And meet you face to face.'

In fair days and in foul
    Round the world and back,
I must hunt my shadow
    And the self I lack.

FIDO, MOPPET AND POPPET
Ah!

INKSLINGER
Say, you can't cook by any chance?

SLIM
Sure.

CHORUS
Can you cook flapjacks?

SLIM
Yes.

CHORUS
Cookies?

SLIM
Yes.

CHORUS
Fish?

SLIM
Yes.

CHORUS
Steaks?

SLIM
Yes.

CHORUS
Are you telling lies?

SLIM
Yes. No. No. No.

CHORUS
You're an angel in disguise.
Sam and Benny get the sack.

1 Slim   *Margaret Harris*   2 Johnny Inkslinger   *Margaret Harris*

Margaret Harris's costume designs for
the first European stage performance on 4th June 1976

3 Ballad singer   *Margaret Harris*   4 Tiny   *Margaret Harris*

5 and 6 Members of the Chorus
Margaret Harris

7 Six Old Trees

Margaret Harris

No 13 BUNYAN'S RETURN

CHORUS

Look, look, the Chief is back.

And look, can I believe my eyes
Is that a girl he's got with him?

Gosh, she's pretty

           And young

                  And trim.

O boy.

           [*Exeunt all but Fido and Inkslinger*]

INKSLINGER

Hello, Fido. Staying to keep me company? That's
mighty nice of you. Say Fido, I want to ask you a
question. Are you happy?
[*Fido shakes his head. Inkslinger goes to the door and looks to see
if anyone is listening*]
Then I'll tell you a secret. Neither am I. May I tell you
the story of my life?
[*Fido nods*]
You're sure it won't bore you?
[*Fido shakes his head but when Inkslinger is not looking stifles a
yawn with a paw*]

No 14 INKSLINGER'S SONG

INKSLINGER

It was out in the sticks that the fire
    Of my existence began
Where no one had heard the Messiah
    And no one had seen a Cézanne.
I learned a prose style from the preacher
    And the facts of life from the hens
And fell in love with the teacher
    Whose love for John Keats was intense
And I dreamed of writing a novel
    With which Tolstoi couldn't compete
And of how all the critics would grovel
    But I guess that a guy gotta eat.

I can think of much nicer professions
    Than keeping a ledger correct
Such as writing my private confessions
    Or procuring a frog to dissect
Learning Sanskrit would be more amusing
    Or studying the history of Spain.
And, had I the power of choosing
    I would live on the banks of the Seine
I would paint St Sebastian the Martyr
    Or dig up the Temples of Crete
Or compose a D major sonata
    But I guess that a guy gotta eat.

The company I have to speak to
    Are wonderful men in their way
But the things that delight me are Greek to
    The Jacks who haul lumber all day.
It isn't because I don't love them
    That this camp is a prison to me
Nor do I think I'm above them
    In loathing the sight of a tree.

O but where are those beautiful places
    Where what you begin you complete
Where the joy shines out of men's faces
    And all get sufficient to eat?

No 14a ENTRANCE OF CHORUS

PETE

I never knew he had a daughter

ANDY

She's much lovelier than I thought her

JOHN

Tiny, what a pretty name

CROSS

I am delighted that she came

PETE

Her eyes

JOHN

        Her cheeks

CROSS

                Her lips

ANDY

                      Her nose

JEN

She's a peach

JOHN

          A dove

PETE

              A rose

[*Enter Tiny*]

No 15a TINY'S ENTRANCE

BEN

Look at me, Miss Tiny: I'm six feet tall.

SAM

Look at me, Miss Tiny: I've the bluest eyes you ever
saw.

CROSS

Feel my biceps, Miss Tiny.

ANDY

I can ride a bicycle.

JOHN

I can spell parallelogram.

ANDY

I've got fifty dollars salted away in an old sock.

JOHN

I'll run errands for you.

SAM

I'll bring your breakfast in bed.

BEN

I'll tell you stories before you go to sleep.

ANDY

I'll make you laugh by pulling faces.

BEN

I'm big and husky. You need someone to look after you.

JOHN
You need someone to look after. I'm sick.

No 15b TINY'S SONG

TINY
Ah!

INKSLINGER
Leave her alone, you fools. Have you forgotten her
mother's just died?

TINY
Ah!

Whether the sun shine upon children playing,
Or storms endanger sailors on the sea,
In solitude or a conversation,
Mother, O Mother tears arise in me.

For underground now you rest who at nightfall
Would sing me to sleep in my little bed;
I turn with the world but grief has no motion;
Mother, O Mother too soon you were dead.

O never again in fatigue or fever
Shall I feel your cool hand upon my brow;
As you look after the cherubs in Heaven,
Mother, O Mother look down on me now.

Should a day come I hear a lover whisper,
Should I stay an old maid whom the men pass by,
My heart shall cherish your guardian image,
Mother, O Mother till the day I die.

CHORUS
The white bone
Lies alone
Like the limestone
Under the green grass
All time goes by
We, too, shall lie
Under death's eye
Alas. Alas.

TINY
Alas.
[Enter Slim]

SLIM
Supper's ready.

TINY
Excuse me, are you the cook?

SLIM
Yes, mam.

TINY
I'm Miss Tiny. Father said I was to help you in the
kitchen.

SLIM
I'm sure you'll be a great help, Miss Tiny.
This way please.

CHORUS [as they exeunt]
1 Did you see how he looked at her?
2 Did you see how she looked at him?
3 I shall take cooking lessons.

REST OF CHORUS
Don't chatter so. Let's go and eat.

[Exeunt]

No 16 INKSLINGER'S REGRET

INKSLINGER [alone]
All the little brooks of love
    Run down towards each other
Somewhere every valley ends
    And loneliness is over
Some meet early, some meet late,
    Some, like me, have long to wait.

VOICE OF PAUL BUNYAN
Johnny.

INKSLINGER
Yes, Mr Bunyan.

PAUL BUNYAN
Has anything happened since I've been away?

INKSLINGER
Keep an eye on Hel Helson. He broods too much by
himself and I don't like the look on his face. And the
bunch he goes around with are a bad bunch.

PAUL BUNYAN
Poor Hel. He was born a few hundred years too late.
Today there is no place for him.
Anything else?

INKSLINGER
Some of the men say they are tired of logging and would
like to settle down. They'd like to try farming.

PAUL BUNYAN
John Shears?

INKSLINGER
He's the chief one but there are many others.

PAUL BUNYAN
I'll look into it. And what about yourself, Johnny?

INKSLINGER
I'm all right, Mr Bunyan.

PAUL BUNYAN
I know what you want. It's harder than you think and
not so pleasant. But you shall have it and shan't have to
wait much longer. Good night, Johnny.

INKSLINGER
Good night, Mr Bunyan.

PAUL BUNYAN
Still *Mr* Bunyan?

INKSLINGER
Good night, Paul.

[Exit Inkslinger]

CHORUS [off]
Good night, Mr Bunyan.

PAUL BUNYAN
Good night. Happy dreams.

No 17 BUNYAN'S GOOD NIGHT (iii)

PAUL BUNYAN
Now let the complex spirit dissolve in the darkness

Where the Actual and the Possible are mysteriously
  exchanged.
For the saint must descend into Hell; that his order may
  be tested by its disorder
The hero return to the humble womb; that his will may
  be pacified and refreshed.
Dear children, trust the night and have faith in
  tomorrow
That these hours of ambiguity and indecision may be
  also the hours of healing.

Act two

Scene one
A clearing

No 18 BUNYAN'S GOOD MORNING

VOICE OF PAUL BUNYAN
The songs of dawn have been sung and the night
watchmen are already in the deep beginnings of sleep.

Leaning upon their implements the hired men pause to
consider their life by the light of mid-morning and of habits
already established in their loosened limbs.
And the aggressive will is no longer pure.

Much has been done to prepare a continent for the
rejoicings and recriminations of all its possible heirs.
Much has been ill done. There is never enough time to do
more than one thing at a time, and there is always either
too much of one thing or too little.

Virtuosos of the axe, dynamiters and huntsmen, there has
been an excess of military qualities, of the
  resourcefulness
of thieves, the camaraderie of the irresponsible, and the
accidental beauties of silly songs.

Nevertheless you have done much to render yourselves
  unnecessary.
Loneliness has worn lines of communication.
Irrational destruction has made possible the
  establishment of a civilized order.
Drunkenness and lechery have prepared the way for a
  routine of temperance and marriage.
Already you have provoked a general impulse towards
  settlement and cultivation.
[*Enter Chorus*]

CHORUS
  What does he want to see us for,
  I wonder what he has in store,
  I never did a thing I shouldn't,
  I couldn't. I wouldn't.
  I'll do my work. I'll never shirk.
  I'll never never grumble any more.

PAUL BUNYAN
  I've been thinking for some time that we needed some
farmers to grow food for the camp, and looking around
for a nice piece of country, the other day I found the very
place. A land where the wheat grows as tall as churches
and the potatoes are as big as airships. Now those who
would like to be farmers: Stand out.

No 18a SHEARS' SONG

JOHN SHEARS
  It has always been my dream
  Since I was only so high
  To live upon a farm and watch
  The wheat and barley grow high.

FARMERS' CHORUS
  The wheat and barley grow high.

PAUL BUNYAN
  Hel Helson.

HEL HELSON
  Yes.

PAUL BUNYAN
  You are in charge while I take our friends to the land of
Heart's Desire. I want you to start today clearing the
Topsy Turvey Mountain. Now boys, if you're ready
we'll start as we have a thousand miles to go before
noon. But if you think farming is a soft job you'd better
stay right here.

No 18b BUNYAN'S WARNING

PAUL BUNYAN
  If there isn't a flood, there's a drought,
  If there isn't a frost, there's a heatwave,
  If it isn't the insects, it's the banks.
  You'll howl more than you'll sing,
  You'll frown more than you'll smile,
  You'll cry more than you'll laugh.
    But some people seem to like it.
      Let's get going.

No 19 FARMERS' SONG

JOHN SHEARS
  The shanty-boy invades the wood
    Upon his cruel mission
  To slay the tallest trees he can
    The height of his ambition.

SECOND SOLO
  The farmer heeds wild Nature's cry
    For Higher Education,
  And is a trusted friend to all
    The best in vegetation.

CHORUS
  I hate to be a shanty-boy
  I want to be a farmer
  For I prefer life's comedy
    To life's crude melodrama.

JOHN SHEARS
  The shanty-boy sleeps in a bunk
    With none to call him Dad, sir,
  And so you cannot wonder much
    If he goes to the bad, sir.

SECOND SOLO
  The farmer sees his little ones
    Grow up like the green willow
  At night he has his Better Half
    Beside him on the pillow.

CHORUS

> I hate to be a shanty-boy
> I want to be a farmer
> For I prefer life's comedy
>   To life's crude melodrama.

NO 19a FARMERS' EXIT

[*The others watch them go and all except Helson and his Four Cronies exeunt*]

CRONIES

1 The Topsy-Turvey Mountain. It's impossible.
2 He's nuts.
3 Just another of his crazy ideas.
4 You are not going to take him seriously, are you, Hel?
1 Why do you go on taking orders from a dope like that?
2 Why don't you run this joint yourself? We'd support you.
3 Sure we would.
4 Hel for Boss.
1 Tell him where he gets off.
2 And that stooge of his, Johnny Inkslinger.
3 You said it. We'll take him for a ride.
4 Stand up for your rights, Hel. You're the only boss around here.

HEL HELSON

Get out.

CRONIES

1 Of course, Hel.
2 Anything you say, boss.
3 We were just going anyway.
4 Don't forget what we think of you.
    [*Exeunt Four Cronies. Helson is left sitting moodily alone*]

NO 20 THE MOCKING OF HEL HELSON

HEL HELSON

> Heron, heron winging by
> Through the silence of the sky,
> What have you heard of Helson the Brave?

HERON

> O I heard of a hero working for wages,
> Taking orders just like a slave.

CHORUS

> No I'm afraid it's too late
> Helson never will be great.

HEL HELSON

> Moon, moon shining bright
> In the deserts of the night,
> What have you heard of Helson the Fair?

MOON

> Not what one should hear of one so handome,
> The girls make fun of his bashful air.

CHORUS

> No I'm afraid it's too late
> Helson never will be great.

HEL HELSON

> Wind, wind as you run
> Round and round the earth for fun,
> What have you heard of Helson the Good?

WIND

> O the old story of virtue neglected,
> Mocked at by others, misunderstood.

CHORUS

> No I'm afraid it's too late
> Helson never will be great.

HEL HELSON

> Beetle, beetle as you pass
> Down the avenues of grass,
> What have you heard of Helson the Wise?

BEETLE

> Oh it's sad to think of all that wisdom
> Being exploited by smarter guys.

HEL HELSON

> Squirrel, squirrel as you go
> Through the forests to and fro,
> What have you heard of Helson the Strong?

SQUIRREL

> Not what one likes to hear of a fighter,
> They say he's a coward, I hope they're wrong.

CHORUS

> Too late, too late, too late,
> He will never, never, never be great.
> *Enter Fido, Moppet and Poppet*

MOPPET

Did you really?

POPPET

Yes, I says, excuse me, I says, but this is my roof, what of it, he says, you're trespassing, I says, and if I am, he says, who's going to stop me, yours truly, I says, scram alley cat, he says, before I eat you, I don't know about alley cats, I says, but one doesn't need to be a detective to see who has a rat in his family tree, and the fight was on.

FIDO

There now, just look. Helson has got the blues again. Dear O dear, that man has the worst inferiority complexes I've ever run across. His dreams must be amazing. Really I must ask him about them. Excuse me.

MOPPET

Nosy prig.

POPPET

He can't help it. Dogs are like that. Always sniffing.

NO 21 FIDO'S SYMPATHY

FIDO [*looking up at Helson*]

> Won't you tell me what's the matter?
>   I adore the confidential role,
> Why not tell your little troubles
>   To a really sympathetic soul?
> [*Helson lunges a kick at him and he bolts*]

POPPET

Dogs have no savoir-faire.

MOPPET

Serve him right. I hate gush.

NO 22 CATS' CREED

MOPPET AND POPPET
Let Man the romantic in vision espy
A far better world than his own in the sky
As a tyrant or beauty express a vain wish
To be mild as a beaver or chaste as a fish.

Let the dog who's the most sentimental of all
Throw a languishing glance at the hat in the hall,
Struggle wildly to speak all the tongues that he hears
And to rise to the realm of Platonic ideas.

But the cat is an Aristotelian and proud
Preferring hard fact to intangible cloud;
Like the troll in Peer Gynt, both in hunting and love,
The cat has one creed: 'To thyself be enough'.

POPPET
Let's go and kill birds.

MOPPET
You've heard about Tiny and Slim? Fido caught them
necking in the pantry after breakfast.

POPPET
Yes, he told me. No one can say I'm narrow-minded,
but there are *some* things that just aren't done till after
dark.

[*Exeunt*]

VOICE OF PAUL BUNYAN
Helson. Helson.
[*Enter Four Cronies*]

CRONIES
1 He's back.
2 He's mad at you.

PAUL BUNYAN
Helson. I want to talk to you.

CRONIES
3 Don't pay any attention to him.
4 Go and settle with him.

PAUL BUNYAN
Helson.

CRONIES
1 You're not going to do what he tells you, are you?
2 Go on, wipe the floor with him.
3 Don't let him think you're sissy.
4 Show him you're an American. Give him the works.

HEL HELSON
I'll kill him.

[*Exit Helson*]

CRONIES
Atta boy.

NO 23 THE FIGHT

[*Chorus rush in*]

CHORUS
What's happening?
What is it?
A fight.
It's Helson.
He's crazy,

He'll kill him.
They're heaving rocks,
That's got him!
No, missed him!
Gosh, did you see that?
Helson is tough
But Paul has the brains.
[*They stream out to watch the fight. Enter Slim and Tiny*]

LOVE DUET

TINY
Slim.

SLIM
Yes, dear.

TINY
Where has everybody gone?

SLIM
I don't know, but I'm glad.

TINY
Darling.
[*They embrace. Thunder and shouts off*]

TINY AND SLIM
Move, move from the trysting stone,
White sun of summer depart
That I may be left alone
With my true love close to my heart.
[*Thunder and shouts off*]

SLIM
Tiny.

TINY
Yes, dear.

SLIM
Did you hear a funny noise?

TINY
I did, but I don't care.

SLIM
Darling.
[*They embrace*]

TINY AND SLIM
The head that I love the best
Shall lie all night on my breast.

TINY
Slim.

SLIM
Yes, dear.

TINY
How do people really know
They really are in love?

TINY AND SLIM
Darling.
Lost, lost is the world I knew,
And I have lost myself too;
Dear heart, I am lost in you.

CHORUS [*off*]
He's got him! Now!
[*Enter Chorus carrying the unconscious body of Hel Helson*]

MOCK FUNERAL MARCH

CHORUS
Take away the body and lay it on the ice,
Put a lily in his hand and beef-steaks on his eyes;
Twenty tall white candles at his feet and head;
And let this epitaph be read:

Here lies an unlucky picayune;
He thought he was a champ but he thought too soon;
Here lies Hel Helson from Scandinavia,
Rather regretting his rash behaviour.

CRONIES
1 We told him not to
We never forgot to

2 Be careful to say
He should obey.

3 'Helson', we said,
'Get this in your head

4 Take orders from Paul
Or you'll have a fall'.

1 and 2
We are all put here on earth for a purpose. We all
have a job to do and it is our duty to do it with all our
might.

3 and 4
We must obey our superiors and live according to our
station in life, for whatever the circumstances, the
Chief, the Company and the Customer are always right.

HEL HELSON
Where am I? What happened? Am I dead?
Something struck me on the head.

CHORUS
It's all right, Hel, you are not dead,
You are lying in your bed.

HEL HELSON
Why am I so stiff and sore?
I remember nothing more.

CHORUS
All right, Hel, don't be a sap
You'd a kind of little scrap,
Don't worry now but take a nap.

HEL HELSON
Who was it hit me on the chin?

VOICE OF PAUL BUNYAN
I'm sorry, Hel, I had to do it,
I am your friend if you but knew it.

HEL HELSON
Good Heavens, what a fool I've been.

PAUL BUNYAN
Let bygones be bygones. Forget the past.
We can now be friends at last.
Each of us has found a brother,
You and I both need each other.

CRONIES
That's what we always told you, Hel.

HEL HELSON
How could I ever have been so blind
As not to recognize your kind.
Now I know you. Scram. Or else.

CHORUS
Scram. Or else.

CRONIES
Ingratitude
A purely selfish attitude
An inability to see a joke
And characteristic of uneducated folk.

CHORUS
Scram. Or else.

CRONIES
Don't argue with them. They're sick people.

CHORUS
Scram, or else!

[*Exeunt Cronies*]

HYMN

PAUL BUNYAN
Often thoughts of hate conceal
Love we are ashamed to feel;
In the climax of a fight
Lost affection comes to light.

CHORUS WITH HELSON
And the prisoners are set free
O great day of discovery!

TINY AND SLIM
Move, move from the trysting stone
White sun of summer depart
That I may be left alone
With my true love close to my heart.

WITH CHORUS
The head that I love the best
Shall lie all night on my breast
Lost, lost is the world I knew
And I am lost, dear heart, in you.

HEL HELSON
Great day of discovery!

CHORUS
Great day!

No 24 THIRD BALLAD INTERLUDE

NARRATOR
So Helson smiled and Bunyan smiled
And both shook hands and were reconciled.

And Paul and Johnny and Hel became
The greatest partners in the logging game.

And every day Slim and Tiny swore
They were more in love than the day before.

All over the States the stories spread
Of Bunyan's camp and the life they led.

Of fights with Indians, of shooting matches,
Of monster bears and salmon catches.

Of the whirling whimpus Paul fought and killed,
Of the Buttermilk Line that he had to build.

And a hundred other tales were known
From Nantucket Island to Oregon.

From the Yiddish Alps to the Rio Grande,
From the Dust Bowl down to the Cotton Land.

In every dialect and tongue
His tales were told and his stories sung.

Harsh in the Bronx where they cheer with zest,
With a burring R in the Middle West,

And lilting and slow in Arkansas
Where instead of Father they say Paw.

But there came a winter these stories say
When Babe came up to Paul one day

Stood still and looked him in the eye;
Paul said nothing for he knew why.

'Shoulder your axe and leave this place:
Let the clerk move in with his well-washed face.

Let the architect with his sober plan
Build a residence for the average man;

OPTIONAL CUT

And garden birds not bat an eye
When locomotives whistle by;

And telephone wires go from town to town
For lovers to whisper sweet nothings down.

We must depart – but it's Christmas Eve –
So let's have a feast before we leave'.

That is all I have to tell,
The party's starting; friends, farewell.

Scene two

No 25 THE CHRISTMAS PARTY

[*Christmas Eve. A full-size pine-tree lit up as a Christmas tree
in the background. Foreground a big table with candles. Chorus
eating dinner. Funny hats, streamers, noises*]

CHORUS
Another slice of turkey,
           Another slice of ham,
I'll feel sick to-morrow, but I don't give a damn.
Take a quart of whiskey and mix it with your beer,
Pass the gravy, will you?
           Christmas comes but once a year.

FIDO
Men are three parts crazy and no doubt always were,
But why do they go mad completely one day in the year?

CHORUS
Who wants the Pope's nose?
        I do.
           French fried if you please.

I've a weakness for plum pudding.
           Would you pass the cheese?
Wash it down with Bourbon.
           I think I'll stick to Rye.
There's nothing to compare with an old-fashioned pie.

MOPPET AND POPPET
Seeing his temper's so uncertain, it's very queer,
He should always be good-tempered one day in the
    year.

CHORUS
Cigars
        Hurrah
             Some nuts
                  I'm stuffed to here
Your health
        Skol
            Prosit
               Santé
                  Cheers
A merry merry Christmas and a happy New Year.
[*Inkslinger bangs on the table and rises*]

INKSLINGER
Dear friends, with your leave this Christmas Eve
    I rise to make a pronouncement;
Some will have guessed but I thought it best
    To make an official announcement.

Hot Biscuit Slim, you all know him,
    As our cook (or coquus in Latin)
Has been put in charge of a very large
    Hotel in Mid-Manhattan.
[*Cheers*]

But Miss Tiny here, whom we love so dear,
    I understand has now consented
To share his life as his loving wife.
    They both look very contented.

THREE SOLOS FROM CHORUS
Carry her over the water
    Set her down under the tree
Where the culvers white all day and all night
    And the winds from every quarter
Sing agreeably agreeably agreeably of love.

FIDO, MOPPET AND POPPET
Put a gold ring on her finger,
    Press her close to your heart
While the fish in the lake their snapshots take
    And the frog, that sanguine singer,
Sings agreeably agreeably agreeably of love.

CHORUS
The preacher shall dance at your marriage
    The steeple bend down to look
The pulpit and chairs shed suitable tears
    While the horses drawing your carriage
Sing agreeably agreeably agreeably of love.

TINY AND SLIM [*rising*]
Where we are is not very far
    To walk from Grand Central Station,
If you ever come East, you will know at least
    Of a standing invitation.
[*They sit down*]

INKSLINGER

And Hel so tall who managed for Paul
    And had the task of converting
His ambitious dreams into practical schemes
    And of seeing we all were working

Will soon be gone to Washington
    To join the Administration
As a leading man in the Federal Plan
    Of public works for the nation.
[*Cheers. Helson rises*]

HEL HELSON

I hope that some of you will come
    To offer your assistance
In installing turbines and High Tension lines
    And bringing streams from a distance.
[*Cheers. He sits down*]

INKSLINGER

And now three cheers for old John Shears
    Who has taken a short vacation
From his cattle and hay, to be with us to-day
    On this important occasion.
[*Cheers. John Shears rises*]

JOHN SHEARS [*stammering*]

I am, I'm not, Er which er what
    As I was saying, the —er,
The er, the well. I mean, O Hell,
    I'm mighty glad to be here.
[*Cheers. He sits down*]

WESTERN UNION BOY [*off*]

Inkslinger! John Inkslinger!
[*Enter Western Union Boy on his bicycle*]

WESTERN UNION BOY

A telegram, a telegram,
    A telegram from Hollywood.
Inkslinger is the name;
    And I think that the news is good.

INKSLINGER [*reading*]

Technical Advisor required for all-star lumber picture
stop your name suggested stop if interested wire collect
stop.

A lucky break, am I awake?
    Please pinch me if I'm sleeping.
It only shows that no one knows
    The future of book-keeping.

CHORUS

We always knew that one day you
    Would come to be famous, Johnny.
When you're prosperous remember us
    And we'll all sing Hey Nonny, Nonny.

INKSLINGER

And last of all I call on Paul
    To speak to us this evening,
I needn't say how sad to-day
    We are that he is leaving.

Every eye is ready to cry
    At the thought of bidding adieu, sir,
For sad is the heart when friends must part,
    But enough – I call upon you, sir.

No 26 BUNYAN'S FAREWELL

VOICE OF PAUL BUNYAN

Now the task that made us friends
In a common labour, ends;
For an emptiness is named
And a wilderness is tamed
Till its savage nature can
Tolerate the life of man.

All I had to do is done
You remain but I go on,
Other kinds of deserts call
Other forests whisper Paul,
I must hasten in reply
To that low instinctive cry
There to make a way again
For the conscious lives of men.

Here, though, is your life, and here
The pattern is already clear
That machinery imposes
On you as the frontier closes,
Gone the natural disciplines
And the life of choice begins.

You and I must go our way
I have but one word to say:
O remember, friends, that you
Have the harder task to do
As at freedom's puzzled feet
Yawn the gulfs of self-defeat;
All but heroes are unnerved
When life and love must be deserved.

No 27 LITANY

CHORUS

The campfire embers are black and cold,
The banjos are broken, the stories are told,
The woods are cut down and the young are grown old.

FIDO, MOPPET AND POPPET

From a Pressure Group that says I am the Constitution,
From those who say Patriotism and mean Persecution,
From a Tolerance that is really inertia and delusion

CHORUS

Save animals and men.

TINY AND SLIM

Bless us, father.

PAUL BUNYAN

           A father cannot bless.
May you find the happiness that you possess.

CHORUS

The echoing axe shall be heard no more
Nor the rising scream of the buzzer saw
Nor the crash as the ice-jam explodes in the thaw.

FIDO, MOPPET AND POPPET

From entertainments neither true nor beautiful nor
    witty,
From a homespun humour manufactured in the city,
From the dirty-mindedness of a Watch Committee

CHORUS

Save animals and men.

HEL HELSON
Don't leave us, Paul. What's to become of America now?

PAUL BUNYAN
Every day America's destroyed and re-created,
America is what you do,
America is I and you,
America is what you choose to make it.

CHORUS
No longer the logger shall hear in the Fall
The pine and the spruce and the sycamore call.

PAUL BUNYAN
Good-bye, dear friends.

CHORUS
                    Good-bye, Paul.

FIDO, MOPPET AND POPPET
From children brought up to believe in self-expression,
From the theology of plumbers or the medical
    profession,
From depending on alcohol for self-respect and self-
    possession

CHORUS
Save animals and men.

INKSLINGER
Paul, who are you?

PAUL BUNYAN
Where the night becomes the day,
Where the dream becomes the fact,
    I am the Eternal guest,
        I am Way,
        I am Act.

Peter Grimes

*An opera in three acts
and a prologue*

by Montagu Slater
derived from the poem of George Crabbe

BENJAMIN BRITTEN OP. 33

CHARACTERS

Peter Grimes *a fisherman*	TENOR
Boy *his apprentice*	SILENT
Ellen Orford *a widow, schoolmistress of the Borough*	SOPRANO
Captain Balstrode *retired merchant skipper*	BARITONE
Auntie *landlady of 'The Boar'*	CONTRALTO
Niece 1 ⎤ *main attractions of 'The Boar'* Niece 2 ⎦	SOPRANO
Robert Boles *fisherman and Methodist*	TENOR
Swallow *a lawyer*	BASS
Mrs (Nabob) Sedley *a rentier widow of an* *East India Company's factor*	SOPRANO
Rev Horace Adams *the rector*	TENOR
Ned Keene *apothecary and quack*	BARITONE
Hobson *carrier*	BASS
Dr Crabbe	SILENT

Chorus of townspeople and fisherfolk

SYNOPSIS OF SCENES

Scene The Borough, a small fishing town on the East Coast

Time Towards 1830

FIRST PERFORMANCE

7 June 1945   *London, Sadler's Wells*

Peter Grimes	Peter Pears
Ellen Orford	Joan Cross
Auntie	Edith Coates
Niece I	Blanche Turner
Niece II	Minnia Bower
Balstrode	Roderick Jones
Mrs Sedley	Valetta Iacopi
Swallow	Owen Brannigan
Ned Keene	Edmund Donlevy
Bob Boles	Morgan Jones
The Rector	Tom Culbert
Hobson	Frank Vaughan
Doctor Thorp	Sasa Machov
A Boy (Grimes's apprentice)	Leonard Thompson

Conducted by Reginald Goodall
Produced by Eric Crozier
Scenery and Costumes by Kenneth Green

Foreword

The opera is derived from George Crabbe's poem, 'The Borough', inasmuch as the story and many of the characters are to be found in Crabbe, but what Crabbe sketched broadly has, of course, been elaborated in the libretto. Textually the libretto bears practically no relation to Crabbe, the only quotations being part of the first and all of the final chorus.

The Borough, as described by Crabbe, is a small fishing and ship-building town on the East Coast. Crabbe sets himself to examine the Borough from all aspects, entitling the main sections of his poem *'The Church'*, *'Sects and Professions in Religion'*, *'Professions (Law, Physic)'*, *'Trades'*, *'Amusements'*, *'Inns'*, *'the Poor of the Borough'*, *'Prisons'*, *'Schools'*, and little by little, character by character, assembling a picture of the whole life of a nineteenth century town.

The main characters of the opera reflect the Borough's activities. The Rector, Mr Horace Adams, is one, Crabbe says, who had

'. . .some desire to rise
But not enough to make him enemies
He ever aimed to please, and to offend
Was every cautious; for he sought a friend;
Yet for the friendship never much would pay,
Content to bow, be silent, and obey,
And by a soothing suff'rance find his way.'

Round him, of course, we find the widows and maiden ladies –

'To ancient females his devoirs were paid . . .
The easy follower in the female train,
Led without love, and captive without chain.'

In the opera, this group of gossips and scandalmongers is typified by Mrs Sedley, sometimes called Mrs Nabob – one who takes an interest in her neighbours:

'While the town small-talk flows from lip to lip;
Intrigues half-gathered, conversation-scraps,
Kitchen cabals, and nursery mishaps.'

Crabbe, in his preface, goes out of his way to apologise for the unfriendliness of his portrait of Swallow, the lawyer, Coroner and wealthy burgher of the Borough.

'The people cursed him, but in times of need
Trusted in one so certain to succeed:
By law's dark by-ways he had stored his mind
With wicked knowledge how to cheat mankind.'

These, with the retired sea-captain Balstrode, a solid, sensible, charitable figure, are the leading citizens of the town.

In the section called 'Inns', Crabbe deals with the Borough's less reputable side, and particularly with 'The Boar', whose landlady is nicknamed 'Auntie', for a good reason.

'Shall I pass by the *Boar*–there are who cry,
"Beware the Boar," and pass determined by:
Those dreadful tusks, those little piercing eyes
And churning chaps, are tokens to the wise.
There dwells a kind old aunt, and there you see
Some kind young nieces in her company;
Poor village nieces, whom the tender dame
Invites to town, and gives their beauty fame.'

'Auntie' has a fellow-tradesman in Need Keene, the apothecary, of whose deluded clients Crabbe says –

'Though he could neither reason, write, nor spell,
They yet had hope his trash would make them well;
And while they scorned his parts, they took his oxymel.'

Among the poor folk of the town is the lovable Ellen Orford, a widow and the Borough schoolmistress, who sums up her own character–

'. . .I look'd around,
And in my school a bless'd subsistence found –
My winter-calm of life: to be of use
Would pleasant thoughts and heavenly hopes produce.'

As for the poor Methodist fisherman, Bob Boles –

'He rails, persuades, explains, and moves the will
By fierce bold words, and strong mechanic skill.'

In this Borough of simple and very ordinary people, Peter Grimes fits uneasily. He is a fisherman – visionary, ambitious, impetuous and frustrated – poaching and fishing without caution or care for consequences, and with only one friend in the town, the schoolmistress Ellen Orford. He is determined to make enough money to ask her to marry him, though too proud to ask her till he has lived down his unpopularity and remedied his poverty.

The Prologue which opens the opera shows Peter under cross-examination – practically on trial – for the death of his apprentice during a recent fishing-trip. The inquest is conducted by Swallow, who clearly shares the general fear and mistrust of Grimes, but dismisses him with a warning from lack of evidence. In Act I, Peter is faced with the impossibility of working his boat without help, but Ned Keene brings news of having found him a new apprentice at the workhouse, and, braving the antagonism of the Borough, Ellen Orford agrees to accompany the carrier in to the Market Town, to bring the boy home to Peter.

The Borough is on that part of the East Coast where the encroachment of the sea makes coast erosion and land-slides a very real danger when gales swell the high tides of the equinox. Peter's troubles are quickly forgotten when a storm breaks, bringing fears of flood and destruction.

The next scene shows 'The Boar' that night, where some of the fisherfolk are sheltering from the storm howling outside. The coast road has been flooded, and the carrier's cart, bringing Ellen and the boy, has been delayed. Peter comes into the pub to wait for them. There are drunken brawls, and the news comes that a landslide has swept part of the cliff away up by Peter's hut. Despite the storm and the floods, the carrier reaches the Borough, and amid the hostile mutterings of the fisherfolk, Peter takes the boy out into the gale to his desolate hut.

Act 2 begins later in the summer, on a Sunday morning, sunlit and calm in contrast with the storm and terror of the previous act. Ellen comes with the boy to sit and enjoy the sun by the sea, outside the parish church, but she soon realises, from tears in his clothing, and bruises on his neck, that Peter has begun to ill-treat him, and when Peter arrives, her questions lead to a quarrel. Ellen is in despair that their plans of re-establishing Peter in the eyes of the Borough by hard work, successful fishing and good care of the boy should have failed, and Peter furiously drives the boy off to launch for a shoal that he has observed out at sea.

The quarrel has roused the Borough – Mrs Sedley has overheard the conversation about Peter's brutality towards the boy – and after an outburst of indignation, the townsfolk follow the Rector and Swallow off to Peter's hut to find out the truth.

The next scene follows immediately, as Peter forces the boy into his hut, roughly ordering him to get ready for fishing. Relenting, he tries to soothe the boy's terror of him, and pictures what their life might be like if all goes well.

His language grows wilder and wilder, foreshadowing his eventual madness, and when the Borough is heard climbing up the road to the hut, he loses his head, and chases the boy out of the cliff-side door. The boy slips and falls: Peter climbs swiftly after him as the men reach the hut. The Rector and Swallow are surprised and taken aback to discover only a neat, empty hut.

Act 3 takes place a few nights later, when the town is gay with a dance in progress at the Moot Hall. There is a steady passage of males between the Hall and 'The Boar', and the nieces are in great demand. Mrs Sedley hails Ned Keene, to tell him her own theories about what has happened to Peter and his boy, who have been missing for some days. She overhears Ellen tell Balstrode about a jersey found washed up on the beach, and summons the men to hunt for Grimes. They scatter, calling and searching for him.

A few hours later, there is a thick fog, and only the calls of the people at their manhunt, and the sound of a fog-horn, break the silence, as Peter staggers in, weary and demented, shrieking back in answer to the voices. Ellen finds him, and tries to soothe him, but he is beyond help: she fetches Balstrode, who tells him to take out his boat, row beyond sight of land, and go down with it. Peter does as he is told, and Balstrode leads Ellen away.

The dawn is breaking as the men come back from their fruitless search, and disperse. A new day begins in the town, with its unchanging routine of tasks. Word comes from the coastguard-station of a boat sinking far out at sea, but nothing can be seen from the Borough, and the people dismiss it as a rumour, and go on with their work.

It remains to add a note on the form of the libretto and its setting. The form – a four-beat line with half rhymes – seemed appropriate for the quick conversational style of the recitatives. The prologue, however, is written in prose.

In the original production by Sadlers Wells we indulged in a calculated inaccuracy in the setting. Historically, Crabbe and the poem belong to the last years of the 18th century: we have set the opera in the early years of the 19th. There is a time-lag between a change of ideas and mode of life and its reflection on costume. If it is thought Crabbe was ahead of his time and anticipated the spirit and problems of the 19th century, then it seems sensible to dress the opera in 19th century clothes.

Prologue

[*Interior of the Moot Hall arranged as for Coroner's Inquest. Coroner, Mr Swallow, at table on dais, clerk at table below. A crowd of townspeople in the body of the hall is kept back by Hobson acting as Constable. Mr Swallow is the leading lawyer of the Borough and at the same time its Mayor and its Coroner. A man of unexceptionable career and talents he nevertheless disturbs the burgesses by his air of a man with an arrière-pensée*]

HOBSON [*shouts*]
Peter Grimes!
[*Peter Grimes steps forward from among the crowd*]

SWALLOW [*reading*]
Peter Grimes, we are here to investigate the cause of death of your apprentice William Spode, whose body you brought ashore from your boat, 'The Boy Billy' on the 26th ultimo. Do you wish to give evidence?
[*Peter nods*]
Will you step into the box. Peter Grimes. Take the oath. After me. 'I swear by Almighty God'

PETER
'I swear by Almight God'

SWALLOW
'That the evidence I shall give'

PETER
'That the evidence I shall give'

SWALLOW
'Shall be the truth'

PETER
'Shall be the truth'

SWALLOW
'The whole truth and nothing but the truth.'

PETER
'The whole truth and nothing but the truth.'

SWALLOW
Tell the court the story in your own words.
[*Peter is silent*]
You sailed your boat round the coast with the intention of putting in at London. Why did you do this?

PETER
We'd caught a huge catch, too big to sell here.

SWALLOW
And the boy died on the way?

PETER
The wind turned against us, blew us off our course. We ran out of drinking water.

SWALLOW
How long were you at sea?

PETER
Three days.

SWALLOW
What happened next?

PETER
He died lying there among the fish.

SWALLOW
What did you do?

PETER
Threw them all overboard, set sail for home.

SWALLOW
You mean you threw the fish overboard? . . .
When you landed did you call for help?

PETER
I called Ned Keene.

SWALLOW
The apothecary here? [*Indicates Ned*] Was there anybody
else called?

PETER
Somebody brought the parson.

SWALLOW
You mean the rector, Mr Horace Adams?
[*The Rector steps forward. Swallow waves him back*]

All right, Mr Adams.
[*He turns back to Peter*]
Was there a certain amount of excitement?

PETER
Bob Boles started shouting.

SWALLOW
There was a scene in the village street from which you
were rescued by our landlady?

PETER
Yes. By Auntie.

SWALLOW
We don't call her that here . . . You then took to abusing
a respectable lady.
[*Peter glares*]

SWALLOW
Answer me . . . You shouted abuse at a certain person?
[*Mrs Sedley pushes forward. Mrs Sedley is the widow of a retired
factor of the East India Company and is known locally as Mrs
Nabob. She is 65, self-assertive, inquisitive, unpopular*]

MRS SEDLEY
Say who! Say who!!

SWALLOW
Mrs Sedley here.

PETER [*fiercely*]
I don't like interferers.
[*A slight hubbub among the spectators resolves itself into a chorus
which is more like the confused muttering of a crowd than
something fully articulate*]

CHORUS
When women gossip the result
Is someone doesn't sleep at night.

HOBSON [*shouting*]
Silence!

SWALLOW
Now tell me this. Who helped you carry the boy home?
The schoolmistress, the widow, Mrs Ellen Orford?
[*Renewed hubbub. Ellen steps forward to Swallow*]

WOMEN'S CHORUS
O when you pay you shut your eyes
And then can't tell the truth from lies.

HOBSON [*shouts*]
Silence!

SWALLOW
Mrs Orford, as the schoolmistress, the widow, how did
you come into this?

ELLEN
I did what I could to help.

SWALLOW
Why should you help this kind of fellow–callous,
brutal, and coarse? [*to Grimes*] There's something here
perhaps in your favour. I'm told you rescued the boy
from drowning in the March storms.
[*Peter is silent*]
Have you something else to say?
No?–Then I have.
Peter Grimes. I here advise you–do not get another boy
apprentice. Get a fisherman to help you–big enough to
stand up for himself. Our verdict is–that William
Spode, your apprentice, died in accidental
circumstances. But that's the kind of thing people are
apt to remember.

CHORUS
But when the crowner sits upon it,
Who can dare to fix the guilt?

HOBSON [*shouts*]
Silence! Silence!
[*Peter has stepped forward and is trying to speak*]

PETER
Your honour! Like every other fisherman I have to hire
an apprentice. I must have help–

SWALLOW
Then get a woman help you look after him.

PETER
That's what I want–but not yet–

SWALLOW
Why not?

PETER
Not till I've stopped people's mouths.
[*The hubbub begins again*]

SWALLOW [*makes a gesture of dismissal*]
Stand down! Clear the court. Stand down!

PETER
'Stand down' you say. You wash your hands.
The case goes on in people's minds
Then charges that no court has made
Will be shouted at my head.
Then let me speak, let me stand trial,
Bring the accusers into the hall.
Let me thrust into their mouths,
The truth itself, the simple truth.
[*He shouts this excitedly against the hubbub chorus*]

CHORUS
When women gossip, the result
Is someone doesn't sleep at night.
But when the crowner sits upon it,
Who can dare to fix the guilt?
[*Against them all Constable Hobson shouts his:*]

HOBSON
Clear the court!
[*Swallow rises with slow dignity. Everybody stands up while he
makes his ceremonial exit.*]

The crowd then begins to go out.
Peter and Ellen are left alone]

PETER
The truth—the pity—and the truth.

ELLEN
Peter, come away!

PETER
Where the walls themselves
Gossip of inquest.

ELLEN
But we'll gossip, too,
And talk and rest.

PETER
While Peeping Toms
Nod as you go.
You'll share the name
Of outlaw, too.

ELLEN
Peter, we shall restore your name.
Warmed by the new esteem
That you will find.

PETER
Until the Borough hate
Poisons your mind.

ELLEN
There'll be new shoals to catch:
Life will be kind.

PETER
Ay! only of drowning ghosts
Time will not forget:
The dead are witness
And Fate is Blind.

ELLEN
Unclouded
The hot sun
Will spread his rays around.

BOTH
My ⎤
Your ⎦ voice out of the pain,
Is like a hand
That ⎡I ⎤
  ⎣you⎦ can feel and know:
Here is a friend.

[*They walk off slowly as the curtain falls*]

INTERLUDE I · DAWN

Act one

Scene one

[*Street by the sea: Moot Hall exterior with its outside staircase,
next door to which is 'The Boar'. Ned Keene's apothecary's shop
is at the street corner. On the other side breakwaters run down to
the sea.*
It is morning, before high tide, several days later.
*Two Fishermen are turning the capstan, hauling in their boat.
Prolonged cries as the boat is hauled ashore. Women come from
mending nets to take the fish baskets from other Fishermen who
now disembark*]

[*Captain Balstrode sits on the breakwater looking out to sea
through his glass. Balstrode is a retired merchant sea-captain,
shrewd as a travelled man should be, but with a general sympathy
that makes him the favourite rentier of the whole Borough. He
chews a plug of tobacco while he watches*]

CHORUS OF FISHERMEN AND WOMEN

CHORUS
Oh hang at open doors the net, the cork,
While squalid sea-dames at their mending work.
Welcome the hour when fishing through the tide
The weary husband throws his freight aside.

FISHERMEN
O cold and wet and driven by the tide,
Beat your tired arms against your tarry side.
Find rest in public bars where fiery gin
Will aid the warmth that languishes within.
[*Several fishermen cross to 'The Boar' where Auntie stands in the
doorway*]

FISHERMAN
Auntie!

AUNTIE
Come in gentlemen, come in.

BOLES
Her vats flow with poisoned gin!
[*Boles the Methodist fisherman stands aside from all this dram
drinking*]

FISHERMAN
Boles has gone Methody! [*Points and laughs*]

AUNTIE
A man should have
Hobbies to cheer his private life.
[*Fishermen go into 'The Boar'. Others remain with their wives at
the nets and boats*]

WOMEN'S CHORUS
Dabbling on shore half-naked sea-boys crowd,
Swim round a ship, or swing upon a shroud:
Or in a boat purloined with paddles play
And grow familiar with the watery way.
[*While the second boat is being hauled in, boys are scrambling
over the first*]

BALSTRODE
Shoo, you little barnacles!
Up your anchors, hoist your sails!
[*Balstrode chases them from the boat. A more respectable figure
now begins, with much hat-raising, his morning progress down
the High Street. He makes straight for 'The Boar'*]

FISHERMAN [*touches cap*]
Dr Crabbe.

BOLES [*points as the swing door closes*]
He drinks 'Good Health' to all diseases.

ANOTHER FISHERMAN
Storm?

A FEW FISHERMEN
Storm?
[*They shade their eyes looking out to sea*]

BALSTRODE [*glass to his eye*]
A long way out. Sea horses.

Kenneth Green 1945

"PETER GRIMES" Project 1.

8 Project 1, a sketch

Kenneth Green

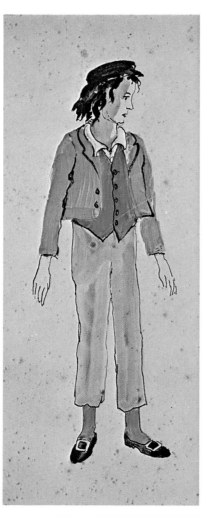

9 Boy

10 Peter Grimes

11 Model of street scene,
   Act III

OPPOSITE

12 A Niece

13 Auntie

14 Model of the interior
   of 'The Boar',
   Act I scene ii

Designer Kenneth Green

9/10

2/13

14

15 Model for the Prologue, inside the Moot Hall *Kenneth Green*

16 Model of the interior of Grimes's Hut, Act II scene ii *Kenneth Green*

The wind is holding back the tide.
If it veers round watch for your lives.

CHORUS OF FISHERS
And if the Springtide eats the land again
Till even the cottages and cobbled walls of fishermen
Are billets for the thievish waves which take
As if in sleep, thieving for thieving's sake—
[*The Rector comes down the High Street. He is followed as
always by the Borough's second most famous rentier, the widow,
Mrs (Nabob) Sedley. From 'The Boar' come the two 'nieces' who
give Auntie her nickname. They stand in front of the pub taking
the morning sun. Ned Keene, seeing Mrs Sedley, pops out of his
shop door*]

RECTOR [*right and left*]
Good morning, good morning!

NIECES
Good morning!

MRS SEDLEY
Good morning, dear Rector.

NED
Had Auntie no nieces we'd never respect her.

SWALLOW
Good morning! Good morning!

NIECES
Good morning!

MRS SEDLEY
Good morning, your worship, Mr Swallow.

AUNTIE [*to Keene*]
You jeer, but if they wink you're eager to follow.
[*The Rector and Mrs Sedley continue towards the church*]

NED [*shouts across to Auntie*]
I'm coming tonight to see your nieces.

AUNTIE [*dignified*]
The Boar is at its patron's service.

BOLES
God's storm will drown your hot desires!

BALSTRODE
God stay the tide, or I shall share your fears.

CHORUS
For us sea-dwellers, this sea-birth can be
Death to our gardens of fertility.
Yet only such contemptuous springtide can
Tickle the virile impotence of man.

PETER [*calls off*]
Hi! Give us a hand!

[*Chorus stops*]

PETER
Haul the boat!

BOLES [*shouts back*]
Haul it yourself, Grimes.

PETER [*off*]
Hi! Somebody bring the rope!
[*Nobody does. Presently he appears and takes the capstan rope
himself and pulls it after him (off) to the boat. Then he returns.
The Fishermen and Women turn their backs on him and slouch
away awkwardly*]

BALSTRODE [*going to capstan*]
I'll give a hand, the tide is near the turn.

NED
We'll drown the gossips in a tidal storm.
[*Grimes goes back to the boat. Balstrode and Keene turn capstan*]

AUNTIE [*at the door of 'The Boar'*]
Parsons may moralise and fools decide,
But a good publican takes neither side.

BALSTRODE
O haul away! The tide is near the turn.

NED
Man invented morals but tides have none.

BOLES [*with arms akimbo watches their labour*]
This lost soul of a fisherman must be
Shunned by respectable society.
Oh let the captains hear, the scholars learn:
Shielding the sin, they share the people's scorn.

AUNTIE
I have my business. Let the preachers learn
Hell may be fiery but the pub won't burn.

BALSTRODE AND NED
The tide that floods will ebb, the tide, the tide will turn.
[*The boat is hauled up. Grimes appears*]

NED
Grimes, you won't need help from now.
I've got a prentice for you.

BALSTRODE
A workhouse brat?

NED
I called at the workhouse yesterday.
All you do now is fetch the boy.
We'll send the carter with a note.
He'll bring your bargain on his cart.
[*Shouts*]
Jim Hobson, we've a job for you.

HOBSON [*enters*]
Cart's full sir. More than I can do.

NED
Listen, Jim. You'll go to the workhouse
And ask for Mr Keene his purchase.
Bring him back to Grimes.

HOBSON
Cart's full sir. I have no room.

NED
Hobson, you'll do what there is to be done.
[*It is near enough to an argument to attract a crowd. Fishermen
and Women gather round. Boles takes his chance*]

BOLES
Is this a Christian country? Are
Pauper children so enslaved
That their bodies go for cash?

NED
Hobson, will you do your job?
[*Ellen Orford has come in. She is a widow of about 40. Her
children have died, or grown up and gone away, and in her
loneliness she has become the Borough schoolmistress. A hard life
has not hardened her. It has made her the more charitable*]

HOBSON
I have to go from pub to pub
Picking up parcels, standing about.
My journey back is late at night.
Mister, find some other way
To bring your boy back.

CHORUS
He's right. Dirty jobs!

HOBSON
Mister, find some other way . . .

ELLEN
Carter! I'll mind your passenger.

CHORUS
You? What! And be Grimes' messenger?

ELLEN
Whatever you say, I'm not ashamed.
Somebody must do the job.
The carter goes from pub to pub,
Picking up parcels, standing about.
The boy needs comfort late at night,
He needs a welcome on the road,
Coming here strange he'll be afraid.
I'll mind your passenger!

NED
Mrs Orford is talking sense.

CHORUS
Ellen—you're leading us a dance,
Fetching boys for Peter Grimes,
Because the Borough is afraid
You who help will share the blame.

ELLEN
Whatever you say . . .
Let her among you without fault
Cast the first stone
And let the Pharisees and Sadducees
Give way to none.
But whosoever feels his pride
Humbled so deep
There is no corner he can hide
Even in sleep!
Will have no trouble to find out
How a poor teacher
Widowed and lonely finds delight
In shouldering care.
[As she moves up the street]
Mr Hobson, where's your cart?
I'm ready.

HOBSON
Up here ma'am. I can wait.
[The crowd stands round and watches. Some follow Ellen and Hobson. On the edge of the crowd are other activities]

MRS SEDLEY [whispers to Ned]
Have you my pills?

NED
I'm sorry ma'am.

MRS SEDLEY
My sleeping draught.

NED
    The laudanum

Is out of stock and being brought
by Mr Carrier Hobson's cart.
He's back tonight.

MRS SEDLEY
Good Lord, good Lord—

NED
Meet us both at this pub, 'The Boar'
Auntie's we call it. It's quite safe.

MRS SEDLEY
I've never been in a pub in my life.

NED
You'll come?

MRS SEDLEY
All right.

NED
Tonight?

MRS SEDLEY
All right.

[She moves off up the street]

NED
If the old dear takes much more laudanum
She'll land herself one day in Bedlam!

BALSTRODE [looks seaward through his glass]
Look! the storm cone!
The wind veers
In from the sea
At gale force.

CHORUS
Look out for squalls!
The wind veers
In from sea
At gale force.
Make your boat fast!
Shutter your windows
And bring in all the nets!

ALL
Now the flood tide
And the sea-horses
Will gallop over
The eroded coast
Flooding, flooding
Our seasonal fears.
Look! The storm cone
The wind veers.
A high tide coming
Will eat the land.
A tide no breakwaters can withstand
Fasten your boats. The springtide's here
With a gale behind.

CHORUS
Is there much to fear?

NED
Only for the goods you're rich in:
It won't drown your conscience, it might
    flood your kitchen.

BOLES [passionately]
God has his ways which are not ours:
His high tide swallows up the shores.
Repent!

NED
And keep your wife upstairs.

OMNES
O Tide that waits for no man
Spare our coasts!
[*There is a General Exeunt—mostly through the swing doors of
'The Boar'. Dr Crabbe's hat blows away, is rescued for him by
Ned Keene who bows him into the pub. Finally only Peter and
Balstrode are left, Peter gazing seaward, Balstrode hesitating at
the pub door*]

BALSTRODE
And do you prefer the storm
To Auntie's parlour and the rum?

PETER
I live alone. The habit grows.

BALSTRODE
Grimes, since you're a lonely soul
Born to blocks and spars and ropes
Why not try the wider sea
With merchantman or privateer?

PETER
I am a native, rooted here.

BALSTRODE
Rooted by what?

PETER
By familiar fields,
Marsh and sand,
Ordinary streets,
Prevailing wind.

BALSTRODE
You'd slip these moorings if you had the mind.

PETER
By the shut faces
Of the Borough clans;
And by the kindness
Of a casual glance.

BALSTRODE
You'll find no comfort there.

When an urchin's quarrelsome
Brawling at his little games,
Mother stops him with a threat,
'You'll be sold to Peter Grimes!'

PETER
Selling me new apprentices,
Children taught to be ashamed
Of the legend on their faces—
'You've been sold to Peter Grimes!'

BALSTRODE
Then the Crowner sits to
Hint, but not to mention crimes,
And publishes an open verdict
Whispered about this Peter Grimes.

Your boy was workhouse starved—
Maybe you're not to blame he died.

PETER
Picture what that day was like
That evil day.

We strained into the wind
Heavily laden,
We plunged into the wave's
Shuddering challenge
Then the sea rose to a storm
Over the gunwales,
And the boy's silent reproach
Turned to illness.
Then home
Among fishing nets
Alone, alone, alone
With a childish death!

BALSTRODE
This storm is useful. You can speak your mind
And never mind the Borough commentary.
There is more grandeur in a gale of wind
To free confession, set a conscience free.

PETER
They listen to money
These Borough gossips
I have my visions
Fiery visions.
They call me dreamer
They scoff at my dreams
And my ambition.
But I know a way
To answer the Borough
I'll win them over.

BALSTRODE
With the new prentice?

PETER
We'll sail together.
These Borough gossips
Listen to money
Only to money:
I'll fish the sea dry,
Sell the good catches—
That wealthy merchant
Grimes will set up
Household and shop
You will all see it!
I'll marry Ellen!

BALSTRODE
Man—go and ask her
Without your booty,
She'll have you now.

PETER
No—not for pity! . . .

BALSTRODE
Then the old tragedy
Is in store:
New start with new prentice
Just as before.

PETER
What Peter Grimes decides
Is his affair.

BALSTRODE
You fool, man, fool!
[*The wind has risen, Balstrode is shouting above it. Peter faces
him angrily*]

PETER
Are you my conscience?

BALSTRODE
  Might as well
Try shout the wind down as to tell
The obvious truth.

PETER
  Take your advice—
Put it where your money is.

BALSTRODE
The storm is here. O come away.

PETER
The storm is here and I shall stay.
[*The storm is rising. Auntie comes out of 'The Boar' to fasten the shutters, in front of the windows. Balstrode goes to help her. He looks back towards Peter, then goes into the pub*]
What harbour shelters peace?
Away from tidal waves, away from storm
What harbour can embrace
Terrors and tragedies?
With her there'll be no quarrels,
With her the mood will stay,
A harbour evermore
Where night is turned to day.
[*The wind rises. He stands a moment as if leaning against the wind*]

CURTAIN

INTERLUDE II · STORM

Scene two

[*Interior of 'The Boar', typical main room of a country pub. No bar. Upright settles, tables, log fire. When the curtain rises Auntie is admitting Mrs Sedley. The gale has risen to hurricane force and Auntie holds the door with difficulty against the wind which rattles the windows and howls in the chimney. They both push the door closed*]

AUNTIE
Past time to close!

MRS SEDLEY
He said half-past ten.

AUNTIE
Who?

MRS SEDLEY
Mr Keene.

AUNTIE
Him and his women!

MRS SEDLEY
You referring to me?

AUNTIE
Not at all, not at all.
What do you want?

MRS SEDLEY
Room from the storm.

AUNTIE
That is the sort of weak politeness
Makes a publican lose her clients.

Keep in the corner out of sight.
[*Balstrode and a Fisherman enter. They struggle with the door*]

BALSTRODE
Phew, that's a bitch of a gale all right.

AUNTIE [*nods her head towards Mrs Sedley*]
Sh-h-h.

BALSTRODE
Sorry. I didn't see you, missis.
You'll give the regulars a surprise.

AUNTIE
She's meeting Ned.

BALSTRODE
Which Ned?

AUNTIE
  The quack.
He's looking after her heart attack.

BALSTRODE
Bring us a pint.

AUNTIE
It's closing time.

BALSTRODE
You fearful old female—why should *you* mind?

AUNTIE
The storm!
[*Bob Boles and other Fishermen enter. The wind howls through the door and again there is difficulty in closing it*]

BOLES
Did you hear the tide
Has broken over the Northern Road?
[*He leaves the door open too long with disastrous consequences. A sudden gust howls through the door, the shutters of the window fly open, a pane blows in*]

BALSTRODE [*shouts*]
Get those shutters.

AUNTIE [*screams*]
O-o-o-o-o!

BALSTRODE
You fearful old female, why do you
Leave your windows naked?

AUNTIE
O-o-o-o!

BALSTRODE
Better strip a niece or two
And clamp your shutters.
[*The two 'Nieces' run in. They are young, pretty enough though a little worn, conscious that they are the chief attraction of 'The Boar'. At the moment they are in mild hysterics, having run downstairs in their night clothes, though with their unusual instinct for precaution they have found time to don each a wrap. It is not clear whether they are sisters, friends or simply colleagues: but they behave like twins, as though each has only half a personality and they cling together always to sustain their self-esteem*]

BOTH NIECES
Oo! Oo!
It's blown our bedroom windows in.
Oo! we'll be drowned.

BALSTRODE
Perhaps in gin.

NIECES
I wouldn't mind if it didn't howl.
It gets on my nerves.

BALSTRODE
D'you think we
Should stop our storm for such as you—
'Oo! Oo!' Coming all over palpitations!
Auntie, get some new relations.

AUNTIE [takes it ill]
Loud man, I never did have time
For the kind of creature who spits his wine.
A joke's a joke and fun is fun
But say your grace and be polite for all that we have
  done.

NIECES
For his peace of mind.

MRS SEDLEY
This is no place for me.

AUNTIE
Loud man, you're glad enough to be
Playing your cards in our company.
A joke's a joke and fun is fun
But say your grace and be polite for all that we have
  done.

NIECES
For his peace of mind.

MRS SEDLEY
This is no place for me.

AUNTIE
Loud man–!
[Some more Fishermen and Women come in. Usual struggle
with the door]

FISHERMAN
There's been a landslide up the coast.

BOLES [rising unsteadily]
I'm drunk. Drunk!

BALSTRODE
You're a Methody wastrel.

BOLES [staggers to one of the Nieces]
Is this a niece of yours?

AUNTIE
That's so.

BOLES
Who's her father?

AUNTIE
Who wants to know?

BOLES
I want to pay my best respects
To the beauty and misery of her sex.

BALSTRODE
Old Methody, you'd better tune
Your piety to another hymn.

BOLES
I want her.

BALSTRODE
Sh-h-h.

AUNTIE [cold]
Turn that man out.

BALSTRODE
He's the local preacher.
He's lost the way of carrying liquor.
He means no harm.

BOLES
No, I mean love!

BALSTRODE
Come on, boy!
[Boles hits him. Mrs Sedley screams. Balstrode quietly over-
powers Boles and sits him in a chair]

BALSTRODE
We live and let live,
And look, we keep our hands to ourselves.
[Boles struggles to his feet, Balstrode sits him down again,
laying the law down]

BALSTRODE
Pub conversation should depend
On this eternal moral;
So long as satire don't descend
To fisticuff or quarrel.
We live and let live, and look
We keep our hands to ourselves.
[And while Boles is being forced into his chair again the
bystanders comment:]

CHORUS
We live and let live, and look
We keep our hands to ourselves.

BALSTRODE
We sit and drink the evening through
Not deigning to devote a
Thought to the daily cud we chew
But buying drinks by rota.

ALL
We live and let live, and look
We keep our hands to ourselves.
[Door opens. The struggle with the wind is worse than before as
Ned Keene gets through]

NED
Have you heard the cliff is down
Up by Grimes's hut?

AUNTIE
Where is he?

MRS SEDLEY
Thank God you've come!

NED
You won't blow away.

MRS SEDLEY
The carter's over half an hour late.

BALSTRODE
He'll be later still: the road's under flood.

MRS SEDLEY
I can't stay longer. I refuse.

NED
You'll have to stay if you want your pills.

MRS SEDLEY
With drunken females and in brawls!

NED
They're Auntie's nieces, that's what they are
And better than you for kissing, ma.
Mind that door!

ALL
Mind that door!
[*The door opens again. Peter Grimes has come in. Unlike the rest he wears no oilskins. His hair looks wild. He advances into the room shaking off the raindrops from his hair. Mrs Sedley faints. Ned Keene catches her as she falls*]

NED
Get the brandy, aunt.

AUNTIE
Who'll pay?

NED
Her. I'll charge her for it.
[*As Peter moves forward, the others shrink back*]

CHORUS
Talk of the devil and there he is
And a devil he *is*, and a devil he *is*.
Grimes is waiting his apprentice.

NED
This widow's as strong as any two
Fishermen I have met.
Everybody's very quiet.
[*No-one answers. Silence is broken by Peter, as if thinking aloud*]

PETER
Now the great Bear and Pleiades
    where earth moves
Are drawing up the clouds
    of human grief
Breathing solemnity in the deep night.

Who can decipher
    In storm or starlight
The written character
    of a friendly fate—
As the sky turns, the world for us to change?

But if the horoscope's
    bewildering
Like a flashing turmoil
    of a shoal of herring
Who can turn skies back and begin again?
[*Silence again. Then muttering in undertones*]

CHORUS
He's mad or drunk.
    Why's that man here?

NIECES
His song alone would sour the beer.

CHORUS
His temper's up.
    O chuck him out.

NIECES
I wouldn't mind if he didn't howl.

CHORUS
He looks as though he's nearly drowned.

BOLES [*staggers up to Grimes*]
You've sold your soul, Grimes.

BALSTRODE
Come away.

BOLES
Satan's got no hold on me.

BALSTRODE
Leave him alone, you drunkard.
[*Goes to get hold of Boles*]

BOLES
I'll hold the gospel light before
The cataract that blinds his eyes.

PETER [*as the drunk stumbles up to him*]
Get out.
[*Grimes thrusts Boles aside roughly and turns away*]

BOLES
His exercise
Is not with men but killing boys.
[*Boles picks up a bottle and is about to bring it down on Grimes's head when Balstrode knocks it out of his hand and it crashes in fragments on the floor*]

AUNTIE
For God's sake, help me keep the peace.
D'you want me up at the next Assize?

BALSTRODE
For peace sake, someone start a song.
[*Keene starts a round. 'That's right, Ned!' says Auntie. The round is:*]

ALL
Old Joe has gone fishing and
Young Joe has gone fishing and
You Know has gone fishing and
Found them a shoal.
Pull them in in handfuls,
And in canfuls,
And in panfuls
Bring them in sweetly,
Gut them completely,
Pack them up neatly,
Sell them discretely,
Oh, haul a-way.
[*Peter comes into the round: the others stop*]

PETER
When I had gone fishing
When he had gone fishing
When You Know'd gone fishing
We found us Davy Jones.
Bring him in with horror,
Bring him with terror,
And bring him in with sorrow!
Oh, haul a-way.
[*This breaks the round, but the others recover in a repeat*]

[*At the climax of the round the door opens to admit Ellen Orford, the Boy and the Carrier. All three are soaking, muddy and bedraggled*]

HOBSON
The bridge is down, we half swam over.

NED
    And your cart? Is it seaworthy?
    [*The Women go to Ellen and the Boy. Auntie fusses over him. Boles reproaches*]

ELLEN
    We're chilled to the bone.

BOLES [*to Ellen*]
    Serves you right, woman.

AUNTIE
    My dear
    There's brandy and hot water to spare.

NIECES
    Let's look at the boy.

ELLEN [*rising*]
    Let him be.

NIECES [*admiring*]
    Nice sweet thing.

ELLEN [*protecting him*]
    Not for such as you.

PETER
    Let's go. You ready?

AUNTIE
    Let them warm up
    They've been half drowned.

PETER
    Time to get off.

AUNTIE
    Your hut's washed away.

PETER
    Only the cliff.
    Young prentice, come.
    [*The Boy hesitates, Ellen leads him to Peter*]

ELLEN
    Goodbye, my dear, God bless you.
    Peter will take you home.

OMNES
    Home? Do you call that home?
    [*Peter takes the Boy out of the door into the howling storm*]

    CURTAIN

Act two

INTERLUDE III · SUNDAY MORNING

[*Scene as in Act one. The Street.
A fine sunny morning, some weeks later, with church bells ringing. Some of the villagers are standing outside the church door. Ellen and the Boy, John, come in against the stream of villagers crossing towards the church. Ellen is carrying a work-basket. She sits down between a boat and a breakwater and takes her knitting from the basket. One or two late-comers cross and hurry into the church*]

ELLEN
Glitter of waves
And glitter of sunlight
Bid us rejoice
And lift our hearts on high.

Man alone
Has a soul to save,
And goes to church
To worship on a Sunday.
    [*The organ starts a voluntary in church, offstage*]
Shall we not go to church this Sunday
But do our knitting by the sea?
I'll do the work, you talk.
    [*Hymn starts in church*]

    CHORUS
    Now that the daylight fills the sky
    We lift our hearts to God on high
    That he in all we do or say
    Would keep us free from harm to-day.

Nothing to tell me,
Nothing to say? Then shall I
Tell you what your life was like?
See if I'm right. I think
You liked your workhouse with its grave
Empty look. Perhaps you weren't
So unhappy in your loneliness?

When first I started teaching
The life at school to me seemed bleak and empty
But soon I found a way of knowing children–
Found the woes of little people
Hurt more, but are more simple.
[*She goes on with her work. John says nothing*]

    CHORUS
    May he restrain our tongues from strife
    And shield from anger's din our life
    And guard with watchful care our eyes
    From earth's absorbing vanities.

John, you may have heard the story
Of the prentice Peter had before.

    CHORUS
    So we, when this day's work is done
    And shades of night return once more
                                    . . . . Amen.

But when you came, I
Said, Now this is where we
Make a new start. Every day
I pray it may be so.

[*Morning prayer begins and the Rector's voice is heard from the church*]

RECTOR
Wherefore I pray and beseech you,
as many as are here present, to
accompany me with a pure heart and
humble voice, saying after me,
Almighty . . . .

CONGREGATION
Almight and most merciful Father;
We have erred and strayed from thy
ways like lost sheep.
[*The church service continues through the ensuing scene*]

There's a tear in your coat. Was that done
Before you came?
　　　Badly torn.
[*Mrs Sedley stops to listen on her way to church*]
That was done recently.
Take your hand away.
Your neck, is it? John, what
Are you trying to hide?

RECTOR AND CHOIR [*in church*]
O Lord, open Thou our lips;
And our mouth shall shew forth thy praise.
O God make speed to save us;
O Lord make haste to help us.
[*Undoes the neck of the boy's shirt*]
A bruise.
　　　Well . . . It's begun.

RECTOR AND CHOIR
Glory be to the Father and to the Son
and to the Holy Ghost;
As it was in the beginning is now . . . .

Child you're not too young to know
Where roots of sorrow are
Innocent you've learned how near
Life is to torture.

RECTOR AND CHOIR
Praise ye the Lord;
The Lord's name be praised.

Let this be a holiday,
Full of peace and quietness
While the treason of the waves
Glitters like love.

Storm and all its terrors are
Nothing to the heart's despair.
After the storm will come a sleep
Like oceans deep.

CHOIR
O all ye works of the Lord, bless ye the Lord
O ye Sun and Moon, bless ye the Lord
O ye Winds of God, bless ye the Lord,
Praise Him and magnify Him for ever.
[*Peter Grimes comes in excitedly from the harbour*]

CHOIR
O ye Light and Darkness, bless ye the Lord
O ye Nights and Days, bless ye the Lord

O ye Lightnings and Clouds, bless ye the Lord
Praise Him and magnify Him for ever.

PETER
Come boy.

ELLEN
Peter—what for?

CHOIR
O ye Wells, bless ye the Lord
O ye Seas and Floods, bless the Lord,
O ye Whales and all that move in the waters
Praise Him and magnify Him for ever.

PETER
I've seen a shoal. I need his help.

ELLEN
But if there were then all the boats
Would fast be launching.

PETER
I can see
The shoals to which the rest are blind.

CHOIR
O all ye Fowls of the Air, bless ye the Lord
O all ye Beasts and Cattle, bless ye the Lord
O ye Children of Men, bless ye the Lord
Praise Him and magnify Him for ever.

ELLEN
This is a Sunday, his day of rest.

PETER
This is whatever day I say it is!
Come boy!

ELLEN
You and John have fished all week
Night and day without a break
Painting boat, mending nets, cleaning fish,
Now let him rest.

PETER
Come boy!

ELLEN
But your bargain . . .

PETER
My bargain?

ELLEN
His weekly rest.

PETER
He works for me, leave him alone, he's mine.

ELLEN
Hush, Peter, Hush!

CHOIR
O ye Servants of the Lord, bless ye the Lord
O ye holy and humble, bless ye the Lord
Ananias, Azarias and Misael, bless ye the Lord,
Praise Him and magnify Him for ever.
As it was in the beginning is now and ever
shall be,
World without end. Amen.
[*The sound dies down. In church the lesson is being read*]
[*Ellen speaks to Peter, away from the boy*]

ELLEN
This unrelenting work
This grey, unresting industry,
What aim, what future, what peace
Will your hard profits buy?

PETER
Buy us a home, buy us respect
And buy us freedom from pain
Of grinning at gossip's tales.
Believe in me, we shall be free!

> CHOIR
> I believe in God the Father Almighty,
> Maker of heaven and earth:
> And in Jesus Christ his only Son our Lord,
> Who was conceived . . . .
> [*Fades into background*]

ELLEN
Peter, tell me one thing, where
The youngster got that ugly bruise?

PETER
Out of the hurly burly!

ELLEN
O your ways
Are hard and rough beyond his days.
Peter, were we right in what we planned
To do? Were we right, were we right?

PETER
[*roughly*] Take away your hand.
[*then quietly*]
My only hope depends on you.
If you—take it away—what's left?
[*Ellen moves unhappily away from him*]

ELLEN
Were we mistaken when we schemed
To solve your life by lonely toil?

PETER [*in anger*]
Wrong to plan?
Wrong to try?
Wrong to live?
Right to die?

ELLEN
Were we mistaken when we dreamed
That we'd come through and all be well?

PETER
Wrong to struggle?
Wrong to hope?
Then the Borough's
Right again?

ELLEN
Peter! You cannot buy your peace
You'll never stop the gossips' talk,
With all the fish from out the sea.
We were mistaken to have dreamed . . .
Peter! We've failed. We've failed.
[*He cries out as if in agony. Then strikes her. The basket falls*]

> CHOIR [*in church*]
> Amen.

PETER
So be it!—And God have mercy upon me!

[*The boy runs from him. Peter follows. Ellen watches. Then goes out the other way*]
[*Behind closed doors and half-open windows neighbours have been watching. Three now emerge. First Auntie, then Ned Keene, finally Boles*]

AUNTIE
Fool to let it come to this!
Wasting pity, squandering tears.

NED
See the glitter in his eyes!
Grimes is at his exercise.

BOLES
What he fears is that the Lord
Follows with a flaming sword.

AUNTIE
You see all through crazy eyes.

ALL
Grimes is at his exercise.

BOLES
Where's the pastor of this flock
Where's the guardian shepherd's hook?

ALL
Parson, lawyer, all at prayers.
[*The service is over and people gradually collect outside the church door*]

NED, BOLES AND AUNTIE
Now the church parade begins,
Fresh beginning for fresh sins.
Ogling with a pious gaze
Each one's at his exercise.
[*Dr Crabbe comes first*]

AUNTIE
Doctor!

NED
Leave him out of it.

MRS SEDLEY [*coming from church*]
What is it?

NED
Private business.

MRS SEDLEY
I heard two voices during psalms
One was Grimes, and one more calm.

BOLES
While you worshipped idols there
The Devil had his Sabbath here.

MRS SEDLEY
Maltreating that poor boy again.

BALSTRODE
Grimes is weatherwise and skilled
In the practice of his trade.
Let him be, let us forget
What slander can invent.

CHORUS
What is it?

AUNTIE, BOLES AND NED
What do you suppose?
Grimes is at his exercise.

[*As people come out two by two they circulate the village green singing their couplets as they reach the centre. First come Swallow and a fellow lawyer*]

CHORUS
What is it? What do you suppose?
Grimes is at his exercise.

FELLOW LAWYER
Dullards build their self-esteem
By inventing cruelties.

SWALLOW
Even so, the law restrains
Too impetuous enterprise.

FISHERWOMAN
Fishing is a lonely trade
Single men have much to bear.

1st AND 2nd NIECES
If a man's work cannot be made
Decent, let him stay ashore.

CHORUS [*over all*]
What is it? What do you suppose?
Grimes is at his exercise.
[*Balstrode pauses by Ned as he walks round*]

RECTOR
My flock—oh what a weight is this
My burden pastoral.

MRS SEDLEY
But what a dangerous faith is this
That gives souls equality!

BALSTRODE
When the Borough gossip starts
Somebody will suffer.

CHORUS
What is it? What do you suppose?
Grimes is at his exercise.
[*During the hubbub Boles climbs a little way up the steps of the Moot Hall*]

BOLES
People—... No! I will speak!...
This thing here concerns you all.

CHORUS [*crowding round Boles*]
Whoever's guilty gets the rap
The Borough keeps its standards up.

BALSTRODE
Tub-thumping.

BOLES
This prentice system's
Uncivilised and unchristian.

BALSTRODE
Something of the sort befits
Brats conceived outside the sheets.

BOLES
Where's the parson in his black?
Is he here or is he not?
To guide a sinful straying flock?

CHORUS
Where's the parson?

RECTOR
Is it my business?

BOLES
Your business to ignore
Growing at your door
Evils, like your fancy flowers?

CHORUS
Evils!

RECTOR
Calm now! Tell me what it is.
[*Ellen comes in. She is met by Auntie who has picked up Ellen's abandoned basket and its contents*]

AUNTIE
Ellen dear, see I've gathered
All your things. Come rest inside.

BOLES AND CHORUS
She can tell you, Ellen Orford
She helped him in his cruel games.

RECTOR [*holding his hand up for silence*]
Ellen please.

ELLEN
What am I to do?

BOLES AND CHORUS
Speak out in the name of the Lord.

ELLEN
We planned that their lives should
Have a new start,
That I, as a friend could
Make the plan work
By bringing comfort where
Their lives were stark.

RECTOR
You planned to be worldly-wise
But your souls were dark.

ELLEN
We planned this time to
Care for the boy;
To save him from danger
And hardship sore, and
Mending his clothes and giving him
Regular meals.

MRS SEDLEY
O little care you for the prentice
Or his welfare!

BOLES
Call it danger, call it hardship
Or plain murder!

KEENE
But thanks to flinty hearts
Even quacks can make a profit!

NIECES
Perhaps his clothes you mended
But you work his bones bare!

AUNTIE
You meant just to be kind
And avert fear!

BALSTRODE
You interfering gossips, this
Is not your business!

HOBSON
Pity the boy!

SWALLOW
You planned to heal sick souls
With bodily care.

ELLEN
O pity those who try to bring
A shadowed life into the sun.

ELLEN, AUNTIE AND BALSTRODE
O Lord, hard hearts!

CHORUS
Who lets us down must take the rap
The Borough keeps its standards up.

OMNES [without Ellen, Auntie and Balstrode]
Tried to be kind!
Murder!
Tried to be kind and to help
Murder!

RECTOR
Swallow—shall we go and see Grimes in his hut?

SWALLOW
Popular feeling's rising.

RECTOR
Balstrode, I'd like you to come.

BALSTRODE
I warn you we shall waste our time.

RECTOR
I'd like your presence just the same.

MRS SEDLEY
Little do the suspects know,
I've the evidence. I've a clue.

CHORUS
Now we will find out the worst.

SWALLOW [points to the Nieces who join the crowd]
No ragtail no bobtail if you please.

BOLES [pushes them away]
Back to the gutter—and keep out of this.

RECTOR
Only the men, the women stay.

SWALLOW
Carter Hobson, fetch the drum.
Summon the Borough to Grimes's hut.

CHORUS
To Grimes's hut!
To Grimes's hut!
[Hobson sounds his drum and the men line up behind Swallow,
the Rector and Mrs Sedley. Balstrode lags behind. Behind them
come the rest of the crowd]

CHORUS
Now is gossip put on trial,
Now the rumours either fail
Or are shouted in the wind
Sweeping furious through the land.

Now the liars shiver for
Now if they've cheated we shall know:
We shall strike and strike to kill
At the slander or the sin.

Now the whisperers stand out
Now confronted by the fact.
Bring the branding iron and knife:
What's done now is done for life.
[The crowd has gone. Auntie, Nieces and Ellen remain]

NIECES
From the gutter, why should we
Trouble at their ribaldries?

AUNTIE
And shall we be ashamed because
We comfort men from ugliness?

ALL
Do we smile or do we weep
Or wait quietly till they sleep?

AUNTIE
When in storm they shelter here
And we soothe their fears away

NIECES
We know they'll whistle their good-byes
Next fine day and put to sea.

ELLEN
On the manly calendar
We only mark heroic days.

ALL
Do we smile or do we weep
Or wait quietly till they sleep?

ELLEN
They are children when they weep
We are mothers when they strive
Schooling our own hearts to keep
The bitter treasure of their love.

ALL
Do we smile or do we weep
Or wait quietly till they sleep?

CURTAIN

INTERLUDE IV · PASSACAGLIA

Scene two

[*Grimes's hut is an upturned boat. It is on the whole shipshape,
though bare and forbidding. Ropes coiled, nets, kegs and casks
furnish the place. It is lighted by a skylight. There are two doors,
one (back centre) opens on the cliff, the other (downstage), opens
on the road. The Boy staggers into the room as if thrust from
behind. Peter follows, in a towering rage. He pulls down the
Boy's fishing clothes which are neatly stacked on a shelf*]

PETER
Go there!
Here's your sea boots. Take those bright
And fancy buckles off your feet.
[*He throws the sea boots down in front of the boy*]

There's your oilskin and sou-wester.
Stir your pins, we must get ready!
There's the jersey that she knitted,
With the anchor that she patterned.
[*He throws the clothes to the Boy. They fall on the floor around him. The Boy is crying silently. Peter shakes his shoulder*]
I'll tear the collar off your neck.
Steady. Don't take fright boy. Stop.
[*Peter opens the cliff-side door and looks out*]
Look. Now is our chance!
The whole sea's boiling. Get the nets.
Come, boy!
They listen to money
These Borough gossips,
Only to money.
I'll fish the sea dry,
Flood the market.
Now is our chance to get a good catch
Get money to choke
Down rumour's throat.
I will set up
With house and home and shop
I'll marry Ellen,
I'll . . .
[*He turns to see the Boy sitting on the rope coil, weeping. He tears off his coat and throws the jersey at him*]
Coat off! Jersey on! My boy
We're going to sea!
[*The Boy is still weeping*]
[*He gives the Boy a shove, which knocks him over; he lies sobbing miserably. Peter changes tone and breaks into another song*]
In dreams I've built myself some kindlier home
Warm in my heart and in a golden calm
Where there'll be no more fear and no more storm.

And she will soon forget her schoolhouse ways
Forget the labour of those weary days
Wrapped round in kindness like September haze.

The learned at their books have no more store
Of wisdom than we'd close behind our door.
Compared with us the rich man would be poor.

I've seen in stars the life that we might share:
Fruit in the garden, children by the shore,
A fair white doorstep, and a woman's care.

But dreaming builds what dream can disown.
Dead fingers stretch themselves to tear it down.
I hear those voices that will not be drowned

Calling, there is no stone
In earth's thickness to make a home,
That you can build with and remain alone.
[*Hobson's drum, at the head of the Borough procession, can be heard very distantly coming towards the hut. Peter doesn't notice*]

Sometimes I see that boy here in this hut.
He's there now, I can see him, he is there!
His eyes are on me as they were that evil day.

Stop moaning boy. Water?
There's no more water. You had the last yesterday.

You'll soon be home
In harbour calm and deep.
[*In the distance can be heard the song of the neighbours coming up the hill*]

CHORUS [*off*]
Now! Now! . . .
[*Peter rises, goes quickly to the street door and looks out*]

PETER
There's an odd procession here.
Parson and Swallow coming near.
[*Suddenly he turns on the Boy, who doesn't move*]
Wait! You've been talking.
You and that bitch were gossiping.
What lies have you been telling?
The Borough's climbing up the road.
To get me. Me! O I'm not scared
I'll send them off with a flea in their ear.
I'll show them. Grimes ahoy!

CHORUS [*off*]
. . . Or are shouted in the wind
Sweeping furious through the land.

PETER
You sit there watching me
And you're the cause of everything
Your eyes, like his are watching me
With an idiot's drooling gaze.
Will you move
Or must I make you dance?
[*The Boy jumps up and begins dragging nets and other tackle up through the cliff door*]

CHORUS [*off*]
Now confronted by the fact.
Bring the branding iron and knife:
What's done now is done for life.

PETER
Step boldly. For here's the way we go to sea
Down the cliff to find that shoal
That's boiling in the sea.
Careful, or you'll break your neck
Down the cliff-side to the deck.
[*Rope in hand he drives the Boy towards the cliff door*]

CHORUS [*off*]
Now the liars shiver, for
Now if they've cheated we shall know:
We shall strike and strike to kill
At the slander or the sin.

PETER
I'll pitch the stuff down. Come on!
[*He pitches ropes and nets*]
Now
Shut your eyes and down you go.
[*There is a knocking at the other door. Peter turns towards it, then retreats. Meanwhile the Boy climbs out. When Peter is between the two doors the Boy screams and falls out of sight. Peter runs to the cliff door, feels for his grip and then swings quickly after him. The cliff-side door is open. The street door still resounds with the Rector's knock. Then it opens and the Rector puts his head round the door*]

RECTOR
Peter Grimes! Nobody here?

SWALLOW
What about the other door?
[*They go and look out. Silence for a moment*]

RECTOR
Was this a recent landslide?

SWALLOW
Yes.

RECTOR
It makes almost a precipice.
How deep?

SWALLOW
Say forty feet.

RECTOR
Dangerous to leave the door open.

NED
He used to keep his boat down there.
Maybe they've both gone fishing.

RECTOR
Yet
His hut is reasonably kept
Here's order. Here's skill.
[*Swallow draws the moral*]

SWALLOW
The whole affair gives Borough talk its—shall
I say quietus? Here we come pell-mell
Expecting to find out—we know not what.
But all we find is a neat and empty hut.
Gentlemen, take this to your wives:
Less interference in our private lives.

RECTOR
There's no point certainly in staying here,
And will the last to go please close the door.
[*They go out—all save Balstrode who hesitates, looks round the hut, sees the Boy's Sunday clothes lying around, examines them, then goes to the path door to shut it. He goes up to the cliff-side door, looks out, and hurriedly climbs down the way Peter and the Boy went*]

CURTAIN

Act three

INTERLUDE V · MOONLIGHT

Scene one

[*Scene as in Act one, a few days later.
The time is summer evening. One of the season's subscription dances is taking place in the Moot Hall which is brightly lit and from which we can hear the band playing a polka and the rhythm of the dancers' feet. 'The Boar' too is brightly lit and, as the dance goes on there will be a regular passage—of the males at any rate—from the Moot Hall to the Inn.
The stage is empty when the curtain rises but presently there is a little squeal and one of the Nieces scampers down the exterior staircase of Moot Hall, closely followed by Swallow. They haven't got very far before the other Niece appears at the top of the Moot Hall stairs.
A barn dance is being played in the Moot Hall*]

SWALLOW [*to Niece 1*]
Assign your prettiness to me,
I'll seal the deed and take no fee,
My signature, your graceful mark
Are witnessed by the abetting dark.

BOTH NIECES
Together we are safe
As any wedded wife.
For safety in number lies
A man is always lighter
His conversation brighter
Provided that the tête-à-tête's in threes.

SWALLOW
Assign your prettiness to me
I'll call it real property:
Your sister shan't insist upon
Her stay of execution.

NIECES
Save us from lonely men
They're like a broody hen
With habits but with no ideas;
But given choice of pleasures
They show their coloured feathers
Provided that the tête-à-tête's in threes.

SWALLOW
I shall take steps to change her mind;
She has first option on my love.
If my appeal should be ignored
I'll take it to the House of Lords.

NIECES
O pairing's all to blame
For awkwardness and shame,
And all these manly sighs and tears
Which wouldn't be expended
If people condescended
Always to have their tête-à-tête's in threes.

SWALLOW
Assign your prettiness to me
We'll make an absolute decree
Of quiet enjoyment which you'll bless
By sending sister somewhere else.

NIECE 2
Ned Keene is chasing me, gives me no peace.

SWALLOW
He went to the Boar to have a glass
Sister and I will join him there.
If you don't want Ned you'd better stay here.
[*He opens the Inn door. Niece is about to enter when−*]

NIECE 1
They're all watching. I must wait
Till Auntie's turned her back.
[*She runs away to join her Sister and leaves Swallow holding the door open*]

SWALLOW
Bah!
[*He goes in 'The Boar' alone.
The Barn Dance stops−applause.
The sisters are half-way up stairs when Ned Keene comes out of the Moot Hall at the top of the stairs. They fly, giggling, and hide behind one of the boats on the shore. Three boats can be seen as at the end of Act one*]

NED [*calls after them*]
Ahoy.
[*He is half-way to their hiding place when a peremptory voice stops him in mid career. Mrs Sedley is at the top of the Moot Hall stairs.
A slow waltz starts from the Moot Hall*]

MRS SEDLEY
Mr Keene! Can you spare a moment?
I've something to say that's more than urgent,
About Peter Grimes and that boy.
[*She is downstairs by now and has him buttonholed*]
Neither of them was seen yesterday.
It's more than suspicion now, it's fact.
The boy's disappeared.

NED
Do you expect me to act
Like a Bow Street runner or a constable?

MRS SEDLEY
At least you can trouble to hear what
I've got to say.
For two days I've kept my eyes open
For two days I've said nothing;
Only watched and taken notes
Pieced clue to clue and bit by bit
Reconstructed all the crime.
Everything points to Peter Grimes:
He is a murderer.

NED
Old woman, you're far too ready
To yell blue murder.
If people poke their noses into others' business−
No! They won't get me to help them−
They'll find there's merry hell to pay!
You just tell me where's the body?

MRS SEDLEY
In the sea the prentice lies
Whom nobody has seen for days.
Murder most foul it is
Eerie I find it
My skin's a prickly heat
Blood cold behind it!
In midnight's loneliness
And thrilling quiet

The history I trace
The stifling secret.
Murder most foul it is,
And I'll declare it.

NED [*who is getting bored, thirsty and angry*]
Are you mad old woman
Or is it too much laudanum?

MRS SEDLEY [*like a cross-examining counsel*]
Has Peter Grimes been seen?

NED
He's away.

MRS SEDLEY
And the boy?

NED
They're fishing, likely.

MRS SEDLEY
Has his boat been seen?

NED
Why should it?

MRS SEDLEY
His hut's abandoned.

NED
I'm dry. Goodnight.
[*The waltz stops.
[He breaks away from her grasp, goes into 'The Boar' and bangs the door after him.
Dr Crabbe emerges from 'The Boar'. Mrs Sedley retires into the shadow of the boats. A Hornpipe starts from the Moot Hall. The Rector and other burgesses come down the Moot Hall stairs*]

BURGESS
Come along, Doctor−[*indicates 'The Boar'*]
We're not wanted there, we oldsters.

BURGESSES
Good night−it's time for bed.
Good night! Good night! Good night, good people,
good night!

RECTOR
I looked in a moment, the company's gay,
With pretty young women and youths on the spree;
So parched like my roses, but now the sun's down
I'll water my roses and leave you the wine.

BURGESSES
Good night! Good night! Good night, good people,
good night!

RECTOR
Good night, Dr Crabbe, all good friends good night.
Don't let the ladies keep company too late!
My love to the maidens, wish luck to the men!
I'll water my roses and leave you the wine.
[*The Rector, Dr Crabbe and the Burgesses gradually disperse to their houses*]

BURGESSES
Good night! Good night! Good night, good people,
good night!
[*The Hornpipe fades out*]

MRS SEDLEY [*still in the boat shadow, goes on with her brooding*]
  Crime, which my hobby is
  Sweetens my thinking.
  Men who can breach the peace
  And kill convention—
  So many guilty ghosts
  With stealthy body
  Trouble my midnight thoughts . . .
  [*Ellen and Balstrode come up slowly from the beach. It is clear that they have been in earnest talk. As they approach Balstrode shines his lantern on the name of the nearest boat: Boy Billy. Mrs Sedley doesn't show herself*]

ELLEN
  Is the boat in?

BALSTRODE
  Yes! For more than an hour.
  Peter seems to have disappeared
  Not in his boat, not in his hut.

ELLEN [*holds out the Boy's jersey*]
  This I found
  Down by the tide-mark.
  [*It is getting dark. To see the garment properly Balstrode holds it to his lantern*]

BALSTRODE
  The boy's?

ELLEN
  My broidered anchor on the chest.
  [*Meditative*]
  Embroidery in childhood was
  A luxury of idleness,
  A coil of silken thread giving
  Dreams of a silk and satin life.
  Now my broidery affords
  The clue whose meaning we avoid.

  My hand remembered its old skill—
  These stitches tell a curious tale.
  I remember I was brooding
  On the fantasies of children
  and dreamt that only by wishing I
  Could bring some silk into their lives.
  Now my broidery affords
  The clue whose meaning we avoid.
  [*The jersey is wet. Balstrode wrings the water out*]

BALSTRODE
  We'll find him, maybe give a hand.

ELLEN
  We have no power to help him now.

BALSTRODE
  We have the power. We have the power.

  In the black moment
  When your friend suffers
  Unearthly torment
  We cannot turn our backs.
  When horror breaks one heart
  All hearts are broken.

ELLEN AND BALSTRODE
  We shall be there with him.

BALSTRODE
  Nothing to do but wait
  Since the solution
  Is beyond life—beyond
  Dissolution.
  [*They go out together. The dance music starts up again. When they have gone Mrs Sedley goes quickly to the inn door*]

MRS SEDLEY [*calling through the door*]
  Mr Swallow, Mr Swallow.
  I want the lawyer Swallow.

AUNTIE [*coming to the door*]
  What do you want?

MRS SEDLEY
  I want the lawyer Swallow.

AUNTIE
  He's busy.

MRS SEDLEY
  Fetch him please, this is official.
  Business about the Borough criminal.
  Please do as I tell you.

AUNTIE
  My customers come here for peace,
  For quiet, away from you
  And all such nuisances.

MRS SEDLEY
  This is an insult.

AUNTIE
  As long as I am here you'll find
  That I always speak my mind.

MRS SEDLEY
  I'll have you know your place.
  You baggage!

AUNTIE
  My customers come here for peace
  They take their drink, they take their ease!

SWALLOW [*coming out*]
  What's the matter?

AUNTIE [*goes in and bangs door*]
  Good night!

MRS SEDLEY [*points dramatically*]
  Look!

SWALLOW
  I'm short-sighted you know.

MRS SEDLEY
  It's Grimes's boat, back at last!

SWALLOW
  That's different. Hey
  [*Shouts into 'The Boar'*]
  Is Hobson there?

HOBSON [*appearing*]
  Ay, Ay, sir.

MRS SEDLEY
  Good, now things are moving; and about time too!
  [*Hobson appears*]

SWALLOW
You're constable of the Borough,
Carter Hobson.

HOBSON
Ay, Ay, sir.

SWALLOW
As the mayor,
I ask you to find Peter Grimes.
Take whatever help you need.

HOBSON
Now what I claims
Is he's out at sea.

SWALLOW [*points*]
But here's his boat.

HOBSON
Oh! We'll send a posse to his hut.

SWALLOW
If he's not there you'll search the shore,
The marsh, the fields, the streets, the Borough.

HOBSON
Ay, Ay, sir.
[*He goes into 'The Boar' hailing*]
Hey, Here! Come out and help!
Grimes is around! Come on! Come on!

MRS SEDLEY
Crime—that's my hobby—is
By cities hoarded.
Rarely are country minds
Lifted to murder
The noblest of the crimes
Which are my study.
And now the crime is here
And I am ready.
[*Hobson comes out with Boles and other Fishermen.
As the dance band fades out, the people crowd out of the Moot
Hall and 'The Boar' and congregate on the green*]

CHORUS
Who holds himself apart
Lets his pride rise.
Him who despises us
We'll destroy.

And cruelty becomes
His enterprise
Him who despises us
We'll destroy.
[*With two Nieces, Mrs Sedley, Boles, Keene, Swallow, Hobson*]
Our curse shall fall upon his evil day. We shall
Tame his arrogance.
We'll make the murderer pay for his crime.

Peter Grimes! Grimes!
[*The people (still shouting) scatter in all directions*]

CURTAIN

INTERLUDE VI

Scene two

[*Scene as in Scene one
Some hours later.
The stage is quite empty—a thick fog. Fog horn and the cries of
the searchers can be heard distantly*]

[*The orchestra is silent*]

VOICES
Grimes!
[*Peter comes in weary and demented*]

PETER
Steady. There you are. Nearly home.
What is home? Calm as deep water.
Where's my home? Deep as calm water,
Water will drink my sorrows dry
And the tide will turn.

VOICES
Grimes!

PETER
Steady. There you are. Nearly home.
The first one died, just died . . .
The other slipped, and died . . .
And the third will . . .
'Accidental circumstances' . . .
Water will drink his sorrows—my sorrows—dry
And the tide will turn.

VOICES
Peter Grimes, Peter Grimes!

PETER
Peter Grimes! Here you are! Here I am!
Hurry, hurry!
Now is gossip put on trial.
Bring the branding iron, aid knife
For what's done now is done for life . . .
Come on! Land me!
'Turn the skies back and begin again.'

VOICES
Peter Grimes!

PETER
Old Joe has gone fishing and
Young Joe had gone fishing and
You'll know who's gone fishing when
You land the next shoal.

VOICES
Peter Grimes!

PETER
Ellen. Give me your hand.
There now—my hope is held by you,
If you leave me alone . . .
Take away your hand!
The argument's finished,
Friendship lost,
Gossip is shouting,
Everything's said.

VOICES
Peter Grimes!

PETER

To hell with all your mercy
To hell with your revenge.
And God have mercy upon you.

VOICES

Peter Grimes, Peter Grimes!

PETER

Do you hear them all shouting my name?
D'you hear them?
Old Davy Jones shall answer:
Come home, come home!

VOICES [close at hand]

Peter Grimes!

PETER [roars back at them]

Peter Grimes! Peter Grimes!
[Ellen and Balstrode have come in and stand watching. Then
Ellen goes up to Peter]

ELLEN

Peter, we've come to take you home.
O come home out of this dreadful night.
See here's Balstrode, Peter don't you hear me?
[Peter does not notice her and sings in a tone almost like prolonged
sobbing. The voices shouting 'Peter Grimes' can still be heard but
more distantly and more sweetly]

PETER

What harbour shelters peace
Away from tidal waves
Away from storms!
What harbour can embrace
Terrors and tragedies?
Her breast is harbour too−
Where night is turned to day.

BALSTRODE [goes up to Peter and speaks]

Come on, I'll help you with the boat.

ELLEN

No.

BALSTRODE [speaking]

Sail out till you lose sight of land, then sink the boat.
D'you hear? Sink her! Good-bye Peter.
[Together they push the boat down the slope of the shore.
Balstrode comes back and waves goodbye. He takes Ellen who is
sobbing quietly, calms her and leads her carefully down the main
street home.
The men pushing the boat out has been the cue for the orchestra to
return. Now dawn begins.

Dawn comes to the Borough by a gentle sequence of sights and
sounds.
A candle is lighted and shines through a bare window. A shutter
is drawn back.

Hobson and his posse meet severally on the green by the Moot
Hall. They gossip together, shake their heads, indicate the
hopelessness of the search, extinguish their lanterns, and while
some turn home, others go to the boats.
Nets are brought down from the houses by Fisherwomen.
Cleaners open the front door of the Inn and begin to scrub the
steps.
Dr Crabbe comes from a confinement case with his black bag. He
yawns and stretches. Nods to the cleaners. The Rector comes to
early morning prayer.
Mrs Sedley follows.
Ned Keene draws the shutters of his shop]

CHORUS

To those who pass the Borough sounds betray
The cold beginning of another day.
And houses sleeping by the waterside
Wake to the measured ripple of the tide;
[Mr Swallow comes out and speaks to the fishermen]

SWALLOW

There's a boat sinking out at sea,
Coastguard reports.

FISHERMAN

Within reach?

SWALLOW

No.

FISHERMAN

Let's have a look through the glasses.
[Fishermen go with Swallow to the beach and look out.
One of them has a glass]

CHORUS

Or measured cadence of the lads who tow
Some entered hoy to fix her in her row,
Or hollow sound that from the passing bell
To some departed spirit bids farewell.

AUNTIE

What is it?

BOLES

Nothing I can see.

AUNTIE

One of these rumours.
[Nieces emerge and begin to polish the brasses outside 'The
Boar']

OMNES

In ceaceless motion comes and goes the tide
Flowing it fills the channel broad and wide
Then back to sea with strong majestic sweep
It rolls in ebb yet terrible and deep.

SLOW CURTAIN

The Rape of Lucretia

An opera in two acts

by Ronald Duncan
*after André Obey's play
'Le Viol de Lucrèce'*

BENJAMIN BRITTEN OP. 37

CHARACTERS

Male Chorus	TENOR
Female Chorus	SOPRANO
Collatinus *a Roman general*	BASS
Junius *a Roman general*	BARITONE
Tarquinius *an Etruscan prince*	BARITONE
Lucretia *wife of Collatinus*	CONTRALTO
Bianca *Lucretia's old nurse*	MEZZO-SOPRANO
Lucia *a maid*	SOPRANO

SYNOPSIS OF SCENES

Act one
Scene one The generals' tent in the camp outside Rome
Scene two A room in Lucretia's house in Rome, the same evening

Act two
Scene one Lucretia's bedroom
Scene two The same as Act one, Scene two, the next morning

FIRST PERFORMANCE

12 July 1946 *Glyndebourne Opera House, Sussex*

Male Chorus	Peter Pears
Female Chorus	Joan Cross
Collatinus	Owen Brannigan
Junius	Edmund Donlevy
Tarquinius	Otakar Kraus
Lucretia	Kathleen Ferrier
Bianca	Anna Pollak
Lucia	Margaret Ritchie

Conducted by Ernest Ansermet
Produced by Eric Crozier
Designed by John Piper

Dedicated to Erwin Stein

Foreword by Benjamin Britten

Many people think that composers can set any old kind of poetry to music; that any pattern of words may start his imagination working. In many cases that is true. Some of the greatest composers have found inspiration in very poor verse (see Schubert in many places) although not many have gone as far as Darius Milhaud in his 'Machines Agricoles'—which is a setting of a catalogue. But I believe that if the words of a song match the music in subtlety of thought and clarity of expression it results in a greater amount of artistic satisfaction for the listener. This applies equally to the large forms—oratorio, cantata and opera. In many oratorios, of course, where the words come from the liturgy or the Bible the composer has the greatest possible inspiration for his music; but with a few exceptions like Metastasio, Dryden, Da Ponte and Boito, few serious poets have provided libretti for these kinds of works. There may be many reasons for this. Opera composers have a reputation of ruthless disregard of poetic values (in some cases rightly)—and all they need is a hack writer to bully and serious poets won't stand for that. Besides it takes a great deal of time to learn the operatic formulae—the recitatives, the arias and the ensembles. The bad enunciation of many singers doesn't seem to provide a suitable show place for a poet's finest thoughts. One of the most powerful reasons for a poet's operatic shyness I suspect to be this. To be suitable for music, poetry must be simple, succinct and crystal clear; for many poets this must be a great effort, and the psychological epic poem to be read (or not read) in the quiet of the study is more attractive. I think they are wrong. Opera makes similar demands of conciseness on the composer. He must be able to paint a mood or an atmosphere in a single phrase and must search unceasingly for the apt one. But this is everlastingly fascinating and stimulating, as it must be to the poet. Similarly fascinating to him should be the problem of continuity, or degrees of intensity, development of character and situation. Also, if he is working together with a sympathetic composer, then the timings and inflections of the dialogue can be fixed exactly and forever—a thing not possible in any other medium.

This 'working together' of the poet and composer mentioned above seems to be one of the secrets of writing a good opera. In the general discussion on the shape of the work—the plot, the division into recitatives, arias, ensembles and so on—the musician will have many ideas that may stimulate and influence the poet. Similarly when the libretto is written and the composer is working on the music, possible alterations may be suggested by the flow of the music, and the libretto altered accordingly. In rehearsals, as the work becomes realised aurally and visually, other changes are often seen to be necessary. The composer and poet should at all stages be working in the closest contact, from the most preliminary stages right up to the first night. It was thus in the case of 'The Rape of Lucretia'.

Act one

Scene one
The generals' tent in the camp outside Rome

[*House curtain rises showing Male Chorus and Female Chorus, reading from books*]

MALE CHORUS
Rome is now ruled by the Etruscan upstart:
Tarquinius Superbus, the Proud, King.
But once servant to the late monarch
Servius. How did Tarquinius reach the throne?
By making his own virtues and his will
Bend to the purpose of determined evil.
In quiet humility he hid his pride;
And running to agree with every faction
Divided the Roman court till each part
Sought him as an ally; and those he murdered,
He would mourn as though a friend had died.
If piety impeded him, he'd pray with it.
If greed, he'd bribe it; and always he'd pay his way
With the prodigious liberality
Of self-coined obsequious flattery;
So he climbed and married the king's own daughter
Whom he murdered; then married her sister,
The self-seeking, self-appointed widow
Who'd poisoned her first husband, the heir.
Once joined in holy wedlock they throttled the king,
And now rule Rome by force and govern by sheer terror.

Whilst their son, Tarquinius Sextus of whom you shall hear,
Leads Roman youth to Etruscan war
And treats the proud city as if it were his whore.

FEMALE CHORUS
It is an axiom among kings, to use
A foreign threat to hide a local evil.
So here the grumbling Romans march from Rome
To fight the Greeks who also march from home;
Both armies fretting under their own generals.
[*Female Chorus closes her book*]
How slowly time here moves towards the date;
This Rome has still five hundred years to wait
Before Christ's birth and death from which Time fled
To you with hands across its eyes. But here
Other wounds are made, yet still His blood is shed.

MALE AND FEMALE CHORUS
While we as two observers stand between
This present audience and that scene;
We'll view these human passions and these years
Through eyes which once have wept with Christ's own tears.
[*Front cloth rises. The scene is a camp outside Rome, with the generals' tent in Foreground*]

MALE CHORUS
Here the thirsty evening has drunk the wine of light;
Sated, the sun falls through the horizon, the air
Sits on their backs like a heavy bear.
Only the noise of crickets alleviates
The weight of this silent evening.
Horses sensing thunder stamp in their stables;
Bull-frogs brag on their persistent note;
Centurions curse their men, the men curse their luck,

As they look towards Rome's distant lights,
Which, bent in the Tiber, beckon through the night.
[*The tent is opened from the inside. Collatinus, Junius and
Tarquinius are seated, drinking*]

COLLATINUS
Who reaches heaven first
Is the best philosopher.
Bacchus jumps there
                                    with a cup,
Reason climbs there
                                    later.

OMNES [*in the tent*]
Oh, the only cup worth filling
Is this! Is this! Is this!

MALE CHORUS
They drink for their time is flowing with the night,
And life is dark except where wine sheds light.
But the officers are not generally drunk so early.

JUNIUS
Who reaches heaven last
Is the worst philosopher.
Logic limps there
                                    on a rule,
Cupid flies there
                                    sooner.

OMNES
Oh, the only girl worth having
Is wine! Is wine! Is wine!

MALE CHORUS
The night is weeping with its tears of stars
But these men laugh—for what is sad is folly.
And so they drink to drown their melancholy.

TARQUINIUS
Who drowns in women's eyes
And then drinks lips of pleasure
Sucks all heaven
                                    in a kiss,
Then thirsts in hell
                                    for ever!

OMNES
Oh, the only wine worth having
Is love! Is love! Is love!

JUNIUS
Love, like wine, spills easily as blood . . .

TARQUINIUS
And husbands are the broken bottles.

MALE CHORUS
Last night some generals rode back to Rome
To see if their wives stayed chaste at home.

JUNIUS
Maria was unmasked at a masked ball.

TARQUINIUS
Celia was not found at all,
Flavius is still searching for her!

JUNIUS
And Maximus found his wife Donata
Had been served by some Sicilian actor!

TARQUINIUS
Sophia's silver chastity belt
Was worn by her coachman—as a collar!

JUNIUS
There Leda lay after a midnight bout,
Too drunk to give a clear account.

TARQUINIUS
Patricia lay naked with a negro.
She told Junius she'd been having massage!

COLLATINUS
You were fools to go at all!
Fools to set the honour of your wives
Against a drunken bet!
I warned you not to go.

TARQUINIUS
Why should you complain?
We found Lucretia safe at home.

JUNIUS
The only wife who stood the test.

TARQUINIUS
And Collatinus has won the bet.
And Junius is a cuckold
A cuckold's a cock
Without a crow,
And Junius is a cuckold!

JUNIUS [*angrily*]
So are you, too,
Tarquinius,
Since you have made
The whole of Rome
Your brothel.
My wife's untrue,
But so is yours.
For you unmarried
Can only know
The constancy
Of whores.

TARQUINIUS [*rising*]
You forget I am the Prince of Rome!

JUNIUS
But I at least am Roman!

TARQUINIUS
With a negro deputy in bed,
It's better to be Etruscan!
[*They brawl*]

JUNIUS
                                                                    Spendthrift!

TARQUINIUS
                                                            Usurer!

JUNIUS
                                                        Lecher!

TARQUINIUS
                                                    Eunuch!

JUNIUS
                                                        Climber!

TARQUINIUS
                                                    Upstart!

JUNIUS

Rake!

TARQUINIUS

Rat!

JUNIUS

You young sot!

TARQUINIUS

You—old man!

JUNIUS

Lewd licentious lout!

TARQUINIUS

Pagan dyspeptic pig!

JUNIUS

Ram reared!

TARQUINIUS

Wolf weaned!

COLLATINUS [*parting them*]
Peace! Peace! save your swords till we meet the Greeks.
Let us drink, Prince Tarquinius, a toast!

TARQUINIUS
To the chaste Lucretia!
To the lovely Lucretia!

OMNES
Lucretia!
[*Junius rushes from the tent, closing the flap behind him*]

JUNIUS
Lucretia! Lucretia!
I'm sick of that name.
Her virtue is
The measure of my shame.
Now all of Rome
Will laugh at me,
Or what is worse
Will pity me.

MALE CHORUS
Oh, it is plain
That nothing pleases
Your friends so much
As your dishonour;
For now they can
Indulge in chatter
And patronise you
With their patter
And if by chance
You lose your temper
They say they tease
In all good humour.

JUNIUS
To-morrow the city urchins will sing my name to school,
And call each other 'Junius' instead of 'Fool'.
Collatinus will gain my fame with the Roman mob,
Not because of battles he has won
—but because Lucretia's chaste
—and the Romans being wanton worship chastity.

MALE CHORUS
Collatinus is politically astute to choose a virtuous wife.
Collatinus shines brighter from Lucretia's fame.
Collatinus is lucky, very lucky . . .

Oh, my God with what agility
does jealousy
jump into a small heart,
And fit
till it fills it,
then breaks that heart.

JUNIUS [*with venom*]
Lucretia! . . .
[*Enter Collatinus from tent*]

COLLATINUS
How bitter of you
How venemous
To vent your rage on her!
Why be so vicious,
Why so jealous?
You're blinded by grief
At Patricia's unfaithfulness.

JUNIUS
The wound in my heart,
Collatinus,
Will drive me to despair.
I ask your forgiveness
For being malicious
When you are so proud
of Lucretia's virtue
[*aside*] or good luck!
[*Collatinus offers Junius his hand*]

COLLATINUS
Dear friend!

JUNIUS
Collatinus!
[*They embrace*]

COLLATINUS
Those who love create
Fetters which liberate.
Those who love destroy
Their solitude.
Their love is only joy
Those who love defeat
Time, which is Death's deceit,
Those who love defy
Death's slow revenge.
Their love is all despair.
[*Tarquinius reels out of the tent*]

TARQUINIUS
Oh, the only girl worth having
Is wine! Is wine! Is wine!
And Junius is a . . .

COLLATINUS [*stopping him*]
Enough, Tarquinius!

TARQUINIUS
A cuckold, a cuckold, a cuckold!

JUNIUS
For God's sake, stop!

COLLATINUS
You disgrace your rank by brawling like a common peasant.

JUNIUS
He's drunk.

COLLATINUS
　That's enough, Junius! Leave
　Quarrelling to those with less
　Important tasks ahead.

JUNIUS
　I'm ready to forget. Give me your hand, Tarquinius.

COLLATINUS
　With you two arm in arm again,
　Rome can sleep secure.
　Good night!
　　　　　　　[*Collatinus goes off towards his tent*]

TARQUINIUS
　Good night!

JUNIUS
　Good night!

TARQUINIUS
　There goes a happy man!

JUNIUS
　There goes a lucky man!

TARQUINIUS
　His fortune is worth more than my Etruscan crown.

JUNIUS
　But he is subject to your crown!

TARQUINIUS
　And I am subject to Lucretia.

JUNIUS
　What makes the Nubian
　Disturb his heavy mountain?
　Why does he ravish
　The rock's austerity
　And powder it to dust
　To find its secret lust,
　Till in his hand he holds
　The cruel jewel?
　　　　　Is this all his hands were seeking?

TARQUINIUS
　What drives the Roman
　Beyond his river Tiber?
　Why do Egyptians dare
　The shark's ferocity
　And grovel in the deep
　To rake its dream of sleep
　Till to his Queen he gives
　The royal pearl?
　　　　　Is this what his eyes were seeking?

TARQUINIUS AND JUNIUS
　If men were honest
　They would all admit
　That all their life
　Was one long search,
　A pilgrimage to a pair of eyes,
　In which there lies
　　　　　a reflection greater than the image,
　　　　　a perfection which is love's brief mirage.

JUNIUS
　It seems we agree.

TARQUINIUS
　But are not of the same opinion!

JUNIUS
　What do you mean?

TARQUINIUS
　I am honest and admit
　As a woman's my beginning,
　Woman's the end I'm seeking.

JUNIUS
　Well . . .?

TARQUINIUS
　But as ambition is your beginning,
　Power's the end you're seeking.

JUNIUS
　That's not true! But don't let's quarrel.
　We're both unfortunate: I, with my unfruitful, faithless
　wife, you . . .

TARQUINIUS
　—With my barren bevy of listless whores.
　Oh, I am tired of willing women!
　It's all habit with no difficulty or achievement to it.

JUNIUS
　But Collatinus has Lucretia . . .

TARQUINIUS
　But Lucretia's virtuous.

JUNIUS
　Virtue in women is a lack of opportunity.

TARQUINIUS
　Lucretia's chaste as she is beautiful.

JUNIUS
　Women are chaste when they are not tempted.
　Lucretia's beautiful but she's not chaste.
　Women are all whores by nature.

TARQUINIUS
　No, not Lucretia!

JUNIUS
　What? . . .
　Already jealous of her honour?
　Men defend a woman's honour
　When they would lay siege to it themselves.

TARQUINIUS
　I'll prove Lucretia chaste.

JUNIUS
　No—that you will not dare! That you will not dare . . .
　Good night, Tarquinius.
　[*Junius goes off: Tarquinius paces slowly up and down*]

MALE CHORUS
　Tarquinius does not dare,
　When Tarquinius does not desire;
　But I am the Prince of Rome
　And Lucretia's eyes my Empire.
　It is not far to Rome . . .
　Oh, go to bed, Tarquinius . . .
　The lights of Rome are beckoning . . .
　The city sleeps. Collatinus sleeps.
　Lucretia! Lucretia!

TARQUINIUS
　My horse! My horse!
　[*Front cloth falls as Tarquinius goes off with sudden resolution*]

INTERLUDE

MALE CHORUS
Tarquinius does not wait
For his servant to wake,
Or his groom to saddle;
He snatches a bridle

And forcing the iron bit
Through the beast's bared white teeth,
Runs him out of the stable,
Mounts without curb or saddle

The stallion's short straight back,
And with heel and with knees
Clicks his tongue, flicks his whip,
Throws the brute into mad gallop.

Impetuous the powered flanks,
And reckless the rider;
Now the Prince and Arab steed
Bend as one for both are speed.

Hear the hoofs punish the earth!
Muscles strain, tendons taut,
Tail held high, head thrust back,
All's compact, nothing's slack.

See, the horse takes the bit
Between his teeth, now no rein
Can impede or stop him,
Yet the Prince still whips him.

Now who rides? Who's ridden?
Tarquinius, the stallion?
Or the beast, Tarquinius?
In both blood furious

With desire impetuous
Burns for its quietus;
With speed aflame through sweat and dust
The arrow flies straight as lust.

But here they cannot cross.
Turn back, Tarquinius;
Do not tempt the Tiber
Try to swim this river!

Stallion rears, hoofs paw the stars,
The Prince desires, so he dares!
Now stallion and rider
Wake the sleep of water

Disturbing its cool dream
With hot flank and shoulder.
Tarquinius knows no fear!
He is across! He's heading here!
Lucretia!
[*Front cloth rises, showing the hall of Lucretia's home. Lucretia is sewing, while Bianca and Lucia work at their spinning wheels*]

Scene two
A room in Lucretia's house in Rome, the same evening

FEMALE CHORUS
Their spinning wheel unwinds
Dreams which desire has spun!
Turning and turning
Twisting the shreds of their hearts
Over and over

LUCRETIA
    till in one word all is wound.
    Collatinus! Collatinus!
    Whenever we are made to part
    We live within each other's heart,
    Both waiting, each wanting.

FEMALE CHORUS
Their humming wheel reminds
Age of its loss of youth;
Spinning and spinning
Teasing the fleece of their time,
Restless, so restless

BIANCA
    till like an old ewe I'm shorn
    Of beauty! of beauty!
    Though I have never been a mother,
    Lucretia is my daughter
    When dreaming, when dreaming.

FEMALE CHORUS
Their restless wheel describes
Woman's delirium;
Searching and searching
Seeking the threads of their dreams
Finding and losing

LUCIA
    till somebody loves her
    from passion or pity.
    Meanwhile the chaste
    Lucretia gives
    Life to her Lucia who lives
    Her shadow and echo.

FEMALE CHORUS
Their little wheel revolves,
Time spins a fragile thread;
Turning and turning,
They spin and then they are spun,
Endless, so endless

LUCRETIA, BIANCA AND LUCIA
    till our fabric's woven
    And our hearts are broken
    Death is woman's final lover
    In whose arms we lie forever
    With our hearts all broken.
[*Lucretia stops the spinning with a gesture*]

LUCRETIA
Listen! I heard a knock. Somebody is at the gate. Lucia, run and see; perhaps it is a messenger. Run, Lucia!
    [*Lucia runs to the door*]

BIANCA
Come and sit down again my child; it is far too late for a messenger. Besides, you have already had two letters from Lord Collatinus to-day.

LUCRETIA

Oh, if it were he come home again! These months we spend apart is time thrown in the grave. Perhaps the war is won or lost. What matters if it's finished?

BIANCA

My child, to hope tempts disappointment.

LUCRETIA

But did you not hear anything?
[*Lucia returns*]
Who was it?

LUCIA

There was no one there, Madam.

LUCRETIA

I was sure I heard something.

BIANCA

It was your heart you heard.

LUCRETIA

Yes, it runs after him with steady beat
Like a lost child with tireless feet.

BIANCA

It is better to desire and not to have than not to desire at all. Have patience, Madam.

LUCRETIA

How cruel men are
To teach us love!
They wake us from
The sleep of youth
Into the dream of passion,
Then ride away
While we still yearn.
How cruel men are
To teach us love!

BIANCA

Madam is tired, it is getting very late.

LUCIA

Shall I put these wheels away, Madam?

LUCRETIA

Yes, and then we'll fold this linen.
[*Lucia and Bianca begin folding the linen*]

FEMALE CHORUS

Time treads upon the hands of women. Whatever happens, they must tidy it away. Their fingers punctuate each day with infinite detail, putting this here, that there, and washing all away. Before the marriage they prepare the feast. At birth or death their hands must fold clean linen. Whatever their hearts hold, their hands must fold clean linen. Their frail fingers are love's strong vehicle, and in their routine is a home designed. Home is what man leaves to seek. What is home but women? Time carries men, but time treads upon the tired feet of women.

LUCRETIA

How quiet it is to-night. Even the street is silent.

BIANCA

It is. I can almost hear myself thinking.

LUCRETIA

And what are you thinking?

BIANCA

That it must be men who make the noise. [*Male Chorus stirs uneasily*] And that Madam must be tired and should go to bed and leave this linen to Lucia and me.

LUCRETIA

O I am not tired enough. It is better to do something than lie awake and worry. But let us light the candles and go to bed.
[*They light candles and prepare to go to bed*]

FEMALE CHORUS

The oatmeal slippers of sleep
Creep through the city and drag
The sable shadows of night
Over the limbs of light.

MALE CHORUS

Now still night to sound adds
Separate cold echo
As hoof strikes hard stones
On worn way, road to Rome.

FEMALE CHORUS

The restless river now flows
Out with the falling tide.
And petals of stars fall out
On to its back and float.

MALE CHORUS

Dogs at heel race and bark,
Sleeping cocks wake and crow,
Drunken whores going home
Turn to curse the Prince of Rome.

FEMALE CHORUS

This city busy with dreams
Weaves on the loom of night
A satin curtain which falls
Over its ancient walls.

MALE CHORUS

Now he's through the city walls!
The black beast's white with sweat,
Blood's pouring from its hocks,
The Prince dismounts; and now he . . .
[*Loud knock on door. In the following scene the characters mime the actions described by the Male Chorus or Female Chorus*]

FEMALE CHORUS

None of the women move.
It is too late for a messenger,
The knock is too loud for a friend.
[*Loud knock repeated*]

FEMALE CHORUS

Lucia runs to the door, hoping that Apollo's called for her.
Anxiety's cold hand grips Lucretia's throat.
She pales with an unspoken fear.

TARQUINIUS [*off*]

Open, in the name of the Prince of Rome!

FEMALE CHORUS

Lucia unbolts the door with excited haste.

MALE CHORUS

Tarquinius enters Lucretia's home.

FEMALE CHORUS

The women curtsey. He is Prince of Rome.

MALE CHORUS
The Prince bows over Lucretia's hand.
His unruly eyes run to her breast,
And there with more thirst than manners rest.

FEMALE CHORUS
Lucretia asks for the news;
Whether her Lord Collatinus is well, or ill
Whether the army's put to flight.
And what brings His Highness here with haste at night?

MALE CHORUS
Tarquinius laughs her fears away and asks her for some
wine.

FEMALE CHORUS
With much relief she pours it.

MALE CHORUS
He claims Lucretia's hospitality. He says his horse is
lame.

BIANCA [aside]
What brings the Prince Tarquinius here at this hour of
the night?

LUCIA [aside]
How can he dare to seek for shelter from Lucretia?

BIANCA [aside]
Oh, where is Lord Collatinus?
He should be here to greet Tarquinius.
His coming threatens danger to us.

FEMALE CHORUS
The Etruscan palace stands only across the city; but
etiquette compels what discretion would refuse, so
Lucretia leads Prince Tarquinius to his chamber, and
with decorum wishes him . . .

LUCRETIA
. . .Good night, your Highness.

FEMALE CHORUS
Then Bianca with that rude politeness at which a
servant can excel, curtseys and says:

BIANCA
Good night, your Highness.

FEMALE CHORUS
Whilst Lucia, standing tip-toe in her eyes, curtseys
lower than the rest, and shyly bids the Prince:

LUCIA
Good night, your Highness.

MALE CHORUS
And Tarquinius, with true Etruscan grace, bows over
Lucretia's hand, then lifts it with slow deliberation to his
lips . . .

TARQUINIUS
Good night, Lucretia.

FEMALE CHORUS AND MALE CHORUS
And then all, with due formality, wish each other a final:

LUCRETIA, LUCIA AND BIANCA
Good night, your Highness

TARQUINIUS
Good night, Lucretia.
[The house curtain slowly falls as the characters leave the stage
    and the Choruses pick up their books and continue reading]

Act two

Scene one
Lucretia's bedroom

[The house curtain rises showing the Choruses reading]

FEMALE CHORUS
The prosperity of the Etruscans was due
To the richness of their native soil,
the virility of their men,
and the fertility of their women . . .,
When the Etruscan Princes conquered Rome
They founded the Imperial City,
Building it in stone.
And the Etruscan builders
Watched the proud Romans sweat
As they toiled in mountain quarry.
Then the victors embellished their palaces
With delicate silver and tapestries
Which they taught the Roman nobility
To weave in the shadow
Of an Etruscan cellar.
Through all their art there runs this paradox:
Passion for creation and lust to kill.
Behind the swan's neck they'd paint a fox,
And on their tombs a wooden phallus stood.

MALE CHORUS
And Tarquinius Superbus ruled in Rome
Relentless as a torrid sun
And the whole city . . .
[At the sound of the off-stage voices, symbolising the unrest in
Rome, Male Chorus and Female Chorus stir uneasily]

COLLATINUS [off]
Now Roman masters become Etruscan servants
And all our city's a bazaar to them

with LUCIA, BIANCA AND JUNIUS [off]
Down with the Etruscans!

LUCIA [off]
They recruit our sons and seduce our daughters
With public processions and Grecian games.

with BIANCA, JUNIUS AND COLLATINUS [off]
Rome's for the Romans!

JUNIUS [off]
God knows it's never been safe to speak one's mind in
    Rome,
But now every whore has the Emperor's ear.

with LUCIA, BIANCA AND COLLATINUS [off]
Down with the Etruscans!

BIANCA [off]
To-day, one either has friends who are officials
Or one goes without and gets kicked around!

with LUCIA, JUNIUS AND COLLATINUS [off]
Down with Tarquinius!

OMNES [off]
Now the she-wolf
    sleeps at night
But each Roman
    Marks his man.
When the she-wolf
    bays at night

Then their throats shall
  know our knife.

MALE CHORUS
  And Tarquinius Superbus ruled in Rome
  Relentless as a torrid sun.
  And the whole city sulked in discontent,
  Hating the foreign aristocrats
  With their orgies and auguries
  And effete philosophies.
  There was whispering
  Behind shuttering
  And every stone that was thrown
  Spoke for the whole of Rome.
  [*Male Chorus closes his book*]
  All tyrants fall though tyranny persists
  Though crowds disperse the mob is never less.
  For violence is the fear within us all
  And tragedy the measurement of man
  And hope his brief view of God.
  Oh, Christ heal our blindness which we mistake for
    sight,
  And show us your day for ours is endless night.

MALE AND FEMALE CHORUS
  While we as two observers stand between
  This present audience and that scene;
  We'll view these human passions and these years
  Through eyes which once have wept
                    with Christ's own tears.
  [*The front cloth rises showing Lucretia asleep in bed, by the side
  of which a candle burns*]

FEMALE CHORUS
  She sleeps as a rose upon the night
  And light as a lily that floats on a lake
  Her eyelids lie over her dreaming eyes
  As they rake the shallows and drag the deep
    For the sunken treasures of heavy sleep.
        Thus, sleeps Lucretia.
  [*Tarquinius is seen stealthily approaching Lucretia's bed*]

MALE CHORUS
  When Tarquinius desires,
  Then Tarquinius will dare.

  The shadows of the night conspire
  To blind his conscience and assist desire.

  Panther agile and panther virile,
  The Prince steals through the silent hall.

  And with all the alacrity of thought
  He crosses the unlit gallery.
  Where a bust of Collatinus
  Stares at him with impotent blind eyes.

  Now he is passing Bianca's door.
  Wake up old woman! Warn your mistress!

  See how lust hides itself!
  It stands like a sentinel, then moves with stealth.

  Perhaps Lucia will hear him?
  Why doesn't he quench his lust with Lucia
  And anticipate her assured consent?

The pity is that sin has so much grace,
It moves like virtue. Back Tarquinius!
[*Tarquinius stands at the head of Lucretia's bed*]

FEMALE CHORUS
  Thus sleeps Lucretia . . .

TARQUINIUS
  Within this frail crucible of light
  Like a chrysalis contained
  Within its silk oblivion
  [*To candle*]
  How lucky is this little light,
  It knows her nakedness,
  And when it's extinguished
  It envelops her as darkness,
  Then lies with her as night.
  [*Sudden anger*]
  Loveliness like this is never chaste;
  If not enjoyed, it is just waste!
  Wake up, Lucretia!

FEMALE CHORUS
  No! sleep and outrace Tarquinius' horse
  And be with your Lord Collatinus.
  Sleep on, Lucretia, sleep on, Lucretia.

TARQUINIUS
  As blood red rubies
  Set in ebony
  Her lips illumine
  The black lake of night.
  To wake Lucretia with a kiss
  Would put Tarquinius asleep awhile.
  [*He kisses Lucretia*]

FEMALE CHORUS
  Her lips receive Tarquinius
  She dreaming of Collatinus.
  And desiring him draws down Tarquinius
  And wakes to kiss again and . . .
  [*Lucretia wakes*]

TARQUINIUS
  Lucretia!

LUCRETIA
  What do you want?

TARQUINIUS
  You!

LUCRETIA
  What do you want from me?

TARQUINIUS
  Me! What do you fear?

LUCRETIA
  You!
  In the forest of my dreams
  You have always been the Tiger.

TARQUINIUS
  Give me your lips
  Then let my eyes
  See their first element
  Which is
      your eyes.

LUCRETIA
  No!

TARQUINIUS
Give me your lips
Then let me rise
To my first sepulchre,
Which is
      your thighs.

LUCRETIA
No! Never!

TARQUINIUS
Give me your lips
Then let me rest
On the oblivion
Which is
      your breast.

LUCRETIA
No!

TARQUINIUS
Give me!

LUCRETIA
No! What you have taken
Never can you be given!

TARQUINIUS
Would you have given?

LUCRETIA
How could I give, Tarquinius,
Since I have given to Collatinus,
In whom I am, wholly;
With whom I am, only;
And without whom I am, lonely?

TARQUINIUS
Yet the linnet in your eyes
Lifts with desire,
And the cherries of your lips
Are wet with wanting.
Can you deny your blood's dumb pleading?

LUCRETIA
Yes, I deny.

TARQUINIUS
Through April eyes
Your young blood sighs;
And denies
refusal
and denial
      of your lips' frail lies.

LUCRETIA
No, you lie!

TARQUINIUS
Can you refuse your blood's desiring?

LUCRETIA
Yes, I refuse!

TARQUINIUS
Lucretia!

LUCRETIA
I refuse!

TARQUINIUS
Can you deny?

LUCRETIA
I deny!

TARQUINIUS
Your blood denies!

LUCRETIA
You lie, you lie!

TARQUINIUS
Lucretia!
[*She turns away from him*]

LUCRETIA
Oh, my beloved Collatinus,
You have loved so well
You have tuned my body
To the chaste note of a silver lute
And thus you have made my blood
Keep the same measure
As your love's own purity.
For pity's sake, please go!

TARQUINIUS
Loveliness like this
Cannot be chaste
Unless all men are blind!
Too late, Lucretia, too late!
Easier stem the Tiber's flood
Than to calm my angry blood,
Which coursing to the ocean of your eyes
Rages for the quietus of your thighs.

LUCRETIA
Is this the Prince of Rome?

TARQUINIUS
I am your Prince!

LUCRETIA
Passion's a slave and not a Prince!

TARQUINIUS
Then release me!

LUCRETIA
What peace can passion find
[*He takes her in his arms*]

TARQUINIUS
Lucretia! Lucretia!

LUCRETIA
Though I am in your arms
I am beyond your reach!
[*She struggles free*]

MALE CHORUS
Go, Tarquinius,
Before the cool fruit of her breasts
Burns your hand
And consumes your heart with that fire
Which is only quenched by more desire.

FEMALE CHORUS [*going near to bed*]
Go, Tarquinius,
Before your nearness
Tempts Lucretia to yield
To your strong maleness.

TARQUINIUS
Beauty is all
In life!
It has the peace
Of death.

LUCRETIA
If beauty leads to this,
Beauty is sin.

TARQUINIUS
Though my blood's dumb
It speaks
Though my blood's blind
It finds.

LUCRETIA
I am his,
Not yours.

TARQUINIUS
Beauty so pure
Is cruel.
Through your eyes' tears
I weep.
For your lips' fire
I thirst.
For your breast's peace
I fight.

LUCRETIA
Love's indivisible.

MALE AND FEMALE CHORUS
Go! Tarquinius,
Whilst passion is still proud
And before your lust is spent
Humbled with heavy shame.
If you do not repent
Time itself cannot
Erase this moment from your name.

TARQUINIUS
I hold the knife
But bleed.
Though I have won
I'm lost.
Give me my soul
Again
In your veins' sleep
My rest.

LUCRETIA
No!

TARQUINIUS
Give me my birth
Again
Out of your loins
Of pain!
Though I must give
I take.

LUCRETIA
For pity's sake, Tarquinius,
Go!
[He pulls the coverlet from the bed and threatens her with his sword]

TARQUINIUS
Poised like a dart

LUCRETIA
At the heart of woman

MALE CHORUS
Man climbs towards his God,

FEMALE CHORUS
Then falls to his lonely hell.
[He mounts the bed]

OMNES
See how the rampant centaur mounts the sky
And serves the sun with all its seed of stars.

Now the great river underneath the ground
Flows through Lucretia andTarquinius is drowned.
[Tarquinius beats out the candle with his sword. The front cloth
falls quickly]

INTERLUDE

FEMALE CHORUS AND MALE CHORUS
Here in this scene you see
    Virtue assailed by sin
    With strength triumphing
All this is endless
    Sorrow and pain for Him.

Nothing impure survives,
    All passion perishes,
    Virtue has one desire
To let its blood flow
    Back to the wounds of Christ.

She whom the world denies,
    Mary, Mother of God,
    Help us to lift this sin
Which is our nature
    And is the Cross to Him.

She whom the world denies
    Mary most chaste and pure,
    Help us to find your love
Which is His Spirit
    Flowing to us from Him.

Scene two
A room in Lucretia's house in Rome, the next morning

[The front cloth rises showing the hall of Lucretia's home flooded
with early sun. Enter Lucia and Bianca]

LUCIA AND BIANCA
Oh! What a lovely day!

LUCIA
Look how the energetic sun
Drags the sluggard dawn from bed,
And flings the windows wide upon the world.

BIANCA AND LUCIA
Oh! What a lovely morning!

BIANCA
And how light the soft mulberry mist
Lifts and floats over the silver Tiber.
It's going to be hot, unbearably hot,
And by evening it will thunder.

LUCIA AND BIANCA
Oh! What a lovely day!

LUCIA
Listen how the larks spill
Their song and let it fall

Over the city like a waterfall.
Oh! This is the day I've grown to.

BIANCA
But look!
Here comes our spendthrift gardener
With all his wealth of flowers.
[*They go to the window and fetch baskets filled with flowers*]

LUCIA
Oh, what lovely flowers!

BIANCA
It is as though the gods threw the stars
Down at our feet.

LUCIA
Let me arrange them royally for Prince Tarquinius.
[*They arrange the flowers*]

BIANCA
Oh, Lucia, please help me fill
My vase with laughing daffodils
And about their stalks I'll bind
  white jasmine
   and eglantine.
Then round the whole I'll wind
  columbine
   and leaves of vine.
So will my little vase contain
The sun's exuberance
     slaked with rain.

LUCIA
Oh, Bianca! Then let me keep
These roses which in scarlet sleep
Dream in tight buds of when
  They'll open
  Be wanton
With the wind and rain and then
  be broken,
   and quite forgotten.
So will my pretty vase enclose
The sun's extravagance
    which is the rose.

BIANCA
What is the age of lavender?

LUCIA
Is the rose young or old?

BOTH
Now earth like a Mother
Holds out her breast to the lips of Spring.

LUCIA
Where shall we put
These violets, lilac and mimosa?
And what shall we do
With all this honeysuckle?
Which cupped like little children's hands
Has begged from God
The precious scent of heaven.

BIANCA
We'll leave the orchids for Lucretia to arrange;
Collatinus' favourite flowers.

LUCIA
Bianca, how long will the Prince stay here?

BIANCA
I think he's already gone. I heard someone gallop out of
the courtyard just before it was light.

LUCIA
That may not have been Tarquinius.

BIANCA
Only a Tarquin would gallop on a cobbled road.

LUCIA
Our Lady Lucretia is sleeping heavily this lovely
morning. Shall I wake her?

BIANCA
No, don't disturb her.
It isn't often she sleeps so well
forever fretting for Collatinus.

LUCIA
I often wonder whether Lucretia's love
Is the flower of her beauty,
Or whether her loveliness
Is the flower of her love.
For in her both love and beauty
Are transformed to grace.

BIANCA
Hush! here she comes.
[*Enter Lucretia*]

BIANCA AND LUCIA
Good morning, my lady.

BIANCA
I hope you had happy dreams?

LUCRETIA
If it were all a dream
Then waking would be less a nightmare.

BIANCA
Did you sleep well?

LUCRETIA
As heavily as death.

LUCIA
Look, what a lovely day it is,
And see how wonderful are all these flowers.

LUCRETIA
Yes, what a lovely day it is.
And how wonderful are all these flowers.
You have arranged them prettily.

BIANCA
But we have left his lordship's favourite flowers
For you to do.

LUCRETIA
How kind of you.
Where are they?

BIANCA
Here, my lady.
The most perfect orchids I have ever seen.

LUCRETIA [*she takes the flowers, then suddenly loses all self-control*]
How hideous!
Take them away!

BIANCA
But, my lady, they are such lovely flowers!

These are the orchids you have grown.

LUCRETIA
Take them away, I tell you!
Oh! Monstrous flower!
Oh! Hideous hour!
Lucia, go send a messenger to my Lord Collatinus.
What are you waiting for, girl? Go!

LUCIA
What message, Madam,
Shall I give the messenger
To take to Lord Collatinus?
[*Lucretia seizes an orchid*]

LUCRETIA
Give him this orchid.
Tell him I find
Its purity
Apt; and that its petals contain
Woman's pleasure and woman's pain,
And all of Lucretia's shame.
Give him this orchid
And tell him a Roman harlot sent it.
And tell him to ride straight to her.
Tell him to come home. Go!
No! Wait, tell the messenger to take my love.
Yes, give my love to the messenger,
Give my love to the stable boy,
And to the coachman, too.
And hurry, hurry, for all men love
The chaste Lucretia.

[*Exit Lucia*]

BIANCA
Shall I throw the rest away, Madam?

LUCRETIA
No, I will arrange them.

BIANCA
Here are the flowers.

LUCRETIA [*She sits and, without being aware of her action, makes a wreath with the orchids*]
Flowers bring to every year
          the same perfection;
Even their root and leaf keep
Solemn vow in pretty detail.
Flowers alone are chaste
For their beauty is so brief
Years are their love
          and time's their thief.

Women bring to every man
          the same defection;
Even their love's debauched
By vanity or flattery.
Flowers alone are chaste.
Let their pureness show my grief
To hide my shame
          and be my wreath.

BIANCA
My child, you have made a wreath.

LUCRETIA
That is how you taught me as a child
To weave the wild flowers together.

Do you remember yesterday
That was a hundred years ago?
Do you remember?

[*Exit Lucretia*]

BIANCA
Yes, I remember!
I remember when her hair
fell like a waterfall of night
over her white shoulders.
And when her ivory breasts
First leaned from her ivory tree.
And I remember how
She ran down the garden of her eyes
To meet Collatinus. Yes, I remember.
[*Enter Lucia*]

LUCIA
You were right. Tarquinius took one of the horses.

BIANCA
What did you tell the messenger?

LUCIA
Lord Collatinus to come immediately.

BIANCA
He must not come. Words can do more harm than
    good.
Only time can heal. Has the messenger gone?

LUCIA
Not yet.

BIANCA
Then go and stop him. Quick, do as I say.

LUCIA
But Lucretia said . . .

BIANCA
Do as I say, quick! Hurry!
[*Just as Lucia goes—a knock*]

BIANCA
Sometimes a good servant
Should forget an order
And loyalty should disobey.
Sometimes a servant
Knows better than her mistress,
When she is servant to her heart's distress.
[*Enter Lucia*]
Did you stop him?

LUCIA
It was too late.

BIANCA
Too late?

LUCIA
Lord Collatinus is here.

BIANCA
Collatinus? Alone?

LUCIA
No, Junius rode with him.

BIANCA
Oh God, why should he come now?
[*Enter Collatinus and Junius*]

17 Lucretia's house   *John Piper*

18 Costume for Lucretia, final scene   *John Piper*   19 Costume for Collatinus   *John Piper*

20 Model of a room
in Lucretia's house

21 Chorale cloth, Act II

Designer John Piper

22 Costume for Lucretia, Act I
John Piper

COLLATINUS
Where is Lucretia?
Tell me,
Where is your Lady Lucretia?

BIANCA
She is well.

COLLATINUS
Then why was the messenger sent to me?

BIANCA
No messenger left here.

COLLATINUS
You're lying.

JUNIUS
Where is Lucretia?

BIANCA
Asleep. My Lady is still asleep.

COLLATINUS
Why did you not come to greet us at the gate?

JUNIUS
Perhaps they were frightened that Tarquinius had come
back.

COLLATINUS
Has Tarquinius been here?
Answer me!

BIANCA
O, do not ask, my Lord.

COLLATINUS
Tarquinius here?

JUNIUS
Last night I heard him gallop from the camp and I
watched for his return, fearing his jealousy of you. He
came back at dawn with his horse foundered, so I came
to warn you.

COLLATINUS
Too late, Junius, too late, too late.
[Lucretia is seen slowly walking towards Collatinus. She is
dressed in purple mourning]

COLLATINUS
Lucretia! Lucretia!
O, never again must we two dare to part.
For we are of one another
And between us,
            there is one heart.

LUCRETIA
To love as we loved
Was to be never but as moiety;
To love as we loved
Was to die, daily with anxiety;

LUCRETIA AND COLLATINUS
To love as we loved
Was to live, on the edge of tragedy.

LUCRETIA
Now there is no sea deep enough
            To drown my shame;
Now there is no earth heavy enough
            To hide my shame;
Now there is no sun strong enough

To lift this shadow;
Now there is no night dark enough
            To hide this shadow.
Dear heart, look into my eyes,
Can you not see the shadow?

COLLATINUS
In your eyes I see
Only the image of eternity
And a tear which has no shadow.

LUCRETIA
Then turn away, for I must tell
Though telling will
Turn your tender eyes to stone
And rake your heart and bring the bones
Of grief through the rags of sorrow.
Last night Tarquinius ravished me
And tore
The fabric of our love.
What we had woven
Tarquinius has broken.
What I have spoken
Never can be forgotten.
Oh, my love, our love was too rare
For life to tolerate or fate forbear from soiling.
For me this shame, for you this sorrow.

COLLATINUS
If spirit's not given, there is no need of shame.
Lust is all taking—in that there's shame.
What Tarquinius has taken
        Can be forgotten;
What Lucretia has given
        Can be forgiven.
[Collatinus kneels to Lucretia]

LUCRETIA
Even great love's too frail
To bear the weight of shadows.
Now I'll be forever chaste,
[She stabs herself]
With only death to ravish me.
See, how my wanton blood
        Washes my shame away!
[She dies]

COLLATINUS [kneeling over the body of Lucretia]
This dead hand lets fall
All that my heart held when full
When it played like a fountain, prodigal
        With love liberal,
        Wasteful.
So brief is beauty.
Is this it all? It is all!
[Junius goes towards the window and addresses the crowd below]

JUNIUS
Romans arise!
See what the Etruscans have done!
Here lies the chaste Lucretia, dead,
And by Tarquinius ravished.
Now let her body be
Borne through our city.
Destroyed by beauty
Their throne will fall. I will rule!

BIANCA AND LUCIA [over Lucretia's body]
She lived with too much grace to be

Of our crude humanity.
For even our shame's refined
By her purity of mind.
Now place the wreath about her head
And let the sentinels of the dead
Guard the grave where our Lucretia lies.
So brief is beauty.
Why was it begun? It is done.

FEMALE CHORUS
Beauty is the hoof of an unbroken filly
Which thundering up to the hazel hedge
  Leaps into the sun,
   And is gone.
So brief is beauty.
Why was it begun? It is done.

MALE CHORUS
They have no need of life to live;
They have no need of lips to love;
They have no need of death to die;
In their love all's dissolved
In their love all's resolved.
O, what is there but love?
Love is the whole. It is all!

OMNES
How is it possible that she
Being so pure should die!
How is it possible that we
Grieving for her should live?
So brief is beauty.
Is this it all? It is all! It is all!
[*Collatinus, Junius, Bianca and Lucia kneel round Lucretia's body. They stay like this till the end of the opera*]

EPILOGUE

FEMALE CHORUS
Is it all? Is all this suffering and pain,
Is this in vain?
  Does this old world grow old
In sin alone?
  Can we attain
      nothing
But wider oceans of our own tears?
  And it, can it gain

     nothing
But drier deserts of forgotten years?

For this did I
  See with my undying eye
His warm blood spill
  Upon that hill
    And dry upon that Cross?

Is this all loss?
  Are we lost?
    Answer us
Or let us
  die in our wilderness. Is it all? Is this it all?

MALE CHORUS
It is not all. Though our nature's still as frail
And we still fall,
  And that great crowd's no less
Along that road,
  endless and uphill;
     yet now
He bears our sin and does not fall
  And He, carrying all
    turns round
Stoned with our doubt and then forgives us all.

For us did He
  live with such humility;
For us did He
  die that we
    might live, and He forgive

Wounds that we make
  and scars that we are.
    In His Passion
Is our hope
  Jesus Christ, Saviour. He is all! He is all!
[*The lights fade on the mourning group. Only Female Chorus and Male Chorus remain lit*]

MALE AND FEMALE CHORUS
Since Time commenced or Life began
Great Love has been defiled by Fate or Man.
Now with worn words and these brief notes we try
To harness song to human tragedy.
     [*The house curtain slowly falls*]

Albert Herring

A comic opera in three acts

by Eric Crozier

freely adapted from a short story by Guy de Maupassant

BENJAMIN BRITTEN OP. 39

CHARACTERS

Lady Billows　　　　　　　　　　　　　SOPRANO
A handsome, elderly autocrat, with greying hair and a glittering eye. Her passion for good works often swamps the recipients with its enthusiasm.

Florence Pike　　　　　　　　　　　　CONTRALTO
Her housekeeper and indispensable companion. A tight-laced, sergeant-major type of woman, a few years younger than her mistress.

Mr Gedge　　　　　　　　　　　　　　BARITONE
Vicar of St Mary's Church. Amiable, forty-fiveish and easygoing.

Superintendent Budd　　　　　　　　　BASS
Superintendent of Police. Heavy, slow-thinking and a good sort.

Mr Upfold　　　　　　　　　　　　　　TENOR
Present Mayor of Loxford. A thin, irritable man, who owns several farms in the district and the local butcher's shop.

Miss Wordsworth　　　　　　　　　　　SOPRANO
Head Teacher at the Church School—aged 38. A simple, enthusiastic person, liked by everybody.

Sid　　　　　　　　　　　　　　　　　BARITONE
The cocky, likeable young assistant from the butcher's shop.

Nancy　　　　　　　　　　　　　　MEZZO-SOPRANO
An attractive girl of 26, who worries about reaching 30 unmarried. This makes her behaviour reckless, though she is naturally modest. She helps her father at the bakery.

Mrs Herring　　　　　　　　　　　MEZZO-SOPRANO
A possessive, narrow-minded widow. She owns a greengrocer's shop in Little Street.

Albert Herring　　　　　　　　　　　　TENOR
A tall, strong boy of 22, who helps his mother run the greengrocer's. No fool, but his mother's mixture of contemptuous bullying and adoration of him have made him extremely shy and awkward—especially when faced with strange people or situations.

Emmie, Cis and Harry　　SOPRANO, SOPRANO, TREBLE
Tiresome village children, aged 15, 13 and 12.

The action of the opera takes place at Loxford, a small market-town in East Suffolk, during April and May of the year 1900.

FIRST PERFORMANCE

20 June 1947　　　　　*Glyndebourne Opera House, Sussex*
　　　　　　　　　　　　　　　　　(E.O.G. production)

Lady Billows	Joan Cross
Florence Pike	Gladys Parr
Miss Wordsworth	Margaret Ritchie
The Vicar	William Parsons
The Mayor	Roy Ashton
The Superintendent of Police	Norman Lumsden
Sid	Frederick Sharp
Albert Herring	Peter Pears
Nancy	Nancy Evans
Mrs Herring	Betsy de la Porte
Emmie	Lesley Duff
Cis	Anne Sharp
Harry	David Spenser

Conducted by Benjamin Britten
Produced by Frederick Ashton
Scenery and costumes by John Piper

Foreword by Eric Crozier

I spent much time with Benjamin Britten when he was planning and writing his operas *Peter Grimes* and *The Rape of Lucretia*. As producer for both works I shared in discussions between composer and poet, and could follow their progress from first ideas to final performance. I tried to profit by this invaluable experience in writing the text for *Albert Herring*.

Albert Herring was conceived in October 1946. We needed a new opera to launch the first independent season of The English Opera Group, in summer 1947. It should be a companion and contrast to *The Rape of Lucretia*, suitable for performance by a small company of singers and twelve soloist musicians.

Our material limitations were clear. They directed our search for a subject, until we settled upon Guy de Maupassant's brilliant short story, *Le Rosier de Madame Husson*, as a starting-point—a subject to match the scale of our plans, and transform practical necessitites into virtues.

We transferred the scene of the story to Suffolk, and centred it upon a small market-town familiar to us both. This brought immediate changes in the treatment of the French story and its characters. Working from our knowledge of English people on one hand, and from the qualities of particular singers on the other, we made our first sketch for a lyrical comedy with twelve characters, in five scenes and three acts. This was written out in scenario form for further discussion.

The next step was to write a longish appreciation of each of the twelve skeleton characters, clothing their bare bones with hints of an individual way of life, personalities, characters and mannerisms. Much of this was finally irrelevant: it served a temporary purpose in bringing the composer and myself to a common view of our town and its people, and gave me material to begin writing the first scene.

Being neither poet nor playwright, I set about my first draft with many misgivings and only three determinations—to be simple, to be sensible, and to be singable. Humble purposes, but I believed then—and believe still—that a librettist is a craftsman working for an artist. He may also be an artist himself, but his main job is not to write as the poet must write, compressing thought and emotion into an inevitable and unchangeable pattern of worlds—but to provide his composer with words, ideas, emotions, actions that are all true to character, true in style, and infinitely capable of formal modification and reshaping to musical ends.

The first draft of Scene One came out more as a play than an opera: it stimulated the composer to ideas of musical forms, and a musical architecture, that demanded the rewriting of my text in a sharper, more crystallised version. This is shown very clearly by the first sentence of the Opera. I wanted to introduce Lady Billows straightaway as a beneficent local tyrant, actively concerned with good works, narrow in her views, and meddling in all the affairs of the town. In my first version, the curtain rose to show Florence, her housekeeper, tidying away the breakfast things. She was interrupted by Lady Billows, who shouted from upstairs and said:—

'LADY BILLOWS [*off*]
 Tell Doctor Jessop the new midwife from Lowestoft mustn't touch illegitimates! She's not to...! I won't have it!'

'FLORENCE
 Very good, milady!'

This speech summed up Lady Billows quickly and economically as a powerful, autocratic character, and prepared the audience for her appearance later on. It stimulated the composer to a musical idea. He has the curtain rise with music illustrating Florence scurrying about the room, clearing breakfast away. A call of 'Florence!' interrupts her, and she goes to listen to an order from Lady Billows expressed in an instrumental phrase, and ending with three words:—

'LADY BILLOWS [*off*]
 ...tell the midwife!'

'FLORENCE
 Very good, milady!'

'LADY BILLOWS [*off*]
 ...She's *not* to...!'

Music has exactly and more vividly expressed the original idea, using six words for Lady Billows instead of eighteen.

This small detail epitomises the collaboration of composer and author. It shows a willing adjustment between a literary and a musical idea that holds good for the writing of an opera in its larger as in its smaller proportions. Both composer and author are working with the same aim—the expression of drama, character, emotion, humour through the infusion of words and music—but the words themselves are only part of a whole whose architectural shape must be determined by musical laws. It is tempting to expand over the possibilities and limitations of this kind of collaboration, but a practical example will illustrate the point more clearly than much theorising.

The third act of *Albert Herring* begins with Albert missing since his coronation the day before: the town is in a ferment of excitement, searching for its lost May King, fearing the worst. The first great climax of the act is the moment when his orange-blossom wreath is found and brought back solemnly to the town. In our first scenario, we described it like this:

'8. Terrible moment. The Super arrives solemnly with the Mayor, carrying a tray on which sits the small wreath of orange-blossom from Albert's hat. This has been picked up on the road to Ipswich, and shows signs of being run over by a cart-wheel. The tray is deposited on a box. At a sign from the Vicar, Nancy pulls down the shop-blind and closes the door. All gather round slowly, and they mourn the passing of Albert in a moving threnody.'

When I came to write the Threnody, we had agreed that each of the nine characters on the stage should have an individual verse of lament, and that all should join in a final quatrain. I wrote nine triplets, of which this is a sample—

'Weep for him whose simple fame
Shone clearly like a candle-flame
Blown bright by the wind, then out again!'

and a final quatrain for all to sing—

'Grief is silent, Pity dumb—,
Despair exclaims in endless pain—
That one so fine should live in vain
And die so young...'

The composer accepted my verses but when he began to plan the musical form of the Threnody he discovered that another verse would be needed—an opening chorus of general grief from which the individual verses of lament could flower. I wrote this new chorus in seven lines. The Threnody grew still clearer in the composer's mind: he wanted only four lines of this verse at the beginning, expanding later to the full seven lines. I then rewrote my chorus, so that lines 1, 2, 6, 7 were a complete statement in themselves–emotionally and formally–capable of being repeated later with lines 3, 4, 5 inserted.

'ALL
> In the midst of life is Death.
> Death awaits us one and all.
> Death beckons us with every breath
> We take, and does not hesitate
> To strike the humble or the great.
> Death attends our smallest step,
> Silent, swift and merciful.

This is not poetry. It is a simple form of verse written and rewritten to meet a particular situation. Its highest ambition is to serve the composer's intention sincerely, neatly and well.

This, I feel, should be the librettist's object. He writes to be sung, not to be read from a printed page. His language must be the spontaneous expression of human feeling. It should aim through the ear to the heart–unlike the current fashion of written verse, which aims at the eye and the brain. Verbal artifice, elaboration, strangeness of diction must all be a means to an end, never an end in themselves.

When a true dramatic or comic poet is willing to collaborate with a composer on these terms and subject his art to the strict discipline of simplicity and aptness for a purpose beyond his own the moment will be ripe for the flowering of the seed of English opera.

Act one

Scene one

[*The breakfast room at Lady Billows' house in Loxford. Florence, the housekeeper, is clearing away breakfast things for one on to a tray. She is interrupted by a commanding shout from offstage, and goes out to hall to listen*]

LADY BILLOWS
Flor—*ence!* . . .
[*The text of her instruction is quite indistinct except for the last three words*]
. . .tell the midwife!

FLORENCE [*shouting in reply*]
Very good, milady!

LADY BILLOWS
She's NOT to . . .!
[*Florence comes back into room, picks up tray and goes out determinedly with it*]

LADY BILLOWS [*off*]
Floren—*ce!*
[*No reply*]
Flor—ence!!
[*Florence hurries back to hall to listen*]

FLORENCE
Here, milady!

LADY BILLOWS [*another indistinct instruction, ending—*]
. . .Make him tear it up!

FLORENCE
Yes, milady!

LADY BILLOWS
DUST-bin!!

FLORENCE
Just on half-past ten . . .
[*She comes back into room, fetches small household book and pencil, and leans over table to write, noting the latest instructions*]
> Doctor Jessop's midwife . . .mustn't touch
> illegitimates
> Advert in chemist's window indecent . . .tear it up!
> Call at Primrose Cottage . . .Must stop
> William making *such* . . .rude noises, or else . . .
> Buy a breakfast cup . . .
[*Checking back on earlier notes*]
> Load of logs for Number Six The Mount–
> Mittens for Mister Pilgrim–Did they count
> How many from the almshouse wanted copies
> Of the Bishop's sermon?–No more poppies
> In altar vases–looks too Roman–Vicar
> Must warn choirboys–make responses quicker . . .
> > One lifetime
> > One brain
> > One pair of hands
> > Are all too few
> > For Lady B.
> >
> > Each day some
> > New idea
> > Makes new demands
> > Upon her sense
> > Of Charity.
> But oh! . . . But oh! . . .

Sometimes I wish . . .
[*As she is about to expand freely, Florence is interrupted by a knock at the door. She straightens her cap and apron and goes to open—she admits:*
Miss Wordsworth, Mr Gedge, Mr Upfold and Police Superintendent Budd]

MISS WORDSWORTH
I hope we're not too early, Florence?

FLORENCE
Oh no, miss. Her Ladyship's expecting you . . .

VICAR
Why, this looks almost like a deputation, eh—?

FLORENCE
Let me take your hats and sticks. I'll say you've come.
[*Florence goes out. The Mayor and the Super are consulting their watches*]

MAYOR
It's just on half-past ten. We're very punctual by that clock.

VICAR
Come and sit here, Miss Wordsworth.

MISS WORDSWORTH [*at window*]
Let me stand till we're ready to begin.

VICAR
As you will—
[*The clock strikes the half-hour*]

SUPER
Ten seconds fast, I make that.

MAYOR
No, you're slow! Exactly right by mine.

MISS WORDSWORTH
Oh I find it so refreshing to escape from school a sunny day like this—

VICAR
Playing truant—?

SUPER [*shaking watch*]
Funny being *slow*! Never known it . . .

MISS WORDSWORTH
. . . Free for a perfect hour or two of liberty . . .

MAYOR
Wonderful weather for April, Mr Gedge!

SUPER
Wants oiling, I expect. Dust in the works . . .

MISS WORDSWORTH
Look! that hedge of rosemary is humming with bumblebees!

VICAR
Quite perfect, Mr Mayor. Promises a splendid May and June.

MAYOR
That it does—

SUPER
'In like a lion, out like a lamb!'—that was true of March this year—

MAYOR
It was—!

MISS WORDSWORTH [*radiant*]
'And lo! the winter is past!'—

VICAR [*joining in*]
'The rain is over and gone. The flowers appear on the earth . . .'

VICAR [*explaining*]
Solomon's Song, you know!

MAYOR [*impatiently*]
Well, since we're here . . .

SUPER
Her Ladyship was very distressed when she heard
About Curtis's daughter—

VICAR
They tell me that's her *third*!

MISS WORDSWORTH
Appalling!

SUPER
She won't confess the father, silly girl!

MAYOR
It's happening far too often!

MISS WORDSWORTH
Lily Jarvis is another problem . . .

SUPER
Twins, if you please!

VICAR
Drunken father—mother a slattern—these
Things breed immorality in the young.

MISS WORDSWORTH
Their *poor* children . . .

MAYOR [*indignantly*]
Something must be done!

SUPER
Hear, hear!

VICAR
A firm stand now before the evil spreads! . . .

MISS WORDSWORTH
Her Ladyship is all for that . . .

SUPER
Though she exaggerates occasionally . . .

VICAR
Strong measures are essential *now*!

MAYOR, MISS WORDSWORTH AND SUPER
Of course they are! *Most* essential! Hear, hear!

VICAR
This Festival idea may help . . .

MAYOR, MISS WORDSWORTH AND SUPER
I'm all for that. I have great hopes. Certainly!

VICAR
Practical measures.

FLORENCE [*bustling in*]
HUSH! she's *here* . . .!

MISS WORDSWORTH
Oh! Her Ladyship–!

MAYOR
Careful now!

SUPER
Here she comes–

VICAR
Ah–Lady Billows!
[*All turn to face the hallway.
Formal musical entrance of Lady Billows, who stalks slowly and
powerfully into the room, her eyes glittering restlessly; then
crosses unexpectedly to the window and pushes it open*]

LADY BILLOWS
Stuffy!
Tobacco stink!
Nasty masculine smell!
[*Her eye flickers accusingly across the Mayor and Super*]

ALL
Good morning, my Lady!

LADY BILLOWS
Good morning.

ENSEMBLE

MISS WORDSWORTH, FLORENCE, MAYOR, SUPER AND VICAR
This is the tenth of April
    The day your Ladyship planned
For our second and final meeting
    To discuss how matters stand.
      For a Queen of the May
      Must be appointed by us today.

LADY BILLOWS
All very punctual! Glad to see it. Early worms!
[*Lady Billows crosses with heavy deliberation to the table and
seats herself*]

ENSEMBLE

MISS WORDSWORTH, FLORENCE, MAYOR, SUPER, VICAR
We've made our own investigations
And bring you our nominees
And we're ready whenever you please.

LADY BILLOWS [*energetically and rapidly*]
Now then! Notebook, Florence! All know why we're
here. Only one item on to-day's agenda–to choose a
Queen of the May.

    May Queen! May Queen!
    There's a lot of simple wisdom in these old
    traditions–
    Like Hallowe'en–Harvest Home–
    Chasing the Old Year out of the Town,–
    And so on. Competition
    To be May Queen
    When I was a girl was amazingly keen!
    Among the village girls, I mean.

    All dressed in white–
    Met on the Green
    At noon on May the First to parade
    Before the Squire.
    Squire picked the winner
    And sat beside her during dinner.

    Oh! you're too young to remember
    How these things were done!

I'm putting up a prize this year. Twenty-five
sovereigns–twenty-five! Consider it my duty. Must
make virtue attractive, exciting, *desirable* for young
people.–Too many goings-on! *Dirty* things–ugh!

    Our birth-rate rises every week:
    Poor Doctor Jessop is run off his feet,
    Delivering new babies to
    Mothers of whom excessively few
    Have taken the trouble of visiting *you*,
    Vicar!
Shocking business! No! I won't have it! Town's in a state
of complete moral chaos. Well, then–all in favour
signify –usual manner . . .?
[*All raise their hands. The clock strikes the three quarters*]
Unanimous! Good . . . Let's hear your
suggestions,–I'm waiting!–FIRST . . .
[*All are a little dazed by Lady Billows' speech. The Vicar
recovers first, while the others bring out their small lists of names.
Florence checks and corrects all names mentioned from her
household book. Lady Billows sits grimly listening, occasionally
heaving from side to side with an expressive snort or interjection*]

BALLAD

VICAR
The first suggestion on my list
    Is a charming local girl
Who takes Communion and never missed
    A Sunday–Jennifer Searl.

FLORENCE
. . .had an affair
with young Tom O'Dare,
           last Christmas . . .

LADY BILLOWS
                      Case dis*missed*!

MISS WORDSWORTH
Of all my pupils from the school
    It gives me particular pleasure
To recommend Elizabeth Newell
    Whose Botany Notes are a treasure.

FLORENCE
. . .was seen in the woods
after dusk with Tom Hood
         last Tuesday. . .

LADY BILLOWS
Cross her name off! No good!

MAYOR
There's Winifred Brown who works in the town
    As assistant to Mrs Bell.
I've asked about her, and people concur
    She behaves on the average quite well.

FLORENCE
Except that she went
With her cousin from Kent
For a trip in a dogcart one Sunday in Lent!

SUPER
Er-humph! Er-humph! Er-

LADY BILLOWS

Speak up, Budd!

SUPER

I've little to say, My Lady,
So I'll make it short and sweet—
The girl in my mind is a treasure, you'll find.
—Her name is Amelia Keats.

FLORENCE

Exposes her ankles
And legs bold as brass.
Her skirt's far too short
For a girl of her class.
None of those four
Seems to me more
Than half up to scratch
As a Queen of the May.

LADY BILLOWS

Won't accept one of them!

Cross them all out!

Can't waste time buttering parsnips!
Want Virgins—Not Trollops . . .

FLORENCE

More names?
[All are rather flustered by the failure of their first suggestions.
They hasten to make others]

VICAR

I have another name or two
I brought with me in case
The first was not acceptable.
—What about Edith Chase?

LADY BILLOWS

Well, what about her?

FLORENCE

Much too flighty . . .

VICAR

She attends my Bible group . . .

FLORENCE

When the postman called
One day, she opened the door in her nightie!

MISS WORDSWORTH

Has anyone thought of the shoemaker's twins
Joyce Mary and her sister?
Most practical girls at Handicrafts . . .

FLORENCE

I've heard of things from Mister
Budd about them both . . .

LADY BILLOWS

Both of them!

SUPER

Take my Bible oath! . . .

FLORENCE

He can't repeat what he caught them at . . .
You'll pardon him, milady . . .

SUPER

There's that

Girl who works at Piper's farm . . .

FLORENCE

Was lost one night and then found in a barn!

MISS WORDSWORTH

Oh, surely there must be one to choose!

MAYOR

The girl from the dairy?

FLORENCE

She won't refuse
Though not ideal by a long, long chalk.

LADY BILLOWS [to Mayor]

Then don't suggest her!

SUPER

People talk
Of Nancy Waters, but I'm not sure . . .

FLORENCE

The baker's daughter?
No! Couldn't have her for Queen of the May!

MAYOR

She runs after Sid, who's my assistant,
And him after her: both very persistent.

VICAR

My mind has scoured the Parish through:
Our lists are finished . . .

MISS WORDSWORTH

What can we do?
Not even one girl whom we can trust?
Not even one in all the town?

SUPER

I reckon that's true . . .

MAYOR

It is!

VICAR

And must
We cast our hopeful glances down?

MISS WORDSWORTH, MAYOR, VICAR AND SUPER

Unhappy? Sad? Defeated? . . .
Before our project is completed?

FLORENCE

You've none of you succeeded!

QUARTET [lamentoso]

VICAR

Oh, bitter, bitter is the fruit
Sprung from the seed of sin:
It feeds on poison at the root
And cankers all within.

MISS WORDSWORTH

I teach my pupils they must strive
For moral grace and truth
But they care little for advice
In headstrong days of youth.

MAYOR

How sad to see a decent town
Lose its good name and sink
Slowly, slowly, slowly down
And hover on the brink.

SUPER
Policemen have a ticklish task
    In stamping out abuses.
For human flesh is only grass
    And darkness has its uses
[*A dismal silence. Florence stands rigid and tight-lipped.
Lady Billows begins to simmer like a volcano and suddenly
erupts*]

LADY BILLOWS

ARIA [*furioso*]

    Is this all you can bring?
        Each single name
    Reeking impurities,
    Exuding moral blame?
    Is there no more than this
    To offer? Not one thing
    But stinks of sensual shame?

FLORENCE [*echoing*]
    . . .but stinks of sensual shame?

LADY BILLOWS
    Are Loxford girls all whores?
        None clean, none sure?
    Lascivious nanny-goats
    Each one, each one impure?
    I'll curb their passions; show
    Them with a whip that laws
    Of morals must endure!

FLORENCE [*echoing*]
    . . .that morals must endure!

LADY BILLOWS
    Is this the town where I
        Have lived and toiled?
    A Sodom and Gomorrah
    Ripe to be despoiled?
    O spawning-ground of horror!
    Shame to Loxford:–sty
    The female sex has soiled!

FLORENCE [*echoing*]
    The female sex has soiled!
[*The clock whirrs and strikes eleven. Lady Billows subsides,
exhausted by her own vehemence. The others are pretty exhausted,
too. After some moments the Super has an idea*]

SUPER
Begging your pardon
I'd like to say–
Has anyone heard
Of a *King* of the May?

FLORENCE
King of the May?

LADY BILLOWS
                Fantastic!

MISS WORDSWORTH
                    I never did . . .

VICAR
Not in East Suffolk . . .

MAYOR
                I suppose you'd crown Sid?

SUPER
Maybe it seems a
Rum sort of notion
But it might help us out
Of the present commotion . . .

LADY BILLOWS
'Rum' it may be; 'helpful' no.
Mere red herring, Budd–

SUPER
                    Just so!
Herring's the name and Herring's the lad!
Fellow we're wanting is there to be had.
Albert Herring! . . .

ALL [*in surprise*]
Albert Herring...

SUPER
                . . .Works for his mother . . .
Has a greengrocer's shop . . .Strong as a horse . . .
Works till he drops . . .Bit simple, of course . . .
but we won't find another . . .

SONG [*in inarticulate excitement*]

    Albert Herring's clean as
        New mown hay;
    Honest, truthful, keen as
        Colman's mustard,
            As they say!

    Never kicks up rough as
        Most boys do–
    Albert's real good stuff, as
        Good as gold, right
            Through and through!

VICAR
I know the boy you mean, but is he quite . . .?

MAYOR
I've seen him since he was a kid. He's always lived next
door to me . . .

MISS WORDSWORTH
When he attended school poor Albert was not bright at
lessons, though quite exceptional for conduct . . .

VICAR
An inoffensive lad–simple, of course . . .

MAYOR
A splendid son to Mrs Herring . . .

LADY BILLOWS
What precisely has a grocer's lad to do with this
discussion? Ridiculous proposal! I'm certain there are
girls–farmers' daughters, maybe–suitable for us.
Florence . . .?

FLORENCE
Hopeless, ma'am. I've been round all the farms and
smallholdings. Shocking results!

[*grimly*]
        Country virgins
        If there be such,
        Think too little
        And see too much

[*It looks as if Lady Billows will erupt again. But the moment passes and she says sombrely*]

LADY BILLOWS
I am a very disappointed woman...[*Pause while that sinks in*]. Either we abandon the Festival–or...

SUPER [*doggedly*]
Albert Herring!

LADY BILLOWS [*with angry distaste*]
Albert Herring!...
[*Seeking help*]
Vicar...?

VICAR
  Virtue
  Says Holy Writ,
  Is–*Virtue*.
  Grace abounding
  Whensoever
  Wheresoever
  Howsoever
  It exists.
  Rarer than
    pearls
      rubies
        amethyst
  Richer than
    wealth
      wisdom
        righteousness!
  Is Albert virtuous?
    Yes? Or no?
  That is all we
    Need to know.

ENSEMBLE

MISS WORDSWORTH
  Albert is virtuous.
    Yes, I know
  He is truly
    Truly so!

FLORENCE
  He's very virtuous
    As boys go:
  Everybody
    Tells me so.

MAYOR
  He's very virtuous.
    Don't you know
  Everybody
    Thinks him so?

SUPER
  What, Albert virtuous?
    That I know.
  Certainly he
    Must be so.
[*After this outburst they all look at Lady Billows, who appears to be asleep in her chair*]

LADY BILLOWS [*subterraneously*]
Albert...What's his name?

ALL [*gently, respecting her mood*]
Herring.

LADY BILLOWS [*scarcely audible*]
Herring. [*with sudden and explosive energy*] RIGHT! We'll have him! May KING! That'll teach the girls a lesson!

FINALE [*vigorously*]

LADY BILLOWS
  May King! May King!
    Remarkable position.
  Cause a great sensation
    On the First of May.

FLORENCE
  Let's go and tell him
    Announcing our decision;
  Warn him to be ready
    On the First of May.

VICAR
  Most satisfactory!
    Magnificent solution
  For the Coronation
    On the First of May.

MISS WORDSWORTH
  So encouraging
    For all our dear young people!
  'Virtue is rewarded
    On the First of May.'

MAYOR
  Urban District Councillors
    All over Eastern Suffolk
  Will envy little Loxford
    On the First of May.

SUPER
  All the police force
    Will have to be on duty
  Keeping things in order
    On the First of May.

ODE [*sung by all–unaccompanied*]

ALL
  Rejoice, my friends, and be exceeding glad!
    Virtue has signalled forth
    Her champion and defender–
      A Village Lad
    Humble in looks, of lowly birth,
    Beneath whose apron beats a heart
  To conquer Sin, repel Temptation, render
    Back to Virtue what she entrusts
    To him without respect of gender–
  Her crown of simple and refulgent splendour!

CURTAIN AND INTERLUDE

Scene two

[*Mrs Herring's greengrocery in Little Street. There is a large sash-window at the back, filled with fruit, vegetables and advertisement cards: through this can be seen the village street. The shop-door stands open: the lower half is connected with a spring-bell, which rings whenever a customer enters. A low counter, with a weighing machine and a sheaf of bags. Behind this, an inner door to the rest of the house.*
Fruit-boxes, baskets, sacks, price-tickets, etc., are plentifully scattered around the shop.

When the curtain rises, the shop is empty. Three children–Emmie, Harry and Cis–are playing outside, bouncing a ball back and forwards against the lower half-door, and chanting a doggerel play-song in time with their game]

SONG

KIDS
Bounce me high
Bounce me low
Bounce me up to Jericho!
Bounce me slow
Bounce me quick
Bounce me to arithmetick!
One . . . two . . . three . . .
[*The ball misses and comes flying in through the top of the door. The song stops. Three heads peer cautiously in, looking around*]

EMMIE
Go on, 'Arry!–the old girl's out!

CIS
She's out!–

EMMIE
We'll help you up. Hold tight!
Watch the bell don't ring–!

HARRY
Mind my trousers! Ow!–

EMMIE AND CIS
All right?
[*The girls shove Harry up to the level of the door. He scrambles over, drops inside, gets the ball and throws it to them: then takes some apples from a barrel, passes them out and begins filling his own pockets.*
All this in silence, except for a few whispered comments]

EMMIE
There it is, by that old box!

HARRY
Catch!

CIS
Give us some too, Harry–Taa!

EMMIE [*dramatic whisper*]
LOOK OUT! S'pose Albert came–?

HARRY
Silly old fool! Can't catch me!

EMMIE
Ooh! What lovely apples!–

HARRY
Here's some more!
[*The girls are so busy watching Harry they don't notice Sid's arrival behind them. He is in butcher's apron and shirtsleeves*]

SID
Come out of that, my lad!
I'll teach you to pinch apples!

EMMIE AND CIS
Look out, it's Sid!

EMMIE AND CIS
Big bully, you!

HARRY
Ow! Leggo!

CIS AND EMMIE
Nosey-Parker, too! Leave 'im be!

HARRY
Leggo of me!

SID
Damn good hiding's
what you need! Empty your pockets!

HARRY
OW!–

SID
Is that the lot? Well then, get *out* . . .*!*

EMMIE AND CIS
We'll tell 'is Dad
Sid from the butcher's knocked 'Arry about!
[*Sid empties Harry's pockets during the struggle, propels him to the door, and kicks him through it, struggling and bellowing with rage.*
Sid dusts himself off, picks up the scattered apples and puts them in his own pocket. Then goes to the inner door and shouts:–]

SID
SHOP!! Hi! . . . Albert!
[*Sid comes back into shop, chooses a good red apple, polishes it on his trousers and takes a bite. There is a dull thud against the inner door. He goes over to it, and guides Albert in backwards by a large sack of vegetables he is carrying*]

SID
There you are!–Just caught young Harry
pinching things.–How d'you carry
a weight like that alone?–Cor–
Must be twenty stone or more!

ALBERT
It's a hundredweight of turnips.

SID
I see!
Strong man act!–Can I have three
Boxes of mixed herbs, please, chum?

ALBERT
Yes–

SID
Got any sage?–

ALBERT
We've some
At threepence a box, same as the mixed.

SID
I'll take three then–that makes six
Boxes at threepence–one and a kick.

ALBERT
That's right.

SID
Toss you–double or quits!

ALBERT
Oh no, Sid, gambling's not in my line.
Mum wouldn't like it . . .

SID
Never you mind!
Heads or tails–Come on–You call!

ALBERT
No, really I won't—thanks all the same—

SID
But why? Because of Mum?
Won't she let you have any fun?—

Did you ever have a pint at the local?

ALBERT
Mum's teetotal . . .

SID
Or go out with a whippet after rabbits?

ALBERT
Strict in her habits . . .

SID
Did you never try taking a girl for a walk?

ALBERT
Do stop this talk! . . .

SID
Or dance to the band in the Jubilee Hall?

ALBERT
. . .I don't like it at all!

SID
You will, once you've broke the apron-strings!

SONG
Tickling a trout
Poaching a hare
Flighting wild geese
Is pretty good sport
For a chap to enjoy.

Living without
A regular share
Of pleasures like these
Is hard to support
For your kind of boy.

But courting a girl is the King of all sports
In a class of its own,
Where there aren't any rules so long as she's caught
And you catch her alone.

Girls mean
Spring six days a week
And twice on Sundays
The whole year round
The winter through.

Girls mean
Games of hide-and-seek
On summer evenings
When someone's bound
To fall for you!

Girls mean
Prowling round in bleak
And wintry weather
Whispering, whispering
'I love you!'

[During this, Albert tries to avoid noticing Sid's remarks by
filling a box from the turnip-sack—on hands and knees]

ALBERT
Sid, I'm sorry
but I've got
a lot to do . . .

SID
Oh! Don't you worry!
I'm just off—
I'm busy too.
[Nancy pokes her head in the door—26, pretty, big smile]

NANCY
Good morning, you two!

SID
Why, look who's here!
Good morning, good morning, good morning!

ALBERT [shyly]
Good morning.

SID
You've just come in time—
We were talking of you.

NANCY
Talking of me—?
You've got a sauce!

SID
It was Albert who started the subject, of course.
You want to watch Albert—he's a very dark horse!

NANCY
You ought to have something better to do
Than gossiping here. Aren't you working to-day?

SID
I've been spinning around like a humming-top
Since I opened the shop at eight o'clock,—
And you know what they say
About work and no play.

NANCY
Well, come and serve me. I'm in a hurry—
I've come for a piece of best English beef.

SID
There's no need to worry! Have a nice peach?

NANCY
Ooh! May I really?

ALBERT
Those are sixpence each!—

SID
Take two—I'll stand the damage.

ALBERT
Two peaches at sixpence—that's a shilling, please.

SID
I think I can just about manage
To squeeze out a bob from the firm's petty cash.

NANCY
I shan't eat them now
They're so ripe they might splash.

SID
You can bring them to-night
And we'll each take a bite,
To flavour our kisses
With a dash of peach bitters.

NANCY
That sounds just delicious—

DUET

SID
Meet me at quarter past eight
    In the street
        Don't be late
Or I'll whistle
Under your window.

NANCY
Yes! If you promise to wait
    In the street
        If I'm late
And not whistle
Under my window.
For Mum will be curious and Dad will be furious
    To hear whistling under our window.

TRIO

SID
Do try to be there
If you possibly can
    For the night will be fine and clear.

NANCY
I'll try to be there
If I possibly can
    For the night will be fine and clear.

ALBERT [aside]
I wish they would clear
Right away from our shop
    For it's hard not to overhear!
There'll be trouble, I fear,
Should my Mother appear
And discover them flirting here!

[Albert retreats behind the counter, leaving Sid and Nancy alone]

NANCY AND SID
We'll walk to the spinney
    Up over the Common
        Arm in arm,
            Your (my) hand
    In my (your) pocket,
Refreshing ourselves in the pleasures of love!

The moon will be shining
    The sky will be starry
        As we walk,
            Your (my) hand
    In my (your) pocket,
Refreshing ourselves in the pleasures of love!

And if it is raining
    We'll share an umbrella
        As we walk,
            Your (my) hand
    In my (your) pocket,
Refreshing ourselves in the pleasures of love!

ALBERT
And I shall be sleeping
    Alone in my attic
        As they walk,
            Her hand

In his pocket,
Refreshing themselves in the pleasures of love!

ALBERT
Excuse me . . .!

SID
Give us a kiss, Nancy!

NANCY
Oh no! Shopping first—kisses afterwards!

SID [impatient]
Come on, then! So long, Albert!

NANCY
                 Goodbye, Albert!

ALBERT
Goodbye!

[They go out. Albert runs after them to the door]

ALBERT
Hi! Sid!! . . . You forgot to pay for the herbs!
[No answer. Albert comes back into the shop]
    He's much too busy
    Even to listen
    Much less to care
    With Nancy there.

    I wonder is he
    Right when he says
    I miss all the fun
    Because of Mum? . . .

    Yes! Mum's uncommon keen
        About the need
    Of living chaste and clean
        In word and deed—
                For what?

    Each morning I get up at six
        And tidy up the stock,
    Enthusiastically fix
        Price-labels round the shop—
                For what?

It's not very thrilling to live among boxes and baskets
Of vegetables, flowers and seasonal fruits:
I'm expert at jobs like weighing up punnets of
raspberries
And knowing when root-crops are likely to shoot—
                For what?

[Meditatively]
    It seems as clear as clear
        Can be, that Sid's ideas
    Are very much too crude
        For Mother to approve.

    And yet I'd really like
        To try that kind of life,
    And see how it compares
        With serving customers.
[Emmie rushes in, breathless and in a great hurry]

EMMIE
Mum wants twopennorth of pot-herbs to make a stew in
a 'urry, Mister!

ALBERT
Where's your basket?

EMMIE
'Aven't got one, bust it! My sister, went an'
lost it—

ALBERT
I'll put 'em in paper—

EMMIE
Taa! That'll be safer than taking 'em loose.

ALBERT
No school to-day?

EMMIE
Got extra holidays!

ALBERT
Whatever for—?

EMMIE
On account of Miss Weaver
Our Botany Teacher
Went camping at Easter
Got scarlet-fever—

She was sharing our tent
When she came out all spotty
So they sent us all home
With a letter explaining
They wouldn't expect us
At school for a week
In case we're infectious.

It sounds a bit potty,
But we're not complaining!—

ALBERT [handing her the parcel]
Tuppence, please! Here you are.

EMMIE
Thanks, Mister! Don't mind farthings, do you?—Taa!
[She dashes off again]

ALBERT
Oh, maybe soon
    I'll have the chance
To get away.
And golly! It's about time.
[He is again interrupted by the arrival of Florence]

FLORENCE
Good morning, young man.

ALBERT
Good morning, Miss Pike.

FLORENCE
I want if I can
To talk to your Mum.

ALBERT
I'll call her at once—
She's washing the clothes.

FLORENCE
The reason I've come
Is more urgent than those!
[Albert calls through the inner door]

ALBERT
Mum! you're wanted!

MUM [off]
                          What? Who is it?

ALBERT
Miss Florence Pike is here on a visit!
[Making conversation]
Just drying her hands—
Would you care to sit down?

FLORENCE
No thank you, I'll stand—
I mustn't stay long.
[Mum bustles in, drying her arms on a towel]

MUM
I'm sorry to keep you
And How do you do?
Nice sunny day
For the time of year, too!

FLORENCE [formal and important]
Her Ladyship is on her way
With Miss Wordsworth and the Vicar,
Messrs Budd and Upfold, too
To visit you here . . .

MUM
                          What did you say?
Visiting us? But they can't come in here!
A shop's not the place for people like them

FLORENCE
We shall get on much quicker
If you will be silent and listen
To me . . .

MUM
And I can't have them into the parlour to-day!
I'm airing the washing there . . .

FLORENCE
                          The decision
They bring concerns Albert, as they
Will explain for themselves . . .

MUM
    Concerns Albert?

ALBERT
                          Concerns me, do you say?

MUM
Oh! don't say that Albert's in trouble some way!

FLORENCE
Be quiet now! Are you ready? Here they come!—
[Lady Billows, accompanied by the Vicar, Mayor, Super, and
Miss Wordsworth, crosses the window and enters]

LADY BILLOWS [enthusiastically]
We bring great news to you
    Upon this happy day!
    Patronage and fame
    Applaud your name!

ALL
    Declaring you
Loxford King of the May!

MUM
They're talking to you, Albert! . . . Oh, Albert!

ALBERT
I don't quite get their meaning–

FLORENCE
You've been chosen as May King.

ALBERT
Chosen as what–? What, me?

FLORENCE
Yes, you! Hush!

LADY BILLOWS
We plan to celebrate
By crowning you upon
May Day afternoon:
That's fairly soon–

ALL
Not long to wait!
Just till April's gone!

MUM
Excuse my asking–What's this crowning for?

ALBERT
I'd like to know that too.

VICAR
In honour of your
Pure, virtuous life–

MISS WORDSWORTH
Reward for chastity!

MAYOR
Official recognition of your modesty!–

ALBERT
Well, I'll be blowed!

SUPER
What costume will he wear?

FLORENCE
White like a swan!

VICAR
A royal crown!

MUM
And where
will *that* come from?

ALBERT
Me dressed in white?
Oh no!

LADY BILLOWS
We'll see to that all right.

FLORENCE
Bring me his sizes in shoes and hats by to-night
To give to the tailor–

MUM
Seems ridiculous to me!–

ALBERT
The whole thing's *daft*!

LADY BILLOWS
Now, Herring, don't be hasty!

VICAR
But before we part
Should we not mention?–

ALL
Of course!–The prize!

LADY BILLOWS
When this great day arrives,
Albert will receive, besides his crown,
A prize in golden coins of five-and-twenty pounds.

MUM
Twenty-five pounds all of his own?
Albert, say Thank you!–as well as a crown!

LADY BILLOWS
In offering this prize,
Our aim is to ensure
Virtue has its just
Reward from us!

ALL
And so goodbye,
Albert! No!–*au revoir*!
[*They go out, Mum escorting them to the door*]

MUM
Good morning to you all!

Well, think of that, my lad,
Being King of the May an' all
And the envy of everyone,
And twenty-five quid in addition!

ALBERT
But I don't want that kind of position
And I don't think I'm going to accept.

MUM
You won't accept? Why ever not?
You can't refuse–!

ALBERT
Oh yes, I can!

MUM
Not while you live with me, young man!
You'll do as you're told–

ALBERT
Now listen, Mum,–

MUM
Don't *listen* me!

ALBERT
Why should they come
And dress me up like a blinking swan,
And make speeches at me like I was stuffed
Instead of flesh and blood?

MUM
Stop shouting at me and fetch me my tape
From the box on the kitchen safe.
I'll measure you up–

ALBERT
Oh no, you won't!

MUM
You heard what I said!–

23 Lady Billows's house
model for Act I scene i
John Piper

24 Mrs Herring's shop
model for Act I scene ii
John Piper

25 The Marquee at the Vicarage
model for Act II scene i
John Piper

26 Mrs Herring's shop   *John Piper*

27 The Marquee at the Vicarage   *John Piper*

28 Lady Billows's house   *John Piper*

29 Loxford, drop curtain   *John Piper*

30 Albert receiving the purse from Lady Billows: Peter Pears, Joan Cross and William Parsons

31 Mrs Herring's shop   *John Piper*

ALBERT
                    I did, and don't
You think I'm willing, 'cos I'm not.

MUM
I'll take a strap to you, that's what!

ALBERT
You try it then!—

MUM
Young devil!

ALBERT
              I'm old enough
To choose for myself—

MUM
                          I brought you up!

ALBERT
You *shut* me up in the shop all day!

MUM
The wicked ingratitude of it! You'll pay
For this, my boy.

ALBERT
                    I'm sick and tired
Of being ordered about—

MUM
                              You little liar!
I won't stand here and be attacked
By a kid who wants his bottom smacked!
Go up to bed and shut the door
And don't you dare to come down before
You're ready to say sorry. Go on!
You devil!
I'll teach you!
[*During the quarrel, the three Kids have collected outside the
shop-window, watching with fascination. As Mum shoves
Albert through the door, they begin chanting a rude variant of
their play-song. Mum turns back, sees them, makes a threatening
move which sends them scuttling off, then back to the door to shout
more insults after Albert*]

KIDS
Albert's Mum
Took a stick
Smacked him on the thingmijig!
Albert hopped
Round the shop,
Squeaking like a tillypig!

MUM
Twenty-five quid! *Twenty-five quid?!!* Bloody little fool!

CURTAIN
END OF ACT ONE

Act two

Scene one

[*Inside a marquee set up in the field adjoining the Vicarage. There
is a trestle-table covered with a cloth, and set for eleven places. A
side-table carries a tea-urn, dishes of fruit, bowls of jelly, cakes,
and other food. The central opening of the marquee shows a view
of hedges and trees, with the Vicarage beyond. Another opening at
one side leads to an annexe used for storage and washing-up.
When the curtain rises, Nancy is bringing in some extra dishes of
food to the side-table. Florence comes in from outside, dressed in
her Sunday-best, and considerably fussed*]

FLORENCE
Isn't he here?

NANCY
Not yet.

FLORENCE
Oh, drat the lad!

NANCY
He promised to come by three . . .

FLORENCE
I'm astonished at him, today of all days! . . .

NANCY
Don't trouble to wait . . .

FLORENCE
I should hate to miss them.

NANCY
There's only the meat to unpack and put out on the
plates. I can easily do that alone.

FLORENCE
The Vicar especially asked me to be there at half-past,
to be took in the photograph group for *The Ipswich and
District Gazette.*

NANCY [*as Sid arrives on his bicycle, with a large box of food*]
Here he is at last!

FLORENCE
And high time too!

NANCY
Hurry up, Sid!

SID [*coming in*]
Am I late?

FLORENCE
Everything's ready but *you!*

SID
Sorry, Miss Pike! Punctured my bike . . .!

FLORENCE
Punctured your bike . . .!

    For three precious weeks
    We've been toiling and scraping,
        Bustling, hurrying,
        Hurrying, scurrying,
    With one aim in sight—
    And at the eleventh hour
        You . . . you . . . *you*
    Keep everything waiting
    Because of your bike!

I think you're lazy and most reprehensible!
Surely you know that the meat's indispensable?
Lateness on May Day is quite indefensible!

NANCY
It's twenty-past . . .

FLORENCE
Then I must fly, or they'll leave me out!
[*Florence hurries out*]

SID [*as she goes*]
You bumble off!—that'll be much more sensible!
[*Looking at table*] That's a fine sight for sore eyes!

NANCY
Don't you think it's a splendid surprise?

SID
And they make all this fuss, 'cos Albert's too shy to go
out on a bust . . .!

NANCY
What were things like down there in the town?

SID
Churchyard's agog with a crowd of folk
    Who couldn't get in for the service:
Seats have been kept for the Band of Hope:
    And each choirboy has got a new surplice.
The Vicar is preaching on 'Living Chaste
    For the Hereafter'—
Some of his listeners are solemn-faced,
    Some near to laughter.

And Albert!—sitting there in his pew,
The poor kid looks on tenterhooks.
He's in the mood to escape if he could.
I'd like to see him go for good!

NANCY
Sid, tell me the truth about why you were late.

SID
What do you mean?

NANCY
You've got some scheme!

SID
How did you guess?

NANCY
I know by the grin
On your face and the gleam
In your eye—Confess!

SID
Can you keep a secret?

NANCY
Mum as an oyster.

SID
Then I'll tell you the plot
While we empty this box.
[*They go out, carrying the box between them.
Miss Wordsworth leads in the three children—Emmie and Cis in
starched white frocks, and Harry in a sailor suit*]

MISS WORDSWORTH
Quickly, children—come along!
Time to try our festive song
Last time through before they come!

EMMIE—
Blimey! Jelly!

CIS
                    Pink blancmange!

HARRY
Seedy cake! Seedy cake!

EMMIE
                         Wiv' icing on!

MISS WORDSWORTH
All stand neatly in a row,
Heads back! Fingers so!
One deep breath and off we go!

EMMIE
Treacle tart!

CIS
                    Sausagey rolls!

HARRY
Trifle! Trifle!

ALL THREE
In a great big bowl!

MISS WORDSWORTH
Food comes later—First we sing
'*Glory to our new May King!*'
Try to make the welkin ring!
Attention now! No fidgeting.
[*She sounds her pitch-pipe*]

There is DOH!
One and two and . . . NO!
When I reach TWO
You *have* to be
Agog to start
On the beat of THREE!

EMMIE
Chicken and ham!

CIS
Cheesey straws!

HARRY
And marzipan!
[*Pitch-pipe again*]

MISS WORDSWORTH
One and two and . . .

CHILDREN [*singing*]
GLORY TO OUR NEW MAY KING

MISS WORDSWORTH
Oh! what a noise!
That's much too shrill,
And Harry, you should
Just *try* to keep still!

One and two and . . .

CHILDREN [*singing*]
GLORY TO OUR NEW MAY KING!
ALBERT, 'AIL, ALL 'AIL! WE SING!

MISS WORDSWORTH
Not 'ail, my dears!
The word is *H a i l*.

A clean, crisp note
From an open throat.
H a i l!!
And insert your aitches
In their proper places.
ALBERT, *H A I L*, ALL *H A I L*! WE SING . . .

CHILDREN
HALBERT, HAIL, HALL HAIL!

MISS WORDSWORTH
Too many now, but
That must do–!
Try the next lines
Fervently through.
Sing with fire!
Beginning on FAH.
You. Emmie, higher–
Your note is LAH.
Doh–ray–me–*FAH!*–soh–*LAH!*–

CHIDREN [*singing a round*]
'EACH SINGLE VOICE
CRIES OUT *REJOICE*
IN HAPPY SONG
BOTH LOUD . . .'

MISS WORDSWORTH
Harry, this is where you always go wrong!–
Just follow Cis, she'll help you along!

HARRY [*hand up*]
Please, Teacher . . .?

MISS WORDSWORTH
Don't take too long!
Our song must begin
Exactly upon
Their coming-in.
[*She shepherds the children out. Sid looks in from the annexe, with Nancy behind*]

NANCY
I don't think you ought!–

SID
Stop spoiling the fun!
Is this where he's sitting?

NANCY
The right-handed one.

SID
Then you begin filling
The glasses all up,
While I add a drop
To His Majesty's cup.
[*Nancy begins pouring lemonade into the glasses all round the table. Sid produces a quarter-bottle of rum from his hip-pocket, and measures a generous tot into Albert's glass*]

NANCY
Don't give him too much!
He mustn't get tight . . .

SID
Just loosen him up,
And make him feel bright.
I think that's all right.
Now add lemonade–

NANCY
It's much the same shade–

SID
Now no-one can smell
There's rum in as well,

NANCY
Excepting for Albert–

BOTH
And he'll never tell!
[*Bells offstage*]

NANCY
Quick, here they are!
Fill up the rest.

SID
We'll stand at the side–
That'll be best.
[*They finish filling all the glasses, just as Miss Wordsworth ushers in the children again, each carrying a bunch of country flowers*]

MISS WORDSWORTH
Here they are, dears! Quickly, come along! Do remember! *Deep* breaths! Nice neat curtsies!
[*The Super and Mum arrive outside the entrance to the tent, with the Mayor and Florence behind*]

SUPER
It's a great day for your son, Mrs Herring!

MUM
Yes, he does look a treat in his white suit,
I couldn't help feeling proud of him too.

MAYOR [*to Florence*]
Today's a big affair for you, Miss Pike.

FLORENCE
For three weeks at least
We've been planning this feast,
Your Worship!
[*The vicar arrives with Lady Billows*]

VICAR
See, virtue triumphs in Albert here.

LADY BILLOWS
Is this the town which I have cherished and loved!
[*Albert follows them. He is dressed in jacket, trousers, shoes of white, with a straw-hat crowned with a circlet of orange blossom. Albert is encouraged to enter the tent, and does so shyly and unwillingly; the others follow and group about him till the Ode is completed. Sid and Nancy watch from the side*]

MISS WORDSWORTH [*sounds her pitch-pipe*]
One and two and . . .

CHILDREN [*joined by Miss Wordsworth*]
GLORY TO OUR NEW MAY KING!
ALBERT, *HAIL! ALL HAIL!* WE SING!
EACH SINGLE VOICE
CRIES OUT *REJOICE*!
IN HAPPY SONG
BOTH LOUD AND LONG!
HAIL! ALBERT! HAIL! WE CRY,
WELCOME TO YOUR MAJESTY!
[*Everyone applauds enthusiastically, breaking into conversation. The children are ushered forward with their bouquets*]

LADY BILLOWS
Quite nicely sung, but rather modern, wasn't it?

MUM
That was splendid! Quite appropriate.

FLORENCE
Thank you, dears. I hope you sang rightly what teacher
intended.

MAYOR
Tuneful and interesting! Very good, I'm sure.

SID
Crikey! What an awful noise!

NANCY
Do be quiet, Sid, they were doing their best.

VICAR
Very harmonious. Did Miss Wordsworth write it?

SUPER
Bravo! Bravo! A fine effort!

MISS WORDSWORTH
Hussh! . . . Harold Wood!
[*Harry is pushed forward to present his flowers to Lady Billows*]

HARRY
My flowers are few
And tender my years
But they are for you
Who Loxford reveres.
[*Applause . . . Harry is hoisted back, and Emmie takes his place
to give flowers to Albert, who doesn't at all know what to do with
them*]

MISS WORDSWORTH
Emmie Spatchett!

EMMIE
Simple Song
Country Flowers
Wish you long
And happy Hours.
[*Applause. Cis is driven nervously into place, to give flowers to
Mrs Herring*]

MISS WORDSWORTH
Now, Cissie Woodger!

CIS
Horray for the–

MISS WORDSWORTH [*sotto voce*]
–Mother–

CIS
–the Mother of–

MISS WORDSWORTH
–Albert–

CIS
Of Albert the–

MISS WORDSWORTH
–King–

CIS
–the King.

CIS [*panicking*]
Hooray!–Hooray!–Hooray!–Hooray!–Hooray!

MISS WORDSWORTH
'Twas yours–'twas yours–'Twas yours to discover–
[*This goes on till Cis bursts into tears and Mrs Herring stops the
rot by taking the flowers firmly, and saying:*]

MUM
Well done, dearie! Very nice, I'm sure . . .

LADY BILLOWS
Thank you, children!–
And thank *you*, Miss Wordsworth! Come, let's sit down
[*All move to the table with general remarks*]

LADY BILLOWS
Albert, come on my right-hand.

MUM
Where d'you think I'd be? I'm the King's Mum

SUPER
Over here, Mrs Herring. Next to me.

MISS WORDSWORTH
That was excellent, children! Sit down quietly–

MAYOR
This me? Where d'you think His Worship sits?

FLORENCE
Food comes *after* speeches! Vicar, you start.

NANCY
Oh, I must stay and listen. This'll be fun.

VICAR
Just a few words of introduction. That will be most
suitable.

CHILDREN
I'm jolly hungry!

ALBERT
Won't somebody take this for me? I don't know what to
do with it!

SID
Chinwagging! What an awful lot of rot!
[*When all are seated, the Vicar rises affably and raps on the
table*]

VICAR
Your Ladyship! . . . Ladies and gentlemen . . . girls
and boys!
I shall not trespass on your time . . . I rise–
Ex officio–
To call upon Her Ladyship,
And ask her if she will
Consent to make a little speech
Before we eat our fill?
[*Much applause. Lady Billows hoists up to her feet*]

LADY BILLOWS
Thank you, Mr Gedge!

I'm full of happiness
To be here in your midst
On such a day as this,
As honoured guest and patroness
Of the Loxford Urban District May-Day Feast.
[*Applause*]

Seated upon my right is Albert Herring–
A young man chosen, marked out, set apart

For honest worth and purity of heart.
You see that in the costume he is wearing—
Virgin white and orange blossom crown.

Dear children! You! The rising generation!
Never forget the meaning of this day!
Treasure its example! Think, oh think
Of Albert! Scorn the sweetmeats of Temptation
Seducing you from straight and narrow ways—
Carnal indulgence!—gambling!—playing
cards!—

Irreligion!
Patriotism is not enough!—D r i n k!
The HAVOC wrought by gin! Oh, never start
That dreadful habit, or you're lost forever!

King and Country! Cleanliness is next to—
God for England and Saint—Keep
Your powder dry and leave the rest to
Nature!—Britons! Rule the deep!
[*Enthusiastic cries of Hooray!*]
Albert! Arise! Stand up to receive
This purse of otterskin—my father shot
The brute in 'Fifty-six on Christmas Eve—
With five-and-twenty sovereigns inside!
Take it, my boy! Take it with joyful pride!
All this is yours—and you deserve the lot!
[*Much applause as Albert takes the purse, and they both sit*]

VICAR [*rising again*]
Magnificent, your Ladyship! Our best thanks to you!
A splendid speech, a splendid prize
    And splendidly deserved!
Now, Mister Mayor, will you please rise
    And add another word?

MAYOR [*reading mechanically*]
As representing the local Council,
I'm happy to declare
Ourselves in full agreement with Her Ladyship,
Thanking her most hearty—heartily—for the ideal
She sets our town in moral leadership.
The repercussions of this Festival
Will travel far, wide, deep and strong—
Like when my Council, acting for the best of all
Its citizens, laid the twelve-inch watermain—
Costing six pounds ten the yard—that runs along
Through Balaclava Avenue—regardless of
objections!—
To guarantee pure water filtered from infections.
Now Loxford leads again by being first, yes!
First in crowning a May King. Well Done!
I hear you cry—*Well Done!* I hear you cry—?
[*Appropriate, if late, cries of 'Well done!'*]
My Council wishes me to mark to-day
By offering this prize to Albert, which they
Have voted from the Entertainment Fund—
This Savings Book in which he'll find five pounds.
[*More applause as Albert rises to take the book, and sits with the Mayor*]

VICAR
Fascinating, Mister Mayor!

A fitting gift indeed
    To store away

For a rainy day
    And keep in case of need.
Miss Wordsworth, you won't disappoint us? Oh! you
have a surprise, I see!

MISS WORDSWORTH [*rising*]
My heart leaps up with joy to see
Virtue and simplicity
Applauded, rewarded, glorified
With heartfelt warmth on every side!
Albert, the Teachers from the School,
Miss Podd, Miss Tuttle, dear Miss Butler and
                                Miss Toole,
Are proud of you, as I am too,—
And profoundly *stirred* by your renown.
Albert! They send this little gift to you
For rainy afternoons—*Foxe's Book of Martyrs*—
In two fine volumes, illustrated,
Inscribed to you appropriately, and dated.
[*Applause. The books are passed along the table to Albert, and
Miss Wordsworth sits*]

VICAR
The Bible, Shakespeare, Foxe's Book of Martyrs—
three cornerstones of our National Heritage!
Thank you, Miss Wordsworth, very much.
    To make our thanks complete,
        One voice is missing!
    Yes—Mister Budd's—
        Last, but hardly *least!*

SUPER [*rising*]
Er . . .! humph! I'm no great shakes as a speechifier,
But my heart's warm enough, if you know what I
    mean!
It's chaps like young Albert keep the British Empire
On top of the world where it has always been.
Good old Albert!—that's my opinion . . .
Good luck to you, boy!
Er . . . humph! before I wind up,
I mustn't forget to thank Mrs Williams
For the loan of her flagpole and two dozen cups.
[*He sits abruptly. Applause just too late for comfort*]

VICAR
Thank you, thank you! Now
I'm certain Albert feels the need
    Of speaking in his turn—
    Returning thanks for gifts received
    Before the feast's begun?

MUM
Go on, Albert!

FLORENCE
Say 'Thank you.'

VICAR
Don't be shy!

MISS WORDSWORTH
Say a word or two!

MAYOR
It's just polite.

SUPER
Don't be scared, old boy!

NANCY, SID
Poor Albert!

LADY BILLOWS
Come along, now!
[*Albert gets to his feet miserably, hesitates a few moments, pulls himself together as if to speak, loses his nerve suddenly, says an abrupt 'Thank You,' and sits down among sympathetic laughter and applause*]

ALL
Oh! Albert! Poor Albert! Bit short, wasn't it? Try again!
He's scared! Short and sweet! That didn't take long!
Better luck next time!

VICAR
Well tried, Albert. We understand—

That modest phrase betrays a heart
   Too full to prate or boast.
Now lift your glasses, everyone,
   And join me in a toast!

Albert the Good!
Long may he reign!
To be re-elected
Again and again.

ALL [*rising and repeating*]
Albert the Good!
Long may he reign!
To be re-elected
Again and again.
[*They all drink except Florence, who is busy whispering to the seated Albert. As they sit, Albert stands and lifts his glass*]

ALBERT
And three cheers for Her Ladyship! Hip–hip–
   (HOORAY!)
Hip–hip–(HOORAY) Hip–hip–(HOORAY!)
[*With clumsy gallantry, Albert raises his glass and drinks to Lady Billows—a good long thirsty drink, which leaves him rocking slightly and smiling. He swoops forward with a long arm to have his glass refilled*]

That's better!–Thirsty!–More, please!–Ur-HIC!
[*Albert suddenly breaks out with a loud hiccup, which is repeated irregularly and surprisingly, however he tries to apologise or smile it away. Various cures are suggested, until the crisis passes*]

MUM
Hiccups!

CHILDREN
Albert's got willups!

LADY BILLOWS
Shall I pat your back?

ALBERT
Beg par . . . ur-HIC!

MISS WORDSWORTH
Most distressing!

FLORENCE
Too much excitement!

SUPER
Count Twenty!

MAYOR
Hold your breath!

ALBERT
I'm trying . . . ur-HIC! . . .

MUM
Pat him harder!

VICAR
Glass of water!

FLORENCE
Lump of sugar!

MAYOR
Soaked in vinegar!

ALBERT
It's almost gone . . . ur-HIC! . . .

NANCY [*sotto voce*]
Do you think it's the rum?

SID [*sotto voce*]
It's got a kick like a gun!

NANCY
Oh, what have we done?

SID
It was only in fun!

ALBERT
. . . ur-HIC! . . . Please don't bothe . . . ur-HIC! . . .
Wate . . . ur-HIC! . . .
[*He makes groping signals for a glass*]

MUM AND OTHERS
Lemonade! Lemonade!

FLORENCE
From the wrong side!–
[*Albert is given a glass to drink from*]

LADY BILLOWS
Sip it–

VICAR AND MUM
Slowly–

MISS WORDSWORTH
Drop by drop–

CHILDREN
He'll go off pop!
[*Pause while he sips from the glass, and straightens up*]

MUM
Better, son?
[*Albert nods*]

VICAR
None too soon!

MISS WORDSWORTH
Oh, well done!–
[*Albert beams his reassurance, and all relax*]

LADY BILLOWS
Well, then, let's begin–!
[*At this signal from Lady Billows, Nancy and Sid begin serving the food, while everyone breaks into conversation, as they help themselves.
The curtain falls on a general roar and babble from the whole table . . .*]

NANCY AND SID
Bring the plates!   Quickly now!
Here you are!   Pass it down.
Will that do?   Plenty more.
Coming now!   This is yours!

FLORENCE
Will you pass up the plates?
Give that to the Vicar.
If you help in that way,
We shall all get served quicker.

VICAR
It's a splendid display!
Quite a banquet, I'd say!
A magnificent spread,
Will the children take bread?

MISS WORDSWORTH
It's coming now, Harry.
They all look so merry!
Sit still and be good, dear,
There's a mountain of food here.

LADY BILLOWS
Put the purse in your pocket
And remove all those books.
Here's a plate of sliced ham—
You can tuck in to that.

ALBERT
I feel brisk like a rocket,
Going up with a *Whoosh!*
Oh! How lucky I am!
Shall I take off my hat?

MUM
I wasn't expecting
Such a wonderful do.
Excuse me for stretching!
Yes, I seem to have two!

MAYOR AND SUPER
Beginning with beef, eh?
Off the sirloin, I'd say.
There's lashings of food.
My! Does that ham look good!

CHILDREN
Cor blimey! I'm aching
To get down to eating.
My tummy is rumbling.
Don't 'arf keep you waiting!

CURTAIN AND INTERLUDE

Scene two

[*Inside the shop later that evening. Dusk has fallen, and light streams through the shop-window from the street-lamp outside. After a few moments, a white shape looms past the window, and there is a fumbling with the latch of the door.*
It opens with a sudden Ting! and Albert lurches through it, humming a version of the toast. He is not exactly drunk, but in a hilarious mixture of excitement and cheerfulness, stimulated by the rum.
He punctuates his little song by banging the door back and forwards, and tingling the bell]

ALBERT
Albert the Good!
Long may he reign.
To be re-elected,
And re-selected,
And re-expected,

and resurrected
Again and again and again and again and AGAIN!

[*Shouting*] Mum! MUM! Yoo-hoo!

It's your little Albert!
Your sugar-plum
Of a prodigal son—
Clean as a whistle,
Sound as a drum,
Home from his Coronat - i - um!

MUM!!!

Stupid! Stupid!

She's gone to call on Auntie Eth
     For a cup of tea and a chat.
Left me coming straight home to bed,
     But I'm blowed if I'm ready for that!

Dark in here!—must find a match—
After that we'll light the gas,
With   e n o r m o u s   care not to break the mantle,
Set fire to the shop or cause a scandal!

Matches?—Matches!—[*calling*] Swan Vestas! . . .
Swan *Vest*as . . .? . . .Ah! . . .
[*He finds a box of matches on the counter*]
That's the chap—
Turn the tap—
Strike the match
Like this—oh drat!
[*He drops the box of matches on the floor, and grovels for them, leaving the gas-jet on*]
Butterfingers! . . . Ooopsadaisy!
[*He stands up, and with great deliberation and slowness prepares to strike the match*]
Open your mouth,
Shut your eyes,
Strike the match
For a nice surprise . . .
[*There is a loud and terrifying report and swoosh of flame from the gas-jet*]
Blast! . . . Dangerous stuff, gas. Smelly, tricky, noisy, dangerous stuff . . .! Leave well alone . . .!
[*He moves away from the gas-jet to the middle of the shop*]
     Phew! . . . it's hot!
     Belt's too tight for tum.
     Loosen it out a notch,
     Relieve my poor old abdom-um
[*Sitting luxuriously on a box*]
     Golly! What a party!
          What a party!
     Talk of eating hearty . . .!
     Dish after dish they brought us: Cakes,
          Different-flavoured
     Jellies, Custard, Chocolate Dates,
     Fruit Salad, Trifle—and they gave us
          Pastries freshly made
     With Cream in, followed by Almond Favours!

But oh! The taste of that lemonade . . .! I wonder how it's made? . . . Nancy knows, I suppose. Nancy will know . . . Pretty name . . .!

Why did she stare
  Each time I looked
    Towards her? . . .

Why was she watching
  Whenever I turned
    Of a sudden? . . .

Why did she blush
  Catching my eye
    As she passed? . . .

What made her stammer
  Speaking to me
    In that manner? . . .

Nancy . . . . . .? No–!

She belongs to Sid, not me:
  We've never talked
    or walked
  Lightheartedly
    through the woods,
Nor shall that I can see.

Girls don't care for chaps like me:
  I'm too shy
    to reply
  Entertainingly
    When they speak,
I lose my nerve and fly.
[*There is a throbbing and inviting whistle down the street*]
  Sounds like Sid serenading
    under her window,
  Impatient at waiting,
  Impatiently aching
  To take Nancy chasing
    love and adventure.
[*The whistle is repeated more urgently*]
  Sid doesn't suffer from shyness,
    timidity,
  Gets what he wants by directness,
    simplicity,
  Aims at his target with shameless
    audacity,
  Trades on the fact of his ruthless
    tenacity.
[*Nancy and Sid appear outside the shop-window, under the lamp-post. Albert sees them, and retreats into shadow*]

NANCY
You oughtn't to whistle. I told you that, Sid!

SID [*aggrieved*]
It's perishing cold standing here in the street. Twenty-five minutes! . . . I'm frozen stiff!

NANCY
I slipped down the stairs as quick as I could . . .

SID
Let's call at the pub for a couple of Ports.
Warm us up quick . . .

NANCY
        Sid, we mustn't! Oh, no!
People will talk . . .!

SID
        They've enough food for chatter
In Albert to-night, so us two won't matter.

NANCY
Poor kid! It does seem wrong
  To show him off to everyone
Like a sort of plaster saint
  Or the village simpleton.

SID
He's all right . . . once he's sown
A few wild oats, he'll live that down.

NANCY
But how can he sow them, tied to his Mum?

SID
I've done my share providing the rum!
Are you volunteering to cheer him
Along the agreeable primrose path?

NANCY
Of course not! Still, I'd like to help.

SID
Heaven helps those who help themselves!

NANCY
It's getting terrible chilly . . . It'll be terrible cold up there on the Common.

SID
You needn't be frightened with me!

DUET

SID
Come along, darling, come follow me quick!
  Time is racing us round the clock,–
  Ticking and tocking our evening away

BOTH
  Which we've hoped for
    and longed for all day.

  Hurry to work and hurry to play,
    Youth must hurry at headlong pace,
  Seizing and squeezing the pleasures of life
    In a cheerful
      and fearful embrace.

SID [*urgently*]
Give us a kiss, Nancy–!

NANCY
Not here in the light!

SID
Kiss me . . .

NANCY
Windows have eyes!

SID
Kiss me . . .
[*A long passionate kiss. Albert emerges from the shadow with horror and embarrassment. The kiss over, they go quickly and happily off, their voices dying away down the street*]

BOTH
  Time is a glutton, Time is a thief,
    Youth must challenge him as he flies,

Catching and snatching its dreams of delight
  Between eight and
    eleven at night!
[*Nancy and Sid have gone. Albert comes out fully into the light;
indignation, excitement and embarrassment combining in him in
a kind of nervous rage*]

ALBERT
'Heaven helps those who help themselves.'

'*Help myself!*' Oh go, go away
And leave me here alone
With doubts and terrors
You have never known . . .!

  Enjoy your evening as you will!
  Kiss and hug your fill! Embrace until
  The stars spin round like Catherine-wheels
  Against the rainbow-covered hills.
  Then hurry home at dawn,
  Proud of what you've done,
  And smile to think I slept alone!

Nancy pities me—Sid laughs—others snigger
At my simplicity—offer me buns
To stay in my cage—parade
Me around as their Whiteheaded Boy—

  Albert the Good! Albert who Should—!
  Albert who Hasn't and Wouldn't if he Could!
  Albert the Meek! Albert the Sheep!
  Mrs Herring's Guinea-Pig!
  Mrs Herring's Tillypig!
  Mrs Herring's —*Prig!*

But?—when?—
Shall I dare and dare again?
How shall I screw
My courage up to do
What must be done by everyone?
The tide will turn, the sun will set
While I stand here and hesitate.
The clock begins its rusty whirr,
Catches its breath to strike the hour
And offers me a final choice
That must be answered *No* or *Yes*.
[*A clinking in his pocket reminds him of the purse. He takes it
out*]
Forgotten those!—
My virgin ransom!

I'll toss for it—and damn the risk!
[*He picks one sovereign from the purse*]
Eeny, meeney, miney mo
Heads for *Yes* and Tails for *No*,
Tails for *No* and Heads for *Yes*—
Spin it up . . .
  . . . *HEADS!*
[*Reflectively*]
Well, you've gone and done it now!
It's very plain
You've burnt your boats
And can't go back again.

[*In sudden fear*] Oh golly! . . . . . .

[*Considering*] But how . . . . . .

[*Far, far down the street there is an echo of Sid's particular
whistle.*
*Albert listens, reflects, grins, and softly tries a whistle of his own
—an elaborate affair outdoing Sid's in trills and flourishes.
He practises it several times—then with sudden resolve, stuffs the
purse in his pocket, snatches his hat, puts an old mac on, goes to
the door, muffles the bell carefully while he opens, and slips
outside. We can see him outside the window, looking up and down
the street both ways before hurrying off. Far down the street, his
whistle rings out triumphant and clear.*
*After a short pause, the door opens and Mum comes in wearily,
locks up, pulls the blinds and goes to call gently at the inner door*]

MUM
  Albert! . . . . . Albert? [*no reply*]
    Fast asleep, poor kid!
    Worn out by all this fuss.
    Sleeping the sleep of the just
    And richer by twenty-five quid!
  [*Yawning*] Ooooaaah! I shan't need rocking myself!
    [*She trudges sleepily up to bed as the curtain slowly falls*]

END OF ACT II

Act three

[*The following afternoon, in the shop.*
*Nancy is alone, occupying herself by miserably polishing the
scales.*
*Suddenly the door clangs open and Emmie comes dashing in
noisily. She remembers, slows down abruptly and finishes the
entrance almost on tiptoe*]

EMMIE [*whispering*]
  Is she asleep?

NANCY
  How could she sleep?
  She's lying upstairs on her bed for a while.

EMMIE
  They've been phoning around to
  Ufford and Orford, Iken and Snape!

NANCY
  Where can he be—?

EMMIE
  Someone was saying
  It's *felo-de-se.*

NANCY
  Felo-de- what?

EMMIE
  Done himself in . . .!
  Unless he's been murdered!

NANCY
  Oh no—! *No*—!
  [*Cis pops her head in through the door*]

CIS
  Come on, Emmie! Got your compass?—
    [*Cis runs on past the shop excitedly*]

EMMIE
  I'm running off now

To join in the hunt
Round Hasketon Hall
With the Peewit Patrol
Ta-ta!
[*Emmie dashes out importantly. Nancy, left by herself, gives way to her unhappiness*]

NANCY
What would Mrs Herring say?
What would everybody think?–
If they knew the trick we played
Giving Albert rum to drink?
  We did it for fun
  Oh we shouldn't have done!
[*Down the street there is a piercing blast on a whistle, and the Mayor's voice is heard shouting*]

MAYOR [*off*]
Hi–i–I! Don't forget the *splints*–!

NANCY
Now he's vanished overnight,
Disappeared without a trace,
And I bitterly regret
What I did in thoughtlessness.
  We did it for fun
  Oh we shouldn't have done!
[*Harry suddenly appears at the window and shouts in*]

HARRY
They're dragging the millpond! With ropes and ruddy great hooks!–
[*He runs on again. Nancy almost breaks down*]

NANCY
Bring him back! Oh bring him back!
Safe and sound in life and limb.
Mrs Herring's heart will break
Losing him–losing him.
  We did it for fun
  Oh we shouldn't have done!
[*Sid arrives, irritable and very muddy round the ankles, shouting back to someone as he comes in*]

SID
What the hell d'you think I am? A human blood-hound?

NANCY
Sid! Thank goodness you've come!

SID
I've spent the whole blooming day
Splashing around,
Up to the neck in water and clay–
  And for all that I found . . .

NANCY
Not . . .!?

SID
. . . one maggotty sheep
Lying dead on the ground!

NANCY
Thank Heavens!

SUPER [*shouting off*]
Any more news about Albert . . .?

MAYOR [*off*]
No . . .!

SID
I'm hungry, I'm tired,
I'm sick of the sound
Of *Albert! Albert! Albert!* all round!

NANCY [*angry*]
You're heartless and selfish and thoughtless and cruel!
No conscience or feelings of kindness at all!
You've ruined poor Albert, you've ruined his Mum,
And I hope you're contented with what you have done!

SID
He isn't the first and he won't be the last
To throw up his heels and kick over the mark!
But why carry on as if Albert had gone
On a one-way excusion to Kingdom Come?

NANCY
Excuses are useless, so don't try them on!
I'm certain as certain we did what was wrong.
I'm sorry we did it–I'm sorry I helped you!
In future, I'll leave you to do things yourself.

SID
You're talking as though I had done all I could
To wipe out the family of Herrings for good!
But all I intended and all that I planned
Was giving young Albert a brotherly hand.
[*The Super comes in with a harrassed air, like one beset with many fools*]

SUPER
Mrs Herring about?

NANCY
She's resting.

SUPER
Ask her down . . . official business . . . won't keep her long.
[*Nancy goes, glad to escape for a moment*]

SID
How's the manhunt?

SUPER [*venting his pent-up irritation*]
Give me a decent murder with a corpse
Give me a clear-cut case of arson
Give me a robbery with force
Or a criminal case of rape.
But God preserve me from these
                          disappearing cases,
Where everyone from the baker to the
                          Nonconformist parson
Turns Sherlock Holmes
And pokes around finding evidence
                          in most unlikely places!

HARRY [*through door*]
Super! Lady Billows wants
you up at her house! Immediate!

SUPER
Lady Billows . . .! Self-appointed Chief Constable!
[*Nancy comes back, supporting Mrs Herring, who is led to a chair, and settled gently with her grief. She is dressed in deep black. Albert's disappearance has knocked all the stuffing out of her*]

MUM
Have you found him?

SUPER
Not yet—

MUM
He's dead and gone, poor Albert's dead and gone . . .

NANCY
Don't say that!

MUM
It's the living truth!—
Dead and gone
In the pride of his youth!

SUPER
I've come to ask
For a photograph
To send round the stations
For identification.

MUM
There's one in a frame
On the whatsisname—
Above the Bible
On the tulipwood table.

[Nancy goes out to fetch it]

MUM
It was took on the Pier at Felixstowe
When his Dad was alive, in a studio—
We paid three-and-six to have it enlarged,
And another three bob for the frame and the glass.
[Nancy returns carrying a large photo of Albert When Young, in bathing-pants and straw-hat, scowling and clutching a bucket and spade. Mum seizes it to her bosom hungrily]

MUM
It's all I have to remember him by!—
All that is left of my darling boy—
All, all, all that remains
Of the baby I bore with such pains!
[The Mayor appears outside the window, and signals to attract attention. The Super and Sid see him and slip out unnoticed by Mum, who is absorbed with her grief]

QUARTET

MUM
All that I did,
All that I planned
Was building in sand,
   For Albert my boy is dead!

Where did he go?
Why was he took?
Wherever I look
The world is full of bitter woe.

Life's become bleak
Life's become bare
Without Albert here
   To ease and relieve my grief.

NANCY
He'll come back again, my dear,
He'll come back to you, I swear,
Trust in that and never fear.

He'll come back before tonight,
He'll repent his sudden flight,

He'll return—you'll see I'm right!
[The Vicar and Miss Wordsworth arrive together to see Mrs Herring]

MISS WORDSWORTH AND VICAR *[joining in quietly and with feeling]*
A grievous torment for a Mother's heart!
A bitter blow to bear alone—
We come to comfort you and ease the smart
With crumbs of Christian consolation.
[Harry thrusts his head violently through the window again]

HARRY *[loudly]*
Hi! *Hi!* Heard the news? There's a Big White Something in Mrs William's well!!!

MUM *[rising]*
Oh God! It's *him* . . .!

NANCY
No . . .! No . . .! I'm sure it isn't him—
[Nancy runs to help Mum as she collapses]

MISS WORDSWORTH AND VICAR
In such an hour
We scarcely dare pretend
We have the power
To help our friend . . .
[Lady Billows surges in—energetic, ruthless, noisy—with Florence behind her]

LADY BILLOWS
Fools! Blundering fools! Budd's the worst!
   I'll ring up Scotland Yard myself!
We must have experts down to help.
A detective-inspector—won't accept less—
Dispatched by the Liverpool Street Express.

NANCY
The Saxmundham Police are out . . .

LADY BILLOWS
Yokels . . .!

VICAR
And the Wickham Market Militia . . .

LADY BILLOWS
Bumpkins—!

MISS WORDSWORTH
If only they could *find* him . . .

LADY BILLOWS
Find him? I'd soon find the wretched boy!
Modern methods—that's what we need. Bloodhounds
   . . . fingerprints . . . electro-magnets . . . water diviners!
Call in Conan Doyle—telegraph the Strand
Magazine . . .! He'll bring him back, dead or alive.

FLORENCE
The whole of the district from Loxford to Ipswich
   Is seeking and searching in vain:
And running around without reason or rhyme,
Wasting their energy, money and time;
Poking their noses into each other's houses,
Snatching at clues that simply confuse
And starting new rumours to keep up the game!

LADY BILLOWS AND FLORENCE
A crisis like this can't be left to the locals.
We must call on expert advice.

[*At this moment the Mayor, the Super and Sid cross the window. They come seriously in through the door. The Mayor is carrying a tray covered with a white cloth.*
Everyone responds to the gravity of the situation. Sid fetches a box for the tray to go on, while Nancy shuts the door and pulls the shop-blind.
Mrs Herring rises in terror, supported by the Vicar and Miss Wordsworth. All are silent, fearing to speak. The Mayor, with infinite pity, looks at Mum, then uncovers the tray. The Super removes his helmet. On the tray sits the little wreath of orange-blossom from Albert's hat, soiled and dirty]

MUM [*screaming*]
My Albert's wreath . . .!
[*She faints*]

MAYOR [*sombrely*]
Found on the road to Campsey Ash . . .

SUPER
Crushed by a cart . . .
[*All draw slowly around the wreath in pitiful homage*]

THRENODY [*sung quietly, simply and with intense feeling*]

ALL
In the midst of life is Death.
Death awaits us one and all.
Death attends our smallest step,
Silent, swift and merciful.

Individual verses, sung above the refrain

VICAR
Sigh for youth that scorns to die
And leaps into eternity
With innocent simplicity.

NANCY
Why was he born who had to run
So short a race and die so young–?
Foredoomed to fall before begun.

MAYOR
He died too soon: Death came before
His bud had blossomed into flower–
And we shall see his like no more.

LADY BILLOWS
Weep for him, whose simple fame
Shone clearly like a candle-flame
Blown bright by the wind, then out again.

SUPER
Heavy-hearted, we ask why
He was chosen for to die–?
But Death's not given to reply.

FLORENCE
These flowers were a joyful sight
And shone with purity and light,
Till Death struck at them overnight.

MISS WORDSWORTH
Yesterday these flowers were fresh
With gaiety and loveliness–
To-day they fade to ugliness.

SID
The grave's a fine and private place
But horribly cold and horribly chaste,
And not attractive to my taste.

MUM
Albert! Albert! My only son!
Flesh of my flesh–Bone of my bone!
Let me die too, now you are gone!

ALL
In the midst of life is Death.
Death awaits us one and all.
He beckons us with every breath
We take, and does not hesitate
To strike the humble or the great.

ALL
Grief is silent, Pity dumb,–
Despair exclaims in endless pain–
That one so fine should live in vain
And die so young.
[*At the climax of the Threnody, Albert, who has been watching through the cautiously-opened top-door in some bewilderment, pushes open the door with a TING! and stands silently there . . . dirty, dishevelled and stained with mud. All are horrified at his interruption and his looks*]

ALL
ALBERT . . .!

ALBERT
What's going on?

ALL [*in furious and righteous indignation*]
Where have you come from? Where have you been?
Wrecking the whole of our daily routine!
Tearing the town from its regular labours
To run up and down and around with the
    neighbours–
Looking for clues, longing for news,
Inspecting, accepting, rejecting reports
That you had been kidnapped, or murdered–or
    worse–
For the twenty-five sovereigns you had in your purse!

ALBERT [*rather inadequately*]
Er . . . I'm sorry about that.
[*His remark is the spark to a powder-magazine*]

LADY BILLOWS
Sorry!?? Sorry!?? He's says he's *SORRY!!!*
As though a *Sorry* could repay
The agony and worry
He has caused us all to-day!

MISS WORDSWORTH, FLORENCE AND NANCY
Where exactly have you been?

MAYOR, VICAR AND SID
Tell us that!

SUPER
Where have you been?

MUM [*balefully*]
Wait till I'm alone with you!
[*Albert is silent. At a signal from Lady Billows, the Vicar steps forward to question him*]

VICAR [*icily*]
You left this house at eight last night?
[*Nod–Yes*]

LADY BILLOWS
Where exactly did you go?
[*No reply*]

FLORENCE
Slipped through the streets and out of sight?
[*Nod–Yes*]

MAYOR AND MISS WORDSWORTH
Were you alone?–Say 'Yes' or 'No'.

ALBERT
Yes.

LADY BILLOWS
Did you remain alone for long?
[*Nod–No*]

VICAR
You met some friends?
[*Nod–No*]

MISS WORDSWORTH
                    Acquaintances?

[*Nod–Yes*]

FLORENCE
Male?
[*Nod–Yes*]

MAYOR
And female?
[*Nod–Yes*]

NANCY
            Oh don't go on!

SUPER
And did you stay with them?–

ALBERT
                    Well, *yes*!

LADY BILLOWS
When you left home, you took with you
Twenty-five sovereigns–

FLORENCE
                In gold–

[*Nod–Yes*]

MUM
How many's left?

ALBERT
            I've twenty-two

MAYOR
So three have disappeared all told!

ALBERT
Yes.

MISS WORDSWORTH
Were they stolen from you?
]*Nod–No*]

SUPER
                    Lost, d'you think?

[*Nod–No*]

MUM
Did you spend three pounds yourself?
[*Nod–Yes*]

VICAR
                        At a shop?

[*Nod–No*]

LADY BILLOWS
At a public-house?
[*Nod–Yes*]

FLORENCE
                All that on *drink*?

[*Nod–No*]

MAYOR
How *did* you spend it?

NANCY AND SID [*breaking in*]
                    For goodness' sake, stop!
Stop prying and poking and probing at him
With your pious old faces delighting in Sin!

OTHERS
We must persist
And insist
On the truth–
However bad it is.

LADY BILLOWS [*bullying*]
Where did that three pounds go?
Tell us the truth!

OTHERS
The truth! At once! Tell us the whole truth!
And nothing but the truth . . .!

ALBERT [*beginning quietly and warming up slowly*]
I can't remember everything but what I can
I'll tell you plain and straight.–It all began
'Cos I suddenly thought it was time I ought
To try a taste of certain things
The Prayer Book catalogues among its sins.
Curiosity killed the cat, they say! Well, if you
    like,
It was curiosity made me pinch a bike
And pedal away to town last night.
Drink was my first experiment. I found a pub,
Ordered some old-and-mild, and drank it up.
Beer tasted queer, so my next idea was rum–
A tumblerful of naval rum, with whisky and gin
    to wash it down!
Before very long, I was pretty far gone–
Reeling about, beginning to shout,
Disgustingly drunk!–a nuisance to everyone!–
So they threw me out of *The Dog and Duck*
To lie in the gutter and sober up!

ALL [*except Nancy and Sid*]
Impossible! Drunk and disorderly? Our May King?

ALBERT
Then I staggered along to the four-ale bar
Of *The Horse and Groom*, which isn't far–
Started a fight 'cos they said I was tight,
Butted the publican, fell on the floor,–
And ended up in the gutter once more!

ALL
Horrible! Stop him! This is revolting! Stop, stop, stop!

ALBERT
You wanted the truth! Do you want some more?
Or will that do as a general sample
Of a night that was a nightmare example
Of drunkenness, dirt, and worse . . . . . .?

MUM
    But how could you do it? How *could* you?

ALBERT [*turning on Mum*]
    You know what drove me . . .!
    You know how I could . . .!
      It was all because
      You squashed me down and reined me in,
      Did up my instincts with safety-pins,
      Kept me wrapped in cotton-wool,
      Measured my life with a twelve-inch rule,–
      Protected me with such devotion
      My only way-out was a wild explosion!

ALL
    Monstrous . . .!

ALBERT
    I've done it now–it wasn't much fun–
    But sooner or later it had to come.

NANCY AND SID
    Good old Albert!

ALBERT
    And I'm more than grateful to you all
    For kindly providing the wherewithal.

ALL
    Preposterous! Wicked boy! He needs a good thrashing!
    Fancy! Young oaf! Turning against his Mother . . .!

ALBERT
    And now I shall take it extremely kind
    If you'll let me get on.

LADY BILLOWS
    You will pay! You will pay
    For your night's holiday–!
    You will pay for your sins of the flesh!
    You will creep to the shade
    Of a profligate's grave–
    A disgrace to your name and your sex!

ALBERT
    Good day, your Ladyship,
    Please let me get on, for I'm all behind.

LADY BILLOWS [*furious*]
    Faugh!
    [*Lady Billows sweeps out in disgust, followed by Florence, the Vicar, Miss Wordsworth, the Mayor and the Super. Albert politely holds the door for them. Mum boils over as they go and attacks Albert in tearful fury*]

MUM
    I'll never forgive you! Not till my dying day!

ALBERT [*facing up to her fair and square*]
                  That'll do, Mum–!

[*Mum gasps, bursts into a wail of sobbing, and flounders noisily off into the house.
Albert has one moment of doubt and turns questioningly to Sid and Nancy*]

ALBERT
    ? . . . I didn't lay it on *too* thick, did I...??
    [*Nancy impulsively throws her arms round him and gives him a smacking kiss, to his complete surprise and astonishment*]

SID
    Hi! That's *my* girl!
    [*Albert, on the recoil, takes the orange-blossom wreath and lets the shop-blind up with a bang to throw it out into the street. The three kids are standing there. When they see Albert, they begin a tentative and half-hearted version of their old song*]

KIDS
    Albert's Mum
    Took a stick
    Whacked him on the thingmijig . . .!
    [*For a moment it is not certain if Albert won't make a dive at them. But he suddenly smiles and invites them in*]

ALBERT
    All right! Come on in! All of you.
    [*The kids obey and creep cautiously and shyly in, not certain what will happen next.
Albert picks up the basket of peaches and offers it*]

ALBERT
    Have a nice peach . . .? Go on! Help yourselves!
    There's plenty for everyone! Put some more in your pockets!
    [*They help themselves eagerly and sing a new version of their song, with Nancy and Sid joining in, while Albert hands fruit all round*]

ALL
      Albert's come
      Back to stay
      Better for his holiday!
      Let's all say
      Hip-hip-hooray!
      Good luck to him, anyway!

ALBERT
    It's nice to be home again.

SID [*picking up the wreath of orange-blossom*]
    Hi! You'd better frame this.

ALBERT
    Chuck it over!
    [*Sid throws the wreath to Albert, who catches it and skims it out over the heads of the audience*]

ALL
    Jolly good riddance!

The Little Sweep

A children's opera in three scenes

by Eric Crozier

BENJAMIN BRITTEN OP. 45

CHARACTERS

Black Bob *a brutal sweep-master*   BASS

Clem *his son and assistant*   TENOR

Sam *their new sweep-boy, aged 8*   TREBLE

Miss Baggott *the housekeeper at Iken Hall*   CONTRALTO

Juliet Brook *aged 14*   SOPRANO

Gay Brook *aged 13*   *the children of Iken Hall*   TREBLE

Sophie Brook *aged 10*   SOPRANO

Rowan *nursery-maid to the Crome cousins*   SOPRANO

Jonny Crome *aged 15*   TREBLE

Hughie Crome *aged 8*   TREBLE

Tina Crome *aged 8*   SOPRANO

*Tom *the coachman*   BASS

*Alfred *gardener at Iken Hall*   TENOR

(*These two parts are doubled with Black Bob and Clem)

The action takes place in the children's nursery at Iken Hall, Suffolk, in the year 1810. The room is large and gaily-decorated, and has two doors, a window and a fireplace. There is a toy-cupboard, an armchair, and a rocking-horse. The room is swathed in dust-sheets, but these will be cleared away before Scene two.

FIRST PERFORMANCE

14 June 1949   *Aldeburgh, Jubilee Hall*

     (E.O.G. production)

Black Bob	Norman Lumsden
Clem	Max Worthley
Sam	John Moules
Miss Baggott	Gladys Parr
Juliet Brook	Anne Sharp
Gay Brook	Bruce Hines
Sophie Brook	Monica Garrod
Rowan	Elizabeth Parry
Jonny Crome	Peter Cousins
Hugh Crome	Ralph Canham
Tina Crome	Mavis Gardiner

Conducted by Norman del Mar

Produced by Basil Coleman

Scenery and costumes designed by John Lewis

Foreword by Eric Crozier

Benjamin Britten and I contemplated writing a children's opera for several years, but it was not until autumn 1948, when we had successfully launched the first Aldeburgh Festival of Music and the Arts, that finding a subject became urgent. One afternoon Britten asked: 'What about Blake's poems—the chimney-sweep?' We hastened to read the two short lyrics that William Blake had written and illustrated (and also printed, hand-coloured and published) in his *Songs of Innocence and of Experience*, 1794. Both were entitled *The Chimney Sweeper*. The first begins 'When my mother died I was very young . . .': the second, 'A little black thing among the snow Crying "*weep!*" "*weep!*" in notes of woe . . .'

Here was our subject, if ever there was one. By that evening we had planned the structure, the action and the characters of a short opera in three scenes. We chose Iken Hall for the setting because it was a large rambling farm-house on a lonely stretch of the river Alde where occasionally we went to visit friends: we took our children ready-made from the sons, daughters and nephews of other friends living at Great Glemham. To them, we added a quintet of professional singers. We also decided that since the audience had responded so enthusiastically to the challenge of singing two hymns in our cantata *Saint Nicolas* at the first Aldeburgh Festival, we would rely on them as chorus.

All this, it must be remembered, was a long time ago. The Aldeburgh Festival was in its infancy, and the idea of an opera for children and audience to perform then seemed highly original. To fill out the evening, we resolved to preface *The Little Sweep* with a play showing children and grown-ups getting ready to perform the opera that they had supposedly written—which would have the added advantage of allowing time for the conductor to rehearse the audience in their songs.

This preliminary play served its purpose at the time, but it does not wear so well as the opera. Ideally, it should be rewritten to suit the local circumstances and characters of any group performing *The Little Sweep*. If the opera alone is to be performed, without the play, it should still be preceded by a short rehearsal of the audience songs.

Scene one

SONG ONE

AUDIENCE

[to be sung before the curtain rises]
1   Sweep! Sweep!
    Saddle your donkey and set on your way!
    There's chimneys need sweeping at Iken today
    Bring brushes and scrapers and baskets and sacks
    To harvest the soot from our chim-in-ey stacks.

2   Black Bob is coming and with him his lad,
    A sullen apprentice as black as his Dad,
    Their cries as they ride through the sharp morning air
    Set partridges drumming and startle the hare.

3   Sam is the white boy, and sweep is his job,
    His father has sold him to cruel Black Bob.
    Today is his black day: today he must climb
    A chim-in-ey stack for the very first time.

4   Snape lies behind them, and over the bridge
    They strike to the left by a narrowing ridge;
    Then follow the wandering dyke where it leads
    Through thickets of rushes and tussocks of reeds.
    [The curtain rises, showing the nursery of Iken Hall. The Sweeps enter, singing]

BLACK BOB AND CLEM
1   Sweep! Sweep!
    Saddle your donkey and set on your way!
    There's chimneys need sweeping at Iken today.
    Bring brushes and scrapers and baskets and sacks
    To harvest the soot from our chim-in-ey stacks.
    [Miss Baggott, the housekeeper, follows the Sweeps into the room. She is elderly and sharp-tongued. Black Bob is the sweep-master, sullen and oafish, carrying a great coil of ropes.
    His son Clem carries an armful of brushes and sacks.
    Last of all comes Sam, looking miserable and tearstained, with three buckets on each arm and a coil of rope slung across his chest. He looks very small and white beside the others. Rowan, the nursery-maid, who is laying dust-sheets over the furniture, is shocked by his wretchedness.
    During the following Quartet, Miss Baggott gives impatient orders, Rowan watches the unhappy Sam, and the two Sweeps assemble their tools]

QUARTET

MISS BAGGOTT
    Sweep this chimney, then next door!
    Hurry, Rowan! don't stand gaping!
    Four more chimneys on this floor.
    Give them all a thorough scraping!

    Filthy rascals, don't you dare
    Spread your soot around my attics!
    Lawks-a-mercy, I declare
    Sweeps are worse than the rheumatics!

ROWAN *[of Sam]*
    Small and white and stained with tears,
    Wrapped in scarecrow rags and patches,
    Faint with terror, full of fears,
    Wretched child whom sorrow catches.

    Torn from play and sold for pay,
    Taught a trade with kicks and curses,
    What can he do but obey–
    Meekly glad of little mercies?

BLACK BOB AND CLEM
    Chimbley-sweepers must 'ave boys,
    Same as poachers must 'ave ferrets.
    Brushes, rods and suchlike toys
    Can't compete with 'uman merits.

    Choose 'em nimble, spry and thin–
    That's the chap for chimbley-sweeping!
    Easy, too, for breaking in,
    Bar a bit of tears and weeping.

SPOKEN DIALOGUE

MISS BAGGOTT
    Hurry, Rowan! Sheets next door!
    [She hurries off]

ROWAN
    Mister Sweep! for mercy's sake, don't send that little white boy up the chimney! He's weeping for fear!

BLACK BOB
    Fear–? Lor' bless you, them's tears of gratitude! He's aching for it, ain't you, Sam?
    [Bob and Clem laugh horribly. Rowan runs from the room in distress. In the next duet the Sweeps turn menacingly on Sam, pull off his clothes, tie a rope round his waist, and despite his struggles, drag him over to the hearth]

DUET

BLACK BOB AND CLEM
    Now, little white boy!
    Shiver-with-fright boy!
    Scared-in-the-night boy!
      Time for your climb!

    Clothes off, my bright boy!
    Don't kick or fight, boy!
    Oh! so you'd bite, boy–?
      Time for your climb!

    Pull the rope tight, boy!
    Kiss us goodnight, boy!
    Climb out of sight, boy!
      Time for your climb!
    [They have lifted poor Sam to the mouth of the chimney to catch the first climbing-rung. Bob hastens him with a terrifying shout]

BLACK BOB *[shouting]*
    Scrape that flue clean, or I'll roast you alive!
    [Sam's legs hurriedly disappear up the flue]

    When he comes back, boy!–
    He'll be a black boy!
    Scraper-and-sack boy!
    Crawl-through-a-crack boy!
    A chimbley stack boy!
    Covered with grime!
    [The Sweeps collect their tools, and go out laughing.
    The room is empty. Only the rope dangling in the hearth shows that the chimney is occupied. There is a distant sound of children's voices]

HIDE AND SEEK

CHILDREN
Juliet! we're coming!
[*The door opens gently. Juliet slips in, shuts it carefully behind her and crosses to an armchair covered with a dust-sheet. Nearer cries from the children*]

BOYS [*far*]
Try the apple room—!

GIRLS [*far*]
No! the linen cupboard—!

TWINS [*near*]
Wait for us!
[*Juliet slips into the chair beneath the sheet. The door flies suddenly open and the Twins pop their heads in*]

TWINS [*speaking*]
She's not in here!

SOPHIE [*far*]
Hughie! Tina!

SOPHIE [*far*]
Tina—!

TWINS
Wait for US—!
[*They disappear hurriedly. Juliet pokes her head above the sheet, emerges and approaches the door. It begins slowly to open. She scurries back to her hiding-place as Jonny peeps in. He makes for her chair*]

CHILDREN [*far*]
Harness-room—!
[*Jonny pulls the sheet from the chair, revealing Juliet*]

JONNY [*speaking*]
Caught you!

JULIET [*speaking*]
Quick, Jonny! You hide, too!
There's lots of room for me and you!
[*They both hide in the chair with the sheet over them*]

CHILDREN [*far*]
Jonny! Jonny! Where ARE you—?
[*Giggles from underneath the sheet. Suddenly the rope in the fireplace begins to waggle violently, and Sam shouts*]

SAM [*from the chimney*]
Help! Help! I'm stuck!

JULIET AND JONNY [*showing themselves*]
What's that?

SAM [*from the chimney*]
Help! Pull me down!

JULIET
It's a sweep-boy!

JONNY
In the flue!

CHILDREN [*near*]
Jonny! Jonny! Where are *you?*

SAM [*from the chimney*]
Help! Help!

JULIET
Call the others quickly, Jon!

CHILDREN [*bursting into the nursery*]
Here we are! What's going on?

JULIET AND JONNY
Sssh!

SAM [*from the chimney*]
Help! I'm suffocating!

JULIET
Pull him down!

JONNY
It's no good waiting!
[*All the children move to the fireplace. Juliet calls up the chimney*]

JULIET
Hold very tight, and don't let go!
We'll pull the rope from down below!
[*The children pick up the rope, ready to pull*]

BOYS
Ready?

SAM [*from the chimney*]
Ready!

SHANTY

ALL CHILDREN
Pull the rope gently until he is free!
    Pull O! Heave O!
Pull the rope gently until he is free!
    Pull O! Heave O!

SAM [*from the chimney*]
No good!

JULIET
Pull harder this time—but not *too* hard!

ALL
    Pull the rope harder and give a good heave!
    Pull O! Strongly O!
    Pull the rope harder and give a good heave!
    Pull O! Strongly O!

SAM [*tearfully*]
I'm still stuck!

JULIET
Try once more!

ALL
Pull the rope smartly with one two three jerk!
    One two, three, jerk!
    Pull the rope smartly with one two three jerk!
    One, two, three, JERK—

SAM
Owwwwwwwwww!!!!!!!!!
[*With a loud scream, Sam descends in an avalanche of soot and stones, and lies flat in the hearth*]

CHILDREN [*scared*]
Oooooohhhh—!!!!

TWINS AND SOPHIE
You've killed him!
[*The children anxiously surround Sam and lift him, bringing out their handkerchiefs to wipe his tears. He is desperate with grief and fear*]

ENSEMBLE

CHILDREN
>Is he wounded? Pease forgive us!
>Are you very much in pain?
>All we wanted was to help you.

SAM
>*Please* don't send me up again!

CHILDREN
>Poor young boy! He's just a baby!
>Weak with toil and wan with strain.
>Fancy making him sweep chimneys!

SAM
>*Please* don't send me up again!

CHILDREN
>Will Miss Baggott let us keep him?
>No, she won't! We'd ask in vain.
>She'd betray him to his master.

SAM
>*Please* don't send me up again!

CHILDREN
>Can't we rescue him from sweeping?
>Hide him safe? And not explain
>Till the sweeps have gone and left him?

SAM
>*Please* don't send me up again!

CHILDREN
>*We* won't give you up again!

RECITATIVE

GAY
>Hide him *here*, among our toys!

JONNY
>Room enough for twenty boys!

OTHERS
>Quickly, then!

JULIET
>>But wait! I say!–
>*They* must think he's run away!

SOPHIE
>Through the window!

TWINS
>>Down the creeper!

BOYS
>Come on, little chimney-sweeper!
>[*The children escort Sam across the room, planting his feet to make tracks on the sheets, while Hughie and Tina stretch the rope with its empty noose pointing towards the window*]

MARCHING SONG

CHILDREN
>Sooty tracks upon the sheet,
>Sooty marks of sooty feet,
>Soot upon the window-seat
>>Make our evidence complete!

>Soot upon the window-sill,
>Soot applied with loving skill,

Soot to blind their eyes, until
>>They'll never see he's with us still!

>Clamber up and smudge the brick!
>Just a little–not too thick!
>There's our disappearing trick...!
>>Someone's coming!
>>>Hide him!
>>>>QUICK!...
>[*The children carry Sam swiftly to the toy-cupboard, bundle him inside, snatch up his ragged clothes, and dive under the shrouded furniture, just as Miss Baggott enters, followed by Bob and Clem, with Rowan behind them*]

SPOKEN DIALOGUE

MISS BAGGOTT
>Quarter-past eleven! Hurry, you idlers! Attics next!

BLACK BOB
>Yaps just like a little old fox-terrier!

CLEM
>Real old blunderbuss, ain't she!

MISS BAGGOTT
>What's this–? Window open–?
>[*They observe the signs of Sam's disappearance*]

MARCHING SONG [*repeated as Trio*]

MISS BAGGOTT, BLACK BOB, CLEM
>Sooty-tracks–upon–the–sheet...
>Soot–upon the–window-seat...
>Sooty-rope and–sooty-noose...
>>After him! Young Sammy's loose...!
>[*Bob runs to the hearth and gives a blood-curdling yell*]

BLACK BOB
>S–A–M————!!!
>[*There is no answer*]

CLEM
>S–A–M————!!!

TRIO FURIOSO

MISS BAGGOTT, BLACK BOB, CLEM
>Wait until we catch him; we'll whip him till he howls!
>We'll teach him to run off and leave his duty!
>Chain him up and kennel him; keep him with the fowls!
>And mortify his pride, the little beauty!
>[*The Sweeps turn and run off, shouting furiously. Miss Baggott follows, calling them back*]

BLACK BOB
>I'll give him *Run Away!* I'll keel-haul 'im round Snape Bridge!

CLEM
>Lily-livered toad! Tar an' feather him!

MISS BAGGOTT
>Come back, you blackguards! Six more chimneys! come back...!
>[*The Sweeps and Miss Baggott have gone. Rowan, thinking herself alone, gives way to her distress for Sammy.*]

SONG

ROWAN

Run, poor sweepboy! Run much faster!
Run with all your might and main!
Close behind you comes your master,
Mad to bring you back again.

Far along the frozen river,
Sharp across the frosty air,
Distant echoes make Sam shiver,
Fill his heart with new despair.

Run, poor boy! O do not slacken!
Black Bob follows swift behind.
See his angry features blacken!
Rage and fury make him blind.

How I wish that I could save you!
I would hide you far away
From those tyrants who enslave you
And torment you day by day!

[*During the last verse of this song the children's heads emerge from under their coverings, unnoticed by Rowan. They watch her in admiration. She gives a gasp of surprise when she realises that they are watching. They stand up and beam at her*]

RECITATIVE

JONNY
Dear Rowan . . .!

SOPHIE
Dear, dear Rowan . . .!

JULIET
Dearest Rowan . . .!

GAY
Dearest, darling Rowan . . .!

TWINS
Dear, dearest, darlingest Rowan . . .!

ROWAN
What does this mean?

CHILDREN [*mysteriously*]
Sssssssh!!

[*They open the cupboard door and beckon. Sam pokes out a timid and very sooty head*]

SPOKEN DIALOGUE

ROWAN
Goodness gracious me! The Little Sweep!

CHILDREN
OUR Little Sweep!

ROWAN
But whatever will Miss Baggott say to him?

GAY
She doesn't know . . .

JONNY
She needn't know . . .

JULIET
And she's *not* to know!

TWINS
He's a Secret!

ROWAN
But what are you going to do with him?

TWINS
Feed him . . .!

SOPHIE
The poor boy's hungry.

JULIET
You see, Rowan, we can't possibly hand him over to those horrible sweeps, can we . . .?
[*Rowan hesitates, so the children answer for her*]

CHILDREN
No—!

JULIET
. . .we can't possibly tell mama, 'cos she's away . . .

GAY
Seeing papa off to join his ship!

JULIET
. . .we can't possibly tell Miss Baggott . . .

TWINS
'Cos she'd turn him out of the house!

JULIET
. . .so you are the only grown-up we can tell!

ROWAN
That's all very well for you, Miss Juliet, and for Master Gay and Miss Sophie, I daresay, but you must remember that your cousins and I are only visitors in your house . . .

JULIET [*interrupting*]
Never mind about cousins and visitors! This is our latest visitor, and when you have a visitor who is cold and hungry and covered with soot from top to toe, what do you do with him . . .?

TWINS
BATH him–!

GAY
Of course you do!

SOPHIE
But what about Miss Baggott?

JONNY
Oh, bother Miss Baggott!

ROWAN
You need not worry for a little. I saw her crossing the courtyard in her clogs.

JONNY
Hooray! She's following the sweeps!

GAY
That gives us an hour to play with . . .

ROWAN
I'm sure I don't know if you are doing right, Miss Juliet . . .

JULIET [*firmly*]
Look at him!–*Does* he need a bath, or doesn't he?

CHILDREN
Yes!

ROWAN
Would you like to have a bath, Sammy?

SAM
Yes, please, Miss!

JULIET
Then you go and fill the buckets, Rowan . . .

ROWAN
There's warm water on the hob . . .

TWINS
We'll fetch the bath from the attic . . .!

SOPHIE
I'll get some clothes from Jonny's box . . .!

JONNY
I'll carry water . . .!

GAY
I'll light the fire . . .!

JULIET
I'll fetch soap and towels . . .! Is that all clear?

ALL
Yes!

JULIET
Then you stay in your cupboard, Sammy, and in five
minutes we'll all be back for the Grand Transformation
Scene!

ALL
Come on—!
[*The children scatter eagerly as the curtain falls*]

END OF SCENE ONE

Interlude

SONG TWO

[*The Conductor invites the Audience to sing the Song of Sam's
Bath*]

AUDIENCE
1   The kettles are singing
       Like midsummer larks,
    The fire is flinging
       A shower of sparks:
    The children run flying
       To fetch what they're bidden,
    For washing and drying
       The sweep-boy they've hidden.

2   They hurry upstairs to
       The nursery hearth,
    Where Rowan prepares to
       Give Sammy his bath:
    With brushes to scrub him,
       With basins to flood him,
    With flannels to rub him,
       With soap-balls to sud him.

3   *Spa-lash!* in he plunges,
       And Rowan lets fly

With sopping-wet sponges
   And sparks in her eye!
She washes and rinses
   And scrubs willy-nilly,
Till poor Sammy winces
   But shines like a lily!

4   And now Sam is gleaming
       Like snow in the sun,
    While Rowan stands beaming
       To see her work done.
    So all who were frightened
       When Sam was benighted,
    Please see how he's whitened
       And show you're delighted!

Scene two

[*The curtain rises.*
All the children are watching the new Sam as he stands clutching
a towel and grinning. Rowan is on her knees beside him. The
children sing the following continuation of the Audience's song,
while Sam finishes drying]

CHILDREN AND ROWAN
5   O Sammy is whiter
       Than swans as they fly,
    O Sammy is brighter
       Than stars in the sky!

6   O Sam is as fair as
       The white-foaming seas,
    Or spindrift in air, as
       Waves challenge the breeze.
    The hateful employment
       He suffered so blindly
    Gives way to enjoyment . .

SAM
             And THANK You all kindly!

SPOKEN DIALOGUE

ROWAN
Quick, children! We must tidy the room before Miss
Baggott comes back.

JULIET
Just one moment, Rowan! Tell me, Sammy, haven't you
any father or mother?

SAM
Yes, Miss.

GAY
Then where are they?

SAM
At home . . .

JONNY
Where's home?

SAM
Little Glemham.

ROWAN
Little Glemham?—But I come from near Glemham
myself! Whose boy are you?

SAM
Dad's name is Sparrow the waggoner.

ROWAN
Josiah Sparrow, from along the ten-acre field?

SAM
That's him, Miss.

JULIET
And he sold you to that wicked sweep . . .?

JONNY
Sold you . . .?

SOPHIE
For money . . .?

GAY
Sold his own son . . .?

TWINS
How *could* he...!

SAM
He didn't want to, but he broke his hip last threshing-time, and there wasn't anything to eat . . .

ROWAN
Poor man!

CHILDREN
Poor Sammy!

SAM
But it's time I began work, they say. I shall be nine next birthday.

CHILDREN [*shocked*]
Only nine . . .!
[*The children are dismayed and unhappy to hear what Sammy has told them. They turn sadly to their task of tidying the room and help Sam into the clean clothes they have found for him.*]

ENSEMBLE

CHILDREN, ROWAN AND SAM
O why do you weep
    Through the working day?
O why do you weep
    At your task, poor boy?
        Father and mother are far away.
        How shall I laugh and play?

O where is the home
    Where your life was gay?
O where is the home
    That you loved, poor boy?
        Home is a hundred miles away.
        How shall I laugh and play?

O what is that voice
    That you must obey?
O what is that voice
    That you fear, poor boy?
        Master is angry again today.
        How shall I laugh and play?

SPOKEN DIALOGUE

JONNY
    I have an idea!

JULIET
    What is it?

JONNY
    Rowan! when will you be packing our trunks?

ROWAN
    Tonight, when you are in bed.

JONNY
    Will you leave an empty space in the top of mine?

GAY
    I see! Put Sammy in the trunk . . .

JULIET
    And take him home with you!

SOPHIE
    Oh, yes!

TWINS
    Hooray!

ROWAN
    But he'll stifle in a trunk . . .!

GAY
    No, he won't.

JULIET
    You can let him out as soon as you are clear of the house.

ROWAN
    I can't think what your father and mother will say to him.

JONNY
    They'll help us, I'm positive they will!

ROWAN
    And where will you keep him for tonight?

GAY
    In the cupboard! It's the only place.

TWINS [*at the window*]
    Quick! Quick! She's coming!

JULIET
    Who's coming?

TWINS
    Miss Baggott!

GAY
    Where?

SOPHIE
    Through the garden gate!

ALL
    Hurry! Hide Sammy! Tidy the room!

HURRY MUSIC—PANTOMIME

[*Sam leaps into the toy-cupboard, Gay and Jonny carry the hip bath out, Sophie takes the towel horse, Rowan and Juliet whisk off the remaining dust-sheets.*
Then the children make a sedate tableau around the fire. The boys are reading, Rowan winds wool from a skein held by Juliet, the Twins are busy with a quiet game.
Miss Baggott comes up to the nursery in hat and boots, irritated, angry and tired, and eager to vent her indignation]

SCENA

MISS BAGGOTT

Ah! . . . Blackguards! Blackamoors! Brutes! . . . Oh! my
poor feet! [*she sits*] The vermin! All the way to Snape and
back! . . . Oh, my joints! . . . Never, *never*—in all my born
days! . . .'Come back!' says I, 'Come back and finish
your lawful work.' Their language! The insults! Drat the
sweeps,—for they that mock shall be a nay-word and a
by-word, and the good shall trample them underfoot! . . .
The insults! . . . Accused me, ME!, of hiding their beastly
boy! I'll hide him, if once I lay my hands on him!
[*Suspicious of the silence, she casts an eagle eye around her*]
Curtain's crooked, Rowan! Carelessness! Slap-dashery!
Help me up!
[*The children assist her to rise heavily from the chair. She moves
slowly round the room and inspects it*]

> Look at the creases in that curtain!
> > Look at the footprints on the floor!
> *You* haven't tidied up, that's certain.
> > Look at that filthy cupboard-door!
>
> Fireplace is grubby, fender *covered!*
> > Bother Black Bob and both his boys!
> Smudges of soot all round the cupboard!
> > Have you arranged the children's toys?
>
> Toys must be tidied up completely.
> > Come over here, you girls and boys!
> Open the door and pack them neatly.
> > Time that you tidied up your toys.

[*Miss Baggott moves determinedly towards the toy-cupboard,
and her hand is out-stretched to grasp the handle and open the
door.
The children are on tiptoe with alarm, when suddenly a loud and
penetrating sigh, like a pricked balloon, distracts her. She turns to
see Juliet collapse full-length on the floor*]

JULIET [*fainting*]
> Aaah ——— hhh!
[*All is confusion as they surround the prostrate girl*]

ENSEMBLE

MISS BAGGOTT
> Help! Help! She's collapsed!
> > A fit of the vapours!
> She's fainted! Stand back!
> > Fetch feathers and tapers!

ROWAN
> Quick! Lift up her head!
> > Rub her hands! Bring some water!
> We'll put her to bed!
> > How lucky you caught her!

CHILDREN [*kneeling reverently*]
> Poor Juliet's ill!
> > Look how she's lying!
> So silent and still—
> > Can she be dying?
>
> Her cheeks are so white—
> > Pale alabaster!
> Oh dear, what a sight!
> > What a disaster!

[*Juliet is lifted and carried into the next room by Rowan and
Miss Baggott, while the children frisk around in a frenzy of
excitement and relief*]

CHILDREN
> Blankets! Feathers! Warming-pan!
> Run as quickly as you can!
> Brandy! Sal volatile!
> Barley water! Cups of tea!
>
> Lift her legs!—no, keep her flat!
> Any simpleton knows that.
> Raise her head! Undo her frock!
> Cold for fever! Warmth for shock!

[*As Juliet disappears through the door among a crowd of over-
zealous helpers, Jonny opens the cupboard door, and calls out—*]

JONNY
> Sit tight, Sammy and tomorrow you're a free man!
[*The children dance with triumph at the way Juliet has saved
them*]

CHILDREN
> Juliet has won the day
> In a very simple way!
> Sam is safe—and he can stay
> In his hiding place—Hooray!
[*The curtain closes on them*]

END OF SCENE TWO

Interlude

SONG THREE

[*The Conductor invites the Audience to sing the Night Song*]

AUDIENCE

GROUP ONE
> The owl, wide-winging through the sky
> In search of mice and lesser fry,
> Repeats his loud, unhappy cry—
> > Tu-whoo! Tu-whoo!

GROUP TWO
> The heron listens, gaunt and still,
> Within his nest upon the hill,
> Then parts a stern and savage bill—
> > Kaah! Kaah!

GROUP THREE
> The turtle dove begins to stir,
> Removes the leaves that shelter her,
> And answers with melodious purr—
> > Prroo! Prroo!

GROUP FOUR
> The chaffinch and his mate rejoice
> To exercise their singing voice.
> They take the descant for their choice—
> > Pink! Pink! Pink!

ALL
> From North and South and East and West
> The birds compete for who sings best,
> But who shall choose the loveliest?
>
> Tu-whoo! Tu-whoo!
> Kaaah! Kaaah!   [*Loudly*]
> Proo! Proo!
> Pink! Pink! Pink!

The night is past, the owl is hoarse,
The finches slumber in the gorse,
The heron stoops, the turtle droops,–

Tu-whoo! Tu-whoo!
Kaaah! Kaaah!   [*Softly*]
Prroo! Prroo!
Pink! Pink! Pink!

Scene three

[*The curtain rises. The following morning. Rowan has just entered the nursery with a breakfast-tray for Juliet, who is wearing a warm quilted dressing-gown. She puts the tray down and they go to the cupboard to fetch Sammy*]

SPOKEN DIALOGUE

ROWAN
Breakfast, Sammy!

JULIET
Ham and eggs!

ROWAN
Stretch yourself–

JULIET
And kick your legs!

ROWAN
Only twenty minutes more
Till the coach is at the door!
[*Rowan hurries off again. Sam stretches himself*]

JULIET
Hungry, Sammy?

SAMMY
Oh yes, Miss!

JULIET
Eat away then, while I unstrap this trunk.
[*Sam sits at the table and begins to eat. Juliet unstraps the trunk, singing*]

SONG

JULIET
Soon the coach will carry you away
    And we shall wave Goodbye! and laugh to see
The little sweep we rescued yesterday
    Set off along the road to liberty.

Black you were, you poor unhappy mite,
    And very ugly too, I must confess!
Today you're guinea-bright and gleaming white,
    And radiant with joy and happiness.

Sammy dear, today at last you're free!
    Your cruel apprenticeship is at an end.
Accept this gift from Sophie, Gay and me
    To show our fondness for our new young friend.
[*Juliet holds out to Sammy three shining half-crowns*]

SPOKEN DIALOGUE

SAMMY
Oh no, Miss! I couldn't accept it, really I couldn't, though it's very kindly meant . . .

JULIET
Please do take it, Sammy!

SAMMY
But I've never seen so much money in my life!

JULIET
Then put it in your pocket and you'll be a rich man!

SAMMY
Oh, but, Miss . . .!

JULIET
Quickly! Here come the others!
[*Juliet goes to the door, and Sam stands ready to hide if need be. The other children rush in, one by one, followed by Rowan*]

ENSEMBLE (Children and Sam)

JONNY
'Morning, Sammy! Lovely weather
For our journey home together!

SAM
'Morning! 'Morning!

SOPHIE
'Morning, Sammy! You look splendid
Now your sweeping-days are ended!

SAM
'Morning! 'Morning!

GAY
'Morning, Sammy! Time to travel!
I hear coachwheels on the gravel!

SAM
'Morning! 'Morning!

TWINS
'Morning, Sammy! We're delighted
That you're safe!–and so excited!

ALL
'Morning, Sammy! 'Morning! 'Morning!

SAM
'Morning! 'Morning!

SPOKEN DIALOGUE

JONNY
The coach is coming–

GAY
Into the trunk with you!

ROWAN
I'll fetch your hats and coats.
[*She goes off to get them*]

JULIET
In you jump!

GAY
Take some bread and butter with you.
[*Sam gets into the trunk and kneels*]

JULIET
Goodbye, Sammy dear, and very good luck!
[*She kisses him*]

SOPHIE
Goodbye, dear Sammy!
[*She kisses him*]

THE BEGGAR'S OPERA
Britten's realization of John Gay's opera was first produced at the Arts Theatre, Cambridge on 24 May 1948

32 Lucy Lockit   *Tanya Moiseiwitsch*   33 Lockit   *Tanya Moiseiwitsch*

34 First Scene: Mildred Watson, Max Worthley, Elisabeth Parry, George James and Gladys Parr

35 Sam, the little sweep, before and after his bath; and Black Bob *John Lewis*

36 Sketch for the nursery *John Lewis*

GAY
Jolly good luck to you, Sammy!
[*Handshake*]

ROWAN [*returning with hats and coats*]
Hurry, children! The coach is at the door!
[*Juliet and Gay hastily strap up the trunk, while Sophie watches
at the door, and Rowan helps Jonny and the Twins into their
travelling clothes*]

SOPHIE
Quickly! Quickly! Quickly! I can hear voices!

GAY
Finished!

JULIET [*kneeling by the trunk*]
Are you all right, Sammy?

SAM [*muffled from inside*]
Yes, thank you, Miss! Very comfortable.
[*The children clap their hands in silent glee*]

MISS BAGGOTT [*off*]
Come along, the pair of you! Mind the paint, or I'll
know the reason why!
[*She enters the room followed by Tom, the coachman from
Woodbridge, who is muffled up in an enormous overcoat, and by
Alfred, the gardener, in apron and leggings. They are not a bit
afraid of Miss Baggott*]

TOM
Whoo! Stairs took me wind away! Whoo!

ALFRED
Terrible old house for stairs, this.

MISS BAGGOTT
That's the trunk and mind the corners!

TOM
Whoa, Missus, whoa! Mustn't flog a willing horse! Easy
does it!

ALFRED
Them stairs catch me a slap in my lumbago.

MISS BAGGOTT
Come along, my men!

TOM
Gently, Ma, gently with the bearing rein!–How's that
strong right arm of yours, Alfred lad?

ALFRED
It's the small of the back does me, Tom. The spirit's
willing, but the small of the back says 'Careful, Alfred,
careful!'

TOM
Shall we take a dab at that little old trunk?

ALFRED
No hurry, Tom. Whenever you're certain of your breath
and suchlike.

TOM
Now let's understand each other, Alfred boy. When I
says *three* we lift, if you take my meaning. One–Two–
Three,' and up she'll come like the morning lark.
[*The two men bend down together and take a grip of the handles,
but find the trunk too heavy to lift*]

TRIO (Tom, Alfred and Miss Baggott)

TOM AND ALFRED
Ready, Alfred? Up she goes!
Gently does it. Mind your toes.

One and two and–Wait for me!
Sorry, Alfred! One, two, three–?

One and two and *three* and lift!
No, the dratted thing won't shift!

What's inside it? Full of books!
Twice as heavy as it looks.

Come along, we'll try once more.
Feels like screwed down to the floor.

Full of stones or sand or such.
Weighs like lead, but twice as much.

MISS BAGGOTT
Heave it up and off you go!
Hurry, carry it below!

What a stupid fuss to make
About a trunk, for goodness' sake!

Can't you lift one little box
Packed with shoes and shirts and socks?

RECITATIVE

TOM
Can't be done, Missus!

ALFRED
Much too heavy!

MISS BAGGOTT
Nonsense! I packed it myself.

TOM
Then you'll have to unpack it.

MISS BAGGOTT
I'll do nothing of the sort.

TOM
Then here she stays!

MISS BAGGOTT
The impertinence!

TOM
Either that there box is unpacked . . .

with ALFRED
. . . or we leave her where she lies!

CHILDREN
Oh, *no!*

ALFRED AND TOM
Oh, yes!

ROWAN
Mister Tom, we'll help you to lift the box!

CHILDREN
Yes, please let us help!

TOM

Well, that's a fair offer, Miss, and kindly meant. What's your view, Alfred?

ALFRED

Very kind indeed!

ROWAN AND CHILDREN

Good!–everyone help lift!
[*All, except Miss Baggott, gather round the trunk*]

ENSEMBLE

ALL

One and Two and Three–hooray!
Up she comes! Hip-hip-hooray!
Many hands make labour light.
Now you'll manage her all right!
[*The men go off with the trunk. Miss Baggott follows them, calling 'Mind the paint! Don't drop it! Easy round the corners!' The children heave a deep sigh of relief*]

SPOKEN DIALOGUE

CHILDREN AND ROWAN

He's gone, thank goodness, on his way!
–And thank you for our holiday!
Goodbye, my dears, goodbye!
[*In great haste Rowan, Jonny and the Twins hurry off, leaving Gay, Juliet and Sophie alone*]

GAY

Quick! Open the window!

JULIET

Look! There's the trunk! They're lifting it into the coach!

SOPHIE

He's safe at last! Sammy's safe!

GAY

There come the others! They're climbing into the coach!

JULIET, GAY AND SOPHIE [*calling*]

Goodbye, Rowan! Goodbye, Jonny! Goodbye, Twins!

VOICES [*off*]

Goodbye! Goodbye!

JULIET, GAY AND SOPHIE [*very quietly*]

And goodbye, Sammy!–dear Sammy!

GAY

Tom's on his box . . .!

JULIET

He's lifting his whip . . .!

ALL

And away they go!
[*The whole cast has come quickly back on stage. They improvise a coach with the trunk, the rocking-horse and a chair or two. The Twins kneel in front twirling parasols for wheels, Sam rides proudly on the horse, Tom the coachman flourishes his whip, and all sway in time with the song as they travel away down the high road*]

SONG FOUR

(Cast and Audience) COACHING SONG

The horses are champing, eagerly stamping,
    Crack! goes the whip, as the coachman lets slip!
        So there! So there! Good brown mare,
        Lead away at a spanking trot.

The gravel is churning. Look! they are turning
    Off to the right, and away from our sight.
        So there! So there! Good brown mare,
        Lead away at a spanking trot.

They swing from the bye-road on to the high-road,
    Gathering pace for the home-again race!
        Ho there! Let me see you canter!
        Canter, canter, good brown mare!

Now Sam has arisen out of his prison,
    Grinning with glee to be happy and free!
        Ho there! Let me see you canter!
        Canter, canter, good brown mare!

Our story is ended. You who've attended
    Join in the song as the coach runs along!
        Go there! Let me see you gallop!
        Gallop, gallop, good brown mare!

        Whoa there! Whoa there! Slacken pace!
        Steady now! You've won the race!

        Time to stop, our journey's done.
        Goodbye to you everyone!

Billy Budd

An opera in four acts

by E. M. Forster and Eric Crozier

*adapted from the story
by Herman Melville*

BENJAMIN BRITTEN OP. 50

CHARACTERS

Captain Vere *of the* Indomitable	TENOR
Mr Redburn *the First Lieutenant*	BARITONE
Mr Ratcliffe *the Second Lieutenant*	BASS
Mr Flint *the Sailing Master*	BASS-BARITONE
John Claggart *the Master-at-Arms*	BASS
Billy Budd *able seaman*	BARITONE
Dansker *an old seaman*	BASS
Red Whiskers *an impressed man*	TENOR
Arthur Jones *another impressed man*	BARITONE
Donald *a sailor*	BARITONE
Squeak *a ship's corporal*	TENOR
The Captain's Cabin boy	SPOKEN
A Novice	TENOR
Novice's Friend	BARITONE

Seamen, Officers, Midshipmen, Petty Officers, Marines, Powder-monkeys, Drummers

SYNOPSIS OF SCENES

Act one

Prologue	Vere
Scene one	The main-deck and quarter-deck of the *Indomitable*
Scene two	The Captain's cabin
Scene three	The berth-deck

Act two

Scene one	The main-deck and quarter-deck
Scene two	The Captain's cabin
Scene three	A bay of the upper gun-deck
Scene four	The main-deck and quarter-deck
Epilogue	Vere

The action takes place on board the *Indomitable*, a seventy-four, during the French wars of 1797.

FIRST PERFORMANCE

1 December 1951   *London, Covent Garden*

Captain Vere	Peter Pears
Billy Budd	Theodor Uppman
Claggart	Frederick Dalberg
Mr Redburn	Hervey Alan
Mr Flint	Geraint Evans
Lieutenant Ratcliffe	Michael Langdon
Red Whiskers	Anthony Marlowe
Donald	Bryan Drake
Dansker	Inia Te Wiata
Novice	William McAlpine
Squeak	David Tree
Bosun	Ronald Lewis
First Mate	Rydderch Davies
Second Mate	Hubert Littlewood
Maintop	Emlyn Jones
Novice's Friend	John Cameron
Arthur Jones	Alan Hobson
Four Midshipmen	Brian Ettridge, Kenneth Nash, Peter Spencer, Colin Waller
Cabin Boy	Peter Flynn

Conducted by Benjamin Britten
Produced by Basil Coleman
Designed by John Piper

Act one

Prologue

[Captain Vere is revealed as an old man]

VERE
I am an old man who has experienced much. I have been a man of action and have fought for my King and country at sea.

I have also read books and studied and pondered and tried to fathom eternal truth.

Much good has been shown me and much evil, and the good has never been perfect. There is always some flaw in it, some defect, some imperfection in the divine image, some fault in the angelic song, some stammer in the divine speech. So that the Devil still has something to do with every human consignment to this planet of earth.

Oh what have I done? Confusion, so much is confusion! I have tried to guide others rightly, but I have been lost on the infinite sea. Who has blessed me? Who saved me? In the summer of seventeen hundred and ninety-seven, in the French wars, in the difficult and dangerous days after the Mutiny at the Nore, in the days when I, Edward Fairfax Vere, commanded the *Indomitable* . . .
[*The lights go up on the main-deck and quarter-deck of H.M.S. Indomitable*]

Scene one

[*Early morning. A cutter has gone to board a passing merchantman. An area of the main-deck is being holystoned by some sailors (the First Party), in the charge of the First Mate*]

FIRST MATE
Pull, my bantams! Pull, my sparrow-legs! That's right! Pull with a will! Bend to it, damn you!
[*He hits one man a crack with a rope's end*]

CHORUS [*First Party*]
O heave! O heave away, heave! O heave!
[*A second party of men, including Donald, arrives downstage, dragging holystones. It is led by the Second Mate*]

SECOND MATE
Here is the spot, men! Look at this main-deck! Stains on the deck of a seventy-four. Get 'em off! Get 'em off, you idle brutes!
[*His men set to work. The First Mate gives orders to his Party*]

FIRST MATE
Belay! Belay! You bantams, belay! Up your anchors and forrard a fathom! Move! Move!
[*The men move painfully to a new patch of deck*]

CHORUS [*First and Second Party together*]
O heave! O heave away, heave! O heave!
[*The Sailing Master comes along the quarter-deck*]

SAILING MASTER
Hi there! You, you're faking your pull!

SAILOR
I'm sorry, sir—hurt me arm.

SAILING MASTER
Can't help that, my man. Can't help that. Life's not all play upon a man-of-war.

CHORUS [*First Party*]
O heave! O heave away, heave! O heave!

SAILING MASTER
Mr Bosun! Mr Bosun!
[*Enter Bosun*]

BOSUN
Yes, sir!

SAILING MASTER
Hands to braces! Man the yards!

BOSUN
Ay, ay, sir!
[*Exit Bosun*]
[*Four young Midshipmen cross the deck, hands on dirks. Some of the men holystoning lift their heads to see what is happening*]

MIDSHIPMEN
Toplights down there, and scrub! Scrub!

FIRST MATE
Toplights down, you swabs! Eyes on deck!

MIDSHIPMEN
Can't idle you know, men. Life's not all play upon a man-of war.
[*The Midshipmen go off jauntily*]

DONALD
Cocky young bastards! Send 'em back to mammy. I'll mammy 'em! Teach 'em to 'play upon a man-of-war'!

FIRST MATE
Pull, my sparrowlegs! Pull! Bend to it, damn you!

SECOND MATE
Toplights down, you bantams! Toplights down! Pull with a will!

CHORUS [*Both Parties*]
O heave! O heave away, heave! O heave!
[*The Bosun's whistle shrills off stage. Two parties of men hurry on stage pulling halyards with them. The Novice is among them*]

MAINTOP [*off*]
All manned above! Yards manned!

BOSUN
Lead those halyards aft—at the double!

DECK
Halyards aft!
[*As the downstage party reaches its position, one of the men, the Novice, accidentally collides with the Bosun*]

BOSUN
Who did that?

NOVICE
I did. I'm sorry.

BOSUN
Damned impertinence, and can't you say 'sir'?

NOVICE
All right, I'm sorry, sir.

BOSUN
Don't you answer an officer back. You take care, I've me eye on you. You need a taste of the cat.

MAINTOP [*off*]
Ahoy there, deck! Lively there!

SAILING MASTER
Stop belly-aching and hoist that yard.

BOSUN
Ay, ay, sir! Take your purchase: and sway!
[*Under the direction of the Bosun, who signals the rhythm with his whistle, the men pull on their lines hand over hand to hoist the yard*]

MEN [*pulling*]
. . . and sway! . . . and sway! . . . and sway!

MAINTOP [*off*]
Belay hoisting, deck!

SAILING MASTER
Belay there. Don't lose!
[*The men stop hoisting. Squeak, a ship's corporal, enters*]

BOSUN
Make fast to braces! Don't lose.
[*The Bosun signals 'Make fast' on his pipe. The two parties of men move to the braces and make off their lines*]

BOSUN
Fall in forrard!
[*The hoisting crews run swiftly off stage. The Novice slips as he runs, and falls*]

BOSUN
You again, you novice! That's done for you! I'll teach you!

NOVICE
I didn't mean to slip, sir. Seems I can't do anything right here.

BOSUN
Squeak!
[*Squeak crosses to them*]

SQUEAK
Yessir.

BOSUN
Take this man away, and list him for twenty strokes. See it's done at once.

SQUEAK
Yessir! Yessir!
[*He seizes the Novice*]

NOVICE
Sir, no!–not me!

SQUEAK
Yes–you.

NOVICE
Don't have me flogged–I can't bear it–not flogging!

SQUEAK
Forrard, you.

NOVICE
Not flogging! Not that!
[*Squeak pulls the Novice out. The Bosun follows them*]

FIRST MATE
Toplights down there! If anyone else wants the cat, he can go slipping. Get forrard!

SECOND MATE
Pay attention, you! Take your Bibles and get forrard!

CHORUS [*both parties*]
O heave! O heave away, heave! O heave!
[*The two parties go out slowly, dragging their holystones. The stage is empty except for the Sailing Master on the quarter-deck*]

MAINTOP [*off*]
Boat ahoy!

VOICE [*off, answering from the distant boat*]
Guard boat! *Indomitable!*

MAINTOP [*off*]
Ahoy, deck! Boarding-party boat to larboard.
[*Four Midshipmen run across the deck and up to the quarter-deck to the Sailing Master*]

MIDSHIPMEN
Sir! Boarding-party boat to larboard.

SAILING MASTER
Ay, ay!
[*The First Lieutenant enters along the quarter-deck*]
Mr Redburn! Boarding-party boat returning. I see we've three recruits.

FIRST LIEUTENANT
Very good, Mr Flint. We'll go on deck.
[*They descend to the main-deck*]

SAILING MASTER
Bosun! Clear gangway! Jump to it.
[*Bosun re-enters with men*]

BOSUN
Gangway, lads, gangway!
[*His men set to work clearing the gangway-rail*]

SAILING MASTER [*to a Sailor*]
Bring table and chairs and muster-book.

MAINTOP [*off*]
Cutter alongside!
[*A Sailor sets a table and chairs for the Officers*]

FIRST LIEUTENANT [*to the Sailor*]
Send for John Claggart! Send for the Master-at-Arms!
[*The Sailor goes. The First Lieutenant and Sailing Master seat themselves at the table on the main-deck*]
Well, what have we got this time?

SAILING MASTER
We seem to have the devil's own luck. Nothing worth having these days. Diseased, hungry grumblers, sweepings of the stews and jails, lackeys and pimps, mechanics and lickspittles.–Ah! [*He thumps the table*] it's wearisome! But it's war, we must be content.
[*Lieutenant Ratcliffe appears at the head of the gangway and salutes. He is followed by three impressed men, Red Whiskers, Arthur Jones and Billy Budd, under guard. They fall in on deck*]

RATCLIFFE
To report having boarded the British merchantman *Rights o' Man*, homeward bound to Bristol. Three men impressed. No resistance.

FIRST LIEUTENANT
Very good, Mr Ratcliffe. We shall proceed at once to question them.
[*John Claggart, the Master-at-Arms, comes on deck, salutes and crosses behind the table*]

FIRST LIEUTENANT
Master-at-Arms, we have three recruits. We require

your assistance.

CLAGGART
Your honour, I am at your disposal. First man forward!
[*Red Whiskers is pushed forward*]

CLAGGART
Your name?

RED WHISKERS
I object, I object! You've no right to press me.

CLAGGART
Your name?

RED WHISKERS
I'm a decent tradesman, I've a wife and family . . .

CLAGGART
Your name? [*He leans forward and threatens him with his rattan*]

RED WHISKERS
No! No! Joseph Higgins. I protest. I object.

CLAGGART
Your age?

RED WHISKERS
I won't give it—I refuse . . .

CLAGGART
Your age?
[*Claggart threatens him again*]

RED WHISKERS
Forty-eight. It's not fair. I'm too old. It's against the law.

CLAGGART
Your trade?

RED WHISKERS
I'm a butcher.

CLAGGART
Your home?

RED WHISKERS
Bristol, and I wish I'd never left it. I'm no sailor.

CLAGGART
Silence! I believe that is all you require, your honour.

FIRST LIEUTENANT
Forepeak, I think, Mr Flint?

SAILING MASTER
Little use to us, but we must keep him. We seem to have the devil's own luck. Take him away.

CLAGGART
Next man.

RED WHISKERS
I protest. I object. I only went to oblige. I'm no sailor.
[*Red Whiskers is hustled away protesting. The second pressed man, Arthur Jones, is pushed forward*]

CLAGGART
Your name?

JONES
Arthur Jones.

CLAGGART
Your age?

JONES
Thirty-four.

CLAGGART
Your trade?

JONES
Weaver.

CLAGGART
Your home?

JONES
Spitalfields.

FIRST LIEUTENANT
Forepeak again, I think, Mr Flint?

SAILING MASTER
Nothing special, but we must be content. Oh, it's wearisome! Next man.
[*Jones is marched away*]

CLAGGART
Next man forward. [*He calls to Billy*] Now you. Come here! Your name?
[*Billy Budd comes forward*]

BILLY
Billy Budd, sir.

CLAGGART
Your age?

BILLY
Don't know, sir.

CLAGGART
'Don't know?' Your trade?

BILLY
Able seaman.

CLAGGART
Can you read?

BILLY
No—but I can sing!

CLAGGART
Never mind the singing.

FIRST LIEUTENANT
This looks better. It'll hearten us.

SAILING MASTER
Better fortune at last, and it's welcome.

CLAGGART
Sound in wind and limb?

BILLY
O yes, sir, yes indeed!

CLAGGART
Where's your home?

BILLY
Haven't any. They say I was a . . . a . . . a . . .

FIRST LIEUTENANT
He stammers! That's a pity. Fine recruit otherwise. Fine recruit all the same.

SAILING MASTER
He stammers. That's a pity. Fine recruit otherwise. There is always some flaw in them. Always something.

BILLY

a . . . a . . . foundling! Ay, it comes and it goes . . . or so the chaps tell me. Don't you worry. Foundling, that's the word. I'm a fou–ou–ou–ou–oundling. found in a basket tied to a good man's door, the poor old man.

FIRST LIEUTENANT [*to the Sailing Master*]

A pretty good find.

BILLY

That's all right, sir.

FIRST LIEUTENANT

What d'you say, Master-at-Arms?

CLAGGART

A find in a thousand, your honour. A beauty. A jewel. The pearl of great price.

FIRST LIEUTENANT

We need many more like him.

CLAGGART

Your honour, there are no more like him. I have seen many men, many years have I given to the King, sailed many seas. He is a King's bargain.

FIRST LIEUTENANT

Now where shall we place him?

SAILING MASTER

Foretop, I think.

FIRST LIEUTENANT

Foretopman, be off and good luck to you. Mind you behave yourself and do as you're told.

BILLY

Thank you, sir. Foretopman! Thank you!
[*Exultant*]
   Billy Budd, king of the birds!
   Billy Budd, king of the world!
   Up among the sea-hawks, up against the storms.
   Looking down on the deck, looking down on the waves.
   Working aloft with my mates. Working aloft in the foretop.
   Working and helping, working and sharing.
   Goodbye to the old life. Don't want it no more.
[*He shouts seawards*]
   Farewell to you, old comrades! Farewell to you for ever.
   Farewell, *Rights o' Man*.
   Farewell, old *Rights o' Man*.
   Farewell to you for ever, old *Rights o' Man*.
[*The Chorus echoes Billy off stage*]

SAILING MASTER, FIRST LIEUTENANT AND RATCLIFFE

What's that? 'Rights o' man'? Down, sir! How dare you? Clear the decks!

CLAGGART

Clear the decks!
                              [*The deck is cleared of Sailors*]

FIRST LIEUTENANT

Dangerous! 'The rights of man' indeed!

SAILING MASTER

Always something, always some defect.
                              [*Exit Sailing Master*]

RATCLIFFE

Fine young chap, but we must keep a watch.
                              [*Exit Ratcliffe*]

FIRST LIEUTENANT

Master-at-Arms, instruct your police. You heard what he called out.

CLAGGART

I heard, your honour.
                              [*The First Lieutenant goes out*]
I heard, your honour! Yes, I heard. Do they think I'm deaf? Was I born yesterday? Have I never studied man and men's weaknesses? Have I not apprenticed myself to this hateful world, to this accursed ship? And oh, the fools! These officers!–they are naught but dust in the wind.
Squeak!
[*Squeak pops on to the main-deck*]

SQUEAK

Yessir.

CLAGGART

Keep an eye on that man.

SQUEAK

Yessir! The one who grumbles.

CLAGGART [*rounding on him*]

Let me finish. Grumblers aren't dangerous.

SQUEAK

No, sir.

CLAGGART

Keep an eye on the big lad with the stammer–Billy Budd.

SQUEAK

Yessir, yessir!

CLAGGART [*bullying*]

'Yessir, yessir.' And how? You hadn't thought, you wouldn't think, you can't think. Now listen! Go and play all your little tricks on this Budd,–tangle up his hammock, mess his kit, spill his grog, splash his soup, sneak about him. And if you see anything of his you fancy–I'll make no trouble.

SQUEAK

Thank you, sir, thank you. Grand!

CLAGGART [*malevolent*]

Look out for his temper. Look out for those fists. You're playing with fire, Squeak, with fire . . .

SQUEAK

Oh, dear!

CLAGGART

He'll kill you if he catches you. Be off!
                              [*Squeak goes, leaving Claggart alone*]
Yes, be off! and be damned! Oh, what a ship! One piece of dirt after another.
[*A Sailor (the Novice's friend) enters and salutes*]
What now?

SAILOR

The flogging, sir. All duly over and King's Regulations observed. But the offender took it badly. He's only a boy and he cannot walk.

CLAGGART
Let him crawl.
[*Claggart goes out along the deck. The Novice comes in half-supported by a small group of Sailors. His Friend goes forward to help him*]

FRIEND
Come along, kid!

NOVICE
I'm done for, I'm done for.

CHORUS
Yes, lost for ever on the endless sea.

FRIEND
The pain'll soon pass.

NOVICE
The shame'll never pass.

CHORUS
Ay, he's lost for ever on the endless sea.

FRIEND
Yer bruises'll heal up, kid.

NOVICE
But my heart's broken!

CHORUS
Ay, he's heart-broken,
We're all broken.

FRIEND
I'll look after you!

NOVICE
They've caught me, my home's gone.

CHORUS
Ay, his home's gone.
They've caught us, they've caught all of us.

FRIEND, NOVICE AND CHORUS
We're all of us lost, lost for ever on the endless sea.
[*The Novice is slowly helped away by his companions. Billy and Dansker, an old seaman, come quickly out of the shadows*]

BILLY
Christ! The poor chap, the poor little runt!

DANSKER
Never seen blood, Baby?

BILLY
I've never seen it shed for no reason.
[*Red Whiskers and Donald follow Billy and Dansker*]

RED WHISKERS
I protest! Let them try it on me!

DONALD
They will, chum, be sure. Wallop!

RED WHISKERS
I'm a respectable tradesman. They dursn't.

DONALD
Wallop! Wallop, wallop!

DANSKER AND DONALD
Only twenty. Fifty . . . hundred sometimes. Hurts!

BILLY AND RED WHISKERS
I'll give no offence, I'll get no punishment.

DONALD
You'll see, Whiskers.

DANSKER
You'll see, Baby.

BILLY
No I won't, and my name ain't Baby, asking your pardon.

RED WHISKERS
No I won't, and my name ain't Whiskers, asking your pardon.

DANSKER AND DONALD
Object to it?

BILLY
Nay.

RED WHISKERS
Yes.

DANSKER
Object to Beauty? Not a bad word, beauty.

BILLY
Me a beauty? There's a name for me. Call me what you like, chum! I don't mind.

DONALD
Whiskers! Pull his bloody whiskers!

RED WHISKERS
Oh! Oh! Lemme go! I won't be pulled around; and I won't be called out of my name.
[*Whistles are heard off. Claggart enters with the Bosun and two Mates and some Sailors*]

BILLY
What's that? What's those whistles?

DONALD
That's changing the watch.

CLAGGART
Come on, get up aloft!

MATES
Come on!

BOSUN
Get up aloft!

CLAGGART [*approaching Billy*]
Foretopman!

BILLY
Me, sir?

CLAGGART
This is a man-o'-war. Take off that fancy neckerchief!
[*He pulls off Billy's scarf*]

BILLY
Very good, sir.

CLAGGART
And . . . Look after your dress. Take pride in yourself, Beauty, and you'll come to no harm.
[*Claggart turns to the Mate*]
Get those men aloft!
[*Claggart, the Bosun and Mates go off. The Sailors begin climbing the shrouds, and the off-duty men descend to the deck*]

BILLY [*to Donald*]
D'you hear that?

DONALD

Ssh! That's the one to study if you want to dodge punishment. That's Jemmy Legs.

BILLY

He seems all right.

DANSKER

Billy, be warned. Keep clear of him.

BILLY

What's the rest like? What's the Captain like?

DONALD

Starry Vere we call him. Starry Vere!

BILLY

Starry Vere you call him?
[*Some sailors gather around Billy and the others*]

CHORUS OF SAILORS

Starry Vere!

RED WHISKERS

That's his name?

DANSKER

He's the best of them all.

DONALD

He's a triumph, and a giant in battle—the one to lead us against the French.

CHORUS

The French, the French!

DONALD

They killed their king, and they'll kill ours.

CHORUS

Ay, ay! Down with them or they'll down us!

BILLY

But Starry Vere'll stop them?

DONALD

Ay, he'll destroy them. He knows all their tricks. He's brave, and he's *good*.

CHORUS

He cares for us, he wishes us well, he cares for us like we are his sons.

BILLY

He's good is he? and goodness is best, and I'm for it, Starry Vere, and I'm for you.

CHORUS [*and the others*]

Starry, Starry Vere! He's the salt of the earth. We'll follow Vere, right thro' the gates of Hell. Starry, Starry Vere! Starry, show us the way.

BILLY

Star of the morning, star of the morning . . .
Leading from night, leading to light . . .
Starry I'll follow you . . .
Follow thro' darkness, never you fear . . .
I'd die to save you, ask for to die . . .
I'll follow you all I can, follow you for ever!

BOSUN [*entering*]

Hi! What do you think you're doing there? Get below decks! Get below there!
[*The Sailors disperse quickly*]
[*Quick Curtain*]

Scene two

[*Captain Vere's cabin. Evening, a week later. Vere is sitting reading*]

VERE

Boy!
[*The Boy enters*]
My compliments to Mr Redburn and Mr Flint, and will they take a glass of wine with me.
[*The Boy goes out. Vere resumes his reading*]
[*He lays down the book*]
Plutarch—the Greeks and the Romans—their troubles and ours are the same. May their virtues be ours, and their courage! O God, grant me light to guide us, to guide us all!
[*The Boy opens the door to admit the First Lieutenant and the Sailing Master*]

BOY [*speaking*]

Mr Redburn and Mr Flint, sir.
[*The Boy sets a bottle and glasses on the table and goes out*]

VERE

Gentlemen, I am glad to see you. Be seated. [*They sit*] Gentlemen, the King!

FIRST LIEUTENANT AND SAILING MASTER

The King!

ALL

God bless him!
[*They drink*]

VERE

Well, my frends, here we are—nearing Finisterre—approaching enemy waters. We may be in action at any time.

FIRST LIEUTENANT

Glad when we are, sir, very glad!

SAILING MASTER

Any moment now, sir, we may sight a French sail and chase her. For show her heels she will to a certainty.

VERE

You are right, Mr Flint, she'll fly from us. We've hard times before us, but there'll be victory in the end.

FIRST LIEUTENANT

May we soon be at 'em. Glad for a crack at the French.

SAILING MASTER

Yes, action's coming. The whole ship's wanting it to start.

SAILING MASTER

Don't like the French. Don't like their frenchified ways.

FIRST LIEUTENANT

Don't like the French. Their notions don't suit us, nor their ideas.

SAILING MASTER

Don't like the French. Don't like their bowing and scraping.

FIRST LIEUTENANT

Don't like their hoppity-skippety ways.

SAILING MASTER

Don't like the French.

FIRST LIEUTENANT
Don't like their lingo.

SAILING MASTER AND FIRST LIEUTENANT
Those damned mounseers!

FIRST LIEUTENANT
England for me. British brawn and beef.

SAILING MASTER
England for me. Home and beauty.

SAILING MASTER
Beg pardon, sir. We ought to express ourselves differently.

VERE
No, gentlemen, I feel as you do. Fill your glasses. Another toast. The French! . . .

FIRST LIEUTENANT AND SAILING MASTER
The French! . . .

ALL
Down with them!
[*They drink*]

FIRST LIEUTENANT
Any danger of French notions spreading this side, sir?

VERE
Great danger, great danger. There is a word which we scarcely dare speak, yet at moments it has to be spoken. Mutiny.

FIRST LIEUTENANT AND SAILING MASTER
Mutiny.

SAILING MASTER
Spithead, the Nore, the floating republic.

FIRST LIEUTENANT
Oh, the Nore! The shame of it! I remember. I served there, those days are clear in my mind. I saw the disgrace and the sorrow. I saw wickedness and its merited punishment. O God preserve us from the Nore!

SAILING MASTER
The Nore!

FIRST LIEUTENANT AND SAILING MASTER
The floating republic!

VERE
Ay, at Spithead the men may have had their grievances, but the Nore—what had we there? Revolution, sedition, the Jacobins, the infamous spirit of France . . . France who has killed her king and denied her God, France the tyrant who wears the cap of liberty, France who pretends to love mankind and is at war with the world, France the eternal enemy of righteousness. That was the Nore. Ay, we must be vigilant. We must be on our guard.

FIRST LIEUTENANT
We are, sir. Claggart is an able one.

VERE
He is indeed a veritable Argus.

FIRST LIEUTENANT AND SAILING MASTER
Beg pardon, sir?

VERE
He has a hundred eyes.

SAILING MASTER
Need of him with that young chap who shouted out 'Rights o'man'.

FIRST LIEUTENANT
Yes—'Rights o' man'! He needs watching. 'The rights o' man' indeed!

SAILING MASTER
Dangerous one. We must be vigilant. 'The rights o' man' indeed!
[*The sound of a shanty is heard from below decks*]

VERE
Oh, that's nothing. I've noted the fellow in question—Budd, Billy Budd, foretopman. Nothing—just youthful high spirits. Don't let that worry us. No danger there, gentlemen. And listen to them singing below decks. Where there is happiness there cannot be harm. We owe so much to them—some torn from their homes.

FIRST LIEUTENANT AND SAILING MASTER
More reason we should watch them.
[*There is a knock at the door. Lieutenant Ratcliffe enters*]

RATCLIFFE
Land on the port bow, sir. Cape Finisterre. Enemy waters!
[*All rise*]

VERE
Gentlemen, you'll be wanting to leave me. Work for us all before long. Good night, my friends.

OFFICERS
Good night, sir.
[*The Officers go out. Vere sits again and takes his book*]

VERE [*reading*]
'At the battle of Salamis the Athenians, with vastly inferior numbers against the power of Xerxes . . . the Athenians . . .'
[*He lays down his book and listens to the men singing between decks*]

                              [*The curtain falls slowly*]

Scene three

[*The berth-deck, showing a vista of gun-bays, in each of which a group of seamen stores its kitbags and slings its hammocks. The same evening*]
[*The watch below is ending a shanty. Billy, Donald, Red Whiskers and Dansker are in the nearest gun-bay*]

ALL
Blow her away. Blow her to Hilo, Riley.
Say farewell, we've a long way to go!

SEMI-CHORUS
Blow her away! Blow her to Hilo, blow her away.
[*The shanty slowly dies out*]

DONALD [*briskly*]
Here, lads! Here, lads! Here! Remember this one?
[*The Semi-Chorus from the other bays crowds round and joins in the chorus of the new shanty*]
We're off to Samoa
By way of Genoa,
Roll on Shenandoah
And up with the line and away,
Up with the line and away. [*With Chorus*]

RED WHISKERS
> We're towing to Malta
> The rock of Gibraltar
> With only a halter
> And Davy Jones lying below,   [*With Chorus*]
> So pray to the Devil below.

BILLY
> We're off to Savannah,
> O sing Polly Anna,
> My lovely Susannah,
> A bird flying high in the sky.
> She's only a bird in the sky.   [*With Chorus*]
> Oh, Anna Susannah!
> I'll find you a bed by and by.

DONALD
> We're off to Nantucket,
> Kick over the bucket,
> So muck it and chuck it
> A dunducket look in the eye.   [*With Chorus*]

RED WHISKERS
> We're riding the ocean,
> A dippetty motion,
> O give me a potion,
> No fish in the locker for me!   [*With Chorus*]

BILLY
> We're off to Bermuda,
> The Sultan of Judah
> Can eat barracuda,
> Including the weevils and all.   [*With Chorus*]

DONALD
> We're anchored off Scilly,
> My aunt willy nilly,
> Was winking at Billy,
> She'll cut up her Billy for pie.

RED WHISKERS, BILLY, DONALD AND CHORUS
> She'll cut up her Billy for pie,
> For all he's a catch on the eye.
> [*The Semi-Chorus go back to their own bays in the distance and intersperse the following dialogue with snatches of the shanty*]

BILLY
Come along, Dansker, and sing!

RED WHISKERS
Come along, Dansker, join the fun!

DANSKER
Na, na, too old for fun, too old for dancing, too old for women. I know how fun ends.

RED WHISKERS
That's no proper thing to say. Don't spoil the sport.

DANSKER
Na, leave me alone. I'm finished. There's only one thing in the world that I want and I ain't got it.

BILLY
What is it, friend?

DANSKER
Bacca, Baby Budd, plug o' bacca.

BILLY
That's easy put right. I'll lend you a chew. I'll give you the whole bar. It's in my kitty. Back in a moment.
[*He goes over to a corner-bay to hunt in his kitbag*]

DONALD
He's a good cuss is Billy.

DANSKER
He's too good. There's his whole trouble.

BILLY
Hi! You . . . a . . . a . . .! [*He stammers*]

DANSKER
What did I tell you?

RED WHISKERS AND DONALD
He's a-stammer! He's upset!

CHORUS
He's a-stammer!
What's up?

SQUEAK
No . . . Ah!

DANSKER
What did I tell you?

RED WHISKERS, DONALD AND CHORUS
Billy's a-stammer!

BILLY
Come out of that!

SQUEAK
No!
[*Billy pulls Squeak forward*]

BILLY
What you meddling there for?

SQUEAK
I warn't.

BILLY
You liar! I caught you.

SQUEAK
Don't, Billy, you're throttling me.

BILLY
Yer stinking little vermin.
[*Billy marches Squeak out into the light*]

CHORUS
Squeak!
Got him at last. He took them ear-rings of mine.
Always at it!
Sneaking swine. Look out!–He's got a knife!

BILLY
So that's it! Very well!
[*Billy and Squeak fight*]

CHORUS
Go it, Beauty! Look out! Careful. Get his knife arm.
[*Billy catches Squeak by the knife arm and struggles to disarm him*]

CHORUS
Oh be careful, Billy! Get him down. Go it, Beauty! O Baby, get him down! Careful! Look out, Baby!
[*Billy chases Squeak round the deck and knocks him down as Claggart appears with his Corporals. Whistles shrill loudly*]

CLAGGART
Avast there!

CHORUS
Look out! Look out! Well done.

CLAGGART
How did this start? Silence! Get back there. Dansker, you speak.

DANSKER
Billy went to his bag. Squeak there. Billy lugged him here. Squeak drew a knife. Billy floored him. That's all.

CLAGGART [to the Corporals]
Seize him.
[They pull Squeak to his feet and hold him]

SQUEAK
I wasn't . . .

CLAGGART
Put him in irons.

SQUEAK
Sir, it was you told me . . .

CLAGGART
Gag him!
[Claggart turns on Billy]
As for you . . .! [He smiles] Handsomely done, my lad. And handsome is as handsome did it, too.
[Distant whistles are heard]
Sling hammocks and turn in. Lights out.
[Claggart turns away. A Boy stumbles against him. He lashes savagely at him with his rattan]

BOY [crying out]
Ah . . .!

CLAGGART [furious]
Look where you go!
[The men sling hammocks in the bays and the battle-lanterns are turned low except for one by the companion-way. Claggart walks slowly along the deck and slowly back again.

CHORUS [off]—TENOR SOLO
Over the water,
Over the ocean,
Into the harbour
Carry me home.

CLAGGART
Handsomely done, my lad. Handsome indeed . . .

CHORUS [a few voices]
Over the water,
Over the ocean,
Into the harbour
Lying at anchor,
Carry me home.
[The deck is silent and dark. Claggart stands alone in the small pool of light by the companion-way]

CLAGGART
O beauty, o handsomeness, goodness! Would that I never encountered you! Would that I lived in my own world always, in that depravity to which I was born. There I found peace of a sort, there I established an order such as reigns in Hell. But alas, alas! the light shines in the darkness, and the darkness comprehends it and suffers. O beauty, o handsomeness, goodness! would that I had never seen you!

Having seen you, what choice remains to me? None, none! I am doomed to annihilate you, I am vowed to your destruction. I will wipe you off the face of the earth, off this tiny floating fragment of earth, off this ship where

fortune has led you. First I will trouble your happiness. I will mutilate and silence the body where you dwell. It shall hang from the yard-arm, it shall fall into the depths of the sea, and all shall be as if nothing had been. No, you cannot escape! With hate and envy I am stronger than love.

So may it be! O beauty, o handsomeness, goodness! you are surely in my power tonight. Nothing can defend you. Nothing! So may it be! For what hope remains if love can escape?

If love still lives and grows strong where I cannot enter, what hope is there in my own dark world for me? No! I cannot believe it! That were torment too keen.

I, John Claggart, Master-at-arms upon the *Indomitable*, have you in my power, and I will destroy you.
[The Novice comes slowly down the companion-way and salutes]

CLAGGART
Come here. Remember your promise. Are you ready?

NOVICE
Yes, sir.

CLAGGART
Tonight—this night—this very minute I've work for you. Will you do it?

NOVICE
Yes, sir, yes, I'll do anything—anything! Oh, the flogging and the misery! and you've said you'll protect me, spoke so fatherly to me when you found me crying. I can't stand any more. I'll do anything you want. Yes, yes.

CLAGGART
Come here. Come nearer. I'll protect you if you don't fail. Squeak has failed.

NOVICE
I shan't fail. I'm not like Squeak. I'm clever. They all said so at home—and then the press-gang caught me. I'll do anything to serve you, anything.

CLAGGART
Would you betray a shipmate?

NOVICE [immediately]
Yes.

CLAGGART
Get evidence against him?

NOVICE [immediately]
I'll get it.

CLAGGART
Come closer. A shipmate who's disloyal—go and talk to him and tempt him. Pretend you're disloyal too, tempt him to join you with this, [he shows some coins] compromise him. Then come and tell me.

NOVICE
I'll do it, trust me. I'll do my best. Who is he?

CLAGGART
Billy Budd. [After a pause] Billy Budd. Why do you hesitate?

NOVICE
Not that one.

CLAGGART
Why?

NOVICE
He's good.

CLAGGART [striking him]
'Good'? What is goodness to you?

NOVICE
No, sir! Don't—don't hurt me again, sir, I can't bear it.
No!

CLAGGART
You've had twenty strokes. Do you want worse? Will
you—or will you not work for me?

NOVICE [blubbering]
Yes, I'll work for you. I've no choice. Give me the
money.
[Claggart hands him the coins and goes]
Why had it to be Billy, the one we all love? Why am I in
this cruel hateful ship instead of safe at home? Oh, why
was I ever born? Why? It's fate, it's fate. I've no choice.
Everything's fate. There's no end to it, and may God
forgive me.
[He pulls himself together and goes to the bay where Billy is
sleeping in his hammock]
Billy! . . . Hist! Billy Budd!

BILLY [asleep]
Dreaming, drowsing . . .

NOVICE
Hist! Billy, wake up!

BILLY
It's a-dreaming that I am—fathoms down, fathoms . . .
Who is it? Can't see your face, and dark, isn't it? Christ,
I dreamt I was under the sea! Who are you? Whatever's
in the wind?

NOVICE
Speak quietly! Don't wake the others. It's a friend. I've
got something to say.

BILLY
Nay, I'm asleep again—I feel it stealing on me now . . .
dreaming . . .

NOVICE
Billy, listen! Come over here.
[Billy climbs from his hammock, aided by the Novice, and they
move into an empty gun-bay]

NOVICE [hurriedly whispering]
It's unjust, it's unfair! These press-gangs are unfair. I
was taken from my home, and you were pressed
too—pressed on a homeward-bound. It isn't fair, it isn't
fair, Billy.

BILLY
Never gave it a thought. Still, you're right in a manner of
speaking. Doesn't seem fair—and you're only a boy.

NOVICE
But you were pressed too, Billy, and there's others like
us too. A whole gang. We can't stand it any more. The
dirt and the stinking food, the floggings and the
lashings . . . It's gone too far. We talk and plan together,
and I thought I'd talk to you, Billy. Couldn't you help us
at a pinch? There's twenty, thirty in our gang, and we're
wanting a leader.

BILLY [fully awake at last]
What do you mean?

NOVICE
Look at this! Guineas! [He holds them up]

BILLY
They twinkle pretty—ay, they twinkle lovely.

NOVICE
Look at them! Touch them! They're for you.

BILLY
Why for me?

NOVICE
Hist, quietly! See the pretty pair . . . Don't they twinkle
lovely in the night-light, shining all gold in the
moonlight. See, they're yours, Billy, and more like them
if you'll lead us.

BILLY
Why, d'ye think I'd . . . a . . . a . . . a . . .

NOVICE
Billy!
[Billy clenches his fist with rage as the stammer chokes his
utterance. The Novice flies in terror. Dansker comes forward from
the hammocks]

BILLY
a . . . a . . . Dansker, old friend, glad to see you!

DANSKER
What's the matter, Beauty? Heard you stammer, saw
that novice slipping away . . .

BILLY
Novice, was he? Thought he might be a sperrit the queer
things he said. Oh, Dansker, keep me company, stay
here a bit!
[Dansker turns up the lantern in the gun-bay and sits]

BILLY
I was dreaming in my hammock—fathoms down,
fathoms . . . and didn't rightly wake until he offered me
them guineas.

DANSKER
Ah!

BILLY
Mutiny, that's what they were for, to make me mutiny—
mutiny! Still I have sent him back where he
belonged . . . (dreaming, drop me deep) . . . Anything
wrong, Dansker? You're so silent. Want anything of
mine? Shall I fetch you another plug?

DANSKER
I want nothing of yours, Baby, no, nothing—not your
youth, no, nor your strength, no, nor your looks nor your
goodness, for Jemmy Legs is down on you.

BILLY
Jemmy Legs?—The Master-at-Arms?

DANSKER
Ay, he's down on you.

BILLY
But Jemmy Legs likes me. He calls me that sweet
pleasant fellow. He gives me the smile and easy order
when we meet. And when I gave Squeak that drubbing,
'Handsomely done' was all he said and he smiled. No,
he likes me. They all like me.

DANSKER
No use—he's down on you.

BILLY
This life suits me. I couldn't wish for better mates. Ay! and the wind and the sails and being aloft and the deck below so small and the sea so wide and the stars seeming all to sway.

DANSKER
Beauty, you'd better go back.

BILLY
I wouldn't go back where I was for nothing. It suits me and I'm suited. And Dansker, old friend, I've heard a tale. I'm to get promotion—captain of the mizzen top. Think of that—near Captain Vere himself, God bless him! Billy Budd, late of the *Rights o' Man*, and soon to be captain of the mizzen!

BILLY
Oh, I'm content, I'm content. Everyone loves me, Jemmy Legs and all. Here's my life, my own world. Here's my friends, and here's you, Dansker, old friend, here's you!

DANSKER
Beauty, you're a fool, and I've told you before. Jemmy Legs is down on you.

[*The curtain falls*]

END OF ACT ONE

Act two

Scene one

[*The main-deck and quarter-deck some days later.
A few men are at work. Vere stands on the quarter-deck with the First Lieutenant and other Officers. He is looking out to sea. The air is grey with mist*]

VERE
I don't like the look of the mist, Mr Redburn.

FIRST LIEUTENANT
No more do I, sir. It may lift, but not for long.

VERE
Time we came to action. Time indeed.

FIRST LIEUTENANT
The men are getting impatient with this long waiting.

VERE
That I well understand.
[*Claggart enters slowly along the main-deck. He stops and removes his cap as a sign that he wishes to speak to the Captain*]

FIRST LIEUTENANT
The Master-at-Arms is here to see you, sir.

VERE
No, I don't like the look of the mist! Send Mr Claggart up.

FIRST LIEUTENANT [*calling*]
The Captain will see you.
[*Claggart ascends to the quarter-deck, cap in hand. The Officers withdraw, but remain in sight*]

VERE
Well, what is it, Master-at-Arms?

CLAGGART
With great regret I must disturb your honour. Duty compels me. I would be failing in my trust unless I came to you at once.

VERE
Speak freely. What is it?

CLAGGART
Your honour, I have served my country long, and have striven in all ways to serve you here upon the *Indomitable*.

VERE
Master-at-Arms, your work is satisfactory. What do you want to say?

CLAGGART
Would that I need not say it, Would I could keep silent, but there is danger, sir, there is danger aboard. Danger from one who . . .
[*He is interrupted by a cry from the maintop*]

MAINTOP [*off*]
Deck ahoy! Enemy sail on starboard bow!
[*The mist begins to lift; the scene brightens*]

BOSUN [*pointing*]
Enemy sail on starboard bow!
[*The Officers hurry forward to where Vere is standing. The Sailing Master and Lieutenant Ratcliffe join them. Claggart

descends to the main-deck, looks for a moment in the direction of the sail, then goes quickly forward]

FIRST LIEUTENANT
The French! The French! And the mist is gone!

SAILING MASTER
Enemy sail! The French! The mist is gone.

RATCLIFFE
By God, the French! And the mist is gone!

CHORUS ON QUARTER-DECK
Enemy sail! The French!
By God, the French! And the mist is gone!

CHORUS ON MAIN-DECK
The French at last!

RATCLIFFE
It's a Frenchman, sure enough.

SAILING MASTER
A frigate fully-rigged!

FIRST LIEUTENANT
She's four miles at least.

SAILING MASTER
No, three.

FIRST LIEUTENANT AND RATCLIFFE
No, four!
[Vere seizes a telescope from the Sailing Master and sights it]

MAIN-DECK CHORUS
We'll blow her from the water! She's a Frenchman, sure enough.

QUARTER-DECK CHORUS
She'll outsail us. She's a fifty-gunner.

VERE *[putting down the telescope]*
A Frenchman, seventy-four and new rigged. Three miles off. Course Nor'-nor'-east. Man the braces, Mr Flint.
[Whistles sound off stage]

SAILING MASTER *[shouting through a megaphone]*
Man the braces! At the double!

BOSUN
Ay, ay, sir.
[A team of haulers rushes in and takes ropes, and hauls with the Bosun]

BOSUN
Come on, you lubbers! . . . and sway!

HAULING PARTY
. . . and sway! . . . and sway! . . . and sway!

CHORUS (TUTTI)
This is our moment,
The moment we've been waiting for,
These long weeks.

VERE
Make all sail!

QUARTER-DECK CHORUS
Make all sail!

SAILING MASTER
Make all sail—set royals and sky-rakers!

VERE, FIRST LIEUTENANT, RATCLIFFE AND SAILING MASTER
O God, keep the mist away and the breeze fresh!

MAIN-DECK CHORUS
A Frenchman at last! A Froggy! Our first fight. We'll blow her from the water.

ALL VOICES
Hooray!

VERE
Action, Mr Redburn. Beat to quarters.

ALL ON QUARTER-DECK
Beat to quarters. Beat to quarters!

ALL VOICES
Hooray!

QUARTER-DECK CHORUS AND MAIN-DECK CHORUS
This is our moment,
The moment we've been waiting for
These long weeks.
[The Gunners run to their guns and start loading]

GUNNERS
Come on, boys! Here she is! Grab the breechings! Back with the guns! Give 'em a taste of good English shot, lads!

QUARTER-DECK CHORUS
Gunners! Ready for loading! Stand by to your guns!
[Seamen run to the nettings with lashed hammocks and stow them as a rough screen against shot]

SEAMEN
Quick, lads, there's a battle in the wind! Fetch your hammocks, stow 'em tight. Quick, lads!

QUARTER-DECK CHORUS
Bring those hammocks forrard! Stow 'em tight!
[Afterguardsmen drag water-tubs amidships and lay matches across their brims. Some scatter sand on deck and bring buckets on ropes for dousing fires]

AFTERGUARDSMEN
Tubs ahoy! Sand the decks! We'll put out the fires!

QUARTER-DECK CHORUS
Monkeys! Where's those monkeys? Double up! Double up! Bring the powder and charges.
[A crowd of powder-monkeys run in with cases of powder over their shoulders]

POWDER-MONKEYS *[chattering]*
Look out! Look out! Make way for the powder-monkeys!

ALL ON MAIN-DECK
Now we'll see action.
We're through with waiting.
Now for the deeds.
[Marines march along the main-deck and up to the quarter-deck]

QUARTER-DECK CHORUS
Hey, Marines!

MARINES
Left right, left right, left right. Marines! Make way for Marines!

QUARTER-DECK CHORUS
Fore-and-afters! Staysails and jibs! Strain by the starboard. Sheet 'em home.

37, 38, 39 Costume designs
Designer John Piper

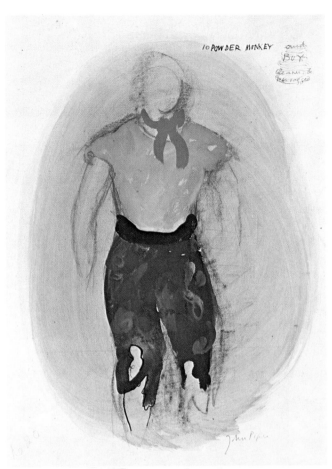

40 Model for Between Decks
John Piper

41 Model for Main Deck and Quarter
Deck
John Piper

42 The final scene on
deck

43 Claggart interrupts the fight between Billy and Squeak, Act i scene iii
     (Act ii scene ii in the original version)

VERE
Volunteers! Call for boarding volunteers!

FIRST LIEUTENANT
Men! Who'll volunteer to board 'em in the smoke?
Who'll be the first on board the Frenchie ship? Sing out
your names! Good men and hearty! Brave men and true!

DONALD
Take me, sir! Donald! I don't mind.

RED WHISKERS
Very well, I'll go too!

DANSKER
Take an old salt. I'll go.

MAIN-DECK CHORUS
Red Whiskers—good for him! And good old Dansker!
Board 'em in the smoke.

DONALD
Good old Dansker! Board 'em in the smoke.

DANSKER
Board 'em in the smoke!

FIRST LIEUTENANT
One more! Four to be the first to board 'em.

BILLY [off]
Here's another. I'm coming down to you. Billy Budd!
I'll come down from the birds.

MAIN-DECK CHORUS
Billy! Billy Budd! He's the one! He's with us! He'll come
down to us!
[Billy climbs down the rigging to the main-deck]

FIRST LIEUTENANT
Fall in there! Budd! Donald! Red Whiskers! Dansker!
Report for arms.

BILLY, DONALD, RED WHISKERS AND DANSKER
Now we'll see action.
We're through with waiting.
Now for deeds!

QUARTER-DECK CHORUS
Report hammocks set, seamen!

SEAMEN
Ay, ay, sir! Ay, ay, sir!

QUARTER-DECK CHORUS
Report tubs and sand, afterguardsmen!

AFTERGUARDSMEN
Ay, ay, sir! Ay, ay, sir!

QUARTER-DECK CHORUS
Report powder ready!

POWDER-MONKEYS
Ay, ay, sir!

QUARTER-DECK CHORUS
Marines! Report muskets loaded!

MARINES
Ay, ay, sir!

ALL VOICES
This is our moment,
The moment we've been waiting for
These long weeks!
Now we'll see action.

We're through with waiting.
Now for deeds!

QUARTER-DECK CHORUS
Report guns ready, gunners!

GUNNERS
Ay, ay, sir!

MAIN-DECK CHORUS
Hooray!

FIRST LIEUTENANT
All guns ready, sir! We wait to fire.

VERE
Wait yet! We're out of range.

SAILING MASTER
Report all canvas set, maintop!

MAINTOP [off]
Ay, ay! All sails set.

SAILING MASTER
All canvas set, sir!

MAIN-DECK [all voices]
Wind, wind, fill our sails! Help our fight!

VERE
Too little for this breeze, I'm afraid. Are we making, Mr
Redburn?

FIRST LIEUTENANT
Barely, sir.

MAIN-DECK [all voices]
Wind, wind fill our sails! Follow us fast!

SAILING MASTER
Maintop! Do you reckon we're making?

MAIN-DECK [all voices]
Bring us victory, now, now, our victory!

MAINTOP [off]
We're making slowly.

MAIN-DECK [all voices]
Wind, wind fill our sails! Help our fight!

VERE
We must be patient.

FIRST LIEUTENANT
We're making, sir!

MAIN-DECK [all voices]
Bring us victory, now, now, our victory!

VERE
Mr Redburn, sight the long eighteens. We'll try a shot.

FIRST LIEUTENANT, SAILING MASTER, RATCLIFFE AND
QUARTER-DECK CHORUS
Stand by, forepeak! Matches ready!

MAIN-DECK [all voices]
We'll send a brace of flying shot to sink the swelling
bastards in their pride!

VERE
Mr Redburn, fire!

FIRST LIEUTENANT, SAILING MASTER, RATCLIFFE AND
QUARTER-DECK CHORUS
By the long eighteens! Are you ready? Fire!

[*There is a tremendous explosion off stage. Smoke drifts aft*]

ALL VOICES
Hurrah!

MAIN-DECK [*all voices*]
This is our moment!

QUARTER-DECK CHORUS
That's got 'em! There's a dumpling for Froggy! Hot from the oven!

MAINTOP [*off*]
Short, deck! Short by half a mile!

FIRST LIEUTENANT
Short, sir! Out of range.

MAIN-DECK [*all voices*]
Ah! Back to our waiting!

VERE
Out of range—and the wind dies.

FIRST LIEUTENANT
Ay! She's dropping.

SAILING MASTER AND RATCLIFFE
Curse the breeze!
[*Slowly the mist closes in round the ship. The scene darkens*]

MAIN-DECK CHORUS
Wind, wind fill our sails! Help our fight!

MAINTOP [*off*]
She's making! The Frenchie's making fast.

GUNNER'S MATE
Carronades ready to fire, sir!

FIRST LIEUTENANT
Wait for orders, deck!

MAIN-DECK CHORUS
Wind, wind, fill our sails!

FIRST LIEUTENANT, SAILING MASTER, RATCLIFFE AND QUARTER-DECK CHORUS
The mist!

MAIN-DECK [*all voices*]
The mist!

VERE
Ay, the mist is back to foil us. The mist creeps in to blind us. Our chase is foolish, gentlemen. Give orders to dismiss.

FIRST LIEUTENANT
Abandon chase, all hands! Down one watch!

SAILING MASTER AND RATCLIFFE
Down one watch!

QUARTER-DECK CHORUS
Down one watch!

MAIN-DECK CHORUS
Ah!
[*The men slowly and gloomily leave action posts and dismiss*]

MAIN-DECK CHORUS
Gone is our moment,
The moment we've been waiting for
These long weeks!
Now we'll see trouble.

Back, back to waiting.
Nothing's done.

FIRST LIEUTENANT
The mist won't break again to-day. We've lost her for good.

QUARTER-DECK CHORUS
Ay, we've lost her!

SAILING MASTER AND RATCLIFFE
It's bad for the men.

QUARTER-DECK CHORUS
They're taking it badly.

RATCLIFFE, SAILING MASTER AND FIRST LIEUTENANT
Day by day things move to the worse.

QUARTER-DECK CHORUS
We must keep a watch.
[*All Officers leave the quarter-deck except the First Lieutenant, Sailing Master and Ratcliffe, who remain in the background, and Vere, who stands thoughtfully in the foreground*]
[*Claggart comes along the emptying main-deck and stands cap in hand as before. Vere sees him*]

VERE
There you are again, Master-at-arms. Come up if the matter's urgent.
[*Claggart climbs the companion-way to the quarter-deck and stands before Vere*]
Now be brief, man, for God's sake.

CLAGGART
As brief, your honour, as my theme allows.
I dare not cut it short. And I must ask your patience.
There's a man on board who's dangerous. I say again—who's dangerous.

VERE
Dangerous? What mean you?

CLAGGART
                    Disaffected, sir,
Ripe for the crimes of Spithead and the Nore.
A common seaman, but a subtle schemer,
Plotting between decks, sapping loyalties,
Corrupting messmates: yes—even in this fight
When all hearts should promote our common purpose:
Fomenting—pardon me the foul word!—mutiny.

VERE
Mutiny? Mutiny? I'm not to be scared by words. Your evidence for this?

CLAGGART
Perhaps your honour would inspect these guineas.
He crept and offered them at dead of night
To a young novice. You will understand
How their bright wonder and pretty twinkling
Would tempt a simple boy. But he held firm
And came at once and handed them to me.

VERE
How came the man by gold?—a common seaman?
Strange story. What's his name?

CLAGGART
                              His name—

Is William Budd.

VERE
Budd, Billy Budd, foretopman?

CLAGGART
The same.

VERE
Nay! you're mistaken. Your police have deceived you. Don't come to me with so foggy a tale. That's the young fellow I get good reports of.

CLAGGART
Ah, pleasant looks, good temper—they are but a mask. He is deep, deep.

VERE
Master-at-Arms, I cannot agree. I have seen many men in my time, and I trust him.

CLAGGART
You do but note his outwards, the flower of masculine beauty and strength. A man-trap lurks under those ruddy-tipped daisies.

VERE
Claggart! take heed what you speak. There's a yard-arm for a false witness.

CLAGGART
Sir! Sir! Your honour!

VERE
No more. I'll see the fellow at once. [He calls] Boy!
[The Boy enters]

BOY [speaking]
Yes, sir?

VERE
You know William Budd, foretopman?

BOY [speaking]
Oh yes, Billy Budd, sir!

VERE
Find him, bring him aft to my cabin. Do you understand?

BOY [speaking]
Yes, sir. [He goes]

VERE
You, Master-at-Arms, when you have seen Budd enter, follow him quietly. I have heard you speak; I wish to speak with him. In a few minutes you will be admitted and confront him.

CLAGGART
Thank you, your honour. I trust that nothing I have done . . .

VERE
Be so good as to leave me!
[Claggart salutes and goes]

VERE
Oh, this cursèd mist!
[The First Lieutenant, Sailing Master and Ratcliffe come forward to Vere]

FIRST LIEUTENANT
Yes, sir, it's got us! It's lost us the Frenchie. The Frenchie's escaped us.

SAILING MASTER
It may lift later, sir, but too late for our purpose.

RATCLIFFE
Sadly disappointing, sir. It's here for good.

VERE
Disappointment, vexation everywhere—creeping over everything, confusing everyone. Confusion without and within.

Oh, for the light, the light of clear Heaven, to separate evil from good!
[The curtain falls]

Scene two

[The Captain's cabin. A few minutes later. Vere is alone]

VERE
Claggart, John Claggart, beware! I'm not so easily deceived. The boy whom you would destroy, he is good; you are evil. You have reckoned without me. I have studied men and their ways. The mists are vanishing—and you shall fail!
[He goes to the door and opens it. Billy enters]

BILLY [radiant]
You wanted to see me. I knew it, I knew I'd be called. Captain of the mizzen! Oh, the honour!—and you telling me! I shouldn't speak so quick, but the talk's got around.

VERE [watching him]
Would you like to be captain of the mizzen, Billy Budd?

BILLY
Yes, or to be your coxswain. I'd like that too.

VERE
Why?

BILLY
To be near you. I'd serve you well, indeed I would. You'd be safe with me. You could trust your boat to me. Couldn't find a better coxswain—that's to say, I'll look after you my best.
I'd die for you—so would they all.

Aren't I glad to be here! Didn't know what life was before now, and O for a fight! Wish we'd got that Frenchie I do, but we'll catch her another day. Sir! let me be your coxswain! I'd look after you well. You could trust your boat to me, you'd be safe with me. Please, sir!

VERE [aside]
And this is the man I'm told is dangerous—the schemer, the plotter, the artful mutineer! This is the trap concealed in the daisies! Claggart, John Claggart, beware!
[To Billy]
You must forget all that for the present. I do not want to see you about promotion.

BILLY [good humoured]
That's all right, sir. I'm content.

VERE
Very well, but now listen to me, Budd. We want to question you—I and the Master-at-Arms.

BILLY
Yes, sir!

VERE
Answer us frankly and show all proper respect. Now stand to attention. [He calls] Boy! Admit Mr Claggart. [The door opens. Claggart enters]

VERE
Master-at-arms and foretopman, I speak to you both. You stand before your Commander as accuser and accused under the Articles of War. Remember both of you the penalties of falsehood. Master-at-arms, stand there. Tell this man to his face what you have already told me.

CLAGGART [staring at Billy]
William Budd, I accuse you of insubordination and disaffection.
William Budd, I accuse you of aiding our enemies and spreading their infamous creed of 'The Rights of Man'.
William Budd, I accuse you of bringing French gold on board to bribe your comrades and lure them from their duty.
William Budd, you are a traitor to your country and to your King.
I accuse you of mutiny!

VERE
William Budd, answer. Defend yourself!

BILLY [unable to speak]
. . a . . a . . a . . a .

VERE
Speak, man, speak.

BILLY
. . a . . a . . a . . a .

VERE
Take your time, my boy, take your time.
[Vere lays his hand on Billy's shoulder. Billy's right fist shoots out, striking Claggart on the forehead]

BILLY
. . a . . a . . a . . . DEVIL!
[Claggart falls and, after a couple of gasps, lies motionless]

VERE
God o' mercy! [He kneels by the corpse] Here, help me!
[Billy does not move. Vere raises the body. It falls back]
He's dead. Fated boy, what have you done? Go in there. Go! God help us! help us all.
[Billy obeys Vere and goes into a small stateroom at the back of the cabin. Vere goes to the door and calls to the Boy]
Boy! fetch my officers at once.

The mists have cleared. O terror! what do I see? Scylla and Charybdis, the straits of Hell. I sight them too late— I see all the mists concealed. Beauty, handsomeness, goodness coming to trial. How can I condemn him? How can I save him? My heart's broken, my life's broken. It is not his trial, it is mine, mine. It is I whom the devil awaits.
[The First Lieutenant, Sailing Master and Ratcliffe enter the cabin hurriedly]
Gentlemen, William Budd here has killed the Master-at-Arms.

FIRST LIEUTENANT, SAILING MASTER AND RATCLIFFE
Great God! for what reason?

FIRST LIEUTENANT
We must keep our heads.

SAILING MASTER
Oh! what unheard-of brutality.

RATCLIFFE
The boy has been provoked.

FIRST LIEUTENANT
Why did he do it? What is the truth?

SAILING MASTER
Claggart is lost to us—we must revenge him.

RATCLIFFE
There's no harm in the boy. I cannot believe it.

FIRST LIEUTENANT
Justice is our duty, justice is our hope.

SAILING MASTER
Claggart, he's dead—give the murderer the rope.

RATCLIFFE
Mercy on his youth—there's no harm in the lad.

FIRST LIEUTENANT
Here and now we'll judge the case.

SAILING MASTER
Neither Heaven nor Hell suffer villainy to rest.

RATCLIFFE
Heaven is merciful—let us be merciful.

FIRST LIEUTENANT
Call him to trial!

SAILING MASTER
We must have revenge, revenge!

RATCLIFFE
Let us show pity, show pity!

VERE
Struck by an angel of God. Yet the angel must hang.

FIRST LIEUTENANT
Sir, command us.

SAILING MASTER
Unheard-of in naval annals.

RATCLIFFE
What's to be done?

VERE
Justice must be done. I summon a drum-head court. The enemy is near. The prisoner must be tried at once. Mr Redburn presides. I myself am present as witness—the sole earthly witness. Gentlemen, the court sits.
[The Officers prepare the cabin for the court-martial. Vere stands rigidly at the side. They carry the body into another stateroom, set table and chairs, and then summon Billy before them]

FIRST LIEUTENANT
William Budd, you are accused by Captain Vere of striking your superior officer, John Claggart, Master-at-Arms, and thus causing his death.
[Billy is silent]

FIRST LIEUTENANT
Captain Vere?

VERE
The Master-at-Arms . . . denounced the prisoner to
me . . . for spreading disaffection . . . sympathy with our
enemies . . . and trying to start a mutiny . . .

BILLY
No, no!

VERE
. . . having French gold for bribes. I asked the prisoner
to reply. He stammered, then struck out, struck John
Claggart on the forehead, and the rest you know.

FIRST LIEUTENANT [to Billy]
Captain Vere has spoken. Is it as he has said?

BILLY
Yes.

FIRST LIEUTENANT
You know the Articles of War?

BILLY
Yes.

FIRST LIEUTENANT
And the penalty?

BILLY
Yes.

FIRST LIEUTENANT
Why did you do it?

BILLY
Sir, I am loyal to my country and my King. It is true I
am a nobody, who don't know where he was born, and
I've had to live rough, but never, never could I do those
foul things. It's a lie.

FIRST LIEUTENANT
Did you bear any malice against the Master-at-Arms?

BILLY
No, no I tried to answer him back. My tongue wouldn't
work, so I had to say it with a blow, and it killed him.

FIRST LIEUTENANT
You stammered then?

BILLY
Ay, it comes and goes.

FIRST LIEUTENANT
Why should the Master-at-Arms accuse you
wrongfully? Why?

BILLY
Don't know, don't know such things. Ask Captain Vere.
Ask him.

FIRST LIEUTENANT
Do you, sir, know any reason?

VERE
I have told you all I have seen. I have no more to say.

FIRST LIEUTENANT
Prisoner, have you any more to say?

BILLY
Captain Vere, save me!

FIRST LIEUTENANT
Go in and wait.

BILLY
Captain, save me!

FIRST LIEUTENANT
Go in.

BILLY
I'd have died for you, save me!

FIRST LIEUTENANT
Go in.

BILLY
Save me!
[The other officers lead Billy back to the small stateroom]

FIRST LIEUTENANT
Poor fellow, who could save him?

SAILING MASTER
Ay, he must swing.

RATCLIFFE
Ay, there's naught to discuss.

TOGETHER
We've no choice.

FIRST LIEUTENANT
There's the Mutiny Act.

SAILING MASTER
There are the Articles of War.

RATCLIFFE
There are the King's Regulations.

TOGETHER
We've no choice.

FIRST LIEUTENANT
Claggart I never liked. Still, he did his duty.

SAILING MASTER
No-one liked Claggart. Still, he's been murdered.

RATCLIFFE
Claggart was hard on them all. How they hated him.

TOGETHER
We've no choice.

FIRST LIEUTENANT
Baby Budd the men called him. They loved him.

SAILING MASTER
Billy Budd! He might have been a leader.

RATCLIFFE
Billy Budd—I impressed him—a King's bargain.

TOGETHER
But we've no choice.

FIRST LIEUTENANT
What, then, is our verdict?

OFFICERS [to Vere]
Sir, before we decide, join us, help us with your
knowledge and wisdom. Grant us your guidance.

VERE
No. Do not ask me. I cannot.

OFFICERS
Sir, we need you as always.

VERE
No. Pronounce your verdict.

OFFICERS
Guilty.

VERE
And the penalty?

OFFICERS
Death.

FIRST LIEUTENANT
Hanging from the yard-arm.

VERE
I accept your verdict. Let the Master-at-Arms be buried
with full naval honours. All hands to witness
punishment at one bell in the morning watch. I will
myself tell the prisoner.

FIRST LIEUTENANT
Gentlemen, the court rises.
                    [*The Officers salute and leave quietly*]

VERE
I accept their verdict. Death is the penalty for those who
break the laws of earth. And I who am king of this
fragment of earth, of this floating monarchy, have
enacted death. But I have seen the divine judgment of
Heaven, I've seen iniquity overthrown. Cooped in this
narrow cabin I have beheld the mystery of
goodness—and I am afraid.

Before what tribunal do I stand if I destroy goodness?
The angel of God has struck and the angel must hang—
through me. Beauty, handsomeness, goodness, it is for
me to destroy you. I, Edward Fairfax Vere, Captain of
the *Indomitable*, lost with all hands on the infinite sea. [*He
goes towards the door of Billy's stateroom*] I am the
messenger of death! How can he pardon? How receive
me?

        [*He goes towards the small stateroom and enters it. The
curtain remains up until the end of the music, and then slowly falls*]

Scene three

[*A bay of the gun-deck, shortly before dawn next morning. Billy
is in irons between two cannon*]

BILLY
                                                    Look!
Through the port comes the moon-shine astray!
It tips the guard's cutlass and silvers this nook;
But 'twill die in the dawning of Billy's last day.
Ay, ay, all is up; and I must up too
Early in the morning, aloft from below.
On an empty stomach, now, never would it do.
They'll give me a nibble—bit of biscuit ere I go.
Sure a messmate will reach me the last parting cup;
But turning heads away from the hoist and the belay,
Heaven knows who will have the running of me up!
No pipe to those halyards—but ain't it all sham?
A blur's in my eyes; it is dreaming that I am.
But Donald he has promised to stand by the plank,
So I'll shake a friendly hand ere I sink.
But no! It is dead then I'll be, come to think.

They'll lash me in hammocks, drop me in deep,
Fathoms down, fathoms—how I'll dream fast asleep.
I feel it stealing now . . .
                            Roll me over fair.
I am sleepy, and the oozy weeds about me twist.
[*Dansker steals in with a mug of grog*]

DANSKER [*whispering*]
Here! Baby!

BILLY
Dansker, old friend! that's kind. [*He drinks*] That's kind.
Gimme a biscuit too—[*He eats*]—I feel better. But you
shouldn't have risked coming to see me. You'll get into
trouble.

DANSKER
All's trouble. The whole ship's trouble . . . and upside-
down.

BILLY
What for?

DANSKER
Some reckon to rescue you, Billy Boy. How they hated
that Jemmy Legs! They swear you shan't swing. They
love you.

BILLY
I'll swing and they'll swing.
Tell 'em that and stop them. [*He puts the mug down*]
Christ! I feel better. Done me a lot of good—a drink and
seeing a friend. Stopped me from thinking on what's no
use and dreaming what needn't be dreamt, and woken
me up to face what must be. What's the day to be?

DANSKER
A fair day.

BILLY
We'd have caught that Frenchie on a fair day. O that
cursèd mist! Maybe you'll still catch her. You better be
going now.

DANSKER
Goodbye, Baby.

BILLY [*holding up his wrists*]
Can't shake hands. Chaplain's been here before you—
kind—and good his story, of the good boy hung and gone
to glory, hung for the likes of me. But I had to strike
down that Jemmy Legs—it's fate. And Captain Vere has
had to strike me down—Fate. We are both in sore
trouble, him and me, with great need for strength, and
my trouble's soon ending, so I can't help him longer
with his. Starry Vere, God bless him—and the clouds
darker than night for us both. Dansker of the *Indomitable*,
help him all of you. Dansker, goodbye!
                                        [*Dansker goes*]
And farewell to ye, old *Rights o' Man*! Never your joys no
more. Farewell to this grand rough world! Never more
shipmates, no more sea, no looking down from the
heights to the depths! But I've sighted a sail in the
storm, the far-shining sail that's not Fate, and I'm
contented. I've seen where she's bound for. She has a
land of her own where she'll anchor for ever. Oh, I'm
contented. Don't matter now being hanged, or being
forgotten and caught in the weeds. Don't matter now.
I'm strong, and I know it, and I'll stay strong, and that's
all, and that's enough.

                                        [*The curtain falls*]

Scene four

[*The main-deck and quarter-deck. Four o'clock the same morning, and first daylight is appearing.*
When the curtain rises the decks are empty, save for a few of the watch on duty and the Marine sentry. The whole crew assembles in silence and in perfect order. They arrive in the following groups:
    Gunners.
    Seamen.
    Afterguardsmen.
    Powder-monkeys (who run in and clamber up the rigging, and on to boats and booms).
    Marines (who march across to the quarter-deck).
    Officers and Midshipmen—on the quarter-deck. Vere, preceded by the First Lieutenant, Sailing Master and Lieutenant Ratcliffe.
When all are in position, Billy enters, preceded and followed by Marine sentries]

FIRST LIEUTENANT [*reading*]
'According to the Articles of War, it is provided as follows:
    If any officer, mariner, soldier or other person in the fleet shall strike any of his superior officers, he shall suffer death.
    It is further provided that if any in the fleet commits murder, he shall be punished by death.'

William Budd, you have been found by the court-martial guilty of striking your superior officer. You have further been found guilty of murder. In accordance with the aforesaid Articles of War, you are condemned to death by hanging from the yard-arm.

BILLY [*suddenly*]
Starry Vere, God bless you!

ALL VOICES [*except Vere and Billy*]
Starry Vere, God bless you!
[*The First Lieutenant closes his book. At this signal, the Marine sentries and Billy turn about and march off towards the main-mast.*
All watch the scene off stage. The light of dawn has grown to a fresh pink.
Captain Vere removes his hat. As he does so, all faces turn slowly upward to follow the body of Billy to the main-yard.

Then begins the sound described by Melville as like the freshet wave of a torrent roaring distantly through the woods, expressing a capricious revulsion of feeling in the crew.
The sound grows and grows, and the whole wedged mass of faces slowly turns in rebellion to the quarter-deck.
There is a growing agitation among the Officers on the quarter-deck, but Vere stands motionless]

FIRST LIEUTENANT, SAILING MASTER AND RATCLIFFE
Down all hands! And see that they go!

QUARTER-DECK CHORUS
Down all hands! Down!
[*The men slowly obey the commands from force of habit and begin to disperse*]

QUARTER-DECK CHORUS
Down all hands! See that they go! Down!
    [*The deck empties by degrees and the light slowly fades*]

Epilogue

[*The light grows and reveals Vere as an old man, as in the Prologue*]

VERE
We committed his body to the deep. The sea-fowl enshadowed him with their wings, their harsh cries were his requiem. But the ship passed on under light airs towards the rose of dawn, and soon it was full day in its clearness and strength.
    . . .For I could have saved him. He knew it, even his shipmates knew it, though earthly laws silenced them.
    O what have I done? But he has saved me, and blessed me, and the love that passes understanding has come to me. I was lost on the infinite sea, but I've sighted a sail in the storm, the far-shining sail, and I'm content. I've seen where she's bound for. There's a land where she'll anchor for ever. I am an old man now, and my mind can go back in peace to that far-away summer of seventeen hundred and ninety-seven, long ago now, years ago, centuries ago, when I, Edward Fairfax Vere, commanded the *Indomitable* . . .

        [*The curtain slowly falls*]

Gloriana

An opera in three acts

by William Plomer

BENJAMIN BRITTEN OP. 53

CHARACTERS

Queen Elizabeth the First	SOPRANO
Robert Devereux, Earl of Essex	TENOR
Frances, Countess of Essex	MEZZO-SOPRANO
Charles Blount, Lord Mountjoy	BARITONE
Penelope (Lady Rich) *sister to Essex*	SOPRANO
Sir Robert Cecil *Secretary of the Council*	BARITONE
Sir Walter Raleigh *Captain of the Guard*	BASS
Henry Cuffe *a satellite of Essex*	BARITONE
A Lady-in-Waiting	SOPRANO
A Blind Ballad-Singer	BASS
The Recorder of Norwich	BASS
A Housewife	MEZZO-SOPRANO
The Spirit of the Masque	TENOR
The Master of Ceremonies	TENOR
The City Crier	BARITONE

Chorus
Citizens, Maids of Honour, Ladies and Gentlemen of the Household, Courtiers, Masquers, Old Men, Men and Boys of Essex's Following, Councillors.

Dancers
Time, Concord, Country Girls, Fishermen, Morris Dancers

Actors
Pages, Ballad-Singer's Runner, Phantom of Queen Elizabeth

Musicians on the stage
State trumpeters, Dance Orchestra, Pipe and Tabor, Gittern, Drummer

Scene England in the time of Queen Elizabeth I.

Time The later years of her reign, which lasted from 1558 to 1603.

NOTE Some of the words put into the mouth of the Queen are quoted or adapted from utterances of Queen Elizabeth I preserved among the records of her life. The words of Essex's second lute-song in Act I, Scene II, 'Happy were he', were written by Robert Devereux, Earl of Essex, himself.

FIRST PERFORMANCE

8 June 1953   *London, Covent Garden*

Queen Elizabeth I	Joan Cross
Earl of Essex	Peter Pears
Lady Essex	Monica Sinclair
Lord Mountjoy	Geraint Evans
Penelope Lady Rich	Jennifer Vyvyan
Sir Robert Cecil	Arnold Matters
Sir Walter Raleigh	Frederick Dalberg
Henry Cuffe	Ronald Lewis
Lady-in-Waiting	Adele Leigh
A blind ballad-singer	Inia Te Wiata
The Recorder of Norwich	Michael Langdon
A Housewife	Edith Coates
Spirit of the Masque	William McAlpine
Master of Ceremonies	David Tree
City Crier	Rhydderch Davies
Time	Desmond Doyle
Concord	Svetlana Beriosova

Conducted by John Pritchard
Produced by Basil Coleman
Designed by John Piper
Choreographed by John Cranko

Act one

Scene one

[*Outside a tilting-ground, during a tournament. Essex, attended by Cuffe, is listening to the proceedings within. Cuffe, at an opening, reports on what he can see*]

CHORUS [*off*]
What champion rides?
Is it Mountjoy?

CUFFE
He throws the gauntlet down!

ESSEX
Who throws the gauntlet down?

CUFFE
He takes it up!

ESSEX
Who takes it up?

CUFFE
My lord Mountjoy.

ESSEX
Oh, if his luck were mine!

CHORUS
He mounts in hope,
With joy we cheer! Mountjoy!

CUFFE
They both salute the Queen.

CHORUS
Hail!

ESSEX
Why do they cheer?

CUFFE
My lord, they love the sight of him.

ESSEX
I hear they do.
If only I were he!

CHORUS
Our joy mounts up,
Our hope, Mountjoy!

CUFFE
They're in the lists, about to charge!
They charge!
A glancing blow—
Will you not watch, my lord?

ESSEX
If I should watch
I could not bear to see
Mountjoy prevail.

CHORUS
Strike anew,
Strike once more!
Mountjoy! Our joy!

CUFFE
They wheel and turn,
He parries with his shield!
A giant thrust! He reels!

ESSEX
Say that he falls,
Say that Mountjoy falls!

CHORUS
Our hope falls!
Mountjoy, our hope sustain!

CUFFE
He does not fall!
Again he wheels for the charge,
Once more they ride.

ESSEX
This time he falls!
This time he's down!

CHORUS
Strike now, Mountjoy!
Mountjoy!

CUFFE
My lord, he's down!

ESSEX
Who's down?

CUFFE
With one great blow
Against his iron breast
The other is unhorsed!

ESSEX
I cannot bear his luck!

CUFFE
Mountjoy has won!

CHORUS
Our champion now
We cheer Mountjoy!
Mountjoy!

CUFFE
There now
The mob has all gone wild
Because Mountjoy has won!

ESSEX
Mountjoy has won!

CHORUS
Mountjoy! Mountjoy!

CUFFE
Now he makes his humble duty
Before the Queen in strength and beauty.

ESSEX
His the place that should be mine!

CHORUS
Mountjoy! Mountjoy!

CUFFE
Now he makes his humble duty
Before the Queen in strength and beauty.

ESSEX
Mine the task to break his pride!

CHORUS
Dismounts with joy,
Salutes the Queen!

CUFFE
He takes a golden prize
Now from the royal hand.

ESSEX
Ah!

CHORUS
Mountjoy!

CUFFE
To the Queen like one they are turning.

CHORUS
Green leaves are we,
Red rose our golden Queen,
O crownèd rose among the leaves so green!
[*Mountjoy emerges from a tent, accompanied by a Page, to whom he hands the golden chessman just presented to him by the Queen, together with a crimson ribbon*]

MOUNTJOY
Boy, bind upon my arm
This my reward.

PAGE
My lord!
[*He does so, with the ribbon*]

MOUNTJOY
I'll wear it as a charm:
No sooner said than done.

ESSEX
'Twas you, my lord Mountjoy,
That won the crowd?
It was. I know it. And I know
Easy applause is loud.

MOUNTJOY
My friend, I boast not.

ESSEX
No,
You need not!

MOUNTJOY
Need not?

ESSEX
What meaneth, may I ask,
That bauble on your arm?

MOUNTJOY	ESSEX
It is a golden queen at chess	You find in that your happiness?
The Queen herself as prize	Mere luck I must despise!
Gave me in great goodwill.	A favour now for every fool!
Take back those words!	Not I!
Unsay it, then!	A favour for a fool, I said!
	Not I!
	Nay!

[*They draw their swords and fight. A fanfare is sounded, off. Essex turns at the sound, and receives a slight wound in the left arm. Enter Trumpeters. Essex's Page binds a scarf round his arm; the scarf at once appears blood-stained. To the sound of the trumpets a procession emerges from the tilting ground, and is followed by a crowd. Essex and Mountjoy kneel as the Queen appears, attended by Raleigh*]

QUEEN [*in surprise and concern*]
Heaven, what have we here?
A wound! My Lord of Essex bleedeth!
[*Seeing at once that the wound is not grave, she turns to Raleigh and speaks ironically*]
One lord weareth a favour,
The other weareth a wound!
How now?

CHORUS
One lord another supersedeth—
Rivals for a lady's favour!
[*The Queen turns to Essex*]

QUEEN
You did not get
That mark in sport!
[*Essex bows and makes no reply*]

QUEEN
The Earl of Essex hangs his head,
Hath lost his tongue, forgot
His courtliness as well. Beware!
I'll not be crossed!

We'll have you both to know
An ancient rule: at court
No man may strike a blow
For any cause at all.
[*She turns to Mountjoy*]
Hearken, my lord Mountjoy:
What penalty should fall
On noble lords who strive
Like ostlers in a brawl?

Explain yourselves!
I'll have the gist!
Your Prince commands!

CHORUS
Her Majesty will hear their case.

QUEEN
I command you!

MOUNTJOY [*to the Queen*]	ESSEX [*to the Queen*]
The honour done me by your Grace	The honour done him by your Grace
Hath been dishonoured in this place!	He came and flaunted in my face!
[*to Essex*]	[*to Mountjoy*]
I flaunted nothing,	A dolt am I
You intruded!	To be deluded?
Meek am I,	Or craven I,
To hear accusings?	To bear abusings?

ESSEX AND MOUNTJOY
The royal presence must subdue
My rightful rage!

QUEEN
Halt! In Heaven's name be dumb!
Even when fishwives wrangle
They must make an end of words.

CHORUS
The Queen will have them know their place!
[*The Queen turns to Raleigh*]

QUEEN
　　Raleigh, what think you
　　Of these pettish lords?

CHORUS
　　Sir Walter takes them both to task.

RALEIGH
　　As your Highness commands,
　　Let me, of riper age,
　　Tell what I see.

　　　　Both lords are younglings, both
　　　　　In glory would appear.
　　　　'Stay,' quoth the first one,
　　　　　'What dost thou here?'
　　　　'Pride,' doth the other answer,
　　　　　'Brings you, my lord, too near.'

　　　　These two are rivals, like
　　　　　The blue fly and the bee:
　　　　'Buzz,' quoth the blue fly,
　　　　　'Hum,' quoth the bee,
　　　　'How can this busybody
　　　　　Take precedence of me?'

　　When head and heart are hot
　　Then tongue and hand are wild:
　　So, Ma'am, it looks to me.

ESSEX AND MOUNTJOY [aside]
　　I curse him for his insolence,
　　And some day I will hurl him down.

QUEEN
　　Raleigh, your wit flies free,
　　We find your judgment mild
　　[She turns to Mountjoy and Essex]
　　Approach, my subjects both,
　　And hear my judgment now.

CHORUS
　　Like Solomon, the wisest Prince,
　　Our Prince her wisdom to her judgment brings.
　　[Essex and Mountjoy approach the Queen]

QUEEN
　　Anger would be too strong
　　Against this youthful sparring:
　　My ruling hear ye both:
　　Forbear from graver warring!

　　God's death, we need your arms!
　　Pray you, good lords, defend us,
　　Our kingdom and our people
　　Against the foes would end us.

　　Fail not to come to court
　　In fine or dirty weather,
　　I'll not neglect you–
　　But see you come together!

　　Rise both, my lords, and see
　　How these good folk respect you:
　　Spurn not their trust; remember
　　Your Princess will protect you.

ESSEX AND MOUNTJOY
　　She'll not neglect us
　　If we will come together.

RALEIGH AND CUFFE
　　Fail not to come to court
　　In fine or dirty weather.

CHORUS
　　Fail not to come to court
　　In fine or dirty weather:
　　She'll not neglect them
　　If they will come together.

　　To our great Queen,
　　Our Queen,
　　Thanks we now give.

ESSEX
　　The wisdom of our Queen
　　Hath made us brothers,
　　Who this day were foes.

MOUNTJOY
　　Our quarrel over, I engage
　　Myself to be his friend.

CUFFE
　　In thankfulness your servant,
　　I stand in a lower place.

RALEIGH
　　All honour to our Queen, who calms
　　The stubborn knights-at-arms.

ESSEX
　　If Gloriana gives me armies to command,
　　My banner will emblazon lasting love.

MOUNTJOY
　　A loyal homage is a lasting love
　　In one that offers life to her.

CUFFE
　　Obeying such a monarch
　　Raiseth a man's esteem.

RALEIGH
　　Each heart from now be dedicate
　　Unto this wise Princess.

CHORUS
　　The wisdom of our Queen
　　Hath made them brothers
　　Who this day were foes.

ESSEX, MOUNTJOY, RALEIGH AND CUFFE
　　Our lives are in your hand,
　　Queen of this island region!
　　Your life is guarded
　　By ours as by a legion
　　We vow this day.

ALL [except the Queen]
　　Long may she keep this realm
　　　From war and war's alarms!
　　Green leaves are we,
　　　Red rose our golden Queen,
　　O crownèd rose among the leaves so green!
　　[Essex and Mountjoy kneel at the Queen's feet. She removes her glove, and gives her hand to Essex, and then to Mountjoy, who both kiss it]

QUEEN
> And now I give you both
> My hand, for your obedience.

ESSEX AND MOUNTJOY
> Your Majesty, a subject kneels
> To thank you for your grace.

QUEEN
> My lords, your quarrel's reconciled,
> And now I end this audience.
> Let trumpets blow!

ESSEX, MOUNTJOY AND RALEIGH
> Let trumpets blow!

QUEEN, ESSEX, MOUNTJOY AND RALEIGH
> Lead on!
> [*The trumpets start a march, and the company moves off in procession*]

CURTAIN

Scene two

[*A private apartment at Nonesuch. The Queen is alone with Cecil. She is seated; he is standing*]

QUEEN
> Too touchy and too hot,
> They fought like boys.
> Lady Rich, Penelope,
> What did she say or do
> When she heard of the fight?

CECIL
> My lord of Essex is her brother;
> My lady was much concerned.

QUEEN
> Concerned for both?

CECIL
> Madam, rumour declares
> Mountjoy and Lady Rich are closely fond.

QUEEN
> 'Tis true, I know: the dark Penelope!
> To have a brother and a lover fight
> Would banish all tranquillity.

CECIL
> The touchier of the two received the wound.

QUEEN
> 'Twas right someone should take
> Our Essex down,
> Or he might grow unruly, and unruled.

CECIL
> The Earl will not be schooled,
> Will never learn restraint.

QUEEN
> My pigmy elf, ah, 'tis for that
> I love the lordly boy!

CECIL
> Ah, Madam, pray take care!

QUEEN
> Hark, sir! This ring
> I had at my crowning:

> With it I wedded
> Myself to the realm.

> My comfort hath been
> That my people are happy:
> Happiness theirs
> Because you are discreet.

> I seek no husband:
> But good Master Ascham
> In my infancy taught me
> Love's better than fear.

CECIL
> And caution is better,
> Sweet Highness, than ruin,
> Than rashness and ruin!
> O Princess, whom your people love
> As their protector, long and long
> My noble father served you:
> O let me serve you now, recite
> The precept that my father taught!

> The art of government
> Is in procrastination and
>   In silence and delay:
> Blazing bonfires left to burn
> Will soon consume themselves away.

> Of evils choose the least:
> Great foes will tumble down in time,
>   Or wither, one by one:
> He that rules must hear and see
> What's openly or darkly done.

> All *that* is not enough:
> There comes a moment when to rule
>   Is to be swift and bold:
> Know at last the time to strike—
> It may be when the iron is cold!

QUEEN
> Your Princess thanks you, trusty elf.

CECIL
> Now if I may obtrude myself,
> The new Ambassador from Spain—

QUEEN
> Is at the old one's tricks again!
> With one care ended, others are begun.

CECIL
> The newest is an old care now renewed.

QUEEN
> What new old care is this?

CECIL
> Word has been brought
> The King of Spain designs
> A new Armada to be sent—

QUEEN
> How soon?
> How nearly can they guess,
> Our faithful eyes and ears?

CECIL
> Perhaps before the spring.

QUEEN
God's death! What men,
What money must be thrown
Into the maw of cannon!

CECIL
Madam, we are in the hands of God.
He at a breath can melt the steel of Spain:
We can but watch and wait.

QUEEN
We can but watch and wait.
[*A stir at the door. Essex's Page enters*]

PAGE [*speaking*]
My lord of Essex!
[*Essex enters, kneels and rises. The Page goes out*]

QUEEN
Welcome, my lord. Sir Robert here,
So wise in counsel, will return anon.
                              [*Cecil bows himself out*]
Cousin, I greet you.

ESSEX
Queen of my life!

QUEEN
Ah, Robin!

ESSEX
Queen of my life!

QUEEN
Cares of State eat up my days.
There lies my lute;
Take it and play.

ESSEX [*taking up the lute*]
      Quick music is best
When the heart is oppressed;
      Quick music can heal
   With dancing, by night and by day.
Hallalloo, hallallay.

      Quick music is best
For the pipe or the strings;
      Quick music can heal
   With dancing, the pleasure of kings.
Hallalloo, hallallay.

QUEEN
Too light, too gay:
A song for careless hearts.
Turn to the lute again,
Evoke some far-off place or time,
A dream, a mood, an air
To spirit us both away.

ESSEX
Happy were he could finish forth his fate
In some unhaunted desert, where, obscure
From all society, from love and hate
Of worldly folk, then might he sleep secure;
Then wake again, and give God ever praise,
Content with hips and haws and brambleberry;
In contemplation spending all his days,
And change of holy thoughts to make him merry:
Where, when he dies, his tomb might be a bush
Where harmless Robin dwells with gentle thrush;
                              Happy were he!

QUEEN
Robin, a melting song: but who
Can this unworldly hermit be?

ESSEX
It might be any man, not one you know.

QUEEN
'Tis a conceit, it is not you.

ESSEX [*putting the lute aside*]
Queen of my life, I cannot tell.

QUEEN
You man of moods!

ESSEX
I know it well!

QUEEN
Victor of Cadiz!

ESSEX
Loser of esteem!

QUEEN
Leader of armies!

ESSEX
Follower of a dream!

QUEEN
Now up, now down, and cautious never!

ESSEX
But to one passion constant ever!

QUEEN
To advance in fortune, as becomes a man.

ESSEX
To advance in favour, as a suitor longs.

QUEEN
Do I not favour thee,
Promote thy pride
And right thy wrongs?

ESSEX
Sovereign most loved—

QUEEN
O heretofore
Though ringed with foes,
I only bled with arrows
   of the spring,
My sense was only
   wounded by the rose:
And I too then could sing:
But years decline and go:
Video et taceo!

ESSEX
What solace more
Can I disclose?
Better than tears the
   faithfulness I bring,
What my heart holds,
   only thy heart knows:
And I too now can sing:
Are tears a sign to show
That we shall reap but as
   we sow?

ESSEX
Ah, Madam, than your voice with me
No song is sweeter.

QUEEN
Then rejoice with me!
I am a woman, though I be a Queen,
And still a woman, though I be a Prince!

ESSEX
      Then let me dare assert
      The man I am, avow

Mine humble duty is
  Far more than duty now:

Call me not malapert
  If from thy feet I start
A subject, who declares
  A more than subject heart—

QUEEN
  Robin, no more!
  Blow not the spark to flame—
  Look, my lord, we are not alone—
  [*She points to the silhouette of Raleigh, suddenly visible through a
  thin curtain*]

ESSEX
  The jackal lurking by the wall,
  How vain his hope the lion will fall!

QUEEN
  Be less impetuous, my lord.

ESSEX
  The jackal waiting in the night,
  He keepeth long his evil spite.

QUEEN
  You wrong Sir Walter Raleigh there.

ESSEX
  Raleigh, Cecil, seek to ban
  My claim to Ireland, if they can.
  I am the man to conquer
  Tyrone. For God's sake let me go!
  I am the man Tyrone to overthrow,
  Sweet Prince, for God's sake let me go!

QUEEN
  Your plainings I can ne'er refuse
  [*She strikes a bell*]
  Robin, I must spare your presence:
  The business of the kingdom waits.
  Make your adieux!
  [*Raleigh's shadow vanishes. Essex kneels, and she gives him her
  hand to kiss. The Page appears, and Essex bows himself out*]

QUEEN [*soliloquizing*]
  On rivalries 'tis safe for kings
  To base their power: but how their spirit longs
  For harmonies and mellowings
  Of discords harsh, of real and phantom wrongs!
  [*thinking of Essex*]
  If life were love and love were true,
  Then could I love thee through and through!
  [*with sudden resolution*]
  But God gave me a sceptre,
    The burden and the glory—
  I must not lay them down:
    I live and reign a virgin,
      Will die in honour,
  Leave a refulgent crown!
  [*In a rapt, exalted mood, she kneels and prays aloud*]

QUEEN
  O God, my King, sole ruler of the world,
  That pulled me from a prison to a palace
  To be a sovereign Princess
  And to rule the people of England:

Thou has placed me high, but my flesh is frail:
Without Thee my throne is unstable,
My kingdom tottering, my life uncertain:
O maintain in this weak woman the heart of a man!

Errors and faults have beset me from my youth,
I bow myself before the curtain of Thy grace:
Forgive and protect me, O God, my King,
That I may rule and protect my people in peace.
                                                    Amen

CURTAIN

45 The Queen, Act II scene i, second costume

46 Sir Walter Raleigh, Act II scene iii

47 Tudor Pillars

Designer John Piper

48 Sketches for eighteen head-dresses   *John Piper*

49 Norwich, Act II scene i   *John Piper*

50 Lady Essex, Act II scene iii second dress
John Piper

51 The Queen   *John Piper*

52 The final scene

53 Mountjoy
Act III scene iii
John Piper

54 Lady-in-Waiting
Act II scene iii
John Piper

55 The Queen's Champion
Act I scene i
John Piper

56 Ante-room at Nonesuch

Designer John Piper

Act two

Scene one

[*The Guildhall at Norwich. The Queen is on progress through the city. She is attended by Raleigh, Cecil, Essex, Mountjoy, and gentlemen of the Court. She is listening to the conclusion of an address by the Recorder in the presence of a crowd*]

RECORDER
And therefore, most gracious Empress, the citizens of Norwich must always pray for Your Majesty's royal person, whom God, now and ever, preserve, to His good pleasure and our great comfort.

QUEEN
I thank you, master Recorder. You have spoken to me from the faithful hearts of my people of Norwich, and I would have them know that they may have a greater or wiser prince, but they shall never have a prince more loving.

CROWD
Hurrah! Hurrah!
[*The Recorder approaches the Queen, who gives him her hand to kiss. In attempting to kneel before her, he stumbles. She helps him to rise*]

QUEEN
Good sir, your homage hath nearly proved your undoing.

RECORDER
Madam, forgive me.
My bones are old;
My heart is old,
But not too old to beat,
And if my knees would bend
I would be kneeling at your feet.

QUEEN
God's blessing on your heart, continue there.

CROWD
Behold! Behold!
Never was a prince more loving!

RECORDER
Madam, it is our hope
You may be pleased to see
A masque, here new devised
To honour you, with song and dance.
[*The Queen signifies her consent, and is conducted to a chair. She is facing a fanciful leafy bower specially made for the occasion*]

ESSEX [*aside*]
Tedious orations, dotards on their knees—
Sir, I for one could yawn myself to death.

CECIL [*aside*]
To be on progress with her Majesty,
Is that no honour to you now, my lord?

ESSEX
An honour, yes, but like a chain
That holds me back.

CECIL
That holds you back, from what?

ESSEX
When will the Queen decide
Her Deputy for Ireland?

CECIL
The masque begins.

THE MASQUE

MASQUERS [*Semi-chorus*]
Melt earth to sea, sea flow to air,
And air fly into fire!
The elements, at Gloriana's chair,
Mingle in tuneful choir.

SPIRIT OF THE MASQUE
And now we summon from this leafy bower
The demi-god that must appear!
'Tis Time! 'tis Time!
[*From the bower springs forth a sunburnt and heroic-looking young man representing Time. He carries a bag slung from one shoulder. Time dances*]

MASQUERS
Yes, he is Time,
Lusty and blithe!
   Time is at his apogee,
Although you thought to see
A bearded ancient with a scythe.

No reaper he
That cries 'Take heed!'
   Time is at his apogee!
Young and strong, in his prime:
Behold the sower of the seed!

QUEEN [*aside*]
And Time it was that brought me here.

ESSEX [*aside*]
And Time hath yet to bring me what is due.

SPIRIT OF THE MASQUE
Time could not sow unless
He had a spouse to bless
His work, and give it life—
Concord, his loving wife!
[*From the bower steps forth Concord, a young woman of placid beauty. She dances*]

MASQUERS
   Concord is here
   Our days to bless
And this our land to endue
With plenty, peace and happiness.

   Concord and Time
   Each needeth each:
The ripest fruit hangs where
Not one, but only two can reach.

SPIRIT OF THE MASQUE
Now Time with Concord dances
This island doth rejoice:
And woods and waves and waters
Make echo to our voice.
[*Time and Concord dance together*]

MASQUERS
From springs of bounty
Through this county
Streams abundant
Of thanks shall flow!
Where life was scanty
Fruits of plenty
Swell resplendent
From earth below!

No Greek nor Roman
Queenly woman
Knew such favour
From Heaven above
As she whose presence
Is our pleasure:
Gloriana
Hath all our love!

RALEIGH [aside]
My lord, hath time brought concord now between
The Earl of Essex and yourself?

MOUNTJOY [aside]
Again we are good friends.

RALEIGH
He loves me not.
Take with a grain of salt,
I beg you, his abuse of me.

SPIRIT OF THE MASQUE
And now, country maidens, bring a tribute of flowers to
the flower of princes all.
[A troop of Young Girls step lightly out from the bower, and
dance]

MASQUERS
Sweet flag and cuckoo-flower,
Cowslip and columbine,
King-cups and sops-in-wine,
Flower-de-luce and calaminth,
Harebell and hyacinth,
Myrtle and bay, with rosemary between,
Norfolk's own garlands for her Queen!

SPIRIT OF THE MASQUE
Behold a troop of rustic swains, bring from the waves
and pastures the fruits of their toil.
[A troop of Rustics and Fishermen appear from the bower. They
dance]

MASQUERS
From fen and meadow
In rushy baskets
They bring ensamples
Of all they grow:
In earthen dishes
Their deep-sea fishes;
Yearling fleeces,
Woven blankets;
New cream and junkets,
And rustic trinkets
On wicker flaskets,
Their country largess—
The best they know!

SPIRIT OF THE MASQUE
Led by Time and Concord, let all unite in homage to

Gloriana, our hope of peace, our flower of grace.
[A final dance, in which all the performers join]

SPIRIT OF THE MASQUE AND MASQUERS
These tokens of our love receiving,
O take them, Princess great and dear,
From Norwich, city you are leaving,
That you afar may feel us near.

QUEEN
Norwich, we never can forget,
Where Time and Concord sweetly met:
Good folk, we thank you from our heart,
And in your time may concord ne'er depart.

CHORUS AND MASQUERS
Behold! Never was a Prince more loving.
O crownèd rose among the leaves so green!
Hurrah! Hurrah!

THE QUEEN'S ATTENDANTS
Long live our rose, our evergreen!

CURTAIN

Scene two

[*The garden of Essex House in the Strand. Evening. Mountjoy is
alone*]

MOUNTJOY
A garden by a river at a trysting
Is perfect in the evening for a pair,
Yet if one for the other long attendeth,
Delay falls like a frost upon the air.

But anguish is exquisite in waiting,
And who, with hope aflame, who feeleth chill?
And O, who can say, when waiting endeth,
There is more joy in hunting than the kill?
[*Lady Rich appears*]
My dark Penelope!

LADY RICH
Mountjoy, I am here at last
For a stolen hour by the Thames:
And stolen love demandeth
Crafty stratagems!

MOUNTJOY
An angel wedded to a brute!

LADY RICH
But could an angel so deceive?

MOUNTJOY AND LADY RICH
Let us walk in the paths of pleasure
And forget the nagging world outside:

MOUNTJOY
My rare one, my ruby, my treasure,
My stealthy, my secret one, my bride!

LADY RICH
Thy words are honey-dew to me:
I never hear their like from my lord.

MOUNTJOY
I'll give thee more than words.

LADY RICH
And more than words I will return thee.

MOUNTJOY
Come to the fountain, my Penelope.

LADY RICH
Yes, I will come with thee.

MOUNTJOY AND LADY RICH
And watch our two reflections kiss:
There in the water we shall see
The double image of our single bliss.
Waters, like mirrors, have no memory
Of any strange encounters they reflect.
[*Essex and Lady Essex appear. They do not see Mountjoy and Lady Rich, but are watched by them*]

ESSEX
Whatever step I take
The Queen will bar my way.

LADY ESSEX
The Queen knows your valour!

ESSEX
She knoweth not
How quick my patience ebbs.

LADY ESSEX
A subject must obey.

ESSEX
Caprice, rebuff, delay—
                    [*Essex and Lady Essex move out of sight*]

MOUNTJOY
Your brother weareth sorrow like a mask.

LADY RICH
He feels his strength unused:
With a great army he would sail
To Ireland, to attack Tyrone:
And he will mope or storm until
The Queen hath let him go.

MOUNTJOY AND LADY RICH
A garden by the river in the evening
Is doleful for a man ill at ease,
With enemies whose envy is more sombre
Than cold unfathomed hollows of the seas.
[*Essex and Lady Essex re-appear*]

ESSEX
Caprice, rebuff, delay—
Far more than enough to bear.

LADY ESSEX
In time she must relent.

ESSEX
In time! I'll break her will! I'll have my way!

LADY ESSEX
Robert, beware! You might be heard!

MOUNTJOY AND LADY RICH [*coming forward*]
Essex,
Brother] you might be heard
By other ears than ours.

LADY ESSEX
Penelope! My lord Mountjoy!

ESSEX
On my own ground,
With my own voice,

To my own wife
I dare indict
Council and Queen,
And Heaven itself . . .

LADY ESSEX
No, my good lord,
You do blaspheme!

ESSEX
'Tis them I hate,
And Cecil first,
The hunchback fox;
Raleigh I curse;
The Queen I blame.

LADY RICH AND MOUNTJOY
My lord, we know you have
Reasons and rights.

ESSEX
By Heav'n, my voice deserveth to be heard!
My birth and rank alone should make me first preferred:
How long am I to wait? The Queen shall know
Delay may turn a sweet affection sour.

LADY RICH
Call on the stars above
To give us one great hour
And the force to shape our fate!
I with the power of love,
You with the love of power,
We can seize the reins of State!

LADY ESSEX
O be cautions, I implore you!
These are treasonable words.
Danger is all about us,
Danger to all we love:

LADY RICH, ESSEX AND MOUNTJOY
The Queen is old, and time will steal
Sceptre and orb from out her hand.
Ours to decide
What other head shall wear the crown;
Ours to maintain
Our hold upon the helm of State.

LADY ESSEX
O pray be cautious, I implore you!
We have great enemies.

LADY RICH, ESSEX AND MOUNTJOY
Yet not so great as our resolve
Ourselves to rule the land.

CURTAIN

Scene three

[*A great room in the Palace of Whitehall at night. An orchestra is playing in the gallery. Courtiers and their Ladies are assembled, and a pavane is being danced. When it ends, the dancers and onlookers converse*]

CHORUS
Pavanes so grave and dignified . . .
Slow and solemn . . .
Too slow for the young . . .
The very harbinger of State . . .

[*Essex and Lady Essex enter, followed by Lady Rich and Mountjoy. Lady Essex is more splendidly dressed than any other lady present, and at once attracts attention*]

LADY-IN-WAITING
In homage to the Queen, no doubt,
My Lady Essex is so fine to-night.

LADY RICH
In homage to the Queen,
To her lord, my brother,
To honour all of us:
And how my lady shines!

MOUNTJOY
Frances, bright star of night,
All eyes to you are turning.

LADY ESSEX
Robert would have me blaze
In all this gaudiness:
But will the Queen approve?

ESSEX
Earl Marshal of England, I require
My lady to appear in state
Befitting her rank and beauty.
[*A tabor in the gallery sounds at a signal from the Master of Ceremonies*]

MASTER OF CEREMONIES
May it please you to dance a galliard!
[*A galliard is danced, in which Essex and Lady Essex take part, and in which Lady Rich is partnered by Mountjoy. As it ends, the dancers and onlookers converse*]

CHORUS
Courtly dancing the heart rejoices . . .
Graceful gliding . . .
Brave looks, noble, noble measure . . .
Nothing is lacking but the Queen . . .
[*The Queen enters, and is received with deep bows and curtsies. She catches sight of Lady Essex and looks her up and down for a perceptible moment*]

QUEEN
On hot nights and for stately moods
Pavanes and galliards are all very well.
To-night the air is chilly,
So let us warm our blood
By dancing high
In the Italian mode.
Command there a lavolta!
[*The tabor sounds as before*]

MASTER OF CEREMONIES
May it please you to dance lavolta!
[*A lavolta is danced, the Queen showing great energy and spirit. As it ends, the dancers and onlookers exclaim with animation, while fluttering fans and mopping their faces with handkerchiefs*]

CHORUS
Lusty leaping! Jump for joy! . . .
Leg over leg, as the dog went to Dover . . .
Gay go up, and gay go down . . .
And the cow jumped over the moon! . . .

QUEEN
High stepping rejoices the sinews
And for a long life the wise decree
A free and frequent sweat.

The ladies will change their linen!
And presently I will rejoin you.
[*The Queen goes out, followed by the ladies who have been dancing, among them Lady Essex. A tiny Morris Dancer, his face blacked, comes in to entertain the company during the interval before the ladies return. The last of the ladies to return is Lady Essex, now wearing a plain dress*]

LADY RICH
Frances, so plain now?
So late and so breathless?

LADY ESSEX
When I was changing
My new court dress vanished:
The maid came running, saying
It was nowhere to be found.

LADY RICH
Some prank has been played on you. Ah!
[*The Queen suddenly returns, unheralded and unattended, and wearing Lady Essex's missing dress. It is much too short for her, and she looks grotesque*]

QUEEN
Well, ladies, how like you
My new-fancied suit?
[*The ladies look at one another in uncertainty and amazement, and curtsey to the Queen. The courtiers bow, murmur among themselves, and shrink back*]

QUEEN [*turning round once or twice, like a mannequin*]
My new-fancied suit!
[*The Queen moves slowly, posturing and turning herself this way and that, towards Lady Essex on the far side of the stage*]
Ah, now, my lady,
And what think you?
Too short, is it not?
And becometh me ill?

LADY ESSEX [*distressed and embarrassed*]
May it please Your Majesty—

QUEEN
It pleaseth me not!
If, being too short,
It becometh not me,
I have it in mind
It can ne'er become thee
As being too gaudy!
So choose we another!
[*She slowly stalks out, amid bowings and curtseyings. Lady Essex turns away and hides her face in her hands. She is a little apart from the rest of the company*]

ESSEX, MOUNTJOY AND LADY RICH [*approaching Lady Essex*]
Good Frances, do not weep.

ESSEX
The Queen upon herself hath brought
Shame, and not upon my lady here.

LADY RICH
Envy and pride inflame the Queen.

ESSEX AND LADY RICH
Good Frances, do not weep.

MOUNTJOY
My lady, in whatever garb
Your sweet grace is clad,

No man on earth dare cast
A slight, or slighting look
Upon an inch of it.

ESSEX
True, my friend,
But no man has done so.

LADY RICH
O see what comes of being ruled——

ESSEX AND MOUNTJOY
By a king in a farthingale!

ESSEX, LADY RICH AND MOUNTJOY
Good Frances, do not weep.

LADY ESSEX
My friends, take care:
Her sudden rage is over now.

ESSEX
Who last year struck me with her hand
Before her Council!
Who taunts my wife before her Court!

LADY ESSEX
She is the Queen!

ESSEX
No spiteful woman ever born
Shall with impunity do this!

LADY ESSEX
Robert, take care:
She is the Queen,
And as the Queen
Hath her conditions.

ESSEX
Conditions! Conditions!
Her conditions are as crooked as her carcass!

LADY ESSEX, LADY RICH AND MOUNTJOY
Ah!

MASTER OF CEREMONIES
My lords and ladies, make way
For the Queen and her Councillors!
[*A march. The Queen returns in state, arrayed now in her own clothes. She is attended by Cecil, Raleigh and Councillors*]

RALEIGH
My lord of Essex, I am commanded by the Queen to summon you hither to her presence that you may hear a matter of great moment.
[*Essex, surprised, uneasy, still enraged, and feeling guilty after his outburst, approaches the Queen with a defiant and truculent air, then abruptly kneels. Cecil hands the Queen a paper*]

QUEEN
My lord of Essex, Knight of our most noble Order of the Garter, Earl Marshal of England, our trusty and well-beloved Cousin. Here in the presence of our Council, of the Captain of our Guard, and our Court assembled, here we acquaint you that by our Letters Patent you are this day appointed Lord Deputy of Ireland. You are to conquer the rebel Tyrone, who encourageth our enemies in Spain and grievously wasteth our substance. [*She hands the paper back to Cecil*] Go! Go into Ireland, and bring back victory and peace! [*She extends her hand, which Essex kisses fervently*]

CHORUS
Victor of Cadiz,
Overcome Tyrone!
All Spain will cower
When the rebel falls!

RALEIGH [*aside*]
So now he has his way,
So goes he to his fate.

CECIL [*aside*]
Exalted high among his peers,
He may at last more steeply fall.

QUEEN
There, Robin, go!

CHORUS
Victor of Cadiz,
Overcome Tyrone!
All Spain will cower
When the rebel falls!

MOUNTJOY AND LADY RICH [*aside*]
Returning soon, O soon,
With armies at his back,
He then will hold
The kingdom in his hand.

LADY ESSEX
At last the Queen
Drives all his cares away.
The load that I have borne
Is not so grievous now.

CHORUS
Go, warlike Earl, for Gloriana, go!

QUEEN
England and England's Queen
Entrust their hopes to you.

CHORUS
Victor of Cadiz,
Overcome Tyrone!
Come back in triumph
To these shouting halls!

ESSEX
Armed with the favour of our gracious Empress, I am armed like a god. My resolve and duty are my helm and sword, the hopes of my countrymen are my spurs. And so into Ireland I go, to break for ever those rebel kerns. With God's help I will have victory, and you shall have peace.

QUEEN
To-morrow to your charge:
To-night we dance.
Strike up the music!

MASTER OF CEREMONIES
May it please you to dance a coranto!

QUEEN
Robert, your hand!
[*Essex leads the Queen in a coranto, and other couples follow*]

CURTAIN

Act three

Scene one

[*An anteroom to the Queen's dressing-room at Nonesuch. At the back a curtain. Early morning. Maids of Honour in conversation*]

FIRST GROUP
What news from Ireland?

SECOND GROUP
Delay, delay: a sorry farce!
The summer wasted, then a truce.

FIRST GROUP
We thought by now to see the rebel's head
Laid at the Queen's feet.

ALL
Her darling Robin hath betrayed her hopes.

SECOND GROUP
The Queen knows more than we.

FIRST GROUP
Knows everything: they say
She used to have a dress
Figured from neck to hem with eyes and ears.

ALL
Ah, she is wary and wise
In the ways of the world!

SECOND GROUP
Those tiring-maids are mighty slow.

FIRST GROUP
As a woman ages
She needeth more artifice
To deck her fading bloom!

ALL
You'll come to it yourself!
[*Enter Lady-in-Waiting in some agitation*]

ALL
What now?

LADY-IN-WAITING
What now? Is the Queen dressed?
There's a great stir below!
Horsemen in haste and urgent words,
Running footsteps and panic fear!
I fear bad news
Or some complot against the Queen . . .

ALL
O God, what's this?
[*Essex bursts in, wild-looking, travel-stained, with his hand on his sword. The Maids of Honour are alarmed and recoil. The Lady-in-Waiting steps forward to meet him and to try and restrain him*]

LADY-IN-WAITING
My lord!

ESSEX
Is the Queen up?
Is the Queen yet dressed?

LADY-IN-WAITING
My lord!

ESSEX
I must see the Queen!

LADY-IN-WAITING
My lord, forbear a while:
The Queen is not yet dressed.

ESSEX
I cannot wait!

LADY-IN-WAITING
The Queen, my lord, cannot receive you now!

ESSEX
She must!
[*The Maids of Honour try to bar his way*]
Ladies, prevent me not!
[*He steps forward and sweeps the curtain back, disclosing the Queen seated at her dressing-table, wearing an old, plain dressing-gown. Two Tiring-Maids are standing beside her, helping her to dress. Her red-gold wig is on a stand before her, among the paraphernalia of the toilet. She has a looking-glass in her hand. Directly she sees Essex she puts the looking-glass down*]

QUEEN
My lord of Essex!
[*Without taking her startled gaze off him, she waves away the Lady-in-Waiting, the Tiring-Maids, and the Maids of Honour. They curtsey and withdraw. Wisps of grey hair hanging round the Queen's face make her look old, pathetic and vulnerable: but it immediately becomes clear that she has not lost command of herself or of the situation*]

QUEEN
Robin!

ESSEX [*kneeling*]
Queen of my life!

QUEEN
What brings you here?

ESSEX
My love and duty.
Day and night from Ireland
I pressed on:
I had to see and hear you:
Madam, forgive me!

QUEEN
But why must I forgive?
Because you catch
An ageing woman unadorned,
You can be called unkind:
But the years pursue us
And the rose must feel the frost:
And nothing can renew us
When the flame in the rose is lost!
[*She makes a tragic gesture, indicating her appearance: then, in the tones of a sad old woman*]
You see me as I am.

ESSEX
No less in majesty.
O give me leave to speak!

QUEEN
O pray, be brief:
The day's not yet begun.
Because you're here
When the larks alone have right of audience:
Because you stand
Besprent with mud and hollow-eyed:

BECAUSE you're here
You must have need to speak.

ESSEX
Because the gale,
The gale of the world has caught me:
Because the world
Is full of lying tongues—

BOTH
Because the world
Must know the truth of things at last—

ESSEX
Madam, give me leave to speak—
You will forgive.
Tyrone I have bound to a truce,
But foes beset me now
Here in England, at home.

QUEEN
What foes are they?
Declare!

ESSEX
Madam, my foes are yours.
My place is at your side.

QUEEN
My foes are over there!
Tyrone is still untouched!

ESSEX
Ah! But the truce—

QUEEN
Were you not required
To break his power down?

ESSEX
Madam, at your command—

QUEEN
Is it at my command
That you are here?

ESSEX
That I am here—

QUEEN
Proves you unfit—

ESSEX
Proves me unfit!

QUEEN
Unfit! Ay, and more—
Proves you untrue!

ESSEX
I, trusty in arms,
The first to defend you,
Am I to be taunted?
O care, O heaviest care!
Against me, me,
They have turned even *you*!

QUEEN
You have failed in my trust,
You have left a wound
In a heart too fond,
In my heart!

ESSEX
Then let me heal you!
Ah, Queen of my life!

ESSEX
O, put back the clock
To the birth of our hope!
The chime as it rang
Told the hour when you gave
Of your grace, when I sang
When my heart was the lute:
Happy were we!

QUEEN
Dear name I have loved,
O, use it no more!
The time and the name
Now belong to the past:
They belong to the young,
And the echoes are mute:
Happy were we!

Ah, Robin, go now!
Eat, drink and refresh you.
Go, Robin, Go!
[*She takes up her looking-glass in her right hand, and extends her left to Essex. He kisses it, and goes slowly out, casting a long look back at the Queen. The two Tiring-Maids return to help her to complete her toilet, and the Lady-in-Waiting leads in the Maids of Honour*]

LADY-IN-WAITING
My lord was early and abrupt.
Deign, Madam—allow our hands
To adorn our Sovereign in peace.
Come, Madam, come.

Lady, to your dressing-table
Turn again, and there descry
Beauty resting, beauty gazing
In her own admiring eye.

ALL
Gazing in the glass or glancing
Like Narcissus on his knees,
Beauty lives by her enhancing
And adoreth what she sees.

LADY-IN-WAITING
Tint with powder, touch with tincture,
Lightly bind a wilful curl,
Fix about the waist a cincture,
In each ear a moony pearl.

ALL
Lady, at your dressing table
With your ladies round you, gaze
Like a goddess in a fable
At the glory of our days!

LADY-IN-WAITING
Pearl and ruby gleam and glisten,
Dews bespangle open roses,
Golden gauzes, sun-rays dazzle
All beholders!
[*Her dressing done, the Queen waves all her attendants away. As they go out in one direction, she rises majestically to greet Cecil, who comes in from another*]

QUEEN

Your presence is welcome, good elf.

CECIL

Burst in upon betimes unmannerly,
Was not your Majesty alarmed?

QUEEN

What fear is, I never knew.
But as we have authority to rule
So we look to be obeyed.
But why is he here? Tell me!
Tell what you know!
What say our faithful eyes and ears?

CECIL

Tyrone is still a rebel
And Ireland not yet ours.
Not ours, but might be Spain's,
Might easily be France's:
For want of forthright action
He forfeited his chances.
And now it is September,
Too late for new campaigning.
And now he's here in England,
With hangers-on unruly,
Armed, and out for trouble,
Madam—I see a certain danger.

QUEEN	CECIL
Think of the waste!	The waste!
Count up the cost!	The cost!
Our orders defied!	Defied!
There an idle force,	
Here a rebel heart!	A rebel heart!
In the eyes of the world	
We now look a fool!	But for a time!
Now is the time for the curb!	The curb!
For the hand on the rein!	The rein!
I trust him no longer!	
Here is my command!	Raleigh awaits your command!

QUEEN

From this hour my lord of Essex
Must be kept under guard.
My Lord Deputy hath defied me;
He flouted my orders.
The Earl Marshal of England
Is himself a rebel:
With his malcontent following
Brought back from Ireland
He endangers my country.
Close watch must be kept!

Ah, my faithful elf, it has come to this!
I have failed to tame my thoroughbred.
He is still too proud;
I must break his will
And pull down his great heart.
It is I who have to rule.

CURTAIN

Scene two

[*A street in the City of London. In front of a tavern sits a blind Ballad-Singer, with a few Old Men grouped about him; at his side sits a young gittern player. A Boy, who acts as his runner and brings him the latest rumours, approaches him and whispers in his ear*]

OLD MEN

News! Give us the news!

BALLAD-SINGER

To bind by force, to hold with bars
    The wonder of this age
They tried in vain, they could not curb
    The lion in his rage:
        Great need had he
        Of liberty,
And now hath bounded from his cage.

FIRST GROUP OF OLD MEN

What can he mean?

SECOND GROUP OF OLD MEN

Essex is out, at large!

ALL

O now we shall see
His followers arm,
And aldermen bolting
Their doors in alarm!
[*The Boy runs out. A rabble of Boys marches in, led by a Man of Essex's following, playing a drum*]

RABBLE

Now rouse up all the City
And join our gallant army
    By noble Essex led:
And join us in our duty,
Make Cecil and make Raleigh
    Both shorter by a head!
        March along with us!
[*The rabble marches off, singing*]

FIRST GROUP

What rabble is this?

SECOND GROUP

Are they rebels or mad?

ALL

Mere idlers and louts
Out to trouble the peace.

BALLAD-SINGER

Whenas the lion roams at large
    And rageth fierce abroad,
Then follow lesser brutes, a mob
    That know him as their lord:
        By day or dark
        Like dogs they bark
And snatch the leavings from the board.

OLD MEN

Poor ravening knaves!
A boy runs mad
When for its bread his belly craves.
[*Drums and a turmoil are heard. Followers of Essex seek with wild cries of 'Saw! Saw! Saw! Tray! Tray!' to enlist the citizens on his side. As the tumult fades, the Boy runs in again and whispers to the Ballad-Singer*]

OLD MEN
News! Give us the news!

BALLAD-SINGER
The raveners grow bold, give tongue,
  All thirsting after prey,
With noise they keep their spirits up,
  As well indeed they may:
    They can't foresee
    What is to be,
The dreadful danger in their way.

OLD MEN
In mortal peril they must go.
[*Cuffe, attended by young rebel Officers, appears, sword in hand,
to harangue the crowd*]

CUFFE
Citizens of London,
The Earl of Essex calls you!

FOLLOWERS
Hear the drums calling,
His enemies are falling!

OLD MEN
Nay, let him call!

CUFFE
Remember Cadiz,
But Spain is still intriguing!

FOLLOWERS
With plots, underminings,
And evil designings!

OLD MEN
He's right! He's wrong!

HOUSEWIFE [*at window above*]
Hey, be off with your bawling!

FOLLOWERS
Down with the Council!

CUFFE
Let Essex save the Queen
From her false advisers!

HOUSEWIFE
Hear the ass braying!

CUFFE
To arms with Essex!

CUFFE AND FOLLOWERS
To arms for England!

HOUSEWIFE
To arms? to the gallows!
Thou rowdy! Sow's ear!
Thou slubberdegullion!
Thou eel's foot!
Rowdy cockerel!
Thou pickthank!
Mongrel! Stool-pigeon!
Thou!

CUFFE
The Queen is old,
Her power fails.
Essex must guard the Crown!

OLD MEN
That we should live into a season
When openly men practise treason!

CUFFE
Old fools, you still have time to learn
That those who deviate will burn!

HOUSEWIFE
Yah, Willy Wet-leg, you won't burn!

CUFFE
Slattern, I'll have your blood!

FOLLOWERS
Come, forward!

CUFFE AND FOLLOWERS
Forward! March!

HOUSEWIFE
I'll damp your courage!
Take that you wastrel!
[*The Housewife leans out and empties a chamber-pot over Cuffe
and his followers as they are marching off*]

CUFFE AND FOLLOWERS [*running out*]
Ah!
[*The onlookers laugh*]

BALLAD-SINGER
Proud man goes strutting forth to slay,
  And brags with might and main,
But Goodwife Joan will jeer at him
  Till Pride itself is slain:
    It is her lot
    To keel the pot
And mock the hero home again.

HOUSEWIFE AND OLD MEN
It is ⎡my ⎤ lot
      ⎣her⎦
To keel the pot
And mock the hero home again.
[*The City Crier with his bell is heard at the end of the street*]

CRIER
Oyez! Oyez! In the name of the Queen! Be it known that
Robert Devereux, Earl of Essex, erstwhile Lord Deputy
in Ireland, having risen against the Crown and Realm of
England, is this day proclaimed TRAITOR. Any man
giving him aid, by word or deed, will be guilty of
TREASON.

FIRST GROUP
Essex a traitor!

SECOND GROUP
Guilty of treason!

FIRST GROUP
There's trouble ahead!

SECOND GROUP
There always is!

ALL
The Queen, the Queen,
What will she do?

BALLAD-SINGER
In all his pride the lion roared
  And sought whom to devour,

But he mistook the time to spring,
  Mistook his pride for power:
    Down in the dust
    Soon fall he must,
For dire is the day, and dread the hour.

ALL
He asked for trouble
And trouble has come.

Trouble has come
And heads must fall—
We told you so!
[*The Ballad-Singer gives the Boy a coin*]

BALLAD-SINGER
Here, Harry boy, a groat—
Fill your belly, wet your throat.
There's work for you, my boy!
Work! Work! Work!
                    [*The Boy runs out*]

CURTAIN

Scene three

[*A room in the Palace of Whitehall. Cecil, Raleigh, and others of the Council*]

RALEIGH
The trial now being over,
The traitor's malice ended—

COUNCILLORS
Essex is guilty and condemned to die!

CECIL
Councillors, take notice of my warning—
Beware of one thing yet!

RALEIGH
Of what?

COUNCILLORS
Essex is guilty and condemned to die!

CECIL
That is our verdict. In the Tower
He awaits the day.

RALEIGH
Wednesday is the day appointed!
He will see no later day!

COUNCILLORS
Essex is guilty and condemned to die!

CECIL
Beware of one thing yet!
The Queen may yet defer the deed.

RALEIGH
The day, but not the deed.

COUNCILLORS
Essex is guilty and condemned to die!

CECIL
She long delayed to seal the doom
Of the Northern Earls and the Queen of Scots:
She may delay once more,
Or even spare his life.

RALEIGH AND COUNCILLORS
Never! Essex can she not forgive!

ALL
Essex is guilty and condemned to die!
[*The Queen enters. All kneel*]

QUEEN
Let me hear the verdict.
Are you all agreed?

CECIL
May it please your Majesty,
The verdict was unanimous.
[*He turns to Raleigh and the Councillors*]

RALEIGH
After trial the court has found
The Earl of Essex guilty of treason.

COUNCILLORS
Guilty of treason and condemned to die!

QUEEN
To die a traitor. Ah!

RALEIGH
Wednesday is the day appointed.

COUNCILLORS
Guilty of treason and condemned to die!

RALEIGH [*proffering the death-warrant*]
Only awaits your royal hand
To ratify his doom.

QUEEN
I will not sign it now!
I will consider it.

CECIL
Madam, I humbly pray, do not defer
This dreadful duty,
Or the people will doubt
If the traitor is guilty
Or the Queen is safe.

QUEEN
Cecil, no prating
To me of my duty!
Silence!
The Council's dismissed!
[*They bow themselves out. The Queen paces up and down*]
I grieve, yet dare not show my discontent;
I love, and yet am forced to seem to hate;
I am, and am not; freeze, and yet I burn;
Since from myself my other self I turn.
[*Raleigh steps boldly into the room*]
Sir Walter, what now?

RALEIGH
Three persons, in humble duty,
Crave audience of their Sovereign.
[*Behind him enters Lady Essex, her face half veiled. She is supported by Lady Rich, and followed by Mountjoy*]

LADY ESSEX, LADY RICH AND MOUNTJOY
Great Queen, your champion in a prison cell
Lies languishing. We come to plead for him.
To intercede for him,
Beseech your pardon, urge your need for him
Whose love and valour may still serve you well.

[*Mountjoy leads Lady Essex forward. She makes an obeisance to the Queen and sinks to her knees*]

MOUNTJOY
To ask your mercy, Madam,
The Countess bows her head and kneels.

LADY ESSEX
Too ill-advised
He greatly erred:
But let the father of my children live!

QUEEN
Hearken, it is a Prince who speaks.
A Prince is set upon a stage
Alone, in sight of all the world;
Alone, and must not fail.

LADY ESSEX
If he must die
I plead for my children,
His!

QUEEN [*gently*]
Frances, a woman speaks.
Whatever I decide—
I have yet to name the day,
To sign his breath away,
His, that betrayed his Queen—
Whatever I decide,
Your children, Frances, will be safe.
[*Lady Essex makes another obeisance, covers her face with her veil, and steps back*]

MOUNTJOY
His sister, Madam, begs to speak.
Deign to hear her pleading.

QUEEN
What! Tears from those bold eyes!
Tears from my Lady Rich!

LADY RICH
The noble Earl of Essex
Was born to fame and fortune,
Yet not his rank alone
Hath made his greatness known.

QUEEN
I gave him honour, gave him power—

LADY RICH
Greatly hath he served the State,
And armies follow him through fire.
Madam, you need him:
Let his greatness be.

QUEEN
He touched my sceptre—
Then he was too great
To be endured.

LADY RICH
Still great he would have been
Without the grace
And favour of a Queen!
Still great!

QUEEN
Woman! How dare you plead
For a traitor's life,
You, an unfaithful wife!

LADY RICH
No traitor he! Not he!

QUEEN
Justice hath found him so!

LADY RICH
Be merciful,
Be wise!

QUEEN
Be dutiful,
Be still!

LADY RICH
He most deserves
Your pardon—

QUEEN
Most insolent,
You dare presume!

LADY RICH
Deserves your love!

QUEEN
Importune me no more!
Out!

LADY RICH [*beside herself with rage*]
God forgive you!
God forgive you!

QUEEN [*to Raleigh*]
Give me the warrant!
I will sign it now!
[*As the Queen takes up a pen to sign the warrant, Lady Rich screams and throws herself into the arms of Mountjoy. The Queen signs the warrant and hands it back to Raleigh, who bows himself out. As Mountjoy leads Lady Rich and Lady Essex away, the stage darkens. The Queen is seen standing alone in a strong light against an indeterminate background. Time and place are becoming less and less important to her*]

QUEEN [*speaking*]
I have now obtained the victory over two things which the greatest princes cannot at their will subdue: the one is fame, the other is over a great mind. Surely the world is now, I hope, reasonably satisfied.

In some unhaunted desert . . .

THE VOICE OF ESSEX [*speaking*]
I am thrown into a corner like a dead carcass and you refuse to hear of me, which to traitors you never did. What remains is only to beseech you to conclude my punishment, my misery, and my life.

QUEEN
There might he sleep secure . . .
[*Cecil appears standing near the Queen*]

CECIL [*speaking*]
The King of Scotland, may he not be told your Majesty's pleasure? Will it not please your Majesty to name the successor to your throne?

QUEEN [*speaking angrily*]
I can by no means endure a winding-sheet held up before mine eyes while yet I live.
[*She dismisses him, Cecil bows and retires. The Queen, standing alone, directly addresses the audience*]

QUEEN [*speaking*]
I have ever used to set the last Judgment Day before mine eyes, and when I have to answer the highest Judge, I mean to plead that never thought was cherished in my heart that tended not to my people's good. I count it the glory of my crown that I have reigned with your love, and there is no jewel that I prefer before that jewel. Neither do I desire to live longer days than that I may see your prosperity: and that's my only desire.
[*Distant cheering. Near the Queen appears a death-like phantom of herself. It approaches and fades*]

QUEEN
Mortua, mortua, sed non sepulta!
[*Cecil appears near the Queen*]

CECIL [*speaking*]
To content the people, Madam, you *must* go to bed.

QUEEN [*speaking*]
The word 'must' is not to be used to Princes! Little man, little man, you durst not have said it, but you know I must die.

CECIL [*speaking*]
I wish your Majesty long life.

QUEEN [*speaking*]
I see no weighty reason that I should be fond to live or fear to die.
[*Cecil disappears, and the Queen is alone again*]

CHORUS [*off*]
Green leaves are we,
Red rose our golden Queen,
O crownèd rose among the leaves so green!
[*The singing fades, and the Queen is slowly enveloped in darkness*]

The Turn of the Screw

An opera in two acts

by Myfanwy Piper

adapted from the story by Henry James

BENJAMIN BRITTEN OP. 10

CHARACTERS

The Prologue	TENOR
The Governess	SOPRANO
Miles and Flora *children in her charge*	TREBLE, SOPRANO
Mrs Grose *the housekeeper*	SOPRANO
Miss Jessel *a former governess*	SOPRANO
Quint *a former manservant*	TENOR

The action takes place at Bly, a country house, about the middle of the last century.

NOTE The line 'The ceremony of innocence is drowned' is taken from 'The Second Coming' by W B Yeats.
The songs 'Tom, Tom, the Piper's Son' and 'Lavender's Blue' are traditional nursery rhymes.
The Latin words used in Act one, Scene six, are schoolboys' rhyming grammatical rules.

FIRST PERFORMANCE
14 September 1954   *Venice, Teatro la Fenice*
                                           (E.O.G. production)

Prologue	Peter Pears
The Governess	Jennifer Vyvyan
Mrs Grose	Joan Cross
Quint	Peter Pears
Miss Jessel	Arda Mandikian
Flora	Olive Dwyer
Miles	David Hemmings

Conducted by Benjamin Britten
Produced by Basil Coleman
Designed by John Piper
Lighting designed by Michael Northen

SYNOPSIS OF SCENES

Prologue

Act one
Scene one	The journey
Scene two	The welcome
Scene three	The letter
Scene four	The tower
Scene five	The window
Scene six	The lesson
Scene seven	The lake
Scene eight	At night

Act two
Scene one	Colloquy and soliloquy
Scene two	The bells
Scene three	Miss Jessel
Scene four	The bedroom
Scene five	Quint
Scene six	The piano
Scene seven	Flora
Scene eight	Miles

Prologue

[*The Prologue is discovered in front of a drop curtain*]

It is a curious story.
I have it written in faded ink—a woman's hand,
governess to two children—long ago.

Untried, innocent, she had gone first to see their guardian
in London; a young man, bold, offhand and gay, the
children's only relative.

The children were in the country with an old housekeeper.
There had been a governess, but she had gone. The boy, of
course, was at school, but there was the girl, and the
holidays, now begun.

This then would be her task.

But there was one condition: he was so much engaged;
affairs, travel, friends, visits, always something, no time at
all for the poor little things—she was to do everything—be
responsible for everything—not to worry him at all—no,
not to write, but to be silent, and do her best.

She was full of doubts.

But she was carried away: that he, so gallant and handsome,
so deep in the busy world, should need her help.

At last
'I will,' she said.

Act one

THEME
Scene one

The journey

[*The lights go up on the interior of a coach. The Governess is in
a travelling dress*]

GOVERNESS
Nearly there.
Very soon I shall know, I shall know what's in store
for me.
Who will greet me? The children . . .the children.
Will they be clever? Will they like me?
Poor babies, no father, no mother. But I shall love
them as I love my own, all my dear ones left at home,
so far away—and so different.
If things go wrong, what shall I do? Who can I ask,
with none of my kind to talk to? Only the old
housekeeper, how will she welcome me? I must not
write to their guardian, that is the hardest part of all.
Whatever happens, it is I, I must decide.
A strange world for a stranger's sake. O why did I come?
No! I've said I will do it, and—for him I will.
There's nothing to fear. What could go wrong?
Be brave, be brave. We're nearly there. Very soon I
shall know. Very soon I shall know . . .

[*The scene fades*]

VARIATION I

Scene two
The welcome

[*The lights fade in on the porch at Bly. Mrs Grose, with the
children dancing about*]

MILES AND FLORA
Mrs Grose! Mrs Grose! Will she be nice?
Mrs Grose! Will she be cross?
Why doesn't she hurry? Why isn't she here?
Will she like us? Shall we like her?

MRS GROSE
Quiet, children!
Lord! How you do tease! Will she be this, will she
be that, a dozen dozen times I do declare.
You'll see soon enough. Now quietly, do!
Miss Flora, your pinafore!
[*She gives Flora a little good-natured tidying shake, pats
Miles's hair into place and smooths down her own apron*]
Master Miles, your hair!
Keep still dearie, or you'll wear me out.
Now show me how you bow.
[*Miles bows*]
How do you curtsey?
[*Flora curtseys. The children continue bowing and curtseying
until Mrs Grose stops them*]
Here she is now.
[*Enter Governess*]

GOVERNESS
You must be Mrs Grose? I'm so happy to see you . . .
so happy to be here.

MRS GROSE [*curtseying*]
How do you do, Miss. Welcome to Bly!

GOVERNESS
This must be Flora? And Miles?
[*Flora curtseys, Miles bows*]

GOVERNESS
How charming they are, how beautiful too. The house
and park are so splendid, far grander than I am used to.
I shall feel like a princess here. Bly, I begin to love you.

MRS GROSE
I'm happy, so happy that you've come, Miss. Miss
Flora and Master Miles are happy, so happy that
you're here too. They're good children, yes, they are,
they're good, Miss. They're lively, too lively for an
ignorant old woman. They wear me out, indeed they
do. My poor head isn't bright enough—the things they
think up! I'm far too old a body for games, Miss, far
too old, and now they'll do better with a young thing as
lively as they are themselves. Master Miles is
wonderful at lessons, and Miss Flora's sharp too. Yes,
they're clever—they need their own kind, they're far too
clever for me! They'll do better now, they'll do better
with a young thing. (Pardon the liberty, Miss.) They'll
do better now you're here!

MILES AND FLORA
Come along! Come along! Do!
We want to show you the house.
We want to show you the park.
Don't stay talking here any more.

MRS GROSE
Quiet, children! Lord! How you do tease.
In a trice they'll be dragging you all over the park.

GOVERNESS
No, they must show me everything!
For Bly is now my home.
[*The scene fades as the children lead the Governess off*]

VARIATION II

Scene three
The letter

[*The lights fade in again on the porch at Bly, to the side of which more of the house is now visible, including a low window. Mrs Grose enters*]

MRS GROSE
Miss! Miss! A letter for you.
[*The Governess enters from the house*]
Here!
[*She hands a letter to the Governess who reads it quietly*]
[*aside*]
A good young lady, I'll be bound, and a pretty one too.
Now all will be well, we were far too long alone!

GOVERNESS
Mrs Grose! He's dismissed his school.

MRS GROSE
Who?

GOVERNESS
Little Miles.

MRS GROSE
Miles?

GOVERNESS
What can it mean—never go back?

MRS GROSE
Never?

GOVERNESS
Never! O, but for that he must be bad!

MRS GROSE
Him bad?

GOVERNESS
—An injury to his friends.

MRS GROSE
Him an injury—I won't believe it!

GOVERNESS
Tell me, Mrs Grose, have you known Miles to be bad?

MRS GROSE
A boy is no boy for me if he is never wild. But bad,
No, no!

GOVERNESS	MRS GROSE
I cannot think him really bad, not Miles. Never!	Never! Not Master Miles. He can be wild, but not bad.

[*They look towards the window where the children are seen playing quietly together*]

FLORA AND MILES
Lavender's blue, diddle, diddle,
    Lavender's green,
When I am King, diddle, diddle,
    You shall be Queen.

Call up your men, diddle, diddle,
    Set them to work,
Some to the plough, diddle, diddle,
    Some to the cart.

Some to make hay, diddle, diddle,
    Some to cut corn,
While you and I, diddle diddle—

GOVERNESS AND MRS GROSE
See how sweetly he plays, and with how gentle a look he turns to his sister. Yes! The child is an angel!
It is nonsense—never a word of truth.
It is all a wicked lie.
[*The window fades*]

MRS GROSE
What shall you do then?

GOVERNESS
I shall do nothing.

MRS GROSE
And what shall you say to him?

GOVERNESS
I shall say nothing.

MRS GROSE
Bravo! And I'll stand by you. O Miss, may I take the liberty?

[*Mrs Grose kisses her. The scene fades*]

VARIATION III

Scene four
The tower

[*The lights fade in again on the house. The tower is now visible. Evening, sweet summer. Enter Governess, strolling*]

GOVERNESS
How beautiful it is. Each day it seems more beautiful to me. And my darling children enchant me more and more. My first foolish fears are all vanished now, are all banished now—
those fluttering fears when I could not forget the letter—
when I heard a far off cry in the night—
and once a faint footstep passed my door.

Only one thing I wish, that I could see him—
and that he could see how well I do his bidding.

The birds fly home to these great trees, I too am at home.
Alone, tranquil, serene.
[*Quint becomes visible on the tower*]

GOVERNESS
Ha! 'Tis he!
[*He looks steadily at her, then turns and disappears*]

Bly, pen and wash sketch

John Piper

Sketch for final design
John Piper

59 Mrs Grose   *John Piper*   60 Flora, Act II   *John Piper*   61 Miss Jessel   *John Piper*

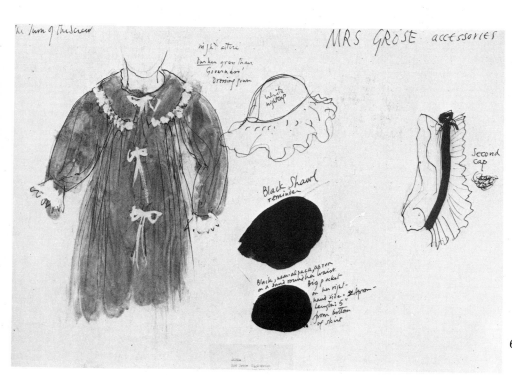

62 Mrs Grose
night attire
John Piper

63 Scene v: Jennifer Vyvyan and Peter Pears

64 Scene viii: David Hemmings

65 Set for Act I

John Piper

The Turn of the Screw
sketch for FLORA
In Act 1 Sc 2

66 Flora
Act I scene ii
John Piper

No! No! Who is it? Who?
Who can it be?
Some servant—no! I know them all.
Who is it, who?
Who can it be?
Some curious stranger? But how did he get in?
Who is it, who?
Some fearful madman locked away there?
Adventurer? Intruder?
Who is it, who?
Who can it be?

[*The scene fades*]

VARIATION IV

Scene five
The window

[*The lights fade in on the interior of the hall at Bly, with window. Flora and Miles ride in on a hobby horse*]

MILES AND FLORA
Tom, Tom, the piper's son
  Stole a pig and away he run.
Pig was eat and Tom was beat,
  Tom ran howling down the street.

MILES
Now I'll steal the pig, I'll steal the pig!

FLORA
Go on, then go on!

MILES AND FLORA
Tom, Tom, the piper's son!
  Stole a pig and away he run—

MILES
Now chase me, chase me!

FLORA
I'll catch you! I'll catch you!

MILES AND FLORA
Pig was eat and Tom was beat,
  Tom ran howling down the street.

FLORA
Let's do it again! Let's do it again!

GOVERNESS [*off*]
Children! Are you ready? Run along then.

MILES AND FLORA
Tom, Tom, the piper's son
          [*They ride off as the Governess enters*]

GOVERNESS
I'll follow.

MILES AND FLORA [*off*]
Stole a pig and away he run. (etc.)
[*The Governess looks about for a moment, picks up a pair of gloves and is about to go out when she looks up and sees Quint appear suddenly in the window. They gaze at one another. He disappears. She runs out and looks through the window as he had done. Mrs Grose enters as the Governess rushes back into the room*]

MRS GROSE
Ah! My dear! You look so white and queer. What's happened?

GOVERNESS
I have been frightened.

MRS GROSE
What was it?

GOVERNESS
A man looked through the window, a strange man. But I saw him before, on the tower.

MRS GROSE
No one from the village?

GOVERNESS
No.

MRS GROSE
A gentleman then?

GOVERNESS
No! Indeed no!

MRS GROSE
What was he like?

GOVERNESS
His hair was red, close-curling, a long, pale face, small eyes. His look was sharp, fixed and strange. He was tall, clean-shaven, yes, even handsome.
But a horror!

MRS GROSE
Quint! Peter Quint!
Dear God, is there no end to his dreadful ways?

GOVERNESS
Peter Quint—who is that?
Tell me. Mrs Grose! Do you know him then? Tell me!

MRS GROSE
Dear God! Is there no end?
[*She weeps*]

GOVERNESS
Mrs Grose, what has happened here, in this house?

MRS GROSE
Quint, Peter Quint, the Master's valet. Left here in charge.
It was not for me to say, Miss, no indeed. I had only to see to the house. But I saw things elsewhere I did not like. When Quint was free with everyone—with little master Miles—

GOVERNESS
Miles!

MRS GROSE
Hours they spent together.

GOVERNESS
Miles!

MRS GROSE
Yes, Miss, he made free with
her too—with lovely Miss Jessel, governess to those pets, those angels, those innocent babes—and she a lady, so far above him.
Dear God! Is there no end!
But he had ways to twist them round his little finger.
He liked them pretty, I can tell you, Miss—and he had his will, morning and night.

GOVERNESS
But why did you not tell your master? Write to him?
Send for him to come?

MRS GROSE
I dursn't. He never liked worries. 'Twas not my place.
They were not in my charge. Quint was too clever.
I feared him—feared what he could do.
No, Mr Quint, I did not like your ways!
And then she went. She couldn't stay, not then.
She went away to die.

GOVERNESS
To die? And Quint?

MRS GROSE
He died too.

GOVERNESS
Died?

MRS GROSE
Fell on the icy road—struck his head, lay there
till morning, dead!
Dear God, is there no end to his dreadful ways?

GOVERNESS
I know nothing of these things. Is this sheltered place
the wicked world where things unspoken of can be?

MRS GROSE
Dear God!

GOVERNESS
Only this much I know: things have been done here
that are not good, and have left a taste behind them.
That man: impudent, spoiled, depraved.
Mrs Grose, I am afraid, not for me, for Miles. He
came to look for Miles, I'm sure of that, and he
will come again.

MRS GROSE
I don't understand.

GOVERNESS
But I see it now, I must protect the children, I must
guard their quiet, and their guardian's too.
See what I see, know what I know, that they may
see and know nothing.

MRS GROSE
Lord, Miss! Don't understand a word of what you say.
But I'll stand by you, Lord, Miss, indeed I will.

[*The scene fades*]

VARIATION V

Scene six
The lesson

[*The lights fade in on the schoolroom. The Governess is hearing
Miles his Latin lesson. Flora is 'helping'*]

MILES	FLORA [*echoing*]
Many nouns in *is* we find	we find
To the masculine are assigned:	are assigned:
Amnis, axis, caulis, collis,	collis
Clunis, crinis, fascis, follis,	follis
Fustis, ignis, orbis, ensis,	ensis
Panis, piscis, postis, mensis,	mensis

Torris, unguis and canalis,	—nalis
Vectis, vermis, and natalis,	—talis
Sanguis, pulvis, cucumis,	and cumis
Lapis, casses, manes, glis.	and glis, and mis
	and lis, and guis
	and nis and ris,
	and tis.
Many nouns in *is* we find	we find
To the masculine are assigned.	are assigned.

GOVERNESS
That's good, Miles, you've learned that well!
Now say for me—

FLORA
Can't we stop now? Let's do history! Boadicea
on her chariot! Look at me!
[*Flora frisks around*]

GOVERNESS
Flora! Don't tease, dear! We must do Miles's Latin.
Come now! What else do you remember? Now think.

MILES
Malo: I would rather be
Malo: in an apple-tree
Malo: than a naughty boy
Malo: in adversity.

GOVERNESS
Why, Miles, what a funny song! Did I teach you that?

MILES
No, I found it. I like it. Do you?
Malo   Malo   Malo.

[*The scene fades*]

VARIATION VI

Scene seven
The lake

[*The lights fade in on the lake in the park. A sunny morning.
Flora and the Governess wander in, Flora with a doll, the
Governess with a book*]

FLORA
O rivers and seas and lakes!
Is this lake in my book?

GOVERNESS
No dear, it's far too small.

FLORA
Small? It's huge! It's a great wide sea!

GOVERNESS
A sea? Then you must name it. Come Flora, what seas
do you know?

FLORA	GOVERNESS
Adriatic and Aegean	Yes.
Baltic, Bosnian and the Caspian,	Good.
Black, and Red and White and Yellow	And—
Medi—medi—terra—nean.	Go on!
And . . . and . . . and . . . the Dead Sea	And this one?
Is the Dead Sea.	Oh!

FLORA
How can a sea be dead?

GOVERNESS
They call it dead because nothing can live in it.

FLORA
Then I wouldn't go in it, and neither would Miles.
[*They settle down, Flora on the ground with her doll, the Governess on a bench with her book*]

FLORA
Go to sleep, my dolly dear. Go to sleep.

GOVERNESS
Sing to her dear, dolly must sleep wherever you choose.

FLORA
Dolly must sleep wherever I choose
Today by the dead salt sea
Tomorrow her waxen lids may close
On the plains of Muscovy.

And now like a Queen of the East she lies,
With a Turk to guard her bed,
But next, when her short-lived daylight dies,
She's a shepherdess instead.

But sleep dear dolly, O sleep, and when
You are lost in your journeying dream
The sea may change to a palace again,
For nothing shall stay the same . . .

That's right, my darling. How good you are.
Go to sleep.
[*During this song Flora has rocked her doll, and put her down. When the song is over she goes on fussing over the doll as she murmurs the last two or three sentences, until Miss Jessel appears on the other side of the lake. Flora silently and deliberately turns round to face the audience away from Miss Jessel. Then the Governess, aware of Flora's silence, looks up and sees Miss Jessel, who at once disappears*]

GOVERNESS
Flora! Come along!
We must go now, go, and find Miles.

MILES [*shouting off*]
Hullo! Where are you, you two?

GOVERNESS
There he is! Go to him! Go to him!

MILES [*off*]
Hullo!   [*Flora runs out*]

GOVERNESS
Miss Jessel! It was Miss Jessel!
She returns too—she too—she too—
And Flora saw, I know she saw, and said nothing.

They are lost! Lost!
I neither save nor shield them.
I keep nothing from them.

Oh I am useless, useless. What can I do?
It is far worse than I dreamed.

They are lost! Lost! Lost!
[*as she goes off*]
                              [*The scene fades*]

Scene eight
At night

QUINT [*unseen*]
Miles! Miles! Miles! Ah, Miles!
[*The lights fade in on the front of the house and the tower. Quint is on the tower. Miles in the garden below him, in his nightgown*]

MILES
I'm here, O I'm here!

QUINT
I am all things strange and bold,
The riderless horse
Snorting and stamping on the hard sea sand,
The hero-highwayman plundering the land.
I am King Midas with gold in his hand.

MILES
Gold, O yes, gold!

QUINT
I am the smooth world's double face,
Mercury's heels
Feathered with mischief and a god's deceit.
The brittle blandishment of counterfeit.
In me secrets and half-formed desires meet.

MILES
Secrets, O secrets!

QUINT
I am the hidden life that stirs
When the candle is out;
Upstairs and down, the footsteps barely heard.
The unknown gesture, the soft, persistent word,
The long sighing flight of the night-winged bird.

MILES
Bird!

QUINT
Miles!

MILES
I'm listening.

QUINT
Miles!

MILES
I'm here.

QUINT
Miles!

MISS JESSEL [*unseen*]   **QUINT**
Flora! Flora! Come!   Miles!
[*The lights now come up on Flora at the window and Miss Jessel by the lake*]

FLORA
I'm here, O I'm here—

MISS JESSEL
Come.

MILES
I'm listening, I'm here.

QUINT
Miles!

MISS JESSEL
Their dreams and ours
Can never be one,
They will forsake us.
O come to me! Come!

FLORA
Tell me, what shall I see there?

QUINT [*to Miles*]
What goes on in your head, what questions?
Ask, for I answer all.

MILES
Oh!

MISS JESSEL
All those we have wept for together;
Beauty forsaken in the beast's demesne,
The little mermaid weeping on the sill,
Gerda and Psyche seeking their love again
Pandora, with her dreadful box, as well.

QUINT
Ask! Ask! Ask!

FLORA
Pandora with her box as well!

QUINT [*to Miles*]
What goes on in your dreams? Keep silent!
I know, and answer that too.

MILES
Oh!

MISS JESSEL
Their knowledge and ours
Can never be one,
They will despise us
O come to me, come!

QUINT AND MISS JESSEL
On the paths, in the woods, on the banks,
by the walls, in the long, lush grass,
or the winter leaves, fallen leaves, I wait—
I shall be there,
you must not fail.

GOVERNESS [*approaching*]   MRS GROSE [*approaching*]
Miles! Where are you?   Flora! Are you there?

QUINT   MISS JESSEL
Come! Miles!   Flora! Come to me!

MILES   FLORA
I shall never fail—   Yes! I shall be there
Yes, I shall be there.   I shall never fail.
[*After these phrases have been repeated over and over again the
Governess appears in the porch. Mrs Grose at the window.
Quint and Miss Jessel disappear. The Governess runs to Miles*]

GOVERNESS
Mrs Grose! Go to Flora!

MRS GROSE
Why, whatever's going on? Miss Flora out of bed!

GOVERNESS
Miles! What are you doing here?
                              [*Mrs Grose takes Flora away*]

MILES
You see, I am bad, I am bad, aren't I?
[*Miles goes into house followed by the Governess as the lights fade*]

CURTAIN

Act two

VARIATION VIII

Scene one
Colloquy and soliloquy

[*The lights fade in on Quint and Miss Jessel; nowhere*]

MISS JESSEL
Why did you call me from my schoolroom dreams?

QUINT
I call? Not I! You heard the terrible sound of the wild
swan's wings.

MISS JESSEL
Cruel! Why did you beckon me to your side?

QUINT
I beckon? No, not I! Your beating heart to your own
passions lied.

MISS JESSEL
Betrayer! Where were you when in the abyss I fell?

QUINT
Betrayer? Not I! I waited for the sound of my own last
bell.

MISS JESSEL
And now, what do you seek?

QUINT
I seek a friend.

MISS JESSEL
She is here!

QUINT
No!—self-deceiver.

MISS JESSEL
Ah! Quint, Quint, do you forget?

QUINT
I seek a friend—
Obedient to follow where I lead,
Slick as a juggler's mate to catch my thought,
Proud, curious, agile, he shall feed
My mounting power.
Then to his bright subservience I'll expound
The desperate passions of a haunted heart,
And in that hour
'The ceremony of innocence is drowned'.

MISS JESSEL
I too must have a soul to share my woe
Despised, betrayed, unwanted she must go
Forever to my joyless spirit bound
'The ceremony of innocence is drowned'.

QUINT AND MISS JESSEL
Day by day the bars we break,
Break the love that laps them round,
Cheat the careful watching eyes,
'The ceremony of innocence is drowned'
'The ceremony of innocence is drowned'.
[*The lights fade out on Quint and Miss Jessel and fade in on the
Governess*]

GOVERNESS
Lost in my labyrinth I see no truth,
only the foggy walls of evil press upon me.
Lost in my labyrinth I see no truth.

O innocence, you have corrupted me,
which way shall I turn?

I know nothing of evil
yet I feel it, I fear it, worse—imagine it.
Lost in my labyrinth which way shall I turn?
[*The scene fades*]

VARIATION IX

Scene two
The bells

[*The lights fade in on the churchyard with a table-tomb and indications of a church*]

MILES AND FLORA [*chanting off*] [*approaching*]
O sing unto them a new song: let the
congregation praise him.
O ye works and days: bless ye the Lord.
[*They walk in like choir boys*]
O ye rivers and seas and lakes: bless ye the Lord.
O amnis, axis, caulis, collis, clunis,
crinis, fascis, follis: bless ye the Lord.
Praise him and magnify him for ever.
[*The children settle themselves on the tomb as the Governess and Mrs Grose enter*]

MRS GROSE
O Miss, a bright morning to be sure.

GOVERNESS
Yes.

MILES AND FLORA
O ye tombstones and trees: praise him.

MRS GROSE
Bright as the Sunday morning bells, how I love the
sound.

GOVERNESS
Yes.

MILES AND FLORA
O ye bells and towers: praise him.

MRS GROSE
And the dear children, how sweet they are together.

GOVERNESS
Yes.

MILES AND FLORA
O ye paths and woods: praise him.
O ye frosts and fallen leaves: praise him.
O ye dragons and snakes, worms and feathered fowl:
rejoice in the Lord.

MRS GROSE
Come Miss, don't worry. It will pass I'm sure.
They're so happy with you. You're so good to them.
We all love you, Miss.

MILES AND FLORA
O Mrs Grose, bless ye the Lord: may she never
be confounded.

GOVERNESS
Dear good Mrs Grose—they are not playing, they
are talking horrors.

MRS GROSE
Oh! Never!

GOVERNESS
Why are they so charming? Why so unnaturally good?
I tell you they are not with us, but with the others.

MRS GROSE
With Quint—and that woman?

GOVERNESS
With Quint and that woman.

MRS GROSE
But what could they do?

GOVERNESS
Do! They can destroy them.

MRS GROSE
Miss! You must write to their uncle.

GOVERNESS
—That his house is poisoned, the children
mad—or that I am? I was charged not to
worry him.

MRS GROSE
Yes, He does hate worry.

GOVERNESS
I shall never write to him.
Can you not feel them round about you? They are
here, there, everywhere. And the children are
with them, they are not with us.

MRS GROSE
Come Miss, don't worry, It'll pass I'm sure.
They're so happy with you, you're so good to
them. We all love you so.
Never you mind, we'll be all right, you'll see.

MILES AND FLORA
O ye paths and woods: bless ye the Lord.
O ye walls and towers: bless ye the Lord.
O ye moon and stars, windows and lakes:
Praise him and magnify him for ever and ever.

MRS GROSE
Come Miss! It is time we went in. Come to church
my dear, it'll do you good. Flora! Miles!
Come along, dears.
[*She collects the children and goes towards the church, but Miles hangs back and turns to the Governess*]

MILES
Do you like the bells? I do.
They're not half-finished yet.

GOVERNESS
No.

MILES
Then we can talk and you can tell me when
I'm going back to school.

GOVERNESS
Are you not happy here?

MILES
I'm growing up, you know. I want my own kind.

GOVERNESS
Yes, you're growing up.

MILES
So much I want to do, so much I might do . . .

GOVERNESS
But I trust you, Miles.

MILES
You trust me, my dear, but you think and think . . .
of us, and of the others.

Does my uncle think what you think?
[*Miles goes off into church. The bells reach their climax and
then stop. The Governess sits down suddenly on the table-tomb*]

MRS GROSE, FLORA AND MILES [*from the church*]
Praise him and magnify him for ever!

GOVERNESS
It was a challenge!
He knows what I know, and dares me to act.
But who would believe my story? Mrs Grose? No—
she's no good. She has doubts.
I am alone, alone.
I must go away now, while they are at church;
away from those false little lovely eyes; away
from my fears, away from those horrors; away from this
poisoned place; away, away!
[*The scene fades as she runs away*]

VARIATION X

Scene three
Miss Jessel

[*The lights fade in on the schoolroom. The Governess enters
immediately. Miss Jessel is sitting at the desk*]

GOVERNESS
She is here! Here, in my own room!

MISS JESSEL
Here my tragedy began, here revenge begins.

GOVERNESS
Nearer and nearer she comes, from the lake,
from the stair.

MISS JESSEL
Ah, here I suffered, here I must find my peace.

GOVERNESS
From the stair, from the passage.

MISS JESSEL
Peace did I say? Not peace but the fierce
imparting of my woe.

GOVERNESS
From the passage, into the very heart of
my kingdom.

MISS JESSEL
I shall come closer, closer, and more often.

GOVERNESS
There she sheds her ghastly influence. She
shall not! She shall not! I won't bear it!

MISS JESSEL
So I shall be waiting, waiting, hovering, ready for the
child.

[*The Governess braces herself to speak directly to her*]

GOVERNESS
Why are you here?

MISS JESSEL [*rises, oblivious*]
Alas! Alas!

GOVERNESS
It is mine, mine, the desk.

MISS JESSEL
Alas! alas!

GOVERNESS
They are mine, mine, the children. I will
never abandon them.

MISS JESSEL
Alas alas, I cannot rest. I am weary and
I cannot rest.

GOVERNESS
Begone! Begone! You horrible, terrible woman!

MISS JESSEL
Alas!
[*Miss Jessel disappears. The Governess sinks down in her place*]

GOVERNESS
I can't go—I can't.
But I can no longer support it alone.
I must write to him, write to him now.
[*She writes. She reads what she has written*]
[*reading*]
'Sir—dear sir—my dear sir—
I have not forgotten your charge of silence,
but there are things that you must know,
and I must see you, must see and tell you,
at once. Forgive me.'
That is all.

[*The scene fades*]

VARIATION XI

Scene four
The bedroom

[*The lights fade in on Miles's bedroom. He is sitting on the edge
of his bed with his shoes and jacket off. He is restless. The room is
lit by a candle*]

MILES
Malo, Malo, than a naughty boy . . .
Malo in . . .
[*The Governess is seen approaching the room*]
I say, what are you waiting for?
[*She comes in*]

GOVERNESS
Why Miles, not yet in bed? Not even undressed?

MILES
O I've been sitting, sitting and thinking.

GOVERNESS
Thinking? Of what were you thinking?

MILES
Of this queer life, the life we've been living.

GOVERNESS
What do you mean by that? What life?

MILES
My dear, you know. You're always watching.

GOVERNESS
I don't know, Miles, for you've never told me,
you've told me nothing, nothing
of what happened before I came. I thought
till today that you were quite happy.

MILES
I am, I am. I'm always thinking, thinking.

GOVERNESS
Miles, I've just written to your guardian.

MILES
What a lot you'll have to tell him.

GOVERNESS
So will you, Miles.
[*Miles changes his position, but does not answer*]
Miles—dear little Miles, is there nothing
you want to tell me?
[*Miles shifts again*]

QUINT [*unseen*]
Miles—are you listening?

GOVERNESS
Miles, what happened at school?
What happened here?
[*Miles turns away from her*]

QUINT [*unseen*]
Miles—I am here.

GOVERNESS
Miles, if you knew how I want to help you, how
I want you to help me save you.

QUINT [*unseen*]
Miles—I'm waiting, I'm waiting, waiting, Miles.
[*Miles shrieks, and the candle goes out*]

GOVERNESS
O what is it? What is it? Why, the candle's out!

MILES
'Twas I who blew it, who blew it, dear!
[*The scene fades*]

VARIATION XII

[*During this variation Quint is seen hovering. He sings*]

QUINT [*unseen**]
So! She has written.
What has she written?
What has she written?
What has she written?

She has told all she knows.
What does she know?
What does she know?
What does she know?

It is there on the desk,
there on the desk.
Easy to take
easy to take
easy to take!

Scene five
Quint

[*Miles is seen hesitating in his room*]

QUINT
Take it!
Take it!
Take it!
[*Miles creeps across the stage and to the schoolroom desk*]

QUINT
Take it!
Take it!
[*Miles takes the Governess's letter across to his bedroom. The
lights fade*]

VARIATION XIII

*Scene six**
The piano

[*The lights fade in on the schoolroom. Miles is sitting at the
piano, playing. The Governess and Mrs Grose are hovering
about, listening. Flora is sitting on the floor, making a cat's
cradle with some string*]

GOVERNESS AND MRS GROSE
O what a clever boy; why, he must have
practised very hard.

MRS GROSE
I never knew a little boy so good.

GOVERNESS
Yes, there is no mistake, he is clever,
they both are.

MRS GROSE
They've come on wonderfully well with you, Miss.

GOVERNESS
My dear, with such children anything is possible.
[*She takes Mrs Grose aside and whispers*]
I've done it! I've written it! It's ready for the post.

MRS GROSE
That's right, Miss. I'm sure that's right.

GOVERNESS [*aloud to Miles*]
Go on, dear. Mrs Grose is enjoying it.
We're all enjoying it.

GOVERNESS AND MRS GROSE
O what a clever boy! I never knew a little boy so good.
[*The Governess stays by the piano hanging over Miles. He
finishes his first piece and turns the pages for the second*]

MRS GROSE [*walks over to watch Flora*]
And Miss Flora, playing at cat's cradle.
There's a nimble-fingered little girl.
[*She settles down near Flora*]

---

* *In the first production, throughout this variation and the following scene, Quint appeared as a silhouette.*

MRS GROSE
Cradles for cats
Are string and air.
If you let go
There's nothing there.
But if we are neat
And nimble and clever
Pussy-cat's cradle will
Go on for ever.

FLORA [*echoing*]

Are string and air.

There's nothing there.

Nimble and clever
Pussy-cat's cradle will
Go on for ever.

FLORA [*During this conversation, Miles begins showing off at the piano*]
Mrs Grose, are you tired?

MRS GROSE
Well, my head do keep nodding. It's this warm room—

GOVERNESS [*softly*]
Ah, Miles! Miles!

FLORA
Shut your eyes then and you shall have a cradle,
a cradle, Mrs Grose's cradle—

MRS GROSE
—and Master Miles's playing

FLORA
Go to sleep! Go to sleep!
[*Flora slips away unnoticed*]

GOVERNESS [*softly*]
Ah, Miles! Miles!
[*Suddenly she stops him*]

GOVERNESS
Flora! Flora! Mrs Grose! Wake up! She is gone.

MRS GROSE
What? Who, Miss?

GOVERNESS
Flora's gone, gone out to *her*.
Come, we must go and find her!

MRS GROSE
Lord, Miss! But you'll leave the boy?

GOVERNESS
O I don't mind that now, he's with Quint!
He's found the most divine little way to keep
me quiet while she went.
Come! Come!
[*They rush off as Miles goes on playing triumphantly and the
scene slowly fades*]

VARIATION XIV

Scene seven
Flora

[*The scene fades in on Flora by the lake, watching*]

MRS GROSE [*off*]
Flora!

GOVERNESS [*off*]
Flora!

MRS GROSE AND GOVERNESS [*off*]
Flora!

MRS GROSE
There she is!
[*runs over to Flora*]
Fancy running off like that, and such a long
way, too, without your hat and coat. You are a
naughty girl, whatever made you leave us all?
[*The Governess slowly walks over to them*]

GOVERNESS
And where, my pet, is Miss Jessel?
[*Miss Jessel appears at the other side of the lake*]

GOVERNESS
Ah! She is there!
Look! She is there! [*pointing*]
Look! you little unhappy thing!
Look! Mrs Grose! She is there!

MISS JESSEL
Flora! Flora!
Do not fail me!

MRS GROSE
Indeed Miss, there's nothing there.

GOVERNESS
Only look, dearest woman, don't you see,
Now! Now!

MISS JESSEL
Nothing shall they know.

MRS GROSE [*to Flora*]
She isn't there, little lady, nobody
is there.

GOVERNESS
But look!

FLORA
I can't see anybody, can't see anything,
nobody, nothing, nobody, nothing; I don't
know what you mean.

MRS GROSE
There's nobody there.

MISS JESSEL
We know all things, they know nothing,
don't betray me. Silence! Silence!

MRS GROSE
She isn't there.
Why poor Miss Jessel's dead and buried,
we know that, love.
It's all a mistake.

FLORA
You're cruel, horrible, hateful, nasty.
Why did you come here?
I don't know what you mean.
Take me away! Take me away!
I don't like her!
[*pointing at the Governess*]
I hate her!

GOVERNESS
Me!

MRS GROSE
Yes, it's all a mistake,
and we'll get home as fast as we can.
There, there, dearie,

we'll get home as fast as we can.

GOVERNESS
Yes! Go! Go! Go!

MISS JESSEL
Ah! Flora, Flora,
do not fail me.
Flora!

FLORA
I can't see anybody, can't see anything,
nobody, nothing.
I don't know what she means.
Cruel, horrible, hateful, nasty,
we don't want you! We don't want you!
Take me away, take me away from her!
Hateful, cruel, nasty, horrible.
[*Flora and Mrs Grose go off, the Governess watches them go and
Miss Jessel slowly disappears*]

GOVERNESS
Ah! my friend, you have forsaken me!
At last you have forsaken me.
Flora, I have lost you.
She has taught you how to hate me.
Am I then horrible?
No! No! But I have failed, most miserably
failed, and there is no more innocence in me.
And now she hates me!
Hates me! Hates me!

[*The scene fades*]

VARIATION XV

Scene eight
Miles

[*The house and grounds. As the lights fade in, Mrs Grose and
Flora appear in the porch, dressed for travelling. Flora has her
doll and a little bag. The Governess walks towards them, Flora
deliberately turns her back. Mrs Grose comes to meet her*]

GOVERNESS
Mrs Grose.

MRS GROSE
O Miss, you were quite right, I must take
her away. Such a night as I have spent—
[*She cries*]
No, don't ask me. What that child has poured
out in her dreams—things I never knew nor
hope to know, nor dare remember.

GOVERNESS
My dear, I thought I had lost you, thought
you couldn't believe me, my dear—

MRS GROSE
I must take her away.

GOVERNESS
Yes, go to their uncle. He knows now that all
is not well, he has had my letter.

MRS GROSE
My dear, your letter never went, it wasn't
where you put it?

GOVERNESS
Miles?

MRS GROSE
Miles must have taken it.

GOVERNESS
All the same, go, and I shall stay and face
what I have to face with the boy.
[*Mrs Grose goes quickly to Flora and takes her off*]
O Miles—I cannot bear to lose you!
You shall be mine, and I shall save you.
[*Miles saunters on*]

MILES
So, my dear, we are alone.

GOVERNESS
Are we alone?

MILES
O, I'm afraid so.

GOVERNESS
Do you mind? do you mind being left alone?

MILES
Do you?

GOVERNESS
Dearest Miles, I love to be with you—what
else should I stay for?

MILES
So, my dear, for me you stay?

GOVERNESS
I stay as your friend, I stay as your friend.
Miles, there is nothing I would not do for
you, remember—

MILES
Yes, yes. If I'll do something now for you.

GOVERNESS
To tell me what it is then you have on your mind.
[*Miles looks round desperately, but cannot see Quint*]

QUINT [*unseen*]
Miles!

GOVERNESS
I still want you to tell me.

MILES
Now?

GOVERNESS
Yes—it would be best, you know.

QUINT [*unseen*]
Beware of her!
[*Miles looks about again*]

GOVERNESS
What is it, Miles? Do you want to go and play?

MILES
Awfully! I will tell you everything. I will!

QUINT
No!

MILES
But not now.

GOVERNESS
Miles, did you steal my letter?
[*Quint appears on the tower*]

QUINT
Miles! You're mine! Beware of her!
[*The Governess sees Quint and pushes Miles around so that he can't see him*]

GOVERNESS
Did you? Did you?

MILES
No. Yes. I took it.

GOVERNESS
Why did you take it?

MILES
To see what you said about us.

QUINT
Be silent!
[*Quint descends the tower*]

GOVERNESS
Miles, dear little Miles, who is it you see?
Who do you wait for, watch for?

QUINT
Do not betray our secrets. Beware, beware of her!

MILES [*desperately*]
I don't know what you mean!

GOVERNESS
Who is it, who? Say—for my sake!
Miles!

QUINT
Miles, you are mine.

MILES
Is he there. Is he there?

GOVERNESS
Is who there, Miles? Say it! Say it!

QUINT
Don't betray us, Miles!

MILES
Nobody! Nothing!
[*Quint comes even nearer*]

GOVERNESS
Who? Who? Who made you take the letter?
Who do you wait for, watch for?
Only say the name
And he will go for ever, for ever.

QUINT
On the paths, in the woods,
remember Quint.
At the window, on the tower,
when the candle is out,
remember Quint
He leads, he watches, he waits, he waits.

MILES [*shrieking*]
Peter Quint, you devil!
[*He runs into the Governess's arms*]

GOVERNESS
Ah, Miles, you are saved, now all will be well.
Together we have destroyed him.

QUINT
Ah Miles, we have failed.   [*Quint slowly disappears*]
Now I must go. Farewell.
[*off*]
Farewell, Miles, farewell.

GOVERNESS
No, what is it? What is it?
Miles, speak to me, speak to me.
Why don't you answer? Miles?
Ah! don't leave me now! Miles?
[*She holds him until at last she realises that he is dead and lays him down on the ground*]
Ah! Miles! 'Malo, Malo!
Malo than a naughty boy
Malo in adversity.'

What have we done between us?
Malo   Malo   Malo   Malo.

Noye's Fludde

The Chester Miracle Play

BENJAMIN BRITTEN OP. 59

CHARACTERS

The Voice of God	SPEAKING PART
Noye	BASS-BARITONE
Mrs Noye	CONTRALTO
Sem, Ham, Jaffett	BOY TREBLES
Mrs Sem, Mrs Ham, Mrs Jaffett	GIRL SOPRANOS
Mrs Noye's Gossips	GIRL SOPRANOS
Chorus of Animals and Birds	CHILDREN
The Congregation	(SATB)

FIRST PERFORMANCE

18 June 1958   Orford Church, Suffolk (E.O.G. production)

The Chester Miracle Play set to music. One act.

The Voice of God	Trevor Anthony
Noye	Owen Brannigan
Mrs Noye	Gladys Parr
Sem	Thomas Bevan
Ham	Marcus Norman
Jaffet	Michael Crawford
Mrs Sem	Janette Miller
Mrs Ham	Katherine Dyson
Mrs Jaffet	Marilyn Baker
The Raven	David Bedwell
The Dove	Maria Spall
Mrs Noye's Gossips	Penelope Allen, Doreen Metcalfe, Dawn Mendham, Beverley Newman,
Property Men	Andrew Birt, William Collard, John Day, Gerald Turner

Conducted by Charles Mackerras
Production and setting by Colin Graham
Costumes designed by Ceri Richards

The medieval Chester Miracle Plays were written to be performed by ordinary people; local craftsmen and tradesmen of the town and their families, with choristers from the local church or cathedral for the children's parts. Each Guild performed one play from the cycle on a cart (called *pageant*). This cart moved around the town from place to place, and on it the performance had to be entirely contained. The scenic devices, though carefully worked out, had to be extremely simple. *Noye's Fludde*, set to music, is intended for the same style of presentation—though not necessarily on a cart. Some big building should be used, preferably a church—but not a theatre—large enough to accommodate actors and orchestra.

The text used in this work was written at the end of the sixteenth century. The old spelling has been retained, but modern pronunciation should be used throughout, except for the indicated sounding of the final *e*'s: for example, *shippë* should be pronounced 'shippe(r)'; *Noye* should be pronounced in the familiar way as 'Noah'.

The text is from 'English Miracle Plays, Moralities and Interludes,' edited by Alfred W. Pollard, by agreement with the Clarendon Press, Oxford.

Three hymns, to be sung by the Cast and Congregation, are included in this work; they are as follows:
'Lord Jesus, think on me'; *words* Bp. Synesius (*tr.* Chatfield), *music* Damon's Psalter.
'Eternal Father'; *words* W. Whiting, *music* J.B. Dykes.
'The Spacious Firmament'; *words* Addison, *music* Tallis' Canon.

Noye's Fludde

THE CONGREGATION [*standing*]
Lord Jesus, think on me,
And purge away my sin;
From earthborn passions set me free,
And make me pure within.

Lord Jesus, think on me,
Nor let me go astray;
Through darkness and perplexity
Point thou the heavenly way.

Lord Jesus, think on me,
When flows the tempest high:
When on doth rush the enemy
O Saviour, be thou nigh.

Lord Jesus, think on me,
That, when the flood is past,
I may eternal brightness see,
And share thy joy at last.
[*During the hymn Noye has walked through the Congregation,*
now seated, on to the empty stage, and kneels there]

GOD'S VOICE [*tremendous*]
I, God, that all this worlde hath wroughte,
Heaven and eairth, and all of naughte,
I see my people in deede and thoughte
    Are sette full fowle in synne.
Man that I made I will destroye,
Beastë, worme and fowle to flye;
For on eairth they me deny,
    The folke that are theiron.
Destroyéd all the worlde shalbe,
Save thou, thy wiffe, and children three,
And ther wiffes also with thee
    Shall saved be for thy sake.
Therefore, Noye, my servante free,
That rightious man arte, as I see,
A shippë now thou shall make thee,
    Of treeyës drye and light;
[*Gradually dying away*]
Three hundreth cubettes it shall be longe,
And fiftie brode, to make yt stronge;
Of heighte fiftie . . . . .
    Thus messuer it aboute.

NOYE [*speaking*]
Three hundreth . . . .
And fiftie brode . . .
Of heighte fiftie . . .
One wyndow worcke through my witte,
A cubitte of lengthe and breadth make itt,
Upon the syde a dore shall sit
    For to come in and oute. [*He rises*]
[*Singing*]
O, Lorde, I thanke thee lowde and still,
That to me arte in suche will,
And spares me and my howse to spill.
[*Calling*]
Have done, you men and wemen all,
Hye you, leste this watter fall,
To worcke this shippe, chamber and hall,
    As God hath bidden us doe.

[*Sem comes running in with an axe*]

SEM
Father, I am all readye bowne[1];
An axe I have, and by my crowne!
As sharpe as anye in all this towne,
    For to goe therto.
[*Ham comes in with a hatchet*]

HAM
I have a hacchatt wounder keeyne,
To bitë well, as maye be seene,
A better grownden, as I wene,
    Is not in all this towne.
[*Jaffett comes in with a hammer*]

JAFFETT
And I can make right well a pynne,
And with this hamer knocke it in:
Goe wee to worcke without more dynne,
    And I am ready bowne.
[*Mrs Sem comes in with a hacking-stock*]

MRS SEM
Hear is a good hacckinge-stoccke,
On this you maye hewe and knocke;
None shall be idle in this floccke;
    For nowe maye noe man fayle.
[*Mrs Ham and Mrs Jaffett come running in*]

MRS HAM [*with the others*]
And I will goe gaither slyche[2]
The shippe for to caulke and pyche[3],
Anoynte yt must be each stiche,
    Borde and tree and pynne.

MRS JAFFETT [*with the others*]
And I will goe gaither chippës heare
To make a fier for you in fere[4],
And for to dightë[5] youer dynner,
    Againste your cominge in.
[*Mrs Noye and her Gossips come in mockingly*]

MRS NOYE [*mock-lamenting*]
And we shall bryngë tymber too,
For we mone nothinge ellsë doe;
Wemen be weeke to undergoe
    Any greate travill.

MRS NOYE AND GOSSIPS [*laughing*]
Ha, ha, ha, ha!

NOYE [*with force*]
Goodwiffe, lett be all this beare[6],
That thou makest in this place heare;
For all they wene thou arte maister,
    And so thou arte, by Sante John!
[*Mrs Noye and her Gossips settle at the side of the stage, drinking*
and mocking, while Noye and all the children start to build the
Ark]

NOYE
Now in the name of God I will begyne
To make the shippë here that we shall in,
That we may be readye for to swyme
[*With the children*]
    At the cominge of the fludde.

Thes bordës heare now I pynne togeither,
To beare us saffë from the weither,

---

¹ *prepared* ² *plaster* ³ *pitch* ⁴ *together* ⁵ *prepare* ⁶ *loud noise*

That we maye rowe both heither and theither,
[*With the children*]
  And saffe be from the fludde.

[*Noye indicates a large palm-tree*]
Of this treey will I make the maste,
Tyed with cabelles that will laste,
With a saile yarde for every blaste,
[*With the children*]
  And iche thinge in their kinde.

[*The three sons fell the tree*]
[*With the children*]
With toppe-castill, and boe-spritte,
With cordes and roppes, I hold all meete[7]
To sayle fourth at the nexte sleete,
  When the shippe is att an ende.
Now in the name of God we make endynge
To make the shippë here that we shall in,
That we may be readye for to swyme
  At the cominge of the fludde.
[*The children put finishing touches to the Ark*]

NOYE [*quietly*]
Wyffe, in this vessell we shall be kepte:
My children and thou, I woulde in ye lepte.

MRS NOYE
In fayth, Noye, I hade as lief thou slepte!
For all thy frynishe[8] fare,
I will not doe after thy rede[9].

NOYE
Good wyffe, doe nowe as I thee bydde.

MRS NOYE
By Christe! not or I see more neede,
Though thou stande all the daye and stare.

NOYE
Lorde, that wemen be crabbed aye,
And non are meke, I dare well saye,
This is well seene by me to-daye,
  In witnesse of you each one.

GOD'S VOICE [*tremendous*]
Noye, Noye, take thou thy company,
And in the shippë hie that you be,
And beastes and fowles with thee thou take,
  He and shee, mate to mate;
For it is my likinge mankinde for to anoy.

Fourtye dayes and fortye nightes
Raine shall fall for ther unrightes,
And that I have made through my mightes,
[*Dying away*]
  Now thinke I to destroye.
[*The first waves appear*]

NOYE
Have donne, you men and wemen alle,
Hye you, lest this watter fall,
That iich beaste were in stalle,
  And into the shippe broughte.
The fludde is nye, you maye well see,
  Therefore tarye you naughte.
[*Two by two, as announced by the children, and heralded by bugle calls, the animals march through the Congregation and into the Ark*]

SEM
Sir! heare are lions, leapardes, in,
Horses, mares, oxen, swyne,
Goote and caulfe, sheepe and kine
  Heare coming thou may see.

ANIMALS   [*Group 1*]
Kyrie eleison!

HAM
Camelles, asses, man maye fynde,
Bucke and doo, harte and hinde,
Beastes of all manner kinde
  Here be, as thinketh me.

ANIMALS [*Group 2*]
Kyrie eleison!

JAFFETT
See heare doggës, bitches too,
Otter, fox, polecats also,
Hares hoppinge gaylie go,
  Bringing colly[10] for to eate.

ANIMALS [*Group 3*]
Kyrie eleison!

MRS SEM
And heare are beares, woulfës sette[11],
Apes and monkeys, marmosette,
Weyscelles, squirelles, and ferrette,
  Eaten ther meate.

ANIMALS [*Group 4*]
Kyrie eleison!

MRS HAM AND MRS JAFFETT
And heare are beastës in this howse,
Heare cattës make carouse,
Heare a ratten, heare a mousse,
  That standeth nighe togeither.

CATS, RATS AND MICE [*Group 5*]–[*squeaking*]
Kyrie eleison!

SEM AND MRS SEM
And heare are fowlës lesse and more,
Herons, owls, bittern, jackdaw,
Swannës, peacokes, them before
  Ready for this weither.

HAM AND MRS HAM
And heare are cockes, kites, croes,
Rookës, ravens, many rows,
Cuckoes, curlues, all one knowes,
  Iche one in his kinde.

JAFFETT AND MRS JAFFETT
And heare are doves, ducks, drackes,
Redshanckes roninge through the lackes,
And ech fowle that noises makes
  In this shippe men maye finde.

BIRDS [*Groups 6 and 7*]
Kyrie eleison!

ALL ANIMALS [*off*]
Kyrie eleison!
[*Noye and the children go into the Ark*]

NOYE AND HIS CHILDREN
Kyrie eleison!

---

[7] *fitting*   [8] *polite*   [9] *counsel*   [10] *cabbage*   [11] *a pair*

NOYE [*calling*]
Wiffe, come in! why standës thou their?
  For feare leste that you drowne.

MRS NOYE
Yea, sir, sette up youer saile,
Rowe fourth with evill haile,
For withouten anye fayle
  I will not oute of this towne.
[*Sem comes down from the Ark*]

NOYE
Sem, sonne, loe! thy mother is wrawe[12]:
Forsooth, such another one I doe not knowe.

SEM
Father, I shall fetch her in, I trowe,
  Withouten anye fayle.
[*He goes to where Mrs Noye is sitting with her Gossips*]
Mother, my father after thee sende,
Byddes thee into yonder shippe wende.
Loke up and see the wynde,
  For we bene readye to sayle.

MRS NOYE [*laughing*]
I will not come theirin to-daye;
Go againe to hym, I saie!
[*She kicks him away, and he runs off into the Ark*]
[*Tenderly*]
But I have my gossippes everyone,
They shall not drowne, by Sante John!
  And I may save ther life.

THE GOSSIPS
The flude comes fleetinge in full faste,
On every syde that spreades full ferre;
For feare of drowninge I am agaste;
  Good gossippes, lett us draw nere.

NOYE
Come in, wiffe, in twentye devilles waye!
  Or elles stand there without.

THE GOSSIPS AND MRS NOYE
Lett us drink or we departe,
For ofte tymes we have done soe;
For att a draughte thou drinkes a quarte,
  And soe will I do or I goe.

JAFFETT
Father! shall we all feche her in?

NOYE
Yea, sonnes, in Christe blessinge and myne!
I would you hied you be-tyme,
  For this flude I am in doubte.
[*Noye's sons go down from the Ark over to Mrs Noye*]

MRS NOYE AND GOSSIPS
Heare is a pottill of Malmsine, good and stronge;
It will rejoyce bouth harte and tonge;
Though Noye thinke us never so longe,
  Heare we will drinke alike.

SEM, HAM AND JAFFETT
Mother! we praye you all together,
For we are heare, youer ownë childer,
Come into the shippe for feare of the weither,
  For his love that you boughte!

MRS NOYE
That will not I, for allë youer call,

But I have my gossippes all.

SEM, HAM AND JAFFETT
In faith, mother, yett you shalle,
  Wheither thou wylte or nought.
[*The three boys pick up Mrs Noye and carry her round the stage into the Ark*]

MRS NOYE
They loven me full well, by Christe!
But thou lett them into thy cheiste[13],
[*The Gossips run off screaming*]
Elles rowe nowe wher thee list,
[*Shouting*] And gette thee a newe wiffe!

NOYE
Welckome, wiffe, into this botte.
[*She boxes his ears*]

NOYE
Ha, ha! marye, this is hotte!
[*Quietly*] It is good for to be still.

[*STORM—with rain, wind, thunder and lightning, flapping rigging, great waves, ship rocking and panic of animals*]
Ha! children, me thinkes my botte removes, . . .
Over the lande the watter spreades;
  God doe as he will.

NOYE, MRS NOYE AND THEIR CHILDREN
A! greate God, that arte so good,
That worckës not thy will is wood.
Nowe all this worlde is on a flude,
  As I see well in sighte.

NOYE
This wyndowe will I shutte anon,
And into my chamber I will gone,
Till this watter, so greatë one,
  Be slackëd through thy mighte.
[*Noye shuts the window of the Ark*]

NOYE, MRS NOYE, CHILDREN AND ANIMALS
Eternal Father, strong to save,
Whose arm doth bind the restless wave,
Who bidd'st the mighty ocean deep
Its own appointed limits keep:
  O hear us when we cry to thee
  For those in peril on the sea.

with CONGREGATION
O Saviour, whose almighty word
The winds and waves submissive heard,
Who walkedst on the foaming deep,
And calm amidst its rage didst sleep:
  O hear us when we cry to thee
  For those in peril on the sea.

O Sacred Spirit, who didst brood
Upon the chaos dark and rude,
Who bad'st its angry tumult cease,
And gavest light and life and peace:
  O hear us when we cry to thee
  For those in peril on the sea.

[*The storm slowly subsides and all the creatures in the Ark go to sleep*]
[*Noye looks out of the window of the Ark*]

NOYE
Now forty dayes are fullie gone,

---

[12] *angry*   [13] *chest (i.e. Ark)*

Send a raven I will anone,
If ought-were earth or tree or stone
    Be drye in any place.
[*The Raven pokes his head out of the window and climbs out*]
And if this foule come not againe
It is a signe, soth to sayne,
That dry it is on hill or playne.
[*The Raven flutters this way and that, flies off, and finally
disappears into the distance*]
Ah, Lorde, wherever this raven be,
Somewhere is drye, well I see;
[*The Dove looks through the window*]
But yet a dove, by my lewtye[14]!
[*The Dove climbs out*]
    After I will send.
[*The Dove starts to fly, hovering here and there, and also
disappears into the distance*]
Thou wilt turne againe to me,
For of all fowlès that may flye
    Thou art most meke and hend[15].
[*The Dove is seen returning with an olive branch in his beak. He
hesitates, looking for the Ark. He alights on the Ark and nestles
up to Noye*]
Ah Lord, blessed be thou aye,
That me hast confort thus to-day;
My sweete dove to me brought has
A branch of olyve from some place.
    It is a signe of peace.
Ah Lord, honoured must thou be,
All earthe dryës now, I see.
[*Noye turns to go back into the Ark*]
But yet tyll thou comaunde me
    Hence will I not hye.

GOD'S VOICE [*quietly*]
Noye, take thy wife anone,
And thy children every one,
Out of the shippë thou shalt gone,
    And they all with thee.
Beastes and all that can flie
Out anone they shall hye,
On earth to grow and multeplye;
    I wyll that soe yt be.
[*The animals two by two leave the Ark, and as they appear they
join in the refrain*]

ANIMALS
Alleluia!
[*Finally Noye, Mrs Noye, Sem, Ham and Jaffett and their wives
come out of the Ark, making a tableau with the Animals*]

NOYE, MRS NOYE AND THEIR CHILDREN
Lord, we thanke thee through thy mighte,
Thy bydding shall be done in height,
And as fast as we may dighte,
We will doe thee honoure.

ALL THE CAST
Alleluia!

GOD'S VOICE [*quietly*]
Noye, heare I behette[16] thee a heste,
That man, woman, fowle, ney beste
With watter, while this worlde shall leste,

I will noe more spill.
My bowe betweyne you and me
In the firmamente shalbe,
By verey token that you shall see,
    That suche vengeance shall cease.
Wher cloudes in the welckine bene,
That ilkë bowe shalbe seene,
In tocken that my wrath and teene
    Shall never thus wrocken be[17]
[*During this speech an enormous rainbow is spread across the
stage behind the Ark*]
The stringe is torned towardes you,
And towarde me is bente the bowe,
That such weither shall never shewe,
    And this behighte I thee.

NOYE'S CHILDREN
The spacious firmament on high
With all the blue ethereal sky
And spangled heavens, a shining frame,
Their great original proclaim.
[*The Sun appears*]

with NOYE AND MRS NOYE
Th' unwearied sun from day to day
Doth his Creator's power display,
And publishes to every land
The works of an almighty hand.
[*The Moon appears*]

ALL ANIMALS
Soon as the evening shades prevail
The moon takes up the wondrous tale,
And nightly to the listening earth
Repeats the story of her birth.
[*The Stars appear*]

with NOYE, MRS NOYE AND CHILDREN
Whilst all the stars that round her burn,
And all the planets in their turn
Confirm the tidings, as they roll,
And spread the truth from pole to pole.

with CONGREGATION [*standing*]
What though in solemn silence all
Move round the dark terrestrial ball,
What though nor real voice nor sound
Amid their radiant orbs be found.
[*Here the Animals, divided into their original groups, each group
led by one of the children or Mrs Noye, walk slowly out in
procession*]

ALL THE CAST AND CONGREGATION
In reason's ear they all rejoice,
And utter forth a glorious voice;
For ever singing as they shine,
'The hand that made us is Divine.' Amen.
[*Noye remains alone*]

GOD'S VOICE [*very tenderly*]
My blessinge, Noye, I give thee heare,
To thee, Noye, my servante deare,
For vengeance shall noe more appeare,
    And nowe fare well, my darlinge deare.
                      [*Exit Noye*]

---

[14] *faith*   [15] *gentle*   [16] *promise*   [17] *that my vengeance shall never more be wreaked*

67 Peacock and Peahen

Ceri Richards

68 The storm

69 Animals wait during rehearsal

70 Curlew

71 Bittern

72 Cockerel

73 Fox

74 Bear and Panda

75 Hart and Hind

Designer Ceri Richards

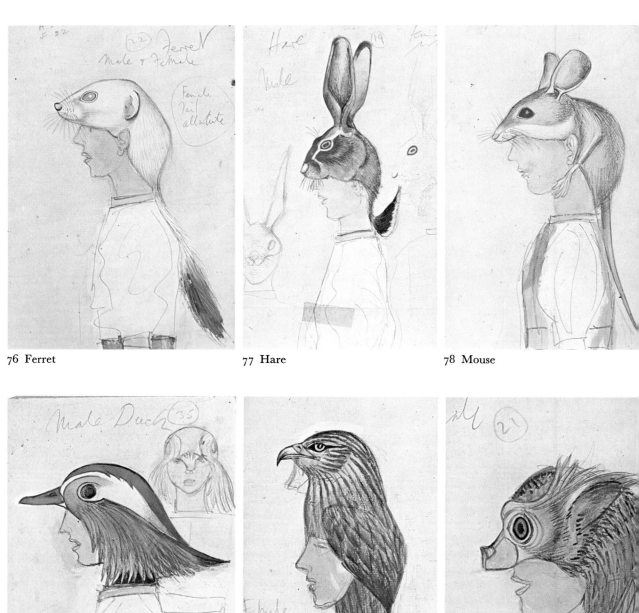

76 Ferret   77 Hare   78 Mouse

79 Duck   80 Kite   81 Monkey

Designer Ceri Richards

A Midsummer Night's Dream

An opera in three acts

by Benjamin Britten and Peter Pears
adapted from William Shakespeare

BENJAMIN BRITTEN OP. 64

CHARACTERS

Oberon *King of the Fairies*	COUNTER-TENOR (OR CONTRALTO)
Tytania *Queen of the Fairies*	COLORATURA SOPRANO
Puck	BOY ACROBAT, SPEAKING ROLE
Theseus *Duke of Athens*	BASS
Hippolyta *Queen of the Amazons, bethrothed to Theseus*	CONTRALTO
Lysander ⎤ *in love with Hermia*	TENOR
Demetrius ⎦	BARITONE
Hermia *in love with Lysander*	MEZZO-SOPRANO
Helena *in love with Demetrius*	SOPRANO
Bottom *a weaver*	BASS-BARITONE
Quince *a carpenter*	BASS
Flute *a bellows-mender*	TENOR
Snug *a joiner*	BASS
Snout *a tinker*	TENOR
Starveling *a tailor*	BARITONE
Cobweb ⎤	
Peaseblossom ⎥ *Fairies*	TREBLES
Mustardseed ⎥	
Moth ⎦	
Chorus of Fairies	TREBLES OR SOPRANOS

SYNOPSIS OF SCENES

Act one	The wood, deepening twilight
Act two	The wood, dark night
Act three	
Scene one	The wood, early next morning
Scene two	Theseus's palace

FIRST PERFORMANCE

11 June 1960   Aldeburgh, Jubilee Hall (E.O.G. production)

Oberon	Alfred Deller
Tytania	Jennifer Vyvyan
Puck	Leonide Massine II
Peaseblossom	Michael Bauer
Cobweb	Kevin Platts
Mustardseed	Robert McCutcheon
Moth	Barry Ferguson
Fairies	Thomas Bevan, Thomas Smyth
Theseus	Forbes Robinson
Hippolyta	Johanna Peters
Lysander	George Maran
Demetrius	Thomas Hemsley
Hermia	Marjorie Thomas
Helena	April Cantelo
Bottom	Owen Brannigan
Quince	Norman Lumsden
Flute	Peter Pears
Snug	David Kelly
Snout	Edward Byles
Starveling	Joseph Ward
Master of Ceremonies	John Perry
Attendant	Jeremy Cullum
Pages	Robert Hodgson, Nicholas Cooper

Conducted by Benjamin Britten
Produced by John Cranko
Scenery and costumes designed by John Piper, assisted by Carl Toms
Lighting designed by William Bundy

Act one

The wood, deepening twilight

[*Enter Fairies (in two groups, Cobweb and Mustardseed with first, Peaseblossom and Moth with second)*]

FAIRIES
Over hill, over dale, thorough bush, thorough brier,
Over park, over pale, thorough flood, thorough fire,
We do wander everywhere, swifter than the Moone's
sphere;
And we serve the Fairy Queen, to dew her orbs upon
the green.

SOLOS
Cowslips tall, her pensioners be,
In their gold coats, spots you see,
Those be rubies, fairy favours,
In those freckles live their savours.

ALL
We must go seek some dewdrops here,
And hang a pearl in every cowslip's ear.

PUCK [*suddenly appearing*]
How now, spirits?
[*The Fairies scatter to the side*]

FAIRIES
Or I mistake your shape and making quite:
Or are you not that shrewd and knavish sprite
Call'd Robin Goodfellow? Are you not he,
That frights the maidens of the villagery,
Skim milk, and sometimes labour in the quern,
And bootless make the breathless huswife churn,
And sometime make the drink to bear no barm,
Mislead night-wanderers, laughing at their harm?
You do the work and they shall have good luck,
They that Hobgoblin call you, and sweet Puck!

PUCK
But room, fairy, here comes Oberon.

FAIRIES
And here our mistress;
Would that he were gone.
[*Enter slowly Oberon and Tytania with her train from opposite sides*]

FAIRIES [*whispered*]
Oberon is passing fell and wrath,
Because that she, as her attendant, hath
A lovely boy stolen from an Indian King,
And jealous Oberon would have the child.

OBERON
Ill met by moonlight,
Proud Tytania.

TYTANIA
Ill met by moonlight,
Jealous Oberon. Fairies skip hence.
I have forsworn his bed and company.
[*The Fairies hide*]

OBERON
Therefore the winds have suck'd up from the sea
Contagious fogs.

TYTANIA
Therefore the ox hath stretched his yoke in vain,

OBERON
The fold stands empty in the drowned fields,

TYTANIA
The crows are fatted with the murrion flock.

OBERON AND TYTANIA
The seasons alter: the spring, the summer,
The childing autumn, the angry winter change
Their wonted liveries, and the mazed world,
By their increase, now knows not which is which;
And this same progeny of evils comes
From our debate, from our dissention
We are their parents and original.

OBERON
Do you amend it then, it lies in you!
Why should Tytania cross her Oberon?
I do but beg a little changeling boy,
To be my henchman.

TYTANIA
Set your heart at rest,
The Fairy land buys not the child of me.
His mother was a votress of my Order,
But she being mortal, of that boy did die,
And for her sake I will not part with him.

OBERON
Give me that boy, and I will go with thee.

TYTANIA
Not for thy Fairy kingdom. Fairies away!
[*Exit Tytania with Fairies*]

OBERON
Well, go thy way: thou shalt not from this grove,
Till I torment thee for this injury.
My gentle Puck come hither; thou rememb'rest
The herb I shew'd thee once,
The juice of it, on sleeping eye-lids laid,
Will make or man or woman madly dote
Upon the next live creature that it sees,
(Be it on Lion, Bear, or Wolf, or Bull,
On meddling Monkey, or on busy Ape.)
Fetch me this herb, and be thou here again,
Ere the leviathan can swim a league.

PUCK
I'll put a girdle round about the earth,
In forty minutes.
[*Puck flies off*]

OBERON
Having once this juice,
I'll watch Tytania, when she is asleep,
And drop the liquor of it in her eyes:
And ere I take this charm from off her sight
I'll make her render up her page to me.
[*Oberon disappears*]
[*Enter Lysander and Hermia, separately, meeting*]

LYSANDER
How now my love? Why is your cheek so pale?
How chance the roses there do fade so fast?

HERMIA
Belike for want of rain, which I could well
Beteem them from the tempest of my eyes.

LYSANDER
Aye me; for aught that I could ever read,

Could ever hear by tale or history,
The course of true love never did run smooth,
But either it was different in blood:

HERMIA AND LYSANDER
O cross!

HERMIA
Too high to be enthrall'd to low.

LYSANDER
Or else misgraffed, in respect of years:

HERMIA AND LYSANDER
O spite!

HERMIA
Too old to be engag'd to young.

LYSANDER
Or else it stood upon the choice of friends.

HERMIA AND LYSANDER
O hell!

HERMIA
To choose love by another's eyes.

HERMIA AND LYSANDER
If then true lovers have been ever cross'd,
It stands as an edict in destiny:

HERMIA
Then let us teach our trial patience.

LYSANDER
A good persuasion; therefore hear me Hermia,
I have a widow aunt, a dowager,
Of great revennew, and she hath no child:
From Athens is her house remote seven leagues,
And she respects me, as her only son:
There gentle Hermia, may I marry thee,
And to that place, the sharp Athenian Law
(Compelling thee to marry with Demetrius)
Cannot pursue us. If thou lov'st me, then
There will I go with thee.

HERMIA
My good Lysander, (if thou lov'st me)
I swear to thee, by Cupid's strongest bow,

LYSANDER
I swear to thee,
By his best arrow with the golden head,

HERMIA
I swear to thee,
By the simplicity of Venus' doves,

LYSANDER
I swear to thee,
By that which knitteth souls, and prospers loves,

HERMIA AND LYSANDER
And by that fire which burn'd the Carthage Queen,
When the false Troyan under sail was seen,

HERMIA
By all the vows that ever men have broke,

LYSANDER
In number more than ever women spoke,

HERMIA AND LYSANDER
I swear to thee . . .   [Exeunt]

[Enter Oberon]

OBERON
(Be it on Lion, Bear or Wolf, or Bull,
on meddling Monkey, or busy Ape).
But who comes here? I am invisible;
I will overhear their conference.
[Enter Demetrius, Helena pursuing him]

DEMETRIUS
I love thee not, therefore pursue me not,
Where is Lysander, and fair Hermia?
The one I'll slay, the other slayeth me.
Thou told'st me they were stol'n unto this wood:
And here am I, and wode within this wood,
Because I cannot meet my Hermia.
Hence, get thee gone, and follow me no more.

HELENA [panting]
You draw me, you hard-hearted adamant,
Leave you your power to draw,
And I shall have no power to follow you.

DEMETRIUS
Do I entice you? Do I speak you fair?
Or rather do I not in plainest truth,
Tell you I do not, nor I cannot love you?

HELENA
And even for that do I love you the more;
I am your spaniel, and Demetrius,
The more you beat me, I will fawn on you.
Use me but as your spaniel; spurn me, strike me,
Neglect me, lose me; only give me leave
(Unworthy as I am) to follow you.

DEMETRIUS
Tempt not too much the hatred of my sprite,
For I am sick when I do look on thee.

HELENA
And I am sick when I look not on you.

DEMETRIUS
I'll run from thee, and hide me in the brakes,
And leave thee to the mercy of wild beasts.
[Exit Demetrius]

HELENA
I'll follow thee, and make a heaven of hell,
To die upon the hand I love so well.
[Exit Helena]

OBERON
Fare thee well nymph, ere he do leave this grove,
Thou shalt fly him, and he shall seek thy love.
[Puck flies in]
Welcome wanderer. Hast thou the flower there?
[Puck gives him the flower and lies at his feet]

OBERON
I know a bank where the wild thyme blows,
Where Oxlips and the nodding Violet grows,
Quite over-canopied with luscious Woodbine,
With sweet musk-roses, and with Eglantine;
There sleeps Tytania, sometime of the night,
Lull'd in these flowers, with dances and delight:
And there the snake throws her enammel'd skin,
Weed wide enough to wrap a Fairy in.
And with the juice of this I'll streak her eyes,
And make her full of hateful fantasies.

Take thou some of it, and seek through this grove;
A sweet Athenian lady is in love
With a disdainful youth: annoint his eyes,
But do it when the next thing he espies
May be the Lady. Thou shalt know the man
By the Athenian garments he hath on.
[Exeunt Oberon and Puck]
[The wood is left empty.]
[The six rustics enter cautiously]

QUINCE
Is all our company here?

ALL
Ay. Ay.

BOTTOM
You were best to call them generally, man by man,
according to the scrip.

FLUTE
First, good Peter Quince, say what the play treats on.

QUINCE
Marry our play is the most lamentable comedy, and
most cruel death of Pyramus and Thisby.

ALL
Of Pyramus and Thisby.

BOTTOM
A very good piece of work I assure you, and a merry.
Now good Peter Quince, call forth your actors by the
scroll. Masters spread yourselves.

QUINCE
Answer as I call you. Nick Bottom the weaver.

BOTTOM
Ready; name what part I am for, and proceed.

QUINCE
You Nick Bottom are set down for Pyramus.

BOTTOM
What is Pyramus, a lover, or a tyrant?

QUINCE
A lover that kills himself most gallant for love.

BOTTOM
My chief humour is for a tyrant. I could play Ercles
rarely, or a part to tear a cat in, to make all split the
raging rocks; and shivering shocks shall break the locks
of prison-gates, and Phibbus' car shall shine from far,
and make and mar the foolish fates. This was lofty.
Now name the rest of the players. This is Ercles' vein, a
tyrant's vein: a lover is more condoling.

QUINCE
Francis Flute the bellows-mender.

FLUTE
Here Peter Quince.

QUINCE
Flute, you must take Thisby on you.

FLUTE
What is Thisby, a wandering knight?

QUINCE
It is the lady that Pyramus must love.

FLUTE
Nay faith, let not me play a woman, I have a beard
coming.

QUINCE
That's all one, you shall play it in a mask, and you may
speak as small as you will.

BOTTOM
And I may hide my face, let me play Thisby too: I'll
speak in a monstrous little voice; 'Thisne, Thisne,' 'Ah
Pyramus my lover dear, thy Thisby dear, and Lady
dear.'

QUINCE
No, no, you must play Pyramus, and Flute you Thisby.

BOTTOM
Well, proceed.

FLUTE *[practising]*
('Ah Pyramus my lover dear, thy Thisby dear, and
Lady . . .')

QUINCE
Robin Starveling the tailor.

STARVELING
Here Peter Quince.

QUINCE
Robin Starveling, you must play Thisby's mother. Tom
Snout the Tinker.

SNOUT
Here Peter Quince.

QUINCE
You, Pyramus's father; myself, Thisby's father;
Snug the joiner, you the Lion's part: and I hope here is a
play fitted.

SNUG
Have you the Lion's part written? pray you if be, give it
me, for I am slow of study.

QUINCE
You may do it extempore, for it is nothing but roaring.

BOTTOM
Let me play the Lion too, I will roar that I will do any
man's heart good to hear me. I will roar, that I will make
the Duke say, Let him roar again, let him roar again.

FLUTE
And you should do it too terribly, you would fright the
Duchess and the Ladies, that they would shriek, and
that were enough to hang us all.

ALL
That would hang us every mother's son.

BOTTOM
But I will aggravate my voice so, that I will roar you as
gently as any sucking dove; I will roar you and 'twere
any nightingale.

QUINCE
You can play no part but Pyramus, for Pyramus is a
sweet-fac'd man, a proper man, and most lovely
gentleman-like man, therefore you must needs play
Pyramus.

BOTTOM
Well, I will undertake it.
[*General satisfaction*]

QUINCE
But masters here are your parts, and I am to entreat
you, request you, and desire you, to con them by
tonight; here will we rehearse anon.

BOTTOM
We will meet, and here we may rehearse most obscenely
and courageously. Take pains, be perfect, adieu.

ALL
Adieu, adieu.

QUINCE
Adieu, at the Duke's oak we meet.

ALL
Adieu, adieu.
                                    [*Exeunt*]

[*The wood is left empty.*]
[*Enter Lysander and Hermia*]

LYSANDER
Fair love, you faint with wandering in the wood,
And to speak troth I have forgot our way:
We'll rest us Hermia, if you think it good,
and tarry for the comfort of the day.

HERMIA
Be it so Lysander; find you out a bed,
For I upon this bank will rest my head.

LYSANDER
One turf shall serve as pillow for us both,
One heart, one bed, two bosoms, and one troth.

HERMIA
Nay good Lysander, for my sake my dear
Lie further off yet, do not lie so near.
So far be distant, and good night sweet friend;
Thy love ne'er alter, till thy sweet life end.

LYSANDER
Amen, amen, to that fair prayer, say I,
And then end life, when I end loyalty:

HERMIA
Amen, amen, say I.
And then end life, when I end loyalty.
[*They sleep. Enter Puck*]

PUCK
Through the forest have I gone,
But Athenian found I none,
On whose eyes I might approve
This flower's force in stirring love.
Night and silence; who is here?
Weeds of Athens he doth wear:
This is he (my master said)
Despised the Athenian maid:
[*He squeezes the juice on Lysander's eyes*]
Churl, upon thy eyes I throw
All the power this charm doth owe:
So awake when I am gone:
For I must now to Oberon.
                                    [*Exit Puck*]

HERMIA [*in her sleep*]
Amen, amen, to that fair prayer, say I.

[*Enter Demetrius and Helena running*]

HELENA
Stay, though thou kill me, sweet Demetrius.

DEMETRIUS
I charge thee hence, and do not haunt me thus.

HELENA
O wilt thou darkling leave me? do not so.

DEMETRIUS
Stay on thy peril, I alone will go.
                                    [*Exit Demetrius*]

HELENA
O I am out of breath, in this fond chase,
The more my prayer, the lesser is my grace,
Happy is Hermia, whersoe'er she lies;
For she hath blessed and attractive eyes.
Alas, I am as ugly as a bear;
For beasts that meet me, run away for fear.
But who is here? Lysander on the ground;
Dead or asleep? I see no blood, no wound,
Lysander, if you live, good sire awake.
[*Lysander awakes*]

LYSANDER
And run through fire I will for thy sweet sake.
Transparent Helena, Nature shows her art,
That through thy bosom makes me see thy heart.
Where is Demetrius? Oh how fit a word
Is that vile name, to perish on my sword!

HELENA
Do not say so Lysander, say not so:
What though he love your Hermia? Lord what though?
Yet Hermia still loves you; then be content.

LYSANDER
Content with Hermia? No, I do repent
The tedious minutes I with her have spent.
Not Hermia, but Helena I love;
Who will not change a raven for a dove?

HELENA
Wherefore was I to this keen mockery born?
When at your hands did I deserve this scorn?
Good troth you do me wrong (good sooth you do)
In such disdainful manner, me to woo.
But fare you well; perforce I must confess,
I thought you Lord of more true gentleness.
                                    [*Exit Helena*]

LYSANDER
She sees not Hermia: Hermia sleep thou there,
And never mayst thou come Lysander near;
And all my powers address your love and might,
To honour Helen, and to be her knight.
                                    [*Exit Lysander*]

HERMIA [*waking*]
Help me Lysander, what a dream was there,
Lysander look, how I do quake with fear:
Methought a serpent eat my heart away,
And you sat smiling at his cruel prey.
[*looking around*]
Lysander, what remov'd? Lysander, Lord,
What, out of hearing, gone? No sound, no word?
Alack where are you? Speak and if you hear:
Speak of all loves; I swoon almost with fear.

Lysander, Lord . . .

                                        [Exit Hermia]

[Enter Tytania, Queen of Fairies, with Cobweb, Peaseblossom, Mustardseed, Moth and other Fairies]

TYTANIA *[distant]*
Come, now a roundel, and a fairy song;
Then for the third part of a minute, hence,
Some to kill cankers in the musk-rose buds,
Some war with reremice, for their leathern wings,
[entering]
To make my small elves coats, and some keep back
The clamorous owl that nightly hoots and wonders
At our quaint spirits: sing me now asleep,
Then to your offices, and let me rest.
[She lies down with the Fairies around her]

SOLO FAIRIES
You spotted snakes with double tongue,
Thorny hedgehogs be not seen,
Newts and blind-worms do no wrong,
Come not near our Fairy Queen.
Philomel with melody,
Sing in our sweet lullaby.

ALL
Lulla, lulla, lullaby, lulla, lulla, lullaby,
Never harm, nor spell, nor charm,
Come our lovely Lady nigh.
So good night with lullaby.

SOLO FAIRIES
Weaving spiders come not here,
Hence you long-legg'd spinners, hence;
Beetles black approach not near;
Worm nor snail do no offence.

[as before]
Philomel with melody, etc.

COBWEB
Hence away, now all is well;
One aloof, stand sentinel.
*[Tytania sleeps. The Fairies (except one standing sentry) slip out
Enter Oberon]*

OBERON
What thou seest when thou dost wake,
Do it for thy true Love take:
Love and languish for his sake.
Be it ounce, or cat, or bear,
Pard, or boar with bristled hair,
In thy eye that shall appear,
When thou wak'st, it is thy dear,
Wake when some vile thing is near.
          [He squeezes the juice on Tytania's eyes and disappears]

CURTAIN

Act two

The wood, dark night

[Tytania lying asleep]
[Enter the six rustics]

BOTTOM
Are we all met?

THE OTHERS
Pat, pat.

QUINCE
And here's a marvellous convenient place for our rehearsal.

THE OTHERS
For our rehearsal.

BOTTOM
Peter Quince?

QUINCE
What sayest thou, bully Bottom?

BOTTOM
There are things in this comedy that will never please. First, Pyramus must draw a sword to kill himself, which the Ladies cannot abide.

THE OTHERS
By'r lakin, a parlous fear.

FLUTE
I believe we must leave the killing out, when all is done.

BOTTOM
Not a whit, I have a device to make all well. Write me a Prologue; tell them, that I Pyramus am not Pyramus, but Bottom the weaver; this will put them out of fear.

SNUG
Will not the Ladies be afear'd of the Lion?

THE OTHERS
The Lion.

FLUTE
I fear it, I promise you.

BOTTOM
Therefore another Prologue must tell them plainly he is not a Lion but Snug the joiner.

QUINCE
But there is two hard things, that is, to bring the moonlight into a chamber: for you know, Pyramus and Thisby meet by moonlight.

STARVELING
Doth the moon shine that night we play our play?

BOTTOM
A Calendar, a Calendar, look in the Almanac, find out moonshine, find out moonshine.

THE OTHERS
Moonshine, moonshine.

BOTTOM
Or else one must come in with a bush of thorns and a lanthorn and say he comes to present the person of Moonshine.

THE OTHERS
    Moonshine.

QUINCE
    Then there is another thing, we must have a wall in the
    great chamber.

SNOUT
    You can never bring in a wall.

ALL
    What say you Bottom?

BOTTOM
    Some man or other must present wall, and let him hold
    his fingers thus, and through that cranny shall Pyramus
    and Thisby whisper.

THE OTHERS
    Then all is well.

QUINCE
    Come, sit down every mother's son, and rehearse your
    parts, every man according to his cue. Pyramus, you
    begin.
    [*Puck flies in*]

PUCK
    What hemper home-spuns have we swaggering here
    So near the cradle of our Fairy Queen?

QUINCE
    Speak Pyramus: Thisby stand forth.

BOTTOM [*as Pyramus*]
    Thisby, the flowers of odious savours sweet . . .

QUINCE
    Odours, odourous.

BOTTOM [*as Pyramus*]
    Odours savours sweet,
    So hath thy breath, my dearest Thisby dear.
    But Hark, a voice; stay thou but here a while
    And by and by I will to thee appear.
                     [*Exit Bottom*]

PUCK
    I'll follow you, I'll lead you about a round.
                     [*Exit Puck*]

FLUTE
    Must I speak now?

QUINCE
    Ay marry must you. For you must understand he goes
    but to see a noise he heard and is to come again.

FLUTE [*as Thisbe*]
    Most radiant Pyramus, most lily-white of hue,
    Of colour like the red rose on triumphant brier,
    Most briskly juvenal, and eke most lovely Jew,
    As true as truest horse, that yet would never tire,
    I'll meet thee, Pyramus, at Ninny's tomb.

QUINCE
    Why, you must not speak that yet; that you answer to
    Pyramus: you speak all your part at once, cues and all.
    Pyramus enter, your cue is past, it is 'never tire'.

FLUTE [*as Thisbe*]
    O, as true as truest horse, that yet would never tire.
    [*Enter Puck and Bottom with the ass-head*]

BOTTOM [*as Pyramus*]
    If I were fair, Thisby, I were only thine.
                     [*Exit Puck*]

THE OTHERS
    O monstrous, O strange. We are haunted, pray masters,
    fly masters, help.
    [*Exeunt Flute, Snout, Starveling, Quince and Snug*]

BOTTOM
    Why do they run away? this is a knavery to make me
    afeard.
    [*Flute reappears*]

FLUTE
    O Bottom, thou art chang'd; what do I see on thee?
                     [*Exit Flute*]

BOTTOM
    What do you see? You see an ass-head of your own, do
    you?
    [*The rustics reappear from behind the trees*]

ALL
    Bless thee, Bottom, bless thee; thou art translated.
                     [*Exeunt*]

BOTTOM
    I see their knavery; this is to make an ass of me, to fright
    me, if they could; but I will not stir from this place, and I
    will sing that they shall hear I am not afraid.
    The woosell cock, so black of hue
    with orange-tawny bill,
    The throstle, with his note so true,
    The wren, with little quill . . .

TYTANIA [*awakening*]
    What angel wakes me from my flowery bed?

BOTTOM
    The finch, the sparrow, and the lark,
    The plain-song cuckoo grey
    Whose note full many a man doth mark
    And dares not answer, nay.

TYTANIA
    I pray thee gentle mortal, sing again;
    Mine ear is much enamour'd of thy note;
    So is mine eye enthralled to thy shape,
    Thou art as wise, as thou art beautiful.

BOTTOM
    Not so neither, but if I had wit enough to get out of this
    wood . . .

TYTANIA
    Out of this wood do not desire to go,
    Thou shalt remain here, whether thou wilt or no.
    I am a spirit of no common rate;
    I'll give thee Fairies to attend on thee;
    Peaseblossom, Cobweb, Moth, and Mustardseed!
    [*Enter Peaseblossom, Cobweb, Moth and Mustardseed*]

PEASEBLOSSOM
    Ready.

COBWEB
    And I.

MOTH
    And I.

MUSTARDSEED
> And I.

ALL FOUR
> Where shall we go?

TYTANIA
> Be kind and courteous to this gentleman,
> Hop in his walks and gambol in his eyes,
> Feed him with apricocks, and dewberries,
> With purple grapes, green figs, and mulberries,
> The honey-bags steal from the humble bees,
> And for night-tapers crop their waxen thighs,
> And light them at the fiery glow-worms' eyes,
> To have my love to bed, and to arise:
> Nod to him elves, and do him courtesies.

ALL FOUR FAIRIES [*bowing to Bottom*]
> Hail mortal, hail!

BOTTOM
> I cry your worships' mercy heartily; I beseech your
> worships' name.

COBWEB
> Cobweb. Hail mortal, hail.

BOTTOM
> I shall desire you of more acquaintance, good Master
> Cobweb. Your name, honest gentleman?

PEASEBLOSSOM
> Peaseblossom. Hail, mortal, hail.

BOTTOM
> I pray you commend me to Mistress Squash, your
> mother, and to Master Peascod your father. Your name,
> I beseech you sir?

MUSTARDSEED
> Mustardseed.
> [*with the others*]
> Hail, mortal, hail.

BOTTOM
> Your kindred hath made my eyes water, ere now. Good
> Master Mustardseed, I desire you more acquaintance.
> Your name, sir?

MOTH
> M . . .

TYTANIA [*interrupting*]
> Come, sit thee down upon this flowery bed
> While I thy amiable cheeks do coy,
> And stick musk-roses in thy sleek smooth head,
> And kiss thy fair large ears, my gentle joy.
> [*Tytania and Bottom settle down on the bank*]

BOTTOM
> Where's Peaseblossom?

PEASEBLOSSOM
> Ready.

BOTTOM
> Scratch my head, Peaseblossom. Where's Mounsieur
> Cobweb?

COBWEB
> Ready.

BOTTOM
> Mounsieur Cobweb, get your weapons in your hand,
> and kill me a red-hipped bumble-bee, and good
> Mounsieur, bring me the honey-bag. Where's
> Mounsieur Mustardseed?

MUSTARDSEED
> Ready.

BOTTOM
> Give me your neaf, Mounsieur Mustardseed. Pray you
> leave your courtesy good Mounsieur.

MUSTARDSEED
> What's your will?

BOTTOM
> Nothing, good Mounsieur, but to help Cavalery
> Cobweb to scratch. I am such a tender ass, if my hair do
> but tickle me, I must scratch. Where's Mounsieur
> Moth?

MOTH
> H . . .

TYTANIA [*interrupting*]
> What, wilt thou hear some music, my sweet love?

BOTTOM
> I have a reasonable good ear in music.
> Let's have the tongs and the bones.
> [*The Fairies take their instruments and start to play*]

BOTTOM
> I have a reasonable good ear in music.
> [*More music. Bottom gets up and begins to dance*]

BOTTOM
> But I pray you let none of your people stir me,
> I have an exposition of sleep come upon me.

TYTANIA
> Sleep thou, and I will wind thee in my arms.
> Fairies begone, and be all ways away.
> [*Exeunt Fairies*]

TYTANIA
> So doth the woodbine, the sweet Honeysuckle
> Gently entwist; the female ivy so
> Enrings the barky fingers of the Elm.
> O how I love thee! How I dote on thee!
> [*They sleep, and it grows dark*]
> [*Enter Oberon and Puck severally*]

OBERON
> How now, mad spirit,
> What night-rule now about this haunted grove?

PUCK
> See, my Mistress with a monster is in love.

OBERON
> This falls out better than I could devise.
> But hast thou yet latch'd the Athenian's eyes
> With a love-juice, as I did bid thee do?
> [*Enter Hermia and Demetrius*]
> Stand close, this is the same Athenian.

PUCK
> This is the woman, but not this the man.
> [*They listen*]

DEMETRIUS
> O why rebuke you him that loves you so?

HERMIA
    If thou hast slain Lysander in his sleep,
    Plunge in the deep, and kill me too:
    Ah good Demetrius, wilt thou give him me?

DEMETRIUS
    I'd rather give his carcase to my hounds.

HERMIA
    Out dog, out cur, oh hast thou slain him then?

DEMETRIUS
    I am not guilty of Lysander's blood.

HERMIA
    I pray thee tell me then that he is well.

DEMETRIUS
    And if I could, what should I get therefore?

HERMIA
    A privilege, never to see me more;
    And from thy hated presence part I so;
    See me no more, whether he be dead or no.
                                    [Exit Hermia]

DEMETRIUS
    There is no following her in this fierce vein,
    Here therefore for a while I will remain.
    So sorrow's heaviness doth heavier grow.
    [Lies down]

OBERON
    What hast thou done? Thou hast mistaken quite
    And laid the love-juice on some true-love's sight;
    About the wood go swifter than the wind,
    And Helena of Athens look thou find.

PUCK
    I go, I go, look how I go,
    Swifter than arrow from the Tartar's bow.
                                    [Puck flies off]

OBERON [squeezing flower on to Demetrius' eyes]
    Flower of this purple dye,
    Hit with Cupid's archery,
    Sink in apple of his eye,
    When his love he doth espy,
    Let her shine as gloriously
    As the Venus of the sky.
    When thou wak'st if she be by
    Beg of her for remedy.
    [Puck flies in]

PUCK
    Captain of our fairy band,
    Helena is here at hand,
    And the youth, mistook by me;
    Shall we their fond pageant see?
    Lord, what fools these mortals be!
    [Oberon and Puck stand aside.]

    [Enter Lysander and Helena]

LYSANDER
    Why should you think that I should woo in scorn?

HELENA
    These vows are Hermia's. Will you give her o'er?

LYSANDER
    I had no judgement, when to her I swore.

HELENA
    Nor none in my mind, now you give her o'er.

LYSANDER
    Demetrius loves her, and he loves not you.
    [Demetrius awakes]

DEMETRIUS
    O Helen, goddess, nymph, perfect, divine,
    To what my love shall I compare thine eyne?
    Crystal is muddy. O how ripe in show
    Thy lips, these kissing cherries, tempting grow!
    That pure congealed white, high Taurus' snow
    Fann'd with the eastern wind, turns to a crow,
    When thou hold'st up thy hand. O let me kiss
    This Princess of pure white, this seal of bliss.

HELENA
    O spite! O hell! I see you all are bent
    To set against me, for your merriment.

LYSANDER
    You are unkind, Demetrius; be not so,
    For you love Hermia; this you know I know.

DEMETRIUS
    Look where thy love comes, yonder is thy dear.
    [Enter Hermia]

HERMIA
    Lysander, why unkindly didst thou leave me so?

HELENA
    Injurious Hermia, most ungrateful maid,
    Have you conspir'd, have you with these contriv'd
    To bait me with this foul derision?
    Is all the counsel that we two have shar'd,
    The sisters' vows, the hours that we have spent,
    When we have chid the hasty-footed time
    For parting us; O is all forgot?
    All school-days friendship, childhood innocence?
    We, Hermia, like to artificial gods,
    Have with our needles created one flower,
    Both on one sampler, sitting on one cushion,
    Both warbling of one song, both in one key;
    Two lovely berries, moulded on one stem,
    So with two seeming bodies, but one heart.
    And will you rend our ancient love asunder,
    To join with men in scorning your poor friend?
    It is not friendly, 'tis not maidenly.

HERMIA
    I am amazed at your passionate words.
    I scorn you not: it seems that you scorn me.

HELENA
    Ay do, persever, counterfeit sad looks,
    Make mouths upon me when I turn my back,
    Wink at each other, hold the sweet jest up:
    But fare ye well, 'tis partly my own fault,
    Which death or absence soon shall remedy.

LYSANDER
    Stay, gentle Helena, hear my excuse,
    My love, my life, my soul, fair Helena.

HELENA
    O excellent!

HERMIA [to Lysander]
    Sweet, do not scorn her so.

DEMETRIUS
If she cannot entreat, I can compel.

LYSANDER
Thou canst compel, no more than she entreat.

DEMETRIUS
I say, I love her more than you can do.

LYSANDER
If thou say so, withdraw and prove it too.

DEMETRIUS
Quick, come.

HERMIA [holds Lysander]
Lysander, whereto tends all this?

LYSANDER
Away, you Ethiope.

DEMETRIUS
No, no, sir, seem to break loose:
You are a tame man, go.

LYSANDER [shaking off Hermia]
Hang off, thou cat, thou burr, vile thing, let loose,
Or I will shake thee from me like a serpent.

HERMIA
Why are you grown so rude?
What change is this, sweet love?

LYSANDER
Thy love? Out, tawny Tartar, out;
Out, loathed medicine: hated potion, hence.

HERMIA
Do you not jest?

HELENA
Yes, sooth, and so do you.

LYSANDER
Demetrius, I will keep my word with thee.

DEMETRIUS
I would I had your bond.
I'll not trust your word.

LYSANDER
What, should I hurt her, strike her, kill her dead?
Although I hate her, I'll not harm her so.

HERMIA
What, can you do me greater harm than hate?
Am I not Hermia? Are not you Lysander?

DEMETRIUS
Lysander, keep thy Hermia, I will none.
If e'er I loved her all that love is gone.

LYSANDER
Ay, by my life; be certain 'tis no jest,
That I do hate thee and love Helena.

HELENA
You both are rivals and love Hermia,
And now are rivals to mock Helena.

HERMIA [to Helena]
O me, you juggler, you canker-blossom,
You thief of love.

HELENA
Fie, fie, you counterfeit, you puppet, you.

HERMIA
Puppet? why so? ay, that way goes the game.
Now I perceive that she hath made compare
Between our statures; she hath urg'd her height,
And with her personage, her tall personage,
Her height (forsooth) she hath prevail'd with him.
And are you grown so high in his esteem,
Because I am so dwarfish and so low?
How low am I, you painted maypole? Speak,
How low am I? I am not yet so low
But that my nails can reach unto thine eyes.

HELENA
I pray you though you mock me, gentlemen,
Let her not hurt me; you perhaps may think,
Because she is something lower than myself,
That I can match her,

HERMIA
Lower? Hark again.

HELENA
O when she's angry, she is keen and shrewd,
She was a vixen when she went to school,
And though she be but little, she is fierce.

HERMIA
Little again? Nothing but low and little?

HELENA
Get you gone, you dwarf,
You minimus of hindering knot-grass made,
You bead, you acorn.

HERMIA
Hark again.
Why will you suffer her to flout me thus?
Let me come to her.

LYSANDER
Be not afraid, she shall not harm thee, Helena.

DEMETRIUS
No sir, she shall not, though you take her part,

LYSANDER
You are too officious
In her behalf that scorns your services.

DEMETRIUS
Let her alone; speak not of Helena,

LYSANDER
Now follow if thou darest, to try whose right
Of thine or mine is most in Helena.

DEMETRIUS
Nay, I'll go with thee cheek by jowl to try whose right
Of thine or mine is most in Helena.
[Exeunt Lysander and Demetrius]

HERMIA
You, mistress, all this coil is 'long of you
Nay, go not back.
Nor longer stay in your curst company.

HELENA
You, mistress, all this coil is 'long of you
I will not trust you, I,
Nor longer stay in your curst company.
Your hands than mine are quicker for a fray,
My legs are longer though to run away.
[Exit Helena pursued by Hermia]

[Oberon comes forward in a rage, dragging Puck]

OBERON

This is thy negligence, still thou mistak'st,
Or else committ'st thy knaveries wilfully.

PUCK

Believe me, King of shadows, I mistook.

OBERON

Thou see'st these lovers seek a place to fight;
Hie therefore Robin, overcast the night,
And lead these testy rivals so astray
As one come not within another's way.
Till o'er their brows, death-counterfeiting sleep
With leaden legs and batty wings doth creep;
Then crush this herb into Lysander's eye.
When they next wake, all this derision
Shall seem a dream, and fruitless vision.
Haste, Robin, haste, make no delay;
We may effect this business yet, ere day.
[Oberon vanishes. A mist descends]

PUCK

Up and down, up and down
I will lead them up and down:
I am fear'd in field and town.
Goblin, lead them up and down.
Here comes one.

LYSANDER *[distant]*

Where art thou, proud Demetrius? Speak thou now.

PUCK *[imitating Demetrius]*

Here, villain, drawn and ready. Where art thou?
Follow me then to plainer ground.

DEMETRIUS *[distant]*

Lysander, speak again.
Thou runaway, thou coward, art thou fled?

PUCK *[imitating Lysander]*

Art bragging to the stars and will not come?

DEMETRIUS

Yea, art thou there?

PUCK

Follow my voice, we'll try no manhood here.
[Exit]

[Enter Lysander]

LYSANDER

He goes before me, and still dares me on.

PUCK *[distant]*

Lysander!

LYSANDER

When I come where he calls, then he is gone,
And I am fallen in dark uneven way,
And here will rest me. Come, thou gentle day.
[Lies down]
For if but once thou show me thy grey light
I'll find Demetrius, and revenge this spite.
[He sleeps]
[Enter Puck]

PUCK

Ho, ho, ho, coward, why com'st thou not?

DEMETRIUS *[distant]*

Abide me if thou darest. Where art thou now?

PUCK

Come hither, I am here.
[Enter Demetrius]

DEMETRIUS

Nay then, thou mock'st me; thou shall buy this dear,
If ever I thy face by daylight see.
Now go thy way; faintness constraineth me
To measure out my length on this cold bed.
By day's approach look to be visited.
[Lies down and sleeps]
[Enter Puck, followed by Helena]

HELENA

O weary night, O long and tedious night,
Abate thy hours, shine comforts from the East,
And sleep that sometimes shuts up sorrow's eye
Steal me a while from mine own company.
[Sleeps]

PUCK

Yet but three? Come one more,
Two of both kinds makes up four.
Here she comes, curst and sad,
[Enter Hermia]
Cupid is a knavish lad
Thus to make poor females mad.

HERMIA

Never so weary, never so in woe,
Bedabbled with the dew, and torn with briers,
I can no further crawl, no further go,
My legs can keep no pace with my desires.
Here will I rest me till the break of day.
Heaven shield Lysander, if they mean a fray.
[She sleeps]
[Enter Fairies, very stealthily]

FAIRIES

On the ground, sleep sound:
He'll apply to your eye,
Gentle lover, remedy.
When thou wak'st, thou tak'st
True delight in the sight
Of thy former lady's eye:
And the country proverb known,
In your waking shall be shown:
Jack shall have Jill,
Nought shall go ill,
The man shall have his mare again,
And all shall be well.
[Exeunt Fairies]
[Puck squeezes juice on Lysander's eyes and exit]

CURTAIN

Act three

The wood

[*Early next morning*]
[*Puck and Oberon appear*]

OBERON
My gentle Robin; see'st thou this sweet sight?
Her dotage now I do begin to pity.
And now I have the boy, I will undo
This hateful imperfection of her eyes.
   Be as thou wast wont to be;
   See as thou wast wont to see.
   Dian's bud, o'er Cupid's flower,
   Hath such force and blessed power.
Now my Tytania wake you my sweet queen.
[*Tytania wakes*]

TYTANIA
My Oberon, what visions have I seen!
Methought I was enamour'd of an ass.

OBERON
There lies your love.

TYTANIA
How came these things to pass?
Oh, how mine eyes do loathe his visage now!

OBERON
Silence awhile. Robin take off his head:
Tytania, music call, and strike more dead
Than common sleep, of all these five the sense.

TYTANIA
Music, ho music, such as charmeth sleep.

OBERON
Sound music; come my Queen, take hands with me
And rock the round whereon these sleepers be.
[*They dance*]
Now thou and I are new in amity
And will this very midnight, solemnly
Dance in Duke Theseus's house triumphantly,
And bless it to all fair prosperity.
There shall the pairs of faithful lovers be
Wedded, with Theseus, all in jollity.

PUCK
Fairy King attend, and mark,
I do hear the morning lark.
   [*Exit Puck. Oberon and Tytania disappear, still dancing*]
[*Distant horns*]

DEMETRIUS [*waking*]
Helena!

LYSANDER [*waking*]
Hermia!

HELENA [*waking*]
Demetrius!

HERMIA [*waking*]
Lysander!

LYSANDER
Are you sure that we are awake? It seems to me
That we yet sleep, we dream.

HERMIA
Methinks I see these things with parted eye,

When everything seems double.

DEMETRIUS
These things seem small and undistinguishable,
Like far-off mountains turned into clouds.

HELENA
So methinks;

ALL FOUR LOVERS

And I have found $\left[\begin{array}{l}\text{Demetrius} \\ \text{Lysander} \\ \text{sweet Hermia} \\ \text{fair Helen}\end{array}\right]$ like a jewel,

Mine own, and not mine own.
Why then we are awake; let's go,
And by the way let us recount our dreams.
   [*Exeunt lovers*]

[*Bottom awakes*]

BOTTOM
When my cue comes, call me, and I will answer. My next is, Most fair Pyramus. Heigh-ho. Peter Quince? Flute the bellows-mender? Snout the tinker? Starveling? God's my life! Stolen hence and left me asleep; I have had a dream, past the wit of man to say what dream it was. Methought I was, there is no man can tell what. Methought I was, and methought I had. But man is but an ass, if he will offer to say what methought I had. The eye of man hath not heard, the ear of man hath not seen, man's hand is not able to taste, his tongue to conceive, nor his heart to report, what my dream was. I will get Peter Quince the carpenter to write a ballad of this dream, and it shall be called *Bottom's Dream* because it hath no bottom; and I will sing it in the latter end of the play, before the Duke. Peradventure, to make it the more gracious, I shall sing it at her death.
   [*Exit*]

[*Enter Quince, Flute, Snout and Starveling*]

QUINCE
Have you sent to Bottom's house? Is he come home yet?

STARVELING
He cannot be heard of. Out of doubt he is transported.

FLUTE
If he come not, then the play is marr'd. It goes not forward, doth it?

STARVELING
It is not possible: you have not a man in all Athens, able to discharge Pyramus but he.

SNOUT
No, he hath simply the best wit of any handicraft man in Athens.

QUINCE
Yea, and the best person too.
[*Enter Snug the joiner*]

SNUG
Masters, the Duke is coming from the Temple. If our sport had gone forward, we had all been made men.

FLUTE
O sweet bully Bottom: thus hath he lost sixpence a day, during his life. And the Duke had not given him sixpence a day for playing Pyramus, I'll be hang'd. He would have deserved it. Sixpence a day in Pyramus, or nothing.

THE OTHERS
He could not have scaped it. Sixpence a day.

BOTTOM [*off*]
Where are these lads? Where are these hearts?
[*Enter Bottom*]

ALL
Bottom, O most courageous day!

BOTTOM
Masters, I am to discourse wonders; but ask me not
what.

ALL
Let us hear, sweet Bottom.

BOTTOM
Not a word of me: all that I will tell you, is that the Duke
hath dined and our play is preferred.

ALL [*except Bottom*]
Our play is preferred. Most dear actors get your apparel
together; good strings to your beards, new ribbons to
your pumps; and ev'ry man look o'er his part.
Let Thisby have clean linen; let not the Lion pare his
nails; eat no onions, eat no garlic, that all may say:
It is a sweet Comedy.

BOTTOM
No more words: to the Palace, away, go, away.
[*Exeunt*]

TRANSFORMATION SCENE TO THESEUS' PALACE

[*Enter Theseus and Hippolyta with their court*]

THESEUS
Now fair Hippolyta, our nuptial hour
Draws on apace: this happy day brings in
Another moon: But oh, methinks, how slow
This old moon wanes; she lingers my desires
Like to a Step-dame, or a Dowager,
Long withering out a young man's revennew.

HIPPOLYTA
This day will quickly steep itself in night;
This night will quickly dream away the time:
And then the Moon like to a silver bow
Now bent in Heaven, shall behold the night
Of our solemnities.

THESEUS
Hippolyta, I woo'd thee with my sword
And won thy love, doing thee injuries:
But I wed thee in another key,
With pomp, with triumph, and with revelling.
[*Enter Lysander, Demetrius, Helena and Hermia*]
[*They kneel*]

ALL LOVERS
Pardon my Lord.

THESEUS
I pray you all stand up.
I know you two were rival enemies.
How came this gentle concord in the world?

LYSANDER
My Lord, I shall reply amazedly;
I went with Hermia thither. Our intent

Was to be gone from Athens, where we might,
Without the peril of the Athenian law.

DEMETRIUS
My Lord, fair Helen told me of their stealth,
And I in fury thither follow'd them;
Fair Helena in fancy following me.
But, my good Lord . . .

THESEUS
Fair lovers,
Of this discourse we more will hear anon.
Hermia, I will o'erbear your father's will;
For in the Temple, by and by with us,
These couples shall eternally be knit.

with HIPPOLYTA
Joy gentle friends, joy and fresh days of love,
Accompany your hearts.
[*The lovers embrace*]

THESEUS
Come now, what masques, what dances shall we have,
Between our after-supper, and bed-time?
[*Enter Quince with play bill. He hands it to Hippolyta and
bows*]

HIPPOLYTA [*reading*]
A tedious brief scene of young Pyramus,
And his love Thisby; very tragical mirth.

LYSANDER
Merry and tragical? tedious and brief?

DEMETRIUS
That is, hot ice, and wondrous strange snow.

THESEUS
What are they that do play it?

HIPPOLYTA
Hard-handed men, that work in Athens here,
Which never labour'd in their minds till now;

THESEUS
I will hear that play.
[*Exit Quince*]
For never any thing can be amiss,
When simpleness and duty tender it.
Take your places, Ladies.
[*Enter the Prologue (all rustics)*]
[*Theseus, Hippolyta and the court take their places*]

ALL RUSTICS
If we offend, it is with our good will.
That you should think, we come not to offend,
But with good will. To show our simple skill,
That is the true beginning of our end.
Consider then, we come but in despite.
We do not come, as minding to content you,
Our true intent is. All for your delight,
We are not here. That you should here repent you,
The actors are at hand: and by their show,
You shall know all, that you are like to know.

THESEUS
These fellows do not stand upon points.

LYSANDER
They have rid their Prologue, like a rough colt:
They know not the stop.

HERMIA

It is not enough to speak but to speak true.

DEMETRIUS

Indeed they have played on their Prologue, like a child on a recorder,

HELENA

A sound but not in goverment.

HIPPOLYTA

Their speech was like a tangled chain; nothing impaired, but all disordered.

THESEUS

Who is next?

PROLOGUE [*Quince*]

Gentles, perchance you wonder at this show,
But wonder on, till truth make all things plain.
This man is Pyramus, if you would know;
This beauteous Lady, Thisby is certain.
This man, with lime and rough-cast, doth present
Wall, that vile Wall, which did these lovers sunder:
This man with lanthorn, dog, and bush of thorn,
Presenteth Moonshine.
This grisly beast is Lion Light by name.
For all the rest,
Let Lion, Moonshine, Wall, and Lovers twain,
At large discourse, while here they do remain.
[*Exeunt all but Wall*]

HELENA

I wonder if the Lion be to speak.

DEMETRIUS

No wonder, fair Lady: one Lion may, when many asses do.

WALL [*Snout*]

In this same Interlude, it doth befall,
That I, one Snout (by name) present a wall:
And such a wall, as I would have you think,
That had in it a crannied hole or chink:
And this the cranny is, right and sinister,
Through which the fearful Lovers are to whisper.

HERMIA

Would you desire lime and hair to sing better?

LYSANDER

It is the wittiest partition, that ever I heard discourse.

THESEUS

Pyramus draws near the Wall, silence.
[*Enter Pyramus*]

PYRAMUS [*Bottom*]

O grim-look'd night, O night with hue so black,
O night, which ever art, when day is not:
O night, O night, alack, alack, alack,
I fear my Thisby's promise is forgot.
And thou O Wall, O sweet, O lovely wall,
That stand'st between her father's ground and mine,
Thou wall, O wall, O sweet and lovely wall,
Show me thy chink, to blink through with mine eyne.
Thanks courteous wall. Jove shield thee well for this.
But what see I? No Thisby do I see.
O wicked wall, through whom I see no bliss,
Curs'd be thy stones for thus deceiving me.

THESEUS

The wall methinks being sensible, should curse again.

BOTTOM

No in truth sir, he should not. *Deceiving me* is Thisby's cue; yonder she comes.
[*Enter Thisbe*]

THISBE [*Flute*]

O wall, full often hast thou heard my moans,
For parting my fair Pyramus, and me.
My cherry lips have often kiss'd thy stones:
Thy stones with lime and hair knit up in thee.

PYRAMUS

I see a voice; now will I to the chink,
To spy and I can hear my Thisby's face.
Thisby?

THISBE

My Love thou art, my Love I think.

PYRAMUS

Think what thou wilt, I am thy Lover's grace.
O kiss me through the hole of this vile wall.
[*They kiss*]

THISBE

I kiss the wall's hole, not your lips at all.

PYRAMUS

Wilt thou at Ninny's tomb meet me straightway?

THISBE

'Tide life, 'tide death, I come without delay.
[*Exeunt Pyramus and Thisbe*]

WALL

Thus have I Wall, my part discharged so;
And being done, thus Wall away doth go.
[*Exit*]

HYPPOLYTA

This is the silliest stuff that ever I heard.

THESEUS

The best in this kind are but shadows, and the worst are no worse, if imagination amend them. Here come two noble beasts in, a man and a Lion.
[*Enter Lion and Moonshine*]

LION [*Snug*]

You Ladies, you (whose gentle hearts do fear
The smallest monstrous mouse that creeps on floor)
Should know that I, one Snug the joiner am
A Lion fell, nor else no Lion's dam:

HERMIA

A very gentle beast, and of a good conscience.

DEMETRIUS

The very best at a beast that e'er I saw.

THESEUS

But let us listen to the Moon.

MOONSHINE [*Starveling*]

This lanthorn doth the horned Moon present:

LYSANDER

He should have worn the horns on his head.

MOONSHINE [*Starveling*]

Myself the man i' th' Moon do seem to be.

THESEUS
The man should be put into the lanthorn. How is it else the man i' th' Moon?

MOONSHINE
This lanthorn doth the horn . . . . . .

DEMETRIUS
He dares not come there for the candle.

THESEUS
Proceed Moon.

MOONSHINE
All I have to tell you is that this lanthorn is the Moon; I, the man i' th' Moon; this thorn-bush, my thorn-bush; and this dog, my dog.

HIPPOLYTA
I am weary of this Moon; would he would change.

ALL
But silence; here comes Thisbe.
[Enter Thisbe]

THISBE
This is old Ninny's tomb. Where is my love?

LION
Oh.
[The Lion roars, Thisbe runs off, dropping mantle]

DEMETRIUS
Well roar'd Lion.

THESEUS
Well run Thisbe.

LYSANDER
Well moused Lion.

HERMIA
Well run Thisbe.

HIPPOLYTA
Well shone Moon.

HELENA
Truly the Moon shines with good grace.
[Exit Lion]

[Enter Pyramus]

PYRAMUS
Sweet Moon, I thank thee for thy sunny beams,
I thank thee Moon, for shining now so bright;
But stay; O spite! but mark, poor Knight,
What dreadful dole is here?
Eyes do you see! how can it be!
O dainty duck: O dear!
Thy mantle good; what stain'd with blood!
Approach, ye Furies fell:
O Fates! come, come: cut thread and thrum,
Quail, crush, conclude, and quell.

HYPPOLYTA
Beshrew my heart, but I pity the man.

PYRAMUS
O wherefore Nature, didst thou Lions frame?
Since Lion vile hath here deflower'd my dear:
Which is: no, no, which was the fairest Dame.
Come tears, confound: out sword, and wound
The pap of Pyramus:
Thus die I, thus, thus, thus,

Now am I dead, now am I fled, my soul is in the sky,
Tongue lose thy light, Moon take thy flight.
[Exit Moonshine]
Now die, die, die, die, die.
[Dies]

DEMETRIUS
With the help of a surgeon, he might yet recover, and prove an ass.
[Enter Thisbe]

THESEUS
Here Thisbe comes, and her passion ends the play.

HIPPOLYTA
I hope she will be brief.

THISBE
Asleep my Love? What, dead my dove?
O Pyramus arise:
Speak, speak. Quite dumb? Dead, dead? A tomb
Must cover thy sweet eyes.
These lily lips, this cherry nose,
These yellow cowslip cheeks.
Are gone, are gone: Lovers make moan:
His eyes were green as leeks.
Tongue not a word: come trusty sword:
Come blade, my breast imbrue:
And farewell friends, thus Thisby ends;
[She stabs herself]
Adieu, adieu, adieu.

THESEUS
Moonshine and Lion are left to bury the dead.

DEMETRIUS
Ay, and Wall too.

BOTTOM
No, I assure you, the wall is down that parted their fathers. Will it please you to see the Epilogue, or to hear a Bergomask dance?
[Bottom (Pyramus) and Flute (Thisby) get up]

THESEUS
No Epilogue, I pray you; for your play needs no excuse. But come, your Bergomask:
[The other rustics come in and arrange themselves for a Bergomask dance. Midnight sounds. The dance stops, and the rustics bow to the Duke and the others, and leave.]

THESEUS
The iron tongue of midnight hath told twelve.
Lovers to bed, 'tis almost fairy time.
I fear we shall out-sleep the coming morn,
As much as we this night have overwatch'd.
Sweet friends to bed.

ALL
Sweet friends to bed.
[Exeunt]

[Enter Fairies]

SOLO FAIRIES
Now the hungry lion roars,
And the wolf behowls the Moon:
Whilst the heavy ploughman snores,
All with weary task fordone.
Now the wasted brands do glow,
Whilst the screech-owl, screeching loud,
Puts the wretch that lies in woe,

82 A waterfall in the wood   *John Piper*

83 The wood, a gauze   *John Piper*

84

85

86

84–88 *Designs by John Piper*

87

88

89 Oberon

Carl Toms

In remembrance of a shroud.
Now it is the time of night,
That the graves, all gaping wide,
Every one lets forth his sprite,
In the church-way paths to glide.
And we Fairies, that do run,
By the triple Hecate's team,
From the presence of the Sun,
Following darkness like a dream,
Now are frolic; not a mouse
Shall disturb this hallow'd house.
[*Enter Puck with broom—he chases the Fairies*]

PUCK
I am sent with broom before,
To sweep the dust behind the door.
[*Enter the King and Queen of the Fairies with all their train*]

OBERON
Through the house give glimmering light,
Every elf and fairy sprite,
Sing this ditty after me,
Sing and dance it trippingly.

TYTANIA
First rehearse your song by rote,
To each word a warbling note.

BOTH
Hand in hand, with fairy grace,
Will we sing and bless this place.

OBERON, TYTANIA AND FAIRIES
Now until the break of day,

Through this house each Fairy stray.
To the best bride-bed will we,
Which by us shall blessed be:
And the issue there create,
Ever shall be fortunate:
So shall all the couples three,
Ever true in loving be.
With this field-dew consecrate,
Every Fairy take his gait,
And each several chamber bless,
Through this Palace with sweet peace,
Ever shall in safety rest,
And the owner of it blest.

OBERON
Trip away, make no stay;
Meet me all by break of day.

[*Exeunt all but Puck*]

PUCK
If we shadows have offended,
Think but this (and all is mended)
That you have but slumber'd here,
While these visions did appear.
Gentles, do not reprehend.
If you pardon, we will mend.
Else the Puck a liar call.
So good night unto you all.
Give me your hands, if we be friends,
And Robin shall restore amends.

QUICK CURTAIN

Curlew River

A parable for church performance

by William Plomer

BENJAMIN BRITTEN OP. 71

CHARACTERS

The Abbot, Eleven Monks, Four Acolytes and Seven
Lay Brothers *who make up the cast of the Parable:*

The Madwoman	TENOR
The Ferryman	BARITONE
The Traveller	BARITONE
The Spirit of the Boy *an Acolyte*	TREBLE
The Leader of the Pilgrims *the Abbot*	BASS
The Chorus of Pilgrims	THREE TENORS THREE BARITONES TWO BASSES

and include

The Instrumentalists *Lay Brothers*

Flute (doubling Piccolo)

Horn

Double Bass

Harp

Percussion*

Chamber Organ

and

Three Assistants *Acolytes*

* 5 small untuned drums, 5 small bells and 1 large tuned
gong

FIRST PERFORMANCE

13 June 1964   Orford Church, Suffolk (E.O.G. production)

The Abbot	John Garrard
The Ferryman	John Shirley-Quirk
The Traveller	Bryan Drake
The Madwoman	Peter Pears
The Spirit of the Boy	Robert Carr
His Voice	Bruce Webb
The Pilgrims	John Barrow, Bernard Dickerson,
	Brian Etheridge, Edward Evanko,
	John Kitchener, Peter Leeming,
	Philip May, Nigel Rogers

Music under the direction of the composer
Production and setting by Colin Graham
Costumes by Annena Stubbs

NOTE

Curlew River is based upon the medieval Japanese *Nō*-play
Sumidagawa, by Jūrō Motomasa.* Grateful acknowledgements are offered to the authoritative translation made by
the Japanese Classics Translation Committee, under the
chairmanship of Dr Sanki Ichikawa, and published in
Tokyo in 1955 by the Nippon Gakujutsu Shinkokai (Japan
Society for the Promotion of Scientific Research).
* 1395-1431

Foreword by Benjamin Britten

It was in Tokyo in January 1956 that I saw a Nō-drama for the first time; and I was lucky enough during my brief stay there to see two different performances of the same play– *Sumidagawa*. The whole occasion made a tremendous impression upon me: the simple, touching story, the economy of style, the intense slowness of the action, the marvellous skill and control of the performers, the beautiful costumes, the mixture of chanting, speech, singing which, with the three instruments, made up the strange music–it all offered a totally new 'operatic' experience.

There was no conductor–the instrumentalists sat on the stage, as did the chorus, and the chief characters made their entrance down a long ramp. The lighting was strictly non-theatrical. The cast was all male, the one female character wearing an exquisite mask which made no attempt to hide the male jowl beneath it.

The memory of this play has seldom left my mind in the years since. Was there not something–many things–to be learnt from it? The solemn dedication and skill of the performers were a lesson to any singer or actor of any country and any language. Was it not possible to use just such a story–the simple one of a demented mother seeking her lost child–with an English background (for there was no question in any case of a pastiche from the ancient Japanese)? Surely the Medieval Religious Drama in England would have made a comparable setting–an all-male cast of ecclesiastics–a simple austere staging in a church–a very limited instrumental accompaniment–a moral story? And so we came from *Sumidagawa* to Curlew River and a Church in the Fens, but with the same story and similar characters; and whereas in Tokyo the music was the ancient Japanese music jealously preserved by successive generations, here I have started the work with that wonderful plainsong hymn 'Te lucis ante terminum', and from it the whole piece may be said to have grown. There is nothing specifically Japanese left in the Parable that William Plomer and I have written, but if stage and audience can achieve half the intensity and concentration of that original drama I shall be well satisfied.

Curlew River

The Scene is set in a church by a Fenland river in early medieval times.

[*The Abbot and his company of Monks, Acolytes and Instrumentalists walk singing in procession to the acting area*]

ABBOT, MONKS, ACOLYTES AND INSTRUMENTALISTS
Te lucis ante terminum,
Rerum Creator, poscimus,
Ut pro tua clementia,
Sis praesul et custodia.

Procul recedant somnia,
Et noctium phantasmata:
Hostemque nostrum comprime,
Ne polluantur corpora.

Praesta, Pater piissime,
Patrique compar Unice,
Cum Spiritu Paraclito,
Regnans per omne saeculum.
            Amen
[*The Abbot comes forward to address the congregation*]

ABBOT
Good souls, I would have you know
The Brothers have come today
To show you a mystery:
How in sad mischance
A sign was given of God's grace.

MONKS
A sign of God's grace.

ABBOT
Not far away
Where, in our reedy Fens,
The Curlew River runs,
Not long ago,
Amid souls akin to you,
A sign was given of God's grace.

MONKS
A sign of God's grace.

ABBOT
As a candle-shine
In a dismal place,
A freshet spilt
In a desert waste,
As innocence
Outshineth guilt,
A sign was given
Of God's good grace.

ABBOT AND MONKS [*exhorting the congregation*]
O pray for the souls of all that fall
By the wayside, all alone.
O praise our God that lifteth up
The fallen, the lost, the least.

ABBOT
Belovèd, attend
To our mystery.
[*The Monks who are to play the Madwoman, the Traveller and the Ferryman are ceremonially prepared*]
[*While the Madwoman and the Traveller leave the acting area*

with their Acolytes, the Monks place benches to one side; then,
with the Abbot, they sit on them, representing a Chorus of
Pilgrims in the ferry boat. The Ferryman is revealed]
[*The Ferryman comes forward*]

FERRYMAN
I am the ferryman.
I row the ferry boat
Over the Curlew,
Our wide and reedy
Fenland river.
In every season, every weather,
I row the ferry boat.

ABBOT AND CHORUS
Between two kingdoms the river flows;
On this side, the Land of the West,
On the other, the Eastern fens.

FERRYMAN
Today is an important day,
Many people need the ferry
To reach the other bank.
There the folk are gathering
To pray before a grave,
As if it were a shrine.
A year ago today
There was a burial;
The river folk believe
Some special grace is there
To heal the sick in body and soul.
Today is an important day,
Mark this well, all of you!
[*He sits in the boat. The Traveller approaches*]

TRAVELLER
I come from the West-land, on a journey.
Far, far northward I must go;
Weary days of travel lie before me.

ABBOT AND CHORUS
Far, far northward he must go;
Weary days of travel lie before him.

TRAVELLER
Behind me, under clouds and mist,
Heaths and pastures I have crossed;
Woods and moorlands I have passed,
Many a peril I have faced;
May God preserve wayfaring men!
[*The Traveller arrives at the ferry*]
Here is the bank of the Curlew River,
And now I have reached the ferry.
[*The Ferryman prepares to cast off*]
I see the ferry boat about to leave.

CHORUS
Between two kingdoms, O River, flow
On this side, the land of the West,
On the other, dyke and marsh and mere,
The Land of the Eastern Fens.

TRAVELLER
Ferryman! Have you a place for me,
A place for me in your boat?
[*The Ferryman rises*]

FERRYMAN
Very well, sir. There is room for you.
Pray get in.

But first may I ask you
What is that strange noise
Up the highway there?

MADWOMAN [*off*]
You mock me
Whither I go.
How should I know?
Where the nest of the curlew
Is not filled with snow,
Where the eyes of the lamb
Are untorn by the crow,
The carrion crow—
There let me go!

FERRYMAN
May I ask, did you see
Who it is that is singing?

TRAVELLER
Yes, the people were watching
A woman in the road
Who seems to be crazy.
They say she comes
From the Black Mountains.
The people were amused
When they heard her singing;
They all began laughing.
She is coming this way.
[*The Madwoman appears*]

FERRYMAN
I will delay the ferry boat.
[*The Traveller sits in the boat*]

MADWOMAN
Let me in! Let me out!
Tell me the way!
How can you say
Why the point of an arrow
Divideth the day?
Why to live is to warm
An image of clay
Dark as the day?
Let me in! Let me out!
I turn me away!

FERRYMAN
I will wait for the madwoman,
I should like to see her.

ALL (Traveller, Ferryman, Abbot and Chorus)
She is coming this way!
We will wait for the madwoman.
We will delay the ferry boat!
We wish to see her.
We wish to hear her singing.
We will laugh at her
Crazily singing.

ALL
She wanders raving, and all alone.
[*She arrives at the ferry and takes a few steps to the left, then to*
the right, as if dancing]

MADWOMAN
Clear as a sky without a cloud
May be a mother's mind,
But darker than a starless night
With not one gleam, not one,

No gleam to show the way.

All is clear but unclear too,
Love for my child confuses me:
Where is my darling now?
Shall I ask these travellers?

ABBOT AND CHORUS
Or will they also laugh at her
As she wanders raving, and all alone?

MADWOMAN
Does he know his mother's grief?
[*She falls to the ground*]

ABBOT AND CHORUS
Dew on the grass
Sparkles like hope
And then is gone.

MADWOMAN
Dew on the grass
Sparkles like hope;
Dew on the . . .
It's here, it's gone!
[*She sinks down*]

ABBOT
Is she to pass her days
Complaining of their bitter taste?

CHORUS
(Dew on the grass—
It's here, it's gone!)
[*The Madwoman raises her head and gazes into the distance*]

MADWOMAN
Near the Black mountains
There I dwelt,
Far in the West,
There I was living
With my only child.

One day alas he vanished:
With silence every room was full,
Full of his absence,
Roaring like the sea!

My only child was lost,
Seized as a slave
By a stranger, a foreigner.

They told me he was taken
Eastward, eastward,
Along the drovers' track
East, east, east.

Clear and unclear in mind
Eastward I wander on,
In longing for my son.
[*She weeps*]

ALL
A thousand leagues may sunder
A mother and her son,
But that would not diminish
Her yearning for her child.

TRAVELLER
Will her search be at an end

Here, at the Curlew River,
Now she has reached the Curlew River?
[*The Madwoman rises*]

ABBOT AND CHORUS
The river flowing between two realms—
On this side, the land of the West,
On the other, the Eastern fens.

MADWOMAN
Ferryman, ferryman,
Let me get into your boat!

FERRYMAN
How can I take you in my ferry boat,
Unless you tell me
Where you have come from,
And where you are going?

MADWOMAN
I come from the Black Mountains!
Searching for, searching for
Someone . . .

FERRYMAN
So you come from the Black Mountains!
I tell you, Black Mountain woman,
Any fool can see
Your feet are wandering,
Your thoughts are wandering too.

MADWOMAN
Let me get into your boat!

FERRYMAN
I will not take you across the Curlew
Unless you entertain us with your
   singing!

FERRYMAN AND TENORS
Unless you entertain us with your
   singing!

TRAVELLER AND BARITONES
We want to hear you singing, crazily
   singing!

ABBOT AND BASSES
Make us laugh with your singing,
   Madwoman!

ALL
Show us what you can do!
Madwoman, sing!

MADWOMAN
Ignorant man!
You refuse a passage
To me, a noblewoman!
It ill becomes you,
Curlew ferryman,
Such incivility.

FERRYMAN
This Black Mountain woman
Uses a high-flown way of talking!

MADWOMAN
Let me remind you
Of the famous traveller
Who once made a riddle
In this very place:

'Birds of the Fenland, though you float or fly,
Wild birds, I cannot understand your cry,
Tell me, does the one I love
In this world still live?'
[*The Madwoman turns, watching the flight of the birds*]
Ferryman, there the wild birds float!
I see the wild birds fly!
What are those birds?

FERRYMAN
Those? They're only common gulls.

MADWOMAN
Gulls you may call them!
Here, by the Curlew River,
Call them, I beg of you,
Curlews of the Fenland.

FERRYMAN
I beg your pardon.
Living in this famous place
I should have known
To call them
Curlews of the Fenland.

MADWOMAN
Instead of gulls.

TRAVELLER
A traveller at this very place cried:

MADWOMAN
'Tell me, does the one I love
In this world still live?'
[*The Madwoman makes as if to follow the birds*]

TRAVELLER
Thinking of his lady love—

FERRYMAN
She too is seeking someone lost.
Searching for a son.

TRAVELLER
—Yearning for a woman.

TRAVELLER AND FERRYMAN
Both derive from longing,
Both from love.
'Birds of the Fenland', she will ask,
But answer they will not.
'Birds of the Fenland, though you float or fly,
Wild birds, I cannot understand your cry'.

CHORUS
Birds of the Fenland, she will ask you too,
'Is the child I love
Still living?'
She will ask, and she will ask,
But answer they will not.
'Tell me, does the one I love
In this world still live?'
[*Coming forward, the Madwoman goes up to the Ferryman and joins her hands in supplication*]

ABBOT AND CHORUS
Birds of the Fenland, she has heard you crying
There in the West, in the mountains, in her home.
How far, how very far,
Birds of the Fenland, comes this wandering soul.

TRAVELLER, ABBOT AND CHORUS
Ferryman, she begs of you
To let her come aboard.
She sees the boat is crowded,
But let her come aboard,
Let her come aboard!

FERRYMAN
This madwoman seems,
Though her mind may be wandering,
To know what she seeks.

Lady, be quick and come aboard!
And you too, traveller.
To navigate the ferry boat
Is not easy
The river is glassy,
But the Devil himself
With strong-flowing currents
Can drag the boat aside,
And carry away
All who are in her.

Be careful and sit still.
God have mercy upon us!

TRAVELLER, ABBOT AND CHORUS
God have mercy upon us!
[*The Madwoman and the Traveller enter the boat*]

FERRYMAN
Hoist the sail!
[*The Acolytes hoist the sail*]
[*The Ferryman plies his pole*]

TRAVELLER, ABBOT AND CHORUS
Curlew River, smoothly flowing
Between the Lands of East and West,
Dividing person from person!
Ah, ferryman,
Row your ferry boat,
Bring nearer, nearer,
Person to person,
By chance or misfortune,
Time, death, or misfortune,
Divided asunder!

TRAVELLER
What are all those people
Crowded on the other bank
Near that yew tree?
[*The Ferryman stops poling*]

FERRYMAN
Today is an important day,
The people are assembling
In memory of a sad event.
I will tell you the story.

It happened on this very day a year ago. There was a stranger in my boat, a Northman, a foreigner, a big man armed with a sword and a cudgel. He was on his way to take a ship to the North-land. [*He poles once*] And not alone. There was a boy with him, a gentle boy, twelve years old maybe, and a Christian. The Heathen said he'd bought him as a slave. The boy said nothing. I could see he was ill. Unused to travelling rough. [*He

90 The Ferryman   *Annena Stubbs*

91 The Madwoman   *Annena Stubbs* 92 The Abbot   *Annena Stubbs*

93 An Acolyte
Annena Stubbs

94 Peter Pears as the Madwoman

95 and 96 Preliminary studies for costume designs

Annena Stubbs

poles once] Poor child. When we had crossed the river, he said he was too weak to walk, and down he lay on the grass near the chapel. [*He poles once*] The Heathen threatened him, swore at him, struck him. He was a man without a heart, and we feared he would kill the boy, but he left the boy where he was, and went on his way. [*He poles twice*]

Abandoned by his master, the boy lay alone. The river people pitied him, took care of him. But he grew weaker and weaker. We asked him who he was, where he was born. 'I was born,' he said, 'in the Western Marches; from my pillow, when I first opened my eyes, I could see the Black Mountains. I am the only child of a nobleman. My father is dead, I have lived alone with my mother. Then, walking alone in our own fields, I was seized by that stranger. He threatened to kill me . . . . But there was no need: I know I am dying . . . . Please bury me here, by the path to this chapel. Then, if travellers from my dear country pass this way, their shadows will fall on my grave, and plant a yew tree in memory of me.' He spoke these words calmly, like a man. Then he said a prayer:

'Kyrie eleison Kyrie eleison!'
And then he died.

TRAVELLER, ABBOT AND CHORUS
Kyrie eleison! Kyrie eleison!
[*The Madwoman weeps*]

FERRYMAN
The river folk believe
The boy was a saint.
They take earth from his grave
To heal their sickness.
They report many cures.

The river folk believe
His spirit has been seen.

TRAVELLER, ABBOT AND CHORUS
Kyrie eleison! Kyrie eleison!

FERRYMAN
There may be some people from the West in this boat.
Let them offer prayers that the soul of that boy may rest in peace.

TRAVELLER, ABBOT AND CHORUS
Kyrie eleison!
[*The Ferryman steers the boat to the bank*]

FERRYMAN
Look! While you were listening to my story, we have reached the bank. Lower the sail!
[*The sail is lowered and the tomb is seen*]

FERRYMAN
Make haste there, all of you! come, get ashore!
[*The Traveller, Abbot and Chorus leave the boat and approach the tomb. The Madwoman remains in the boat*]

TRAVELLER, ABBOT AND CHORUS
Curlew River, smoothly flowing
Between the Lands of East and West,
Dividing person from person.
Ah, Ferryman, row your ferry boat!
Bring nearer, nearer,
Person to person,
By chance or misfortune,

Time, death or misfortune,
Divided asunder!

TRAVELLER
I'll remain here today.
I cannot journey on today.
Though I never knew the boy
I'll offer up a prayer for him.

ABBOT AND CHORUS
Though he never knew the boy
He'll offer up a prayer for him.
[*The Ferryman turns and looks at the weeping Madwoman*]

FERRYMAN
Come along there, you crazy soul!
It's time to land,
So get out of the boat.
Come along there,
Get out of the boat!
You must be soft-hearted
To weep at my story,
To weep so bitterly.
Make haste there, step ashore!

MADWOMAN
Ferryman, tell me,
When did it happen,
This story you have told us?

FERRYMAN
Last year, at this time,
On this very day, a year ago.

MADWOMAN
Ferryman, how old was the boy?

FERRYMAN
I told you, he was twelve.

MADWOMAN
What was his name?

FERRYMAN
But I told you all about him!
I told you what he was,
And how he came here.

MADWOMAN
Ferryman, pray tell me,
Tell me what his name was.

FERRYMAN
Oh, how should *I* know?
His father was a nobleman
From the Black Mountains.

MADWOMAN
And since then have neither
Of his parents been here?

FERRYMAN
No one of his family.

MADWOMAN
Not even his mother?

FERRYMAN
Not even his mother!

MADWOMAN
No wonder no one
Came here to look for him!

He was the child
Sought by this madwoman.

TRAVELLER
The boy was her child,
The child she was seeking!
He who died here
Was this poor woman's child.

FERRYMAN
Who could have dreamed it?
The boy who died here!
Her sad search is ended.
It is ended after months of weary searching.

ABBOT
The madwoman was his mother!
Him she was seeking
Was not to be found.

MADWOMAN
Am I dreaming?
Is this a dream?

CHORUS
[*Tenors*]
He was her child!
She has found his grave here by the river.
[*Baritones*]
She was his mother!
She has only found sorrow!
[*Basses*]
Is this a dream?
Or is it true she was his mother?
[*The Madwoman rises*]

MADWOMAN
O Curlew River, cruel Curlew,
Where all my hope is swept away!
Torn from the nest, my bird,
Crying in empty air.
Now the nest of the curlew is silent with
    snow,
And the lamb is devoured by the carrion
    crow . . .
The innocent lamb . . .
The heathen crow!
Good people, where shall I turn?
Tell me now!
Take me back . . .
Chain on my soul, let me go!
[*She sinks down*]
O River Curlew, O curlew, cruel bird!

ABBOT AND CHORUS
Here, where the Curlew
Separates for ever
On that side, the Land of the West,
And here, the Eastern Fens.
Here where the River
For ever divides them
Her sad search is ended.

FERRYMAN
Who would have guessed that
The boy was her child?

TRAVELLER
This madwoman was his mother.

FERRYMAN
Lady, I pity you!

TRAVELLER
I pity you!

BOTH
We pity you!

MADWOMAN
Let me in! Let me out! Let me in!

FERRYMAN
Your sad search is ended!
[*The Ferryman and Traveller move to help the Madwoman out of the boat*]

FERRYMAN
Now let me show you
Where the boy is buried.
I beg you,
Please step this way.
Lady, come with me.
[*The Ferryman leads the Madwoman to the tomb*]
This is the grave of your young child.
That his young soul may rest in peace,
We all can pray.
May Heaven receive it!
For his young soul's repose, lady,
Your prayer is best.

TRAVELLER, ABBOT AND CHORUS
Lady, let him guide you to the tomb,
The place where your wandering steps
    have brought you.
This is the grave of your young child.
That his soul may rest in peace,
We all can pray.
May Heaven receive it!

MADWOMAN
[*She turns away from the tomb*]
Hoping, I wandered on,
Hoping to find my son.
I have come alone
To the reedy land of Fens,
Where all is strange to me,
Only to learn
In all this earth, no road
Leads to my living son.
Hoping, I wandered on—
I have come to a grave!
Did I give birth to him
To have him stolen
And carried far away,
Here to the Eastern Fens
To end as dust by the road?

O, good people, open up the tomb
That I may see again
The shape of my child,
His face, his well-belovèd face!
[*She claws hopelessly at the tomb, then sinks down weeping*]

ABBOT AND CHORUS
He whose life was full of promise
Promised, and is gone.
She who feels her life is passing,
She is left alone.

Left alone, and weeping:
May her weeping cease!
[*An Acolyte tolls the bell*]

FERRYMAN
What is the use of tears?
Whom can your weeping help?
No, rather say a prayer
That in the other world
The soul of your child
May rest in peace.

MADWOMAN
Cruel!
Grief is too great,
I cannot pray,
I am struck down.
Here, on the ground,
All I can do is weep.

TRAVELLER
This is not right.
Lady, remember,
All of us here
May pray for your child:
But *your* prayer is best
To rejoice his young soul.

MADWOMAN
What you say is true:
I'll say a prayer
For the soul of my lost child.
Deafened by his silence,
Roaring like the sea.
[*She turns and faces the tomb*]

ABBOT AND CHORUS
The moon has risen,
The river breeze is blowing,
The Curlew River
Is flowing to the sea.
Now it is night
And time to pray.

MADWOMAN
I pray with the others
Under the white light
Of the cloudless moon.

FERRYMAN
And her prayers go straight to Heaven.

TRAVELLER
Her prayers go to Heaven.

FERRYMAN AND TRAVELLER
And, O, to the numberless
Holy and glorious
Saints and martyrs,
All the company
Holy and glorious
There in the blessèd
Abode of eternal
Peacefulness, happiness.
All angels, all martyrs,
All saints, pray for us.
Christ have mercy upon us.
[*The Abbot and Chorus kneel, facing the tomb*]

ABBOT AND CHORUS
Custodes hominum psallimus Angelos,
Naturae fragili quos Pater addidit
Caelestis comites, insidiantibus
Ne succumberet hostibus.

Nam quod curruerit proditor Angelus,
Concessis merito pulsus honoribus,
Ardens invidia, pellere nititur
Quos caelo Deus advocat.
[*The Ferryman and Traveller kneel, facing the tomb*]
[*The Madwoman turns from the tomb and gazes into the distance*]

MADWOMAN
From the river
I hear voices,
Like souls abandoned
Curlews are calling.

'Birds of the Fenland, though you float or fly,
Wild birds, I cannot understand your cry.
Tell me, does the one I love
In this world still live?'

FERRYMAN, TRAVELLER, ABBOT AND CHORUS
Huc custos igitur pervigil advola,
Avertens patria de tibi credita
Tam morbos animi, quam requiescere
Quidquid non sinit incolas.
[*The voice of the Spirit of the Boy is heard from inside the tomb*]

SPIRIT AND THE REST
Sanctae sit Triadi laus pia jugiter . . .

MADWOMAN
I thought I heard
The voice of my child.

SPIRIT AND THE REST
Cujus perpetuo numine machina . . .

MADWOMAN
I thought I heard him
Praying in his grave.

SPIRIT AND THE REST
Triplex haec regitur, . . .

FERRYMAN
We also heard it,

TRAVELLER
The voice of the child.

SPIRIT AND THE REST
. . .cujus in omnia . . .

FERRYMAN
We shall keep silent.

TRAVELLER
Say your prayer alone, lady.

FERRYMAN
Say it alone.

ABBOT, CHORUS AND SPIRIT
Regnat gloria saecula.
[*All except the Madwoman withdraw from the tomb*]

MADWOMAN
O but if only
I might hear it,
Hear his voice once again,
The voice of my son,
Hear the voice of my son!

SPIRIT
Amen.
[*The Spirit of the Boy appears in full view above the tomb*]

ALL [*except Madwoman and Spirit*]
Hear his voice!
See, there is his shape!

MADWOMAN
Is it you, my child?
[*The Spirit circles slowly round the Madwoman, who appears transformed*]
[*He returns to the tomb*]

SPIRIT [*off*]
Go your way in peace, mother.
The dead shall rise again
And in that blessèd day
We shall meet in Heaven.

ABBOT AND CHORUS
Amen.

SPIRIT
God be with you all.

FERRYMAN AND TRAVELLER
Amen.

SPIRIT
God be with you, mother.

MOTHER [*now freed from her madness*]
Amen.

SPIRIT
Amen.
[*The Mother bows her head. The Monks come forward and hide her from view. She, the Ferryman, and the Traveller resume their Monks' habits.*]
[*The Abbot comes forward and addresses the congregation*]

ABBOT
Good souls, we have shown you here
How in sad mischance
A sign was given of God's grace.

MONKS
A sign of God's grace.

ABBOT
A vision was seen,
A miracle and a mystery,
At our Curlew River here.
A woman was healed by prayer and grace,
A woman with grief distraught.

MONKS
With grief distraught.

ABBOT AND MONKS [*exhorting the congregation*]
O praise our God that lifteth up
The fallen, the lost, the least;
The hope He gives, and His grace that heals.

ABBOT
In hope, in peace, ends our mystery.
[*The Abbot moves away from the acting area, and the Monks, Acolytes and Instrumentalists form a procession after him*]

ALL
Te lucis ante terminum,
Rerum Creator, poscimus,
Ut pro tua clementia,
Sis praesul et custodia.

Procul recedant somnia,
Et noctium phantasmata:
Hostemque nostrum comprime,
Ne polluantur corpora.

Praesta, Pater piissime,
Patrique compar Unice,
Cum Spiritu Paraclito,
Regnans per omne saeculum.
Amen

The Burning Fiery Furnace

Second parable
for church performance

by William Plomer

BENJAMIN BRITTEN OP. 77

CHARACTERS

The Abbot, Twelve Monks, Five Acolytes and Eight Lay Brothers *who make up the cast of the Parable:*	
Nebuchadnezzar	TENOR
The Astrologer (The Abbot)	BARITONE
Ananias	BARITONE
Misael	TENOR
Azarias	BASS
The Herald and Leader of the Courtiers	BARITONE
The Chorus of Courtiers	THREE TENORS TWO BARITONES TWO BASSES
Five Attendants	TREBLES

including Angel, Tumbler, Entertainers, Pages, etc.

The Instrumentalists *Lay Brothers*

Flute (doubling Piccolo)

Horn

Alto Trombone

Viola

Double Bass (doubling Babylonian Drum)

Harp (doubling Little Harp)

*Percussion**

Chamber Organ (doubling small Cymbals)

*5 small untuned drums, anvil (small untuned steel plate), 2 tuned wood blocks, lyra glockenspiel, Babylonian drum, multiple whip

FIRST PERFORMANCE

9 June 1966   Orford Church, Suffolk (E.O.G. production)

The Astrologer (the Abbot)	Bryan Drake
Nebuchadnezzar	Peter Pears
Ananias	John Shirley-Quirk
Misael	Robert Tear
Azarias	Victor Godfrey
The Angel	Philip Wait
Entertainers and Pages	Stephen Borton, Paul Copcutt, Paul Davies, Richard Jones, Philip Wait
The Herald and Chorus Leader	Peter Leeming
Chorus of Courtiers	Graham Allum, Peter Lehmann Bedford, Carl Duggan, John Harrod, William McKinney, Malcolm Rivers, Jacob Witkin

Music under the direction of the composer
Production and setting by Colin Graham
Costumes and properties by Annena Stubbs

Foreword by William Plomer

The Burning Fiery Furnace develops the convention invented by Benjamin Britten for *Curlew River*. For those who have not yet seen and heard *Curlew River* it may be helpful to say something of its origin and nature.

The work was generated by the strong response, at quite different times, of the composer and the librettist to performances in Japan of the medieval *Nō*-plays, upon one of which its story is based. It would have been impossible to transpose or imitate either the highly stylised Japanese production or the traditional subtleties of the *Nō*. But it was found possible to adapt the use of a small, projecting, curtainless stage; the functioning together operatically of performers and orchestra without a conductor; and a formalised production. By devising 'a parable for church performance' it was possible to present the work in an atmosphere fitting its religious, legendary nature.

The success of what was by no means an easy experiment and the experience gained from it have enabled the composer to allow himself, in this second 'parable', greater freedom and richness of texture within the prescribed limits. And whereas *Curlew River* required the transmuting of a Far Eastern, Buddhist legend into a Western, Christian ideology, *The Burning Fiery Furnace* has not involved that need. It is directly based upon the familiar Biblical story of Shadrach, Meshach and Abednego, which is to be found in the third chapter of the Book of Daniel. It may be felt that in this new version the character of Nebuchadnezzar, the cult of 'the god of gold', and the resistance movement—ultimately triumphant—of the three young Jewish exiles are not without some relation to our own times.

The Burning Fiery Furnace

The action of the parable takes place in Babylon in the Sixth Century BC.

[*The Abbot and his company of Monks, Acolytes and Instrumentalists walk singing in procession to the acting area*]

ABBOT AND ALL
Salus aeterna,
indeficiens mundi vita,
lux sempiterna,
et redemptio vere nostra,

Condolens humana
perire saecla
per tentantis numina,
non linquens excelsa
adisti ima
propria clementia.
Salus aeterna,
indeficiens mundi vita,
(lux sempiterna,
et redemptio vere nostra).

Mox tua spontanea
gratia,
assumens humana,
quae fuerant perdita
omnia
salvasti terrea,
ferens mundo gaudia.
(Salus aeterna,
indeficiens mundi vita,)
lux sempiterna,
et redemptio vere nostra.

ABBOT
God be with you all!
[*The Abbot comes forward to address the congregation*]

ABBOT
Good people, in His holy name
We come to perform
A mystery.
We show how three young men
Of Israel
By steadfastness
Rose in a single day
Into the light of lasting fame.

MONKS
The calm pure light of endless fame.

ABBOT
To that imperial city, Babylon,
These three were brought,
Sons of princes
Chosen out to rule
Three provinces in Babylon.

MONKS
In that great empire, Babylon.

ABBOT
Their fathers blest them,
Only made one rule
Binding upon them all:

They never must in any way
Betray their faith.
How could they know
What testing lay ahead?

MONKS
God give us all
The strength to stand
Against the burning,
Murderous world!

ABBOT
Now we all shall play our parts,
And I, your Abbot, must appear
A heathen, and an evil man:
It is all for the glory of God.

MONKS
Amen!
[*The Abbot, who is to play the Astrologer, and the two Monks who are to play Nebuchadnezzar and the Herald are ceremonially prepared. So are Ananias, Misael and Azarias. Nebuchadnezzar and the Astrologer leave the acting area. The Chorus, representing Courtiers, take their places. The Herald comes forward*]

HERALD
By the Royal Command
Of the great King of Kings,
Nebuchadnezzar,
Great King of Babylon,
This day we are to feast
In honour of three young men,
Brought here from Israel,
Chosen out of all the world
For knowledge and skill,
To take high rank in Babylon.
Ananias! Misael! Azarias!
We welcome you and acclaim you.
[*The Three bow in acknowledgment*]

HERALD
To mark the esteem
In which he holds your virtues
The great King himself
Has declared his purpose
To be present at this feast.
[*He bows and joins the Courtiers*]

COURTIERS
O joyful occasion,
The King gives a feast!
And we are invited
As guests at his table,
To share the King's meat
And drink to his joy,
His power and long life,
In the King's precious wine.
[*A flourish proclaims the ceremonious arrival of Nebuchadnezzar. As he approaches, together with the Astrologer, all join to welcome him with an anthem*]

COURTIERS WITH ANANIAS, MISAEL AND AZARIAS
Great King, whom all you rule,
Greet and salute,
Great King of Babylon,
All-wise and absolute,
Greet and salute!
We bow deeply before you,

Lord and Giver of life,
Greet and salute!
We praise you and adore—
Greet and salute!

ASTROLOGER [*coming forward*]
The King commands you all
To take your places,
And before the feast begins
To hear his gracious words.
[*All seat themselves*]

NEBUCHADNEZZAR
Adept in magic though our sage
Chaldeans be,
Our own foresight has brought these
chosen strangers here
For special cause. Pre-eminent in wisdom
Beyond their years, they drank in with
their mothers' milk
Authority!
Authority we give them now
Over three provinces in Babylon to rule,
Viceregally to rule, to rule, and be
obeyed.

ANANIAS, MISAEL AND AZARIAS
Great King, accept, we pray,
Our homage and our thanks.
Our humble duty, and our thanks.

All honoured with your royal trust
We pledge ourselves
To serve you faithfully
In Babylon the great.

NEBUCHADNEZZAR
See that you do,
See that you do. And now it is our royal
wish,
And in accordance with the ruling of the
stars,
That you be given Babylonian names,
instead
Of those outlandish names you bring from
Israel.
Astrologer, tell them how they are
called.

ASTROLOGER
You Ananias,
Hear your new name.
Shadrach.

COURTIERS
Shadrach!

ASTROLOGER
Misael, take note.
Your name is now
Meshach.

COURTIERS
Meshach!

ASTROLOGER
Azarias, learn your new name.
You are to be called
Abednego.

97 Ananias, Misael and Azarias

Annena Stubbs

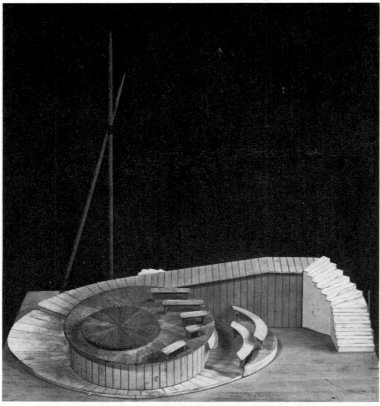

98 Model of stage for the Church Parables. The curved benches are for the instrumentalists

99 and 100 Production photographs including the Image of Gold

101 Nebuchadnezzar and the Astrologer   *Annena Stubbs*

COURTIERS
    Abednego!
    Shadrach! Meshach! Abednego!

NEBUCHADNEZZAR
    Now, let the feast begin.
    Good appetite, good cheer!

COURTIERS
    Good cheer, good cheer,
    Indeed, good cheer.
    If every change of name
    Leads to a royal feast,
    We'll ask the King
    To give us all new names,
    New names,
    And all grow fat.
    [*All sit down and begin feasting, except the Three, who politely
    refuse what is handed to them. Attention is distracted from this by
    the Entertainers, who dance and sing.*]

ENTERTAINER 1
    The waters of Babylon,
        The flowing waters,
            All ran dry.
        Do you know why?

ENTERTAINER 2
    Of course I do!

ENTERTAINER 1
                And so do I!

COURTIERS
    Good cheer indeed!

ENTERTAINER 2
    The gardens of Babylon,
        The hanging gardens,
            Grew like mad.
        Do you know why?

ENTERTAINER 1
    Of course I do!

ENTERTAINER 2
                And so do I!

COURTIERS
    Good cheer indeed!

ENTERTAINER 1
    The people of Babylon,
        The thievish people,
            Ate the figs,
    They ate the melons and ate the grapes—
    The thievish people of Babylon ate the
        grapes—
        Do you know why?

ENTERTAINER 2
    Of course I do!

ENTERTAINER 1
                And so do I!

ENTERTAINERS 1 AND 2
    The reason the waters all ran dry
    Was that somebody had monkeyed with
        the water supply;
    The reason the gardens grew like mad
    Was because of all the water they'd had:

The reason they gobbled up the melons
    and grapes and figs
Was that Babylonians are greedy pigs!
    If pigs had wings then pigs would fly
    Far above Babylon. Babylon, goodbye!

COURTIERS
    Good cheer, good cheer!
    If every change of name
    Leads to a royal feast . . .

ENTERTAINERS
    Goodbye!

COURTIERS
    Good cheer indeed!
    [*Suddenly the Astrologer notices that the Three are not eating and
    drinking, and addresses them*]

ASTROLOGER
    Sirs, what is this?
    Not eating? not drinking?
    Does this mean you disdain
    The King's hospitality?

COURTIERS
    We'll ask the King to give us all new
        names
    And all grow fat!

ASTROLOGER
    This is no time for abstinence!
    There may be in your country
    Bad behaviour at table,
    But here in Babylon
    Our guests do not insult us.
    [*He turns to Nebuchadnezzar*]
    Sir, this is an outrage!

NEBUCHADNEZZAR
    Come Shadrach, Meshach,
    Come, Abednego,
    My welcome guests, where are your
        appetites?
    This is no time for modesty. Fall to,
        fall to.
    Show us that Israelites
    Can be good trenchermen!
    Come, Shadrach! Meshach! Abednego!
        Come, come!
    [*The Three rise*]

ANANIAS
    Great King! We value deeply
    All your gracious favours—

MISAEL
    We feel honoured vastly
    To be here at your table—

AZARIAS
    Guests at this royal table
    Of the great King of Babylon.

ALL THREE
    But we beg your Majesty
    To excuse our frugality.
    We are very small eaters.

NEBUCHADNEZZAR
    You are very small eaters?

Do you live then on air?
When in Babylon, dine,
Dine as the Babylonians dine.

ALL THREE
Sir, pray excuse us.

NEBUCHADNEZZAR
Come now, we cannot have you living
only
On your excellent reputations.
Never, never be it said
We let our guests go empty.

ASTROLOGER
Why are they not eating?

COURTIERS
They are making excuses.

ASTROLOGER
They are not even drinking.

COURTIERS
Not drinking—they are not even
drinking!

NEBUCHADNEZZAR
Come, fill up the goblet!

COURTIERS
Good cheer, indeed!
. . .and all grow fat!
[*The Three refuse*]

NEBUCHADNEZZAR
What, you refuse even to drink with us?
Take care lest you offend us.

AZARIAS
O King, though greatly tempted
By this royal meat and wine—

MISAEL
So graciously pressed on us—

ANANIAS
Your Majesty will understand—

ALL THREE
Partaking is forbidden
By the sacred laws of Israel.
[*The Three draw apart*]

ASTROLOGER
O King, you are insulted.
See what comes of preferring
These aliens in Babylon.

COURTIERS 1
Young Jews, a bunch of foreigners!
Foreigners, foreigners,
Never trust foreigners!

COURTIERS 2
O what are you saying?
They are strangers—
Do not treat them harshly!

ASTROLOGER
Has your Majesty forgotten
My timely warning?
Always faithful to my duty,
Always faithful to my King,

I warned you,
I warned you
The stars were against you.
This rash innovation,
Invasion of immigrants,
Puts Babylon in danger.

NEBUCHADNEZZAR
The stars are against me!
If the stars are against me
Then how can I govern?
My best intentions
Lead only to confusion and danger!
Dangerous! Advise me!
Have I angered the heavens?
Have I defied the stars?
What must I do?
[*Nebuchadnezzar rises and leaves in panic, attended by the Astrologer; the Courtiers follow*]

COURTIERS 1
Babylon in danger!
The wise man knows best!

COURTIERS 2
He is jealous,
The young men are harmless.

NEBUCHADNEZZAR
Have I defied the stars?
What must I, must I do?

ASTROLOGER
I warned your Majesty.

COURTIERS 1
Babylon in danger!
Down with the foreigners!

COURTIERS 2
To them we are the foreigners,
These strangers are innocent.

NEBUCHADNEZZAR
How can I now take back, take back my
own decree?

ASTROLOGER
I consulted the stars.

COURTIERS 1
Down with them!

COURTIERS 2
Be not over-hasty—

NEBUCHADNEZZAR
Come with me—advise me—

ASTROLOGER
Danger, sir!

COURTIERS 2
Be not over-hasty!

COURTIERS 1
Out with them!

NEBUCHADNEZZAR
Have I done right or wrong?

ASTROLOGER
I warned you!

COURTIERS 1
  Danger . . .

COURTIERS 2
    Hasty . . .

ASTROLOGER [off]
  Merodak!

NEBUCHADNEZZAR [off]
  Merodak?
  [The Three are left alone]

ANANIAS, MISAEL AND AZARIAS [severally]
  We do not lack enemies.

  We might have known jealousy
  Would work against us here.

  Our foreign blood, our Jewish faith,
  Enrage the Astrologer,
  And our more active brains.

  He sees us here in Babylon
  As rivals to his power.

  We must be careful.
  He has aroused the King against us.

  They have given us new names
  To disguise our true natures,
  Shadrach, Meshach, and Abednego!
  But names cannot change us.

  What we are, we remain.

ALL THREE [together]
  And so must continue,
  Children of Israel,
  Servants of Jehovah.
  Lord, help us in our loneliness.
  We rejoice in declaring
  Our trust in thy power.
  Lord, help us in our loneliness.
  The idols of the heathen
  Are silver and gold,
  But Jehovah, Most High,
  Has armed us with salvation.
  In the armour of faith
  Lord, help us in our loneliness.
  We defy our enemies.
  Lord, help us in our loneliness.
  [They settle down calmly to rest. The Herald comes forward]

HERALD
  By the Royal decree
  Of the great King of Kings,
  Nebuchadnezzar,
  There shall be set up
  In the province of Babylon
  An image of gold,
  Of height three score cubits,
  The breadth thereof six cubits.
  An image of Merodak,
  The great god of Babylon.
  O people, nations and languages,
  At what time ye hear the sound of the cornet,
  Flute, harp, sackbut, psaltery, dulcimer,
  And all kinds of music,

  Ye fall down and worship the image of gold.
  Whoso falleth not down and worshippeth
  Shall be cast into the midst
  Of a burning fiery furnace.
  [The Three pray aloud and are interrupted by the
  Instrumentalists preparing for the procession]

ALL THREE
  Blessed art thou, O Lord God of our fathers,
  Let thy name be glorified for evermore.
  For our sins we are in the hands of an unjust king,
  But thy ways are just and true.
  O deliver us not up wholly,
  Cause not thy mercy to depart from us.
  They shall not be confounded
  That put their trust in thee.
  Lord, help us in our loneliness.
  [Led by the Herald the Musicians circulate in procession, then
  return to the acting area where the Courtiers have gathered. The
  Image rises in the background, and Nebuchadnezzar and the
  Astrologer come towards it]

ASTROLOGER
  O hearken, all ye people!
  I speak for the King of Kings.
  Now fall ye down and worship—
  Worship the image of gold—
  Or fear the penalty!
  [While the Three remain aloof, still praying to their own God, all
  the others worship and sing a hymn of adoration to the Image]

ASTROLOGER
  Merodak!
  Lord of Creation,
  We bow down before you,
  Adore you, implore you
  To glorify our nation,
    Our nation!

NEBUCHADNEZZAR AND COURTIERS
  Merodak!
  Make our enemies fear us,
  Yes, fear and respect us,
  Destroy them! Protect us!
  Merodak, O hear us,
    O hear us!

COURTIERS
  Merodak!
  Those who disobey you
  Crush, punish, erase!
  God of gold, whom we praise,
  Defend us, we pray you,
    We pray you!

NEBUCHADNEZZAR AND ASTROLOGER
  God of gold!
  Gold is our God,
  Fall down and worship it!
  Obey the decree, obey!
  Curse our enemies, curse!
  Curse them in your songs of hate!
  Sing! Louder!
  All ye people, shout! Shout!

NEBUCHADNEZZAR AND COURTIERS
  Merodak!
  We bow down before you!
  [The Astrologer approaches Nebuchadnezzar]

ASTROLOGER
O King, live for ever!
Those Jews whom your Majesty
Hath set in authority
Have not regarded you.

NEBUCHADNEZZAR
Must you disturb me while I pray?
Let me alone!

NEBUCHADNEZZAR AND COURTIERS
O Merodak!
We adore you, implore you
To glorify our nation—

ASTROLOGER
Sir, those Jews disobey you,
They are openly rebellious—
I beg you, sir, be firm with them.

NEBUCHADNEZZAR
Must you bring complainings at this time?
Go away! Go away!

NEBUCHADNEZZAR AND COURTIERS
Merodak!

ASTROLOGER
Sir, they serve not your god,
Nor worship the image
You have set up.

NEBUCHADNEZZAR
Nor worship the image I have set up?
Bring them here before my Majesty!
[*The Three are brought before Nebuchadnezzar*]

NEBUCHADNEZZAR
Is it true, O Shadrach,
Meshach and Abednego,
You do not serve my god, the god of
    gold, of Babylon?
Is it true, O Shadrach,
Meshach and Abednego,
At the sound of the cornet,
Flute, harp, sackbut, psaltery, dulcimer,
And all kinds of music, you fall not down
    and worship
The image I have made?
Have you not heard,
O Shadrach, Meshach and Abednego,
You shall be cast at once
Into the burning fiery furnace?
And who is that god
Shall deliver you out of my hands?

NEBUCHADNEZZAR AND ASTROLOGER
Shadrach, Meshach, Abednego, answer!

COURTIERS
Shadrach, Meshach, Abednego!

ANANIAS, MISAEL AND AZARIAS
O King, Nebuchadnezzar,
Our God whom we serve is able to deliver us.
If he wishes, he will deliver us—
Out of thy hands,
But, if not—
We would not offend you, O King.
We will not serve thy god,
Nor worship the image of gold

Which you have set up, in Babylon the
Great.
[*Nebuchadnezzar is enraged, and the glow of the Furnace is seen*]

NEBUCHADNEZZAR
Ah! Heat the burning fiery furnace!
Heat the furnace! Heat the furnace!
Make it seven times hotter, hotter,
Than it ever was before.

ASTROLOGER
See what happens to the foreign traitors,
See what happens when they disobey their King.

NEBUCHADNEZZAR
Take those men,
Traitors to Babylon.
Let them now be straightway cast
Into the burning fiery furnace.

ASTROLOGER
See what happens
To the proud Israelites.
See what happens
When they disobey
Merodak, god of gold, god of Babylon.

NEBUCHADNEZZAR AND ASTROLOGER
Let them be straightway cast
Into the burning, fiery furnace.
[*The Three are dragged to the Furnace, into which they are cast,
and they disappear*]

COURTIERS 1
See them all
Go up in smoke!
Let them learn what sevenfold heat is
In the burning fiery furnace.

COURTIERS 2 AND ASTROLOGER
Burn the foreigners!
Burn the traitors to Babylon!
See them burning
To the glory
Of Merodak!
[*Those who cast the Three into the Furnace are overcome by the
heat, but the Three are seen standing unhurt in the fire, with a
fourth figure among them*]

ANGEL
O . . .

ANANIAS, MISAEL AND AZARIAS
O all ye Works of the Lord, bless ye the
Lord.

NEBUCHADNEZZAR
Did we not cast three men bound
Into the midst of the fire?

ASTROLOGER
True, O King.

ANGEL
O . . .

ANANIAS, MISAEL AND AZARIAS
Praise him and magnify him for ever!

NEBUCHADNEZZAR
But I see four men free,
Walking in the midst of the fire,
And they are unharmed.

ASTROLOGER
True, O King.

ANGEL
O . . .

ANANIAS, MISAEL AND AZARIAS
O ye Angels of the Lord, bless ye the
Lord.
O ye Heavens, bless ye the Lord,
Praise him and magnify him for ever.

NEBUCHADNEZZAR
And the form of the fourth
Is like the Son of God.

COURTIERS
The form of the fourth
Is like the Son of God.

ASTROLOGER
True, O King.

ANGEL
O . . .

ANANIAS, MISAEL AND AZARIAS
O ye Waters that be above the firmament, bless ye
the Lord.
O ye Sun and Moon, bless ye the Lord.
O ye Stars of Heaven, bless ye the Lord.
O ye Showers and Dew, bless ye the Lord.
O ye Winds of God, bless ye the Lord.
O ye Fire and Heat, bless ye the Lord,
Praise him and magnify him for ever!
[Nebuchadnezzar steps forward, cautiously, because of the heat]

NEBUCHADNEZZAR
Shadrach, Meshach, Abednego,
Ye servants of the most high God,
Come forth, and come here.

ANGEL
O . . .

ANANIAS, MISAEL AND AZARIAS
O, blessed be the God
Who hath sent his angel
And delivered them
Who put their trust in him.
[The fourth figure disappears. The Three come out of the
Furnace. Nebuchadnezzar examines them to see whether they are
untouched by the fire]

NEBUCHADNEZZAR
But the sevenfold heat
Of the burning fiery furnace
Has not even scorched you!
Since time began was there ever such a wonder!

COURTIERS
Since time began was there ever such a wonder!

NEBUCHADNEZZAR [turning on the Astrologer]
And you, Chaldean,
What have you to say?
Consulter of the stars,
Pretentious fraud,
Where is your wisdom now?

ASTROLOGER
Always faithful to my duty,
Majesty, you wrong me.

In such complexity
The stars revolve,
Stars do not easily
Yield their secrets.

NEBUCHADNEZZAR
So then you invent them,
And mislead your monarch?
Go, leave me.

ASTROLOGER
Majesty, you wrong me.
[He cringes and withdraws]

NEBUCHADNEZZAR
O blessed be the God
Who hath sent his angel
And delivered them
Who put their trust in him.
[Nebuchadnezzar beckons to the Three to stand beside him]
Hear my decree:
There is no god except this God,
The God of Shadrach, Meshach and
Abednego.
Down with Merodak,
Down with the god of gold.
[The Image falls]

ATTENDANTS
O . . .

NEBUCHADNEZZAR, ANANIAS, MISAEL AND AZARIAS,
COURTIERS [severally and together]
O ye Winter and Summer, bless ye the
Lord,
Praise him and magnify him for ever.
O ye Nights and Days, bless ye the Lord.
O ye Light and Darkness, bless ye the
Lord.
O let the Earth bless the Lord.
Yea, let it praise him and magnify him
for ever.
O ye Seas and Floods, bless ye the Lord.
O all ye Fowls of the Air, O ye Whales and all that move
in the waters, O ye Beasts and Cattle, bless ye the
Lord.
O ye Children of Men, bless ye the Lord.
O ye Priests of the Lord, bless ye the
Lord.
O ye Servants of the Lord, bless ye the
Lord.
O ye Spirits and Souls of the Righteous,
ye holy and humble men of heart,
O Ananias, Azarias, and Misael, bless ye
the Lord.
Praise him and magnify him for ever.
[The Monks come forward to help Nebuchadnezzar and the other
characters to disrobe; they resume their monks' habits. The Abbot
enters, now in his own robes, and addresses the congregation]

ABBOT
Good people, we have shown you here
The burning trial of faith.
Over that great city, Babylon,
That mighty place,
A new light shines.

MONKS
A new light shines.

ABBOT
Friends, remember!
Gold is tried in the fire,
And the mettle of man
In the furnace of humiliation.

ABBOT AND MONKS
God give us all
The strength to walk
Safe in the burning furnace
Of this murderous world.

ABBOT
Good friends, so ends our mystery.
[*The Abbot moves away from the acting area, and the Monks,
Acolytes and Instrumentalists form a procession after him*]

ABBOT AND ALL
Salus aeterna,
indeficiens mundi vita,
lux sempiterna,
et redemptio vere nostra,

Condolens humana
perire saecla
per tentantis numina,

non linquens excelsa
adisti ima
propria clementia.
Salus aeterna,
indeficiens mundi vita,
(lux sempiterna,
et redemptio vere nostra).

Mox tua spontanea
gratia,
assumens humana,
quae fuerant perdita
omnia
salvasti terrea,
ferens mundo gaudia.
(Salus aeterna,
indeficiens mundi vita,)
lux sempiterna,
et redemptio vere nostra.

ABBOT
God be with you all.

ALL
Amen.

The Prodigal Son

*Third parable
for church performance*

by William Plomer

BENJAMIN BRITTEN OP. 81

CHARACTERS

The Abbot, Monks, Acolytes and Lay Brothers *who make up the cast of the Parable:*

Tempter *Abbot*	TENOR
Father	BASS-BARITONE
Elder Son	BARITONE
Younger Son	TENOR
Chorus	
Servants (8)	THREE TENORS
Parasites (8)	THREE BARITONES
Beggars (8)	TWO BASSES
Young Servants and Distant Voices	FIVE TREBLES

The Instrumentalists *Lay Brothers*

Alto Flute (doubling Piccolo)
Trumpet (in D)
Horn
Viola
Double Bass
Harp
Percussion*   *Percussion**
Chamber Organ

*5 small untuned drums, small Chinese cymbal, conical gourd rattle, large tuned gong, 2 tuned wood blocks, high-pitched wood block.

On stage
Small drum (tambour), pair of small cymbals, tambourine, sistrum (jungle rattle), small bell-lyra

FIRST PERFORMANCE

10 June 1968   Orford Church, Suffolk (E.O.G. production)

The Tempter (the Abbot)	Peter Pears
The Father	John Shirley-Quirk
The Elder Son	Bryan Drake
The Younger Son	Robert Tear
Chorus of Servants, Parasites and Beggars	Paschal Allen, Peter Bedford, Carl Duggan, David Hartley, Peter Leeming, John McKenzie, Clive Molloy, Paul Wade
Young Servants and Distant Voices	Robert Alder, John Harriman, Peter Heriot, Richard Kahn, David Morgan

Music under the direction of the composer
Production and setting by Colin Graham
Costumes and properties by Annena Stubbs

Foreword by William Plomer

The Prodigal Son is the third of Britten's church operas, or Parables for Church Performance. The first of them, *Curlew River*, based upon one of the medieval *Nō*-plays of Japan, involved the transmuting of a remote Buddhist legend into Western, Christian ideology, at the same time retaining a formalized, hieratic production. The second, *The Burning Fiery Furnace*, presented, within the completely new convention devised for *Curlew River*, the dramatic Old Testament story of Shadrach, Meshach, and Abednego.

Of all the parables in the New Testament, none has had quite such a universal and ever-renewed appeal as that of the Prodigal Son. A long list could be compiled of painters, writers, and composers whose imaginations have been stirred by it, from Rembrandt (whose supreme painting of the subject hangs in the Hermitage) to Debussy and Gide.

With its unforgettable climax of reward and rejoicing being lavished not upon virtuous correctness but upon a sinner, this parable celebrates the triumph of forgiveness. The story seems to bring into the clearest possible focus the Christian view of life. And it is worth remarking that, like Christianity itself, all three of these church operas are ultimately of Asian derivation. Plot and production make this plain enough, and the music itself has not been uninfluenced by the composer's travels in Asia.

Those familiar with the first two of these works will be able to discern how *The Prodigal Son*, while remaining within similar limits, has in various ways developed beyond them, notably in the much fuller function given to the chorus.

The Prodigal Son

[*The Monks, Acolytes and Lay Brothers walk singing in procession to the acting area*]

ALL VOICES [*except the Abbot*]
Jam lucis orto sidere,
Deum precemur supplices,
Ut in diurnis actibus,
Nos servet a nocentibus.

Linguam refraenans temperet,
Ne litis horror insonet:
Visum fovendo contegat,
Ne vanitates hauriat.

Sint pura cordis intima,
Absistat et vecordia:
Carnis terat superbiam
Potus cibique parcitas.

Ut cum dies abscesserit,
Noctemque sors reduxerit,
Mundi per abstinentiam
Ipsi canamus gloriam.
                    Amen
[*The Abbot, disguised as the Tempter, is heard from the opposite end of the church, at a distance*]

TEMPTER
Amen, Amen!
[*The Tempter appears; the Monks, hearing him, turn away*]
Ah—you people, listening here today,
Do not think I bid you kneel and pray.
[*The Tempter slowly moves past the congregation towards the acting area*]
I bring you no sermon,
What I bring you is evil.

You are about to see
A country patriarch,
A father with his family.
With property and progeny
In order,
So orderly, so dutiful,
He enjoys
The harvest of a well-spent life.

Ah—what a worthy family!
What a quiet life!
Habit has made them dull,
Dull and self-satisfied.
[*The Tempter arrives at the acting area and faces the congregation*]
Here you will see them!
Father, servants who obey
His least command,
Two sons, the elder stern,
The younger full of life,
He is the one I'll use
To break this harmony.
What perfect harmony!
See how I break it up.
[*He passes the acting area, and goes out behind the stage. The Monks slowly turn*]

See how I break it up!

MONKS

Deliver us, O Lord, from the evil man
Who imagines mischief in his heart,
Adders' poison is under his lips,
Like a hunter he has laid a snare for us.
Preserve us, O Lord, from the wicked man,
Let not the ungodly have his desire.
Amen

[*The Monks who are to play the Father and the two Sons are
ceremonially prepared.
The Chorus, representing the Servants, the Elder Son and the
Younger Son are gathered round the Father*]

FATHER [*seated*]

I am father to you all,
Hear what I have to say.
[*He rises*]
The earth is the Lord's
And all of us are His.
For He, the Lord,
Has made us what we are.

This is our life
He has ordained for us.
He has given us peace,
Seed-time and harvest,
Life-giving sun,
The cool and fruitful rain.
[*The Father sits again*]
This is our home
Where each needs all,
And all need each of us.
This is our peaceful life,
Our life we maintain
By love and toil.

Evil lurks everywhere
Watching for idleness,
When evil is lurking
Repel it by work.

Sin is for idle hands,
We must gain our daily bread.
Men, to the fields!
[*The Father rises*]
And you, my elder son,
My right hand whom I trust,
Son, go with the men.
[*The Elder Son rises*]

ELDER SON AND SERVANTS

To the fields, the fields we go,
There in the burning day
To till the ground, and hoe
Rank weeds away.

FATHER

And you, dear younger son,
Child of my later years,
My son, go with the men.

ELDER SON AND SERVANTS

May the fields, the fields we sow
Grow up so green in spring,
May the miles of harvest laugh,
Laugh and sing.

FATHER

And God go with you all.

ELDER SON

Come, all of you.
Men, to the fields away.
You know what waits to be done,
To the west, in the olive grove,
To the east, in the barley field.
[*The Elder Son and the Servants go to the fields. The Younger Son
follows slowly*]

ELDER SON AND SERVANTS

To the west we go, to the east we go
To tend the master's lands,
The Devil fears the work
Of toiling hands.
[*The Tempter comes forward and confronts the Younger Son*]

TEMPTER

Forgive my asking you,
Have you not had enough
Of this quiet life you lead?

YOUNGER SON

Who are you? This quiet life?
I do not understand you.

TEMPTER

Ah, but I think you do.
A lusty youth like you
Is a prisoner here at home.
You are letting life go by.

YOUNGER SON

What right have you to speak?
You, a stranger to me,
To tell me how to live!

TEMPTER

I am no stranger to you,
You know me very well,
I am your inner voice, your very self.

When quite alone
Have you never thought
'If I go on
Living this life
Of long monotonous days,
When shall I ever know
The strong sweet taste
Of life outside?'
[*The Younger Son turns to the Tempter*]

YOUNGER SON

What right have you—?

TEMPTER

What right have *you*
To keep yourself locked up
In this desert here
Of stupid family life?
[*He comes very close to the Younger Son*]
Imagine, imagine,
What you are missing.
Imagine, imagine,
Before it's too late,
High living, secret delights,
And beauty, beauty
To kindle your senses,

While you are young, still young,
While you are young.

Imagine, imagine!

YOUNGER SON
How can he be informed
Of my most secret longings in this way,
Giving them shape as I have never dared to do?

TEMPTER
Act out your desires!
[*The Tempter begins to withdraw as the Elder Son and Servants
are heard singing at their work*]

TEMPTER
Act out your desires!

ELDER SON AND SERVANTS
There is time, there is time when young
To live inside a dream,
    Before things show themselves
        Not what they seem.

YOUNGER SON
Why should I not, before it is too late?
But what will my father say? I hardly dare . . .
Ah, but he loves me, he will understand,
I will go to him now.
[*The Younger Son approaches his Father*]

YOUNGER SON
Father, may I speak to you?

FATHER
My son, there is no need to ask.
I see you are troubled.
If it is in my power
I will help you.

YOUNGER SON [*kneeling*]
Father, I hesitate,
I am ashamed.
You are so good to me.

FATHER
You are not contented here.

YOUNGER SON
How did you know?

FATHER
I have been young myself,
Therefore I understand.

YOUNGER SON [*rising*]
My discontent is this,
While I am living here
Life is passing by.

FATHER
Life bears tempting fruit
Not to be gathered at home.
But oh, my son . . .

YOUNGER SON
Father, if I could now
Have my inheritance!
I need my freedom,
I have to see the world.
If I could have my portion!
If I could have it now!

FATHER
If I were to dissuade you, that would be foolish,
What is forbidden inflames desire.
Think of the dangers of the journey,
Leaving without guide or friend
You might learn little save what is bad.
Think of the hazards,
Perils to your fortune, snares, temptations,
Poisons to your health, your virtue, and your life.

YOUNGER SON
Father I beg you,
If I could have my portion,
If I could have it now!
I am grown to manhood.

FATHER
My son, to content you
I will give you your portion.

YOUNGER SON
Father! My father!
[*The Elder Son and Servants return from their work*]

ELDER SON AND SERVANTS
It is work, it is work that keeps
By night as well as day
    From idle hands all sly
        Tempters away.
[*The Servants gather round the Father; the Elder Son hangs
back*]

FATHER [*rising*]
Come, hearken to me!
While you were in the fields
A change has taken place.
My son, my younger son,
Will now be leaving us.
He wishes to see the world,
A world that is not ours.

SERVANTS
Abandon your childhood,
    Quiet days must end,
Go out in the mad world
    And look for adventure,
        Do what you intend.
[*The Young Servants bring in a symbolic robe to indicate the
Younger Son's share of his inheritance*]

FATHER
Take your due portion.
Go your way safely
And may the Lord God defend you.
[*The Younger Son is robed*]

SERVANTS
Go then, if you must go,
    Quiet days must end,
We see you departing
    Without a protector,
        Without any friend.
[*The Elder Son comes forward*]

ELDER SON
Father, tell me
Why are you doing this?
What are you giving him?

FATHER
Your brother is leaving us,
Going out in the world.
He has asked for his freedom,
I give him his portion.

ELDER SON
You give him his portion?

No word of this
Was uttered to me.
He will go jaunting
While I stay and work.

Never a word of it
Uttered to me,
Turns his back on us,
Strolls off and out.

FATHER
Son, be calm,
He will be wiser for his journey.

YOUNGER SON
Brother, do not think ill of me,
Wish me farewell.

ELDER SON
Farewell, brother, fare you well.
[The Elder Son withdraws]

YOUNGER SON
Friends, I am leaving you.
I wish you farewell.

SERVANTS
Farewell, young master,
Fare you well.
[The Servants withdraw]

YOUNGER SON
Father, to leave you saddens me,
Yet I wish you farewell.

FATHER
Farewell, O my son,
Fare you well.
[The Father withdraws; the Younger Son starts on his journey]

SERVANTS
Go, if you must go,
    Young son and young master,
Out into the wide world
    Where dangers are vaster.

Wherever you wander,
    Whatever beset you,
Good fortune go with you,
    We shall not forget you.

May your innocent footsteps
    Avert all disaster,
Go, if you must go,
    Go safely, young master.

FATHER
May the Lord bless and keep you,
My wandering son.
The younger son departing!

ELDER SON
So he goes jaunting,
Goes off with his share.
The younger son departing!
Just turns his back,
Away, off, and out.
The younger son departing!
[The Younger Son goes on walking; the rest are now out of sight. The Tempter swiftly joins the Younger Son]

TEMPTER	YOUNGER SON
Free! Free!	Free! Free!
At last you are free!	At last I am free!
Be what you want to be,	Be what I want to be,
Do what you want to do,	Do what I want to do,
Be guided by me.	Be guided by you.
From now on please yourself,	From now on please myself,
Ask nobody's pardon,	Ask nobody's pardon,
The world's all before you,	The world's all before me,
One great pleasure-garden.	One great pleasure-garden.
You have longed for this day,	I have longed for this day,
All joys await you.	All joys await me.

[They stop walking and the Younger Son turns to the Tempter]

YOUNGER SON
Come, my guide,
You must show me the way.

TEMPTER
Look ahead, there lies the city.

YOUNGER SON
Do I see the tall towers?

TEMPTER
You see the tall towers.
[They walk again]

ELDER SON   YOUNGER SON

YOUNGER SON	TEMPTER
And when I get there	When you get there,
Will doors open for me?	Doors open for you.

TEMPTER
Open doors, open arms,
Handsome unforeseen boy!
[They arrive at the city]

YOUNGER SON
Do I see the great gates?

TEMPTER
You see the great gates.

TEMPTER	YOUNGER SON
The great gates are wide open,	The great gates are wide open,
Open for you!	Open for me!

[The Parasites surge forward and surround the Younger Son]

PARASITES
Welcome, welcome stranger!
The great gates are open,

We beg you to enter.
We are here to serve you,
The great city is yours!

Welcome, welcome stranger!
To you we surrender
The keys of desire,
The great city is yours!

DISTANT VOICES [*off*]
Drink the wine we offer,
Taste the joys untasted.
Drink long and gladly,
And forget the time you've wasted.

YOUNGER SON
What do these strange voices mean?

TEMPTER
You are tired from a long journey. They ask you to rest
and refresh yourself. Now you are free, now you are rich,
they ask you to enjoy yourself. Go and taste the wine
your new friends offer you. Enjoy yourself!

PARASITES [*offering wine*]
Come and try, come and taste,
Taste and drink, and drink again,
Float for ever on the flowing
Stream of glad forgetfulness.
[*The Younger Son and the Parasites fall in a drunken stupor*]

TEMPTER
Your pleasures must be paid for.
Pay what is due.
[*They remove the first part of his portion robe*]

DISTANT VOICES [*off*]
Nights of ecstasy,
Joys of fierce completeness,
Beauty offers
Pangs of piercing sweetness.

YOUNGER SON
What are these strange promises?

TEMPTER
Your senses have been freed by the pleasures of wine,
but you have not yet begun to learn what pleasure
means. Now you are offered the delights of the flesh,
what you have been praying for. My boy, indulge
yourself! Show yourself to be a man!
[*The Parasites advance, beckoning*]
[*The Younger Son is hidden from view*]

PARASITES
Nights are days, days are nights,
Come and taste dark delights.
Life is strong, and love is sweet.
You are young, and both are yours.
[*The Younger Son reappears, exhausted*]

TEMPTER
You have learned by experience that
Experience has its price.
[*They remove the second part of his portion robe*]

DISTANT VOICES [*off*]
Fingers handling coins of gold,
You will gamble, you will win.
Hearts beat quick, winnings blaze,
Dazzling gold like suns expanding.

YOUNGER SON
What is all this talk of gold and gambling?

TEMPTER
You have only a little gold left, so now is the time to
enjoy the games of chance. Suppose by throwing a dice
or playing a card you could recover your fortune, and
double it, what a triumphant end to your wonderful
time in this city of pleasure!
[*The Parasites advance, enticingly*]

PARASITES
Never mind your gold is short,
Come to us, be quickly taught
Bidding, betting, how to rake in
All the gold you'll ever need.
[*The Younger Son gambles with the dice*]
Cards and dice and heavy betting,
You will gamble, you will win.
Good luck is on your side.
Gold! Gold! rake it in.
[*The Younger Son loses the game*]

TEMPTER
You have gambled and lost,
Now you must pay.
[*They remove the last piece of robe*]
Now you have nothing.
You are nothing.
[*The Tempter turns away*]

YOUNGER SON
I have drunk and I have diced,
Gold pieces I gave with delight
To harlots with eyes
The darkness of night.

I have done what I wanted,
Acted out my desires,
I am now at the end
Of what I began.

Where are the friends that I drank with?
Why am I now all alone?
[*The Tempter comes forward*]

YOUNGER SON
You it was taught me, brought me
Out into the world.
To taste what it offered
I gave all I had.

You are my guide,
Now where do I go?

TEMPTER
Fool that you are,
You've had your good time.
Did you think it would last?
Now you must learn
After plenty comes poverty,
Now you must pay!

DISTANT VOICES [*off*]
Oh, woeful want!
We are starving, starving,
We are dying, dying,
Pity our need!

TEMPTER
Have you not heard
Of the country-wide famine?
Everyone now
Is out for himself,
Begging or stealing
A mouthful of food.
[*The Beggars slowly walk round the acting area and disappear at the back*]

BEGGARS
We are starving, starving.
For the love of God
Give us bread, pity our need!
We are dying, dying.

YOUNGER SON
What, must I join them?

TEMPTER
Yes, join them!

YOUNGER SON
Am I brought down to begging?

TEMPTER
Yes, begging!

YOUNGER SON
But how am I to live?

TEMPTER
Go and work as a swineherd,
Consort with the swine!

YOUNGER SON
What, be a swineherd?
Consort with the swine?

TEMPTER
You might get the leavings
Of whatever the swine eat.

YOUNGER SON
No, no!
[*He falls to the ground*]
[*The Tempter turns to the congregation*]

TEMPTER
Now—
I have done
What I said I would do.

I showed you a family,
A patriarch
With property and progeny in order.
So quiet, such harmony.

I have broken up that family
Before your eyes.

See how I broke it up!
[*Gracefully bowing, the Tempter leaves the stage*]

YOUNGER SON
With joy I sowed, my harvest is despair,
The end is bitterness, this is the end.
While I lie here and slowly starve,
My thoughts keep turning home.

While I have sinned, and wasted what I had,

I think of home and slowly starve to death,
While even my father's servants can eat,
The end is bitterness, this is the end.
[*He rises to his feet and starts his journey home*]
I will arise!
I will arise and go,
I will go to my father
And will say to him,
'Father, I have sinned against God
And against you.
I am no more worthy
To be called your son.
Father, let me be,
Oh let me only be
One of your servants,
Let me work for hire.'
[*The Younger Son journeys home*]
[*The Father appears in the distance and comes to meet him. They embrace*]

FATHER
My son.

YOUNGER SON [*kneeling*]
Father, I have sinned against God
And against you,
And am no more worthy
To be called your son.

Father, let me be
One of your servants.
Let me work for hire.
[*The Father raises the Younger Son, and holding him by the hand, calls to the Servants, who enter gradually*]

FATHER
Attend to me, all of you!
This is a great day,
See, the young master
Has returned to us all.
Bring him my best robe
For him to put on.
Put a ring on his hand
And shoes on his feet.

Go, you, give orders,
Kill the fatted calf,
Let us eat and be merry,
With singing and dancing.
For this son of mine was dead
And is alive again,
Was lost and is found.
[*The Servants dress the Younger Son in the Father's best robe*]

SERVANTS
Was dead and is alive again,
Was lost and is found.

FATHER
Now, take up your instruments and play
To welcome the young master,
To welcome my son.
[*The Servants begin to circulate, singing, round the Father and Younger Son; the Young Servants accompany the dance on their instruments*]

SERVANTS
O sing unto the Lord a new song,

For he hath done marvellous things.
Show yourselves glad unto the Lord, all ye lands,
Make a loud noise, sing and rejoice.
O show yourselves joyful before the Lord,
Sing unto the Lord God with the harp.
With trumpets also and the sound of shawms,
The harp, and the voice of a psalm.
Let the sea roar and the fullness thereof,
The round world and they that dwell therein.
Let the floods clap their hands, let the hills
Be joyful together before the Lord.

FATHER
O my son!

YOUNGER SON
My father!
How joyful this day

FATHER
Your returning to me.

FATHER AND YOUNGER SON [*together*]
The Younger Son is home again!
A ⎤
Your ⎦ wandering son
Now to wander no more.

No music so dear
As your voice reheard.
The Younger Son is home again!

FATHER, YOUNGER SON AND SERVANTS
O sing unto the Lord *etc.*
[*The Elder Son appears*]

ELDER SON
Stay! What does this mean?
Why are you rejoicing?

FATHER
My son, come and join us.
My friends, continue.
[*The dance continues*]

ELDER SON
Delay, while I learn
The cause of your joy.

FATHER
Come forward, I will tell you.
Your brother has come home to us,
Safe and sound.
[*The Elder Son comes forward*]

ELDER SON
The waster is back, wearing
My father's best robe?

FATHER
Because he has come home to us
I have ordered rejoicing.

ELDER SON
What, for this waster!

I have slaved for you
Like a dutiful son.
I have cared for your property.
Obeying your orders,
But you take me for granted.

You have ordered the killing
Of our fatted calf.
You never gave me
So much as a kid
To feast with my friends.

You lavish rewards
On this ne'er-do-well waster,
Who has spent all he had
On drinking and harlots.

FATHER
My son, you are ever beside me,
You are my right hand,
All that I have is yours.

ELDER SON
Father!

FATHER
You and I have shared troubles,
Let us all share this joy.
For thy brother was dead, and is alive again,
Was lost, and is found.
[*The Elder Son and the Younger Son are reconciled*]

FATHER, SONS AND SERVANTS
He was dead, and is alive again,
Was lost, and is found.
[*The disrobing ceremony begins. The Abbot (The Tempter) returns to the acting area*]

ABBOT
My children, you have seen
A worthy family.
The father,
A just and upright man,
His willing servants,
Both his sons,
The elder, stern and dutiful,
The younger
By evil led astray
(Have you not seen me,
Did I not tempt him
Craftily away?)
And prodigal come home.

MONKS
And prodigal come home.

ABBOT
O my children, understand,
More joy shall be in heaven
Over one repenting sinner
Than over ninety-nine
With nothing to repent.

Be not self-righteous, do not say
'Thank God I am not like
Another I could name.'
He that so exalts himself
Shall be cast down.

ABBOT AND MONKS
Remember the story of the Prodigal Son,
Remember his Father's forgiveness.

ABBOT
And may the Lord
Bless and keep you.

[*The Abbot leaves the acting area, and the Monks, Acolytes and Instrumentalists form a procession after him*]

ABBOT AND ALL VOICES
Jam lucis orto sidere,
Deum precemur supplices,
Ut in diurnis actibus,
Nos servet a nocentibus.

Linguam refraenans temperet,
Ne litis horror insonet:
Visum fovendo contegat,
Ne vanitates hauriat.

Sint pura cordis intima,
Absistat et vecordia:
Carnis terat superbiam
Potus cibique parcitas.

Ut cum dies abscesserit,
Noctemque sors reduxerit,
Mundi per abstinentiam
Ipsi canamus gloriam.
          Amen

Younger Son
Return

Prodigal Son

Annena Stubbs 68

102 The Prodigal Son, after his return

Annena Stubbs

103 The Tempter triumphs over the Prodigal Son's downfall

104 The Parasites welcome the Younger Son as he arrives at the city

OPPOSITE

105 The Elder and Younger Sons
Annena Stubbs

Two
Sons

106 and 107 First performance by the Vienna Boys' Choir

The Golden Vanity

A vaudeville for boys and piano
after the old English ballad

by Colin Graham

BENJAMIN BRITTEN OP. 78

CHARACTERS

The boys should be equally divided into two groups, representing the ship's company of *The Golden Vanity* and the pirates of the *Turkish Galilee*. In the first group the soloists are the Captain (alto), the Bosun (treble) and the Cabin-boy (treble), and in the second group the Pirate Captain (alto) and the Pirate Bosun (treble). The rest of the boys make up the crews of the two ships (trebles and altos).

The Vaudeville should be given in costume but without scenery. When the choruses move apart as the two ships, each group should stand or sit in a boat-like formation, thus fulfilling the functions of both ship and crew. A bench could be used as the core or bridge of each ship and the soloists could stand on these.

The action—swimming, cannon-firing, drowning etc.—should be mimed in a simple way and only a few basic properties, such as telescopes and a rope, are needed: each boat should carry a pennant, suitably designed, which can be hoisted at the right moment. A drum should be used for the sound of cannon fire.

Stage directions are only given where the action is not obvious from the text.

FIRST PERFORMANCE

3 June 1967   *The Maltings, Snape*
Vienna Boys' Choir

Foreword by Benjamin Britten

Vaudeville was originally the name given to the songs sung in the valleys (*vaux*) near *Vire* by Olivier Basselin in the 15th century, of a satirical nature and often about current events. In the 17th century this name was given to topical verses fitted to well-known ballad tunes, sung around the towns (a possible second derivation of the name is *voix de ville*). These often became inserted into dramatic pieces, particularly those given by strolling players. Later still *vaudevilles finals* were used to end plays—each character in turn singing a verse to the same tune. The name was also given to plays in verse and parodies of opera.

The Golden Vanity was written in answer to a request from the boys of the Wiener Sängerknaben themselves, to perform on their tours. They particularly asked that they should not have to play girls' parts.

The Golden Vanity

[*The boys march in*]

ALL VOICES
> There was a ship came from the North
>   Country,
> A gallant ship, yes, a gallant ship was she,
> Her name (I believe) was the Golden
>   Vanity
>   And she sailed upon the Lowland, Lowland,
>   She sailed upon the Lowland Sea.

[*The first group becomes the Golden Vanity*]
> So one fine day in summer (I am told)
> She sailed from port with a cargo in the hold
> A treasure of ducats—both silver and gold
>   To carry on the Lowland Sea.

[*The second group becomes the Turkish Galilee*]
> She'd not sailed a league, or a league only three,
> When up she came with a Turkish Galilee
> That had no business (I'm sure you will agree)
>   On the waters of the Lowland Sea!

[*The Skull and Crossbones is run up on the Turkish Galilee*]

THE CREW OF THE GOLDEN VANITY
> The Captain turned pale, and the Bosun was aghast
> When the Skull and Crossbones ran up the foreign
>   mast:

CAPTAIN [*on the lookout*]
> I'm sure we shall be taken,
> Taken by the foe!
> And think of all the treasure
> Lying here below!

PIRATE CAPTAIN
> Ha, ha, ha, ha!
> Ho, ho, ho, ho!
> They think they'll escape—
> No, never, no, no!

CAPTAIN
> Turn about, or we'll be taken,
> Taken you shall see!
> Oh, whoever heard of Turkeys
> Upon the Lowland Sea?

PIRATE CAPTAIN AND BOSUN
> Ha, ha, ha, ha!
> Ho, ho, ho, ho!
> We'll follow them close
> Wherever they go!

THE GOLDEN VANITY (ALL)
> Full sail and let us fly,
> Fly before the foe!
> Oh think of all the treasure
> Lying here below!

PIRATES (ALL)
> Ha, ha, ha, ha!
> Ho, ho, ho, ho!
> They think they'll escape—
> No, never, no, no!

CREW (G V)
> Then up spake the Bosun, up spake he:

BOSUN (G V)
> Never shall the Turkeys take the Golden Vanity!

CREW
Huzzah!

CAPTAIN (G V)
Brave fellow! What do you suggest?

BOSUN
To shoot 'em from the water with a broadside would
be best—
Let us quickly man the cannon and put them to
the test!

CREW
Huzzah! Huzzah! Huzzah!

CAPTAIN
Brave fellow!
We'll do as you suggest,
We'll put them to the test!
Gently now!

CREW
Huzzah! Huzzah!
[*The Golden Vanity turns broadside on to the Turkish Galilee*]

CAPTAIN
Mr Bosun, we'll try a shot!
[*The Captain is hoisted on to the shoulders of one of the crew*]

BOSUN
Stand by! Matches ready!

CAPTAIN, BOSUN AND CREW
Fire!
[*The cannon fires*]

THE GOLDEN VANITY (ALL)
But alas! the brave attempt sadly came to
naught:
For the range was too great and the shots they fell
too short,
And while they were re-loading the Pirates swang
to port!
[*The Turkish Galilee, unharmed, swings broadside on to the
Golden Vanity*]

PIRATE CAPTAIN
Belay there! Let's give 'em a shot!
[*The Pirate Captain is hoisted on to the shoulders of one of the
crew*]

PIRATE BOSUN
Stand ready! We'll show 'em how!

PIRATE CAPTAIN, BOSUN AND CREW
Fire!
[*The Pirate cannon roars*]

PIRATE CREW
Huzzah!
[*The Golden Vanity's Captain falls backwards and is caught by
the Bosun*]

ALL VOICES
And with their superior Turkish Strategy
They shot away the mast of the Golden Vanity!
There was weeping, wailing, so dreadful for to see
As she floundered on the Lowland Sea!

CAPTAIN (G V)
I know we shall be taken,
Taken with the gold;
And into Turkish slavery

We shall all be sold.

CREW
All of us be sold,
Into Turkish slavery
We shall all be sold.
[*The Cabin-Boy comes forward shyly*]

CREW
Then up spake the Cabin-boy, up spake he:

CABIN-BOY
Sir . . . Your Honour . . . Magnificence . . . Your
Worship . . . My Lord . . .
What will you give me if I sink the Turkish
Galilee?

CREW
What will we give you if you sink the Turkish
Galilee?
And the officers and men, they chortled in their
glee.

CAPTAIN
Be silent!
Very well . . .let's hear what *you* suggest, herrumph—
now—What's-yer-name?

CABIN-BOY
What will you give me if I sink the Turkish Galilee?

CAPTAIN [*taken aback*]
What will I give you?

CABIN-BOY
Yes, what will you give me?

CAPTAIN
What will I give *you*?

CABIN-BOY
Yes, *what* will you give *me*?

CAPTAIN
I see—well—let me think now—
I will give you silver, I will give you gold,
Enough and more to keep you till you grow old.

CABIN-BOY
With nothing to warm me but silver and gold,
What joy shall I find me in growing me old?

CAPTAIN
I will give you too what's worth a good deal more:
My pretty little daughter that lives upon the shore.

CABIN-BOY
For love of your daughter that lives upon the shore,
I'll venture this and love her evermore.

CAPTAIN
You'll venture this and love her evermore.

CAPTAIN AND CABIN-BOY
You'll
I'll   think of a way to defeat the enemy
And sink him in the Lowland Sea.

CREW
But the Bosun turned away and heaved a bitter sigh,
For on the Captain's daughter he had set his eye!
[*The Bosun turns away as the Captain and Cabin-boy shake
hands. The Cabin-boy strips, shivers a little, and dives into the
water*]

THE GOLDEN VANITY
(ALL BUT THE CABIN-BOY)
Casting his clothes off he dived into the sea,
And swam like a fish so gallantly did he—
He swam till he came to the Turkish Galilee
As she lay in the Lowland Sea.

PIRATES
The Vanity lay at anchor like a fish upon a line;
The Pirates laughing merrily then settled down to dine.

THE GOLDEN VANITY
Meanwhile unseen the boy arrived, surfaced for a
moment, then dived again below the Pirate brig,
and with a little spike three holes began to dig.

PIRATES
The Pirates, filling up with rum, did little know the hold
was filling up with water down below.

THE GOLDEN VANITY
He came up for air, then once more took his chance,

PIRATES
While overhead the Turkeys sang their song and then
began to dance.
[*The Pirates dance on their ship*]

PIRATES
Ripe for plucking like a plum upon a tree
Is the treasure on the Golden Vanity!

Ho, ha, hum!
And a one, and two, and three!
Ho, ha, hum! . . . etc.

THE GOLDEN VANITY
Some played cards and others played dice,
while the Cabin-boy pierced the vessel thrice—
and the water flowed in and dazzled in their eyes!

ALL VOICES
Confusion struck into the foreign horde,
They climbed into the rigging and there with terror
roared—
And all for the boy and the little holes he'd bored—
And they sank beneath the Lowland, Lowland . . .
[*The Crew of the Golden Vanity laughs, and the Pirates scream
as the Turkish Galilee sinks beneath the billowing main: the
Pirates thereafter become waves surrounding the Golden Vanity*]

PIRATES
Gurgle, gurgle, gurgle—
Must we all drown?
The waters gurgle up
And the Turkeys gurgle down.
Gurgle, gurgle, gurgle—

THE GOLDEN VANITY
The Pirate ship no longer did annoy
The Golden Vanity who laughed and cried for joy—
And in their mirth they forgot the Cabin-boy
Adrift in the Lowland Sea.

CABIN-BOY
Oh, Bosun, Oh, Captain, take me up on board,
And give me my fee as good as your word!
Throw a rope! for I've sunk the Galilee,
As she sailed upon the Lowland Sea.

CAPTAIN
I won't take you up—there is no reward—

BOSUN
His daughter for a cabin-boy? No, that he can't afford!

CAPTAIN AND BOSUN
We'll not throw a rope nor take you up on board,
Nor prove to you as good as our word!
[*Apart*]
To protect our gold no promise was too great,
But now our gold is safe, our promise we forget!

CREW
His strength began to falter and most bitterly he cried—
And he leant upon his breast and swam round the side—

CABIN-BOY
I am drifting, I am failing, oh, pull me up the side!
Oh, messmates, take me up for I'm sinking with the tide,
Sinking in the Lowland Sea!

CREW
He slipped beneath a wave but he bore him up with
hope;
And he bore him up with courage, till no longer could he
float.
And then, but only then, did the crew throw out a
rope.
[*The Crew of the Golden Vanity hauls the Cabin-boy on board*]

CREW
They laid him on the deck, but on the deck he died.

His messmates brushed away a tear and heavily they
sighed.
He'd saved them and was murdered for the Captain
and his gold!
As cold and cruel as the Lowland Sea!

CAPTAIN AND BOSUN [*coming forward*]
We both turned away but found we couldn't weep,
Ashamed of the promises we never did keep—
For the thought of the Cabin-boy no more shall we sleep,
While we sail on the Lowland Sea.
[*The Crew of the Golden Vanity comes forward carrying the dead
Cabin-boy*]

CREW
They gently took him up from the deck where he died.
They wrapped him in his hammock that was so large
and wide.
They sent him overboard to go with wind and tide,
And then to sink in the Lowland Sea.
[*The rest come forward*]

ALL VOICES (EXCEPT CABIN-BOY)
Now should you pass today o'er the spot where he died,
You still can hear the Cabin-boy as on the day he cried:
Oh, messmates take me up for I'm sinking with the tide!

CABIN-BOY [*unseen*]
Sinking in the Lowland Sea!

ALL VOICES
As you sail upon the Lowland Sea!

ALL (WITH CABIN-BOY)
I'm sinking in the Lowland Sea!

[*The boys march out*]

Owen Wingrave

An opera in two acts

by Myfanwy Piper
based on a short story by Henry James

BENJAMIN BRITTEN OP. 85

Owen Wingrave *the last of the Wingraves* BARITONE

Spencer Coyle *who runs a military cramming establishment* BASS-BARITONE

Lechmere *a young student with Owen at Coyle's establishment* TENOR

Miss Wingrave *Owen's aunt* DRAMATIC SOPRANO

Mrs Coyle SOPRANO

Mrs Julian *a widow and dependant at Paramore* SOPRANO

Kate *her daughter* MEZZO-SOPRANO

General Sir Philip Wingrave *Owen's grandfather* TENOR

Narrator *the ballad singer* TENOR

Distant Chorus TREBLES

The scene takes place in London, at the Coyles' military cramming establishment in Bayswater; at Miss Wingrave's lodgings in Baker Street, and in Hyde Park; in the country at Paramore, the Wingrave family seat. The time is the late nineteenth century.

FIRST PERFORMANCE

Commissioned for television by the British Broadcasting Corporation and first transmitted by them 16 May 1971. First stage performance 10 May 1973, London, Covent Garden

Owen Wingrave	Benjamin Luxon
Spencer Coyle	John Shirley-Quirk
Lechmere	Nigel Douglas
Miss Wingrave	Sylvia Fisher
Mrs Coyle	Heather Harper
Mrs Julian	Jennifer Vyvyan (BBC)
	Janice Chapman (Covent Garden)
Kate Julian	Janet Baker
General Sir Phillip Wingrave	Peter Pears
Colonel Wingrave, and Ghost (BBC)	Peter Pears
Young Wingrave, and Ghost (BBC)	Stephen Hattersley
Young Wingrave's Friend (BBC)	Geoffrey West
Narrator	Peter Pears

The Wandsworth School Boys' Choir, directed by Russell Burgess

Conducted by Benjamin Britten (BBC)
    Steuart Bedford (Covent Garden)

Directed by Brian Large and Colin Graham (BBC)

Produced by Colin Graham (Covent Garden)

Scenery designed by Tony Meyerscough-Jones (BBC)
    John Piper, assisted by Edward Piper (Covent Garden)

Costumes designed by Charles Knode

Act one

Prelude: The family portraits at Paramore. Ten are seen, of which the fifth is a double portrait.

Scene one

[*Like an eleventh portrait, Owen appears. He is then seen to be with Lechmere in the study at Coyle's cramming establishment. There are military maps, engravings and weapons on the walls, and a globe*]

COYLE
You've got your maps there?
You've marked the dispositions of both armies?
A supreme example of how to lose a battle
by lack of imagination and false conclusions,
in fact the allied army fell into the trap.
After an easy victory here,
[*pointing to map*]

LECHMERE
Where's that, sir?

COYLE
here—Telnitz, Napoleon's right.

LECHMERE
I see, sir.

COYLE
They crossed the Goldbach river,
their troops massed in the defiles
between the two frozen lakes and the stream,
General Van Damme fell on them from above.
Result: disorder, panic, defeat.

LECHMERE
And the losses, sir?

COYLE
Napoleon eight thousand,
the Allies fourteen thousand killed, wounded or
    drowned
and eighteen thousand taken prisoner.
As you can imagine, Napoleon was radiant.
Thank you, gentlemen. That will be all for this morning.
[*Lechmere bangs his books shut and stands up*]

LECHMERE
'The Minstrel Boy to the war is gone
In the ranks of death you'll find him—'

OWEN
The Wingraves all went too . . .
And didn't they love it!

LECHMERE
And so they should, it's a glorious life.
[*He takes a weapon off the wall and brandishes it*]
Ah! you beauty, how many vile heads, vile foreign heads
have you rolled into the dust?
Chop, chop, chop!

COYLE
Put it down, you silly boy, or you'll break something.

OWEN
Violence, violence,
how you all rejoice in violence!

LECHMERE
What is the enemy for but to be routed and killed?

OWEN
You forget, you are the enemy too.

LECHMERE
Too bad. That's the luck, the glorious luck of battle.
Selfless, reckless, you charge into the enemy's ranks.
Death or Victory ahead, no matter which,
I feel it, long for it.
How long, sir, how long before we're in the thick of it?

COYLE
Four years, if you pass in.

LECHMERE
We will, we will—Owen will at any rate.
Four years, Lord, what a time!

COYLE
The conduct of war is a science,
the commanding of men is an art.
These things must be learnt by those who would lead.
No general can win without this knowledge,
no officer perform his duty.

OWEN
Duty! Ruffians all:
Hannibal, Caesar, Marlborough,
Napoleon—I'd hang the lot.

COYLE
And Wellington?

OWEN
Wellington, for all his warlike glory,
remember what he said: 'Next to a battle lost the
    greatest misery
is a battle gained.'

LECHMERE
It didn't stop him winning, all the same.
But cheer up! I'm off to grind.
Hurrah for glory, 'La Gloire c'est tout.'
[*Exit Lechmere*]

OWEN
Is it? Is glory everything?

COYLE
You're in a strange mood, Owen. Too much work?
You, at least, have no fear of failure.

OWEN [*calmly*]
Sir—I can't go through with it.

COYLE
What's that?

OWEN
I can't go through with it.

COYLE
You can't—

OWEN
Be a soldier I mean.

COYLE
You must be off your head.

OWEN
My head's all right. I don't like war.

COYLE
Impossible. You're not serious!

OWEN
I am. I'm sorry. I know you're angry.
The fear of this kept me from speaking sooner.

COYLE
You should have spoken sooner.
You should have spoken months ago.

OWEN
I had to be certain, know for certain—
that is what took the time.

COYLE
Impossible! What do you suppose your family will say,
your family at Paramore?

OWEN
They'll be angry, furious; I'm ready for it.
I mind your disapproval more.
I'll do anything for you—but not that,
not be a soldier.

COYLE
But, dear boy, that is why you're here,
to learn to be a soldier.

OWEN
I know, it's a waste.
But you'll get over it . . .in the end.

COYLE
You'll get over it rather faster I suppose.

OWEN
I know I'm right, I've thought so long.

COYLE
You know, at your age, better than us all,
better than your soldiering forbears,
better than your sacrificing family,
better than your father,
better than your country's leaders!

OWEN
I know their fighting and their sacrifice.
I will have none of it,
I despise a soldier's life.

COYLE [*angry*]
Despise! Come, think before you speak.
Say what right have you to despise,
to despise far better men than you,
men who fought to make your country what it is?

OWEN
I shall not change.

COYLE
You must change.

OWEN
No.

COYLE
Have you broached this folly to your aunt?

OWEN
I thought I'd tell you first.

COYLE
Someone must see her, someone must talk to her.

OWEN
You go—she's in London now.

COYLE
Very well, I'll go.
As for you, clear your mind of all this nonsense.
Take a walk, you're over-wrought.
Mind you, I don't accept it,
no, not for a moment.

OWEN
Oh you will, you know.

[*Exit Owen*]

COYLE
Oh! I thought I knew them all, the foibles of the young.

Straight out of school they come to me, full of
      themselves,
impatient of advice, careless, hot-headed and rash—
      mere boys.
My task is to instil a needed discipline,
a core of ordered facts to set reality
beside their gallant dreams,
and yet not cool the heroes' blood
that makes me choose to teach them.

But Owen, the most gifted, heroic, of them all,
is moved by some new ferment, unknown to me.
Owen, whom I delight in, in whom I believe,
surely he must retract—though I fear his mood.

How shall I tell Miss Wingrave?
What will they all say at Paramore?
Soldiering's their life, and their religion,
Owen their hope, heir to the Wingrave flag of glory.

[*Exit Coyle*]

[*Interlude: regimental banners wave brilliantly*]

Scene two

[*In this scene Owen is in Hyde Park, sitting with Shelley's poems
in his hand; and Miss Wingrave is with Coyle in her London
lodgings*]

OWEN [*in the Park*]
At last it's out.
No doubt but old Coyle will rage,
      but in the end
he'll see I'm strong, not mad
      or weak—
strong against war, unwilling
      to prepare
my mind and body for destruction.
One little word: no! no! no! no!
And I am released for ever
from all the bonds of family and
      war.

MISS WINGRAVE [*in her lodgings*]
He won't go in for it?
It's in his blood.

COYLE
He denies his blood.

MISS WINGRAVE
    Wingraves are soldiers,
    they go when they are called.

COYLE
    He will not go.

MISS WINGRAVE
    Protectors of their Country's right,
    protectors of God's given truth,
    always and everywhere.

COYLE
    He will not, ever.

MISS WINGRAVE
    Owen, the last of the Wingraves,
    Owen will follow,
    he may not choose.

COYLE
    He *does* choose, misguided boy,
    with all the force of his intelligence.

MISS WINGRAVE
    We're all intelligent,
    we're an intelligent family,
    we understand our duty
    and rejoice in it.

OWEN
    I'm not afraid.
    Courage in war is false,
    courage in peace,
    the kind the poets know,
    wins everything.
    [*Horse Guards gallop by; Owen and Miss Wingrave have a common image of military glory*]

OWEN
    Ah! Ah, that rippling, sweet,
        obedient well-being.

MISS WINGRAVE
    Ah! Glorious, glorious, the glory
        and pride of England.

COYLE
    Ah! Yes, he would have made a
        brilliant soldier.

OWEN
    So easy to conform to,
    so easy to accept.

MISS WINGRAVE
    Would have? *Will.* This fancy must
        be stopped.
    [*Owen imagines a scene of military carnage*]

OWEN
    See them fall!
    Strike and be struck!
    And all for what? Glory?
    An illusion.

COYLE
    It is no fancy. He is not a child.
    He despises the profession,
    thinks it is beneath him.

MISS WINGRAVE
    Despise! Beneath!

Send him to us—
    he shall be straightened out at Paramore.

OWEN [*picking up his book*]
    No, it is false,
    false plumes and pride,
    obedience that ends in destruction
    and murder.
    [*Interlude: old tattered flags as a background to Owen reading from Shelley: 'Queen Mab'*]

OWEN
    'War is the statesman's game, the priest's delight,
    The lawyer's jest . . .

    And to those royal murderers, whose mean thrones
    Are bought by crimes of treachery and gore . . .

    Guards, garbed in blood-red livery surround
    Their palaces, participate the crimes
    That force defends . . .

    These are the hired bravos who defend
    The tyrant's throne—the bullies of his fear . . .

    The refuse of society, the dregs
    Of all that is most vile . . .

    They cajole with gold,
    And promises of fame, the thoughtless youth
    Already crushed with servitude—he knows
    His wretchedness too late . . .

    Look to thyself, priest, conqueror or prince!
    Whether thy trade is falsehood . . .'

Scene three

[*A room at Coyle's establishment. Coyle, Mrs Coyle and Lechmere are met before dinner: they are expecting Owen. Lechmere is handing round sherry*]

LECHMERE
    Your sherry, Mrs Coyle.

MRS COYLE
    Thank you, my boy.
    No, I don't believe it,
    it makes no sense to me.
    Next you'll be saying
    Lechmere gives up too.
    [*Coyle indicates that Lechmere should help himself*]

LECHMERE
    Oh thank you sir. No ma'am!
    I wouldn't throw my hand in,
    not for a million pounds.

COYLE
    His heart and hopes are simple,
    he'll never suffer doubts.
    [*Lechmere offers the sherry again*]

MRS COYLE
    No more sherry my dear.

COYLE [*to Mrs Coyle*]
    But your favourite Owen,

it seems has questioned all,
throws up his whole career.

MRS COYLE [*to herself*]
Is he my favourite? Owen my favourite?
So many boys come here
and I rejoice in all.
After the long day with their books they come to me
and charm me with their new-found grown-up ways.
They are all sons to me.
Had I a son I could not bear to think of his bright life
banished to some dreadful battle-field.
And yet, our son, like them, would have to serve
whatever way seemed right.

But Owen, I'll admit
he has a special place,
we cannot let him miss
his whole life for a whim.

LECHMERE [*sips his sherry excitedly*]
I'll tell you what, he shan't—
I—we—why, we won't let him—
shan't have such strange ideas.

COYLE
He must not have ideas.
It is his duty to be a soldier
and as a soldier to obey.

LECHMERE
Right you are, sir.
I'll go for him and tell him,
tell him it's a shame.

MRS COYLE
Shame and Owen—no!

COYLE
More than shame, disgrace!

MRS COYLE
Disgrace and Owen—no!

LECHMERE
Owen must command, have a great career.

MRS COYLE
Have a great career.

COYLE
No! but press the point,
as a comrade plead with him.

MRS COYLE
You should be proud to do it,

LECHMERE
He is so true, so bold.

COYLE
People won't think so now.

LECHMERE
No-one will think so now.

MRS COYLE
You'll talk him round, I'm sure.

LECHMERE
Oh sir, I'll tackle him
I'll bring him round.

COYLE
You'll bring him round, I'm sure.

MRS COYLE
We'll bring him round.
[*During this ensemble Owen has come in quietly and listened to the conversation*]

OWEN
You'll never bring me round, my mind's made up.

COYLE
Your reflection, then, has brought no change?

OWEN
It has made me more determined.
I have not changed.

COYLE
Neither, my boy, have I.

OWEN [*to Mrs Coyle*]
I know, but *you're* not angry with me, are you?

MRS COYLE
I don't know what to think,
it seems so strange.

OWEN
Please think that I am serious.

COYLE [*aside*]
And a fighter too.

Come, Lechmere, to your duty.
[*Lechmere fills the glasses*]

COYLE [*serious*]
I drink to your future, Owen, wherever that may lie.

LECHMERE
Hurrah!

MRS COYLE
I drink to our faith, Owen, our faith in you.

LECHMERE [*over-excited*]
Hurrah, Owen. Here's to the future we planned.
My friend, my comrade, Hurrah!

COYLE
Lechmere!

OWEN
To you all, my friends,
here's to the fight, my fight!

LECHMERE [*aside*]
Hurrah!
[*All drink. The Coyles go to the door: Owen follows*]

OWEN
Mr Coyle, sir, did you see her?
Did you see my aunt?

COYLE
You are to go home to the country at once.
They'll straighten you out, she says, at Paramore.
[*Coyle and Mrs Coyle go out*]

LECHMERE
Owen, you can't mean it—
it's mad, it's your whole life.

OWEN
It's my whole life, that's why I mean it.

LECHMERE
But—your family—they'll never stand for it—

a Wingrave who is not a soldier.

OWEN
They will learn.

LECHMERE
What will you do, Owen?
I can't imagine Paramore a farmer's place.

OWEN
Oh, I dread it, I dread going there.

LECHMERE
Are they so very terrible?

OWEN
Grandfather looks quiet enough,
a formal, stiff old man.
Bue he has a smouldering eye,
red-rimmed with the glint of far-off battles;
he knows no other life than war.
His son, my father, died, a sabre cut
dashed him from hope and love and life.
My mother died bereft, bearing my dead-born brother.
Kate's father, and her uncle too (Aunt Wingrave's
    lover),
slaughtered while the empty banners flew.
And in those deaths, and countless other deaths,
the Wingraves see their sacrifice,
their glory and their good.

LECHMERE
And for those deaths there must be some revenge; how
    well I understand their need to fight, and you must too!

OWEN
I'll none of it! I'll break it!
I'll fight it to the end.
                                        [*They go out*]

[*Interlude: Paramore*]

Scene four

[*Paramore. Mrs Julian, Kate and Miss Wingrave are waiting
for Owen's arrival*]

MRS JULIAN
Oh, how unforeseen, how unforeseen.
Oh, how we are dogged, dogged by misfortune.
Goodness knows I have struggled, struggled to educate
    my child on charity.
But we Julians are far too proud to tolerate a shirker.
The poor Wingraves, the poor, poor Wingraves.
What is their pride to them now?
The very house seems to groan.
Surely when he comes he will listen to the house.

KATE
How strange to abandon the dreams of our childhood:
he has been too long away and he reckons without me.
I'll not allow him his treacherous thoughts,
he shall not carry out so infamous a plan.
He'll change his mind when he gets here,
into the house of his ancestors.
It is too strong, asks for too much,
stands for too much from all of us.
Once here he will listen to the house.

MRS JULIAN
Surely he will listen to the house.

MISS WINGRAVE
Wingraves are soldiers,
they go when they are called;
protectors of their country's rights,
protectors of God's given truth,
always and everywhere.
Owen, the youngest and last, Owen will follow them.
They asked no questions, nor did we,
but sent them willing to their fate.
Thus will it be with Owen,
he will listen to the house.
He cannot choose but listen to the house.

MRS JULIAN
Surely he will listen to the house.

KATE
Once here he will listen to the house.
[*The ladies come together. They see Owen from the window*]

KATE
There he is!
He's just walked through the lodge gates.

MRS JULIAN
Why, he looks almost jaunty—how dare he?

MISS WINGRAVE
We'll not be there, ladies, until he's well inside.

KATE, MRS JULIAN AND MISS WINGRAVE
There'll be no hero's welcome,
let him speak first to his ancestors.
[*They go off. Owen is seen arriving at the house, relaxed, quite
cheerful*]

OWEN [*outside*]
And now, to face them, all of them,
the living and the dead.
[*He comes into the empty hall*]

OWEN [*calling*]
Hullo!
No-one to greet me? Not even Kate? No-one here?
All silent? Silence, yes.
Good soldiers in a mist, we're told, keep silence—
no friendly murmurs, no scream of pain
betray their position to the enemy.
The enemy! How strange!
Here in my own house I stand an enemy.
I say, where is everyone?
[*Enter Mrs Julian*]

OWEN
There you are, Juli—where are the others?
Where's Kate? Is anything wrong?

MRS JULIAN
Wrong? Wrong? You know what's wrong—
Sir Philip not well, not well at all.
And, oh your aunt—
I've never known her quite so put about.

OWEN
And Kate?

MRS JULIAN
Poor Kate! Owen, how could you go against everything,
upset everything, be so selfish?

OWEN
Come, Juli, *you* aren't cross?

MRS JULIAN
No, don't coax me,
I'm most upset.
What's good enough for all your family
is surely good enough for you.

OWEN
And if I say not good enough?
[*Kate comes downstairs and answers him herself*]

KATE
I'd say that you weren't good enough.

OWEN
Kate! I missed my welcome, Kate.

KATE
You come to betray us—
you ask for a welcome!

OWEN
Oh Kate, don't say that you're shocked too.

KATE
I'm not shocked, nor is Miss Wingrave shocked.
As for the **General**,
would he treat a pinprick as a gaping wound?

OWEN
And I'm not shocked by girlish talk.
I'll make you understand, Kate.
We'll have this out,
you shan't dismiss my plans, my new ideals.

KATE
We're not shocked by childish talk.
As I see it, there is nothing to understand.
I have my loyalties and I stick to them.
What new ideals can we need at Paramore?
We need no teaching from a boy,
a silly, thoughtless boy.
[*Kate flounces out*]

OWEN
Oh Kate, Kate, you too?
[*talking to the family portraits*]
Is there not one of you to help me—you? you?
You are all silent too,
but your eyes, your nostrils speak.
Turn your eyes away from me.
I refuse your censure,
I refuse your demands.
I am a boy, but resolute.
Father! Father! *You* must understand.
I am as resolute as you at Kandahar.
[*Miss Wingrave has appeared at the top of the stairs*]

MISS WINGRAVE
I heard you speaking to your Father.
He laid down his life for Queen and country,
something it seems
you do not care to do.

OWEN
I . . .

MISS WINGRAVE
I will not parley with you now,
the General awaits you in his room.
[*She opens a door into the study and Sir Philip appears, glaring at Owen*]

SIR PHILIP
Sirrah! How dare you!

[*Blackout*]

Scene five

[*An abstract scene: a week passes during which Owen is under constant attack from his relations and friends*]

SIR PHILIP, KATE, MISS WINGRAVE AND MRS JULIAN
How dare you!

SIR PHILIP
It is an ill-considered jape.
You won't admit that you are wrong?

MISS WINGRAVE
It is idle talk,
ill-afforded money thrown away.

MRS JULIAN
Shirkers are not tolerated here.
What can you be thinking of?

KATE
You must be mad, I cannot understand you.
Who have you been talking to?

SIR PHILIP
Insulting the family,
dragging our name in the dirt—
disgusting!

MISS WINGRAVE
Public dishonour to Wingraves,
our noble name scorned—
obscene!

KATE
Scion of fighting men,
fighters for England's glory.

MRS JULIAN
What would your father say
and your poor mother
who's better dead!

MISS WINGRAVE
Heroes since Domesday,
heroes of Agincourt,
of Crécy!

SIR PHILIP
Heroes of the Mutiny,
Lucknow, Cawnpore!

KATE
Heroes of Sebastopol, of Waterloo—
wherever our flag flies.

MRS JULIAN
Heroes in every quarter of the globe.

SIR PHILIP, KATE, MISS WINGRAVE AND MRS JULIAN·
Dare you reject them?

SIR PHILIP
Ha! They'll never stand for it.
You say you'll not fight, ha!
Insulting the family,

insulting the flag,
insulting your Queen and country!

KATE
You cannot reject them,
oh, you are no gentleman!
What will your ancestors say?
What will tradition say?
What will the past say?

MRS JULIAN
But now you are insulting her,
a soldier's daughter.
An insult to a soldier's widow—an insult!

MISS WINGRAVE
They'll turn in their graves, I say.
They'll have their revenge, see!

KATE
I used to love, admire you.
How can you betray our ambitions?

MRS JULIAN
You used to be such a brave little boy,
so like your gallant father.

MISS WINGRAVE
How disappointing after all your young promise!

SIR PHILIP [weeping]
Ah!

SIR PHILIP
I'll court-martial you,
turn you out for less—
you hypocrite, traitor, you dog!

MISS WINGRAVE
We'll not have shirkers here.
Serpent in our midst—
unworthy, unworthy.
You're a scoundrel.

KATE
Oh, go away from here.
I can't bear you,
you poor creature!

MRS JULIAN
How can you be so selfish?
You're not worthy of Paramore,
not worthy to be here!

SIR PHILIP, KATE, MISS WINGRAVE AND MRS JULIAN
How dare you!
[Blackout]

Scene six

[Coyle and Mrs Coyle, just arrived at Paramore, come
downstairs to the hall]

MRS COYLE
Coyle! I wish I had not come.
It's horrible.

COYLE
Uneasy, that I grant you.

MRS COYLE
Uneasy! Gruesome rather.

That poor boy, surrounded with these ghouls,
the living and the dead,
and all against him.
What a week he must have had.

COYLE
They're ranked, I must say.

MRS COYLE
And this house,
it's haunted, I'm sure.

COYLE
That goes without saying.

MRS COYLE
You mean there *is* a ghost?

COYLE
If I'd said, you wouldn't have come.

MRS COYLE
That I shouldn't . . .but a ghost?

COYLE
There's a story:
old Colonel Wingrave and the boy.
[looking at the double portrait]
That's the one!

MRS COYLE
And that strange girl,
oh, what a very important personage!
So rude, so high and mighty, so possessive.

COYLE
And handsome too!

MRS COYLE
Pshaw!

COYLE
He's putting up a fight, it seems,
just as I thought he would.
Not one of them can credit him with thought
or real conviction.

MRS COYLE
Coming from you my dear,
that does sound strange.

COYLE
I own to a deep interest in the boy.
What he thinks right I may deplore,
but cannot conscientiously dismiss.
[Enter Owen, followed by Lechmere]

MRS COYLE
Ah! Owen!

COYLE
Owen!

OWEN
How good of you to come to this sad house.
And Lechmere too,
quite like the gay old times.

MRS COYLE
You don't look very gay, my dear.

LECHMERE
But Owen has such sad ideas.

OWEN
Sad they may be, but I believe them.

COYLE
You've thought yourself into this trouble.

OWEN
But you trained me to use my mind.

COYLE
To make you understand what war means,
what war is.

OWEN
Too well you made me understand.

MRS COYLE AND LECHMERE
Too well you made him understand.

COYLE
War stems from mankind's triple nature;
his elemental passion,
the ranging freedom of his soul,
his power of reason.

OWEN
A fearful trinity of hatred,
and the play of chance and politics.
I know the noble theories and I hate them.

MRS COYLE
I hate the thought,
so fine, so handsome,
such a rare young man,
should have to be a soldier.

LECHMERE
I hate the thought,
my friend, and comrade,
cleverer far than I
will never be a soldier.

COYLE
I hate the thought,
these months of teaching
so promising a lad,
should not produce a soldier.
[*Coyle puts his arm through Owen's, leads him aside. Mrs Coyle and Lechmere go off*]

COYLE
Was it bad?

OWEN
It was awful, far worse than I thought possible.

COYLE
I feared as much.
[*Coyle notices Miss Wingrave in the gallery. He withdraws his arm*]

COYLE
But I've not come down to give you sympathy,
I've come, since they asked me,
to make one last appeal.

OWEN
Oh sir, do you think I'm one to surrender?
I'm in a state of siege;
bombarded with horrible words,
blockaded by the past,
starved by lack of love.

COYLE
Oh my dear boy, the pity is you are a fighter.

OWEN
Ugh! We're tainted all.
[*looking round at the portraits*]
I've roused up all the old ghosts.
The very portraits seem to glower.
They won't let me alone, none of them.
The servants, my old friends, know I'm in disgrace.
[*Interlude: the preparation for dinner. Servants lay the table and light the candles*]

Scene seven

[*The family comes formally to the dinner-table: Sir Philip brings Mrs Coyle–Coyle, Miss Wingrave–Lechmere, Kate–Owen, Mrs Julian. They pause behind their chairs*]

SIR PHILIP
May God bless the Queen,
and this house.
[*They all sit down*]

MRS COYLE
How noble this room looks by candlelight, Sir Philip.

SIR PHILIP
Noble? There were some noble fellows here long ago.

KATE
How good to see you well enough to dine, Sir Philip.

MISS WINGRAVE
He was not ill,
he didn't choose to come.
He did not like the company.

KATE
Am I not good enough?

SIR PHILIP
Oh, Kate, Kate, you keep me young.

LECHMERE
Oh sir, she would–Miss Julian keep anyone young.

KATE
Heavens, I wouldn't want to keep *you* quite so young.

COYLE
No compliments for you from Kate, Lechmere!

OWEN
Only grandfather gets compliments from Kate.

KATE
You'll get none from me, that's certain.

MRS COYLE
I see Miss Julian keeps you all in order!
[*Uncomfortable pause as the dishes are cleared away. The characters betray their thoughts*]

MRS COYLE
Oh, how uneasy this is–
we can do no good here–
what can Coyle do?

KATE
Does he think I shall plead with him–
he is mistaken!

Child
identical

1850.

108 Preliminary costume notes

Charles Knode

109 Model for the first stage production   *John Piper*

110 Old Man and Boys of the ballad   *Charles Knode*   111 Mr Coyle   *Charles Knode*

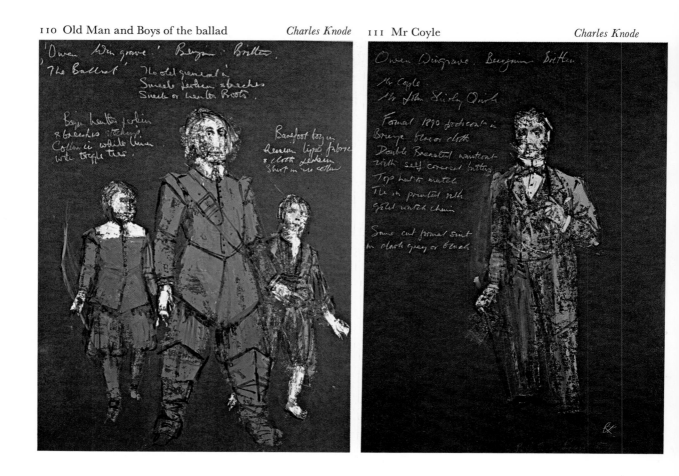

112 Kate, dinner dress   *Charles Knode*   113 Sir Phillip, first costume   *Charles Knode*

114 Mrs Coyle, night attire   *Charles Knode*   115 Kate, night attire   *Charles Knode*

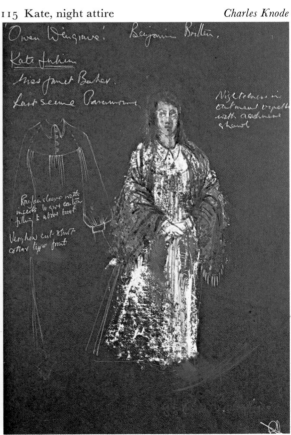

116 Preliminary costume notes

Charles Knode

117 Rough sketches for Kate's costumes

Charles Knode

LECHMERE
If anyone can bring him round she will—
I could not bear her disapproval.

MISS WINGRAVE
Can he be my brother's son?
I begin to doubt it.

MRS JULIAN
Ah, what will come of it all?
Can nothing be done?

SIR PHILIP
We breed soldiers, centuries of them.
He must do what we all have done—obey!

OWEN
Obey! Believe! Accept!
That is all I need to do,
but the orders are wrong.

COYLE
All my life I have taught the art of war,
but for war in the family
there's no answer in the books.

COYLE [breaking the spell, to Sir Philip]
I've never understood, sir,
our troops' disposition, Bhurtpore, '23

SIR PHILIP
Aha! I was there—
I've all the battle array in my head.
I well remember the joy of riding to battle.

MRS COYLE
Coyle will ride his hobby-horse:
strategy, Sir Philip, is his life.

OWEN
He makes it come to life like no-one else.

COYLE
Ah, you've a grasp of it.
To teach him, Sir Philip, Madam,
to teach young Owen here has been a luxury.

MISS WINGRAVE
Soldiering's no luxury to us.
His time with you is a necessity.
Mr Coyle, do not flatter him,
he must be made to see his fault.

SIR PHILIP
Aha! The years have seen the fighting Wingraves
time out of mind.
Halberds, pistols, daggers are their company.
Lances, sword-thrusts, parted them from life,
all fighting men, so long ago.
May their souls fight on—
for right and England.
[He chokes at the remembrance of the present situation]
But he—my—can I call him anything of mine?—
chooses to back out,
to reject the life,
our life, his life,
the life we owe to England.

MRS COYLE [gently]
Ah! Sir Philip, Owen has his scruples.

SIR PHILIP, MISS WINGRAVE, MRS JULIAN AND KATE
Scruples! Scruples! Scruples!

SIR PHILIP
Say what right has he to have scruples?

MISS WINGRAVE
His not to question but obey.

KATE
Might is right, the soldier's truth.

MRS JULIAN
Scruples are for milksops.

SIR PHILIP
Scruples are for women.

KATE
Scruples are for parsons.

MISS WINGRAVE
Scruples are for weaklings.

SIR PHILIP, MISS WINGRAVE, MRS JULIAN AND KATE
Scruples are for adolescent boys.

COYLE
Yes, he has scruples,
but not to save his skin, I'm sure.

SIR PHILIP
Aha! What good are scruples when the enemy charges?
When the garrison's dying,
women, children gasping for food and water?

KATE, MISS WINGRAVE AND MRS JULIAN
Scruples!

MRS COYLE
But, Sir Philip, you are too cruel!

SIR PHILIP, MISS WINGRAVE, MRS JULIAN AND KATE
You have scruples, scruples, scruples!

OWEN [standing]
Yes, and more—
I'd make it a crime to draw your sword for your country,
and a crime for governments to command it.

SIR PHILIP [rising]
There's no more to be said,
I'll leave you now.
[Sir Philip turns his back and hobbles off helped by a man-
servant: the others follow slowly. Owen is left alone]

END OF ACT ONE

Act two

Prologue

[*A ballad singer is heard alternating with a distant chorus and trumpet*]

NARRATOR
There was a boy, a Wingrave born,
A Wingrave born to kill his foe,
Far away on sea and land
The Wingraves were a fighting band.

CHORUS
Trumpet blow,
Paramore shall welcome woe.

NARRATOR
And with his friend young Wingrave played,
Young Wingrave played with tautened bow,
And when the games were won or lost
The two of them began to boast.

CHORUS
Trumpet blow,
Paramore shall welcome woe.

NARRATOR
'My father has a thousand fields,
A thousand cattle through them go',
'The timber from my father's trees
Sails on a thousand far-off seas'.

CHORUS
Trumpet blow,
Paramore shall welcome woe.

NARRATOR
'You lie,' he said, 'Not I,' 'Then fight',
His friend said 'Fight, and prove it so'.
With folded arms young Wingrave stood
And watched the hawk above the wood.

CHORUS
Trumpet blow,
Paramore shall welcome woe.

NARRATOR
Then silently he walked away,
He walked away with head hung low.
His father at the window wide,
Looked down and saw him turn aside.

CHORUS
Trumpet blow,
Paramore shall welcome woe.

NARRATOR
'Craven', he cried, 'you shame our name,
The Wingrave name to answer "No".'
And grimly marched him up the stair,
To his small chamber waiting there.

CHORUS
Trumpet blow,
Paramore shall welcome woe.

NARRATOR
He struck him on his tender head,
His tender head with blood did flow,
Until a corpse upon the floor
He never ran nor breathed more.

CHORUS
'There was a boy, a Wingrave born,
A Wingrave born to kill his foe.
Far away on sea and land
The Wingraves were a fighting band.'

NARRATOR
They called for him to toll the bell,
The bell was for the child he slew,
They found him lifeless on the ground
Of that same room without a wound.

CHORUS
Trumpet blow,
Paramore shall welcome woe.

Scene one

[*The gallery at Paramore. Coyle and Owen are looking at the double portrait of the old man and the boy of the ballad*]

OWEN [*joining the voice of the Narrator*]
The bell was for the child he slew.
They found him lifeless on the ground of that same
room . . .
What caused his death they never found out.

COYLE
Was it remorse?

OWEN
Not him! The blow was justified!
Wingraves do not refuse to fight . . .ever.

COYLE
Rough justice—horrible—a frightening face.

OWEN
It is the Wingrave look . . .even the boy.

COYLE
You take it hard, this legend of the house.

OWEN
Oh sir, he was my ancestor in every sense.
For me it is not the past, but now,
renewed with every thought and breath.
I can't forget them, the bully and the boy
stalking their way to the room which saw their deaths.
[*They move along the gallery to the door of the haunted room*]

COYLE
And this is the very room.

OWEN
Yes.

COYLE
A place of tragedy, a place of ghosts.

OWEN
Walking, walking—these two:
the old man and the boy,
for ever in each other's company.
[*They gradually move back along the gallery. They see Lechmere and the ladies talking below and slowly descend to join them*]

LECHMERE [*to Mrs Julian*]
I envy you this fine old house.

MRS JULIAN
Do not envy us what is not ours.

MRS COYLE [*quickly*]
Lechmere means your living in it as your home.

LECHMERE
You need never go, you'll stay here always, I am sure.

MRS JULIAN
Our friends are very kind, but we are not secure,
no, ours is not an enviable state, young man.
[*Coyle and Owen come up to the group*]

MRS COYLE
Ah, Coyle, Owen!

COYLE
I have been hearing the legend of the house,
a curious heritage.

MRS JULIAN
We think it noble—do we not Kate?

OWEN [*half to himself, but overheard by Kate*]
Noble?
Ruffians all! Given the chance I'd hang the lot.

KATE [*to Owen*]
What you would do and what you think
has ceased to interest us.

MRS COYLE [*to Kate*]
Miss Julian you are very young,
do not, I pray you, be too hasty.
A man can only do his duty as he sees it.
If we have trusted in the past
we must trust still
and try to understand.

KATE
I understand too well.

MRS COYLE
I think not,
brought up as we have been—
oh yes, my family were soldiers too—
it is hard to understand, hard even to forgive
so total a rejection.

KATE
I do not want to forgive.

MRS COYLE
Take time, forgive me if I urge once more,
take time.
To be led by those we love
is our privilege, my dear.

KATE
I could not be led by anyone
who did not think as I do.
No! I should feel degraded.
[*All are startled by the sudden appearance of Sir Philip, shuffling out of his room and glaring*]

SIR PHILIP
Aha!

COYLE, MRS COYLE, KATE, MRS JULIAN AND LECHMERE
Sir Philip!

MISS WINGRAVE
Father! You want something?

SIR PHILIP
I'm ready—send the traitor in!

[*Sir Philip turns his back abruptly and Owen follows him into his room. Coyle, watching, is aware of the similarity between the old general and the youth and the other old man and the boy of the legend*]

COYLE [*after they have disappeared*]
'Paramore shall welcome woe!'
[*Sir Philip's voice can be heard off-stage until Owen's reappearance*]

SIR PHILIP [*half heard words*]
Here's my last word . . . I'll not
accept it . . . You have disgraced
yourself . . . you must obey . . . What
is there left to be said . . . Can
you deny your behaviour's unmanly . . .
God save us all . . . can it be true . . .
can I believe my ears . . . can I believe
my eyes . . . I've told you before . . . and
I must tell you once again . . . you must be ready . . .
to behave yourself . . . and do your duty . . . never . . .
never . . . never . . . never . . . return. Ha!

COYLE
If we hold our breath we may hear,
in spite of closed doors,
the boom of the cannonade.

MISS WINGRAVE
There will be no fighting, Mr Coyle,
there will be orders, and obedience.

COYLE
I wonder if we do not underestimate
the strength of Owen's will.

MISS WINGRAVE
I fail to understand you.

COYLE
The boy has spirit, you will admit.

MISS WINGRAVE
No Wingrave lacks spirit.

COYLE
Then may he not be guided by his beliefs?

MISS WINGRAVE
His beliefs should be those of his family;
there is no life but soldiering for him.

COYLE
Are you so keen to send him to be killed?

MISS WINGRAVE
Is it not your job to encourage fighting men?

COYLE
He is, in the highest sense, a fighting man.

MISS WINGRAVE
What use are fighting men, who will not die in battle?

KATE
My father died in battle, just like his.
Should I, a soldier's orphan,
suffered in this house,
should I, rejected by my playmate,
praise his mutiny?

LECHMERE
But Kate, does he reject you?

KATE [*turns towards Lechmere*]
Owen throws his destined life away and so, throws me.
[*Sir Philip's door opens*]

SIR PHILIP
Begone!
[*Owen reappears*]

COYLE, MRS COYLE, MRS JULIAN, KATE AND LECHMERE
Well?

MISS WINGRAVE
Owen! You've had your orders?

OWEN
It's over,
I'm disinherited.
He turns me out for ever!
[*Miss Wingrave hurries from the room to see the old man*]

MRS JULIAN [*sobbing*]
Disinherited!
Deprived of all his patrimony—
oh my girl, my girl—
deprived of Paramore.
Oh what selfishness!
That ever it should come to this.

KATE
Mother, be quiet, you shame us!

MRS JULIAN
All I have planned for, striven for,
shattered in one blow.

KATE
Mother! Control your tears.

MRS JULIAN
Oh, come Kate, come, my only child,
out into the world together,
we have no-one but each other now.
Your chosen mate has left you.
Out into the world,
farewell to Paramore!

LECHMERE [*to Owen*]
I'm sorry, Owen, it's too bad.

KATE
Sorry for him! Oh no,
he doesn't need our sympathy:
he's lost all interest in comrades now.

LECHMERE
But not in you!

KATE
I tell you it's over,
the habit broken.
From now I must rely upon myself.

LECHMERE [*eagerly*]
But Kate, everyone loves *you*!

MRS COYLE
Oh, Coyle, can't you stop him?

KATE
But can I rely on you, could *you* defend me?

LECHMERE
With all my heart, defend you to the last.

MRS COYLE
The puppy!

COYLE
The silly fellow is besotted!

KATE
Ah, my friend, you'll make a splendid soldier.

COYLE
She has no reticence, I must say.

KATE
For me a man must be bold.

LECHMERE
I would be bold.

KATE
My choice must offer his life.

LECHMERE
I would offer my life.

KATE
Offer his heart and his soul to his country with no
thought of gain.

LECHMERE
My gain would be you.

For you I'd follow the flag.

KATE
Our unsullied flag.

LECHMERE
Proudly with you as my wife.

KATE
A true soldier's wife.

LECHMERE
I would seek glory with you as my wife with no thought
of gain.

KATE
My gain would be you.

KATE AND LECHMERE
For me a man/girl must believe.

MRS COYLE
I am amazed . . .

KATE AND LECHMERE
A soldier's life is the best.

MRS COYLE
She is callous, unkind . . .

KATE AND LECHMERE
When I/you become one without thought of gain,
my gain will be you!

MRS COYLE
Oh my poor Owen.

KATE
Knights must perform a task, what will you do?

LECHMERE
Anything—to prove my worth to you.

KATE
Would you sleep in the haunted room?

LECHMERE
What! I should say so!

KATE
Are you sure? Owen wouldn't.

COYLE
Nor will you, my boy, that's certain,
your work comes first,
and while in my care
I'll see you'll lose no sleep.

LECHMERE
Oh sir, she wants . . . Kate wants me to.

KATE [*losing interest*]
It's of no importance.
Come mother–calm yourself, we'll go to bed.
[*Miss Wingrave reappears to usher them to bed*]

OWEN [*bitterly*]
'And with his friend young Lechmere played . . .'

MISS WINGRAVE
Mr Coyle, Madam,
Sir Philip will not reappear tonight.
He wishes me to thank you both
for your civility in coming here,
no less because it is of no avail.
The Wingraves have seen reverses, suffered much,
their spirit does not flag.
The renegade is now as if he had not ever been
a member of our valiant family:
Paramore will still survive.
I bid you all good-night.
[*Owen comes forward now as if to perform his usual duty of
lighting the ladies' candles but is snubbed by his aunt who turns
deliberately to Lechmere*]

MISS WINGRAVE
Mr Lechmere, would you please light the ladies'
candles?
[*As they wish each other 'Good-night', Miss Wingrave starts the
procession upstairs. Owen stands aside*]

MRS COYLE [*to Owen*]
Good-night, my dear boy.
May Heaven direct you right.

COYLE
Now Lechmere, off with you.
Good-night ladies. Mrs Julian,
please do not distress yourself unduly.

MRS COYLE [*to Coyle*]
Coyle, come to bed, I'll not go up alone.

COYLE
I'll follow, my love.
[*Coyle goes to Owen*] I feel for you.

OWEN
Yes.

COYLE
I even feel for them, you know.

OWEN
Yes, I know.

COYLE
Although I think their action harsh, unjust.

OWEN
Oh that: that's nothing.
I half thought the old man would knock me down –
or worse.
Now I feel I have escaped,
only I am so tired.

COYLE
Then sleep now, and–God bless you.
[*Coyle goes upstairs: Owen walks about and looks at the
portraits*]

OWEN
Now you may save your scornful looks
and turn your faces to the wall.
You heard her words:
        'The renegade
is now as if he had not ever been
        a member of our valiant family'?

I was surrounded with love,
nursed in hope,
spoiled with admiration,
but all for the image they made of me,
for the man they planned to make of me.
Now I am nothing, I bid you all farewell.
[*Turns away from the portraits*]
In peace I have found my image,
I have found myself.
In peace I rejoice amongst men
and yet walk alone,
in peace I will guard this balance
so that it is not broken.

For peace is not lazy but vigilant,
peace is not acquiescent but searching,
peace is not weak but strong like a bird's wing
        bearing its weight in the dazzling air.
Peace is not silent, it is the voice of love.

Oh you with your bugbears, your arrogance, your
        greed,
your intolerance, your selfish morals
and petty victories,
peace is not won by your wars.

Peace is not confused, not sentimental, not afraid.
Peace is positive, is passionate, committing–
        more than war itself.
Only in peace can I be free.
And I am finished with you all.
[*Apparitions of the old man and the boy of the portrait appear to
Owen*]
[*speaking*]
Ah,
I'd forgotten you!

Come on, then,
come on, I tell you.

You two will never walk for me again.
I'm rejected,
the Wingraves have turned me out
and you don't belong to me,
nor I to you.

[*to the boy*]
Poor boy,
you made your stand too young—
but I have done it for you—for us all.
Tell the old man, tell your fearful father,
your fate and his no longer frighten me.
Tell him his power has gone
and I have won,
[*The apparitions disappear into the haunted room*]
and at last I shall have peace.
[*And he sinks into a chair in the shadows*]
[*Kate comes down the stairs sadly. She does not see Owen*]

KATE
Ah, Owen, what shall I do?
Can nothing move you now?

His lost inheritance,
the fields that once he loved don't move him now.
The Wingraves' pride, and mine,
our country's cause
won't move him now.
My love, my hate, my scorn!
Will nothing move him now?

Ah, Owen, what shall I do?
[*Owen moves forward to her*]

OWEN
Kate, you've come back.

KATE [*sadly*]
Yes, I've lost something—
a jewel from my brooch.

OWEN
You've lost more than that, Kate.

KATE
I came to look for the Owen that I knew.

OWEN
Oh Kate! All our lives we've shared
the same strange life.

KATE
Here in this brave, old house,

OWEN
These silent rooms,

KATE
the mist on the grass,

OWEN
owls in the dark,

KATE
The broken branches in the park,

OWEN
the dry click-click of antlers,

KATE
the rival stags fighting for their chosen hind.

OWEN
You loved that sound—

KATE
Persistent, wild, exultant.

OWEN
But I wept for the loser's wound,

and searched for him.

KATE AND OWEN
But only found the blood-soaked bracken
and trampled grass.

KATE
Owen! Why can't we go on?
Why did you spoil it all?

OWEN
I spoil it? To you at least
I looked for sympathy.
We two, the only young things here,
could build a new life.
Kate, come with me.
It's not too late.

KATE
I can't, I can't.
I was prepared to sacrifice my life to you, and your fate;
even in death your glory would be mine.

OWEN
Unreal, ridiculous! You would sacrifice
to a false idea of glory.

KATE
What was good enough for our fathers
is good enough for us.
Give your life for England's glory.

OWEN
But think, Kate, think,
that's a childish . . a schoolgirl's dream.

KATE
You're wrong, you're wrong,
everyone knows you're wrong—
even Lechmere, your friend, knows it.

OWEN [*in a sudden passion*]
How dared you flirt with Lechmere,
heartless, thoughtless,
careless of all feelings but your own.

KATE
How dare you scold me—
coward that you are.

OWEN
What! What did you dare to say?

KATE
Coward that you are!
[*Lechmere appears in the background*]

OWEN
That I'm not,
even you don't dare believe it.

KATE
How do I know?

OWEN
You *do* know.

KATE
Then prove it.

OWEN
Tell me what you want.
Some drunken officer's trick?
Thrust my sword through my hand?

Pin it to the table,
to amuse the gaping ladies?

KATE
No.

OWEN
What then?

KATE
No.

OWEN
What then?

KATE
Sleep in the haunted room.

OWEN
Ah! I thought I'd done with that,
with the Wingraves and the house
Would you drag me back?

KATE
I see your brave heart fails you.

OWEN [*going upstairs*]
No. If that is your idea,
I'll do it.

KATE [*following him*]
You won't last out the night!

OWEN
Then lock me in.
Oh Kate! What childish dares are these.
As if to sleep
under that heartless roof
could prove my worth.

KATE
Why do you tremble like a boy,
the first time in the field?

OWEN
Not fear but passion makes me tremble.
The anger of the world is locked up there,
the horrible power that makes men fight:
now I alone must take it on,
I must go in there.
[*They are both outside the door of the haunted room*]

KATE
Ah Owen, Owen, give in,
for your sake and for mine,
say you'll be a soldier!

OWEN
No. I can't believe in it.

KATE
Oh your beliefs! Why was I not a man?

OWEN
Come, turn your key.
[*He goes into the room: Kate locks the door, brushes past
　　　　　　　　Lechmere and goes back to her room*]

Scene two

[*Later that night: the Coyles' bedroom. Mrs Coyle is in her
négligée, looking anxious*]

MRS COYLE
Is that you, Coyle?–
[*Coyle comes in*]
I heard you go out.
Where have you been?

COYLE
To see that Lechmere has not disobeyed.

MRS COYLE
Surely not!

COYLE
No, he's in his room.
I didn't go in.

MRS COYLE
I thought him heartless, thoughtless,
and wrong to flirt with her.

COYLE
She led him on,
he's never met a Kate before.

MRS COYLE
I'm glad I've not–a hateful girl.

COYLE
Not hateful–only young.

MRS COYLE
I took her aside, tried to talk to her, tried to calm
　　her down,
but she would have none of it,
wouldn't listen to me.
Oh she's an arrogant girl.

COYLE
Go to sleep now, you'll feel better:
I shall read a while.
[*The lights fade to indicate a passage of time; Coyle is reading*]

MRS COYLE [*calling*]
Coyle, I've been thinking–
what will Owen do?

COYLE
I don't know.
Downstairs he seemed resigned,
in a strange way,
as if he were at peace.

MRS COYLE
But we must help him!

COYLE
Never mind now, sleep.

MRS COYLE
Ugh! I shall be glad to leave here,
I feel stifled.
These people . . . even the house–
creaks and rustles, groans and moans,
I hate it, hate it.

COYLE
Oh come, you're getting fanciful.
Go back to bed, do.

[*Another passage of time; Coyle has a book in his hand, but is not reading. There is a knock at the door*]

COYLE [*irritably*]
Come in.

LECHMERE
It's me, Lechmere.

COYLE
Come in, come in, what *is* all this?

LECHMERE
Excuse me, sir,
I couldn't sleep.
I came out for a smoke
and saw your light.

MRS COYLE
Coyle! What's happening?
Who's there?

COYLE
It's only Lechmere,
he says he couldn't sleep.
[*Mrs Coyle joins them in her dressing gown*]

LECHMERE
I had to speak to someone.

COYLE
I should not have brought you here.

LECHMERE
She—she's pushed him into it.

COYLE
Into what? Who?

LECHMERE
Kate, she's made him sleep in that room.

COYLE
How d'you know?

LECHMERE
I heard. I went back to talk to him,
they were quarrelling.
She taunted him, said he wouldn't stick it out.
He said, 'Then lock me in'.

MRS COYLE
Oh that horrible girl,
why couldn't she let him alone?

LECHMERE
I think she likes him.

MRS COYLE
What a way to show it!

COYLE
If he's really there,
if he agreed to go there,
I think I'm glad—
it puts them so in the wrong.
He's still the dauntless boy.

MRS COYLE
All the same, I'm worried about him,
all alone in that wicked room.
Coyle, go to him, see that he's all right.

LECHMERE
Yes go, please go, and

I'll come with you, we'll go together.
[*Kate's voice is heard, crying from outside the haunted room*]

KATE [*off*]
Ah, Owen, Owen you've gone!

LECHMERE
It's Kate, it's her voice. Kate!

MRS COYLE
I knew it, I knew something terrible would happen.

COYLE [*leaving*]
Come, come this way! The sound came from here.
[*Coyle, Mrs Coyle and Lechmere hurry out of the bedroom.
Blackout*]

KATE [*off*]
Gone with the old man and the boy.

MRS JULIAN
Kate, what's happening, are you hurt?

MISS WINGRAVE
What is all this noise?
You'll disturb Sir Philip.
[*The scene changes to outside the haunted room. Kate is fallen in the doorway. The other characters approach along the galleries*]

KATE [*nearer*]
Ah, why have you left me now?

LECHMERE
Oh Kate! What has she done?

COYLE
These foolish children, these children!

MRS COYLE
I fear for Owen.

MRS JULIAN
Oh dear, oh dear!

MISS WINGRAVE
No, father, I'll see to it.
[*All have arrived at the door of the haunted room. Kate is sobbing hysterically, and pointing*]

MRS COYLE, MRS JULIAN, MISS WINGRAVE, LECHMERE
AND COYLE
Kate! What is it?

KATE
Ah, Owen, Owen,
it's my fault.
I shut him in there.
I came back, I was sorry,
and Owen—he's dead!

SIR PHILIP
My boy!
[*He pushes open the door. Owen is lying dead on the ground. The others are frozen on the spot. The ballad singer's voice is heard with the distant chorus and trumpet as before*]

NARRATOR
There was a boy, a Wingrave born,
A Wingrave born to face his foe.
He did not change, nor did he yield,
A soldier on the battle field.

CHORUS
Trumpet blow,
Paramore shall welcome woe!

Death in Venice

An opera in two acts

by Myfanwy Piper
based on the short story by Thomas Mann

BENJAMIN BRITTEN OP. 88

CHARACTERS

SINGERS

Gustav von Aschenbach *a novelist*	TENOR
The Traveller *who also sings*	BASS-BARITONE

   The Elderly Fop
   The Old Gondolier
   The Hotel Manager
   The Hotel Barber
   The Leader of the Players
   The Voice of Dionysus

The Voice of Apollo	COUNTER-TENOR
Hotel Porter	TENOR
Strawberry Seller	SOPRANO
English Clerk *in a travel bureau*	BARITONE
Two Strolling Players	SOPRANO AND TENOR

CHORUS *generally*
Youths and girls, hotel guests and waiters, gondoliers and boatmen, street vendors and touts, citizens of Venice, choir in St Mark's, Followers of Dionysus.

DANCERS

The Polish mother
Tadzio, her son
Her two daughters
Their governess
Jaschiu, Tadzio's friend
Other boys and girls, Strolling Players, beach attendants

SYNOPSIS OF SCENES

Act one

Scene one	Munich
Scene two	On the boat to Venice
Overture	Venice
Scene three	The journey to the Lido
Scene four	The first evening at the hotel
Scene five	On the beach
Scene six	The foiled departure
Scene seven	The Games of Apollo

Act two

Scene eight	The Hotel Barber's shop (i)
Scene nine	The pursuit
Scene ten	The Strolling Players
Scene eleven	The travel bureau
Scene twelve	The Lady of the Pearls
Scene thirteen	The dream
Scene fourteen	The empty beach
Scene fifteen	The Hotel Barber's shop (ii)
Scene sixteen	The last visit to Venice
Scene seventeen	The departure

FIRST PERFORMANCE
16 June 1973   *The Maltings, Snape, Suffolk*

Gustav von Aschenbach	Peter Pears
The Traveller	John Shirley-Quirk

   The Elderly fop
   The Old Gondolier
   The Hotel Manager
   The Hotel Barber
   The Leader of the Players
   The Voice of Dionysus

The Voice of Apollo	James Bowman
The Polish Mother	Deanne Bergsma
Tadzio	Robert Huguenin

and members of the English Opera Group, The Royal Ballet, and children of the Royal Ballet School.

Conducted by Steuart Bedford
Produced by Colin Graham
Choreographed by Sir Frederick Ashton
Scenery designed by John Piper
Costumes designed by Charles Knode
Lighting designed by John B. Read

Act one

Scene one
Munich

[*Aschenbach is walking in the suburbs of Munich on a spring evening*]

ASCHENBACH
My mind beats on
and no words come.
Taxing, tiring,
unyielding, unproductive—
my mind beats on.
No sleep restores me.

I, Aschenbach,
famous as a master-writer,
successful, honoured,
self-discipline my strength,
routine the order of my days,
imagination servant of my will

My mind beats on,
why am I now at a loss?

I reject the words called forth by passion
I suspect the easy judgement of the heart—
now passion itself has left me
and delight in fastidious choice.

My mind beats on,
and I am at an end.
O tender leaves and tardy spring refresh me!
[*He stops before the entrance to a cemetery*]
How solitary it is here—
the silent graveyard,
and the silent dead.
[*He notices the texts on the façade of the mortuary chapel*]

CHORUS
'They enter into the house of the Lord'.

ASCHENBACH
Yes! From the black rectangular hole in the ground.

CHORUS
'May light everlasting shine upon them'.

ASCHENBACH
Light everlasting?
Would that the light of inspiration had not left me.
[*He is suddenly aware of the Traveller standing on the steps of the chapel. They stare at each other*]
Who's that? A foreigner, a traveller no doubt—
from beyond the Alps by his looks.
How he stares: a rude, insolent fellow.
I won't, don't want to notice him.
[*He turns away, sunk in thoughts called up by the Traveller*]

TRAVELLER
Marvels unfold!
A wilderness, swollen with fearful growth,
monstrous and thick,
and heady flowers
crowd in the steaming marsh.
Trees, distorted as a dream,
drop naked roots

into a glass-green pool,
where float great milk-white blooms
and at the stagnant edge
huge birds stand hunched and motionless.

ASCHENBACH
Strange—strange hallucination,
inexplicable longing.

TRAVELLER
See! in the knotted bamboo grove
(O terror and delight) a sudden
predatory gleam,
the crouching tiger's eyes.

ASCHENBACH
What is this urge that fills my tired
heart, a thirst, a leaping, wild unrest,
a deep desire!

TRAVELLER
Marvels unfold!
No boundaries hold you,
Go, travel to the South.
Great poets before you
Have listened to its voice.
[*Aschenbach looks for the Traveller, but he is nowhere to be seen*]

ASCHENBACH
Gone, he's gone, as suddenly as he came—
the traveller from beyond the Alps.

Should I go too beyond the mountains?
Should I let impulse be my guide?
Should I give up the fruitless struggle with the word?
[*He takes from his pocket a small book, the symbol of his novelist's trade*]
I have always kept a close watch over my development
as a writer, over my behaviour as a man. Should I now,
without thought, break my habit, my summer of work in
the mountains, to holiday in the warm and lovely south?
The break can be justified of course by this growing
fatigue, that no one must suspect and that I must not
betray by any sign of flagging inspiration. Yes, it can be
justified—but the truth is that it has been precipitated by
a sudden desire for the unknown.
[*He puts his book away*]
So be it!
I will pursue this freedom
and offer up my days
to the sun and the south.
My ordered soul shall be refreshed at last.

Scene two
On the boat to Venice

[*Some youths lean over the boat rail and shout to their girl friends on shore*]

YOUTHS
Hey there, hey there, you!
You come along with us,
come along do!

GIRLS [*on shore*]
Not with you, not very likely, not with you!

ONE YOUTH
Aren't you old enough to leave home?
[*They all laugh*]

TWO GIRLS
You be quiet!

YOUTHS
'Serenissima, Serenissima'

ONE BOY
Let the girls alone,
there are plenty where we're going.

ANOTHER
. . .plenty where we're going.

GIRLS
Look out for the girls over there!
They'll hook you, they will!
They'll trap you, they will!
They'll get you, they will! They will!

ONE YOUTH
Thanks, we can look after ourselves!
[*The youths are joined by their friend, the Elderly Fop*]

GIRLS
Ho! Here comes young Casanova,
there, him with the hat.
He'll make trouble.

ELDERLY FOP
Me Casanova?
Me make trouble?
I don't know what trouble is, do I boys?

YOUTHS
Doesn't know what trouble is, does he boys?

ELDERLY FOP [*going up the gangway*]
Come on, cara mia!
We'll be nice to you.

YOUTHS [*following him*]
Hi, come back!

ELDERLY FOP
Leave me alone, boys!
[*They struggle with him and pull him back as the hooter sounds and the boat leaves*]

ELDERLY FOP
I say, we're off! Addio!

YOUTHS [*on boat*]
We're off, thank goodness, Addio!
We're off. Hurrah for Serenissima. Addio!

GIRLS [*on shore*]
You're off! Too late! Be careful do! Addio!
They're off, good riddance too. Addio!
[*The Elderly Fop stops the 'Addios' and starts the song*]

ELDERLY FOP AND YOUTHS
We'll meet in the Piazza,
The flags will be flying,
And outside San Marco
The girls we'll be eyeing.
[*Aschenbach comes on to the deck*]

ELDERLY FOP
Hush boys, quiet!
We have a noble companion on board.

YOUTHS
We'll sit in the Piazza,
The band will be playing,
But inside San Marco
They're singing and praying.

ELDERLY FOP [*to Aschenbach*]
Greetings, Conte!
Bound for Serenissima I'm sure.
[*Aschenbach starts as he sees he is not young, but elderly, rouged and wrinkled*]

ASCHENBACH
Why, he's old!
He's not young at all.

ELDERLY FOP
But you look doubtful?
Pray don't change your mind, you won't regret it!
Venice—an excellent choice,
you'll find everything you're wanting—
won't he, boys?
[*laughs*]

YOUTHS
The bells of San Marco
Call us to our duty
But I'll leave the Piazza
And follow my beauty.
[*They run off*]

ASCHENBACH
Ugh! How can they bear that counterfeit
that young-old horror.
A wretched lot, a wretched boat.
[*A Steward comes forward with a chair*]

STEWARD
Do you want a chair, Signore?

ASCHENBACH
Yes, put it there, away from the young men.
[*To himself*]
What romantic notion
made me want to come by sea?
[*The Steward puts the chair down and Aschenbach settles himself*]

YOUTHS [*off*]
'Serenissima'

ASCHENBACH
Low-lying clouds, unending grey

YOUTHS [*off*]
'Serenissima'

ASCHENBACH
Beneath the sombre dome
the empty plain of the sea.
[*He dozes*]
[*The Elderly Fop crosses in front of Aschenbach*]

YOUTHS [*off*]
'Row us over to Serenissima'

ELDERLY FOP
Hush boys, the Conte is dreaming!
Dreaming of love and Serenissima.
[*He goes off*]
[*Aschenbach gets up and looks towards the shore of Venice now visible*]

YOUTHS [*off*]
'Serenissima'

ASCHENBACH
Where is the welcome
that my Venice always gave me?
[*The boat arrives and the Elderly Fop and the Youths, by now
rather drunk, come running on*]

ELDERLY FOP AND YOUTHS
Here we are, here we are!

ELDERLY FOP
Wait for me, I'm coming too
I want my beauty, Hurrah!

YOUTHS
Hurrah for the Piazza
The pride of the city
All hail to San Marco
Hurrah for my beauty!
[*They all rush on shore, followed slowly by Aschenbach*]

ELDERLY FOP [*to Aschenbach*]
Au revoir, Conte!
Pray keep us in mind
and, by the way,
our love to the pretty little darling—
don't you know!

OVERTURE · VENICE

Scene three
The journey to the Lido

[*Aschenbach is in a gondola rowed by the Old Gondolier*]

ASCHENBACH
Ah Serenissima!
Where should I come but to you
To soothe and revive me
Where but to you
To live that magical life
Between the sea and the city?
What lies in wait for me here,
Ambiguous Venice,
Where water is married to stone
And passion confuses the senses?
Ambiguous Venice.

GONDOLIER [*to himself*]
Passengers must follow
Follow where I lead
No choice for the living
No choice for the dead.
[*Aschenbach suddenly realises the Gondolier is rowing out to the
Lido*]

ASCHENBACH [*to Gondolier*]
Where is the man going?
[*To Gondolier*]
I want to go to Schiavone.

GONDOLIER
The Signore is going to the Lido.

ASCHENBACH
Yes, by vaporetto.

GONDOLIER
The Signore cannot go by vaporetto,
the vaporetto does not take baggage.

ASCHENBACH
That is my affair; you will turn round.

GONDOLIER [*to himself*]
Nobody shall bid me
I go where I choose
I go my own way
I have nothing to lose.

ASCHENBACH [*to himself*]
Is it money he's after?

GONDOLIER
The Signore will pay.

ASCHENBACH
I will pay nothing
if you do not take me where I want to go.

GONDOLIER
To the Lido.

ASCHENBACH
But not with you.

GONDOLIER
I row you well.

ASCHENBACH [*to himself*]
True, he rows well.
I shall leave him alone,
go back to my dreams,
to the sway of the boat
and the indolent lapping waves.

GONDOLIER [*to himself*]
They know how I row them
They take what I give
But nobody shall bid me
Not while I live.
[*A boatload of boys and girls singing is heard in the distance*]

CHORUS [*off*]
Serenissima, Serenissima
Row us over to Serenissima

GIRL	BOY
Bride of the sea	True bride for me
GIRLS	BOY
Gossip and stroll	Eye every girl
GIRL	BOY
Choose the right one	Make her your own
GIRLS	BOYS
If she won't come	Leave her alone
GIRLS	GIRLS
Loiter and play	Tease every boy
BOYS	BOY
You play too long	I'll change my song

BOYS AND GIRLS
Serenissima
Bride of the sea
True bride for me.
[*As the boatload comes nearer Aschenbach throws them money*]

ALL
Mille grazie, Signore.
Tanti auguri.
Addio, addio . . .
[*Fading away*]

GONDOLIER [*to himself*]
   Nobody shall bid me
   I do what I want to
   I'm not out to please.
   [*The gondola arrives at the Lido quayside. Aschenbach gets up and is helped ashore by a Boatman and the Hotel Porter*]

BOATMAN
   Buon giorno, Signore. Piano, piano!

PORTER
   This way, Signore, prego.

ASCHENBACH
   One moment please, I have not paid the gondolier.
   [*He turns to pay the Old Gondolier, who has disappeared*]
   Why, he's gone, gone without his money.

PORTER
   He made off, Signore,
   A bad lot.

BOATMAN
   He was recognised here,
   a bad lot.

PORTER
   A man we don't trust.

BOATMAN
   A man without a licence.

BOTH
   But the Signore is lucky,
   he had his gondola ride for nothing.
   [*Aschenbach tips the Boatman. The Hotel Porter picks up his baggage and carries it off, Aschenbach walking slowly behind him*]

ASCHENBACH
   Mysterious gondola,
   a different world surrounds you,
   a timeless, legendary world
   of dark, lawless errands
   in the watery night.
   How black a gondola is—
   black, coffin black,
   a vision of death itself
   and the last silent voyage.
   Yes, he rowed me well.
   But he might have done for me,
   rowed me across the Styx
   and I should have faded
   like echoes in the lagoon
   to nothingness.

Scene four
The first evening at the hotel

[*The Hotel Manager welcomes him*]

MANAGER
   We are delighted to greet the Signore
   to our excellent hotel.
   [*Aschenbach nods*]
   We trust the Signore had a pleasant journey;
   he will have a pleasant sojourn I am sure.
   [*Aschenbach nods*]
   The Signore was wise to come to the Lido by gondola,
   not so fast as the boat, but pleasanter, far pleasanter.

ASCHENBACH
   That was not my intention.

MANAGER
   Just so, but a happy chance none the less.
   And here is the room, as you commanded,
   and look Signore, the view!
   The view of the beach from our rooms is superb,
   from this one especially.

ASCHENBACH
   Thank you, it will do very well.

MANAGER
   And here, Signore, outside your room,
   but private, unfrequented,
   you may sit and see the world go by.
   For men of letters, like the Signore,
   take pleasure in the contemplation of their fellows—

ASCHENBACH
   Thank you.

MANAGER
   —for the Signore is well-known in our country.

ASCHENBACH
   Thank you, very nice, quite satisfactory.

MANAGER
   Prego, egregio Signor von Aschenbach.
   [*The Hotel Manager bows himself out*]

ASCHENBACH [*with book*]
   So I am led to Venice once again—egregio
   Signor von Aschenbach; the writer who has found a
   way to reconcile art and honours,
   the lofty purity of whose style has been officially
   recognised and who has accepted, even welcomed the
   austere demands of maturity. Yes, I turned away from
   the paradox and daring of my youth, renounced
   bohemianism and sympathy with the outcast soul, to
   concentrate upon simplicity, beauty, form—upon these
   all my art is built. Now, in this beautiful, agreeable
   place, I intend to give myself to the leisured world for a
   spell. A pleasant journey did he say? The whole
   experience was odd, unreal, out of normal focus. Was I
   wrong to come, what is there in store for me here?
   [*He puts his book away*]
   But there is the sea
   and near by Serenissima
   though the sky is still grey,
   the air heavy, a hint of sirocco.
   [*He gets up and looks out to the sea and the beach*]
   How I love the sound
   of the long low waves,
   rhythmic upon the sand.
   [*The Hotel Guests with their children begin to process before dinner and Aschenbach turns to watch them*]

ASCHENBACH
   But here the sound is of another kind.

GUESTS [*all*]
   The Lido is so charming, is it not.

FRENCH GIRL
   Maman, le dîner quand sera-t-il servi?
   Je meurs de faim.

FRENCH MOTHER
   Tais-toi, Bérénice c'est assez!

ALL
And this hotel is all that one could wish.

TWO AMERICANS
FIRST
That was a most interesting excursion.
SECOND
Most interesting.
FIRST
We should have Mario guide us again tomorrow.
SECOND
Mario? Mario!

ALL
And Venice is so close one is not bored beside the sea.

GERMAN FATHER AND MOTHER
Komm' mein Kindchen, lass' uns hören
was die Wellen dir erzählen.*

ALL
One meets one's friends from everywhere–
from Warsaw!

A POLISH FATHER [to his son]
Jeśli jutro będzie pogoda to
pojedziemy na wyspy.*

ALL
and Denmark!

DANISH LADY
Det er så varmt.*

ENGLISH LADY [replying]
What was that you said, dear?

ALL
and Moscow!

RUSSIAN NANNY [to her children]

Тары-бары-растабары,
Снежки белы выпадали,
Серы зайцы выбегали,
Охотнички выезжали,
Ты постой,стой,стой,стой...

RUSSIAN PARENTS [interrupting her]

При {Маме Папе} надо вести себя прилично ! *

ALL
So civilised, quite so.
So elegant, quite so.
So 'comme il faut', don't you know.

HOTEL PORTER AND WAITER
Signori! Il ristorante, al vostro servizio.
[All the guests, repeating their individual phrases, go towards the dining room]

ASCHENBACH
United in their formal ways
in the ease that wide horizons bring.
Well-mannered murmurs of a large hotel.
[The Polish family (Governess, two girls and Tadzio) enter. Aschenbach notices them]

ASCHENBACH
Poles, I should think,
Governess, with her children–
a beautiful young creature, the boy.
    Surely the soul of Greece

Lies in that bright perfection
A golden look
A timeless air,
Mortal child with more than mortal grace.
[Tadzio's mother comes in. The family gets up, bow and curtsey, and they all move off into the dining-room]

ASCHENBACH [with book]
How does such beauty come about?
What mysterious harmony between the individual and the universal law produces such perfection of form? Would the child be less good, less valuable as a human being if he were less beautiful? The fact is that in that disciplined family, beauty dominates. The severe, plain little girls must be quiet, demure; the elegant boy may show off his grace. No doubt Mama with her fabulous pearls indulges herself in a pampering partial love–just as I indulge myself in these novelist's speculations. There is indeed in every artist's nature a wanton and treacherous proneness to side with beauty.

Scene five
On the beach

[Aschenbach and hotel guests]

ASCHENBACH
The wind is from the West
a lazy sea,
the sky overcast,
a stagnant smell from the lagoon.
My temples throb, I cannot work
O Serenissima, be kind,
or I must leave,
just as once I left before.
[A group of children play at beach games. Aschenbach watches them]
[A Strawberry Seller wanders across the beach. The children stop and watch her]

STRAWBERRY SELLER
    Le bele fragole,
    La bela, bela ua.
Fine strawberries, Signori, fresh today.
[The game continues. The Seller goes to Aschenbach who buys some strawberries]

STRAWBERRY SELLER
Grassie, Signore . . .
Bellissime!

ASCHENBACH
I'll stay, I cannot leave.
What can be better than the sea?
What can be better than this?
[With book]
Ah, how peaceful to contemplate the sea–
immeasurable, unorganised, void. I long to find rest in perfection, and is not this a form of perfection?
[Aschenbach raises his head to see Tadzio coming on to the beach]
Ah here comes Eros–his very self.
I was not mistaken, it is very good.
[A little pantomime of Tadzio's hatred of the Russian family]
So the little Polish god is proud,
proud like all his race.
He is human after all.

There is a dark side even to perfection.
I like that.
[*Tadzio goes and sits down with his family. His friends call him to join them*]

CHORUS [*off*]
Adziù! Adziù!

ASCHENBACH
What is it they call him, Adziù! Adziù?
They call him Adziù!
[*Children's games with Tadzio as ringleader. They play in the water. Tadzio runs back wet to his mother*]

CHORUS [*off*]
Adziù! Adziù!

ASCHENBACH
Tadziù, Tadziù! that is it . . .
from Thaddeus, short for Thaddeus.
Tadzio.
[*Tadzio joins the children again. They acknowledge him as their leader. He then walks back to his mother. She presents him to some of her friends, and he smiles rather self-consciously*]

ASCHENBACH
So, my little beauty,
you notice when you're noticed,
do you?
[*With book*]
As one who strives to create beauty, to liberate from the marble mass of language the slender forms of an art, I might have created him. Perhaps that is why I feel a father's pleasure, a father's warmth in the contemplation of him. Yes, Aschenbach, you have grown reserved, self-sufficient since the death of a wife and marriage of an only daughter—dependent not upon human relationships but upon work, and again—work. How much better to live, not words but beauty, to exist in it, and of it. How much better than my detached and solitary way.

Scene six
The foiled departure

[*Aschenbach crosses to Venice in a gondola*]

GONDOLIER
Aou'! Stagando, aou'!
Aou'!
[*At the landing place, Aschenbach gets out and starts walking through the streets. He looks unhappy and uncomfortable. Vendors and beggars cry to him from all sides*]

A GUIDE
Guida, guida! Let me guide the Signore.
I can find him places he does not know,
places to delight him.

ASCHENBACH
While this sirocco blows
Nothing delights me.
My head is heavy,
My eyelids ache.

A LACE SELLER
Guardi, Signore, see the beautiful silks and lace.

Tutto a buon mercato.
[*Many times repeated*]

A GLASSMAKER
Venga qui, Signore, look at my beautiful glass.
Tutto a buon mercato.
[*Many times repeated*]

ASCHENBACH
Foul exhalations rise
Under the bridges,
Oppress my breathing,
Dispel my joy.

BEGGAR WOMAN [*with her child*]
La carità, la carità!
Il padre is sick,
the bambini are hungry,
la carità.

A RESTAURANT WAITER
Provi, Signore!
Vongole, granseole, aragosta,
gamberetti, mazanette,
calamaretti molto buon'.
Provi, Signore!

BEGGAR WOMAN
La carità,
il padre is sick,
bambini hungry,
la carità.

ASCHENBACH
The rubbish stirs in gusts
Over the piazzas.

GLASSMAKER
Venga qui, Signore, look at my beautiful glass.
Tutto a buon mercato.
[*Many times repeated*]

ASCHENBACH
Every doorway
Harbours feverish fears.

LACE SELLER
Guardi, Signore, see my beautiful lace.
Tutto a buon mercato.
[*Many times repeated*]

ASCHENBACH
O Serenissima,
I fear you in this mood.

GUIDE
Guida, guida, Signore!
I can find places you do not know,
places to delight you.
[*Aschenbach has now arrived back at the landing stage*]

ASCHENBACH
Enough, I must leave, I must go away.
Back to the mountains—
and the fresh mountain air.
[*He gets into the gondola*]
But where? where shall I go?
I must leave this unfriendly lagoon
horrible, evil, nauseous.
I must go elsewhere
I must find a clearer sky
a fresher air.

118 Study of Venice   *John Piper*

119 Study of Venice *John Piper*

118 Study of Venice *John Piper*

121 Exterior of St Mark's   *John Piper*

122 Interior of St Mark's   *John Piper*

123 The Lido Beach (vocal score cover)

John Piper

GONDOLIER
Aou'! Aou'!

ANOTHER GONDOLIER [*off stage*]
Aou'! De longo aou'!
[*The gondola arrives at the Lido. Aschenbach gets out*]
[*Passage of time*]
[*Aschenbach is revealed in the hotel hall*]

MANAGER
Naturally, Signore, I understand.
How regrettable, unfortunate.
We shall be sorry to lose you,
but of course if the Signore has reasons
then he must go.
[*Aschenbach nods*]
No doubt the Signore will return to us
in his own good time.
[*Aschenbach nods*]
Meanwhile our deepest respects
and please keep us in mind.
Arrivederci, Signore!
[*Aschenbach nods*]
[*Calling*]
Giulio, veni qui.
The Signore's baggage. Presto.

PORTER
Sì, pronto! Sì, sì.
It is here.
[*To Aschenbach*]
The motor-boat is waiting.

ASCHENBACH
It is too soon,
you allow too much time,
I will not be hurried.
I will follow by gondola.

PORTER
Bene, Signore.
[*He goes off with the baggage*]

ASCHENBACH
Yes, I must go—
but does it seem fresher this morning?
Can the wind have changed?
[*Tadzio walks through the hall*]
For the last time, Tadziù,
it was too brief, all too brief—
may God bless you.
[*Tadzio glances at Aschenbach*]

[*Passage of time*]

[*Aschenbach in the gondola*]

GONDOLIER
Aou'!

ANOTHER GONDOLIER [*distant*]
Premando aou'!

ASCHENBACH
Shall I never see these columns rise again?
Never see the marble brows
upon each curving bridge?
O Serenissima!
Why did I yield so quickly to my fears?
[*The gondola arrives in Venice. The Hotel Porter comes to the side of the quay and calls to Aschenbach*]

PORTER
There you are, Signore, just in time.

ASCHENBACH
You have my baggage?

PORTER
Safe, Signore, gone on the train to Como.

ASCHENBACH
Gone to Como?
That is not where I'm going.

PORTER
Sorry, Signore.
Mi dispiace, Signore.

ASCHENBACH
You must find it—get it back—
Without it, I cannot go.
You understand? I cannot go.
I shall return to the hotel.
Arrange for the baggage to be sent back there.

PORTER
Very good, Signore.
In the twinkling of an eye it shall be back.
[*Calling*]
Gondoliere, to the Lido at once!
[*The Gondolier starts rowing back to the Lido*]

ASCHENBACH
I am become like one of my early heroes, passive in the face of fate. What do I really want? First I am grief-stricken but must go because of the danger to my health, then I am furious because I am forced to return, but secretly I rejoice. Vacillating, irresolute, absurd.

GONDOLIER [*very distant*]
Aou'!

ASCHENBACH [*continuing*]
The whole experience has been disruptive to my thoughts and to my work; yet in spite of it I feel my spirits rise. Often what is called disruptive is not directed against life, but is invigorating, a renewal . . .
[*At the hotel the Manager greets him*]

MANAGER
A thousand apologies to the Signore,
I would not have discommoded him for the world.
And now the Signore will find the wind
is blowing from the healthier quarter,
the wind blows sweetly from the east.
[*The Manager takes Aschenbach to his room and opens the window on to the beach*]
Now the Signore
can holiday at ease,
he can enjoy
what he thought to have left
for ever.
[*The Manager leaves. Aschenbach remains looking wearily out on to the beach. Tadzio, Jaschiu, and a few other boys are seen playing in the distance*]

ASCHENBACH
Ah, Tadzio, the charming Tadzio,
that's what it was,
that's what made it hard to leave.
[*The boys run off. Aschenbach lifts his hands in a gesture of acceptance*]

So be it. So be it.
Here I will stay,
here dedicate my days to the sun
and Apollo himself.

Scene seven
The Games of Apollo

[*The Lido beach. Aschenbach is in his chair*]

CHORUS [HOTEL GUESTS]
Beneath a dazzling sky
The sea rolls silken-white,
Calm morning hours drift on
To scented dusk and melting night
Day after carefree day
The idle minutes run
While he transported to the antique world
Lives in Elysium.

THE VOICE OF APOLLO
He who loves beauty
Worships me.
Mine is the spell
That binds his days.
[*Tadzio 'drives' a group of boys on to the beach*]

CHORUS
No boy, but Phoebus of the golden hair
Driving his horses through the azure sky
[*They form a pyramid and Tadzio climbs to the top*]
Mounting his living chariot shoulder high,
Both child and god he lords it in the air.
[*The boys dismount*]
No boy, but Phoebus of the golden hair.

VOICE OF APOLLO
Now in my praise
They tell again
Olympian tales
Of rivalry.
[*Jaschiu and another boy vie for Tadzio's attention, watched by Tadzio's mother*]
[*While the Chorus sings, the appropriate actions take place. Jaschiu shows off his acrobatic skill, Tadzio imitates him. The other boy tries to attract Tadzio with his skill, the two boys compete. Tadzio is accidentally knocked down. They carry him across to his mother, who comforts him.*]

CHORUS
Come, see where Hyacinthus plays
Basking in Apollo's rays,
Careless sun that gilds his love
With beauty that will fatal prove.
But a rival watches there
With envious pangs too strong to bear.
Jealous Zephyr's angry breath
Guides the blow that brings his death.
Poor broken boy as on the ground you rest
The curled flower springs immortal from your breast.

VOICE OF APOLLO
Love that beauty causes
Is frenzy god-inspired
Nearer to the gods
Than sanity.
[*Formal solo for Tadzio*]

OPTIONAL CUT

CHORUS
Phaedrus learned what beauty is
From Socrates beneath the tree:
Beauty is the only form
Of spirit that our eyes can see
So brings to the outcast soul
Reflections of Divinity.

VOICE OF APOLLO
At the feasts of the sun
See my devotees contest
In strength, agility and skill
The body's praise.
[*The boys compete in a variety of sports*]
(1 Running)

CHORUS
First, the race!
Run, run,
get ready go,
foot by foot,
outpace one another,
with flashing forms
legs, thighs, working arms.
[*Tadzio is first*]
(2 Long jump)
Next, to the pit.
Try your skill
turn by turn
heaving breath—
Go!
Springing high
gather limbs
time the moment—
Go!
Now release
shooting forward
legs and arms
flinging forth
skim, and land
with thudding heel.
Go!
[*Tadzio has jumped furthest*]
(3 Throwing the discus)
Now, the throw!
Young discobolus
tensing body bent
weighs the swelling stone
firm upon the hand
swinging back and up
gathering all his force
arching wider still
hurling now,
hurling the discus.
Young discobolus!
[*Tadzio has thrown furthest*]
(4 Throwing the javelin)
On tip-toe rise!
Up and over
graceful turn and drop
higher each one
the heavens attempt
triumphant flying,
free in weightless flight.
Yet to the earth at last
the shaft is bound.
[*Tadzio has thrown furthest*]

(5 Wrestling)
　　For skill and strength
　　this is the final test!
　　Measure to fight,
　　face your man
　　forehead to forehead
　　fist to fist
　　limbs coiled round limbs
　　panting with strain
　　tear apart and close again
　　immobile now—tensing, tensing!
　　Panther-like, a shoulder throw.
　　[*Tadzio is winner of the Pentathlon*]

CHORUS
　　Who is the victor?
　　Tadzio has won.
　　Crown him with olive!
　　[*Tadzio comes forward; the boys dance round him*]
　　Tadzio has won,
　　Tadzio is victor.
　　[*Many times repeated*]

VOICE OF APOLLO
　　Praise
　　Praise my power.
　　Beauty is the mirror of spirit.
　　[*The Hotel Guests and all the children retreat to the distance (the chorus still singing) leaving Tadzio alone. Aschenbach rises and comes forward, very excited*]

ASCHENBACH
　　The boy, Tadzio, shall inspire me.
　　His pure lines shall form my style.
　　The power of beauty sets me free
　　I will write what the world waits for
　　rejoicing in his presence.

　　When thought becomes feeling, feeling thought . . .

　　When the mind bows low before beauty . . .

　　When nature perceives the ecstatic moment . . .

　　When genius leaves contemplation for one moment
　　　of reality . . .

　　Then Eros is in the word.
　　[*Tadzio, sauntering, approaches Aschenbach*]
　　Ah Tadzio, the victor, the admiration of all,
　　I must say well done.
　　I must speak to him,
　　we will become friends,
　　it is easy, nothing more natural.
　　[*Tadzio passes Aschenbach who turns away*]
　　Too late, I couldn't . . . couldn't do it . . .
　　this is frenzy, absurd.
　　The heat of the sun must have made me ill.

　　So longing passes back and forth
　　between life and the mind.
　　[*Tadzio's mother comes back with her family to collect him. As Tadzio passes Aschenbach on the way into the hotel he smiles*]
　　Ah, don't smile like that!
　　No one should be smiled at like that.
　　[*Then realising the truth at last*]
　　I—love you.

Act two

ASCHENBACH [*with book*]
　　So, it has come to this. I can find no better description of my state than the hackneyed words 'I love you'. Overcome by beauty I tried, quite simply to use the emotion released for my own creation. What I wrote was good, quite what was expected of me; to the point, yet poignant. But when it was done I felt degraded—as if I had taken part in an orgy.

　　Then I was moved to put this relationshp—if so onesided an affair can be called a relationship—on to a natural footing. I would hail the boy, exchange a few words with him: I couldn't do it. My beating heart and trembling limbs refused to obey my will. So I had to mock myself as the crestfallen lover.

　　Who really understands the workings of the creative mind? Nonetheless 'so be it'. This 'I love you' must be accepted; ridiculous but sacred too and no, not dishonourable even in these circumstances.
　　[*Passage of time*]

Scene eight
The Hotel Barber's shop (i)

HOTEL BARBER
　　Guardate, Signore!
　　Va bene, Signore?
　　[*Aschenbach is revealed in the barber's chair*]
　　Move the head to the left.
　　Yes, the weather is idyllic.
　　Too hot? O, just a trifle.
　　The hotel guests are fewer?
　　[*The Barber holds up a mirror*]
　　Guardate, Signore!
　　Va bene, Signore?
　　Your head down, if you please.
　　But what was that you're saying?
　　you hear less German?
　　Ah! your compatriots are always very careful
　　but so nice.
　　Take the von Becks!
　　I've tended Her von Beck for many summers,
　　a splendid head of hair if I may say so,
　　remarkable for someone in his middle years,
　　and such a youthful skin!
　　(Guardate, Signore!)
　　Each year they spend the summer with us,
　　(va bene, Signore?)
　　but now after ten days they have gone,
　　gone back to the cold unwelcoming north.
　　(Head up just a little!)
　　The Signore is not leaving us?
　　He does not fear the sickness, does he?

ASCHENBACH [*sharply*]
　　Sickness! what sickness?

BARBER
　　Nothing, I know nothing.

ASCHENBACH
　　But you mentioned it.

BARBER
It is not important, it is nothing.

ASCHENBACH
You must know what you mean.

BARBER
Take no notice, sir, it is not important.
You fancy this oil, sir?
A delectable scent, sir,
the Signore now takes little interest in such things,
I know.
That is it, Signore.
[*Aschenbach gets up from the chair*]
Next week at the same time?
Va bene, Signore, egregio Signore.
Prego, prego!
[*Aschenbach comes forward as the Hotel Barber and his chair fade*]

ASCHENBACH
Sickness, what sickness?
More than a malaise from the sirocco?
A sickness to drive people away?
[*Passage of time*]

Scene nine
The pursuit

[*Aschenbach is crossing to Venice*]

ASCHENBACH
Do I detect a scent?
A sweetish medicinal cleanliness,
overlaying the smell of still canals?

GONDOLIER
Aou'!

ANOTHER GONDOLIER [*off stage*]
Aou'!
[*The gondola stops and Aschenbach gets out. There are many people standing about*]

ASCHENBACH
How quiet the city is!
What can they all be looking at?

CITIZENS [*reading from a notice*]
Citizens are advised to take precautions against
  infection.
Citizens are warned not to eat shellfish in this unusually
  hot season.
Citizens must not use the canal waters for household
  purposes,
People are warned . . . warned . . .

ASCHENBACH
warned . . . warned . . .

CITIZENS
Everyone is warned.

ASCHENBACH
What is all this?
The city fathers are seldom so solicitous.
[*Moving to talk to some shopkeepers*[
What is this sweetish smell
that pervades the air, my friends?

SHOPKEEPERS
Scusi?

ASCHENBACH
What are these warnings?

GLASSMAKER
Just a formal precaution, sir.

RESTAURANT WAITER
Police regulations, sir, with which we must conform.

LACE SELLER
The air is sultry, the sirocco blows.

A GUIDE
No, quite unimportant, sir, precautionary–
Let me guide the Signore,
I can find him . . .

ASCHENBACH
Basta! Basta!
[*He turns away*]

SHOPKEEPERS
Scusi, Signore!

BEGGAR WOMAN [*pursuing him*]
La carità! The bambini are sick.

NEWSPAPER SELLER [*entering*]
La Stampa! Giornali tedeschi . . .
Il Mondo! German newspapers . . .

ASCHENBACH
Das Tagblatt, grazie.

NEWSPAPER SELLER [*goes out*]
Grazie, Signore . . . La Stampa!
Giornali inglesi . . . Il Mondo!
La Stampa! Giornale, giornale . . .

ASCHENBACH [*reading*]
Let me see what my countrymen say.
'Rumours of cholera in Venice officially denied.
Rumours of an incipient plague in Venice, officially
denied.'

Ah, here it is. 'We doubt the good faith of the Venetian
City fathers in their refusal to admit to the cases of
cholera in the city. German citizens should return as
soon as possible.' Ugh! rumours, rumours. They should
be silent. The city's secret, growing darker every day,
like the secret in my own heart.
[*The Polish family appears*]
They must receive no hint.
They must not be told.
They must not leave.
[*Aschenbach begins following the family*]
And now I cannot let them out of sight,
daily I watch and wander.
Strange times of chance encounters, painful hopes,
and silent communion.
[*The family is sitting at a café table in the piazza. Aschenbach
sits near them. The café orchestra plays. Tadzio's mother
deliberately gets up and places herself between her son and
Aschenbach*]
[*The family leaves and starts walking. Aschenbach follows*]
Careful search now leads me to them,
cunning finds him out.
[*The family approaches and enters St Mark's*]

My eyes are on him even at his prayer,
incense and sickness mingle in the air.
[*Aschenbach follows. Tadzio kneels a little apart from the others. Aschenbach stands amongst the casual populace away from the family. There is a service going on. Bells*]

CHORUS
Kyrie eleison, Christe eleison.
[*Tadzio is aware of Aschenbach's presence*]
Christe audi nos, Christe exaudi nos.
Sancte Marce ora pro nobis.

PRIEST
Ite, missa est.
[*The service is over, the family leaves. Aschenbach follows them down the Merceria*]

ASCHENBACH
When I am near, he knows.
As for me a calm untroubled face
hides a panic fear—
yet am I driven on . . .
[*The citizens gradually appear*]

CHORUS
Fewer guests from smart hotels
come to walk about our streets.

ASCHENBACH
Yet am I driven on.

CHORUS
We who live by summer's trade
guard the city's secret.

ASCHENBACH
Yet am I driven on.

CHORUS
There's no danger if we watch
and do as we are told.

ASCHENBACH
Yet am I driven on.

CHORUS
Under a burning sky
The sirocco still blows.
[*Aschenbach suddenly comes face to face with the family. He bows, raises his hat and turns away*]

ASCHENBACH
O voluptuous days,
O the joy I suffer:
feverish chase,
exquisite fear,
the taste of knowledge,
time gained by silence
while the echoing cries answer
from the labyrinth.
[*The family gets into a gondola*]

ASCHENBACH [*calling to a gondolier*]
Follow them!
[*He gets into his own gondola and follows them through the canals*]

GONDOLIERS [*in the two boats*]
Aou'! De longo aou'!

THIRD GONDOLIER [*from a distance*]
Aou'!
Chiamate! Aou'!

FIRST AND SECOND GONDOLIERS
Stagando aou'!
[*The family gets out of their gondola. Aschenbach follows them*]

ASCHENBACH
Ah, Tadzio, Eros, charmer,
see I am past all fear,
blind to danger,
drunken, powerless,
sunk in the bliss of madness.
[*The family enters the hotel, followed by Aschenbach*]
Ah, Tadzio, Eros, charmer.
[*Tadzio disappears into his bedroom. Aschenbach remains some time leaning against the door post. He then slowly goes to his room*]
[*Shaken but excited, he calls himself to order*]

ASCHENBACH [*with book*]
Gustav von Aschenbach, what is this path you have taken? What would your forebears say—decent, stern men, in whose respectable name and under whose influence you, the artist, made the life of art into a service, a hero's life of struggle and abstinence?
[*He pauses, smiles to himself*]
Yes, but when heroes have flourished Eros has flourished too. It was no shame to them to be enthralled, rather it brought them praise, it brought them honour.

Scene ten
The Strolling Players

[*On the terrace outside the hotel after dinner. The Hotel Porter and Waiter are ushering the guests*]

PORTER
This way for the players, Signori!

WAITER
Please come this way.

PORTER
A rough lot of course, but you'll enjoy it.

WAITER
A rough lot.

PORTER [*answering a guest*]
Yes, they come each year; it is the custom.
Take your places, Signori.

WAITER
Take your places, Signori.
[*The Hotel Guests take their places*]

GUESTS
The players are here,
Where are our places?
The players are here
To charm and delight us
With quips and grimaces,
With old songs new turned
With new antics learned
To please and excite us
To woo and invite us
The players are here,
We're in our places!
[*The Strolling Players begin. A boy and a girl come forward: two acrobats mime the instruments (flute and guitar)*]

BOY AND GIRL

O ⌈mio carino⌉ how I need you near me
  ⌊mia carina⌋

BOY

Just as the Siren needs the salt sea water

GIRL

Dearest I weep when you're not near to hear me

BOY

And in my veins the blood begins to falter.

BOTH

Better by far if we had met and parted

GIRL

I knew the Creed, but now I can't get started,

BOY

Can't say the Gloria nor l'Ave Maria,

BOTH

How shall I save my soul, l'anima mia?
[*Aschenbach takes his place, apart from the other guests*]
Dearest my life is guided by your beauty
[*Tadzio is visible on the terrace*]
Just as the North star guides the storm-tossed sailor.

BOY

For you forgotten honour work and duty.

BOY AND GIRL

Carina, ⌉ how shall I save my soul?
L'anima mia,⌋

[*The Leader of the Players comes forward, an acrobat mimes the trumpet*]

LEADER OF THE PLAYERS

La mia nonna always used to tell me
'Leave the blondes alone, Sonny–
Sono tutte vagabonde!'
La mia mamma always used to tell me:
'Don't you choose brunettes, Sonny–
Sono tutte traditore!'
Padre mio always used to tell me:
'Never touch a redhead, Sonny–
sono tutte . . . sono tutte . . .'
So I shall never be able to marry–
Evviva la libertà.

[*The Leader goes among the guests with his hat. Aschenbach calls to him*]

ASCHENBACH

A word, please.

LEADER

Signore?
[*During this conversation the two acrobats amuse the guests*]

ASCHENBACH

Why are they disinfecting Venice?

LEADER

Orders, just orders.

ASCHENBACH

So there is no plague in Venice?

LEADER

Ha! That's a good one,
perhaps the sirocco's a plague?
Or the police, *they* are a plague!

No, you've got it wrong, Signore,
it's the heat, the heat and the weather.
Basta! Basta!
[*He tries to go on with his collecting but is intercepted by the Hotel Porter*]
Here, hands off!

PORTER

What did you say to the German Signore?

LEADER

Nothing, let go!

PORTER

What did you say?

LEADER

Told him he was talking a lot of nonsense
that's what I told him.

PORTER

Go on then, they're waiting,
and mind you, not a word.
[*The Leader runs back to the other players and starts the laughing song. Aschenbach and Tadzio never join in the laughter*]

LEADER

*Fiorir rose in mezo al giasso
e de agosto nevegar.

CHORUS

Ha, ha, ha, ha,
How ridiculous you are!

LEADER

Trovar onde in terra ferma
e formighe in mezo al mar.

(Chorus)

Giovinoto che e na vecia
tanti basi ghe vol dar.

(Chorus)

Bela tosa che se voia
co un vecio maridar.

(Chorus)

Oseleto un fià stracheto
che sia bon da sifolar.
[*To the audience*]
What a lot of fools you are!

CHORUS

How ridiculous you are!
Ha, ha, ha, ha.
[*General laughter, led by the Leader, grows in intensity until he stops it with a gesture. He then takes the players off amidst applause. The Leader then starts his antics, ending with a wild gesture. He puts his tongue out at the Hotel Guests, who start leaving uneasily*]

ASCHENBACH [*tenderly*]

Ah, little Tadziù,
we do not laugh like the others.
Does your innocence keep you aloof,
or do you look to me for guidance?
Do you look to me?

[*Tadzio remains quietly for a moment, then leaves. The Hotel Porter and Waiter bustle the Leader off*]
[*Musing*]
So the moments pass;
And as they dwindle through the fragile neck
Dividing life from death I see them flow
As once I saw the thread of sand slip through
My father's hour glass.
[*Passage of time*]

A YOUNG ENGLISH CLERK [*from the distance*]
One moment if you please.
[*Nearer*]
One moment if you please.

Scene eleven
The travel bureau

[*A Young English Clerk is coping with a crowd of Hotel Guests*]

CLERK
One moment, if you please.

GUESTS [*singly*]
We must go today, no later.

My ticket please.

CLERK
One moment, if you please.

GUESTS
Information please, it is most urgent.

Please pay attention to me.

CLERK
One moment, if you please.

GUESTS
Four places in the Wagon-lits for tonight,
four places—first class.

But my dear young man, I said today.

CLERK
One moment, if you please.

GUESTS
A hotel overnight, near the station.

Called to France—urgent business—I cannot wait— I must go.

Will you help me please.

CLERK
I'm sorry, Signori, we are closed.
[*The Hotel Guests leave in confusion. Aschenbach comes forward*]

ASCHENBACH
Young man, why do all these people hurry to leave?

CLERK
The end of the season, sir.

ASCHENBACH
What are these warnings all over the city?

CLERK
The city always takes precautions in this weather.

ASCHENBACH
Is that the truth?

CLERK
Sir, that is what they say,
what we are told to believe. But . . .

ASCHENBACH
The truth!

CLERK
In these last years, Asiatic cholera has spread from the delta of the Ganges: to Hindustan, to China, Afghanistan and thence to Persia. They thought it would travel westwards by land, but it came by sea, to the southern ports—Malaga, Palermo . . . Last May, two dead bodies were discovered here in Venice with signs of the plague. It was hushed up. In a week there were ten more—twenty—thirty. A guest from Austria went home and died; hence the reports in the German newspapers. The authorities denied it—the city had never been healthier, they said. Sir, death is at work, the plague is with us. It flourishes, redoubles its powers. It is violent, convulsive, suffocating, few who contract it recover. The Ospedale Civico is full. The traffic to San Michele is continuous. And Sir, the authorities are not moved by scruples, or by international agreements. They fear for their pockets—if there should be panic or blockade . . . Meanwhile the city is demoralised. Crime, drunkenness, murder, organised vice—evil forces are rife. Sir, take my advice. The blockade cannot be far off. Rather than put it off till tomorrow, you would do well to leave today.

ASCHENBACH
Thank you, young man.

CLERK
Good night sir, it is true, every word.

Scene twelve
The Lady of the Pearls

[*Aschenbach walks up and down agitatedly*]

ASCHENBACH
So it is true, true, more fearful than I thought.
I must warn them, warn the lady of the pearls,
speak to her now.
'Madame', I will say,
'allow a perfect stranger to give you a warning'.
'Madame', I will say, 'Go away, at once,
you are in danger.
Venice is in the grip of the plague.
Do you not see how everyone is leaving?
You must go too, with your daughters,
and with . . . Tadzio, your son'.
'Madame', I will say, 'Madame' . . .
[*The lights go up on the Hall of the hotel. Tadzio's mother walks into the Hall. Aschenbach makes as if to speak to her. She comes right up to him but he turns aside into his room*]

ASCHENBACH [*with book*]
So—I didn't speak! Once again I have failed to make everything decent and above board, missed the opportunity to become myself again, missed the opportunity to regain my reason, my self-possession. But what *is* self-possession? What is reason, moral sense,

what is art itself, compared to the rewards of chaos. The
city's secret, desperate, disastrous, destroying, is my
hope. I will not speak.
What if all were dead, and only we two left alive?

Scene thirteen
The dream

[*A dark stage. Aschenbach is faintly discernible asleep*]

THE VOICE OF DIONYSUS
Receive the stranger god.

THE VOICE OF APOLLO
No! Reject the abyss.

DIONYSUS
Do not turn away from life.

APOLLO
No! Abjure the knowledge that forgives.

DIONYSUS
Do not refuse the mysteries.

APOLLO
No! Love reason, beauty, form.

DIONYSUS
He who denies the god, denies his nature.

APOLLO
No! Be ruled by me and by my laws.

DIONYSUS
Come! Beat on the drums.

APOLLO
No!

DIONYSUS
Stumble in the reeling dance.

APOLLO [*fading*]
No!

DIONYSUS
Goad the beasts with garlanded staves,
seize their horns,
ride into the throng.
Behold the sacrifice!

APOLLO [*distant*]
I go, I go now.
[*The Followers of Dionysus appear, dancing*]

FOLLOWERS
Aa-oo! Aa-oo!

DIONYSUS
Taste it, taste the sacrifice.
Join the worshippers,
embrace, laugh, cry,
to honour the god,
I am he!

FOLLOWERS
Aa-oo! Aa-oo!
[*The Dionysiac dance reaches a climax and slowly fades*]

ASCHENBACH [*in his sleep*]
Aa-oo, aa-oo!
[*He suddenly awakes*]

[*Spoken*]
It is true, it is all true.
I can fall no further.
O the taste of knowledge.
Let the gods do what they will with me.

Scene fourteen
The empty beach

[*Aschenbach slowly moves to his chair on the beach where Tadzio
and a few friends are mooning about. They begin a desultory
game. It breaks off. They begin another, but soon run off*]

ASCHENBACH
Do what you will with me!

Scene fifteen
The Hotel Barber's shop (ii)

[*Aschenbach is revealed in the chair and the Hotel Barber is
attending to him*]

BARBER
Yes, a very wise decision, if I may say so.
One should not neglect oneself in one's middle life.
Everyone should make a stand against advancing years.
[*Holding up the mirror*]
Guardate, Signore, egregio Signore!
Grey? O just a trifle,
due to lack of interest,
you would not neglect your health? your teeth?
Then why refuse the use of cosmetics?
Nothing ages a man like grey hair,
permit me to aid it just a little?
[*The Barber works on his hair with lotions etc.*]
Very wise,
magnificent,
all the difference,
va bene, Signore?
Now if we were to tone up the skin?
O just a little, a very little . . .
[*The Barber works on Aschenbach's skin*]
Signore, my forte . . .
to bring back the appearance of youth . . .
Va bene, Signore?
Give some brilliance to the eyes—
nothing brightens a face like the eyes!
[*The Barber works on Aschenbach's eyes*]
Head back, Signore . . .
quite, quite still . . .
an excellent subject, if I may say so.
[*Holding up the mirror*]
Guardate, Signore! va bene, Signore?
Prego, prego.
A masterpiece, a masterpiece!
Now the Signore can fall in love with a good grace.
Prego, prego,
[*Accepting Aschenbach's tip*]
Addio, Signore, egregio Signore!

124 The Governess   *Charles Knode*

125 Tadzio, scene x   *Charles Knode*

126 Tadzio's two sisters   *Charles Knode*

127 American Hotel Guests   *Charles Knode*

128 The Traveller   129 The Elderly Fop   130 The Gondolier

131 The Hotel Manager 132 The Hotel Barber

133 The Strolling Player

Designer Charles Knode

134 Aschenbach, scene ii *Charles Knode*

135 The Mother, scene v *Charles Knode*

136 The Strawberry Seller *Charles Knode*

137 The Acrobats *Charles Knode*

Scene sixteen
The last visit to Venice

[*Aschenbach (with his new appearance) is seen getting gaily into a gondola*]

ASCHENBACH
Hurrah for the Piazza
The pride of the city
All hail to San Marco
All hail to my beauty
[*The gondola stops and Aschenbach gets out*]
'the pretty little darling don't you know'.
[*He sees the Polish family walking in front of him and starts distractedly following them. Tadzio detaches himself from the rest of his family and waits for Aschenbach. He looks full at Aschenbach, who turns away*]

ASCHENBACH
He saw me, he saw me, and did not betray me.
[*Tadzio joins his family. Aschenbach continues to follow but loses sight of them. Aschenbach leans exhausted against a well-head. The Strawberry Seller comes by*]

STRAWBERRY SELLER
Le bele fragole,
La bela, bela ua,
Fine strawberries.
[*Aschenbach buys some fruit*]
Grassie tante a voi, Signore.
[*She goes out singing*]
Signore, fresh today.

ASCHENBACH
Ugh, they are soft, musty, over-ripe!
[*He sits down, tired and ill*]
Chaos, chaos and sickness.
What if all were dead
and only we two left alive?
O Aschenbach . . .
Famous as a master . . .
Self-discipline . . . your strength . . .
All folly, all pretence–
O perilous sweetness
the wisdom poets crave.
Socrates knew, Socrates told us.

Does beauty lead to wisdom, Phaedrus?
Yes, but through the senses.
Can poets take this way then
For senses lead to passion, Phaedrus.
Passion leads to knowledge
Knowledge to forgiveness
To compassion with the abyss.
Should we then reject it, Phaedrus,
The wisdom poets crave,
Seeking only form and pure detachment
Simplicity and discipline?
But this is beauty, Phaedrus,
Discovered through the senses
And senses lead to passion, Phaedrus
And passion to the abyss.

And now, Phaedrus, I will go.
But you stay here
and when your eyes no longer see me,
then you go too.
[*Passage of time*]

Scene seventeen
The departure

[*The Hotel Hall leading to the beach. The Hotel Manager is standing waiting. The Hotel Porter is fussing around*]

MANAGER
The wind still blows from the land,
the air is not good, it is hot and unnatural.
The time of politeness and welcome
to our excellent hotel is over.

PORTER [*gaily*]
First one goes,
then another goes–è capo?
Soon we shall be all alone–è capo?

MANAGER
Be silent!
Where is the baggage of the lady of the pearls?
Were you not told to bring it down?

PORTER
First one goes,
then another goes,
then five go–è vero, capo?

MANAGER
Begone!
[*The Hotel Porter goes off*]

MANAGER
When guests arrive at my splendid hotel
I welcome them,
I show them the view.
And when they go,
by choice or chance,
I'm here to say addio!

PORTER [*returning with baggage*]
First one goes,
now they all go.
[*He puts the baggage down*]
And the writing gentleman?

MANAGER
Be silent–
who comes and goes is my affair.
[*Aschenbach comes in wearily. He looks at the baggage*]
Buon giorno, Signor von Aschenbach.

ASCHENBACH
More departures?

MANAGER
Signore, it is the time of departure.

ASCHENBACH
Our Polish friends?

MANAGER
Precisely, Signore,
the lady and her family
now return to their home
in the cold, cold north
beyond the mountains.

ASCHENBACH
When?

MANAGER
After luncheon, to be sure.
[*Aschenbach nods*]

Yes, Signor von Aschenbach
the season comes to an end,
our work is nearly done.
No doubt the Signore
will be leaving us soon?
We must all lose
what we think to enjoy the most.
[*The Hotel Manager watches Aschenbach go out to the deserted
beach. He goes to his usual chair. Tadzio, Jaschiu, a few other
boys, and Tadzio's sisters come on to the beach. Tadzio and
Jaschiu start a game together; the other children watch. The game
becomes rougher with Jaschiu dominating. The other children
become frightened. Jaschiu gets Tadzio down: he kneels on his
back. The children cry out. Jaschiu presses Tadzio's face into the
sand. The other children run off*]

ASCHENBACH [*trying to get up*]
  Ah, no!
  [*Jaschiu suddenly lets Tadzio go and runs off. Tadzio slowly
  gets up as he is called*]

CHORUS [*off*]
  Adziù! Adziù! Adziù!

ASCHENBACH
  Tadziù!
  [*At a clear beckon from Tadzio, Aschenbach slumps in his chair.
  Tadzio continues his walk far out to sea*]

---

* *Translations*

GERMAN FATHER AND MOTHER
  Come my child, tell us what
  the waves are saying.

A POLISH FATHER
  If tomorrow is fine then we will go to the islands.

DANISH LADY
  It is so hot!

The RUSSIAN NANNY'S song is a nonsense rhyme

RUSSIAN PARENTS
  In Mummy's/Daddy's presence one must
  behave properly!

Laughing Song
  Do roses flower in the midst of ice.
  Does snow fall in August.
    (Chorus)

Are there waves upon dry land,
or ants in the middle of the sea.
  (Chorus)

Does a young man want
to give an old woman kisses.
  (Chorus)

Does a pretty girl wish
to marry an old man.
  (Chorus)

Can a tired bird whistle.
  (Chorus)

Select Bibliography

Blythe, R. (ed.) *Aldeburgh Anthology* Snape Maltings Foundation and Faber Music, London, 1972

Britten, B. *On Receiving the First Aspen Award* Faber & Faber, London, 1964 (new edn Faber Music, 1978)

Benjamin Britten, A Complete Catalogue of his Published Works Boosey & Hawkes and Faber Music, London, 1973; Boosey & Hawkes, New York, 1963

Crozier, E. (ed.) *Peter Grimes*: with contributions by Benjamin Britten, E. M. Forster, Montagu Slater and Edward Sackville-West. Sadler's Wells Opera Books, No. 3, John Lane The Bodley Head, London, 1945

Evans, P. *The Music of Benjamin Britten* Dent, London, and Minnesota University Press, 1979

Gishford, A. (ed.) *Tribute to Benjamin Britten on his Fiftieth Birthday* Faber & Faber, London, 1963; Humanities Press, New York, 1963

Holst, I. *Britten* (Great Composers series) 3rd edn Faber & Faber, London, 1979; Thomas Crowell, New York

Keller, H. *The Rape of Lucretia, Albert Herring* Covent Garden Operas, Boosey & Hawkes, London, 1947

Mitchell, D. & Evans, J. *Benjamin Britten: Pictures from a Life* 1913–1976 Faber & Faber, London and Charles Scribner's Sons, New York, 1978

Mitchell, D. & Keller, H. (eds) *Benjamin Britten: A Commentary on his works from a group of specialists* Rockliff, London, 1952, (Greenwood Press reprint, USA, 1972)

Porter, A. *Music of Three Seasons* Farrar, Straus & Giroux, New York, 1978; Chatto & Windus, London, 1979

The Rape of Lucretia: a symposium by Benjamin Britten, Ronald Duncan, John Piper, Henry Boys, Eric Crozier and Angus McBean, with reproductions in full colour of the original designs by John Piper. The Bodley Head, London, 1948

White, E. W. *Benjamin Britten: His Life and Operas* Faber & Faber in association with Boosey & Hawkes, London, 1970; University of California Press, 1970

Index to main text

139 Tadzio   *Charles Knode* 140 Tadzio   *Charles Knode*